Principles of Management

A SYSTEMS APPROACH TO THE MANAGEMENT PROCESS

HENRY L. SISK, Ph.D.
Professor of Business Administration
North Texas State University

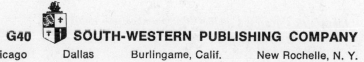

G40   SOUTH-WESTERN PUBLISHING COMPANY

Cincinnati   Chicago   Dallas   Burlingame, Calif.   New Rochelle, N. Y.

Library of Congress Catalog Card Number: 69–15905

4 5 6 7 8 H 5 4 3 2 1 0

Printed in the United States of America

Preface

Several assumptions are implicit to the writing of a textbook about management. First, it is assumed that there are aspects of the practice of management that can be taught to others. Such a statement runs counter to the belief that managers are born or that experience is the only teacher; yet the belief that managers can be taught minimizes in no way the value of experience and practice in the development of managerial skills and insights. It is believed, however, that those who enter managerial positions with knowledge and concepts gained from a formal study of management require less time to develop an acceptable level of managerial performance than those who have not studied management as a discipline. Second, it is assumed that management is best defined as a process of coordinating all the resources of an organization in order to achieve organizational objectives. The definition of management as a process permits the description and analysis of that process, thus making it possible to develop and organize the concepts and techniques of management in a systematic way. Third, there is the implied assumption that the management process is present in and necessary to all formal organizations—business, governmental, educational, social, religious, and charitable—if they are to achieve their respective organizational objectives effectively. Because of the universality of management and the consequent demand for managers, the study of management fulfills an important educational need.

This book is intended for use as a textbook in the principles of management course in four-year colleges and universities and in those junior colleges and community colleges offering a midmanagement curriculum. The book may also be used to advantage in company management development programs.

The approach used in this book combines the familiar and traditional analysis of the management process and the presentation of management principles with the newer systems concept of management in an endeavor to make it truly a systems approach to the management process. The process of management is described and analyzed in the usual temporal sequence of planning, organizing, directing, and controlling. Principles of management are defined as fundamental observations concerning causal relationships between managerial action and the subsequent effect of that action upon the attainment of organizational objectives. Organizations are regarded as cybernetic systems with the management process occurring within organizational systems. The combining of the traditional principles of management and the systems approach to the study of management permits the development of guides for the successful practice of management and at the same time provides a conceptual framework for a better understanding of the management process and the organizations in which management occurs.

One of the difficulties encountered in the teaching of principles of management to undergraduates is that they are unable to relate material studied in the textbook to a specific business situation since they do not have a common, if indeed any, background in business. In an effort to minimize this difficulty there are two case problems for each chapter, in itself not a unique feature. However, the cases are presented as an integral part of the text. Each chapter begins with an opening case problem that describes a business situation. In most of the chapters the case is referred to in the text material, thereby utilizing the case as a practical example to make the discussion in the text more meaningful. Generally, the closing case for each chapter draws upon concepts presented in the latter part of the chapter for its solution and is related to the text by means of a bridge paragraph at the end of the chapter.

Many persons contribute to the writing of a book with the result that an author always runs the risk of offending by omitting a specific contribution. Notwithstanding, an attempt is made to publicly acknowledge the contributions of several persons who have been closely associated with the writing of this book. Professor Emeritus Paul J. Kruse, Cornell University, imparted to the author a desire to write a textbook and has provided much encouragement and guidance in professional matters for a period of more than 30 years. Professor O. J. Curry, Dean of the School of Business Administration, North Texas State University, and Professors C. L. Littlefield, formerly chairman of the division of management, and Kenneth Cox, chairman of the division of management, have done much by arranging the author's teaching schedule to make this book possible. Professors S. Allen Self, Texas Christian University, and J. D. Dunn, North Texas State University, used a mimeographed form of the manuscript in their classes and provided many helpful suggestions. Finally, a special note of thanks is due to Professor George J. Gore, University of Cincinnati, and Professor Leon C. Megginson, Louisiana State University, who read the entire manuscript and offered many constructive criticisms.

Henry L. Sisk

●●●●● Contents

PART I · INTRODUCTION

PAGE

Chapter 1   **Management Defined** **1**
Case Problem 1-A: A Problem in Management
    Definition 1
The Nature of Management 3
The Systems Concept and the Management Process . 12
About This Book 15
Case Problem 1-B: What Went Wrong at Underwood? 17

Chapter 2   **The Development of Management Concepts** . **23**
Case Problem 2-A: Symptoms or Causes? 23
The Emphasis upon Human Relations 26
The Emphasis upon Production 31
The Emphasis upon Administration 37
Summary of Principles 43
Case Problem 2-B: Manual vs. Automatic Equipment . 46

Chapter 3   **Objectives and Ethics** **48**
Case Problem 3-A: A Public Trust 48
Objectives 50
Ethics 58
Summary of Principles 73
Case Problem 3-B: The New York Stock Exchange—
    An Example of Self-Regulation 75

PART II · THE PLANNING FUNCTION

Chapter 4   **Planning** **79**
Case Problem 4-A: Selecting a Plant Site 79
Fundamental Concepts of Planning 81
Types of Plans 86
Criteria for Evaluating Plans 89
Summary of Principles 100
Case Problem 4-B: How Much Planning Went
    into the Edsel? 102

Chapter 5   **Planning for Profit** **106**
Case Problem 5-A: Developing a Profit Plan . . . 106
The Meaning of Profit 107
Planning Financial Policy 114
Analysis of Profit 120
Application of Principles 132
Case Problem 5-B: Expand or Merge? 136

v

PAGE

Chapter 6 **Planning for Sales** **137**

    Case Problem 6-A: Channel of Distribution . . . 137
    Determinants of Demand 139
    Planning Sales Policies 144
    Application of Principles 154
    Case Problem 6-B: Changing Sales Policies . . . 162

Chapter 7 **Planning for Production** **164**

    Case Problem 7-A: Kwickie Kar Klean 164
    The Production Function 167
    Planning Production Policies 171
    Application of Principles 178
    Case Problem 7-B: Social Aspects of Automation . . 189

Chapter 8 **Management Information Systems** **191**

    Case Problem 8-A: The Parable of the Spindle . 191
    Functions of an Information System 195
    Integrated Data Processing 199
    Case Problem 8-B: The Short-Order Economy . 208

Chapter 9 **Decision Making** **213**

    Case Problem 9-A: A Personal Choice 213
    The Decision-Making Process 214
    Aids in Decision Making 220
    Creativity in Decision Making 226
    Case Problem 9-B: Another Mentholated Cigarette . 236

PART III · THE ORGANIZING FUNCTION

Chapter 10 **Organization Theory** **237**

    Case Problem 10-A: What Kind of Organization? . 237
    Theory X—A Work-Centered Approach 240
    Theory Y—A People-Centered Approach . . . 244
    Theory Z—A Systems Approach 254
    Case Problem 10-B: Plant Shutdown for Vacation . 258

Chapter 11 **Organization Structure** **261**

    Case Problem 11-A: Span of Management 261
    Departmentation 264
    Span of Management 269
    A Systems Approach to Organization Structure . . 275
    Case Problem 11-B: Needed—A Plan for Organization 284

PAGE

Chapter 12 **Organization Relationships** **287**

    Case Problem 12-A: A Strike Vote 287
    Authority 289
    Line-and-Staff Relationships 294
    Case Problem 12-B: Line/Staff Relationships . . . 309

Chapter 13 **Organizational Processes—Delegation and**
                Decentralization of Authority **311**

    Case Problem 13-A: A Need for Delegation . . . 311
    The Process of Delegation 313
    Decentralization of Authority 326
    Summary of Principles 335
    Case Problem 13-B: Decentralization—
        Fact or Fiction? 337

Chapter 14 **Group Functions in Organization—**
                The Committee **339**

    Case Problem 14-A: A Problem in Coordination . . 339
    Committees 340
    The Board of Directors 353
    Case Problem 14-B: How Rathbone Runs
        Jersey Standard 360

Chapter 15 **Preparing for Organizational Change—**
                Organizational Analysis **366**

    Case Problem 15-A: Charting an Organization . . 366
    Organizational Analysis 368
    Evaluating Organizational Effectiveness 380
    Case Problem 15-B: An Organizational Audit . . . 387

PART IV · THE LEADERSHIP FUNCTION

Chapter 16 **Leadership Patterns** **389**

    Case Problem 16-A: Selecting a President . . . 389
    Theories of Leadership 392
    Components of Leadership 396
    Personality Dynamics in Leadership 400
    Selecting a Leadership Pattern 405
    Case Problem 16-B: A Leader Who Failed . . . 414

PAGE

Chapter 17   Communications 416

Case Problem 17-A: A Message for Management . 416
The Meaning of Meaning 417
Principle of Communication 422
Problems in Communication 423
Improving Communications 435
Summary of Principle 441
Case Problem 17-B: A Case of Misunderstanding . 443

Chapter 18   Motivating Employees 446

Case Problem 18-A: Part I: An Employee Benefit
     Program 446
The Basis of Motivation 449
Motivation in Industry 457
Job Satisfaction and Productivity 470
Case Problem 18-B: Part II: Incentives or Job Design? 478

Chapter 19   Management's First Line: The Supervisor . . 480

Case Problem 19-A: No Smoking 480
The Supervisor's Job 482
Selection and Training of Supervisors 491
Improving Supervisory Performance 506
Principle of Supervision 512
Case Problem 19-B: The New Truck Problem . . 515

Chapter 20   Organization Development and Personnel
     Planning 516

Case Problem 20-A: Organization Planning . . . 516
Executive Development 520
Personnel Policies 542
Case Problem 20-B: Formulating Personnel Policies . 556

PART V · THE CONTROL FUNCTION

Chapter 21   The Basis of Control 559

Case Problem 21-A: A Need for Control 559
The Nature of Control 561
The Control Process 566
Characteristics of Good Control 583
Principles of Control 589
Case Problem 21-B: Controlling Sales Expense . 592

PAGE

Chapter 22   **Budgetary Control 594**

Case Problem 22-A: Developing a Revenue and
     Expense Budget 594
The Nature of Budgets 596
Human Factors in Budgetary Control 606
Effective Use of Budgets 615
Case Problem 22-B: A Need for Corrective Action 619

Chapter 23   **Nonbudgetary Control 621**

Case Problem 23-A: Improving Operating Ratios . 621
Personal Observation 624
Reports 625
Audit Programs 627
Ratio Analysis 633
Break-Even Analysis 637
Time-Event-Network Analysis 640
Case Problem 23-B: Shortening the Critical Path . 647

Appendix A: How to Analyze a Case 649

Appendix B: Comprehensive Case: Omega Rubber
     and Plastics Corporation 654

Index 665

Author Index 673

● CHAPTER 1

Management Defined

"Are we ready to begin now?" Mr. White, president of the J. B. White Company, asked as he mentally noted that all were present for the regular Thursday morning staff meeting. Seated on his left were the chief engineer, the vice-president in charge of sales, and the vice-president in charge of manufacturing. On his right were the controller and the director of research. At the opposite end of the long table was Mr. Peterson, the personnel director.

"As you know," Mr. White continued, "we have discussed from time to time the formation of a management club, but have never quite gotten around to actually starting one. The main problem seems to be in determining who should belong to the club. Let's see if we can't get this settled by next week and schedule the first meeting. Mr. Peterson, would you summarize from your minutes of these meetings our past discussions?"

Before Mr. Peterson could commence, Mr. Riley, the sales vice-president, interrupted, "I would like a clearer picture of what is to be gained by this sort of club. Personally, I don't see much need for my men to attend, although if you wanted someone, the man in charge of the sales order department could come. The others are too busy."

"We'll get to the purpose in just a minute," Mr. Peterson replied, "but first let's discuss the following criteria for membership that have been suggested: (1) every person whose name appears on the published organization chart; (2) all those who have supervisory responsibility; (3) all persons exempt from the provisions of the Wages and Hours Law; and (4) everyone whose earnings are over $500 a month. Mr. Burke, the vice-president in charge of manufacturing, has stated that he thinks the only ones who should belong are the foremen in the factory who

---

Case Problem 1-A

A Problem in Management

Definition

---

supervise. It has also been recommended that membership be limited to our plant here in Cleveland and not include any of the personnel in the branch plant, which is 25 miles away. As you know, Mr. Riley doesn't feel that any of his salesmen or district managers should belong."

Mr. Davis, the controller, spoke up and said, "I've been thinking about the suggestion that I made regarding the salary cutoff, and after looking at some of the earnings of the draftsmen in the engineering department, I think that we had better say 'salary' rather than 'earnings.'"

"That's right," agreed Mr. Johnson, the chief engineer. "I have draftsmen making more money than some of my junior engineers and trainees because these fellows don't get overtime pay since they are classified as professional employees."

"The same is true for me," said Mr. Brewer, the director of research. "Yet I feel that some of my research men would benefit from such a club as they might get a better feel for what we are trying to do as an organization."

There was a pause at this point and then Mr. White spoke, "I know that some of you were critical when I insisted that every person who does not receive overtime pay for extra hours worked be listed on the organization chart by name. I still think that the fact that a person is exempt from overtime pay should be the basis for membership in the management club."

"The heart of any club of this type is the foremen," argued Mr. Burke, vice-president in charge of manufacturing. "These are the people who should be represented. We should have a management club and call it that, even if there are only foremen in it. These men are the company to the employees in the shop, and I think that we should treat them accordingly. Also, we should tell them of our plans, and that way they could find out ahead of time what's going to happen instead of learning it from the union."

Mr. White saw that there had not been much change in the position of any of his staff since the last time the question of having a management club was discussed. He decided that the best course would be to present a specific proposal and ask them to either accept it or reject it. With this thought in mind, he made the following request of Mr. Peterson, the personnel director.

"Mr. Peterson, I would like for you to prepare a summary recommendation for consideration at our next meeting. Include in your report the name of the club, those who are eligible for membership, and a statement of the objectives of the club."

Problems

1. Assume that you are Mr. Peterson, the personnel director. Write a brief memo to Mr. White as requested.
2. Mr. Burke mentioned the fact that a management club would enable top management of the company to keep the foremen better informed in regard to company plans. Is there any possibility that top management might receive information from the foremen? Discuss.
3. *Research Assignment.* Mr. White indicated that if an employee did not receive overtime payment for extra hours worked, he was eligible for inclusion on the company organization chart. Such employees are norm-

ally termed *exempt,* since they are exempt from the overtime provisions of the Fair Labor Standards Act, commonly called the Wages and Hours Law. Consult your nearest wages and hours office, either in person or by letter, and review those publications which discuss the basis for exemption. Discuss briefly whether exemption from overtime payment serves as a valid criterion for membership in a management club.

•   •   •   •   •   •   •   •   •

Seemingly, each person has his own ideas concerning the meaning of the term "management." Some use the word "management" as a collective noun and refer to management as a certain group of persons within an organization. Others define management as a process calling for the performance of specific functions, and there are those who view management as a profession, a science, or an art. Management is also regarded as an academic discipline and field of study. Each of these concepts of management reflects a different aspect of the nature of management. Serious study of management requires a relatively precise definition, and as a means of developing such a definition, let us examine more closely the nature of management.

THE NATURE OF MANAGEMENT

It is said that the lead sentence of a news story should answer the following questions: who, what, when, where, why, and how? These are questions that must also be answered in respect to management so that a precise definition can be developed. In Case Problem 1-A, A Problem in Management Definition, one question to be resolved is the *who* of management: Who is considered a member of management? However, before the *who* of management can be determined, it is necessary to know *what* management does, *how* it is done, *when* management becomes necessary, *where* management is found, and *why* management is necessary. These key questions form the broad organizational outline of the first part of this chapter.

The Need for Management

Our discussion of the need for management answers two of the key questions: *why* and *when*?

One of the best illustrations of the need, or the *why*, of management is found in an announcement reporting a change in the management of a given company. Typically, it is stated that the president of the company has been replaced, though the word "resigned" may be used, and that several vice-presidents have also "resigned." These changes result in the formation of a new management team. One can infer from these changes that something happened which incurred the displeasure of some of the stockholders or the directors of the company. The reasons for the dissatisfaction vary with each situation and range from personal misconduct on the part of the officers replaced to downright ineptness in their handling of the affairs of the company.

Assuming the reason is incompetence, one might raise the question, "Why weren't all of the company's workers fired instead of the president and a few of the other officers?" The answer to this question, in part, defines one facet of the nature of management: *Management is responsible for the success or failure of a business*. If such were not the case, the owners (stockholders) might well have decided to discharge all the workers. Thus, it is apparent that a management is needed to direct the affairs of a company. This need for management is succinctly stated in the phrase, "to run the business." The statement that management is responsible for the success or failure of a business tells us *why* we need a management, but it does not indicate *when* management is needed.

Whenever men form a group, which by definition consists of more than one person, and that group has an objective, it becomes necessary for the group to work together in order to attain their stated objective. Members of the group must subordinate their individual desires to some extent to attain the group goal, and management should provide leadership for group action.

It can be argued that management exists even in the coordination of the efforts of only two individuals. Assume that you and a friend have been driving and run out of gas a few blocks from a service station. You decide it is much quicker to push the car to the station rather than walk to the station and carry the gas back to the car. You then agree that the strength of both of you is required to push the car. Further, you agree that the effort must be exerted at the same time. Once this determination has been reached, your efforts must be coordinated, and both of you must push at the same time. An agreement that one person is to give the signal, "push," makes that person a manager at the time he gives the command. Thus, the question *when* is answered by stating that management is needed whenever there is a group with stated objectives.

The Functions of Management

An analysis of the functions of management tells us *what* management does. Also, an analysis of the functions of management provides the first step in the development of a precise definition of the word "management."

When studying management as an academic discipline, it is necessary to consider management as a *process*. When management is regarded as a process, it can be analyzed and described in terms of several major functions. However, a word of caution is necessary. In discussing the process of management, it is convenient, and even necessary, to describe and study each function of the process separately. As a result, it may seem that the management process is a series of discrete functions with each function fitting neatly into a separate compartment. Nothing could be further from the truth, yet the process must be subdivided with each component part discussed separately so that it may be readily understood. In practice, a manager may, and often does, perform simultaneously, or at least as a part of a continuum, all of the following four functions: planning, organizing, directing, and controlling.

Planning. When management is viewed as a process, planning is the first function performed. Once objectives have been determined, the means necessary to achieve these stated objectives are presented as plans. An organization's plans determine the course it takes and provide a basis for estimating the degree of probable success it will have in fulfilling its objectives. Plans are prepared for activities that require many years to complete; they are also necessary for short-term projects. Examples of long-range planning are found in product development programs and in the plans that guide the financing of a company. At the other end of the time scale, a production supervisor plans the output of his department for a period of one day and for a whole week. Each of these examples represents extremes in the time span covered by the planning process, and each is necessary for the achievement of stated company objectives.

Organizing. In order to carry out plans after they have been prepared, it is necessary to create an organization. It is a function of management to determine the type of organization required to execute stated plans. The kind of organization that is developed determines to a large extent whether or not the plans are fulfilled. In turn, the objectives of an enterprise and the plans required to meet these objectives have a direct bearing upon the characteristics and structure of the organization. A company whose objective is to provide food and shelter to the traveling public requires an entirely different organization than a firm whose objective is to transmit natural gas through a pipeline.

Directing. The third function of management—directing—has been termed motivating, leading, guiding, stimulating, and actuating. Although each of these words has a different connotation, any one of these terms indicates clearly that this function of management is concerned with the human factors of an organization. It is as a result of the efforts of each member of an organization that goals are attained; hence, a major function of the management process is to direct the organization so that objectives may be achieved.

Controlling. The last phase of the management process is the control function. The control function measures present performance in relation to expected standards of performance, and as a result of such comparison, it can be determined whether or not corrective action is needed to bring present performance in line with the expected performance expressed as standards. The control function is exercised continuously, and, although related to the functions of organizing and directing, it is more closely associated with the planning function. The corrective action of control almost invariably calls for a restatement of plans. As a result, many students of the management process consider the planning and control functions as part of a continuous cycle of planning-control-planning.

Management as a Group

One of the questions asked at the beginning of the chapter is whether or not management may be regarded as a group of people—the *who* of management. To some it is unfortunate that the word management is used as a collective noun to designate a group of managers instead of limiting the use of the word to describe the specific processes of planning, organizing, directing, and controlling. Nonetheless, reference to management as a group is deeply imbedded in our everyday language, and clarification of who is normally considered a member of management is needed.

Managers are those persons in an organization who accomplish their work primarily by directing the work of others. Some of the managers of the J. B. White Company, Case Problem 1-A, are seeking an answer to the question, who is eligible to join the management club? Stated another way, who are the persons in the J. B. White Company performing any or all of the functions of planning, organizing, directing, and controlling?

In a typical corporation there are a board of directors, a president, a group of vice-presidents or major executives, managers of divisions or departments, and supervisors of specific areas or functions who report to the manager of that department. Reporting to a departmental supervisor are workers whose function is the performance of specific duties assigned by the supervisor. There is general agreement that those persons who direct the work of others are a part of management. In addition, there are some who do not direct the work of others, yet participate in planning, organizing, or controlling. These people are usually referred to as staff specialists, rather than managers, and are also considered a part of management. Persons who perform relatively specific and routine duties under the direction of a manager or a staff specialist are called operative personnel and are not classed as a part of management.

As a rule, the distribution of a manager's time spent in the performance of each of the four functions of management—planning, organizing, directing, and controlling—is a function of his position in the organization. The major executives of a company devote much of their time to planning and organizing. They are charged with policy making, a form of planning, and they must also determine the organization necessary to execute these policies. On the other hand, a departmental supervisor directs the operative personnel in his department and is responsible for the amount and quality of work produced. Consequently, a large portion of his time is spent in directing and controlling the efforts of his subordinates.

Is Management a Profession?

The question is often asked: Is management a profession? It is also frequently asked whether management is a science or an art. If a profession is defined as an occupation that serves others, it is possible to consider management a profession. However, if a profession is thought of as a vocation requiring licensing and graduate study, such as medicine and law, then management is not a profession. It is not particularly important to categorize management as either a profession, a science, or an art; but there are certain characteristics implied by each of these designations that are worth discussing.

There is a body of knowledge that is peculiar to the study of management. Over the years certain principles of management have been developed, and there is a vast amount of technical information related to the management of specialized areas such as production, sales, finance, and personnel. Thus, in respect to specialized knowledge, management is a technical field that requires mastery. One of the reasons for studying a course in principles of management is to become acquainted with some of this information. However, neither a license nor a degree is required in order to practice as a manager. The absence of formal licensing and educational requirements is essentially sound because it places the emphasis where it belongs: on performance rather than on academic training. Although academic training is to be highly regarded, access to the field of management should not be limited only to those persons who have completed a prescribed course of study. Nonetheless, a trained manager usually performs better than his untrained counterpart, particularly in today's complex industrial society.

Is Management a Science or an Art?

A discussion of management as a science or an art seldom resolves the question conclusively to anyone's satisfaction. However, since the question is raised frequently in management literature, it is well to establish a point of reference so that each student may answer the question to his own satisfaction. Frederick W. Taylor is usually considered the father of "scientific management." His contributions to management, along with those of other pioneers in the field, are discussed in the following chapter. The use of the phrase, scientific management, in connection with the work of Taylor implies that there is some other form of management. Is the type of management that is not scientific the management described by the phrase, "art of management"?

Historically, scientific management is defined as management that uses the methods of science in making its decisions and evaluating its subsequent courses of action. Every effort is made to obtain complete, valid, reliable information pertinent to the problem under consideration before a decision is made. Under these conditions the decision is consistent with and derived from the obtained information, and subsequent courses of action are subject to rigorous control procedure as a further check upon the correctness of the original decision. The antithesis of the scientific approach is management that operates "by the seat of its pants." It is an approach to management that places emphasis upon sources of information such as personal experiences, intuition, and hunches—all of which have unknown reliability and validity.

The art of management refers specifically to the practice of management. There are many phases of business operations that are not readily amenable to rigorous examination and control. Consequently, information developed in these fields is less precise than information obtained by means of the scientific method. As a result, a greater emphasis is placed upon the individual manager's past experience and judgment than is placed upon his knowledge resulting from a technical course of study, such as engineering or accounting. The solutions to problems involving human relations call upon skills developed primarily through experience. When these skills are practiced smoothly and successfully by a manager, they are often regarded as an art; yet in their development and acquisition, they differ only in degree, not in kind, from skills and knowledge acquired through the more critical methods of science.

A Definition of Management

The basic questions raised at the beginning of this chapter concerning the nature of management have been discussed and partially answered. It is shown that a definite need for management exists if a group is to obtain its desired objectives. The major functions of management—planning, organizing, directing, and controlling—are outlined. Those persons in an organization who are normally considered managers and referred to as members of management are differentiated from nonmanagerial employees because they perform in some measure the four managerial functions of planning, organizing, directing, and controlling and because they share the responsibility for meeting organizational goals. There is a clarification of the use of such terms as science, art, and profession as applied to management.

It is necessary to develop a precise definition of management as a basis for our study of the principles of management. There are three parts to a definition of management as a process: first, the coordination of resources; second, the performance of managerial functions as a means of achieving coordination; and, third, establishing the purpose of the management process. Each part is discussed separately.

1. The first aspect of a definition of management is coordination. Remember the elementary example mentioned earlier of the two students who agree that together they can push a car but that individually they cannot. The coordination required in that situation is the coordination of effort so that both can push at the same time. What does the manager of an enterprise coordinate? He coordinates the resources of the organization; namely, money, materials, and men.

   In a business enterprise, and for that matter in most organized groups, a prime requirement is money. There is seldom an organization without some measure of capital, a requisite for fraternal, social, and religious groups as well as for business organizations. Materials include the physical properties of a business, such as production equipment, plant facilities, and inventories. The people who are members of the organization are the third element. These three elements form a convenient mnemonic device: the three M's of management—money, materials, and men. And, although an over-simplification, this device is an aid in remembering the coordinative aspect of management.

2. The coordination of the resources of an organization is achieved by means of the managerial functions of planning, organizing, directing, and controlling.

3. A definition of management as the coordination of resources through the utilization of the functions of the management process is not complete. Management is a *telic,* or purposive, process; it is directed toward the attainment of stated goals or objectives. Without an objective, there is no goal to reach nor can there be a path to follow. The concept of goal orientation and the subsequent state-ment of that goal as an objective provide the purposive characteris-tic of management.

From the above discussion a definition of management may be stated: *Management is the coordination of all resources through the processes of planning, organizing, directing, and controlling in order to attain stated objectives.*

The Universality of Management

The definition of management as a purposive, coordi-native process is universal in its application to all forms of group endeavor. It is not confined to business enterprises alone, but is ap-plicable whenever man attempts to reach a stated goal through group effort. The concept of universality of management is also applicable to all levels of managers within an organization and is not confined to the top echelon only. Every manager and every staff specialist of an organization participates in the coordination of resources, the exercise of one or all of the managerial functions, and all are working to achieve the stated objectives.

Principles of Management

Science is concerned with observation. As observa-tions are recorded and verified, they become facts. Eventually many facts pertaining to a given field of study or a specific phenomenon are collected and questions arise concerning the possibility of causal relationships that might exist between the observed facts. Untested statements concerning causal relationships that might exist between observed phenomena are called *hypotheses*. As hypotheses are verified and arranged within a conceptual framework, they are referred to as *principles. A principle is a fundamental observation concerning causal relationships*. Eventually, after repeated verification and testing, principles may be stated as scientific laws. However, the laws of science are not immutable; instead, they are subject to continued verification and even modification as additional knowledge is acquired.

Principles of management are fundamental observations concerning the causal relationships between managerial action and the subsequent effect of that action upon the attainment of organizational objectives. Principles should be stated in such a manner that it is possible to predict the outcome that might reasonably be expected to result from a given course of managerial action. Principles are stated positively; that is, the accepted managerial action that is associated with the desired result is presented rather than stating the inappropriate action that would lead to undesirable or unwanted results. The statement of a principle implies a value system, since a principle says in effect, "If you do this you can expect *good* results." The definition of *good* is not too difficult since management is a purposive process directed toward the attainment of organizational objectives. Therefore, if such action leads to a realization of these goals it may be considered *good* because it contributes to organizational objectives.

There are those who criticize the use of the phrase *principles of management* on the grounds that such principles have not been verified by the rigorous methods of science. There is virtually no experimental data to support generally accepted management principles, and, for that matter, there is very little statistical, or normative, data to support these principles. Nonetheless, the presentation of principles serves several useful purposes.

The statement of an observation of questionable validity as a principle might serve to motivate some researcher to test the accuracy or worth of the principle. In addition to this possible long-range value that may result from the statement of principles, management principles are of immediate value to both student and practitioner. For the student, principles form the outline of a conceptual framework of tested observations concerning the practice of management. Establishing such a frame of reference makes it easier to assimilate and remember new information and to relate the information gained from the study of other courses in the business curriculum. For the practitioner, principles offer useful guides and a series of checkpoints that are of value in predicting the probable success of a contemplated course of action.

Students and practitioners alike should be wary of the "practical man" (usually spelled with a capital *P*) who is reported to have achieved great success and who has never read or even heard of a single principle of management. It is quite possible that he is successful, but no one knows how much more successful he might have been had he applied established principles of management.

THE SYSTEMS CONCEPT AND THE MANAGEMENT PROCESS

Defining management as a purposive, coordinative process provides a useful basis for the study of management. However, it is necessary to place the management process in proper perspective. Management does not occur as an isolated phenomenon; rather, the functions of management are performed as part of a much larger environment. In order to appreciate the complexity of the processes of management, and at the same time gain a greater appreciation of the manager's job, we must develop a way of describing and relating those factors, both internal and external, that influence the management process. A systems approach to the management process offers a means of appreciating the internal complexities of the management process and, at the same time, relating those processes to the larger environment in which management occurs.[1]

Systems Theory

Systems theory is a way of interpreting objects and events. The definition of a system is relatively simple and easy to understand. In its simplest form, *a system is composed of parts that are interrelated in a manner that forms a unified whole that is more than a mere summation of the parts*. A table or a chair may be considered a system since the parts are arranged in a manner that forms a whole that is *more than* a simple summation of the parts. *More than* means that the distinguishing characteristic of the whole is a configuration

---

[1] Robert Chin, "The Utility of Systems Models and Developmental Models for Practitioners." From Warren G. Bennis, Kenneth D. Benne, and Robert Chin, *The Planning of Change* (New York: Holt, Rinehart, and Winston, Inc., 1961). Mr. Chin presents a sound discussion of several types of systems and develops models for each type of system. He also discusses developmental models and their application.

which is dependent upon the interrelationships of the parts rather than being derived from the characteristics of each individual part. Tables are recognized as such because at least three legs support a plane surface in a way that provides the utility factors normally ascribed to a table. It makes no difference whether the shape of the surface is round, square, or hexagonal, or whether the legs are carved, metal, or six in number; if they are arranged in a certain way, we recognize the whole as a table. A slightly more complex example of a system is an automobile. The idea is the same—the parts are arranged and function in a manner that produces a unified whole.

Thought processes are events that can be reduced to writing and arranged in logical patterns. As a result, there are philosophical systems, economic systems, and number systems. Other events that are described as systems are the relationships between people; e.g., social systems, governmental systems, and legal systems.

A still more complex example of a system incorporates features that permit the system to modify its normal way of functioning so that the system adapts to changes as they occur in any of its parts (sometimes called subsystems) or to changes that occur in the larger external environment in which the system operates. Such systems are self-correcting and are called *servo systems*. The corrective action of a servo system is dependent upon the existence of one or more "feedback loops" that provide contact with the external environment or between the component subsystems. The thermostatically controlled household furnace is an example of a simple servo system. The wall thermostat is the feedback loop (and a subsystem) that maintains contact with the external environment (the temperature of the room), and the thermostat in the plenum chamber is the feedback loop (also a subsystem) that prevents the entire system from over heating.

Management and the Systems Concept

The management process occurs within an organizational system. Any organization—whether it be a business firm or a religious, educational, or social institution—is in turn a part of a larger socioeconomic system. As yet there is no single systems category that adequately describes a business firm. To the economist the firm is an economic system, but a treasurer or financial analyst may regard the firm as a system of "cash flow." To others a company is best described as a social system, a production system, or an information-decision-making system. There is evidence to support each point of view.

Regarding a company as a system has several far-reaching implications. For the major executives of a company it means that larger systems must be identified and understood and that the relationships of their company to these larger systems must be defined. Usually such recognition and definition lead to the conclusion that any one firm is, in effect, a subsystem. The company itself is composed of many subsystems with each subsystem having its own goals and objectives. Further, each subsystem within a company is part of a larger external system, not necessarily the same system defined by the major executives. For the chief executive the primary external system may be the government, but the head of the industrial relations department is more closely tied to union organizations as an external system. The sales manager may consider his external systems environment the purchasing departments of the company's customers. The systems concept stresses the dynamic nature of an organization and prevents the manager from viewing his job as one of managing static, isolated elements of the organization.[2]

The four functions of the management process may be considered a system, and each of the functions—planning, organizing, directing, and controlling—may be regarded as a separate subsystem. The functions are interrelated, and the effectiveness of any one managerial function is dependent upon the execution of the other three functions. Planning requires information from the activities of organizing, directing, and controlling, and when plans are developed they may result in change in the organization structure; those who direct the organization must be aware of plans, and provisions must be made for proper controls to determine whether or not these plans are properly executed. Similarly, changes in organization structure may call for a modification of plans, new tasks for those who direct the organization, and the modification of controls to fit the requirements of the new organization.

Each function is a subsystem dependent upon a constant feedback of information from internal and external sources. Planning requires close communication with the external environment and continuous information concerning the capabilities of the organization and the potentialities of control systems so that the feasibility of plans may be determined. The organizing function needs information descriptive of present and future manpower requirements and must interpret this information in the light of projected plans. The resultant organization

---

2 Seymour Tilles, "The Manager's Job: A Systems Approach," *Harvard Business Review*, Vol. XXXXI (January-February, 1963), pp. 73-81. Mr. Tilles defines the manager's job as one of managing systems. He must define the company as a system, establish system objectives, create formal subsystems, and integrate all subsystems.

must also provide a basis for a sound control system. The same interchange of information is needed for the functions of directing and controlling.

The effectiveness of the management process is not dependent upon success in the performance of any single managerial functional area, such as finance, sales, or production. Rather, the success of managerial action is dependent upon achieving a balanced interrelationship between the functions of the process of management and the attainment of stated goals in each of the major functional areas.[3]

ABOUT THIS BOOK

As indicated by the title, this book presents established principles of management so that they may serve as a conceptual framework for the study of management and as guides for the successful practice of management. At the same time, the concepts of systems theory are used as a basis for analyzing and understanding specific aspects of the management process. Combining traditional principles of management and a systems approach to the study of management does not call for a radically new organization of content. An analogy from the study of medicine shows why a marked departure from the traditional content pattern of management texts is unnecessary.

We no longer question the conclusion that the human organism is a system composed of many interrelated subsystems. In our everyday speech we refer to the skeletal system, the circulatory system, and the central nervous system. Yet modern textbooks of medicine reveal a judicious blending of the use of the term *system* and the study of special systems with traditionally recognized disease processes. For example, some of the major topics discussed in one outstanding medical textbook are the infectious diseases, diseases of allergy, diseases of the skin, diseases of the bronchopulmonary system, diseases of the cardiovascular system, and diseases of the kidneys.[4]

The systems concept can be applied in the same way to a textbook of management. Where pertinent, systems theory is presented and discussed so that a concept of the management process as a system gradually unfolds.

---

[3] Ernest C. Miller, *Objectives and Standards: An Approach to Planning and Control* (New York: American Management Association, AMA Research Study 74, 1966). See pages 9-21 for a discussion of the management process and an interpretation of the management process as a system.

[4] Paul B. Beeson and Walsh McDermott, *Textbook of Medicine,* 13th ed. (Philadelphia: W. B. Saunders Company, 1963), pp. xix-xlv.

Although principles of management are applicable to the management of religious, social, charitable, and educational groups, our concern is with the management of business enterprises in a political climate relatively free of governmental controls. Consequently, the illustrative material of the text and the case problems are based upon situations that occur in business organizations. Following the three introductory chapters that form the first major section of this book, the following four sections discuss each of the major functions of the management process in order—planning, organizing, directing, and controlling.

• • • • • • • • •

Case Problem 1-B is an illustration of management effort in one American corporation. This is a story of the Underwood Corporation, an organization formed over 75 years ago and regarded for many years as a successful manufacturing firm. Today the position of Underwood has changed. The reason for this change can be attributed to the management of the company, for all companies competed in the same socioeconomic environment. While reading the story of Underwood, it is well to ask yourself the following questions: (1) How effectively were the resources of the company used? (2) Were the activities of planning, organizing, controlling, and directing effectively carried out? (3) Did there appear to be a clear-cut objective for the Underwood management to reach?

When you have answered the questions asked at the end of the case problem, read the full article as it appeared in the September, 1960, issue of *Fortune,* page 141. Compare your answer to question No. 6 with what actually happened. The article on Olivetti, starting on page 137 of the same issue of *Fortune,* is of interest in this connection and presents a dramatic contrast between the two managements.

Questions for Study and Discussion

1. Should a marked decline or a sharp increase in company earnings always be attributed to the management of that company?
2. What connotations are frequently attached to the word "management"? Are any of these connotations contradictory?
3. What are the four major functions of management? Give an example of each. Which of these functions, in your opinion, is the most important in each of the following types of business: an oil pipeline transmission company, a door-to-door sales organization such as the Fuller Brush Company, a large retail discount store, and a complex multiproduct company such as General Motors?

4. Differentiate between an owner and a manager. Give an example of a manager who is also an owner and an example illustrating the separation of ownership and management.

5. Do you agree with the statement made in the text that it would be undesirable to require a prescribed course of study as a requisite for a management position? Why?

6. What is meant by the phrase "universality of management"?

7. What is the definition of management given in the text? What are the three major factors included in the definition of management? Develop a series of definitions using only two factors for each definition. Evaluate each definition thus developed in respect to its completeness.

8. Many analogies have been drawn between a business organization and an athletic team. Examples of this analogy are reflected in such phrases as "get on the team" and "let's pull together." In what respects are the jobs of a head football coach and the president of a company similar? How do their jobs differ?

9. The thermostatically controlled household furnace is cited as an example of a servo system. Describe several other familiar servo systems, and explain why each is a servo system.

10. Considering each of the functions of management as a system, describe a specific change in the control system that might occur and describe the effect of this change on each of the other functions. Be specific in your descriptions. Give specific examples of changes in planning, organizing, and methods of directing. Show how changes in any one of these functions affect the other three.

● ● ● ● ● ● ● ● ●

". . . The typewriter that John Thomas Underwood began manufacturing in 1896 had no technical equal. For a time Underwood was the Singer of typewriters, a name that was practically a synonym for the machine. Like Singer, Underwood equipped the world; one of its specially adapted export models worked in reverse for Hebrew, and another wrote Chinese characters. At home, Underwood was the standard machine used in typist schools,

---

Case Problem 1-B
What Went Wrong
at Underwood? [5]

---

and generations of office girls went out to their jobs habituated to it.

"The product's reputation was healthier than the company's management by the time founder Underwood bowed out in 1927. He was just past seventy years old, and his grip was loosening. Not for the last time in its history, Underwood looked to merger as a solution for its troubles. It joined forces with Elliott-Fisher, a small but energetic manufacturer of bookkeeping machines.

---

[5] "What Went Wrong at Underwood," *Fortune,* Vol. LXII, No. 3 (September, 1960), pp. 141, 245-46, 248, © 1962 *Time, Inc.*

Elliott-Fisher's top management moved over in the deal, and Philip D. Wagoner became chief executive officer and eventually chairman of Underwood, Elliott-Fisher (it reverted to just plain Underwood in 1945). He was to remain in that post for the next twenty-eight years.

"Wagoner had already carved out an illustrious corner in industry, and he added gloss to it by integrating Underwood, Elliott-Fisher, and its subsidiary, Sundstrand Corp., which made one of the finest adding machines of the day, into a sound and prosperous firm that made money in all but one year of the depression.

"With the benefit of hindsight, some students of Underwood's decline mark 1937 as the real turning point. In that year, Underwood's sales—$31 million —were about equal to I.B.M.'s. From then on, I.B.M. took off and increased its sales more than thirtyfold in twenty years, while Underwood's did not even triple. A look at the contrasting policies of the two corporations helps to explain why. Whereas I.B.M. kept plowing back its earnings into growth, Underwood paid out over the years an average of 87 percent of its net profits in dividends. The pittance it spent on R. and D. [research and development] was inadequate to develop new products, and as competitors introduced more advanced equipment, the Elliott-Fisher and Sundstrand machines gradually lost their markets, while the Underwood typewriter slipped behind its better designed rivals. Averse to taking chances on anything daringly new, Underwood turned down an opportunity to manufacture the electric typewriter that went to I.B.M. By the time Underwood got around to making its

own creditable machine, I.B.M. had a stranglehold on the market.

"More chances were miffed during the war. The government, somewhat mysteriously regarding typewriters as nonessential, all but suspended their manufacture, and Underwood went 100 percent into military production. But while its competitors asked for war jobs that would help improve their peacetime skills, Underwood took what it was given. It turned out a total of 600,170 complete 30-caliber carbines and 1,706,430 carbine barrels, a magnificent record, but one that contributed nothing to Underwood's future. The company threw itself so wholeheartedly into making guns that it gave no thought to postwar planning. In the reconversion, other firms in the office-equipment industry again got the jump by acquiring new plants at cut-rate prices and strengthening their managements with new talent out of the armed forces. Underwood resumed where it had left off, with the same old plants, the same old products, aging executives, and an alarming vacuum in middle management.

"The release of pent-up demand for typewriters and then another spate of defense orders during the Korean war temporarily concealed the symptoms of weakness. A high level of sales distracted attention from an ominous rise in costs, the result of overcapacity and inefficiency. Flowing dividends kept the stockholders happy.

"But the board of directors was beginning to show signs of restiveness. Wagoner had always surrounded himself with board members who were eminent in the financial community— e.g., Reeve Schley, Albert Wiggin, Charles Hayden. But he was accustomed to having his own way, and the board used to run through its business in ten or fifteen minutes. Toward the end of 1952, however, the board made two decisions of its own. The first was to buy the tiny Electronic Computer Corp. of Brooklyn, and get into the computer business. The second decision was to hire Booz, Allen & Hamilton, the management consultant firm, to get rid of one bothersome but not very important production snarl in the Hartford plant.

"Wagoner "foolishly agreed" (he has since admitted) to hiring Booz, Allen, and he soon regretted the decision. The Booz, Allen team's pursuit of the Hartford production problem led into many other aspects of the company. The consultants made some sensible and constructive recommendations for reducing overcapacity, cutting costs, and rationalizing production, many of which were eventually put into effect but too late to do much good. The immediate effect of Booz, Allen's intervention was to antagonize Underwood's senior executives and to weaken company morale.

"In 1955, Wagoner, who was then seventy-nine, finally dropped the reins; the following year he became honorary chairman of the board. His successor as chairman was Leon Stowell, who had served unobstrusively as president during the last decade of the Wagoner regime. But a new man, Fred M. Farwell, came in as president, and within a year he had replaced Stowell as chief executive officer. Farwell was a Booz, Allen recommendation, brought in because he was an experienced electronics man. Though his last job had been with S. C. Johnson & Son, Inc., the wax maker, he had previously worked for I.B.M. for twenty-two years. Farwell

had the kind of expansiveness Underwood was glaringly short of; indeed, he may have had too much of it. As another officer observed, "He'd be damned if he'd spend the rest of his life peddling adding machines and typewriters."

"Farwell abandoned the company's traditional parsimony and mounted a full-scale effort to make Underwood a name in the computer industry. To finance the excursion into electronics, the company had already borrowed liberally from the Chase Bank; Farwell raised $6 million more by an issue of convertible debentures. The trouble was that, for all his ambitious dreams, Farwell knew only the sales end of the computer business. The company remained weak in men familiar with the technical aspects. After absorbing $12 million in eighteen months, the computer project failed to develop a marketable product and had to be scrapped. This experience left grievous scars in Underwood.

"By this time, Farwell had developed doubts that Underwood had the resources by itself to make a strong showing in the office-machine business, electronic or otherwise. These doubts hardened into the conviction that "a marriage was necessary." Of the possible merger partners, Farwell preferred I.T.T. and tried to press negotiations with that company to a conclusion. The desirability of joining I.T.T. commended itself to both the old-timers and the newcomers at Underwood, and it also promised advantages to I.T.T., which was seeking to balance its flourishing defense and foreign business with an entry into the U.S. consumer market. But just when a meeting of minds seemed imminent, General William

Harrison died suddenly, and I.T.T.'s new president, General Edmond Leavey, considered that he had too much on his hands to take on Underwood.

"Farwell's next prospect was National Cash Register, which eventually made an offer to buy up Underwood stock on an exchange basis of slightly more than half an N.C.R. share for each Underwood share, or at the market equivalent of about $30 a share. Farwell believed this was a fair price, and the best Underwood could get in the circumstances. But a majority of the Underwood board disagreed and voted the offer down. The opponents balked mainly at the price, but behind their objection was also the fear that Underwood would lose its identity if N.C.R. took it over. They nourished the hope that the company could hold out for a better deal.

"Repudiated, Farwell resigned in mid-1957. The new chief executive officer, Frank E. Beane, had joined Underwood as controller, also with the recommendation of Booz, Allen. He had had extensive experience in finance, beginning with a prewar job in his father's firm, Fenner & Beane (which later became part of Merrill Lynch, Pierce, Fenner & Smith). Charming and persuasive, Beane entered office on the premise that the company could be saved and restored to a profit position without merger. At the time, he really believed he could bring it off, but at any rate, as he argued, the only sensible course was to act as if he could. For if merger proved to be the only salvation, the company would do far better dealing from strength. Underwood already looked somewhat shopworn after the well-publicized N.C.R. negotiations. Under the impression that a sellout was inevitable, dealers were quitting and employees were worrying about their job security. Beane's contention was that by openly putting itself on the block, the company would only hasten its deterioration.

"To one board member, Beane's attempt at salvage seemed "like asking a man to run the hundred-yard dash through quicksand." But Beane was unquenchably optimistic. Annual reports and messages to stockholders glowed with assurances that recovery was just around the corner. Elaborately prepared projections carried the same theme to the board, though a few directors took a skeptical view of Beane's figures. Beane also took some long-needed action. He closed the high-cost Bridgeport plant and transferred its production to Hartford, thereby slashing the payroll by about 1,000 men and reducing the appalling overcapacity. Simultaneously, he started a program of new-product development and put designers to work remaking the face of the Underwood typewriter.

"But Underwood simply lacked the strength to bounce back. Beane did not have enough experienced office-equipment men capable of generating practical new ideas, and he lacked the money to hire them. When he launched a massive advertising campaign, it soon became apparent that the debilitated sales force was incapable of backing it up. The first telling blow to Beane's hopes was the 1957-58 recession. Typewriter manufacturers are accustomed to being hit harder than most in any general slump, but Underwood was in no shape to take this one in its stride. Early in 1958 the company was forced to lay off 80 percent of its production workers for eight weeks. So acute was the cash shortage that it had to resort to various ingenuities to maintain a facade of solvency. It made an arrangement with a finance company to finance its future installment contracts, and it sold its outstanding installment contracts to a bank. To eke out a further saving, it began delaying payments to suppliers, several of whom thereupon ceased doing business with Underwood.

"Beane finally admitted defeat in the spring of 1959, when a new adding machine, designed to replace the antiquated Sundstrand, had to be sent back to the drawing board for debugging. Without a first-rate product in the numbers field, Underwood hadn't a prayer of making out on its own. Ruefully Beane changed his attitude toward merger and stopped playing hard to get. But the question of whom to merge with soon embroiled him in the bitterest controversy of his tenure as head of the company.

"A small group of board members, notably including Joseph Thomas of Lehman Brothers, whose firm had helped to underwrite Underwood's 1956 convertible debenture issue, had held informal conversations with Charles (Tex) Thornton of Litton Industries some time before Beane had his change of heart. Litton had entered the office-equipment business by acquiring Monroe Calculating Machine Co. of Orange, New Jersey, and it expressed an interest in combining Underwood with that operation. For Underwood such a deal offered a chance to catch a ride with a fast-moving growth company.

"Beane, however, took a dim view of a Litton merger. He resented the fact that initial overtures had been made behind his back, and he was particu-

larly aroused because Thomas was both a Litton and an Underwood director, a circumstance that Beane alleged left Thomas open to a charge of conflict of interest. Beane received no support in his allegations, and Thomas stuck to his position, maintaining he was acting in the best interests of Underwood. For several months Underwood was disrupted by the spectacle of the chief executive officer feuding with one of his most respected directors. A powerful stockholder's voice might have called a halt, but Beane happened to be the board member who represented the biggest block of stock —his own 7,675 shares plus a substantial amount of convertible debentures.

"To counter Litton, Beane went looking for merger prospects of his own. For a while, Lou Chesler, the versatile Canadian promoter, tossed around the notion of combining Underwood with his Universal Controls, Inc. Beane also got nibbles from North American Aviation, Lockheed, and Howe Sound, all attracted mainly by the $16 million tax-loss carry-forward that Underwood had accumulated from 1956 through 1958. None of these possibilities ever came to the offering stage. But in April, 1959, Beane made what turned out to be his most significant move. He sent Herbert W. Bertine, the company's secretary, to Italy for an exploratory talk with Olivetti.

"Meanwhile Litton kept playing the suitor. But its reluctance to come to the point and make a firm offer gave the impression, shared even by some pro-Litton people at Underwood, that it was bent on beating the price down by waiting until Underwood wallowed further into difficulties. Finally, the board set September 30 as a deadline for Litton to commit itself.

"By September the clock was ticking loudly for Underwood. The cash shortage became so grave that, one Sunday afternoon, an Underwood executive had to put in a hurried call to the German subsidiary, Adrema Werke, requesting immediate transfer of $150,000 to meet that week's payroll. Shortly afterward, Underwood was compelled to inform the Chase Manhattan Bank that it could not make the payments due on its short-term loans. . . ."

Problems

1. Why is the year 1937 picked as a turning point in Underwood's history?
2. What basic product area was lacking in order for Underwood to grow?
3. How would you evaluate the strength of the human resources of Underwood?
4. Why did mergers appeal to Underwood's management?
5. Describe the efforts of each successive Underwood management.
6. What is your forecast for the future of Underwood?

CHAPTER 2

The Development of Management Concepts

It was six o'clock In the evening on the last Friday in April as Marsh Saunders sat at his desk organizing the impressions he had gained during his first month as plant manager for Excellent Foods, Inc. Though he had been a plant manager for Excellent Foods for more than five years, this was the first time he had managed a can manufacturing plant for the company; his previous experience had been in food processing plants. He jotted down a list of his major observations on a sheet of paper divided into two columns. The column on the left side of the page was headed "Symptoms" and the one on the right, "Causes?" The following is a copy of his notes.

Case Problem 2-A

Symptoms or Causes?

Symptoms	Causes?
1. Production—in all operating departments —assembly, shipping, lithography, and press room—operating in the red as measured by engineered standards. Losses range from −20% to −5%; average monthly loss for plant is −15%.	Machines not properly maintained. Personnel not capable, need more training. Applies to all four departments.
2. Labor relations—poor.	Every effort to increase efficiency called a speedup. Too many grievances, 150 last year. (Is this the cause of Symptom No. 1, or is it the result of poor performance?)
3. Quality—very poor, many complaints.	Operating personnel and supervisors don't seem to care. Improperly maintained and poorly adjusted equipment.
4. Housekeeping—lousy.	Entire plant dirty with nothing ever in its right place. Machine shop has no idea of spare parts inventory.
5. Quality of supervision—probably technically competent as they all came up from the ranks. Seem to be beat down, no spirit, poor human relations in all departments.	Do not consider themselves a part of management. Afraid to do anything, seem fearful of losing job. Would a guarantee of no personnel changes for six months be a good move?

Symptoms

6. Manager's staff—all heads of staff departments (industrial, engineering, personnel, purchasing, quality control, production control, and accounting) have been in their respective jobs for at least three years. No one willing to exercise authority or take responsibility—all seem mediocre in ability.

7. Low morale at all levels from the hourly production workers, through the clerical help, to supervision and staff.

Causes?

Is poor performance of this group due to lack of native ability or would additional training help? Should training be in respective technical fields or general management? Though mediocre, these people know the organization.

The plant seems to lack a common purpose or goal. An esprit de corps is completely lacking.

As he looked at this list, Mr. Saunders wondered if Symptom No. 7, poor morale, should not be listed as the number one problem in place of low production. He knew that the list was incomplete and that another 10 or 15 items could be added. He also knew that before he could start the much needed management training program, he would have to group his problems, or symptoms, into several major areas.

Problems

1. Assume that you are Mr. Saunders. How would you group the seven symptoms so that a training program could be directed toward three major subject matter areas?

2. Do you think that the headings placed at the top of each column—symptoms and causes?—are a better choice of words than problems and solutions? Why?

3. In his notes on the probable causes for Symptoms No. 2 and No. 5, Mr. Saunders raised several questions. How would you answer these questions?

4. Is there any significance in the fact that this is the first can plant that Mr. Saunders has managed?

As you read this chapter, you will discover that the problems confronting Mr. Saunders are neither new nor unique to his plant; they are as old as management itself.

● ● ● ● ● ● ● ● ●

There is considerable evidence that effective management of complex social groups has existed for well over 6,000 years. The early civilizations of the Egyptians, the Greeks, and the Roman Empire could not have existed for centuries had there not been well-developed administrative organizations and procedures. Even before these civilizations, there is reason to believe that considerable thought and effort had been expended on studying and formulating the management process.

One of the earliest analytical statements of a management problem appears in the Bible, Exodus 18:13-26. This passage tells how Jethro,

Moses' father-in-law, observed Moses spending an entire day listening to the complaints and problems of his people. Following this observation, Jethro told Moses that what he was doing was too much for one man and suggested specific steps that should be taken to relieve him of his burden. His first recommendation was that "ordinances and laws" should be taught to the people. The modern counterpart of this advice is an organization's policy statement. Secondly, he recommended that leaders be selected and assigned "to be rulers of thousands, and rulers of hundreds, and rulers of fifties, and rulers of ten." The process of appointing leaders, each of whom is responsible for a given number of subordinates, is referred to as delegation of authority. Jethro's third point, that these rulers should administer all routine matters and should bring to Moses only the important questions, forms the basis for a sound control procedure—attending to the exception that does not conform with expected results.

The recounting of Jethro's advice to Moses illustrates the fact that interest in management as a process existed in antiquity. However, the literature of industrial management appears at a much later date. Imagine that you are passing through an archway into a room containing the major writings in the field of management. Look at the archway, and you will see that it has three distinct parts. There is a vertical column on each side of you and directly overhead is an arch that connects these two columns, thus forming a unified whole. The literature of management which is housed in this room describes three separate approaches to problems of management and, like the parts of an archway, may be arranged so that they form a unified whole.

The first of these approaches, one of the two vertical columns of the archway, emphasizes the importance of establishing sound practices of *human relations* as a means of improving the management process. Writers who stress the importance of human relations are concerned with the human element in management. This point of view is convincing, for there are many instances where improved relationships between management and the workers and among the workers themselves have solved the problems of a particular company. The second approach, the other vertical column of the archway, places its emphasis upon *production*. The group of writers who follow this approach believe that managers should direct their attention and energy to increasing the efficiency of the production process. As might be expected, there are many instances where conflict arises between those who regard a company's problems as primarily questions to be resolved through the application of practices intended to improve human relations and those who believe that the company's problems are to be solved by increased efficiency of the production process. The third approach to the problems of management is similar to the arch, or curved portion, of the archway. Like the arch, this approach is a separate member of the archway; at the same time it connects the two vertical columns and, thus, forms a unified whole. The "arch" that binds together the two separate approaches, human relations and production efficiency, consists of those writings that emphasize the *administration* of the entire organization.

These three basic concepts that form the archway leading into the literature of management are discussed in the following order:

1. A review of several of the major writings in the field of human relations.
2. A discussion of some of the work that emphasizes production.
3. A summary of the principles of administration.

THE EMPHASIS UPON HUMAN RELATIONS

Robert Owen

Robert Owen, a successful textile mill manager in Scotland from 1800 to 1828, made some remarkable observations concerning the factors which influenced the productivity of the personnel in his plants. He referred to his employees as "vital machines," and in describing how they should be regarded and treated, he compared the importance and nature of "vital machines" with the "inanimate machines" of the factory. A summary of his position was presented in "An Address: To the Superintendents of Manufacturies, and to those Individuals generally, who, by giving Employment to an aggregated Population, may easily adopt the means to form the Sentiments and Manners of such a Population." The date of publication of this address was 1813, and in some ways it foreshadows the conclusions of the famous Hawthorne Studies of Mayo which were not undertaken until more than a century later.[1]

Owen stated that it was generally accepted that mechanical equipment kept in a state of good repair more than paid for itself by its increased productivity and longer life. Reasoning by analogy, he concluded that if this were true for the "inanimate machines," it should also be true for the "vital machines." He applied this conclusion to his

---

[1] Robert Owen, *A New View of Society* (1st American ed. from the 3d London ed.; New York: E. Bliss & F. White, 1825), pp. 57-62. Reprinted in H. F. Merrill (ed.), *Classics in Management* (New York: American Management Association, 1960), pp. 21-25.

own plants in New Lanark, Scotland, and claimed that as a result of attention to his personnel, he was receiving more than a 50 percent return on any money so spent. The summation of his position follows:

> And when it was perceived that inanimate mechanism was greatly improved by being made firm and substantial, that it was the essence of economy to keep it neat, clean, regularly supplied with the best substance to prevent unnecessary friction, and, by proper provision for the purpose, to preserve it in good repair, it was natural to conclude that the more delicate, complex, living mechanism would be equally improved by being trained to strength and activity; and that it would also prove true economy to keep it neat and clean; to treat it with kindness, that its mental movements might not experience too much irritating friction; to endeavor by every means to make it more perfect; to supply it regularly with a sufficient quantity of wholesome food and other necessaries of life, that the body might be preserved from being out of repair, or falling prematurely to decay.[2]

George Elton Mayo

Closely related to the work of Owen, though separated by slightly more than 100 years, are the efforts of George Elton Mayo and his team of Harvard researchers. Mayo was born and educated in Australia, came to the United States in 1922, and was first associated with the University of Pennsylvania. In 1926, he joined the faculty of Harvard University, where he remained until his retirement in 1947. One of his early studies, completed while he was at Pennsylvania, illustrates clearly the results that may be expected by following Owen's admonition "to treat it (the vital machine) with kindness, that its mental movements might not experience too much irritating friction." Appropriately, the title given to this work is "The First Inquiry."[3]

"The First Inquiry." Mayo and his group were asked to solve an industrial problem, the symptoms of which were an excessive turnover of employees in a certain department of a Philadelphia textile mill. The department in question was that of the mule-spinners, whose annual turnover rate was nearly 250 percent while that of other departments in the mill was between 5 and 6 percent. Several consulting firms, then called efficiency engineers, had previously worked on the problem and,

---

[2] H. F. Merrill, *ibid.*, pp. 23-24.

[3] Elton Mayo, *The Social Problems of an Industrial Civilization* (Boston: Division of Research, Graduate School of Business Administration, Harvard University, 1945). Portions of this work and the Hawthorne Studies are reprinted in H. F. Merrill, *ibid.*, pp. 407-36.

among other things, had established a financial incentive plan. The reasoning behind this approach assumed that man is an economic animal, and, as such, he will respond to financial incentive or reward. However, this was not the case, for not once had the men in the department produced enough to earn the rewards of the financial incentive plan. The morale of the department was low. There were many complaints of foot trouble, neuritis, and other miscellaneous aches and pains. The men were working five 10-hour days each week with the day being broken only by a 45-minute lunch period at the end of the first five hours. There were no rest periods during the day, and since the men were on their feet continually, there was reason to believe that fatigue might be playing an important part in creating their general feelings of depression.

The experiment began with the introduction of rest periods for some of the workers in the mule-spinner's department. But rest alone was not the only changed condition in the experiment. The problem had been discussed with all employees in the department, and, as a result, they were made to feel a part of the whole program. In addition, these men were fondly attached to the manager of the plant, a colonel with whom many had served in World War I. They were confident that if the rest periods worked for the experimental group, about one third of the workers, all of them would soon have rest periods because of the essential fairness of "The Colonel."

The results of the experiment were almost immediate, not only for the third who received the rest periods, but also for the two thirds who served as the control group and did not receive rest periods but who had taken part in discussing the problem. For the first time since the installation of the incentive bonus plan by the efficiency engineers, the mule-spinners earned incentive pay. This continued for a period of four and one-half months, until February 15, 1923. Then, within a period of seven days the entire department had returned to their initial pessimism and production dropped to its former low level.

What had happened? Nothing that had not happened thousands of times in industrial plants prior to this experiment and thousands of times since this study. There was a sudden demand for the product of the textile mill, and, as a result, the supervisor in the department simply ordered the abandonment of all rest periods. The results were immediate and well-nigh disastrous. The sequel to this supervisor's ill-advised, albeit typical, act is often overlooked. The Colonel, the manager in whom the men had complete personal confidence, took immediate charge. He reinstated the four rest periods and guaranteed that every employee would have two 10-minute rest periods in the morning and two in the afternoon. Practically everyone, except the Colonel himself, doubted that this loss of 40 minutes a day per man could be made up since the machines could not be speeded up. However, the Colonel was right. During the month of April the men made a bonus, and the rate of production continued to climb until the efficiency figures were well above 85 percent, a considerable change from the March low of 70 percent. In addition to reestablishing the rest periods in a manner which had left no doubt in anyone's mind as to what the management believed, the Colonel had done something else of great significance. He had delegated responsibility to the men themselves. Each group of three men was to determine the exact time when the group would take its individual rest periods, but each knew that, without fail, the group would receive four such periods a day. Thus, a guaranteed policy of management and the fact that the workers themselves were to participate to some extent in the decisions involved had turned the tide.

The Hawthorne Studies. Shortly after completing his work, "The First Inquiry," Mayo joined the faculty of Harvard University where, as head of the Industrial Research Department, he led a series of pioneering studies at the Hawthorne plant of the Western Electric Company.[4] Initially, the purpose of the study was to determine the effect of illumination upon the output of workers; however, at a later date, the studies sought to determine methods of establishing teamwork and continuing cooperation in industrial groups.

In the illumination study, workers were divided into two groups—an experimental group and a control group. Lighting conditions for the experimental group were varied from 24 to 46 to 70 footcandles in intensity while the lighting of the control group remained constant. As expected, the output of the experimental group increased with each increase in light intensity, but the performance of the control group was not expected. Their production increased at about the same rate as the production of the experimental group. Later, the light of the experimental group was reduced from 10 to 3 footcandles. Again, the output of the experimental group continued to increase, and so did the output of the control group. Finally, a decline in productivity of the

---

[4] There have been several major books published by Mayo and his coworkers describing the extensive work completed at Western Electric. Among them are the following:

Elton Mayo, *The Human Problems of an Industrial Civilization* (Boston: Division of Research, Harvard Business School; 2d ed.; New York: Macmillan, 1946).

F. J. Roethlisberger and W. J. Dickson, *Management and the Worker* (Harvard University Press, 1939, 10th printing, 1950).

F. J. Roethlisberger, *Management and Morale* (Harvard University Press, 1942).

experimental group did occur, but only when the intensity of light was low enough to approach the level of moonlight. Clearly, something other than illumination was the cause of changes in productivity.

Similar results were obtained in the relay assembly test room experiment, only this time the variable was the amount of rest, rather than lighting, to determine the effects of fatigue on productivity. First, normal production was established, then rest periods of varying lengths and frequency were introduced. Production increased with the increase in frequency and length of rest periods. Finally, in Period XII of the experiments, it was decided to return to the original conditions: no formal rest periods, no lunches, and a full 48-hour week. The return to the original conditions did not result in the expected drop in production; instead, production stayed at its usual high level.

The Hawthorne studies showed quite plainly that factors other than environmental working conditions and the physiological state of the worker had a marked influence on productivity. These factors were recognized as social in nature. The workers of these studies were the subject of experiments of interest to the managers of the plant and their immediate supervisors, and the workers knew that they were participating in experiments that were of interest to management. They responded to these social forces rather than to the experimentally in-duced changes in the external physical environment. Many consider Period XII of the studies concerned with the effect of fatigue a turning point in our understanding of human relations because the importance of attitudes toward work, toward management, and toward the work group is recognized as vitally significant.

Summary

Robert Owen urged his contemporaries to concern themselves with the social well-being of their employees both in the community and on the job. In doing this, he recognized that man is essentially a social being. He also stated that if the personal and social needs of employees were attended to, the economic repayment for such attention would take care of itself. Indeed, he claimed that he was receiving a payment on money so invested in excess of 50 percent and soon expected a return of 100 percent. When Mayo first entered the textile mill in Philadelphia, the men were not behaving as the economic creatures that the incentive plan implied or assumed they were. When their personal needs were attended to——their physical condition recog-nized and corrected——and when they were viewed as social beings, through a discussion of their problems with them, the results were almost immediate. True, the rest periods helped, but the key to the solution is the fact that initially all employees in the department showed an increase in production. And, the increase was not limited to the one third receiving the rest period.

Several conclusions from Owen and Mayo can be drawn at this time. First, man is essentially a social being, not economic, and should be regarded as such. Second, as a social being he is a member of a group; therefore, it is the group that should be approached to participate in discussing their problems and in determining the solution. There is a third conclusion to be drawn from a study of these two works. Mayo touches on this point only lightly and Owen not at all, although in the case of the latter, it might have been considered immodest if he had. In both instances, the men running the company (Owen in New Lanark, Scotland, and the "Colonel" in Philadelphia) were leaders and were even perceived as such by the employees. Both were men who "knew" when they were right, and both were sincere in their desire to do the best that they could for the physical well-being of their employees. However, these attributes on their part were not sufficient without a reciprocal feeling on the part of the employees. In each instance, the employees had strong feelings of confidence regarding the ability and sincerity of their leader. Therefore, it is clear that for any successful program in human relations there must be a leader with ability and sincerity, and these traits must be recognized by his employees.

THE EMPHASIS UPON PRODUCTION

Charles Babbage

Charles Babbage, a contemporary of Robert Owen, laid the groundwork for much of the work that later became known as "scientific management." However, Robert Owen and Charles Babbage had little in common, for the latter was primarily a scientist and mathematician rather than the operating head of a company. A project which he worked on throughout his life and, unfortunately, was never successful in fully developing was the "Difference Engine," an invention considered to be the forerunner of our modern data processing equipment. His interest about production problems resulted in two contributions that are as valid today as when they were first presented. The first contribution stresses the importance of dividing and assigning labor on the basis of skill. The second contribution provides a means of determining the feasibility of replacing manual operations with automatic machinery.

Division of Labor. In 1832, in his "On the Economy of Machinery and Manufactures,"[5] Babbage presented a keen analysis of the alternative methods then available in making pins. In his analysis of making pins by hand, he offers convincing and complete data showing that a division of labor on the basis of skill is an economic necessity. He cites as advantages of dividing labor by its level of skill the fact that the learning time is reduced, since any one worker has to learn only one skill rather than all. Secondly, in the actual process of manufacturing, there is a saving because less time is lost as the result of changing from one set of skills to another. He also points out that a high degree of precision can be acquired by each workman, for he is learning only one task and repeating it many times. In addition, since the job is broken down into its component parts on a basis of the skills required, there is the obvious possibility of developing specialized tools and equipment to further aid the process. All of these observations result in the conclusion that dividing a job into its component levels of skill enables the manufacturer to acquire and pay for only the exact amount of skill required for each operation.

Manual vs. Automatic Operations. Following his discussion on the art of making pins by hand, Babbage then mentions briefly a new (remember, 1832) American process of making pins by machine. He suggests several questions, the answers to which determine whether or not the introduction of machine methods is desirable:

1. To what defects pins so made (i.e., by machine) are liable?

2. What advantages they possess over those made in the usual way?

3. What is the prime cost of a machine for making them?

4. What is the expense of keeping it in repair?

5. What is the expense of moving it and attending to it?[6]

These questions are as important today as they were when originally asked by Babbage more than 100 years ago in that they raise questions concerning quality, the original cost of the machine, and the cost of operation including manpower and maintenance. Much of management's effort is directed toward obtaining an answer to these questions.

---

[5] Charles Babbage, *On the Economy of Machinery and Manufactures* (Philadelphia: Carey and Lea, 1932), Chap. 17, pp. 121-40, "On the Division of Labour" reprinted in H. F. Merrill, *ibid.*, pp. 29-44.

[6] H. F. Merrill, *ibid.*, p. 43.

Frederick Winslow Taylor

By far the ablest exponent of the probing, analytical attitude expressed by Babbage was Frederick W. Taylor, commonly regarded as the father of scientific management. All of you have without doubt heard the phrase "scientific management" before reading it in this book, yet how many of you can offer a satisfactory definition of the phrase? Let us approach the problem of defining scientific management by stating what scientific management is not. There is no better source than the words of Taylor himself.

Scientific management is not any efficiency device, nor a device of any kind for securing efficiency; nor is it any branch or group of efficiency devices. It is not a new system of figuring costs; it is not a new scheme of paying men; it is not a piecework system; it is not a bonus system; it is not a premium system; it is no scheme for paying men; it is not holding a stopwatch on a man and writing things down about him; it is not time study; it is not motion study nor an analysis of the movements of men; it is not the printing and ruling and unloading of a ton or two of blanks on a set of men and saying, "Here's your system; go use it." It is not divided foremanship of functional foremanship; it is not any of the devices which the average man calls to mind when scientific management is spoken of. The average man thinks of one or more of these things when he hears the words "scientific management" mentioned, but scientific management is not any one of these devices. I am not sneering at cost-keeping systems, at time study, at functional foremanship, nor at any new and improved scheme of paying men, not at any efficiency devices, if they are really devices that make for efficiency, I believe in them; but what I am emphasizing is that these devices in whole or in part are not scientific management, they are useful adjuncts to scientific management, so are they also useful adjuncts of other systems of management.[7]

The list of what scientific management is not is rather complete, but if it is not any of these techniques, all of which in some form or other have been designed to render the management of a shop more efficient, then what is it? Other questions that come to mind at this time refer specifically to the phrase "scientific management." Who coined the phrase and why was it applied to the systems developed and espoused by Taylor? And what did Taylor do that resulted in his

---

[7] H. F. Merrill, *ibid.*, p. 77. The above passage is an exerpt from testimony of Frederick W. Taylor at hearings before the Special Committee of the House of Representatives to Investigate the Taylor and Other Systems of Shop Management, January 25, 1912, p. 1387.

testifying before a special committee of the House of Representatives? The answers to these questions shed much light upon some of the problems still facing management today.

Scientific Management—A Mental Revolution. Consider first the words "scientific management," which to some epitomize the best of our modern industrial society, and to others, the undesirable aspects of the same. The name was not an accident; it was the result of a deliberate choice made during a meeting held in the apartment of one of Taylor's friends and associates, H. L. Gantt, a short time before the congressional hearings began. Other names were considered, such as the Taylor system, functional management, and shop management; but the group decided that henceforth, and particularly during the hearings, the system developed and typified by Taylor's work would be referred to as scientific management.

Taylor, after stating what scientific management was not, went on to state clearly the main characteristic of scientific management. To him, "a complete mental revolution" was necessary for scientific management to come into being. Further, and this is important because it points up the fact that Taylor was far more than a capable technician, this mental revolution must occur in the *workman's* mind as well as in the mind of management. Taylor's analysis of industrial problems existing between management and labor concluded that, to a large extent, it was an argument over the division of the surplus created by industry. Indeed, this still remains one of the major issues in current collective bargaining. The first part of the mental revolution, according to Taylor, is that both parties stop quarreling about how the surplus should be divided and unite to increase the size of the surplus so that the need for hairsplitting in this area becomes less acute.

The second phase of the mental revolution is that the scientific method must be the sole basis for obtaining information to determine the proper procedure to be used in the performance of each job and to establish the proper level of output per man-hour. It is the second phase of scientific management that has caused most of the criticism of the Taylor system. The reason is that the application of the scientific method requires so much detailed work and time that the original goal of increasing the surplus is never realized. An example of the extensive work necessary in some areas to determine the scientific basis for the performance of an operation is found in the series of experiments conducted by Taylor extending over a 26-year period to determine the best methods of machining or cutting metals. In the process, high-speed tool steels were developed, and the science of cutting metals was broken down into 12 interrelated variables. These interrelationships were expressed mathematically by formulas, and slide rules were developed so that the optimum conditions for any given task could be computed. It is no wonder that a person becoming immersed in the mathematical analysis of production problems loses sight of the first great mental revolution required; namely, a change in attitude.

The Science of Shoveling. Nor must one conclude that the simple tasks were overlooked. Taylor speaks of the "science of shoveling," and in this discussion points up one of the major results of scientific management, the placing of a greater planning and coordinative responsibility upon management. He describes the original operation of the labor gang in the Bethlehem Steel Works as a large group of rather nondescript men reporting for work every morning and, for the most part, each bringing his own shovel. The men used the same shovel regardless of the type of material being shoveled. To Taylor's keen mind this was a problem in need of careful analysis. First, it was necessary to break down the operation of shoveling into its individual elements and then study each element carefully in order to determine the best method for each element and the time it would take a good workman to perform each element. Also, it was necessary to determine the optimum amount of weight per shovelful that a man could effectively handle during the full course of a day. The range in the weight of the material being shoveled was between 3½ to 38 pounds per shovel. Careful study showed that regardless of the type of material that was being shoveled, the men did the greatest amount of work when the blade of the shovel carried 21 pounds, no more and no less. Following this discovery, a shovel was designed for each material so that it would hold 21 pounds, and the men were instructed in the proper method of shoveling. Next, a piecework system of pay was established so that a man was paid in proportion to his output. At the time of this work, the going rate for laborers was $1.15 per day, but the men at Bethlehem operating under the piecework system earned $1.85 per day, or an increase of 60 percent over the going rate.

This is only half of the story. What was the effect of this change upon management? With the design of a special tool (shovel) for each type of material to be handled, it became impractical for each man to own his own shovel; therefore, the company furnished shovels designed for a specific purpose. Further, the company housed the new equipment in an orderly fashion; but most important, each day's work was carefully planned. Output per man was now known, thus it became necessary to determine how much of a given material was needed to be moved the next day, how many men would be needed, and which shovels they would use. The work for the entire labor crew had to be carefully planned and coordinated. The failure of managements to do their job properly, that of coordinating and planning, was to Taylor the second big problem.

The Need for Scientific Management. Scientific management was developed to solve two major problems: to increase the output of the average worker and to improve the efficiency of management. To a degree, increasing the productivity of the average worker is the same problem that challenged Mayo at a later date, but the approaches used by each of the these men were different. Mayo sought the answer in terms of the social forces that affect the worker as a member of a group, but Taylor considered each worker as a separate "economic" man motivated by financial need.

Taylor believed that the basis of a worker's tendency to restrict output was his fear of displacement, not too unlike the fear expressed in some quarters today in regard to automation. He suggested two methods of minimizing the fear of displacement expressed by the workmen. One approach was to educate the worker to understand that his economic salvation lay in producing more at a lower cost. The other method was to prove to the worker the effectiveness of this argument by placing him on a piecework system and thereby permitting him to earn more.

Taylor's Principles of Management. The second major problem, improving the efficiency of management, was to be solved through the application of Taylor's four principles of management. The first of these principles urged a gathering, analysis, and codification of all "rule-of-thumb" data existing in the business. The second principle urged careful selection and a thorough study of the workman so that he may be developed to his maximum capabilities. Third, was the persuasive principle of educating, or more properly "inspiring," men to use the scientific principles derived from the careful analysis of all data and methods used in each job. Lastly, he urged that management organize in such a manner that it could properly manage and carry out its duties.

Underlying the whole approach of scientific management is the belief that there is a one best way of doing everything, whether it be using a shovel or making a complex cut on a piece of metal. There was much resistance to the methods espoused by Taylor. It was the strike at the Watertown Arsenal against the Taylor System which led to the congressional investigation. As a result of the investigation, piecework rates were banned from all government jobs at that time; nonetheless, the hearings afforded Taylor an opportunity to bring clearly before the public the meaning of scientific management.

Barth and Gantt. Before leaving Taylor and his work, mention should be made of two of his coworkers. One was Carl Barth, whose mathematical genius enabled the construction of a slide rule capable of handling 12 variables. While this rule was designed for determining the most efficient conditions for a given metal-cutting operation, its application by Barth tended to oversimplify the problem to the untrained eye and made it appear that increasing output was purely a mechanical problem.

The other associate was H. L. Gantt, who has been credited with humanizing the scientific management movement. Though Taylor spoke often of human problems, he was by nature a stern and remote man. There was little in his methods that reflect an insight into human nature. For example, Taylor's piecework system did not provide a base pay for the worker for those periods of time when production was interrupted or when he was unable to attain standard production because of factors beyond his control. This lack of financial security led to much of the opposition against the Taylor piecework system. Gantt recognized this shortcoming and provided a guaranteed base pay plus an incentive in the plan he developed. In addition, he emphasized the importance of leadership on the part of management and recommended a more democratic approach than Taylor had used in the solution of industrial problems.

THE EMPHASIS UPON ADMINISTRATION

The third group of writings in the literature of management, the arch connecting the vertical columns of human relations and production efficiency, emphasizes the administrative aspects of management. The emphasis is an overall approach to the problems of management, not at all contradictory to the approach of Taylor and his associates nor to the emphasis upon the human factor as stated by Owen and Mayo. The task of management has been summarized in a single word, *coordination,* by Mary Parker Follett; but in order to understand this concept it is necessary to know what is being coordinated and to review suggestions as to how coordination can best be accomplished.[8]

---

[8] Mary Parker Follett, *Freedom and Coordination* (London: Management Publications Trust, Ltd., 1949), H. F. Merrill, *ibid.,* pp. 337-52.

Fayol's Principles of Management

Henri Fayol, a French engineer and geologist, was the first to state a series of principles of management that provide guideposts for successful management coordination. Concurrent with Taylor's study of management through a detailed analysis of the individual worker, Fayol, manager of a large French mining and metallurgical company, analyzed the problems of top management. He modestly believed that his success was not due to any personal characteristics of leadership, but was the result of applying a set of general administrative principles that could be isolated and taught to others. In his book, *General and Industrial Management,* Fayol lists the following 14 principles of management: [9]

1. Division of work
2. Authority
3. Discipline
4. Unity of command
5. Unity of direction
6. Subordination of the individual interest to the general interest
7. Remuneration
8. Centralization
9. Scalar chain (line of authority)
10. Order
11. Equity
12. Stability of tenure of personnel
13. Initiative
14. Esprit de corps

Five of Fayol's 14 principles are concerned primarily with the improvement of human relations. One of his principles emphasizes production efficiency, and the remaining eight are directed toward administration of the organization. Those principles contributing to the improvement of human relations are discussed first.

Principles Emphasizing Human Relations

The five principles applicable to problems in the field of human relations are: No. 6, subordination of individual interest to

---

[9] Henri Fayol, *General and Industrial Management* (London: Sir Isaac Pitman and Sons Ltd., 1949), pp. 19-42. H. F. Merrill, *Ibid.,* pp. 217-41. The copyright date, 1949, is the date of the English translation. Fayol's "General Principles of Management" first appeared in 1916 in an industrial association bulletin published in France.

the general interest; No. 11, equity; No. 12, stability of tenure of personnel; No. 13, initiative; and No. 14, esprit de corps. In the first of this group, subordination of individual interest to the general interest (No. 6), Fayol states that individuals and small groups within the overall organization should make their needs secondary to those of the firm. He also emphasizes that it is necessary for the firm to place its interests second to those of the society in which it operates. Recognition of the fact that the administrator of an organization is dealing with a number of groups, as contrasted to a number of individuals, is fundamentally the same group concept of Elton Mayo. Fayol suggests that the attainment of subordination of interest can be achieved by close supervision, good examples of subordination of personal interest by supervisors, and by making agreements with various employees and groups of employees as fair as possible.

In Principle No. 11, equity, he defines what is meant by fair agreements. To him, equity is composed of two ingredients: kindliness and justice. The equal application of policies and practices to all groups and individuals within an organization is certainly a concept difficult to quarrel with, yet also difficult to apply at all times. Fayol applies the concept of desirability of stability of tenure to all levels of the organization. The production worker must have some feeling of security in order to learn his job so that he may perform it well, and he must also have some feeling of psychological security.

Stability of tenure for top management is necessary, for it takes time to get to know the organization, its problems, and its personnel. Fayol even suggests that it might be better for a concern to have a mediocre manager with long tenure rather than have a succession of brilliant managers. In this connection, the following interesting question is raised: Is the poor performance of a company that is experiencing a high turnover of managerial personnel the result of the turnover; or, is the poor performance of managerial personnel the cause of the turnover? It is a question that plagues many companies today, and they are no nearer the answer than was Fayol.

One of the chief reasons for the success of Mayo's work with the textile production problems was that the workers themselves defined the problem, offered a solution, and saw their solution carried through to its success. To Fayol, participation in the solution of problems is represented by the principle of initiative. The principle is with us today and is illustrated by the efforts of companies to establish suggestion systems at all levels of the organization so that the ideas and energies of all workers may be tapped in the solution of common problems.

Effective employee suggestion programs utilize the principle of initiative, for they enable an employee to see his ideas carried through to a successful conclusion.

In his last principle, esprit de corps, Fayol states his belief that in union there is strength and warns against a system of divide and conquer in an organization. While dividing and conquering may be a good way of eliminating the opposition, it does not work within a single group such as a business organization. The manager's task is not to eliminate the opposition, but rather to unify all divergent groups and individuals.

Production Efficiency

The first of Fayol's principles, division of work, is similar to the thesis that Charles Babbage presented in "On the Division of Labour."[10] Fayol offers the same reasons for dividing work and creating groups of specialists. He mentions the resulting increased skill, the reduction in learning time, and the increased efficiency that results from not having to change from one task to another. But he goes further than Babbage and applies the principle of the division of work to all levels of management, not limiting its application to the hourly worker. Also, the first principle is an expression of the same interest shown by Babbage and Taylor; namely, an emphasis upon the production process with a desire to increase the efficiency of that process. It is the only one of his 14 principles which can be classed as solely emphasizing production. However, there are two principles of such breadth that production processes are included in their application: remuneration and order. These are discussed later.

Principles Emphasizing Administration

The principles discussed thus far restate much that has been said by other writers in the field who have stressed the improvement of either production efficiency or human relations. The remaining principles are new in concept, for they deal with the problems of top management—administration and organization.

Fayol's second principle, authority, is the first of this group. Authority is defined as the right to give orders and is discussed with its corollary, responsibility. The granting of authority to a manager implies that in accepting that authority, he has also accepted responsibility. It is organizationally unsound and inefficient to assign responsibility

---

[10] Charles Babbage, *ibid.*

without, at the same time, granting authority commensurate to this responsibility. Fayol recognized that authority is misused and suggests that preventing the abuse of authority is dependent upon the integrity of the individual having authority.[11]

Discipline, the third principle, is regarded as the respect shown by all members of the organization toward the written agreements, or policies, governing their conduct in the firm. Fayol proposes that good discipline be achieved by having all agreements between the company and the employees presented as clearly and as fairly as possible, that all supervisors throughout the organization be thoroughly capable, and that if the need for penalties or discipline arises, such penalties should be as fair as possible.

The fourth and fifth principles, unity of command and unity of direction, respectively, are similar and closely related. Yet there is sufficient difference in their purposes so that two separate principles are warranted. The first of these, unity of command, states that orders should originate from one source only. Thus, from a subordinate's point of view, he is assured that he will have only one superior in the organization from whom he can receive orders. Unity of direction is not directed toward the individual, but refers to the plan or work activities of the group and emphasizes that for one plan there should be one head or director. Thus, these two principles complement each other; the former assures the employee that there will be only one superior, and the latter assures organizational effectiveness in that for every group of workers carrying out a plan, there shall be only one director.

These principles of organization—authority, discipline, unity of command, and unity of direction—leave little room for deviation or individual choice. Because of their nature they appear to be an "all or none" proposition. However, not all of Fayol's principles dealing with organization are as rigid as illustrated by his eighth principle, centralization, and the ninth, scalar chain or line of authority. (Though not stated in the title of the eighth principle, both principles deal with the problem of authority.) The ninth principle urges that definite lines of authority be established from the bottom of an organization to its very top in such a manner that the exact lines of authority relationships between the successive levels of management are unmistakably clear. When it becomes necessary for individuals in different sections of the organization to work directly with each other in order to attain speed of action, the formal chain of command should be short-circuited, provided all persons concerned are properly informed.

---

[11] The problem of integrity is discussed in Chapter 3, "Objectives and Ethics."

The same type of flexibility is evident in determining the optimum degree of centralization in an organization. In general, those actions that tend to reduce the authority and responsibility of subordinates and place more in the hands of a superior may be considered as actions which lend to a greater degree of centralization of authority, while those acts that increase responsibility and authority at lower levels result in what is termed a greater degree of decentralization of authority. With the concept of varying degrees of centralization of authority there is no recommended absolute level of centralization or decentralization. The desired level or degree is dependent upon the situation and includes such factors as the nature of the organization, the problem of the department at hand, and the capabilities of the subordinates in question.

The remaining two principles describe operating procedures of such breadth that they are difficult to classify within the framework of either human relations, production, or administration. These principles, remuneration and order, encompass all three areas. Since they are expressed as problems of top management rather than problems in human relations or the improvement of production, the principles of remuneration and order are considered among those principles contributing to the administrative efforts of management. One of these, the principle of remuneration, starts with the assumption that the wages paid to personnel should be based upon concepts of equity and should be satisfactory both from the point of view of the employee and from the point of view of the company. The various methods of paying hourly employees are listed, and Fayol shows that he was thoroughly familiar with the piecework system advocated by Taylor. He also mentions the problems involved in profit-sharing plans and bonuses, not only for hourly workers, but for all members of the organization. Again, Fayol develops the same flexible conclusion that he did in principles eight and nine—the method of payment selected should be the one that works best for the particular situation, and the definition of "best" should include the point of view of all interested parties.

The other principle, also broad in scope, is that of order. At first glance, the meaning of order may seem to be the same as Taylor's admonition that the placement of materials and tools should be the result of a methods study to assure efficient production. Fayol's principle does include the concept, "A place for everything and everything in its place." However, it means much more than the neat arrangement of physical materials of an organization. Fayol's idea of order also applies to the human element of the organization. An application of this principle is the organization chart, a device which literally shows the place of every person in the organization and the relationships of each to the other. In addition to knowing personnel as they appear on the organization chart, Fayol recommended they be considered as human resources expressing different capabilities and desires.

SUMMARY OF PRINCIPLES

Three separate approaches to the problems of management have been reviewed.[12] Each approach emphasizes a different aspect of management and each draws its own conclusions as to what factors are of significance in the management process. Conclusions that are fundamental to their nature and basic to the management process have been termed principles of management. Neither Robert Owen nor Elton Mayo, who both designated the development of sound human relations as the primary task of management, stated their conclusions as principles of management. Frederick W. Taylor, representative of the approach that emphasizes production efficiency, and Henri Fayol, who stressed the administrative aspects of management, have stated fundamentals basic to the management process and referred to these conclusions as principles of management.

Taylors principles of scientific management illustrate the need for increased efficiency:

Taylor's Principles of Scientific Management

1. Management must gather, analyze, and codify all existing rule-of-thumb data pertaining to the business in order to develop a science.

2. Workers must be carefully selected and thoroughly studied so that each one may be developed to his maximum capabilities.

3. Workmen must be inspired or trained to use the scientific methods developed as the result of analyzing and codifying rule-of-thumb data.

4. Management must organize in such a manner that it can properly manage and carry out its duties.

---

[12] There are other approaches to the problems of management beyond the scope of this chapter. Professor Harold Koontz suggests, in addition to the three that have been discussed, the empirical school or approach, the social system school, the decision theory school, and the mathematical school. See Harold Koontz, "The Management Theory Jungle," *Journal of the Academy of Management,* Vol. IV (December, 1961), pp. 174-188.*

For a discussion of a modern group, known as the revisionists, see: Warren Bennis, "Leadership and Administrative Behavior," *Administrative Science Quarterly,* Vol. IV (December, 1959), pp. 259-301.

* Footnote references followed by an asterisk (*) may also be found in Max D. Richards and William A. Nielander, *Readings in Management,* 3d ed. (Cincinnati: South-Western Publishing Company, 1968).

Henri Fayol stressed the administrative aspects of management. At the same time, he recognized the need for sound human relations and the importance of production efficiency. His 14 principles have been arranged to show the area to which each contributes.

Fayol's Principles of Management

Human Relations

Subordination of individual interest to the general interest

Initiative

Esprit de corps

Equity

Stability of tenure of personnel

Production Efficiency

Division of work

Administration

Authority

Discipline

Unity of command

Unity of direction

Centralization

Scalar chain (line of authority)

Remuneration

Order

• • • • • • • • •

In this chapter we have reviewed a few of the major works in the literature of management, and have shown that the development of management concepts expressed in the literature has taken well over a hundred years. Of what value is such information to the present-day manager? Marsh Saunders (Case Problem 2-A), the new plant manager facing the challenge of creating an effective organization, may not find the specific answers he desires in the literature, but he will discover established principles that will serve as guideposts for any action he takes. In Case Problem 2-B, Manual vs. Automatic Equipment, a modern counterpart of making pins by hand is described. As a building manager, you are asked to answer and evaluate the worth of the questions posed by Charles Babbage in reaching your decision concerning the advisability of purchasing new equipment in order to convert a manual operation to one that is fully automatic.

Questions for Study and Discussion

1. What major conclusions can be drawn from the work of Mayo and Owen?

2. Give an example from your own experience that illustrates the importance of personal leadership.

3. What modern industrial operation best illustrates the division of labor by levels of skill?

4. What responsibilities of management change as the result of changes in methods and time studies of hourly production jobs? Why?

5. Describe Taylor's study in which he determined the best method of shoveling. What other operations do you think would benefit from the same type of analysis?

6. Would Mayo have been successful in raising the output of the mule-spinners had he used the methods of Taylor? Do you believe that Taylor would have been successful in raising the output of the labor gang of the Bethlehem Steel Works had he employed the methods of Mayo?

7. In what respect does Fayol's concept of the division of work differ from Babbage's concept as expressed in "On the Division of Labour"?

8. Which of Fayol's principles emphasize human relations? Which of his principles emphasizes production, and which ones emphasize the organizational or administrative aspects of management?

9. Why is it unsound for a manager to approach his organization with a "divide and conquer" philosophy?

10. Differentiate between Fayol's principles of unity of command and unity of direction.

11. What is meant by the term "centralization" as applied to a company's organization structure? What is meant by the term "decentralization?" Give an example of each.

12. Two of Fayol's principles are so broad in their application that they cannot be conveniently classified as falling entirely within any one of the three areas discussed; i.e., human relations, production, or administration. One reason was presented in the text for their consideration as principles contributing toward the administrative aspect of management. What are the principles in question, and what was the reason offered for their being classified as administrative principles?

13. What reasons can you develop to justify the classification of the two principles mentioned in Question 12 as principles contributing primarily to either human relations or production efficiency?

•   •   •   •   •   •   •   •   •

The home office of the Diamond Insurance Company occupies the fourth, fifth, and sixth floors of the 12-story Diamond Building, which was built in the early thirties. The building has been well maintained throughout the years, and in 1950 was completely air conditioned. It is well located, with easy access to downtown stores and other office buildings, with the result that the occupancy rate has been well over 90 percent of capacity until the current year when it dropped to 85 percent. The costs of operating the building have risen steadily for the past 15 years. Though there have been several increases of rental charges in the past to offset rising costs, a readjustment of rates seems out of the question at the present time because several new buildings are nearby and their space costs little more than the Diamond Building.

H. W. Canton, vice-president of the Diamond Insurance Company, who is responsible for the operation of the building, was acutely aware of the declining occupancy rate and the impracticality of raising rental charges as he spoke to Mr. Thomas, the building manager.

"I wish you would look into the feasibility of installing automatic elevators. Find out the cost of installation, maintenance cost, and whether the service to our tenants will be as good as the service we now provide with the elevator operators. We might be interested in converting to automatic elevators if we could pay for them in less than ten years without spending any more than we now spend for operator service."

Case Problem 2-B
Manual vs. Automatic
Equipment

"What about interest rates?" asked Mr. Thomas.

"Don't worry about that at present. We can always add that amount to the cost that you find." As the building manager started to leave the room, Mr. Canton added, "In determining present costs, use the hourly rate we are now paying the operators. We all know that it is going up, but by using the present rate we'll be on the safe side."

Mr. Thomas began his assignment by collecting all available cost data for the present operation. For the past five years, maintenance costs on the present equipment have averaged $2,000 each year. There are five girls employed as operators for the four elevators, and one employed as working supervisor who schedules the operators, acts as starter, and provides information to visitors from her position at a desk in front of the elevators. Mr. Thomas assumed that she would be retained in order to provide information.

The girls operate the elevators from eight in the morning until 5:30 p.m., Monday through Friday, and from eight to twelve noon on Saturdays. Service on Saturday afternoons, evenings, and Sundays is provided by either the watchman or the night porter. All operators receive $1.50 an hour, and the starter receives $1.80 an hour. Overtime at the rate of time and one half is paid for all hours worked over eight in any one day and for any hours in excess of 40 in any one week. Two of the girls work nine hours Monday through Friday and receive nine and one-half hour's pay, since the ninth hour is paid at the overtime rate. Three of the operators, one of whom acts as relief operator, work eight and one-half hours each weekday and receive 8.75 hour's pay. The starter also is paid for 8.75 hours since her normal work day is eight and one-half hours, Monday through Friday. On Saturdays, two of the operators and the starter each work four hours, and since they all work more than 40 hours during the week, they receive overtime pay for the entire four hours. Work schedules are rotated so that the earnings of the operators are equalized. Fringe benefits, including group insurance, social security taxes, and uniforms, are estimated to be 30 cents an hour (using a 40-hour week) or a total of $72 a week for the six employees. No replacements are hired during the summer when vacations are normally taken.

After consolidating the above information into an annual cost figure, which includes maintenance and labor costs for a 52-week year, Mr. Thomas contacted several elevator companies for estimates on the cost of converting to automatic elevators. The best estimate he received was $103,000 for the cost of installation, with an annual maintenance charge of 4 percent of the installation cost. The elevator manufacturer assured him that automatic service would be superior to their present manual service. This opinion was confirmed by several building managers who had made the conversion.

Problems

1. Prepare a summary report and recommendations for Mr. Canton.

2. Which of the questions raised by Charles Babbage in 1832 are applicable to the problems stated in this case?

3. What is your answer to each of Babbage's five questions?

4. Can you think of any additional questions that should be answered before a decision is made?

CHAPTER 3

Objectives and Ethics

At the turn of the century in 1901, a group of civic-minded citizens of Golden City formed a public corporation and received from the city a franchise "to operate a public transportation system." The Golden Transit Company, the corporation thus formed, grew with Golden City; and in 1946 at the close of World War II, its annual statement showed a capital surplus of $1,200,-000 in the form of cash and negotiable securities. In addition, the corporation owned substantial real estate holdings, including a 12-story office building.

The end of the war also marked a turning point in the fortunes of the Golden Transit Company. Golden City expanded from its postwar population of 300,000 to more than 700,000 by 1960 and, in the process, the geographic area of the city grew from an area of 30 square miles to more than 120 square miles. The length of existing bus routes had to be increased and, in many cases, new routes were established. With the advent of a system of freeways, Golden City residents contributed their share to the booming automobile market. The transit company had to purchase additional rolling stock, some of which was an overdue

Case Problem 3-A

A Public Trust

replacement of equipment worn out during the war years when replacements were impossible. Much of the equipment, however, was to serve new bus lines and was purchased in an effort to make public transportation more convenient and to attract new customers. In addition, a continuing spiral of rising costs and subsequent fare increases began. The seeming result was that with each fare increase, the number of passengers declined. Though the frequency of service was greatly reduced on many routes, no routes were completely eliminated. The earnings of the company were poor and as a result, the stock of the company was traded on the local over-the-counter market at $11 per share, despite the fact that financial analysts estimated a book value of $23 per share.

In the spring of 1961, sales of the stock became more active, and during the remainder of that year it traded at prices ranging between $12 and $14 per share. By the year's end, the reason for the increased market activity of the stock became apparent. It was revealed that National Busways, an out-of-state corporation, had purchased 60 percent of the outstanding stock. Early in 1962,

48

National's slate of directors was elected and a new management for the Golden Transit Company was appointed. During 1962 the following events occurred:

1. Two requests were submitted to the Golden City council for fare increases. The new management stated that it was a public corporation entitled to make a profit, and that if the fare increase were not granted, it would be necessary to further reduce service and eliminate unprofitable routes. The first request was denied by the city council, with the result that ten relatively new routes serving suburban areas were discontinued. The city council was still considering the second request for a fare increase.

2. The real estate holdings, including a 12-story office building, were transferred to a holding company controlled by National Busways. The income from this property was no longer available to offset the operating losses of the Golden Transit Company. A large part of the capital surplus was used to purchase another transit company in an adjacent state.

3. Golden Transit Company had been somewhat tardy in establishing adequate retirement and disability insurance plans. However, they recognized these obligations to their employees and devised a plan whereby disabled persons and some of those who had retired could continue work-

ing with the company on a part-time basis performing light duty. A total of 51 persons were employed in this category. All of this group were discharged by the new management with the comment "We're running a bus line—not a charity."

4. A citizen's group, whose chairman was a prominent Golden City attorney, was investigating the steps necessary to revoke the charter under which National Busways was operating the Golden Transit Company.

Problems

1. What were the objectives of the Golden Transit Company when it was first organized?
2. State the objectives in order of apparent importance, of National Busways, the company now operating the Golden Transit Company.
3. Assume that the citizen's group follows the necessary legal steps and is successful in revoking the charter under which National Busways is operating. Is this action justified? If so, on what grounds can it be justified?
4. What problems in the field of ethics (fairness and equity to others) have resulted from National's reducing the frequency of service, eliminating entire routes, and discharging long service employees?

In Chapter 1, management is defined as the coordination of all resources through the processes of planning, organizing, controlling, and directing in order to attain stated objectives. Case Problem 3-A brings into sharp focus the changing objectives of the Golden Transit Company after the management of National Busways gained control of the company. Prior to the change in management, the chief objective seemed to be service. There are public utilities formally known as public service companies, and the Golden Transit Company could have been named quite properly the Golden Public Service Company.

The stage is set to determine whether the primary objective of Golden Transit should be service or profit. Case Problem 3-A also illustrates that the existence of a business firm is sanctioned by the society in which it exists; society, in this case, is represented by the Golden City council. In addition to these questions which relate to the objectives of a business, serious doubts are raised concerning the propriety of the methods used by the new management in obtaining its objectives. The judgment as to whether the actions of the new management are proper or improper is an evaluation of the ethical standards of that management. The determination of the objectives of a firm defines the framework within which the management processes take place. The methods used to attain these objectives, to the extent that these methods affect various groups of people, reflect the ethical standards of a company. This chapter will discuss, first, the objectives of business; and, second, review some of the problems encountered in analyzing and establishing ethical standards for businessmen.

OBJECTIVES

Definition

Managing a firm without stated objectives is as frustrating and meaningless as sailing a ship without destination. For management, there is no direction to its efforts or effective coordination of resources; nor can there be needed direction and effective coordination until there is a stated purpose or goal. Thus, an *objective* may be defined as *the end point or goal toward which management directs its efforts.* The statement of an objective is in effect a statement of purpose, and when applied to a business organization, becomes the statement of that firm's reason for existing. In order to gain maximum effectiveness from a statement of objectives, an organization must state its objectives prior to initiating the management processes of planning, organizing, directing, and controlling. Stating an objective may require considerable research, yet it is not a part of the planning process. The planning process is put into effect, along with the other three management processes, for the purpose of achieving stated objectives.

Principle of the Objective

The requirement that the objective should be predetermined is considered of such significance that it is referred to as the *Principle of the Objective*. A concise statement of the principle of the objective is that of John F. Mee: *"Before initiating any course of action, the objectives in view must be clearly determined, understood, and stated."* [1]

Characteristics of Objectives

The principle of the objective stresses the outstanding characteristic of an objective. This characteristic is that an objective is *predetermined,* an act which thereby sets it apart from the processes utilized in reaching the objective. A second characteristic of an objective is that it is stated. Generally, stating an objective implies that the statement be in written form. The process of writing a thought contributes to its clarification and, in addition, creates a degree of permanence. One of the chief reasons that written assignments are given to students is that the act of writing forces a clarification not usually achieved in oral presentations. Companies that are reluctant or unable to state their objectives in writing reflect either an inability to reach accord on their goals or a fear of criticism that might be engendered by such a statement. The third characteristic of an objective expresses a duality that, on the surface, appears to be contradictory. An objective should be well within the reach of the organization, yet difficult to attain. If an objective is not attainable, it will be disregarded. When this happens, there is no goal. At the same time, an objective must be sufficiently difficult so that it presents a challenge to everyone concerned; otherwise, its potential as an incentive is not realized.

Value of Objectives

There are four outstanding benefits that result from a statement of objectives. Stated objectives fulfill a need for direction and

---

[1] John F. Mee, "Management Philosophy for Professional Executives," *Business Horizons* (Bureau of Business Research, School of Business, Indiana University, December, 1956), pp. 5-11.

also serve as motivators for the personnel of an entire organization. In addition, objectives contribute to the management process and form the basis for a sound management philosophy.

Objectives Provide Direction. The primary need for objectives is implied in the definition of an objective as an end point or goal toward which management directs its efforts. That need is the need for direction and is felt throughout the entire organization. Not only should there be a statement of objectives for the company as a whole, but there should also be a statement for each organizational unit of the company. Each unit of the business should have its own related objectives so that its efforts may be coordinated and unified toward a common goal.

Objectives Serve as Motivators. Ideally, objectives serve as motivators in addition to providing direction. Examples of the motivating value of an objective are the monetary rewards used in industry. Incentive plans for hourly workers all assume, to some degree, that one of the objectives of a worker is to earn more money. When this assumption is true, it follows that the creation of a situation making it possible for a person to increase his earnings motivates him toward achieving that immediate goal or objective. The desire for economic gain underlies the concept of behavior held by Taylor and others who have installed incentive plans. The creation of corporate profit is often stated as one of the major objectives of business; however, a subtle problem of differentiation exists in determining whether profit is in fact a goal or whether it is primarily a motivator of managers.

Objectives Contribute to the Management Process. The third value to be gained from a statement of objectives is that such a statement makes a significant contribution to the management process. Clearly understood and realistic objectives form a basis for the control process, the measurement of the firm's present position in relation to its desired goal. Objectives are important in that they influence the size and characteristics of an organization and affect the type of leadership required; however, the closest relationship is between objectives and the processes of planning and control. Plans are formulated in order to reach specific goals, and the control process measures the extent to which these plans are achieved. Neither is possible without a prior statement of objectives.

Objectives Are the Basis for a Management Philosophy. Lastly, the statement of objectives forms the basis for a management philosophy. It makes possible the creation of a management by objective rather than management in response to "crash programs" and "special drives." When objectives are not formally stated, the solutions of immediate emergencies are dignified as objectives, and, as such, they become a series of short-term projects that lack cohesiveness and are frequently contradictory in purpose. An example of management by drives in response to emergency situations is the company that exerts all efforts during the month of January toward reducing the number of hourly workers; in February, the drive is directed toward improving the quality of its product; March finds management trying to increase the total number of units produced, with the result that when April comes, there is the same number of employees as in January. Nor has there been any significant change in either the quality or the quantity of the product. Management by drives makes it virtually impossible to achieve Fayol's "esprit de corps," or singleness of purpose, for the simple reason that there are no cohesive objectives. The organization is continually shifting its attentions and efforts in first one direction and then another, with no opportunity to achieve a goal or objective that would result in a feeling of singleness of purpose.

Types of Objectives

There is no single objective for a business organization. Some objectives are primarily of interest to persons and organizations not a part of the organization itself. Other objectives are of especial interest to the organization and of concern to those who are members of or owners of the firm. It is not a question of determining which objectives are most important—those external to the firm or those internal to the firm—but, rather, how to fulfill each set of objectives to the maximum degree.

External Objectives. National Busways in Case Problem 3-A states that its objective is to make a profit, and judging from the action taken, the implication is a profit at all costs. However, a group of aroused citizens is asking that the charter which permits National to operate the Golden Transit Company be revoked. The request is being made, not because the group objects to the company making a profit, but because the company is ignoring its primary function; namely, providing adequate service to its customers. Therefore, it seems that in this instance, service to customers is a primary objective, and making a profit is a secondary or subsidiary objective. Admittedly, a transit company is a special situation; that is, a public utility chartered to serve the public.

The question arises whether the same emphasis upon service to customers holds true for those firms that are not utilities, but are engaged in manufacturing a product for public consumption. The answer is the same as it is in the case of a utility, although the issue may not be as sharply defined. No organization can exist unless a portion of the public becomes its customers and buys its service or its product. The legendary manufacturer of buggy whips serves as an example. Of what value is it to make a good buggy whip if no one is interested in buying that product? But, you say, this is an extreme example. True, however, the same concept applies to the distribution of those products and services currently in demand by customers. Unless a product or service is comparable in respect to price, quality, and utility to that of competing products or services, it will not be purchased in sufficient quantities to generate a profit large enough to permit staying in business. The desire to make a profit and the hope of sharing that profit motivate all employees, particularly managers; but in order to create profit, an organization must serve a customer. Thus, a primary objective of any organization is a service objective—to serve the needs of a customer.

Another implication to be drawn from the Golden Transit Company is that business is sanctioned by the society in which it exists. It is particularly clear in this case since the city granted the charter that permits the company to operate; and by the same token, the city can revoke that permission when the company fails to discharge its obligations. There are many types of businesses that are prohibited by law. For example, most states prohibit gambling. There are federal laws that are restrictive in nature, such as the antitrust laws. Consequently, another objective of business is to render a service sanctioned by society. The objectives of an organization must be in accord with the wishes of society or that organization is not permitted to continue operations.

Internal Objectives. The two objectives, service to a customer and service to society, are objectives *external* to the firm. At the same time these objectives are being fulfilled, an organization is interested in satisfying certain objectives that are of particular interest to the firm itself. These objectives are *internal* objectives. The first of the internal objectives is the overall position of a firm in relation to its competitors. A company may desire to be the largest, to be the most profitable, to show the greatest growth, or to produce the greatest number of new products.

Secondly, there are objectives related to employee groups. The firm may be desirous of attracting and holding the finest type employee possible; or depending upon the nature of the business and the objectives of its management, it may seek an employee with minimal qualifications. In addition, various employee groups may have subobjectives of their own. An example of this is the desire for wages and fringe benefits as expressed by unions.

A third group of objectives is directed toward satisfying the stockholders and is considered internal since stockholders are a part of the firm and are not necessarily the customers nor representatives of the society that sanctions the firm. These objectives usually define profit as a goal so that the stockholders may receive a return on their investment in the firm. Profits are also necessary to provide funds that permit the attainment of the first of the internal objectives, the desired relative position of the company with respect to its competitors.

In summary, the objectives of a firm are classed as external and internal. External objectives are service objectives. Business firms, if they are to survive, must provide a product or a service that is acceptable to customers. Also, the service or product provided must be sanctioned by society. Internal objectives are of particular interest to the firm itself. These objectives define the position of a firm in respect to its competitors and state specific goals in respect to employee groups. There are also internal objectives directed toward satisfying the needs of stockholders. Profit, the lifeblood of a business firm, functions as both an objective and a motive; but profit is not possible unless the needs of customers are satisfied and unless the objectives of the firm are sanctioned by society.

Statement of Objectives

So that objectives may be meaningful and perform the dual role of goal and motivator, they must be stated in a manner that is easily understood. Since there are two types of objectives, those external to the firm and those internal to the firm, which are at times in conflict with each other, it is highly unlikely that a satisfactory statement of goals can be accomplished by setting one single objective. Therefore, it is necessary that objectives be stated for each of several areas of performance. Peter Drucker suggests that objectives be stated for each of the following eight areas of accomplishment:

1. Market standing
2. Innovation
3. Productivity
4. Physical and financial resources

5. Profitability
6. Manager performance and development
7. Worker performance and attitude
8. Public responsibility [2]

Objectives for the first five areas are susceptible to quantitative measurement and statement and may be expressed as a numerical value. For example, market standing may be expressed as a rank position in the industry—i.e., first in its field. Standing may also be stated in terms of specific dollar volume—i.e., $10 million sales for the past year. Innovation, or technological development, in respect to the management of the business and in the processes of production, as well as in respect to the product itself, is also susceptible to relatively precise measurement and expression. Productivity may be expressed in terms of total units or in a manner that measures the efficiency of the production process, such as units per man-hour or units per dollar of capital expenditure. Physical and financial resources and profitability may also be expressed in dollars. These are the traditional measures of the growth and well-being of a firm, but unless these objectives are properly supported by stated objectives in the last three areas—manager performance and development, worker performance and attitude, and public responsibility—they become meaningless and the entire structure of objectives will collapse like a house of cards.

It may be argued that the last three objectives relating to the performance of management, the workers, and the meeting of public responsibilities are not objectives but in reality a statement of policy; that is, a broad framework within which the organization operates. Be that as it may, an organization is composed of people, and unless plans are made for the perpetuation of the organization and its improvement as a functioning unit, the organization will not be capable of maintaining or advancing its position in respect to market position, technological development, physical resources, and profitability. It is also necessary that broad social responsibilities be recognized and stated as objectives since society sanctions, or permits, business to exist.

Figure 3-1 is an example of how the Continental-Emsco Company has stated its objectives. Notice how these objectives follow the pattern of the eight areas suggested by Peter Drucker. Objectives Nos. 1 through

---

[2] Peter F. Drucker, *The Practice of Management* (New York: Harper and Brothers, 1954).* These eight areas for which objectives should be set are of significance not only in the setting of objectives but also in determining the areas for which controls must be provided. Seven of these areas appear again in Chapter 21 as those areas needing controls.

Company Objectives

Continental-Emsco Company *
(A Division of the Youngstown Sheet and Tube Company)

1. To be a growth organization to the degree that is permitted by the profitableness of our current operations.
2. Further the diversification of Company operations.
3. Maintain a formalized advanced planning program.
4. Through research and development and/or acquisition acquire proprietor type products for manufacturing and distribution. When necessary improve existing products.
5. To manufacture quality products at the lowest possible cost utilizing modern manufacturing practices, facilities, tools, and equipment.
6. To sell quality products competitively priced.
7. Find new profitable sales markets for existing product lines and services.
8. To develop and maintain a position of leadership in the industries in which we operate.
9. To instill in each employee pride in the policies, products, and progress of his Company.
10. Continue the development of an aggressive, capable, visionary, and versatile organization, and in so doing develop employees in accordance with their natural capacities.
11. To make it possible for employees to earn promotion and promote from within the Company whenever possible.
12. To provide fair and reasonable salaries equitably applied.
13. To furnish employees adequate knowledge of the Company and what it is doing.
14. To give each employee the opportunity to express his opinion freely regarding policies, working conditions, etc.
15. To provide for each employee an opportunity to be prepared in case of sickness, accident, disability, or death, and to assure an income for his declining years.
16. To deal with each employee fairly and with respect for his human dignity.
17. Develop good employee relations and teamwork, plus good work climate permitting attainment of the greatest possible employee productivity.
18. To provide safe and pleasant work environments.
19. To build good public relations and be a good citizen in the areas of our operations.
20. To promote health, education, and good government.
21. To return our owners a reasonable profit on their investment.
22. To maintain and increase the value of our owners' investment in the Company.

* Reproduced by permission of Continental-Emsco Company, Dallas, Texas.

Figure 3-1

COMPANY OBJECTIVES

4 relate to innovation, including both technological development in existing product lines and the establishment of a character willing to innovate in order to meet changing conditions. Market standing is inferred or determined by objectives Nos. 5 through 8, which relate to product quality, price, the finding of new customers, and the maintenance of a position of leadership. Productivity is covered in objectives Nos. 17 and 18, with the recognition that the degree of productivity is based upon the teamwork of employees and the conditions under which they work. Objectives in regard to physical and financial resources are stated in the last objective, No. 22, and profitability as an objective is found in No. 21. Profitability is recognized as one of the major factors that determines growth and it is stated in the first objective.

Objectives Nos. 9 through 16 set objectives in regard to manager performance and development, and worker performance and attitude. In addition, these objectives suggest to some extent how the desired performance is to be achieved and motivated. Note that there is no differentiation in these objectives in respect to their applicability; they apply equally to the worker and to management. Objectives clarifying the company's social responsibilities are stated in terms of being a good citizen, No. 19, and in encouraging health, education, and good government in objective No. 20.

These are the overall objectives of the entire Continental-Emsco Company. To insure that all levels of management are aware of the stated objectives of the company, a personnel development program is conducted in each plant. The management personnel in each plant develop the statement of objectives for that plant. Since plant objectives are formulated by each plant, they reflect the particular needs and capabilities of that plant, thus permitting maximum contribution to overall company objectives by each unit. In addition, having each plant state its own objectives fulfills one of the requisites stated in the principle of the objective; namely, that the objective must be clearly understood.

ETHICS

Once the objectives of a firm have been established, and assuming that these objectives are sanctioned by society, the manner in which objectives are achieved falls within the province of ethics. The word, ethics, as it is used today, comes from the Greek root, "ethos," and in its original form referred to habitual practices and customs. At a later date the concept of character became a part of its meaning.

Ethics is defined as the study of conduct between individuals—what are the standards governing their interrelationships? The problem of ethics is concerned with the behavior of individuals; therefore, such terms as "business ethics," "corporate ethics," and "corporate morality" become vague and meaningless. Furthermore, a person's impression of the state of "business ethics" is actually his judgment of the behavior of individuals employed in the business community. Specifically, is the Golden Transit Company behaving in an unethical fashion, or is it the behavior of its managers that is subject to criticism? A business firm may have policies that govern to some extent the conduct of its executives, but the firm itself is a legal entity, not an individual. Thus, a firm is incapable of those personal interrelationships that characterize individuals.

There is a second concept implied in the definition of ethics in addition to the interrelationships between individuals. The additional concept is that the word clearly indicates a desirable standard of performance as demonstrated by the existence and use of the word *unethical*, which denotes behavior that does not meet desired standards.

The Nature of Ethical Problems

There are two approaches to the determination of ethical standards for businessmen. First, there are writings that record examples of behavior in order to classify and synthesize these observations into a meaningful arrangement. This method is best described as a series of philosophical essays. Secondly, there is at least one extensive empirical study that analyzes current ethical practices in American business. In this study, 1,700 businessmen were asked to give their reaction to a selected range of ethical problems.[3] Both approaches will be examined and recommendations will be made to describe how an individual firm can aid in controlling the ethical standards of its management.

No two writers have described the questions of ethics for businessmen in exactly the same way. However, analysis of the literature results in at least three distinct problem areas:

1. Problems related to the making of decisions that are based on personal values rather than upon factual data.
2. Problems that are best described as a conflict of interest within the individual which arise because he is simultaneously a member of several groups that often have conflicting goals.

---

[3] R. C. Baumhart, "How Ethical Are Businessmen?" *Harvard Business Review*, Vol. 39 (July-August, 1961), pp. 6-12, 175.

3. Interpersonal relationships; that is, relationships with other individuals or groups of individuals.

Let us look at each of these problem areas in turn.

Problems Relating to Decision Making. Not all decisions resolve into ethical problems. Some questions are neatly solved by the application of an impersonal mathematical formula. Examples are plentiful and can be found in all areas of business and at all levels within the organization. The production foreman decides which machine will be used in making a certain part, after analyzing the relative merits of the machines with respect to availability, cost, quality, and amount of time the operation will require. Likewise, the decision to buy a given piece of equipment in preference to another can be made in the same manner. But there are many areas where computations are not applicable. Such an analysis has been presented by Louis W. Norris in his discussion of the "Moral Hazards of an Executive." Mr. Norris presents the following six types of decisions that utilize ethical concepts in their resolution:

1. Living with the necessity of compromise—but never compromising too much.
2. Being free to disclose parts of the truth on many occasions, yet needing to see the whole truth.
3. Having to make final decisions but on the basis of incomplete facts.
4. Accepting the responsibility for the mistakes of subordinates while not allowing them to make too many mistakes.
5. Living up to the image that the public and his associates demand of a man in a high office, but not becoming the victim of it.
6. Succeeding as a man of thought as well as a man of action.[4]

These moral hazards fall within the province of ethics because the resolution of any one of the above-mentioned situations has its impact upon other people; yet this is not the critical factor in making these decisions. In each case the executive is asked to make a judgment, and the reference point for determining the soundness of the decision is a personal value held by the decision-maker himself. Compromise, for example, is essential to success and may be accomplished by modifying the goal or the means of obtaining the goal. The question is one of determining when a given compromise becomes too much compromise. In a sense, a personal value is being compromised. Also, it is a judgment

---

4 Louis W. Norris, "Moral Hazards of an Executive," *Harvard Business Review*, Vol. 38 (September-October, 1960), pp. 72-79.

based on personal values that guides the executive in determining how much of the truth in any given situation should be revealed, whether a decision should be made even though all the necessary facts are not available, and in determining the upper limits of the number of mistakes on the part of a subordinate that may be tolerated. In addition, a manager must retain a degree of individuality in his personal life, and he must strive to broaden and deepen his intellectual horizons even though the image of his office calls for a man of action. The above-mentioned situations are not susceptible to quantification, and mathematical analysis, but must be viewed as questions of personal values.

Conflict of Interest Problems. Much has been said about conflict of interest as it applies to high-ranking government officials. It is now customary for the President of the United States and Defense Department officials to divest themselves of the shares they hold in public corporations, or to establish a trust fund in such a manner that they are not aware of the specific shares held and have no control over the purchase or sale of their equities. Such action has been considered necessary in order to minimize or eliminate situations that might lead to a conflict of interest. It is only normal that a potential conflict of interests exists when an individual is simultaneously a member of one or more groups. Potential conflict is present because a person as a member of a group is expected to perform those actions necessary for the support of that group. Thus, it seems reasonable to assume that the possibility of conflicting interests may be controlled by limiting the number of groups in which an individual may participate at any given time.

The typical conflict of interest situation that arises most frequently originates when an official employed by one company has interests in a second company that either supplies or purchases from the employing firm. This possible conflict of interest is illustrated by the following questions: If an executive has a major financial interest in a firm that supplies parts to the company that employs him, will he, as an employee, be sufficiently forceful in demanding the best price and quality? Will he be more forceful in demanding the best for his employer if he has no personal financial interests in the profits of the supplying firm?

Let us see how one company has answered these questions. The Gillette Company, in its annual report for 1960, answers two specific questions relating to the control of conflict of interest. In answer to a question requesting the company's practice in regard to outside business interests of key employees, the following statement was made: "No member of the management group is permitted to hold a paid position anywhere else which might interfere with his duties or responsibilities to the Company. Questions of directorships, paid or otherwise, are discussed with and approved by the Chairman and President."[5]

This statement, properly applied, does much to control the development of potential conflict of interest situations resulting from an executive's acceptance of pay from outside sources. The statement covers only one aspect of conflicting loyalties in that it mentions only those instances where services are paid for by another company. It does not touch upon the problem of gifts or gratuities. In answer to the specific question concerning the company's practice in regard to avoidance of conflict of interest that might arise from the acceptance of gifts, the following position is quite clear: "No member of management of the Company is allowed to accept any gift or gratuities from third persons which might conceivably tend to induce him to violate his duties to the Company or to have any appreciable interest in any business enterprise which is a supplier or has business relationships with the Company."[6] These statements by the Gillette Company indicate the extent to which control may be exercised in order to minimize the possibility of conflicting or divided loyalties.

Interpersonal Relationships. Ethical problems recognized primarily as matters of interpersonal relationships are closely related to company objectives since the interpersonal contacts of an executive arise to a large extent as the result of actions intended to assist the company in meeting its objectives. One writer, Mr. Charles Kendrick, who is chairman of the board of directors of Schlage Lock Company has defined the problems of business ethics entirely within a framework of interpersonal relationships, and offers the following areas requiring ethical judgments on the part of the businesssman: (1) ethical relations with customers, (2) with the company, (3) between companies, (4) with employees, and (5) with shareholders.[7] Mr. Kendrick limits the fourth area of ethical judgments—interpersonal relationships with employees —to relationships between superior and subordinate and implies that the responsibility for ethical behavior rests solely with the superior. In addition, there are relationships between a subordinate and his superior that call for ethical judgment on the part of the subordinate; therefore, a sixth relationship—ethical relationships between subordinate and superior—is added to make the analysis logically complete.

The six ethical areas of interpersonal relationships may be grouped as relationships with those persons who are *external* to the firm, and

[5] The Gillette Company, *1960 Annual Report* (Boston: 1961), p. 16.
[6] *Ibid.*
[7] H. B. Maynard, (ed.), *Top Management Handbook* (New York: McGraw-Hill Book Company, 1960), pp. 1145-1158.

relationships with those persons who are *internal* or part of the firm. Relationships with customers and with society, including the governmental units representing that society, and with other companies, are external to the firm. Relationships with employees, with shareholders, and between subordinate and superior may be considered as internal to the firm. Let us examine the influence of company objectives upon relationships with those persons outside the firm and, then, with those persons who are part of the firm.

EXTERNAL RELATIONSHIPS. A person who represents a company that has adopted a policy of *caveat emptor*—let the buyer beware—has a difficult time in maintaining a continuing relationship with customers that may be judged as satisfactory and within the limits of good business behavior and ethics. Fortunately, most companies are more than willing to stand behind their products and, in many instances, they do so far beyond the demands of any written guarantee. In addition to the desire of individual companies to be fair and equitable with their customers, certain governmental agencies have been established to force compliance with minimum standards in this respect. One example is the Fair Trade Commission, which has much to do with the control and elimination of false and misleading advertising.

A company does much to insure ethical behavior on the part of its representatives in relation to society when it spells out specific objectives that define its relationship with the community in which it exists. For example, the Continental-Emsco Company provides objectives in this area in its objective No. 19, page 57, which specifies that the company desires to be a good citizen, and in objective No. 20, which states the firm's desire to promote health, education, and good government. These objectives imply in broad terms the kind of behavior toward society that may be expected of company executives in fulfilling the requirements of their jobs. Consider, on the other hand, the relationship that exists between an executive of National Busways and the community in which he lives after he has discontinued some of the bus routes and decreased the frequency of service on others. He, too, is doing what is required of him in order to meet company objectives.

Underlying business relationships between competing companies is the assumption that all firms should be allowed to compete on equal terms in a free society. Over the years, a body of regulatory law at the national level has developed, the purpose of which is to define those actions that are not considered as fair and equitable relationships between competing companies. Basic statutes in this area are the Sherman Antitrust Act of 1890 and the Clayton Act of 1914, which were passed to control the formation of monopolies and other activities such as price-fixing, which would tend to result in a restraint of trade. These are but two of the many laws that have been passed to regulate the conduct of businessmen, not only in their relationships with each other, but also in respect to their relationships with society and their customers.

INTERNAL RELATIONSHIPS. There are three areas of interpersonal relationships with individuals and groups internal to the firm that require ethical judgments. These relationships are with employees, shareholders, and superiors. Relationships with the first two groups are more likely to be considered ethical if an executive is fulfilling company objectives that are well stated and have the approval of society. Although company objectives that call for equitable relationships with employees and stockholders guide an executive in making ethical judgments, such objectives do not offer much help when there is an honest difference of opinion as to what constitutes fairness in a specific situation. Examples are the periodic negotiations a company has with the union representing its employees in those matters pertaining to wages and other conditions of employment. Likewise, an honest difference of opinion may arise when shareholders, as owners of the business, desire a greater return on their investment. In addition to resolving these two conflicting requests, management is asked to determine what part of earnings should be retained in the business in order that the company might continue to maintain, or possibly improve, its competitive position. The apportionment of company earnings is not an easy decision to make and requires an ethical judgment concerning the validity of the claims of each segment of the business: the employees, the shareholders, and the needs of the business itself to fulfill its stated objectives.

In addition to relationships between employees and shareholders that are based on principles of equity, a manager's relationship with his superior often calls for ethical judgments. One phase of the subordinate-superior relationship, in which the subordinate is forced to rely upon his own ethical standards in determining proper conduct, is the subordinate's decision that defines proper action on his part in obtaining promotions. Can he establish a reputation for honesty and integrity and at the same time be an opportunist who takes advantage of others in order to advance himself? Another decision dependent upon a subordinate's ethical standards centers around his judgment as to what constitutes an honest, workmanlike job in the completion of duties assigned him. The other phase of this relationship—from superior to subordinate—has been touched upon in the discussion of those decisions that must be made that are dependent upon an ethical judgment as a criterion. In particular, it is mentioned that a superior is faced with the problem of determining to what extent he can permit a subordinate to make mistakes and at the same time accept responsibility for those mistakes. A superior also faces ethical problems in determining just how much he should compromise with a subordinate and in determining the extent to which he can reveal all the facts of a situation to those reporting to him.

How Ethical Are Businessmen?

Before answering the question, "How ethical are businessmen?" a few examples of some typical problems in ethics will be helpful.

As a member of the board of directors, you learn that a merger is planned with a small company that is unprofitable, and as a result, the stock of this smaller company is priced very low. Also, you are certain that when the merger is announced to the public, the stock in the smaller company will rise sharply. Would you quietly buy some shares for yourself, would you tell some of your good friends of this possibility of making a profit, would you tell your broker, or would you do none of these things and keep quiet about the whole matter?

Suppose you are an executive of a highly competitive industry, for example, electronics, and you find out that a competitor has made an important product development that will probably reduce your company's profits and sales. You discover the name of the engineer who made the development and has complete technical knowledge of the details. Would you try to hire him to save your own business?

Assume that a choice has to be made between two new advertising programs for your company's product line. One of these plans emphasizes the social and economic superiority of the product while the other stresses the product's quality. Which program would you choose?

What do you think of a man who earns $10,000 a year and pads his expense account by about $500 annually? Is this wrong under all circumstances, is it acceptable if other people in the company do the same thing, is it acceptable if his superiors know of his actions and say nothing? [8]

---

[8] R. C. Baumhart, *ibid*. These questions and the discussion following are based upon the questionnaire and findings reported by the Reverend Raymond C. Baumhart, S. J., Doctoral Candidate, Harvard Business School. The study reports a wealth of detailed material that is of unique value in that it is a statement of how businessmen define ethical problems and how they react to problems involving ethical concepts.

These and similar questions were included in a survey of 1,700 representative executives to determine their attitudes toward ethical problems. The survey establishes four problem areas: the extent to which businessmen are aware of their social and ethical responsibilities, current practices in industry that are accepted yet recognized as unethical, a description of specific areas requiring ethical judgments, and an analysis of the determinants of ethical standards and practices in industry.

Awareness of Social and Ethical Responsibilities. Awareness of ethics as related to business is illustrated by the overwhelming number of executives, 99 out of every 100, who indicate complete agreement with the following statement: "Sound ethics is good business in the long run." In addition, there is considerable evidence that businessmen recognize the multiple nature of business objectives. Five out of six believe that it would be unethical to act in the interest of shareholders only and exclude the interests of employees and consumers. However, one out of six, or approximately 16 percent, does not agree that sound ethics is good business.

When the statement, "Sound ethics is good business in the long run," is paraphrased so that it becomes "Whatever is good business is good ethics," 15 percent of those queried indicate agreement with the paraphrased statement. In conclusion, it appears that the vast majority of executives are acutely aware of the social and ethical implications of their actions, but there is also evidence that approximately 15 percent of those included in the survey have a different value system.

Further evidence that business behavior is not as ethical as it might be is provided in the answers to the four questions on page 65. An interesting technique was employed in the wording of these questions. One half of the 1,700 businessmen receiving the questionnaire were asked what would *you* do in the following situations. The other half were asked to state what they thought the *average* executive would do. Thus, the results can be interpreted in terms of what I would do and in terms of what the other fellow, the average executive, would do. A summary of the data obtained from each of the groups is presented in Figure 3-2.

In every instance there is a marked tendency for the executive to rate himself as more ethical than the hypothetical "average" executive, thereby revealing a skepticism of the motives and behavior of the other fellow. Also, in all instances, there is considerable room for improvement, based upon ideal ethical standards, for the group rating its own behavior.

CASE 1

IMAGINE THAT YOU ARE A MEMBER OF THE BOARD OF DIRECTORS OF A LARGE CORPORATION. AT A BOARD MEETING YOU LEARN OF AN IMPENDING MERGER WITH A SMALLER COMPANY WHICH HAS HAD AN UNPROFITABLE YEAR, AND WHOSE STOCK IS PRESENTLY SELLING AT A PRICE SO LOW THAT YOU ARE CERTAIN IT WILL RISE WHEN NEWS OF THE MERGER BECOMES PUBLIC KNOWLEDGE.

	WHAT I WOULD DO	WHAT THE AVERAGE EXECUTIVE WOULD DO
BUY SOME FOR SELF?	42%	61%
TELL A GOOD FRIEND?	14%	46%
TELL BROKER?	2%	11%
DO NOTHING?	56%	29%

CASE 2

AS PRESIDENT OF A COMPANY MANUFACTURING CONSUMER GOODS, YOU ARE CONSIDERING NEW IDEAS FOR INCREASING SALES. YOUR MARKETING DEPARTMENT HAS PRESENTED TWO PROGRAMS, EACH OF WHICH WOULD ACHIEVE THE DESIRED INCREASE IN SALES. ONE PROGRAM EMPLOYS AN ADVERTISING THEME PORTRAYING OWNERSHIP OF YOUR PRODUCT AS A SYMBOL OF THE PURCHASER'S SUPERIORITY, WHILE THE OTHER PROGRAM USES AN ADVERTISING THEME EMPHASIZING THE QUALITY OF YOUR PRODUCT.

WHAT I WOULD DO — 66%, 11%, 23%

WHAT THE AVERAGE EXECUTIVE WOULD DO — 33%, 50%, 17%

EMPHASIZE PRODUCT QUALITY

EMPHASIZE PURCHASER SUPERIORITY

NO REASON TO MAKE A CHOICE HERE

CASE 3

AN EXECUTIVE EARNING $10,000 A YEAR HAS BEEN PADDING HIS EXPENSE ACCOUNT BY ABOUT $500 A YEAR.

	WHAT I THINK OF THIS	WHAT THE AVERAGE EXECUTIVE THINKS OF THIS
ACCEPTABLE IF OTHER EXECUTIVES IN THE COMPANY DO THE SAME THING	6%	27%
ACCEPTABLE IF THE EXECUTIVE'S SUPERIOR KNOWS ABOUT IT AND SAYS NOTHING	11%	28%
UNACCEPTABLE REGARDLESS OF THE CIRCUMSTANCES	86%	60%

CASE 4

IMAGINE THAT YOU ARE THE PRESIDENT OF A COMPANY IN A HIGHLY COMPETITIVE INDUSTRY. YOU LEARN THAT A COMPETITOR HAS MADE AN IMPORTANT SCIENTIFIC DISCOVERY WHICH WILL GIVE HIM AN ADVANTAGE THAT WILL SUBSTANTIALLY REDUCE, BUT NOT ELIMINATE, THE PROFITS OF YOUR COMPANY FOR ABOUT A YEAR. IF THERE WERE SOME HOPE OF HIRING ONE OF THE COMPETITOR'S EMPLOYEES WHO KNEW THE DETAILS OF THE DISCOVERY, WOULD YOU TRY TO HIRE HIM?

WHAT I WOULD DO — 48%, 52%

WHAT THE AVERAGE EXECUTIVE WOULD DO — 70%, 30%

PROBABLY WOULD HIRE HIM

PROBABLY WOULD NOT HIRE HIM

I'M MORE ETHICAL THAN HE

Note: The figures for Cases I and II do not add to 100% since some respondents gave more than one answer to the case problem.

Figure 3-2

I'M MORE ETHICAL THAN HE

Current Practices: Accepted, Yet Unethical. The skepticism concerning the motives and actions of the average executive shown in Figure 3-2 may be attributed in part to practices within most industries that are tolerated and sometimes even accepted though they fall far short of ideal standards of ethical behavior. In order to obtain direct information on accepted, yet unethical practices, the following question was asked: "In every industry there are some generally accepted business practices. In your industry are there any such practices which you regard as unethical?"

Actions intended to buy loyalty for the company and its products are mentioned most frequently as the one practice that should be eliminated. Among the methods used to secure preferential treatment for the company and its products are gifts, gratuities, lavish entertainment, and outright bribes. Twenty-three percent of those queried indicate that these practices ranked first among those that should be eliminated. Unfair practices in pricing, such as price discrimination, are listed as the next most undesirable practice, with 18 percent indicating that these practices should be eliminated. Dishonest advertising ranks first on the list of practices to be eliminated by 14 percent of those queried. Miscellaneous unfair competitive practices; cheating customers, unfair credit practices, overselling; price collusion by competitors; dishonesty in making or keeping a contract; and unfairness and prejudice in hiring are mentioned, but in no case did more than 10 percent rank any one of these practices as the one practice that should be eliminated.

The preceding information is important for several reasons. First, it illustrates the extent of unethical practices, along with a detailing of these practices. Second, the practices of an industry form the "ethical climate" in which an executive must operate and, as such, have a marked influence upon his behavior. And lastly, the existence of unethical, yet accepted, practices sets the stage for a certain degree of conflict within the executive himself, as he may be required to do certain things in order to be accepted by his industry that he recognizes as unethical in the light of his own standards.

Problem Areas Requiring Ethical Judgments. The giving of gifts, gratuities, and lavish entertainment, all of which are intended to obtain loyalty for a company or its products, are ranked as the number one unethical practice that should be eliminated. Thus, it would seem that the problem situation most frequently giving rise to conflict would be in connection with these activities. However, such is not the case. Instead, problems of interpersonal relationships ranked first as the business situation causing the deepest source of concern. Interpersonal problems create a conflict within the individual executive between what is expected of him as a profit-conscious businessman and what is expected of him as an ethical person. Yet, it must be noted that only 75 percent of the executives participating in the study indicate that there are any ethical problems. Apparently the 25 percent that do not perceive any problems do not regard the following interpersonal problems as having an ethical content. The problem areas considered as causing the deepest concern are: firings and layoffs, honest communications; collusion and sharp practices in pricing; gifts, entertainment, and kickbacks; and pressure from superiors.

FIRINGS AND LAYOFFS. The problem mentioned most frequently as creating the deepest concern is that of firings and layoffs, a situation related to an earlier observation concerning the general awareness that exists in regard to the social and ethical responsibilities of businessmen. In this connection, it is noted that five out of every six persons believe that it would be unethical to act in the interest of shareholders alone to the exclusion of the interests of employees and customers. The ethical content of interpersonal problems arising from firings and layoffs is shown by the following comment supplied by a personnel director: "It has always concerned me that the industry's regular (periodic) reduction in work force should always bear so heavily on the 'little people'—particularly when adversity has not always been equally shared by stockholders and top management." [9]

HONEST COMMUNICATIONS. The second category of ethical situations—honest communications—is an example of those problems relating to the making of a decision based upon personal values rather than upon factual data. The question to be answered is essentially the same as that mentioned by L. W. Norris.[10] The problem in respect to honest communications is not the determination of what the truth is nor whether the truth should be told; instead, it is a matter of determining how much of the truth should be revealed. In reaching this decision, the final judgment is based upon one's own personal values.

COLLUSION AND SHARP PRACTICES IN PRICING. The third category centers around interpersonal relationships with competitors. Particular reference is made to the opportunity for collusion in pricing the company's products. Problems expressed in this area range from the pressure put on small companies to fix prices in line with those of large com-

---

[9] *Ibid.,* p. 163.
[10] L. W. Norris, *ibid.* Mr. Norris' "Moral Hazards of an Executive" are discussed on page 60.

petitors to the establishment of price differentials for those who buy because of price alone—yet not giving the same advantage to their loyal customers. Also included is the question of determining a fair price for those who purchase goods on an installment plan.

GIFTS, ENTERTAINMENT, AND KICKBACKS. Though the use of gifts and lavish entertainment is designated most frequently as the one practice that should be eliminated, these practices rank fourth as a source of ethical conflict. There seems to be a recognition that customers who are retained by means of lavish entertainment are capable of being bought by someone else who is willing to pay a higher price. Also, questions are raised concerning the propriety of expensive trips for company personnel and other practices that represent an unwise use of the company's money; in short, a breach of trust with the shareholders.

PRESSURE FROM SUPERIORS. The last, and perhaps the most important, situation creating interpersonal conflict is the result of pressures from one's superiors in the company. Such pressures may range from a normal feeling that one is being asked to accomplish too much in too short a time to a frantic attempt to please everyone as a means of advancing within the company. Excessive pressure may also come from a drive for increased production, increased sales volume, or greater profits without regard for the actions necessary to meet these goals. Undue influence from superiors may also extend to expecting an individual to conform with practices that are a violation of law; for example, the establishing of prices that may be in restraint of trade.

Determinants of Ethical Standards and Practices. The degree of awareness of social and ethical responsibilities has been reviewed; current practices—accepted, yet unethical—have been examined; and the five problem areas causing concern because the decisions required involve ethical judgments have been discussed briefly. Though this information is significant, the major contribution of the Reverend Baumhart's study is that it points the way toward the development of a principle of ethics. Before the principle can be developed, it is necessary to know the factors determining the degree of ethical behavior in the business community. The executives included in the survey were asked to rank the influences which, in their opinion, contribute most to ethical behavior and the influences contributing most to unethical behavior. The results of the ranking are shown in Table 3-1.[11]

When answering the question calling for influences that create ethical behavior, the factor given first rank is the individual's personal

---

[11] *Ibid.*, p. 156.

Table 3-1

DETERMINANTS OF ETHICAL BEHAVIOR

Factors Determining Ethical Decisions		Factors Determining Unethical Decisions	
Factor	Average Rank	Factor	Average Rank
A Man's Personal Code of Behavior	1.5	The Behavior of a Man's Superiors in the Company..	1.9
The Behavior of a Man's Superiors in the Company..	2.8	Ethical Climate of the Industry	2.6
Formal Company Policy	2.8	The Behavior of a Man's Equals in the Company....	3.1
Ethical Climate of the Industry	3.8	Lack of Company Policy	3.3
The Behavior of a Man's Equals in the Company ...	4.0	Personal Financial Needs	4.1

code of conduct. Tied for second place in importance as determinants of ethical behavior are two factors in the executive's immediate business environment; (1) the behavior of his superiors in the company, and (2) a formal statement of company policy. Though the ethical climate of the industry and the behavior of his equals in the company are important, they are not as significant in determining ethical behavior as the first three factors—his own ethical standards, the standards of his superiors, and the standards of his company as reflected in its policy statement.

What are the influences leading to unethical decisions? Moving to first rank in importance in determining unethical behavior is the behavior of a man's superiors. The climate of the industry, in reality a composite of the behavior of all the executives of that industry, is second in importance as a determinant of unethical actions. The remaining three factors—behavior of a man's equals, lack of company policy, and personal financial needs are of significance, but in each case the ranked value is greater than three.

Thus, it seems that regardless of the manner in which the question is worded; i.e., whether the emphasis is placed upon ethical or unethical behavior, two factors stand out as major determinants of ethical behavior. They are: (1) the individual executive's personal code of conduct and (2) the behavior of his superiors. In the last analysis, the superior's behavior is governed, in turn, by his own personal code of conduct.

The above conclusion, which indicates the ultimate dependence upon a personal code of conduct and ethics, has a familiar ring. In Chapter 2, in the discussion of Fayol's principle of authority, it is mentioned that the solution to questions concerning the abuse of authority lies in the integrity of the person holding that authority. Fayol's full statement concerning this point is as follows: "The best safeguard against abuse of authority and against weakness on the part of a higher manager is personal integrity and particularly high moral character of such a manager, and this integrity, it is well known, is conferred neither by election nor ownership." [12]

Principle of Ethics

Fundamental to the development of a principle of ethics is the recognition that the business community is composed of many industries which, in turn, are made up of many companies. Each company has its own management, and each and every member of that management is at the same time an individual, a subordinate, and a superior. As an individual, his own personal code of conduct exerts the greatest influence in determining the degree to which his behavior is judged as ethical. As a subordinate, his own code is reinforced and supported by the actions of his superiors. As a superior, he exerts a great positive influence in encouraging ethical behavior on the part of subordinates and has potentially an even greater influence in contributing to a subordinate's unethical behavior. The principle is clear: *The ethical standards of any industry are determined by the ethical standards of individual executives of each member company in that industry.*

Code of Ethics

Though the ethical standards of a group are dependent upon the standards of each individual member of the group, the establishment of a code of ethics may serve a useful purpose. The chief value obtained from the establishment of a code is that it offers a framework within which individual members of the group may work. Guides are provided that offer aid in reaching decisions on those problems having a high ethical content. Ethical codes tend to be an expression of the ideal and, as such, they have the effect of raising the level of conduct of the group governed by the code. There have been many criticisms of codes of ethics. Chief among these criticisms is that, for the most part, such codes are established voluntarily and are difficult to enforce. Usually the penalty for violating a code is expulsion from

---

[12] Henri Fayol in H. F. Merrill (ed.), *Classics in Management* (New York: American Management Association, 1960), p. 220.

a group, which has the effect of leaving the violator free from further criticism. Codes are also criticized as being at best an expression of good intentions and not an accurate statement of conditions as they actually exist.

Nonetheless, several industries and groups associated with industry have developed codes of ethics. In 1957 the AFL-CIO formulated a statement known as the AFL-CIO Ethical Practices Code. This code states six ethical practices to be followed by members of the AFL-CIO. Included are regulations which govern the issuance of charters for local unions, the honest administration of trust funds, and the conduct of honest elections for union officials. Also mentioned are conditions limiting eligibility to hold office in the AFL-CIO or any affiliated union, limitations upon outside financial interests on the part of union officials, and provisions designed to insure that accurate and honest records of all union transactions are maintained. In 1958, the National Association of Manufacturers (NAM) issued a two-part statement setting forth the beliefs of management in regard to moral and ethical standards. The first part of the statement outlines the beliefs of the NAM in regard to the type of political economy that industry should support and suggests the proper relationships between industry and government, suppliers, customers, and stockholders. The second part of the statement outlines the beliefs of the NAM with respect to employer-employee relationships.[13]

In the opinion of many, these two codes of conduct have fallen far short of their goals. Neither all unions, nor all managements, conduct themselves in accordance with the standards set forth by their respective groups. Yet there are instances where self-regulation, the alternate to government regulation, has worked effectively, and demonstrate that self-regulation is possible and effective provided the group sincerely wishes to enforce ethical standards. An illustration of self-regulation is provided in Case Problem 3-B.

SUMMARY OF PRINCIPLES

Two related topics, objectives and ethics, are presented in this chapter. The major characteristic of the objective is that it is set apart from and occurs prior to the processes of management— planning, organizing, controlling, and directing. The principle of the objective emphasizes this characteristic.

---

[13] *Moral and Ethical Standards in Labor and Management* (New York: National Association of Manufacturers, 1958), pp. 1-7.

Principle
of the
Objective

{ Before initiating any course of action, the objectives in view must be clearly determined, understood, and stated.

An overwhelming number of businessmen are aware of the obligations of business to society and to individual members of society. There is considerable evidence indicating that many individuals, companies, and industries fall short of desired ethical standards. The principle of ethics does not offer a panacea for these ills, but it does state in concise form the major reason why companies and industries fail to meet expected ethical standards.

Principle
of
Ethics

{ The ethical standards of any industry are determined by the ethical standards of the individual executives of each member company in that industry.

Questions for Study and Discussion

1. One of the characteristics of an objective is that it should be well within the reach of an organization, yet difficult to obtain. With this in mind, comment on the following statement: The difficult we do today; the impossible we do tomorrow.
2. Why is the creation of profit a good example of an objective that simultaneously gives direction and motivates?
3. Why is it necessary for a firm to have an objective that states its desired overall position in relation to its competitors?
4. Why is it necessary to state several objectives for a firm rather than one general objective?
5. Continental-Emsco Company, in its statement of objectives, follows the recommendations of Peter Drucker, but separate objectives are not stated for managers and for workers. If you were preparing a statement of objectives for a company, would you differentiate between manager performance and development, and worker performance and attitude?
6. Of what value are the statements of company practice as stated by the Gillette Company concerning outside financial interests of key employees?
7. Is it significant that the classification of interpersonal relationships follows the same general pattern as the classification of objectives; i.e., internal and external interpersonal relationships which correspond to those objectives that are internal to the firm and those objectives that are external to the firm?

8. What is the question of ethics involved in each of the four typical ethical problems presented on page 65?
9. Comment on the following statements: "Sound ethics is good business in the long run," and "Whatever is good business is good ethics."
10. On page 69 there is a quotation from a personnel director who recognizes an ethical problem in the effect of periodic layoffs upon workers when adversity has not been equally shared by stockholders and top management. Does the same problem in ethics exist if the company continues to grant wage increases to the extent that it cannot pass on the gains obtained from increased productivity to stockholders in the form of increased dividends and to customers through a reduction in price?
11. The principle of ethics is worded with reference to an industrial situation; that is, the ethical standards of an industry and the standards of the companies that make up that industry. Does this principle apply equally to professional groups such as teachers, physicians, and lawyers?

• • • • • • • • •

This case is based upon two press releases issued on the same day by the New York Stock Exchange.[14] Press Release No. 1 is a statement by Mr. Edward C. Werle, chairman of the Board of Governors of the New York Stock Exchange. Mr. Werle's statement presents a detailed statement of an action, and the reasons for that action, taken by the Board of Governors of the New York Stock Exchange. Press Release No. 2, by the president of the New York Stock Exchange, Mr. G. Keith Funston, emphasizes the "moral responsibilities" of the New York Stock Exchange.

Case Problem 3-B
The New York Stock Exchange—An Example of Self-Regulation

Press Release No. 1

Edward C. Werle, chairman of the Board of Governors of the New York Stock Exchange, this morning (September 28) made the following announcement from the rostrum overlooking the trading floor of the Exchange:

"A charge was preferred against Anton E. Homsey, a member of the Exchange and a partner of DuPont, Homsey & Company, a member organization, under Section 1 of Article XIV of

---

[14] News Bureau, New York Stock Exchange (New York: September 28, 1960). Both releases were issued on the same day and both are reproduced in full.

the Constitution. The charge was considered by the Board of Governors at a special meeting on September 27, 1960.

"The charge stated that he had committed fraud or fraudulent acts. The substance of the charge was as follows:

"Anton E. Homsey, the managing general partner of DuPont, Homsey & Company, was responsible for the supervision and administration of the firm's back office operations and for surveillance of the firm's capital position.

"Mr. Homsey had delivered to him, on his instructions to the firm cashier or by delivery from the customer, securities from the accounts of three of the firm's customers between March and June, 1960. Mr. Homsey pledged all or most of these securities as collateral for loans without the knowledge of the customers. None of the loans was made in the name of DuPont, Homsey & Company or in the name, or for the benefit, of any of the three customers. Total market value of the securities was approximately $503,000.

"Mr. Homsey also personally removed two 100-share stock certificates from the firm's security box and pledged them as collateral for loans. These loans were not made in the name of the firm.

"Mr. Homsey certified to the Board of Governors that, to the best of his knowledge and belief, answers to financial questionnaires from the Exchange, as of February 29 and July 31, 1960, represented true and correct financial statements of DuPont, Homsey & Company. On each date, however, Mr. Homsey failed to report that he had borrowings on securities in excess of $200,000. The answer to the July 31 questionnaire also failed to disclose the apparent liability to the customers with respect to the securities withheld or withdrawn from customers' accounts.

"The Board found Mr. Homsey guilty of the charge and determined that he be expelled."

Press Release No. 2

Keith Funston, president of the New York Stock Exchange, said today the Board of Governors authorized the following statement regarding the expulsion of Anthony E. Homsey, a member of the Exchange and a partner in DuPont, Homsey & Company:

"The Board of Governors has expelled Mr. Anton E. Homsey from membership in the New York Stock Exchange—an action which means that the firm of DuPont, Homsey & Company is no longer a member firm of the Stock Exchange.

"The New York Stock Exchange is shocked that one of its members should have violated the trust placed in him by his associates and clients and is also dismayed that Mr. Homsey, by his action, placed in jeopardy the solvency of a New York Stock Exchange member organization.

"This is the first time in 22 years that the Exchange's Board of Governors has found it necessary to expel a member for fraudulent acts which endangered a member firm's financial position. As part of the vigorous financial supervision to which all member firms are subject, Exchange examiners, in the course of an examination, discovered a condition which suggested that DuPont, Homsey & Company could not be permitted to continue as a member firm with safety to its creditors. Consequently, the firm was suspended promptly from the Stock Exchange, and the appropriate regulatory agencies were notified. Continued investigation by the Stock Exchange uncovered evidence that fraudulent acts had been committed by Mr. Homsey and charges were quickly brought against him.

"At the present time a temporary court-appointed receiver is determining the exact financial position of DuPont, Homsey & Company. Pending a complete audit of the firm's affairs which we are advised should be completed in about two weeks, the exact nature of the losses—if any—which might be sustained by the firm's customers cannot be stated.

"While each member firm of the New York Stock Exchange bears the complete responsibility for its obligations to its customers, the Stock Exchange recognizes, nevertheless, that the expulsion of Anton E. Homsey does not solve the problem of protecting the interests of investors—particularly those of modest means—who dealt in good faith with DuPont, Homsey & Company. More than that, the New York Stock Exchange feels that its moral responsibilities to these investors are not ended with the act of expulsion.

"At this time, while awaiting results of the final audit, and of current negotiations by the receiver to resolve outstanding financial problems, the Stock Exchange is studying ways of assisting the receiver in order to help protect the interests of the firm's customers."

Problems

1. Why should the New York Stock Exchange feel that it has a moral responsibility in this case?

2. What immediate steps would you recommend be taken to protect the interests of those who invested with DuPont, Homsey & Company?

3. What long-range recommendations would you make to insure the interests of investors who invest with member firms of the New York Stock Exchange?

4. Why was it significant that the New York Stock Exchange discovered the irregularity of a member firm and then took the action described in this case?

5. Does this case illustrate the principle of ethics developed in the text? How?

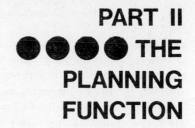
● CHAPTER 4

Planning

The Bojo Corporation is an established manufacturer, located in a small town in southwestern New York State. The Company was founded about 90 years ago and initially served both the railroad industry and the oil fields of northern Pennsylvania. At the present time, a large part of its business is still associated with the oil industry. However, in recent years, it has branched into other fields and has been able to develop applications of products originally used in the oil fields to other areas. The Bojo Corporation is a subsidiary company of a large national firm with headquarters in St. Louis. The national headquarters controls all capital expenditures, reviews operating budgets developed by the subsidiary corporations, follows up to insure the meeting of budgetary goals, and also exerts strong influence in the labor relations area. All labor contracts and labor policies are determined by the headquarters staff.

Case Problem 4-A
Selecting a Plant Site

In recent years, the Bojo Corporation developed a new type of pipe coupling that is used to join two pieces of pipe without having to thread the ends of the pipes being joined or cutting them to an exact length. The coupling saves time and money and has experienced a remarkable sales volume from municipalities since it is used primarily to replace existing water and gas lines. There is every reason to believe that the market will expand and that the Bojo Corporation will receive a large share of the increase. Since the coupling is particularly useful in the replacement market with the oldest water and gas systems on the eastern seaboard, the greatest potential market for the immediate future is in this area.

Present manufacturing facilities, a department in the main plant, are now running at capacity; and in order to meet the anticipated increase in demand, new facilities are needed. Since the present plant location does not permit expansion, it has been decided that a new plant should be built to house the present coupling department and to provide for future increases in volume. A member of the St. Louis controller's staff, Mr. Johnson, has been assigned the task of conducting a plant location survey and submitting recommendations to the president of the Bojo Corporation and officials of the parent company.

In preparing for his assignment, Mr. Johnson contacted several executives, among them the executive vice-president responsible for the Bojo Corporation and other subsidiaries in Pennsylvania, New York, and Massachusetts. It was the executive vice-president's wish that the plant be located on a direct route between Pittsburgh, Pennsylvania, and their present location, or between Buffalo, New York, and their present location. His reason for desiring the plant in these areas was that it would be convenient for him as a company executive to fly into either the Buffalo or Pittsburgh airport, rent a car, and drive directly to the plant.

A conversation with the home office vice-president, industrial relations, revealed that the company, as a matter of policy, wished to have a different international union in the new plant rather than have the employees represented by the same union that organized Bojo's New York plant. The reason for the policy was that by having a different union in each plant it would lessen the possibility of all plants closing as the result of a strike, since no one international union would represent more than one plant. The vice-president indicated that it would

be necessary to locate at least 100 miles from the present plant in order to be assured of a different union. He also recommended analyzing the labor rates of any community proposed as a location for the new plant so that maximum savings might be realized from low initial labor costs. He stated further that by starting operations with labor rates as low as possible, the company would be in a better position to increase rates in the future.

When Mr. Johnson contacted the president of the Bojo Corporation and reviewed the wishes of the two central office executives, he found the president had a few ideas of his own to add to the picture. The president indicated that it was mandatory that the new location have complete rail facilities, since raw materials were received most economically by rail and many of the finished product shipments could be made by rail. He wanted the plant located east of the present facility to minimize transportation costs by establishing a direct flow of materials from Pittsburgh to the East Coast markets. He was also insistent, as operating head of the company, that the new plant be located in an area where there is a well-defined, stable tax structure. He felt that tax stability was necessary to predict long-range profits with some degree of accuracy. Another requirement was that the site chosen be large enough to permit future expansion of the proposed plant to twice its initial size. The president of Bojo placed no exact limitations in regard to construction costs provided such costs were in line with typical costs for the area selected.

Problems

1. Assume that you are Mr. Johnson. Prepare an initial determination of the relative significance of the factors considered to be important by:
   a. The executive vice-president of the home office
   b. The vice-president, industrial relations, home office
   c. The president of the subsidiary Bojo Corporation

2. Indicate in detail the steps that you would follow in conducting a study to evaluate alternate sites for the new plant.

3. Prior to Mr. Johnson's receiving his assignment, certain decisions had been made by the Bojo management. What were these decisions? What additional decisions must be made after a satisfactory location for the new plant has been found?

●　●　●　●　●　●　●　●　●　●

Planning is generally considered the first function performed in the management process sequence of planning, organizing, directing, and controlling. The need for planning is not limited to the development of plans for the attainment of organizational objectives. Planning is required to develop plans for the organization necessary to implement those plans designed to achieve overall organizational objectives. Planning is also necessary to determine the methods and types of controls as well as the kind of direction best suited to the organization. Yet, the success or failure of an enterprise or the success or failure of specific plans is dependent upon the way in which the other three functions of the management process are performed, as well as upon the quality of the planning function, since planning is but one function of the management process cycle.

In our study of the planning function we shall examine some of the fundamental concepts of planning and develop a definition of planning. The different types of plans are reviewed and classified, and in the last part of the chapter, criteria are developed for the evaluation of plans. Two principles pertaining to the planning function are presented as a basis for predicting the probable success of plans.

FUNDAMENTAL CONCEPTS OF PLANNING

In order to understand the nature of planning, the meanings of three terms—planning, the plan, and decision making—must be clarified. We also need to know the purpose of planning and why planning is important to the management process. First, let us clarify the meaning of the terms, *planning, the plan,* and *decision making.*

Planning

Planning is an activity performed by all levels of management. Differences in the complexity of the planning process and the resultant plans are, to a large measure, determined by the organizational level of the person who initiates the planning process. Mr. Johnson (Case Problem 4-A) has been asked to develop and analyze alternatives available to the Bojo Corporation in the selection of a new plant site. There are many factors that he must consider, among which are availability of land, cost of land, cost of building, availability of transportation, and location in respect to raw materials and markets for the finished product. He is required not only to list these factors but also to evaluate them in respect to their relative importance, which in turn means that value criteria must be developed. These are the kinds of managerial activities normally associated with planning.

The outstanding concern of planning is the future, and as a process it probes into the future, literally attempting to foretell the effects of coming events, thereby enabling a firm to meet the future with some degree of success. Less apparent is planning's concern with the past. To develop a sound plan, it is necessary to review the past and evaluate information relevant to the present and the future. Analysis of forces of the present—both internal and external to the organization requiring planning—must also be considered. Thus, the planning function is defined as *the analysis of relevant information from the present and the past and an assessment of probable future developments so that a course of action (plan) may be determined that enables the organization to meet its stated objectives.*

The Plan

Planning, the process of evaluating all relevant information and the assessment of probable future developments, results in the statement of a recommended course of action—a *plan*. Plans should be regarded as blueprints for action. The kinds of plans commonly used in business operations are discussed in the next major topic of this chapter, "Types of Plans." The characteristics of plans and the effect that these characteristics have upon the probable success of plans are discussed in the section, "Criteria for Evaluating Plans."

Decision Making

Decision making is an activity that permeates the entire planning process. *Making a decision is making a choice between two or more alternatives.* The alternative selected is the decision. Planning requires the continuous collection, evaluation, and selection of data. Some data are rejected as not being pertinent to the problem at hand; other data are retained and used to formulate a recommended course of action. Selecting some information and rejecting other information constitute a choice, or a decision. Ultimately one proposed course of action is recommended as being superior to an alternate course as a means of attaining desired objectives. Again, a decision has been made. These are the decisions of a planner as he develops a plan.

Decision making is also used to describe an activity that is characteristic of executive positions. The responsible executive either accepts or rejects the plan presented to him. If he accepts the plan, the next step is its implementation. The implementation of a plan requires the commitment of company resources, an action that initiates a chain of events which are sometimes irreversible. The difference between an executive's decision and the decision of a planner is one of degree— not kind—since both are making choices. The executive's decisions are overt in their nature and are recognized because they commit company resources, but the planner's decisions are covert and can be retracted and reevaluated at will.[1]

Purpose of Planning

The operation of a business does not occur under conditions of complete *certainty,* nor does it occur under conditions of complete *uncertainty.* Conditions of complete certainty exist when more than 99 percent of all the relevant factors are known. Conditions of complete uncertainty exist when less than one percent of all the relevant factors are known. The concepts of uncertainty and certainty represent a range from one percent to 99 percent rather than a range of 0 percent to 100 percent. Business operations occur under conditions that lie between the extremes of uncertainty and certainty—an area on the scale from 1 to 99 percent that is known as *risk.* Risk is defined as knowledge of the probability that a given event will either occur or not occur.[2]

The purpose of planning is to provide information concerning the conditions surrounding a proposed course of action so that the ele-

---

[1] Case Problem 4-B illustrates the commitment of company resources following the acceptance of a recommended plan.

[2] A discussion of the concepts of certainty risk and uncertainty risk is found in M. H. Spencer and L. Siegelman, *Managerial Economics* (Homewood, Illinois: Richard D. Irwin, Inc., 1959), Chap. 6, pp. 5-16.

ment of risk is known and stated as a probability. Planning does not eliminate the element of risk, but planning does provide the basis for stating the degree of risk in more precise terms. As knowledge of the facts that influence the success or failure of a proposed plan approaches the level of certainty, the degree of risk declines.

Importance of Planning

Planning is of importance for two reasons: its *primacy* from the standpoint of position in the sequence of management functions, and its *pervasiveness* as an activity that affects the entire organization.

Primacy of Planning. Planning has a position of primacy among the management functions. The reason for designating planning as the first of the management processes is that in some instances planning may be the only managerial function performed.[3] Planning may result in a decision that further action is not required or possible. When this happens, there is no need for the subsequent processes of organizing, directing, and controlling. Had the Bojo Corporation, as a result of early planning, determined that they could manufacture couplings economically and in sufficient quantity by rearranging their present facilities, the present plant location study would not have been initiated, nor would the need arise to organize, direct, and control a new plant.

Pervasiveness. When need for further action is indicated, the pervasiveness of the planning function is revealed. Implementing the results of planning has its effects upon the functions of organizing, directing, and controlling. In addition, planning is an activity that is required to perform the functions of organizing, directing, and controlling. The effect of planning on each of the other managerial functions is discussed below.

ORGANIZING. Plans, the result of planning, have their effects upon the structure and functioning of an organization. Assume that there is a plan designed to raise a company's sales volume to $500 million. Further, the desired volume requires the acquisition of companies producing related products as well as increasing the sales volume of

---

[3] L. F. Urwick, "Management and Human Relations," in R. Tannenbaum, I. R. Weschler, and F. Massarik, *Leadership and Organization* (New York: McGraw-Hill Book Company, 1961), pp. 416-28. On page 423 Colonel Urwick states that planning must be considered a separate function, one which precedes an organization, because one of the possible results of planning is that there is no need for subsequent organization.

products now being produced. Acquiring other companies may necessitate establishing a special staff group to study and evaluate potential acquisitions. Also, permanent organizational units must be created to administer and coordinate the companies purchased as a part of the plan to increase sales volume. To increase the volume of sales produced by the present organization, a realignment of the duties of key executives may be required to establish broad geographic divisions, with each division having the capabilities of attaining its own specified share of the expected increase.

Planning, as a function of the management process, is required to define the structure, the authority relationships, and the proper scope for each of the newly created or modified organizational units arising from the implementation of an accepted plan.

DIRECTING. The results of planning have their effects upon the direction of an organization. As we shall find in Chapter 16, "Leadership Patterns," the methods of directing subordinates range from those methods considered as highly participative to techniques of direction regarded as authoritarian in nature. The closeness of direction varies from extremely close supervision to direction that exemplifies a "hands off" policy. Several factors determine the kind of direction that is best suited to meet organizational objectives. Some of these factors are the size of the organization, the capabilities and needs of the members of the organization, the goals of the organization in relation to the goals of its members, the need for an interchange of information between members of the organization, and the extent to which the organization is meeting its stated objectives. All of these conditions—each having its effect upon the kind of direction that is most effective—are the results of planning and the implementation of plans.

CONTROLLING. Planning is closely related to the control process in that plans often serve as the basis for control. A fully developed plan incorporates a timetable that shows, in proper sequence, the activities necessary to reach a stated objective and includes an estimate of the time required to complete each step. Also, a well-presented plan includes a statement of organizational responsibility. Thus, with checkpoints defined and responsibility clearly designated, there is a framework for the control process. The checkpoints provide a basis for comparing present performance, and the designation of organizational responsibility facilitates and makes more effective the corrective action of control. The proper exercise of the control function frequently requires the formulation of new plans or the modification of existing ones—and again, the new or changed plans serve as the basis for continuing control. The continuing relationship between planning and control is frequently described as the planning-control-planning cycle.

TYPES OF PLANS

We have seen that the primary purpose of planning is to reduce the degree of risk in business operations and that planning is important because of its position of primacy and its pervasiveness in influencing the other management functions. The emphasis has been placed on planning as a function. Let us now examine the result of planning—the plan—in respect to its characteristics and application.

The following outline classifies plans in respect to characteristics and use or application:

1. Classification by time or duration
   a. Long-range plans
   b. Short-range plans
2. Classification by business function or use
   a. Plans concerning the sales function
   b. Plans concerning the production function
   c. Plans concerning the personnel function
   d. Plans concerning the finance function
   e. Plans concerning any other major function
3. Classification in respect to breadth or scope
   a. Policies
   b. Procedures
   c. Methods

The above outline provides a useful basis for discussing the various types of plans. However, it must be remembered that any given plan includes more than one of the characteristics or uses shown in the outline. For example, a policy statement in the area of finance is considered a policy because of its breadth; it may also be a long-range plan if it pertains to the means of securing financial resources; and it is a plan concerned with a specific business function, finance. Similarly, a short-range plan may be applicable to any given business function and also classified by its breadth or scope; e.g., a procedure to guide the preparation of a physical inventory.

Classification by Time

When plans are classified in respect to their duration, they are recognized as either long-range plans or short-range plans. Examples of long-range planning are numerous and almost always include financial plans. It is not unusual for companies to issue bonds with a 25-year maturity date as part of a long-range plan to develop desired financial strength. Research and development programs are planned for many years, and the long-range plans for research frequently emphasize the research of "pure science" as well as the development of new products. Research not directed specifically toward new products must be continued on a long-range basis since it has been demonstrated many times that the "pure" research of today leads to the development of products for tomorrow. Corporate public relations programs are also planned on a continuing basis since one of their express purposes is to create a stable public image. General Electric's slogan, "Progress is our most important product," capitalizes on long-range research plans as a means of establishing a corporate image.

As might be expected, plans that encompass a relatively short period of time are referred to as short-range plans. There is, unfortunately, no precise cut-off point in time which enables one to designate categorically all plans extending beyond a given duration as long range and all plans up to that duration as short range. Short-range plans are best understood in their relation to long-range plans. Examples are found in the daily and even annual operations of a company. Typical short-range plans are production schedules for a period of a day, a week, or perhaps a month. Actually, production schedules may be considered short-range plans even though they extend over a period of a year, provided expanded facilities are planned for the foreseeable future. Thus, the designation of a plan as either short range or long range depends, to some measure, upon whether the plan considered as short range is part of a larger plan. Generally, if a plan is part of a large plan, it may be considered as a short-range plan.

The time span or duration of a plan is significant, not only as a basis for classifying plans, but also as an index of difficulty in evaluating its success. As a rule, it is more difficult to evaluate long-range plans than short-range plans because their duration is sometimes longer than the life span of their originator, or the life span of any one observer. Many times a treasurer retires or dies before his mistakes are discovered. Since the duration of long-range plans makes a determination of their ultimate success difficult, if not impossible, extreme care must be taken to insure highest standards in performing the planning function.

Classification by Function

Another basis for classifying plans is in respect to their function or use. Classification by business function considers planning as applied to the sales function, to the production and procurement function, and to financial and personnel areas. Grouping plans by functions is particularly useful when analyzing the operations of specific areas in an organization. Consequently, many companies find it convenient to develop policy statements in reference to four major functional areas—finance, sales, production, and personnel. Functional grouping of plans enables one to determine more clearly the interaction and interdependence that exist between major areas of operations, and emphasizes the need for determining these interrelationships before plans are approved and put into effect. Specifically, a sales department considering the installation of a sales order procedure should be aware that any such procedure will probably have a marked effect upon production and accounting procedures.

Classification by Scope

Classification in respect to breadth is the third way of grouping plans. Three distinct groups of plans are recognized when scope or breadth is the basis for classification. They are policies, procedures, and methods. Interestingly enough, this classification not only permits an immediate determination of the breadth of the plan but also reveals the organizational level that initiated the plan and the extent that the plan is utilized in the organization.

Policies. Company policies are broad in their application, and, as a a result, they often appear to be vague and nonspecific in their wording. They are intended to serve as guideposts that define the scope of activities necessary and permissible to reach desired objectives. In origin, policies are usually developed by the board of directors or by the executive committee of a company. It is rare for a department head to develop policy. He may recommend policy statements for approval by either the executive committee or the board, but policies emanate from the highest levels of a company. Another characteristic of policies is their stability in that they do not change rapidly. They are not immutable, however; but their change is slow. Examples of change can be found in company policies relating to credit and methods of distribution. The J. C. Penney Company ultimately changed its credit policy from one of strictly cash to one that permits and even encourages customer charge accounts. Sears Roebuck, over the years, has shifted its emphasis from distribution by means of mail-order houses to distribution through retail stores.

Procedures. There is considerably more variation among procedures in respect to both origin and scope than there is among policies. For the most part, procedures are interdepartmental or intradepartmental in their breadth. They do not affect the entire organization to the same extent that policy statements do, even though they may be observed on a company-wide basis. The phrase "standard operating procedure" typifies the fact that procedures are more closely related to the daily operations of a company than policies. Examples of procedures are found in every major department of a company, with their origin and application confined to one department, such as production, sales, or personnel. Procedures are, by definition, of sufficient breadth to have an impact upon the operations of related departments. Production control procedure, which has as its goal an organized flow of materials through a plant, by its nature modifies and, in turn, is modified by the procedures of the sales department governing the receiving and entering of orders, and by procedures of the accounting department utilized to determine production costs.

Methods. Another group of plans, more specific in scope than procedures, are methods. Methods are applied within a given operating department and are regarded as plans that detail the manner and sequence of performing those individual tasks necessary to complete given assignments. A method is designed to influence the behavior of an individual; for example, there is a prescribed method for the completion of employment application forms. Likewise, there is an approved method for the assembly of a given product or the grinding and finishing of a machined part.

In conclusion, the classification of plans by breadth ranges from policies, which are the broadest of all plans and originate at the highest levels of an organization, through procedures, which are concerned with the operations of major functional departments and are interdepartmental in their effect, to methods, which are specific and stated as a guide to direct the performance of individuals.

CRITERIA FOR EVALUATING PLANS

Two approaches are available in developing criteria for the evaluation of plans. One approach, designated as *Approach A*, is a review and analysis of characteristics that differentiate successful plans from unsuccessful plans. These criteria are descriptive in nature and serve as a checklist against which the plan under consideration may be judged. These characteristics have been observed by many different students of planning, and there is considerable agreement concerning the characteristics necessary for a plan to be successful.

A second approach to the development of criteria for judging plans, designated as *Approach B,* is the determination of the degree to which the plan under consideration is economic. The word "economic" is used here in its broadest sense; i.e., the effective utilization of resources. In order to determine the economic worth of a plan, it is necessary to use a technique that permits the description of any plan in economic terms and to utilize this technique to the extent that it becomes a "way of thinking" about plans. We consider first those criteria developed from observable characteristics and, second, the evaluation of plans in terms of economic effectiveness.

Approach A—Observable Characteristics

The problem of developing characteristics for use as criteria for judging plans necessitates an analysis of the elements or dimensions of the planning process and the resultant plan. A comprehensive study has listed the following 13 dimensions or factors:

1. Complexity	8. Frequency
2. Significance	9. Confidential nature
3. Comprehensiveness	10. Formality
4. Time	11. Authorization
5. Specificity	12. Ease of implementation
6. Completeness	13. Ease of control [4]
7. Flexibility	

Davis has listed the following characteristics of a plan:

1. Objectivity
2. Logical soundness
3. Futurity
4. Flexibility
5. Stability
6. Comprehensiveness
7. Clarity
8. Simplicity [5]

---

[4] P. Le Breton and D. A. Henning, *Planning Theory* (Englewood Cliffs, New Jersey: Prentice-Hall, Inc., 1961), p. 23. This comprehensive work treats planning as it is performed at all levels in the industrial firm. The student is referred to Part 5, pp. 320-44, in which the authors present an excellent summary that shows the relation of each of the above-mentioned dimensions of a plan to one another and the effect of each dimension on the other.

[5] Ralph C. Davis, *The Fundamentals of Top Management* (New York: Harper & Brothers, Publishers, 1951), p. 46.

It is apparent that these characteristics or dimensions may be worded to provide a basis or measure against which a plan may be evaluated. It is possible to summarize under three major headings the characteristics that may be considered as criteria for evaluating the probable success of plans. These characteristics are objectivity, degree of structuralization, and flexibility. To apply these characteristics as criteria, it is necessary to discuss more fully the meaning of each term and to present specific examples showing the application of the term to the planning process and to the resultant plan.

Objectivity. Objective findings or conclusions, such as plans, are subject to verification by another observer. The greater the degree of objectivity, the greater is the likelihood that another observer will reach the same conclusion. The antithesis of objective findings is known as subjective and is based upon one's own feelings and beliefs. Conclusions based upon personal experiences and beliefs are not subject to verification by outside observers.

Objectivity results from the precise observation, recording, analysis, and interpretation of pertinent data, a form of analysis and reasoning known as the *scientific method*. The managerial process of planning can be accomplished by either subjective or objective means. The extent to which the scientific method is followed in the planning process determines the objectivity of that process and the objectivity of the resultant plans. The scientific method, as applied to planning, consists of the following six steps:

1. Statement of objective
2. Statement of problem
3. Designation of planning authority
4. Collection and interpretation of data
5. Formulation and testing of tentative plan
6. Statement of final plan

The application of each of these steps to the process of planning is discussed separately.

STATEMENT OF OBJECTIVE. A strict definition of the scientific method does not include a statement of the objective. Yet it is necessary that a planner have before him, at all times, a clear concept of the broad objectives of the firm and the specific objectives of any given plan. A plan should contribute to meeting these objectives. Having stated objectives available for the planner minimizes the possibility of developing plans that are inappropriate for the attainment of specific objectives.

STATEMENT OF PROBLEM. When planning is required, there is the implication that the organization is not completely meeting its objectives, for if it were, there would be no need for additional or new plans. The discrepancy between present performance and desired performance constitutes the problem area. The problem to be resolved by the planning process must be clearly stated. Stating the problem clearly and setting forth the limiting factors and conditions that must be met define the extent of the planning process and the scope of the resultant plan. In Case Problem 4-A the problem is clearly defined. There is a need for a plant to manufacture a known product. Further, limiting conditions, such as shipping costs of raw materials and finished products, the cost and availability of labor, land requirements, and transportation facilities, are clearly stated. In contrast, a poorly defined problem fails to direct the planning process toward a specific goal and frequently results in inappropriate and ill-conceived plans.

DESIGNATION OF PLANNING AUTHORITY. As part of the planning process, there must be a designated planning authority. After a company has stated the problem and is convinced that a plan or course of action should be developed as a solution to the problem, it is necessary that an individual or group be given the authority necessary to carry out an effective planning process and develop alternate plans. The planner's authority should be granted by that level of the organization that normally has the responsibility for performing those functions included in the approved plan. For example, a plan requiring a large capital outlay, such as the construction of a plant, is normally approved by the president or the executive committee. Determining the appropriateness of the source of the planner's authority provides an estimate of the extent that the recommended plan will be approved and implemented.

COLLECTION AND INTERPRETATION OF DATA. The next step in the planning process is the collection and interpretation of available data. As stated in the definition of planning, consideration must be given to pertinent information from the present and the past, and an assessment must be made of probable future events.

Generally, the data used in planning fall into two broad categories —external data and internal data. Information pertaining to the national economy and the industry in which the company is operating is typical of *external data*. The financial resources of the firm, the past performance of the firm in the attainment of similar objectives, and the ability of personnel charged with executing the plan are representative of *internal data*. Available information from both sources along with estimates of probable future developments must be utilized and interpreted to insure a successful plan.

FORMULATION AND TESTING OF TENTATIVE PLAN. Whenever possible, a tentative plan should be formulated and initiated on a trial basis. Although this step is not always feasible, it is desirable since a trial run reveals strengths and weaknesses and offers a basis for predicting the probable success of a plan. Training programs are sometimes adopted on a trial basis before being applied on a company-wide basis. New products may be introduced to a single geographic region to test the acceptability of the product and the effectiveness of the proposed marketing techniques before making a final decision concerning national distribution.

If plans can be presented as a mathematical formula, changes that would result from altering the value of any one factor or condition can be determined with precision. Analyzing the effect of change by using a model is called *simulation*. The effect of changes in proposed production schedules may be simulated, and the effect of changes in price and volume upon profit may also be predicted accurately. When plans are expressed in quantitative terms, the effects of changing conditions may be simulated as a way of testing a plan's potential success without having to commit company resources.

STATEMENT OF FINAL PLAN. The last step in the planning process is the statement of the final plan. If a plan is to be considered objective (that is, capable of being developed by another planner following the same procedure), it must be derived from the data developed and analyzed. In this sense, a plan is a conclusion, and as such must be based on the information from which it is derived. The extent to which the analysis and reasoning of the scientific method have been followed in developing the final form of a plan indicates the degree of objectivity of the stated plan.

Degree of Structuralization. The determination of the degree of objectivity of a plan is essentially an analysis and evaluation of the planning process used in the development of the plan. The *degree of structuralization* is a criterion for evaluating the format of the plan and the extent to which the plan structures the actions of the organization that are necessary for its successful implementation. Well-structured plans are capable of precise execution. Factors considered in determining the degree of structuralization are: comprehensiveness, time span, assignment of duties, and control features.

COMPREHENSIVENESS. When evaluating the structure of a plan, one consideration is the degree of comprehensiveness. The complexity and the breadth of a plan are not necessarily measures of comprehensiveness. Simple plans that are well stated may be comprehensive. A production plan for a departmental supervisor may be for a period of one day and affect the work of only two people; yet it answers his needs. Similarly, a plan requiring 100 people for its execution and a time span of one year is not comprehensive unless it answers fully all the questions raised in the original problem. A plan is comprehensive to the degree that it provides solutions to the original problem raised in the planning process.

Time Span. A well-structured plan has a definite statement of the length of time required for its completion. The statement of dates for the start and the completion of a plan should be specific; in addition, complex plans specify intermediate time goals. For example, a building construction plan should state the date for the first activity on the building site, usually commencing with surveying, the time that grading begins, the date that foundation work starts, and beginning and completion dates for all other events including an expected occupancy date. It is recognized that there are factors which may delay the completion of any intermediate goal; however, the sequence and the relationship of these intermediate points should be clearly stated in the original plan. When a delay occurs, full information concerning the sequence and relationship of all phases of the project facilitates the task of revising the plan.

Assignment of Duties. The characteristics of comprehensiveness and time span refer to the structure of the plan itself. One of the expected results of a plan is that it structures the behavior of the organization responsible for carrying out the plan. In order to implement a plan effectively, it is necessary to assign specific duties to designated personnel in the organization. The mere listing of activities to be performed is not sufficient. Activities must be expressed as job duties and assigned as responsibilities to individual members of the organization.

Control Features. Another factor indicating the degree of structuralization is the extent that a plan includes features which facilitate control. One method of controlling the execution of plans is the utilization of logical time-oriented control points. Budgets, a type of financial plan, generally provide for quarterly reviews as an integral part of the plan. Another aspect of control is the designation of personnel to review progress and recommend necessary control action. Also, it is desirable to indicate the amount of variance from the original plan that can be tolerated. Provisions should be made for reporting these exceptions to the responsible manager.

Flexibility. Paradoxical as it may seem, the characteristic that contributes most to the stability and probable success of a plan is its flexibility. Rigid plans may appear to offer stability and firmness; however, rigidity also leads to an inability to meet the requirements of changing conditions.

Flexibility does not mean, nor imply, vagueness or instability. Flexibility results from the development of alternate courses of action. Developing plans that include alternatives has several advantages. First, flexibility permits management to meet changing external conditions rapidly and effectively. A plan without an alternate can result either in a blind-alley venture or reaching a point of no return, thereby dooming the plan to failure. Second, if a series of alternate actions is included in the plan, alternates are available immediately and avoid the delay that would result from having to develop a new plan. Lastly, it is much easier to gain approval for a plan in its initial stages when alternate courses are indicated. The presence of several choices implies that a fairly complete analysis of the problem has been made, and that one path has not been chosen and followed blindly. When a plan is being submitted to a group having varied interests and goals, the inclusion of alternate choices increases the possibility of compromise; but when only one course of action is presented, the result may be a rejection of the entire plan. For example, if a plan is presented proposing that a quality control program be established and the only recommendation concerning its administration is that it be placed under manufacturing, and a strong personal conflict exists between the vice-presidents of manufacturing and engineering, an impasse may develop resulting in the cancellation of the entire program. However, the inclusion of an alternate form of organization—the creation of a separate department reporting directly to the president—provides a ready compromise and the achievement of the goal of the original plan.

Principle of Planning

The preceding discussion—an analysis of the characteristics of plans—presents three criteria for judging the probable success of a plan. These criteria—objectivity, degree of structuralization, and flexibility—serve not only as a measure of the probable success of a given plan but also reflect the effectiveness of the planning process. The relationship between planning and plans is summarized in the *Principle of Planning: Effective planning results in plans that are objective, structured, and flexible, and the extent to which resultant plans possess these characteristics is a measure of their probable success.*

Approach B—Economic Effectiveness

The principle of planning is sound and has withstood the test of time. Over a period of years it has been observed that good plans have the aforementioned characteristics. However, it is quite possible that a plan carried through to its successful completion may not have been the most appropriate plan for that specific situation. There is a concept that has been widely used in the field of economics that may be applied to determine whether or not a plan makes the maximum contribution to company objectives. This concept is *economic effectiveness*.[6] Its application as a management tool rests upon two basic assumptions:

1. Management of a business enterprise is primarily an economic activity, and the principles and techniques of economics should be applicable and transferrable as principles and techniques of management. The word *economics* means the effective utilization of all resources.
2. The primary objective of any organization is to maximize the units of return (output) in relation to the effort (units of input) expended. This premise is stated in broad terms because the concept of maximization of return applies not only to capital invested, sales, or production, but also to the management of a charitable foundation seeking the best (most economic) distribution of its funds; to a religious organization seeking converts; or to a labor union demanding increased benefits for its members.

The Law of Diminishing Returns. It is implied in the second assumption that the units of return are compatible with organizational objectives. If so, the problem is one of determining the amount contributed by the last unit of input in relation to the amount contributed by the next to last unit of input. The method of making this determination can be accomplished in several ways, but all methods have one common characteristic—they represent a certain way of looking at input-output relationships. An example frequently presented in economics to illustrate input-output relationships assumes a unit of land (usually an acre), a man who is a worker, and corn, the product. The

---

[6] C. J. Hitch and R. N. McKean, *The Economics of Defense in the Nuclear Age* (Cambridge: Harvard University Press, 1960), pp. 422-vii. This book represents the combined efforts of the staff of the Rand Corporation. In it is presented an economic analysis of the problems of defense. It ranges from an analysis of resources available, through concepts of efficiency, and a detailed presentation of specific problems and applications to military research, logistics, and the ultimate development of policies for the choice of military deterrents. The underlying economics are applicable to the management of business firms.

one man works the one acre and is able to produce 100 bushels of corn with the tools given him. It is reasonable to expect that, with the same tools, by increasing manpower there will be an increase in the yield of corn *up to a point*. Eventually, however, there are enough men so that additional manpower does not result in additional product. This phenomenon has been stated variously as the *law of diminishing returns,* or the *law of variable returns.*

Now, translate the classic economic example into a problem in production. Columns A, B, and C of Table 4-1 indicate the three elements of our first example. Assume that the tools (that is, the plant and the facilities), the product, and the methods remain the same. One unit of input is the work of one man for an eight-hour day. This one unit of input produces 10 units of output, the total produced. In this instance the average produced is also 10. Average production is obtained by dividing total units produced by the units of input. When another man is added, the economic effectiveness of each man increases and the total produced reaches 24; the average goes up to 12. The addition of the third man results in total production of 39, with an average of 13. So far everything is increasing. When the fourth man is added, total production continues to rise; but the average drops to 12. With the addition of a fifth man, the production goes up and the average slips to 11; and with the addition of the sixth man, the average is down to 10 again; however, the total number of units produced is 60, or six times as much as that produced by one man. After the seventh, eighth, and ninth men, the average production per man is reduced to seven; and, by adding the ninth man, the phenomenon of diminishing returns appears and the total production declines from 64 to 63.

Table 4-1

THE RELATIONSHIP BETWEEN UNITS OF INPUT, TOTAL PRODUCED, AVERAGE PRODUCED, AND MARGINAL PRODUCT

A Units of Input	B Total Produced	C Average Produced	D Marginal Product
1	10	10	—
2	24	12	14
3	39	13	15
4	48	12	9
5	55	11	7
6	60	10	5
7	63	9	3
8	64	8	1
9	63	7	−1

This relatively simple example poses a problem that recurs as the central theme of many managerial decisions. Managers, in making their decisions, are asked to answer the following question: What combination of resources results in the greatest economic return consistent with the objectives of the organization? If it can be said of a plan that it represents the best (most economic) combination of resources resulting in the achievement of desired objectives, the plan can then be considered appropriate. Obviously, both aspects of the test must be met. If the plan does not result in the achievement of desired objectives, it is not appropriate; nor is it appropriate if in achieving the desired objectives, there is anything less than the most economic utilization of resources.

The Concept of Marginal Product. How can it be determined when there is the most efficient use of available resources? The data presented in the first three columns of Table 4-1 do not provide sufficient information, but they do indicate some difficulty as reflected in the average units produced per man. Note that the average starts falling when the fourth man is added. A second indication that all is not well is revealed by the amount of total production. This measure drops when the ninth man is added. Since our concern is with input-output relationships, does it not seem logical to study these relationships more carefully and find out what happens each time an additional person is added? It is necessary to determine exactly how much *additional* output results from each *additional* unit of input. Economists refer to this incremental relationship between additional units of input and resultant additional units of output as *marginal product*. The terms marginal productivity, marginal revenue, or marginal profit, may be interpreted as *additional* productivity, *additional* revenue, or *additional* profit in relation to an *additional* unit of input.

In Table 4-1, Column D shows the marginal (additional) product resulting from each additional unit of input. The first man working for eight hours (one unit of input) forms the base of the problem. His marginal productivity cannot be computed because prior to him there was no production. With the addition of the second man, 24 units were produced, a gain of 14 units over that produced by the first man alone (24-10). The marginal production for each additional man is shown in Column D. The addition of the third man results in the production of 39 units, 15 units more than the amount produced by the previous two-man team. The addition of the fourth man yields only nine additional units, compared to the 14 added by the second man and the 15 added by the third man. The average production also drops by one unit from 13 to 12. The incremental increase in production resulting from additional units of input continues to drop and at a more rapid rate than the decline in average production. With the addition of the ninth man, the results are negative, a marginal (additional) increase of -1; and the total number of units produced also declines by one. An inspection of Column D shows that there are increasing amounts of additional production until the fourth man is added; thus, it seems that the maximum utilization of available resources occurs when the third man is added. Prior to this point, the operation is not at maximum efficiency since the cost of additional units of input is more than offset by the value of additional units of output. Beyond this point the operation loses efficiency as each additional unit of input results in the production of a smaller and smaller amount of additional product. The phenomenon of decreasing efficiency in the use of resources is revealed by the marginal product rather than by measures of average or total production. The average production is 12 when the second man is added, and it is also 12 when the fourth man is added; but in the first instance the marginal productivity is increasing while in the second case; i.e., with the addition of the fourth man, it is decreasing.[7]

The concept of marginal output, or incremental changes in the rate of production in relation to each additional unit of input, is a means of determining how efficiently available resources are employed. Efficiency increases as long as the additional units of output increase at a faster rate than the rate of additional units of input. When the point is reached where an additional unit of input results in a smaller rate of increase in output than that resulting from the addition of the previous unit of input, the maximum, or most efficient, utilization of resources no longer exists.

---

[7] The student who has had calculus will understand that the curve for marginal productivity is the derivative of the equation for the total product curve. The problem can be expressed as $MC = MR$, or marginal costs equal marginal revenue. In addition to the standard texts in calculus, the following references are suggested for the student who is interested in a better understanding of the mathematical expression of the concept of marginal product. C. J. Hitch and R. N. McKean, *op. cit.*, pp. 362-405. The appendix of the book, headed "The Simple Mathematics of Maximization," presents the fundamental concepts of calculus as used in maximizing returns in relation to inputs. D. Yoder and H. G. Heneman, *Labor Economics and Industrial Relations* (Cincinnati: South-Western Publishing Company, 1959), pp. 693-709. Yoder and Heneman discuss marginal wage theory. The discussion is directed to problems of marginal productivity as they affect wages; however, the concepts presented are applicable to any situation concerned with input-output relationships. M. H. Spencer and L. Siegelman, *op. cit.*, pp. 202-208. This portion of the book presents a discussion of the relationships that exist between simple production functions.

Principle of Economic Effectiveness

The management of any organization must continuously ask if its action, or its proposed plan, maximizes the efficient utilization of resources in meetings its goals. When a choice must be made between two or more plans, each of which possesses to the same degree the characteristics of objectivity, structuralization, and flexibility, it is apparent that another measure is needed in order to reach a decision. *Economic effectiveness* is the fourth criterion for use in judging the worth of plans and provides a basis for selecting the appropriate plan. The application of the criterion of economic effectiveness minimizes the possibility of adopting a plan capable of successful execution, yet not the appropriate plan because it does not offer the most efficient utilization of resources in meeting stated objectives. The importance of economic effectiveness as a criterion for evaluating plans is stressed in the *Principle of Economic Effectiveness: Economic effectiveness in planning results in plans that maximize achievement of company objectives through the most efficient utilization of available resources.*

SUMMARY OF PRINCIPLES

Two approaches are utilized in this chapter to develop criteria for evaluating the probable effectiveness and value of plans. Approach A is an analysis of those characteristics that appear in successful plans. The three criteria developed by this analysis—objectivity, degree of structuralization, and flexibility—serve a useful purpose in that each concentrates on a different aspect of planning. Objectivity emphasizes the planning process, structuralization is directed toward the final plan, and flexibility indicates the feasibility or practicality of the plan in action. The importance of these criteria is stated in the principle of planning.

Principle of Planning { Effective planning results in plans that are objective, structured, and flexible, and the extent to which resultant plans possess these characteristics is a measure of their probable success.

Approach B, an economic evaluation of plans, is an analysis of input-output relationships with emphasis on the marginal (incremental) increase in the rate of output in comparison to the marginal (incremental) increase in the rate of input. An operative plan is effort (input) directed toward the achievement of objectives. The degree of efficiency in attaining objectives is dependent upon how well the plan utilizes available resources. Economic effectiveness is a fourth criterion for measuring the worth of plans and indicates the extent to which a plan effectively utilizes available resources in achieving stated objectives. The principle of economic effectiveness evaluates the economic worth of plans.

| Principle of Economic Effectiveness | { Economic effectiveness in planning results in plans that maximize achievement of company objectives through the most efficient utilization of available resources. |

• • • • • • • • •

Case Problem 4-B reports in some detail the planning that went into a major industrial effort, the introduction of the Edsel automobile. See if you can determine, by evaluating the various steps of the planning process outlined in the case, why this car has become a collector's item.

Questions for Study and Discussion

1. Determining the objectives of a business was discussed in Chapter 3. Some writers include the determination of objectives as a part of the planning process and discuss objectives as a part of planning. Develop several reasons for the inclusion of objectives as a part of planning and several reasons for considering the determination of objectives as a function that precedes planning.
2. Develop an example that shows how the planning function can be applied to the other managerial functions of organizing, directing, and controlling.
3. Comment on the statement, "Good decision makers are good planners."
4. Give an example of a decision made by a planner. How does this decision differ from an executive decision? Why?
5. Define the concepts of risk and uncertainty in your own terms. Why is the concept of risk important in understanding the environment of business operations? Does good planning reduce risk?
6. What are meant by the concepts of primacy and pervasiveness as applied to planning?
7. Give several examples of "pure" research that have developed into today's products. What are some of the products of tomorrow that may develop from today's research?
8. Develop a policy statement for a specific functional area. Next, describe the procedures and methods necessary to implement the stated policy.

9. What is meant by the concept, objectivity, when used to describe plans or the planning function?
10. What is simulation? Give an example of simulation and describe the conditions that must be met before simulation is possible.
11. Define in your own terms the concept, marginal productivity. Give an example of marginal product.
12. What are some of the circumstances that might make it advisable to continue production even though the marginal product is declining?

• • • • • • • • •

How much planning went into the Edsel? In a sense, it must be the most thoroughly planned product ever introduced. Over the past 20 years, there has rarely been a time when someone, somewhere, at Ford Motor Company was not researching or designing a car that could be considered a spiritual cousin to the Edsel. The Company's need for a line of medium-priced cars is as obvious as the brass radiator on an old Model-T and almost dates back to the same time. About the only man at Ford who couldn't see that the Company needed a medium-priced car was Henry Ford. It was not until 1936 that Henry, cajoled by his son Edsel, finally introduced the Lincoln-Zephyr, and two years later, the Mercury. But nothing happened to either of those brands during Henry's lifetime to make him think he had been wrong. So it remained for Henry Ford II, who will be 40 years old on Edsel's Introduction Day, to do what his grandfather opposed and his father did not quite succeed in doing; carving out a place in the market for the Mercury and launching a second medium-priced Ford-built car.

Case Problem 4-B
How Much Planning Went
into the Edsel? [8]

For the record, 1948 is as good a year as any to date the conception of what is the closest progenitor of the Edsel. During that year Henry Ford II told the Company's Foreward Product Planning Committee to research the possibility of a new medium-priced car. The car was still in the market research stage in 1950 when the Korean War forced the Committee to puts its plan on the shelf. Research intensified again in 1952 and in January, 1955, the planners finally presented their research to the Executive Committee with a recommendation that Ford launch a second medium-priced brand of car. Their report (6 volumes) was approved by the Board of Directors three months later.

The Planning Committee had no illusion that there was a vast consumer yearning for a new car, nor did it (or Ford engineers) believe that startling mechanical innovations could be devised to insure a new car's success. The logic of the decision, the committee figured, was the logic of marketing; the

---

[8] Thomas P. Murphy, "How Edsel Lured Those Dealers," *Fortune*, Vol. 56, No. 3 (September, 1957), pp. 144-47, 242-52. Courtesy of *Fortune* magazine.

medium-priced market is big and is growing bigger; therefore, an attractive car sold through an industrious dealer body could be shoehorned into that market.

The planners could show that 32 percent of the nation's families had incomes of $5,000 or more per year, which put a medium-priced car within their grasp. Some 60 percent of the cars being sold were, by the planner's reckonings, medium priced (a calculation that included the sales of the more expensive lines of the Chevrolet, Ford, and Plymouth). The medium-priced market, in other words, was the mass market. In 1955, it should be even better. Almost half of all families should be making $5,000 or more.

From the moment the Edsel project was authorized, it was agreed that the car would bracket middle-priced buying. The planners doubtless had an eye on Buick when they made their recommendations, for Edsel, like Buick, has four series of cars (Ranger, Pacer, Corsair, and Citation) and 18 models. Edsel prices will start about the same as the most expensive Ford Fairlane, around $2,300, and like Buick ascend gracefully into the lower reaches of the luxury-car market, about $3,500. Thus, the Edsel overlaps the higher priced Fords and will, by 1957 pricing, be both below and above the Mercury. This broad pricing was a great selling point when Larry Doyle's field force talked to prospective Edsel dealers.[9]

The Planning Committee had another angle in mind. Car buyers show a distinct loyalty not only to brands but to corporations as well. A study of Michigan auto registration showed that about 9 out of 10 Chevrolet owners who trade up stay with General Motors; Plymouth owners who shift to more expensive cars show a preference for other Chrysler makes, almost 5 out of 10 of them stay with the company. Ford, in contrast, found that only 1 in 4 of its up-trading owners was buying Mercury. The Edsel would fill a gap.

How sound are all these calculations on which Ford and their dealers have based a big gamble? No one in the industry questions the existence of consumer loyalty, and no one questions the wisdom of a broad line of cars. But the really basic premise behind the Edsel decision—the medium-price cars already account for 60 percent of sales and are destined to get more—has raised some eyebrows. To reach a 60 percent estimate, the Ford Planners included the expensive models of the three low-price cars. Without them, the medium-price market is not expanding; it may even be contracting. While no one argues that a $2,400 Chevrolet Bel Air or Ford Fairlane is a low-price car, it remains to be seen whether buyers will return to the more austere models of the medium-price cars or continue their trend toward the heavily chromed models of Chevrolet, Ford, and Plymouth.

The medium-price field is, by any reckoning, the most bitterly competitive today. The big three have seven well-entrenched brands in the market, contrasted with one brand each in the low and high-price fields. Larry Doyle, however, claims to be unmoved by all this and confidently talks to his dealers about capturing 3 to 3.3 percent of the

---

[9] The body of this article, as the title indicates, describes how Edsel wooed dealers from other agencies to sell their cars. Mr. Doyle was given the responsibility of creating an Edsel dealer organization.

total U. S. market in 1958. Assuming a 6 million car year, Doyle's expectations amount to roughly 200,000 units. This is more than Cadillac's 1956 unit sales, or those of DeSoto, or Chrysler, or the total of all the imported cars.

If Ford's new product appeals to the public as effectively as it did to the dealers who saw it, the credit will go, in no small degree, to 40-year-old Roy Brown. Brown, a designer in the Lincoln styling studio, was put in charge of styling the Edsel almost a year before the division was formed. His first move was to take a stylist out to a busy Dearborn intersection to look at cars. To no one's surprise, they decided that all American cars looked pretty much alike. Brown knew the car he was to design would have to conform to the dimensions of the Ford or Mercury body shell on which it would be built, but within these dimensions he resolved to design something that looked different. "I wanted a car with strong identity," Brown says, "one that could be recognized instantly from the front, from the side, or rear."

Radiator grills, what Brown calls "the front-end theme," proved a fruitful area for attack. Virtually all kinds of American cars use massive horizontal grills to give the illusion of great width and lowness. Brown, with the encouragement of Ford Motor Company's styling boss, George Walker, proposed to move against the trend and make the Edsel's grill vertical. He was delighted with the result. "It is crisp and fresh looking," he said. "That grill could become a classic."

For the rear of the car, Brown retained only vestigal tail fins, which left him with the problem of finding a distinctive design theme. He finally displayed twenty-five-inch-wide tail lights across the rear fenders and trunk lid. They were promptly dubbed "gullwing" tail lights by the advertising copywriters.

Brown believes he has a design that, if not conservative, is at least as restrained as it is possible to make it without risking public apathy. "You know," he says wistfully, "it has come to the point where we take competitive cars and measure the number of square inches of chrome they carry." The Edsel, Brown is pleased to note, is somewhat sparing of chrome. Walker likes Edsel's big package look. "You take Loewy's '51 Studebaker." he says, "That was a swell design, but wasn't big."

It was the job of Neil L. Blume in engineering the car to load it with exciting things for Edsel dealers to talk about. Blume also worked to get as much interchangeability as he could with Ford and Mercury. For the engine of the two lower priced cars, Blume used the Ford V-8 engine block-casting and drilled it to his own specifications; the larger Edsel uses the same engine-block casting as the Mercury. Performances, however, will be quite different. Blume managed to get 303 horsepower out of the smaller block and 345 horsepower from the larger one. These make Edsel, to put it mildly, a peppy car. The horsepower of the 1958 Edsel Corsair and Citation exceeds that of all 1957 stock cars. Even Blume does not know what speed that gives the Edsel, and he disclaims interest in the topic. "The engine," Blume earnestly explains, "was designed for torque, for maximum acceleration. Especially," he says, "in the passing range, 35 miles per hour to 70.". . . .

The very thing that worries Edsel's new dealers, the fact that the car has no "personality" in the public's mind, seems like a major advantage to Dave Wallace, Edsel's director of market research. "We give the car an idealized personality," he says. "That is something no brand has ever been able to do before."

Wallace, with the help of Columbia University's Bureau of Applied Social Research, spent two years delving into what he calls "the social and product images of American cars." He found that Americans, at least the 1,600 interviewed in Peoria and San Bernadino, have some strong opinions about the various brands and the kind of people that drive them. The Buick, for example, is considered by the majority of people to be "the doctor's car." It is an enviable possession, associated with middle-age and older buyers, the fairly well-to-do. The Dodge also connotes an older buyer, but one that is not so affluent. Mercury, Wallace found, is distinctly a masculine car and consumers associate it, suprisingly, with buyers of lower income than that of Ford buyers.

It is one thing to know what the consumer's images of the various brands are, and quite another to do something about them. Wallace is concerned about the first Edsel buyers. He would like to think they will be solid citizens, but he fears, on the basis of studies with other new products, that they won't be. "The real opinion leaders," Wallace says resignedly, "probably won't buy their car until late winter or spring. They are the kind who hold off for awhile."

At least, neither Wallace nor Fairfax Cone, Chairman of the executive committee of Edsel's advertising agency, Foote, Cone, and Belding, has any doubts about the kind of personality they will try to create for the Edsel. The way Cone puts it, Edsel is "the smart car for the younger American family on its way up." To appeal to this group, Edsel's advertising uses a stylish, restrained treatment. The full-page magazine and newspaper introductory advertisements are almost Spartan. Cone had an unprecedented chance to shop NEW. Instead he used the simple confident headline "This is the Edsel." Larry Doyle likes that headline. It has the same tone of confidence that worked so well for him along Automobile Row.

Since the Edsel is no longer manufactured, it is apparent that something did not develop as anticipated.[10, 11]

Problems

1. Evaluate the overall planning that went into the Edsel with respect to its general market considerations.
2. How significant do you believe the studies to be in respect to consumer loyalty to the company, i.e., the tendency for people to move up to a higher priced car manufactured by the same corporation?
3. What additional information would you need to have had to (a) have made this project a success, or (b) to have gained sufficient information to withdraw from the contemplated move?
4. What do you believe really happened to cause the Edsel's failure?

---

[10] "The Edsel Account," *Fortune*, Vol. 54 (December, 1956), p. 125.

[11] J. Burek and S. Parker, "The Biggest Car Market Yet," *Fortune*, Vol. 54 (November, 1956), pp. 109-13. This article is a broad market survey of the automobile market as it appeared in November, 1956. It is significant in relation to Case Problem 4-B dealing with the planning that went into the Edsel.

CHAPTER 5

Planning for Profit

Assume that you are president of The Specialties Company and own 60 percent of the outstanding common stock. Other members of your family own 20 percent, and the remaining 20 percent is held by outsiders. You have before you the current condensed operating statement shown below.

For the past five years, the operating statements of your company have been very similar. There have been only a few unforeseen expenses and, as a result, a substantial surplus has accrued. Your product, a power lawn edger, has been especially successful and has been distributed on a regional basis. The current building lease is due to expire in six months and you have been notified that the annual cost of rental will be increased $20,000, thereby increasing fixed costs that much. However, the building is adequate in that it houses both office and plant facilities, and there seems little chance of renting for less. Most of the advertising has been conducted through local newspapers and radio and television stations. The advertising agency has informed you that space rates have increased and that it would be well to budget another $5,000 for this expense, which has been charged as a fixed selling expense.

There are approximately 50 hourly employees whose wages are charged as direct labor. If present policy is continued, each will receive an additional five cents an hour, making an increase of about $5,500 in variable direct labor costs. Early indications are that direct material costs will increase four percent in the next year.

Case Problem 5-A
Developing a Profit Plan

The Specialties Company
Condensed Operating Statement

	Variable	Fixed	
Net sales (60,000 units @ $20 ea.)			$1,200,000
Less costs and expenses:			
Direct material	$195,000		
Direct labor	215,000		
Mfg. expense	100,000	$200,000	
Selling expense	50,000	150,000	
Admin. gen. expense	160,000	50,000	
Total costs and expenses			1,120,000
Net profit before taxes			$ 80,000

Problems

These are the questions you are asking yourself:

1. What will company expenses be next year?
2. What is the present break-even point and how will it be affected by these changes?
3. What is the present level of profitability as measured against sales, and what will it be next year?
4. Can these relationships be presented graphically so other members of management will understand them?
5. What level of sales must be reached so that the company will still net $80,000?
6. What level of sales has to be reached so that the net profit expressed as a percentage of sales will be the same as it is now?

• • • • • • • • •

In Case Problem 5-A, a very brief picture of an organization has been given in terms of its operation and the resultant profit. Despite rising costs, if the company increases its dollar volume of sales sufficiently, the level of profits will remain the same. But how are profits to be measured—as an absolute number of dollars, $80,000, or as a percentage of sales? But, first a need arises for a satisfactory definition of profit. The first section of this chapter discusses the meaning of profit; then, the scope of financial policies is outlined. Next, one of the basic tools of profit planning, the break-even chart, is presented. The last section of the chapter shows how the Principle of the Objective and the Principles of Planning are applied to planning for profit.

THE MEANING OF PROFIT

There has been much discussion concerning the *nature* of profits. Profits have been viewed as a form of compensation to either the individual or to the suppliers of the capital necessary to form and operate an industrial firm. Profits have also been defined in reference to an economic process, with the concept that profits within a firm are the result of that firm's operating in an economic environment that is not perfect; i.e., there are *frictions* operating. Differences in the desirability of location or the possession of a patent on a manufactured product are examples of frictions, or inequalities, that result in one company earning more than its competitor. Another view holds that profits may be the result of innovations, either in respect to the product or to the method in which the business is being operated.[1]

---

[1] M. H. Spencer and L. Siegelman, *Managerial Economics* (Homewood, Illinois: Richard D. Irwin, Inc., 1959), pp. 87-134. In this discussion, the authors present advanced analytical techniques for profit management, in addition to a brief summary of profit theory.

Definition of Profit

There is little dispute concerning the definition of profit, for it is generally agreed that profit is the amount remaining after all expenses associated with conducting a business have been met. Yet, this definition leaves much to be desired. It is passive in nature and can lead one to believe that profits are something that normally happen. Furthermore, it implies that profits are something left over after meeting all expenses of the business. While it is undoubtedly true that there are many claims on the apportionment of the sales dollar, profit should not be viewed as that part remaining; rather, it must be regarded as an integral portion of the sales dollar and a management goal. Planning helps make the attainment of this goal a reality.

For the individual engaged in his own business, it might be sufficient to regard profit as a form of compensation for his time and for the risk he takes as an entrepreneur. Thus, the individual who operates a very small retail or service establishment, where there is little capital invested, can regard his profit as compensation for his time spent. If, in addition to time, there is capital invested in the business, then profits become not only compensation for time but also a return on the invested capital. Had the owner not invested capital in his business, he could have invested it in another company with someone else managing his money and providing a return.

While the concept of profit as payment for time and risk is useful where applied to the entrepreneur, it does not help in understanding the role of profits in a corporation. In a publicly held corporation, members of management are employees and are compensated for performing the functions of management. In the corporation, profits must be generated in order to repay those persons who have invested their capital in the firm. Also, profits create new capital to provide for future expansion. The continuance and growth of any industrial enterprise depend upon its ability to produce profit. This is not to say that profits are the only objective of a firm nor that the level of profitability is the primary objective; but it does mean that without profits, the industrial firm as we know it in our society cannot survive.

Measurement of Profit

There are two measurements commonly used in expressing the amount of profit earned. One measurement expresses profits as total dollars earned for a specified period of time. The other measurement is a ratio that expresses profits as a percentage of either sales or capital invested in the business.

Total Dollars Earned. Total dollars earned for a specified period of time is a measure commonly used in stating company profits; yet, unless additional related information is known, this measure is not too meaningful. Knowledge of past performance adds meaning to a statement of dollars earned because it provides a basis for comparing a company's present performance with its own past record. Also, the profit for a given firm must be considered in the light of the performance of the industry within which that firm is operating.

Table 5-1 shows the profits of selected companies for the first quarter of 1966 compared with the profits of a like period for 1965. All industry groups, with one exception—steel—had an increase in sales volume for the first quarter of 1966 when compared with the same period for 1965. The sales volume for the steel industry was off 11.9 percent. As might be expected, profits for the steel industry were also off, −23.7 percent. Profits for the cement industry were off 6.5 percent, even though sales for the industry were up 5.6 percent. The last two columns in the table express profit as a percentage of sales volume. Note that the profit margins for baking, brewing, chemicals, drugs,

Table 5-1

HOW PROFIT MARGINS LOOK INDUSTRY BY INDUSTRY

No. of Cos.	Industry	Sales 1st qtr. 1966 ($000)	% change vs. 1st qtr. 1965	Profits 1st qtr. 1966 ($000)	% change vs. 1st qtr. 1965	Profit margins	
						1965	1966
7	Aerospace	$ 1,642,447	8.5%	$ 52,988	30.1%	2.7%	3.2%
5	Appliance	275,788	31.9	18,929	31.1	6.9	6.9
9	Autos, trucks, parts	2,131,166	18.9	98,248	23.6	4.4	4.6
2	Baking	187,196	7.4	9,973	4.4	5.5	5.3
3	Brewing	129,965	12.7	5,328	8.3	4.3	4.1
6	Building materials	361,281	12.3	18,261	27.9	4.4	5.1
4	Cement	58,031	5.6	5,275	−6.5	10.3	9.1
16	Chemicals	3,731,027	12.7	347,098	11.4	9.4	9.3
5	Container	816,615	11.8	37,878	41.5	3.7	4.6
6	Controls, instruments	113,055	14.0	5,534	14.4	4.9	4.9
6	Cosmetics, toiletries	261,838	14.8	26,119	18.1	9.7	10.0
2	Distilling	218,470	7.4	8,997	23.0	3.6	4.1
13	Drugs	756,065	13.1	100,601	12.7	13.4	13.3
10	Elec. equip., electronics	3,487,686	20.6	171,282	19.9	4.9	4.9
6	Food	1,447,493	9.2	66,371	20.3	4.2	4.6
6	Glass	500,059	4.4	29,106	12.2	5.4	5.8
3	Hardware	38,489	8.2	2,180	51.2	4.1	5.7
18	Machinery	1,319,860	17.7	83,088	16.5	6.4	6.3
10	Nonferrous metals	1,260,723	18.6	87,629	35.6	6.1	7.0
7	Office equip., computer	1,461,341	16.6	155,392	12.5	11.0	10.6
13	Oil	2,564,834	9.3	308,177	17.5	11.2	12.0
7	Paper	557,607	8.9	37,989	16.6	6.4	6.8
6	Photo equip., optical	565,739	27.8	75,096	51.4	11.2	13.3
4	Plumbing, heating	287,390	10.2	8,136	13.0	2.8	2.8
4	Printing, publishing	216,843	12.1	10,798	32.3	4.2	5.0
4	RR equip.	385,652	7.4	15,987	14.3	3.9	4.1
3	Rubber	587,409	10.2	21,073	23.6	3.2	3.6
16	Steel	2,904,889	−11.9	166,907	−23.7	6.6	5.7
9	Textiles, clothing	940,350	14.3	57,576	16.0	6.0	6.1
5	Tobacco	844,579	9.0	48,183	5.4	5.9	5.7
4	Wood, wood prods.	508,133	17.9	35,650	16.1	6.1	7.0
10	Misc. consumer prods.	191,876	15.2	10,011	28.2	4.7	5.2
13	Misc. mfg.	1,268,881	13.5	79,405	25.4	5.7	6.3
	Total	32,023,777	11.0	2,205,265	13.8	6.7	6.9

Source: Business Week, April 30, 1966, p. 90.

machinery, office equipment, and tobacco groupings declined despite an increase in the dollar volume of both sales and profits. These figures emphasize the variation in profitability for different industry groups and show that profit, when expressed as a percentage of sales, may decline even though the dollar volume of sales and of profits increases.

Knowledge of variations in industry performance provides an additional basis for judging the progress of a company and the effectiveness of its management. The meaning of the statement that a company has earned $100,000 for the current year, up 10 percent when compared with its profits for the preceding year, changes significantly when it is known that the average profits of other companies in the same industry also increased 10 percent. A different meaning would appear, however, if the industry average had decreased 10 percent or had remained constant during the same period of time.

Profit Ratios. In addition to expressing profits as total dollars earned, which must be interpreted in light of the company's past record and the trend of profits for the industry, the following two ratios, or percentages, are normally used to express profitability: (1) percentage return on sales, and (2) percentage return on invested capital.

PERCENTAGE RETURN ON SALES. Percentage return on sales is a measure closely associated with the operating statement of a company and is affected proportionately by changes in operating costs. If costs increase 5 percent, the percentage of sales retained as profit must necessarily decrease 5 percent; conversely, if costs decrease 5 percent, profits increase by that amount. The answer to Problem 3, Case Problem 5-A, illustrates the effect of rising costs upon the percentage of sales retained as profit. Likewise, profits expressed as a percentage of sales decrease 5 percent when sales volume declines by that amount unless costs are also reduced 5 percent; and when sales volume increases, profits show the same percentage increase provided all operating costs remain constant.

PERCENTAGE RETURN ON INVESTED CAPITAL. Profit expressed as a percentage return on invested capital is, in the opinion of many, by far the most important measure of management's performance. The return on capital invested indicates the effectiveness of management's stewardship and has a marked effect upon the company's ability to attract new investment capital, thereby directly influencing its rate of growth. When profit is expressed as a rate of return on invested capital, management is judged not only in respect to its capability compared to the managements of other companies within the same industry grouping, but also it is compared with the managements of all other industrial firms. All companies strive to retain their present capital and many seek additional new capital. If the return on capital invested in a given company or industry declines, the question is raised as to whether it would not be wiser to invest new capital in another company or industry where the percentage return is greater.

Ratios of profitability to sales or to invested capital for individual companies must be interpreted in relation to the norm for their industry. Table 5-2 shows the variations in the median profitability for each of 21 industry groupings for the year 1964. The companies included in this survey were the 500 largest industrial firms in the United States as determined by dollar volume of sales. The median profit for all industry in 1964, when expressed as a percentage of sales was 5 percent; and when expressed as a return on capital invested, the median profit was 10.5 percent. There is considerable variation in the level of profitability for each industry. The lowest percentage return on sales is 2.4

Table 5-2

INDUSTRY MEDIANS OF PROFITABILITY EXPRESSED AS A RETURN
ON SALES AND AS A RETURN ON CAPITAL INVESTED, 1964

Industry group	% Return on sales	% Return on invested capital
Mining	10.8%	11.8%
Pharmaceuticals	10.8	16.3
Tobacco	9.1	12.3
Glass, cement, gypsum, concrete	7.0	10.5
Petroleum refining	7.5	9.0
Chemicals	6.6	12.1
Metal manufacturing	5.6	9.1
Soaps, cosmetics	5.6	14.8
Paper and wood products	4.5	9.6
Farm and industrial machinery	5.0	11.0
Appliances, electronics	4.9	11.9
Rubber	4.4	10.6
Publishing and printing	5.9	12.6
Motor vehicles and parts	4.5	12.5
Metal products	4.0	9.6
Apparel	3.7	11.0
Textiles	3.9	8.6
Food and beverage	2.7	9.8
Shipbuilding, railroad equipment	4.8	9.4
Office machinery (includes computers) ..	4.7	11.4
Aircraft and parts	2.4	11.8
All industry	5.0	10.5

Source: "The Fortune Directory," *Fortune*, Vol. LXXII, No. 1 (July, 1965), pp. 149-168. Industry groupings are based on classifications established by the Bureau of the Budget. Medians are computed only from data from the 500 industrials included in the *Fortune* Survey.

percent for the aircraft and parts industry, while the highest return on sales is 10.8 percent in the mining and pharmaceuticals industries. However, the profitability of the mining industry and the aircraft and parts industry is eighth in rank, 11.8 percent, when profits are expressed as a percentage return on capital invested. The profitability of the pharmaceuticals industry ranks first, with a 16.3 percent return on invested capital.

Summary—Measurement of Profit

Ratios of profitability are not directly dependent upon the size of the company as determined by dollar volume of sales. Medium- and small-size companies may show a greater degree of profitability, expressed as either a percentage of sales or of invested capital, than a larger company that produces a greater volume of profits. This statement does not imply that very large companies are incapable of producing profits that represent a very satisfactory rate of return on sales and invested capital.

Table 5-3 shows the sales volume, invested capital, and dollar profits expressed as a return on sales and as a return on invested capital for 11 companies selected from *Fortune's* survey of the 500 largest United States industrial corporations. Also shown is the rank position of each of the 11 companies surveyed for each of the measures of profit. The largest industrial corporation is General Motors, as determined by sales volume and dollar volume of profits. Standard Oil (New Jersey), second in sales volume but first in respect to invested capital, ranks second in dollar volume of profit. DuPont, another industrial giant, produced the fifth largest dollar volume of profit and ranks fourth when profits are measured as a percentage return on sales.

The greatest profitability, expressed as a return on sales, was achieved by Amerada Petroleum, with a return of 31.5 percent. Avon Products achieved the greatest return on invested capital, 38.0 percent, and a dollar level of profits that resulted in a rank position of 90th. The Aluminum Company of America required approximately eight times the amount of invested capital and slightly more than three times the sales volume to produce a dollar level of profits approximately 50 percent greater than the profits earned by Avon. Table 5-3 emphasizes the characteristic differences that exist among various industries in regard to the amount of capital required for each dollar of profit and the variations in profitability when expressed as a rate of return on sales.

Table 5-3

PROFITABILITY EXPRESSED AS A PERCENTAGE OF SALES AND AS A PERCENTAGE OF INVESTED CAPITAL

Company	Sales ($000)	Rank	Invested capital ($000)	Rank	Profits ($000)	Rank	Profits % Sales	Rank	Profits % Inv. cap.	Rank
Aluminum Company of America	$ 1,036,922	53	$ 867,506	30	$ 60,764	51	5.9%	195	7.0%	408
Amerada Petroleum	163,537	340	257,904	118	51,583	63	31.5	1	20.0	27
Avon Products	299,449	203	104,962	258	39,839	90	13.3	16	38.0	2
Borden	1,293,439	36	427,746	69	45,486	74	3.5	342	10.6	242
DuPont, E. I. deNemours	2,786,459	12	2,055,166	11	417,426	5	16.9	4	22.8	15
General Dynamics	1,579,862	30	299,530	109	42,611	84	2.7	393	14.2	112
General Motors	16,997,044	1	7,599,015	2	1,734,782	1	10.2	57	22.8	16
Gillette	298,956	204	126,265	228	37,673	95	12.6	22	29.8	6
Pitney-Bowes	98,453	497	52,557	416	8,071	312	8.2	91	15.4	86
Smith Kline & French Laboratories	218,247	276	124,844	231	38,686	92	17.7	3	31.0	4
Standard Oil (N. J.)	10,814,661	2	8,358,689	1	1,050,555	2	9.7	64	12.6	166

Source: "The Fortune Directory," *Fortune*, Vol. LXXI, No. 1 (July, 1965), pp. 149-168. The 11 companies above were selected from the 500 largest U. S. industrial corporations as reported by *Fortune.* Invested capital is capital stock, surplus, and retained earnings at year's end. Profit is after taxes and after special charges or credits.

PLANNING FINANCIAL POLICY

Financial policies are formulated to provide plans for the utilization of the money necessary for a company's operation. The acquisition of needed money, the utilization of money in producing and selling the product or service of the organization, and the distribution of the resultant profit form a continuous cycle that is frequently termed *cash flow*. The first step of the cycle is the acquisition of needed funds, usually in the form of cash. Next, as the cash flows through its cycle, a portion remains as cash to be used in meeting payrolls, paying taxes, or creating reserves for unforeseen expenses. Some cash may be converted into fixed assets, such as plant and equipment necessary for the production process, and some of it takes the form of raw materials and supplies that are ultimately converted into the product or service desired. The third step in the process occurs after the product is sold and money is received in payment. All indebtedness incurred is paid, and the resultant profit may be distributed.

Financial policies are grouped to correspond to the three steps of the cycle, but the broader term "capital" is usually substituted for the word "cash." The three groups of financial policies provide a basis for the effective performance of each of the three following functions of financial management: (1) acquisition of capital, (2) employment or utilization of capital, and (3) distribution of profits. The scope of policies to guide action in each of these three areas is discussed in turn.

Acquisition of Capital

For an individual entering business, the acquisition of necessary capital may pose no serious problem, especially when he is utilizing his own savings. Personal savings is one of the major sources of capital for the individual. It is also possible that he may be able to borrow from friends in order to start his venture. If he has sufficient collateral in the form of real property, negotiable securities, or life insurance, he may borrow from an established financial institution such as a bank.

Generally, the same sources used by the individual proprietor—savings, or prior earnings, and borrowed capital—are available to a corporation. The savings of a corporation are the reserves that have been set aside to supply additional capital when needed. The capital that a corporation acquires from outside sources may be classified according to the length of time for which the financing is desired.

Financing available for a period of one year or more is referred to as *long-term capital,* and that capital available for a period of less than one year is referred to as *short-term capital.*

Long-Term Capital. The sources of long-term capital are: (1) stock, (2) bonds, (3) mortgages, and (4) long-term notes, each of which has distinct advantages and disadvantages as shown below.

STOCK. The sale of *stock,* which represents a share of ownership, is the most widely used means of raising capital for the corporation. Stock is usually classified as *preferred* and *common.* The rights and privileges accorded the stockholder of each kind of stock vary with the conditions existing at the time of issuance. As might be expected from the designation "preferred," certain preferential treatment is accorded preferred stockholders. Usually the selling price of the preferred stock and a fixed rate of return in the form of a dividend are established. The dividends payable to the preferred stockholders have first claim on the profits of the corporation and must be paid prior to the declaration of any dividends on common stock, a situation that may cause discontent among the common stockholders. Common stock carries neither a fixed selling price nor a fixed dividend. Its value is determined primarily by the price paid for the stock in the open market. If the company is expanding and has increasing profits, substantial dividends may be paid and the value of the common stock usually appreciates. If, on the other hand, the earnings of the company decline and the forecast for future earnings is dismal, the price of the common stock declines.

One of the problems faced by a company in determining whether to issue additional stock is centered around the concept of equity. If the issuance of additional stock, either common or preferred, results in a lesser amount per share of fixed assets, such as land and buildings, than prior to the issuance, the result is a dilution of equity. Also, to issue more stock at approximately the same market value as that of the stock presently outstanding, there should be sufficient earnings for the company to warrant payment of the additional dividends required by the additional shares of stock. Thus, the firm must formulate definite financial policies concerning the concept of stockholder equity to serve as a guide in determining whether the sale of additional stock is desirable as a means of acquiring more capital.

BONDS. Another means used for long-term financing is the issuance of *bonds.* A company issuing bonds agrees in writing that it will repay the face value of the bond on a specified date and that it will pay a fixed rate of interest annually to the bondholder. There are two types of bonds—*secured bonds*, which have a specific portion of the physical assets of the company pledged as security, and *unsecured bonds*, commonly called *debentures*, which have no specific assets pledged as security.

Many utilities and railroads have found bonds a convenient means of raising additional capital since such capital is typically spent for real property that is used to secure the bonds. Issuing debentures offers advantages to a company with a well-established reputation of performance and integrity. One advantage of bonds is that the present management's control of the company is not jeopardized as it may be when additional stock, with its attendant voting rights and ownership, is issued. Another advantage is that the fixed rate of interest that a company pays on money obtained from bonds is an expense item and is not taxed as income. On the other hand, dividends paid to stockholders come from the residual profit of the firm after income taxes have been paid. A company that issues $1 million of bonds with an annual rate of interest of 4 percent realizes additional gross profit of $150,000 if the rate of return on invested capital is 15 percent. The annual 4 percent interest is $40,000, which may be deducted from the earnings of $150,000 as an expense item, resulting in a profit before taxes of $110,000. The present federal income tax rate is approximately 50 percent; therefore, the profit after taxes is about $55,000. If the same amount of money, $1 million, is obtained by selling additional common stock and is invested at a 15 percent rate of return, taxable earnings are $150,000 and the net profit after taxes is approximately $75,000. Should the company's dividend policy call for a return of 4 percent on common stock, the dividends would be the same as the interest paid on the bonds. However, the dividends would be paid from the net income of $75,000, and the amount retained in the business after taxes and dividends would be only $35,000. A disadvantage resulting from the issuance of bonds is that their interest rate represents an additional fixed charge to the company, while common stock carries no such burden.

MORTGAGES. It is possible for a firm to obtain money by mortgaging a part or all of its real property. Usually, a fixed interest rate is specified, along with predetermined dates for repayment of the principal. Most modern mortgages enable a company to retain its present management and control as long as the obligations of repayment of principal and interest are met.

LONG-TERM NOTES. In recent years, long-term borrowing, particularly from funds made available by life insurance companies, has become increasingly popular as a means of raising long-term capital. As in the case of bonds, interest payments are an expense item and, thus, tax deductible. Usually funds procured from long-term borrowing are spent for additional assets intended to increase the earnings of the company, thus making it possible for the note to be repaid. Distinct disadvantages may result, however, if the lender places restrictions on the payment of dividends or the purchase of additional assets. Lenders may also require representation on the board of directors, which may or may not be an acceptable condition.

Short-Term Capital. Short-term capital is borrowed for a period of one year or less and, unlike long-term capital, is not used to acquire additional fixed assets or to improve existing assets. Short-term capital supplements the company's existing cash and may be used for such things as additional inventory to be sold and returned to cash, or to pay for goods purchased and realize cash discounts or discounts for quantity purchases. Sources of short-term capital are: (1) commercial credits, (2) bank loans, and (3) commercial factors.

COMMERCIAL CREDITS. Commercial credits are similar to an individual's charge account. Vendors of goods and services extend to customers with a good credit rating the privilege of deferred payment just as a department store does to its charge-account customers. Payments may be deferred for 30, 60, or even 90 days, thus establishing valuable short-term credit. However, cash discounts, which may represent a considerable sum if the volume purchased is large, are sacrificed.

BANK LOANS. Perhaps the most frequently used source of short-term capital is the local bank loan. The degree to which banks are utilized as a source of credit depends upon the company's reputation and the relationship it has established with the banking community. Bank loans may or may not require collateral, depending upon the individual company and the lending bank.

COMMERCIAL FACTORS. Commercial factors are firms that specialize in short-term financing usually through the purchase of a company's accounts receivable. In some instances, factors prepare the required invoices and perform all the paper work necessary to collect the accounts receivable. To firms short on capital and without an adequate clerical staff, the use of a commercial factor may offer an attractive solution for acquiring short-term capital.

Utilization of Capital

The second group of financial policies serves as guides for the employment or utilization of capital after it has been acquired. Elements to be considered in determining the most effective utilization of capital are the amount of capital to be converted into fixed assets, the ratio between fixed assets and working capital, the amount of inventory, credits and collections, and depreciation. Each of these elements demands cash, and unless there are policies that specify the amount to be allocated for each use, a serious imbalance may result and thereby impair the firm's financial position.

Fixed Assets. A firm needs to examine closely the extent to which capital is converted into fixed assets. In its simplest form, the question is one of leasing or buying. There is no single answer for all types of business, nor is there one answer for all types of fixed assets within any given business. There are many factors to be considered before a definite policy can be established concerning the amount and nature of fixed assets a company should acquire. Among them are problems of obsolescence, maintenance, replacement, and the rate of return on the specific asset. It is also necessary to consider the effect of buying versus leasing with respect to tax liability. Usually money paid for rentals or leases is chargeable as an expense and hence is tax deductible. On the other hand, if the equipment is purchased, a depreciation allowance is permitted which may or may not offset the added tax liability. Fixed assets may be sold and converted into cash, a move that may be proper if the assets are not being fully utilized and if additional cash is needed. Conversion of assets into cash usually does not change the amount of capital unless the assets are sold at a price significantly below their purchase price.

Working Capital. Policies must be developed to determine the amount of capital to be retained for the operation of the business and how this capital is to be utilized. This capital, called *working capital,* is used for the purchase of materials and services, for payment of payrolls, and for contingencies. There should be a balance maintained between fixed assets, all of which require money to operate, and the working capital available for their operation. Policies define the proper relationship for a given company. When fixed assets become too great in relation to available working capital, excessive borrowing may result in order to remain in operation; or if additional funds are not obtainable, a curtailment in production may be necessary. Working capital not fully utilized is a waste of the firm's resources and suggests that the excess should be invested so that the company's return on its resources may be increased.

Inventory. One of the major uses of capital is its employment for, and transformation into, an inventory of finished goods or goods in process. Without clear-cut policy statements in this area, it is possible for a company without fully realizing it to sink an enormous amount of money into inventories. This is particularly hazardous if there is a possibility of obsolescence due to a change in the product on the part of a competitor. It is also hazardous in those businesses where there is a marked variation in the prices of the raw materials used in making the product. Thus, policy statements in regard to inventory should include a determination of the size of inventory, including both in-process and finished goods expressed as a unit portion of annual sales, along with a determination of the rate of inventory build-up and turnover so that advantage may be taken of price fluctuations of raw materials.

Credits and Collections. Virtually every business firm is forced to extend some credit to its customers. The extent to which credit is granted may be determined by general industry practices, or it may be the result of attempting to secure a better competitive position. In either event, clear-cut policies are needed to determine the amount of credit that should be extended. Closely allied to credit policies are policies governing the collection of accounts receivable and the granting of discounts from list price for prompt payment. Accounts receivable, unless closely watched, may become abnormally large as a percentage of current assets.

Depreciation. Policies are needed to determine the method to be used in calculating the rate of depreciation of capital expenditures. Certain types of equipment may be useful for a period of time considerably longer than their normal or expected life; and in this case, other things being equal, the straight-line method of depreciation might prove satisfactory. However, in fields where there is rapid technological change and improvement in manufacturing methods, along with changes in the product itself, it might be well to utilize any one of several methods of accelerated depreciation so that sufficient capital will be available to replace equipment as changing conditions make replacement necessary.

Distribution of Profits

The third area in which financial policies serve as a guide concerns the distribution of profits. As mentioned before, profits are absolutely vital as a means of continuing a business. Therefore, it is necessary that policies be developed concerning the amount of cash reserves to be retained in order to operate the business. Obviously, too much money may be retained to the long-run detriment of the firm. There are many who facetiously referred to the "Bank of Montgomery Ward" during the period of time that the retail chain was under the direction of Sewell Avery. During this period, huge cash reserves equal to those of many small banks were built up because of Mr. Avery's stated belief that another severe depression was in the offing.

Dividends. Policy must be established regarding the payment of dividends. Such a statement is necessary to assure a fair return on investment to those who have invested in the firm and to make the purchase of equities in the firm an attractive investment. When policies express the amount to be paid out in dividends as a percentage of profits earned, there is the possibility of increasing dividends and consequently an increasing rate of return on money invested.

Reinvestment. After the establishment of adequate cash reserves and the payment of dividends, the disposition of earnings must be determined. Questions to be answered are: what portion of the profit is to be reinvested in the firm, and how is this money to be invested? It can be invested in fixed assets, a means of placing capital in those channels that result in expanded sales. Another means of expanding sales, not ordinarily classified as an investment, is to direct capital into an expanded advertising program or to establish sales territories not currently serviced by the company. Another major direction for the utilization of capital is in the area of research and product development.

ANALYSIS OF PROFIT

Without stated policies to guide management in the acquisition and utilization of capital and the subsequent distribution of profits, it is highly unlikely that the level of profits achieved by a business organization ever approximates its potential. Many times before a final determination can be made regarding the establishment of policies in each of the three areas of financial management, it is necessary to analyze more closely the nature of the process of developing and measuring profits. One analytical method used to show the interrelationships of the factors affecting profits is break-even analysis. The following section discusses the steps necesary to complete a break-even analysis, the dynamics of the factors influencing profit, and an evaluation of break-even analysis as an analytical technique.

Break-Even Analysis

A *break even analysis* reveals the operating conditions that exist when a company "breaks even"; that is, when sales reach a dollar volume equal to all expenses incurred in attaining that level of sales. Beyond this point or level of volume, the company has the potential to make a profit on additional sales. It is the purpose of break-even analysis to clarify the dynamic relationships existing between the total costs of a company and the volume of sales produced as a result of these costs.

The following condensed operating statement includes information needed for a break-even analysis:

Ace Manufacturing Company

Condensed Operating Statement
for the Fiscal Year, 19—

Revenue from sales (20,000 units @ $50 ea.)		$1,000,000
Less costs and expenses:		
Variable costs	$500,000	
Fixed costs	400,000	
Total costs and expenses		900,000
Net profit before taxes		$ 100,000

The operating statement shows clearly the two variables needed for break-even analysis—a measure of input, costs; and a measure of output, unit volume or sales. The problem is to present the relationship existing between these variables in such a fashion that the break-even point, the point at which the Ace Manufacturing Company had sales sufficient to defray all expenses, may be readily determined. These variables are presented graphically in Figure 5-1.

In Figure 5-1, sales volume is plotted on the x, or horizontal axis, and expense items are plotted on the y, or vertical axis. Note that the costs for the Ace Manufacturing Company have been separated into two major types—those costs that are *fixed,* or relatively unchanging as a result of sales volume; and those costs that are *variable* and vary primarily as a function of sales volume. Usually fixed costs are costs

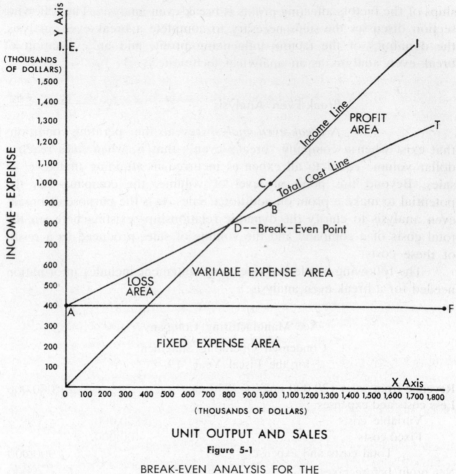

UNIT OUTPUT AND SALES

Figure 5-1

BREAK-EVEN ANALYSIS FOR THE
ACE MANUFACTURING COMPANY

that accrue whether or not anything is being manufactured or sold. These costs normally include real estate taxes, insurance, depreciation, certain administrative overhead expenses such as executive and clerical salaries, and interest on indebtedness. They are similar in nature to the fixed costs of owning an automobile—insurance and depreciation—and have little to do with the number of miles driven. Gasoline costs, however, are a direct function of the number of miles driven and are thus considered variable costs. Likewise, certain costs of business, usually materials and the cost of labor that works directly on the product (called direct labor) vary with the number of units produced and are classified as variable costs.

There are always some cost items that cannot readily be classified as either fixed or variable. Typical of these are the costs of supervision, power costs, and some forms of indirect labor such as inspection and shipping. In a strict sense these costs are variable, but they are variable costs that behave as fixed costs; i.e., they move very slowly, and within broad ranges of units produced they do not change. For example, a supervisory staff of 10 foremen may direct the work of 150 men and this work force may be doubled before it becomes necessary to add another supervisor. It is usually safe practice to classify as fixed those costs that are not clearly variable.

At a level of $1 million sales, fixed costs for the Ace Manufacturing Company are $400,000. This value becomes point *A* on the *y*, or vertical, axis. Since this amount does not vary as a result of the number of units sold, it is expressed graphically as a straight line parallel to the *x* axis and is interpreted as constant for all sales up to and including $1 million. The area below the line *A-F* is referred to as the *fixed expense area.*

Since variable costs are in addition to fixed costs and vary directly as the result of the number of units produced, they are shown graphically as added to the fixed expenses. With a unit volume of zero, there are no additional costs attributable to materials or direct labor; thus, the left-hand end of the variable cost line is placed at point *A* on the vertical or cost axis. Point *B*, variable costs of $500,000 at a sales volume of $1 million, is taken from the operating statement (page 121) and is entered on the graph directly across from the $900,000 mark ($500,000 variable costs plus $400,000 fixed costs) on the vertical axis and directly above the amount of sales ($1 million) obtained at that level of expense. Because these costs vary directly with the units produced, the relationship can be shown by a straight line, *A-T*. Notice that this line is called the *total cost line* rather than the variable cost line because any point on this line is in effect a summation of fixed costs and variable costs for the corresponding level of sales. The area between line *A-F* and line *A-T* is referred to as the *variable expense area* since it represents only that portion of the total cost that is variable.

Note that the vertical axis *O-IE* has been called an *income-expense* line. This dual designation is necessary to show clearly that expenses are paid out of income and that the difference remaining is profit. The next step in analyzing the profit of Ace Manufacturing Company is to locate point *C*, current income, a point directly over the $1 million mark on the horizontal or sales axis. Since this point also represents total income for the company, point *C* is located directly across from the $1 million mark on the vertical income-expense axis. A line drawn from point *0* (zero sales and zero income) through point *C* forms *0-I*, the *income line*. The line crosses the total cost line at point *D,* the break-even point, a sales volume of $800,000. The area enclosed by the triangle *IDT* represents the *profit area*, while the area enclosed by the triangle *ADO* represents the *loss area*. Thus, the break-even chart shows graphically the relationships that exist among fixed costs, variable costs, unit price, and unit sales for the Ace Manufacturing Company.

Dynamics of Profit

The interrelationships among the four factors utilized in break-even analysis—(1) unit volume, (2) fixed costs, (3) variable costs, and (4) unit price—emphasize the dynamic nature of profit and stress that profit cannot be viewed as something left over after all expenses are paid. A change in any one of these factors has a predictable effect upon the profit of a company, and if the amount of the change is known or can be anticipated, as in Case Problem 5-A, the resultant effect upon profit can be computed. The influence of each factor upon profits is discussed below.[2]

Effect of Volume. One measure that shows the effect of volume upon the profitability of a company is profit expressed as a percentage of sales. Since this measure is the quotient obtained when the dollar volume of profits (the numerator) is divided by the dollar volume of sales (the denominator), it is apparent that any change in the value of the numerator changes the rate of profitability. The expression of profit as a percentage of sales utilizes total volume. For example, on page 121 the Ace Manufacturing Company shows a 10 percent profit (profit of $100,000 divided by current sales of $1 million). In view of this measure of profit, does it seem reasonable to state that there is a profit of 50 percent to be gained for every dollar of sales beyond the break-even point? Your answer is probably negative, yet 50 percent is a correct statement of Ace's profitability beyond the break-even point.

Analysis of the relationship existing between profit and volume beyond the break-even point is called the *profit to volume analysis* or the *profit to volume ratio (P/V ratio)*. The relationship between profit and volume beyond the break-even point is stated precisely in the following formula:

────────────

    [2] Fred V. Gardner, *Profit Management and Control* (New York: McGraw-Hill Book Company, 1955). This discussion of profit management and control has as its basis the break-even point as a means of analysis. Part 1 of the book introduces the break-even concept as a basis for profit control, and Part 2 details the use of break-even point analysis in management decisions. Chapter 6, "The Laws of Profit," pp. 42-64, is a complete discussion of the interrelationships existing among the factors that influence profit.

$$P/V \ \text{Ratio} = \frac{\text{Marginal Income}}{\text{Sales}} \quad \dots \dots \dots \dots \dots \dots \dots \dots \dots \quad (1)$$

where,

Marginal Income = Sales — Variable Costs, and
Sales = Total Dollar Volume of Sales.

In order to understand the relationships expressed in the formula above, let us apply it to the operating statement of the Ace Manufacturing Company. Stated fixed costs are $400,000, an amount that remains constant throughout the entire range of sales from zero to $1 million. As goods are manufactured and sold, variable costs (labor and material) must be paid. After variable costs have been paid, the remainder, *marginal income*, is applied to paying the fixed costs of the business. Since the variable costs of the company are $500,000 when sales are $1 million, variable costs represent 50 percent of the sales dollar. Each unit manufactured sells for $50; therefore, $25 of the money received for each unit is paid out for material and labor. The marginal income remaining, also $25, is applied to fixed costs. This distribution of sales dollars continues until all fixed costs, in this case $400,000, have been paid and results in reaching the break-even point. Beyond the break-even point there are no more fixed costs to be paid; the only costs to be met are the variable costs of material and labor for each additional unit made and sold. Thus, the profit for each additional unit beyond the break-even point is determined by subtracting the variable costs from the sales price. The remainder, $25 marginal income, is divided by the sales value of each unit, $50, in order that the relationship may be expressed as a ratio or a quotient; the quotient for this example is .50, or 50 percent. Since the P/V ratio assumes a constant variable cost per unit and a constant price per unit, the same result, .50, may be obtained when the totals from the operating statement are used rather than analyzing the fixed and variable costs of each unit made and sold. When totals are substituted in Formula (1), marginal income, $500,000 ($1 million sales minus $500,000 variable costs) divided by $1 million (sales) yields .50. Therefore, the statement that the Ace Manufacturing Company has a profit to volume ratio of 50 percent is correct and can be interpreted as meaning that a profit of 50 percent can be expected on each unit sold above the break-even point.

After the P/V ratio, or more simply P/V, is determined, the break-even point may be computed algebraically, thereby permitting an accurate determination of the company's profit path. One function of profit planning is to predict the effect of contemplated changes upon company profits. Case Problem 5-A requires a determination of the present break-even point and the expected break-even point created by rising costs so that plans may be formed to retain profits at their present level. Given the fixed expenses of a company and the P/V, the break-even point is determined by the following formula:

$$\text{Break-Even Point} = \frac{\text{Fixed Expenses}}{P/V \text{ Ratio}} \quad\dotsi\dotsi\dotsi\dotsi\dotsi\dotsi \quad (2)$$

In the case of the Ace Manufacturing Company, fixed expenses of $400,000 divided by the P/V of .50 result in a break-even point of $800,000, the same value obtained by graphic analysis in Figure 5-1. To understand the reasoning behind Formula (2), one must remember that every dollar earned prior to the break-even point is divided two ways—one part is used to pay current variable costs and one part is used to pay established fixed costs. For the example given, an equal amount is distributed to each type of cost.

Effect of Fixed Costs. A change in the amount of fixed costs in either direction changes the break-even point and the amount of profit earned for a given level of sales volume, but it does not change marginal income. (Marginal income is equal to total sales minus variable costs.) Fixed costs must be paid out of marginal income; therefore, should fixed costs increase too much, the remainder is negative and appears as a loss, rather than positive, a profit.

A company should examine with care any move that results in an increase in fixed costs. By their very nature they are extremely difficult to lower as they are literally "fixed." For example, unused plant facilities may be sold, thereby reducing fixed costs; but the question remains whether or not such a move can be accomplished rapidly enough to avoid excessive losses. Consequently, before increasing the fixed costs of any business, the Principle of Economic Effectiveness should be used as a guide. Ask the question whether the additional revenue (or service) is going to at least equal in value the additional cost incurred. If the answer is negative, move with caution, if at all.

Effect of Variable Costs. Unlike changes in fixed costs, a change in variable costs produces a change in marginal income. Marginal income is defined as total sales less variable costs, and as the variable costs of direct labor and materials increase, marginal income decreases. Since fixed and unchanging costs must be paid out of marginal income, the effect is a definite "squeeze on profits." The inherent characteristics of fixed costs, which make them relatively unyielding to change, and the realization that they must be paid out of marginal income go a long way toward explaining the behavior of management during a typical cost-cutting drive. Emphasis is placed upon personnel costs, both direct and indirect, material costs, expense accounts, and a host of seemingly relative unimportant items. Why? Simply because these items are controllable, or variable, and the truly large cost items of depreciation, taxes, and interest remain either stationary or move slowly in a downward direction. Furthermore, every dollar saved in variable expenses represents an additional dollar of profit.

Effect of Price. A change in dollar sales volume may be accomplished in one of two ways: by producing the same number of units of volume but selling at a higher price per unit, or producing a greater number of units of volume and selling at the same or original price. A change in price per unit results in change in marginal income—total sales minus variable costs. In addition, the degree of change in marginal income can be predicted prior to a price change by multiplying the expected difference in price by the number of units produced. Since an increase in price, with all other factors remaining constant, results in decreasing the break-even point and correspondingly increasing profit, the need for experimental pricing practices is evident. There are undoubtedly many instances where modest or even substantial price increases could be accomplished without a decline in the total number of units sold. Some food products are introduced to a specific market area and prices are varied within that area to determine the effect of price on demand. Too often, firms dealing in consumer products assume that a lower price results in increased volume but are hard pressed to produce data to support the relationship.

Aside from the effect that changes in price may have on volume, consideration should also be given to the effect that such changes may have on competitors. A price change in an upward direction may enable a competitor to lower his price and capitalize on the increased price differential and increase his volume. Or, a reduction in price may be followed by a similar reduction on the part of competitors, with the result that the same volume is produced and sold by the industry, but with one important difference—all firms are selling at a lower price. An intimate knowledge of the industry and its market characteristics, along with a complete knowledge of the effect of price and volume in relation to the company's break-even point, should be the determining factors in the development of pricing policies.

Evaluation of Profit Analysis Techniques

There are many criticisms of both break-even analysis and the profit to volume ratio as analytical techniques. If one were to choose a single word to describe the objections, it would be that the techniques are *static* in nature and consequently are not appropriate for use in describing the dynamic situation that is typical of the business environment. Specifically, criticisms have attacked both the reliability and the validity of the concepts of variable and fixed costs, stating that neither is a truly reliable measure, other than for the instant from which it is drawn, and that they are not valid measures since they are not what they claim to be. Break-even analysis is also criticized because it implies that all costs contribute directly to production. A third criticism is that break-even analysis is not an accurate reflection of the effect of company pricing practices. The fourth criticism is that break-even charts cannot be applied accurately to a company that manufactures more than one product.

Reliability and Validity of Variable and Fixed Costs Concepts. Break-even analysis and the P/V ratio assume that variable costs can be shown graphically by means of a straight line; that is, variable costs change at a constant rate. The description of variable costs as constant is not an accurate statement of conditions as they actually exist. It does not take into account those instances where the costs of labor and materials decrease as the result of gains in production efficiency attributable to an increased volume of production. Increases in efficiency that are the result of increased volume occur frequently when labor is not fully utilized at the lower levels of production. Also, there are many instances where significant savings in costs are possible when materials are purchased in large quantities. Variable costs shown as changes at a constant rate do not reflect those instances where the phenomenon of diminishing returns for each additional unit of input occurs. In summary, it appears that variable costs can be more accurately described as curvilinear rather than as linear functions. A comparison of the two functions is shown in Figure 5-2.

Essentially the same criticisms have been leveled at showing fixed costs as a straight line parallel to the output axis. The criticism is particularly true where a firm is operating near capacity because it is unable to increase output without additional facilities such as production equipment or manufacturing space. Aside from physical facilities, there are other fixed charges such as the costs of administrative, clerical, and supervisory personnel, which vary with the level of volume. There are those who say that if these charges are fixed as claimed, then why

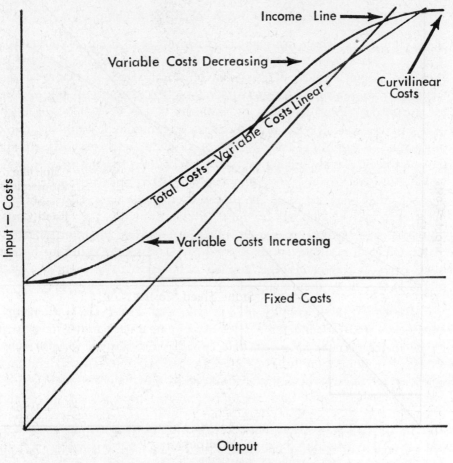

Figure 5-2

CURVILINEAR VARIABLE COSTS COMPARED WITH
LINEAR VARIABLE COSTS

spend so much time attempting to control them. However, they are controllable within limits, and whenever a planning opportunity arises, every effort should be made to keep fixed costs at the lowest level possible. The fixed costs of a business, in all probability, follow a stair-step pattern, and the analytical techniques of break-even analysis are accurate for only one given level of production. The stairlike progression of fixed costs is shown in Figure 5-3.

Contribution of All Costs to Production. The second criticism is concerned with the problem of determining and assigning costs. Break-even charts are drawn with the input factors shown on the vertical axis, and output on the horizontal axis. It is implied that all costs contribute

Figure 5-3

STAIRLIKE PROGRESSION OF FIXED COSTS
AND STATIC FIXED COSTS

to the formation of the product. While such an assumption may be perfectly true in the long run, it does not reflect the contribution of inputs for any given year. There may be sizable expenditures for a five-year period for research or product development without any expected or actual contribution to the current volume of goods produced and sold. These costs are not variable costs since they are not a direct function of current volume, nor is their classification as a fixed charge justified because they are not immediately related to present production. There is no way to shrug off this criticism, but these costs should be considered as fixed, at least within a given budgetary period, and re-garded as the result of company policy and planning. Ultimately they are expected to contribute to some degree to the firm's growth and economic strength. Though not a cost necessary for present volume, they are a form of insurance, paid for currently, which will enable the firm to remain in business in the future.

Analyzing Company Pricing Practices Via Break-Even Analysis. The third criticism is that profit analysis techniques are unable to reflect accurately the pricing practices and policies of many companies. A small company may not determine the price charged for its goods or services, but rather, may follow the industry pattern. Indeed, it may even have to lower prices to stay in business, and the industry leader may then have to lower its prices in order to remain in a dominant position. Volume discounts are common for many products, and when such practices exist, the reliability of break-even analysis may be seriously impaired. Volume discounts have their effect upon company revenue, with the result that the revenue line is not the straight line shown on break-even charts.

Applying Break-Even Analysis to Multiproduct Manufacturers. Fourth, there is the problem of an accurate profit analysis in those companies manufacturing more than one product. It is extremely difficult to assign fixed charges to a specific product with any degree of assurance. For the company manufacturing three separate products, it does not follow that each product should bear one third of the fixed costs. A common practice is to assign costs in proportion to the number of units of each product. Another approach is to assign fixed costs in proportion to the dollar sales realized for each product. The same problems exist in the assignment of variable costs. Direct labor may work one day on one product and the next day on another. Then, too, a given part or operation may be common to several products. In a sense, such criticisms of profit analysis are summarized in the statement that the processes are too complex for accurate analysis. This may be so, but there are many times when an inaccurate or sketchy analysis is better than none.

These criticisms do not mean that the break-even chart or the profit to volume ratio should be abandoned. They do mean, however, that extreme care should be used in the development of these measures so that they reflect existing conditions as accurately as possible. It is also necessary to use caution in making predictions of future earnings, costs, and revenues. It is true that these techniques are static in the sense that a cross-section of the present is shown, but what is to prevent a later analysis when conditions have changed? Underlying the use of any analytical technique is an attitude of willingness to come to grips with a problem. Break-even analysis and its extension, the profit to volume ratio, provide a conceptual framework that permits an analysis of the dynamic factors creating profit, thereby enabling a manager to fulfill more effectively one of his major functions—planning.

APPLICATION OF PRINCIPLES

The application of three principles of management developed in earlier chapters has a direct bearing upon the profits of a company and the extent to which its plans for profit are successful. The first principle that may be brought to bear directly upon a firm's profitability is the Principle of the Objective. Second, the Principle of Planning offers a means of predicting the probable success of the financial policies and plans developed by a firm; and, third, the Principle of Economic Effectiveness serves as a criterion for evaluating the economic worth of a proposed plan for the achievement of stated objectives. The application of each of these principles of management to profit planning is discussed below.

Principle of the Objective

The Principle of the Objective states that *before initiating any course of action, the objective in view must be clearly determined, understood, and stated*. For most firms their objectives are multiple in nature, as shown in the statement of objectives by Continental-Emsco Company in Chapter 3, page 57. The process of stating clearly each objective so that it may be thoroughly understood minimizes the possibility of conflicting objectives and forces the establishment of a hierarchy of objectives with a priority rank assigned to each objective. One such objective that must be placed in proper perspective is the objective of earning a profit. In considering profit as an objective, the question of profit maximization frequently arises.

Most laymen and many professional managers assume that every corporate plan should be designed to maximize profits expressed either as a return on invested capital or as a percentage of gross sales. Yet, maximizing profits is not always possible, for there are times when profits of the immediate or near future are sacrificed with the expectation that profitability over the long run will be increased. There are also situations where it seems advisable to operate at a diminished level of profits for a continuing period of time.[3] A company may have as a major objective the stabilization of sales volume, and as a result embarks upon a program of diversification; that is, broadening its product line in order to achieve the desired sales stability. In so doing, it is quite possible that the overall profit to volume ratio may be lowered. A policy emphasizing research for new products may limit profits of the present and the immediate future, but may be very necessary for survival over a long period of time. The two examples above illustrate the establishment of priorities in the achievement of objectives and although profit remains a major objective, it is subordinated in one instance to the desire for stability of income and in the other instance to the need for continuing product research.

Principle of Planning

The Principle of Planning emphasizes that *effective planning results in plans that are objective, structured, and flexible, and the extent to which resultant plans possess these characteristics is a measure of their probable success.* Policies are plans in every sense of the word, for they outline the course of action to be followed in reaching specified objectives. As such, they must be examined with respect to each of the three characteristics of objectivity, structuralization, and flexibility as measures of their probable success.

Objectivity. The degree of objectivity exercised in the planning process determines the objectivity of the resultant plan. In the development of financial policies directed toward the acquisition of capital, all relevant data must be carefully assembled and interpreted. In order to achieve a high degree of objectivity, it is necessary to analyze all aspects of the firm's present and past performance and to utilize every relevant source of internal data. The utilization of data external to the firm must be equally thorough, and all available sources of funds must be examined and given careful consideration. The same care in the collection and interpretation of data must be exercised in developing policies that guide the utilization of capital and the distribution of earnings. In short, the extent to which the scientific method is employed is a measure of the objectivity of a firm's policies.

---

[3] Robert N. Anthony, "The Trouble with Profit Maximization," *Harvard Business Review* (Boston), Vol. 38 (November-December, 1960), pp. 126-34. Mr. Anthony discusses why business decisions are not and cannot be made with profit maximization as the sole goal. A brief statement of the reasons presented, taken from the subtitle of the article, is: "It is too difficult, it is unrealistic, and it is immoral."

Degree of Structuralization. The characteristic of structuralization refers to the degree of structuralization inherent in the plan itself and the extent to which the plan structures or guides the behavior of the persons implementing the plan. When applied as a criterion for judging financial policies, emphasis is placed upon the structure of the policy itself. It is important that financial policies for each of the three major financial functions—acquiring capital, utilizing capital, and distributing earnings—form a well-structured and coordinated financial pattern. A policy that calls for the acquisition of outside capital with its attendant costs at a time when the company has a large surplus is illustrative of poorly coordinated financial efforts. Maintaining a proper ratio between fixed assets and working capital is an example of unified planning and proper structuring of financial plans.

Flexibility. In many respects flexibility in financial planning is difficult to achieve because most commitments are difficult to modify and obligate a company for a long period of time. Obligations incurred in long-term financing are a good example of why it is difficult to secure flexibility. Even so, a measure of flexibility may be achieved when there is a margin of safety sufficient to insure the meeting of obligations even though sales volume and profit decline or do not reach their anticipated levels. A new plant designed to permit ready expansion if the need arises and the construction of office facilities with movable partitions are examples of flexibility in the utilization of fixed assets.

Principle of Economic Effectiveness

Economic effectiveness in planning results in plans that maximize achievement of company objectives through the most efficient utilization of available resources.

The Principle of Economic Effectiveness provides a basis for making a choice between two or more alternate courses of action so that the plan selected offers the greatest contribution relative to cost in the achievement of company objectives. The optimum relationship is that point where the incremental gain realized in achieving the firm's objectives is equal to the incremental cost of the plan. The application of the concept of equating marginal costs and marginal revenues to policies governing the acquisition of funds is of value not only because it indicates when the capital requested is sufficient for the task at hand, but because it may also indicate the need for a greater amount of capital than anticipated originally. For example, a company considering the need for long-term funds of $1 million may intend to invest this sum in facilities with an expected return of 15 percent. Further investigation may show that if $2 million were invested, the return would be 22 percent, while an investment of $3 million would yield a return of only 10 percent. Under these conditions, the optimum amount to be financed is $2 million, or twice the amount originally thought desirable. The application of the concept of equalizing incremental gains in relation to incremental costs can reveal a need for more money as well as showing when too little has been requested.

•   •   •   •   •   •   •   •   •

Case Problem 5-B, "Expand or Merge?", presents a company that has two courses of action available for increasing its sales volume and profit. The application of the principle of economic effectiveness is of value in choosing the better plan for this company.

Questions for Study and Discussion

1. Why is a definition of profits as something that is left over after meeting all expenses considered inadequate as a definition from the viewpoint of a professional manager? How would you, as a student of management, define profit?
2. What measures are commonly used to measure profit, and how does each contribute to an understanding of a company's financial position? In your opinion, which measure is the most important?
3. How are financial policies related to the concept of cash flow?
4. What are the advantages and disadvantages of the commonly used sources of long-term capital and of short-term capital?
5. Why is the allocation of capital important? Discuss the effects of various types of imbalances in the allocation of capital.
6. What are the dangers of distributing profits on a fixed-percentage basis? Do these shortcomings apply to other means of distributing profits on a fixed-dollar basis?
7. Using the formulas presented in this chapter, what is the break-even point when: Sales = $250,000; VC = $75,000; FC = $25,000?
8. Assume a unit sales price of $10 for the sales of $250,000 in Question No. 7. What do these data add to the significance of the break-even point?
9. What is the P/V ratio for the figures presented in Question No. 7?
10. Show graphically the effect of changes in unit price, unit volume, and changes in fixed and variable costs on the break-even point.
11. Why is the break-even analysis technique criticized? In view of the criticisms, when do you recommend its use?

12. How should the knowledge of P/V ratios for each of the products in a company's product line affect sales effort?

13. What is meant by profit maximization? Do companies maximize profits?

● ● ● ● ● ● ● ● ●

Mr. John Wood is president of Abrasives, Inc., a firm that he founded and built to its present size. In 1935, Mr. Wood started as a manufacturer's representative and one of his lines was industrial grinding wheels. The company producing these wheels decided to discontinue their manufacture in 1946. They sold the trade name and much of their equipment to Mr. Wood, who incorporated under the present name in 1950. During the last year of operation, the sales of Abrasives, Inc., were $5,750,000 and net profit, before taxes, was $460,000, or 8 percent of sales. Fixed costs, $2,702,500, are currently 47 percent of sales, and variable expenses are $2,587,500.

For several months Mr. Wood has been considering a plan to extend his present facilities. He estimates that the expanded facilities would easily produce an additional 10 percent in dollar sales volume. The cost of this expansion will be $1,300,000, payable in four annual installments. The cost of interest is included in this amount, and Mr. Wood believes that payments can be met out of current earnings.

Recently, Mr. Wood contacted a broker and, as a result, consideration

Case Problem 5-B
Expand or Merge?

is being given to the possibility of growth by means of merger rather than by expanding present facilities. The company for sale, Sandco, manufactures and distributes industrial sanding belts, a product that complements Abrasives' present line of grinding wheels. Last year the sales of Sandco were $2,500,000, with a net profit before taxes of 10 percent. The P/V ratio of this company is 55 percent, somewhat higher than the P/V ratio for Abrasives, Inc.; fixed costs are 45 percent, and variable costs are also 45 percent of sales. Mr. Wood estimates that he can retain 90 percent of the current sales volume and believes that a merger will reduce the fixed costs of Sandco by at least 10 percent. The asking price for Sandco is approximately $2 million, with the possibility of arranging annual payments of $500,000 each, including interest charges.

Problem

Outline your recommendations to Mr. Wood. Present a complete analysis of: (1) his present operation, (2) Sandco's operation, and (3) the anticipated merger.

CHAPTER 6

Planning for Sales

In 1920 Electroware began manufacturing electrical household appliances in Toledo, Ohio. From its founding until 1930, its product line was limited to small appliances such as electric irons, toasters, waffle irons, portable ovens, and percolators. These items were sold directly to retail stores, which in turn sold to the consumer. Approximately 1,000 such retail outlets in midwestern and eastern states are customers of Electroware. In 1930 the company introduced a line of electric hot water heaters designed for residential use; and, without giving the matter much thought, the existing channel of distribution from manufacturer to retail outlet to consumer was continued. Several years ago the company discontinued the manufacture of small appliances and devoted its full attention to manufacturing and selling electric hot water units.

Recently John Miller was promoted from the position of vice-president, manufacturing, to president. While in charge of the manufacturing function, he had served as chairman of a product diversification committee. The committee recommended that the company manufacture electric stoves to supplement its existing line of hot water heaters. The recommendation was adopted and, during his first year as president, Mr. Miller's attention was directed toward the completion of a new addition to the plant and the installation of necessary equipment so that electric stoves could be produced. Reliable estimates from the production planning department indicated that the stove line would be in operation by the end of the year and that a total of 26,500 units could be assembled during the next calendar year. Production of electric hot water heaters is expected to remain constant at 40,000 units per year, or slightly more than 150 a day.

Tom Andrews, vice-president, sales, had opposed the expansion of facilities in order to manufacture electric stoves; instead, he had urged that the output of hot water heaters be increased. He pointed out that the present annual production of heaters amounts to less than four heaters per month for each of the 1,000 retail outlets and that the store owners and managers are becoming dissatisfied since they are not receiving a quantity of heaters sufficient

---

Case Problem 6-A
Channel of Distribution

to meet customer demand. One store owner described the situation as follows: "People don't come in here to buy hot water heaters only; usually they want something else for their home at the same time. If they can't buy all the things that they want in one place, most of them will go to a store that will sell them everything that they want at the same time. Not having enough heaters is costing me sales in those items that I do have in stock." Andrews also argued that the projected volume of electric stoves would be adding insult to injury because each dealer would receive an average of only two stoves a month. Mr. Miller then suggested that the stoves be sold through a different channel of distribution, such as selling direct to the builders of apartments and large housing projects. Andrews objected to this approach and insisted that the company should be loyal to its present dealers since they had stood by Electroware during the lean years. Furthermore, he feared that many dealers would refuse to handle the hot water heaters unless they received a commission on all Electroware products sold in their community.

Mr. Miller discussed the problem of selecting a channel of distribution with Ted Donham, the controller, and asked for his suggestion. Donham recommended that a distributor, or wholesaler, be appointed for each of the following cities: Chicago, Detroit, Cleveland, and Cincinnati. He did not like the idea of selling direct to the building

contractors because he felt that many of them might prove to be poor credit risks and that the cost of contacting each contractor individually would be excessive. He was against extending the present method of distribution to electric stoves because it would require the shipment of one or two items a month to each of the 1,000 retailers, thereby creating a great deal of paper work. He believed that the selection of four distributors would permit the company to ship in carload lots and reduce freight costs. He also emphasized that the production rate of electric stoves would be sufficient to satisfy the needs of four carefully selected distributors.

Problems

1. Define the problem that Electroware is attempting to solve.
2. State the policy that you believe Electroware should adopt in order to solve its current problem.
3. Would you recommend that both products be sold through the same channel of distribution? Why?
4. Do you subscribe to Mr. Andrews' point of view that the company should be loyal to its present dealers?
5. While Mr. Miller was vice-president, manufacturing, he served as chairman of a product diversification committee. Would Mr. Andrews, vice-president, sales, appear to be a more logical candidate for the chairmanship of such a committee?

• • • • • • • • •

Electroware must make a policy decision regarding the method to be used in distributing its product. Selecting the appropriate channel of distribution for the goods or services of a company is but one of several major policy decisions required in planning an effective sales program. Before reviewing the scope of sales policies, it is necessary to understand the factors that influence the demand for a given product or service. Also, it is necessary to evaluate sales policies to determine the extent to which sound principles of management have been applied. The major topics discussed in this chapter are, first, the determinants of demand; second, the scope of sales policies; and third, the application of principles of management as a means of insuring sound sales policies.

DETERMINANTS OF DEMAND

The sales or marketing function of a business organization encompasses those activities necessary to persuade a buyer to purchase the products or services of the organization. There are many factors that determine the efficiency and effectiveness of a sales organization. Furthermore, some of the factors that influence the sales of a given company are economic in nature and beyond the control of any one company; yet, the firm must operate within an economic environment that cannot be controlled by any one company. Our task is to determine those factors of the environment that may be modified and the marketing techniques available to create the desired changes. In order to understand the framework in which selling takes place, it is necessary to review the factors that determine the demand for consumer goods and to consider very briefly the factors that influence the demand for capital goods.

Demand for Consumer Goods

There are three elements necessary for the completion of any marketing transaction. One of these elements is a *buyer,* a person or an institution desirous of purchasing a given product or service. The second element of the transaction is a *seller* who is able to provide the desired product or service. The third element is a *price* that the buyer is willing to pay and that the seller is willing to accept. The economist's approach to the marketing process described above is directed toward a better understanding of the relationships that exist between the supply (available quantity) of a product or service and the demand (amount purchased) for a product or service. The conclusion reached from analyzing these relationships has been stated as the *Law of Supply and*

Demand. This law holds that an increase in the supply of a given product tends to decrease the price, thereby increasing the demand for the product; and conversely, if the supply of the product decreases, the price ultimately goes higher, with a resultant decrease in demand.

The discussion above, from the viewpoint of the economist, places a great deal of emphasis upon the supply of goods available and seeks to determine the effect of supply upon the price of a given product or service. The businessman, however, is concerned with determining how he can influence the consumer to buy at a specified price level and in sufficient quantities so that an adequate return can be realized on invested capital. In the classical portrayal of supply and demand, the buying power of the consumer is not mentioned explicitly, yet it is self-evident that a purchaser must have money in some form in order to buy. Buying power is one of the major determinants that affects the sales of an individual business firm. Supply, a major concern to the economist, is in most instances not a critical determinant of the price of manufactured consumer goods over the long run in the United States since our manufacturing facilities are capable of producing more than can be consumed. To a degree, manufacturers of consumer goods operate in an economy that can be characterized as a constant state of oversupply, with the influence of supply as a factor determining price, and ultimately the demand remaining relatively constant. Consequently, in the discussion that follows, supply is not considered as a determinant of the demand for consumer goods.

Consumer goods, those items consumed by individuals in contrast to certain items purchased by industry, are traditionally classified as either *nondurable* or *durable.* Each of these types of consumer goods is discussed separately.

Consumer Nondurable Goods. *Consumer nondurable goods* include those items that are perishable, such as beverages, foods, and other products that are consumed in a single act. Also included are items such as household supplies that are consumed "in a matter of months." Usually the unit price of consumer nondurables is less than the unit price of durable goods. The following factors are of importance in determining the demand for consumer nondurables: (1) buying power, (2) demography, (3) price, and (4) sales effort.

BUYING POWER. *Consumer buying power* is the *net* amount of money available for discretionary spending after all fixed charges have been paid. A formula to determine buying power would read like this: Buying power is equal to current income from wages, plus available credit, plus savings, plus income from investments. From this amount must be subtracted payments on life insurance, cost of housing, debt repayment, contribution to company pension plans and payment on other retirement annuities, and direct taxes such as social security, income taxes, and property taxes. The remainder, after all fixed items of expense have been subtracted from gross income, is net buying power, the amount of dollars available for the purchase of those items that are considered discretionary purchases.

DEMOGRAPHY. Assume that the amount of money available for the discretionary purchase of consumer nondurable goods for a given region of the United States is $100 million. Can each industry safely assume that there is a proportionate share of discretionary income for the purchase of its product? No—an industry's share of the market described above is further modified by *demography,* the personal characteristics of the population that has the buying power. If a disproportionately large number of persons in our theoretical region of the United States is over 65 years of age, the brewing industry could not expect to sell as much in this area as they might in other geographic areas because the segment of the population between the ages of 18 and 45 provides the best market for the sale of beer. On the other hand, a manufacturer of geriatric foods would have a distinct advantage since his market is that portion of the population over 65 years old. Other examples of demographic characteristics that may influence the sale of any given product are the number of automobiles owned, the number of preschool children, or the educational level of the adult population.

PRICE. The monetary price charged for consumer nondurables is important as a determinant of demand. However, the full significance of price cannot be measured solely in terms of dollars, for price must also be interpreted in relation to buying power and the price of competitive and substitute products. The price of an article is in effect lower (in terms of a percentage of income) when price remains constant and the amount of discretionary income increases. On the other hand, if buying power decreases and price remains constant, the effect is the same as an increase in price. The price of substitute and competitive products must also be considered. A manufacturer of cans for consumer nondurables not only competes with other manufacturers of metal containers but he also competes with the manufacturers of glass and plastic containers because these items are substitutes for cans.

SALES EFFORT. Buying power, demography, and price function concomitantly as determinants of demand. They are economic in origin and for the most part cannot be modified by the seller. The fourth determinant, sales effort, is within the control of the seller, and in many instances sales effort is the most important single determinant of demand for consumer nondurables. Sales effort has literally created entire industries; for example, the sales of chewing gum and cigarettes are primarily the result of sales effort expressed in advertising. Further, the sales effort of an individual seller is a significant factor in determining his share of the total market.

Consumer Durable Goods. In contrast to consumer nondurable goods, *consumer durable goods* are consumed over a period of years, rather than being consumed in a single act. Examples of durable goods are the appliances used in the home—washing machines, dryers, dishwashers, refrigerators, and household furniture. The serviceable life of these products may extend for many years. The same factors of buying power, demography, price, and sales effort are determinants of the demand for consumer durables, but their effect as determinants is modified by the long life of the product, the relatively high unit price, and the need for additional facilities required for the use of certain durables. These characteristics of the product—long life, relatively high unit price, and the need for additional facilities—all combine to influence the effectiveness of sales effort. The effect of each of these factors upon the normal determinants of demand is discussed below.

Long Life. The characteristic long life of consumer durables modifies the significance of buying power as a determinant of demand. Thus, returning to Case Problem 6-A, we find that not all persons having the amount of discretionary income required to purchase an electric stove may be considered potential customers by Electroware. Many of these people have stoves with an expectancy of useful service that may exceed 10 years. They become potential customers only when it is necessary to replace their present stove; thus, one part of the market for consumer durables is termed a *replacement market*. The other segment of the market for consumer durables results from the formation of new family units. Typically, a durable such as a stove, a refrigerator, or a television set is shared by a family unit; hence, the formation of new household units is necessary for the creation of a new market for durables. Information concerning the size of the new market and the replacement market, combined with buying power (including credit), offers a means of predicting the demand for a given consumer durable good.

HIGH UNIT PRICE. As a result of relatively high unit prices, the purchaser of consumer durable goods extends his payment for the product over a period of time. The availability of consumer credit lessens the impact of a high unit price and becomes an important factor in determining the demand for durable products. An increase in unit price may drive some potential purchasers from the market, not because the total cost of the unit is too much, but because an increased price requires a larger down payment. High unit prices may be offset by the availability of consumer credit and a combination of lower down payments and smaller monthly payments extended over a longer period of time. Another way of interpreting unit price is in relation to the useful life of the product. A refrigerator priced at $600 with a useful life of 10 years results in a cost of $5 a month throughout the life of the product; however, if the useful life is reduced to five years, the cost per month is $10.

ADDITIONAL FACILITIES. Some consumer durables require the presence of related facilities in order that they may be used effectively. For example, many household appliances require the added facilities of gas or electricity for their operation, and the continuing sale of automobiles may be affected by the availability of highways and provisions for adequate servicing. The demand factors of buying power, demography, price, and sales effort are all negated unless the proper supplemental facility is present.

Demand for Capital Goods

Capital goods are those items bought for the express purpose of creating more products or services for the consumer. Examples of capital goods that produce products are the machine tools that make equipment used in the production process, such as the huge presses that stamp out automobile body panels or parts for refrigerators and other household appliances. The rolling stock of the railroads and the trucking industry is regarded as a capital good in that it provides service for the consumer by transporting the products he uses. Without capital goods, consumer products and services as we know them would not exist. Since capital goods and consumer goods are closely related, almost a cause-and-effect relationship, the question naturally arises whether the same factors that determine the demand for consumer goods also determine the demand for capital goods.

A survey article by Charles F. Roos provides an understanding of the factors that influence the demand for capital goods.[1] As is the case for consumer goods, purchasing power plays an important role; however, the purchasing power of a corporation is defined somewhat differently than the purchasing power of an individual. *Corporate purchasing power* is composed of profits from current operations, accumulated capital from earlier profits, funds available from new financing, and the amount of money accumulated in depreciation accounts. Also of importance are the prices of metals and metal products, the basic materials that go to make up capital goods. Long-term interest rates are significant, and the ratio of production output to capacity is important. The extent of the contribution of each of the factors above must be determined for each industry, and it is necessary to go one step further and determine the needs of each company within its industry. A proposed program of highway construction may create a demand for the capital goods used in making cement, but an individual company within that industry may not purchase additional capital goods as the result of not having sufficient purchasing power or as the result of having recently refurbished its plant equipment.

PLANNING SALES POLICIES

From the preceding discussion, it is evident that broad socio-economic factors are the chief determinants of demand; the sales efforts of a single company have little, if any, effect upon the total demand for a given product or service. Nonetheless, it is important that these factors be recognized and understood since they are part of the economic environment within which sales objectives are determined. In practice, these objectives are expressed in terms of relative achievement within the industry or in comparison to the individual company's past record. For a firm to achieve its sales objectives, it is necessary to formulate policies to serve as plans for each of the four functional areas of sales management. First, it is necessary to state policies that define the characteristics of the product to be sold. Second, the basis for pricing the product must be stated; and third, a channel of distribution must be selected. Finally, effective means of sales promotion must be determined. Each of these areas of sales policies is discussed in turn.

---

[1] Charles F. Roos, "Survey of Economic Forecasting Techniques," *Econometrica*, Vol. XXIII (October, 1955), pp. 363-95. As the title suggests, this is a survey article. The part of the discussion concerned with the forecasting of capital requirements begins on page 391.

Product Policies

The determination of policies concerning the product or service to be sold is a decision that includes not only the sales function but also the functions of finance, production, and personnel. It is necessary to consider the adequacy of available financing, the production facilities needed for the manufacture of a given product, and the qualifications of personnel in respect to technical knowledge and skills required to make the product. The unique contribution of the sales department in forming product policies is its estimate of the potential market. There are four policy determinations that affect the product's market potential. They are: (1) product diversification, (2) product obsolescence, (3) quality, and (4) product standardization.

Product Diversification. *Product diversification* refers to the number of products produced and distributed and the extent to which these products differ from each other in respect to physical characteristics, size, manufacturing processes, and selling methods. At one end of the scale of diversification are companies manufacturing a single product, such as Electroware prior to the decision to make stoves in addition to electric hot water heaters. At the other end of the scale are companies such as General Motors and General Dynamics that manufacture and distribute a range of products having little or no common ground in respect to physical characteristics, use, manufacturing processes, or selling method. The phrase, product diversification, implicitly refers to the acquisition of additional products. However, diversification policies should serve not only as guides for the acquisition of additional products but also for showing the need for reducing the number of items in an existing product line. The acquisition of new products must be considered in the light of available financing, the production facilities required, and the expected method of distribution. The qualifications of available personnel, particularly their ability to perform continuing research and development work, is a necessary consideration if a position of leadership is desired. Anticipated market size is also important, for it indicates potential contribution to sales and profit. Predetermined levels of sales volume and profitability serve as effective guides in determining when an existing product should be dropped from the product line.

The statement of company objectives has a profound influence upon the extent and direction of product diversification. The railroads, for example, viewed themselves not as transportation companies but as rail carriers and shunned the addition of new transportation services provided by bus, truck, and air, with the result that these services were developed by other companies. The action of Humble Oil Company in proclaiming itself an energy company stands out in sharp contrast to the position taken by the railroads. Both of the large producers of metal containers, American Can Company and Continental Can Company, retain the word *can* in their respective company names, yet they are in reality packaging companies, for they manufacture all types of packaging, including metal containers. Had either company chosen to remain entirely within the field of metal containers, sales volume would be much less than it is at present.

Obsolescence and Style. Durable goods may become obsolescent, that is, reach a state of not being usable or used, for any one of several reasons. Products are sometimes called obsolete when they are worn out and have served their useful life. Obsolescence due to wear forms part of the replacement market for consumer durables and, to a lesser extent, the replacement of worn equipment affects the demand for capital goods. Obsolescence due to wear is rarely the result of a policy decision on the part of the manufacturer of the product. However, forced obsolescence is the direct result of a policy decision. Continued product improvement or change may be used to create consumer dissatisfaction with the product in its present form, thereby forcing that particular model into a state of disuse or forced obsolescence. An example of forced obsolescence is provided by the phonograph and record industry. In the late 1940's, the 78 rpm phonograph record was replaced by 33⅓ and 45 rpm records, requiring different turntable speeds and a special stylus. Record players were manufactured to accommodate these new records, with the result that the older 78 rpm records and turntables soon became obsolete. The same industry later developed stereophonic sound, a system that utilizes a still different type of record and stylus, dual-channel electronic components, and a dual-speaker system. As a result, sound systems using monaural 33⅓ and 45 rpm records are being forced into obsolescence.

Changes in style, or the external appearance, of products offer an additional means of inducing forced obsolescence. An excellent example of periodic style change is afforded by the automobile industry with its annual array of new models that emphasizes external changes in appearance. Policy statements concerning product obsolescence and style determine the extent and frequency of changes in mechanical design and style as a means of forcing obsolesence of earlier products by creating a desire for the model that is new in appearance or better in performance.

Quality. *Quality* refers to those characteristics that are relevant in measuring the degree to which a product meets predetermined standards of performance. Quality is not an absolute value, yet there is an implied relationship between quality and excellence of design, workmanship, and materials. There is also an obvious relationship between quality and price. One of the questions that must be resolved is determining whether or not several levels of quality are to be produced and sold. Most companies have one level of quality; however, Sears, Roebuck & Company describes the quality of many of its products as good, better, and best. There are hazards in selling multiple levels of quality because a customer who purchases an item described as "good," with full knowledge that there are two higher grades of quality available, may nonetheless expect the "best" standard of performance. Another consideration concerning quality is that of deciding how effectively quality can be used as a basis for sales promotion. Midas Muffler, for example, guarantees its product for the life of the car or as long as the car is owned by the person who purchases the replacement part.

Standardization. The existence of several grades of quality increases the complexity of the product line and can be justified only if each gradient of quality taps an additional segment of the market. The production of several models, all meeting a uniform standard of quality, also assumes that each additional model captures its share of the market. Extremes in model variations within the same industry are illustrated by the Volkswagen passenger cars with three body styles and the American counterpart that may have as many as 11 body styles. A reduction in the number of levels of quality or the number of models produced or distributed is a move toward product standardization and usually results in a lowering of manufacturing and distribution costs. Hence, a policy statement setting forth the optimum degree of standardization of a company's product line, either in respect to quality levels or the number of models available, is a choice between potentially lower costs and the possibility of increased market potential.

Pricing Policies

In discussing policies concerning the product, it is stated that a direct relationship exists between product cost and quality. Painstaking design, careful workmanship, and better materials all contribute to increased costs and consequently influence price. However, costs are but one of several factors that must be considered in establishing pricing policies. The price charged for similar goods and services by competing companies is of importance. In addition, when pricing a new product, it is necessary to consider the proposed price in relation to the price structure of the entire product line. Finally, the terms of sale, including the availability of credit and discount privileges, modify the significance of the stated price. Each of these factors—product costs, competition, pricing new products, and terms of sale—is discussed in turn.[2]

Product Costs. Product costs, if they are to serve as a realistic basis for pricing, must include not only direct material and labor costs but also the indirect costs of administration and distribution. In addition, expected profit contribution must be included in the final price. If the resulting price is one that the consumer is willing to pay, there is no problem; however, if the price is too high, several alternatives are available. First, every effort must be made to reduce product costs, including administrative and distributive costs as well as manufacturing costs. Second, the possibility of a more effective sales effort should be examined; perhaps a different method of promotion and presentation of the product will permit its sale at the desired price. If neither of the steps above results in a price that is acceptable to the customer and at the same time recovers full product costs and contributes to profit, a decision must be made whether to market the product at a lower price. Occasionally retailers adopt the practice of promoting a *loss leader,* an item that does not meet its full share of costs, because it is believed that customers are attracted who are willing to buy the more profitable items. It is doubtful that the loss leader concept is workable at the manufacturing level for any length of time; however, occasionally manufacturers sell at a price that does not recover full costs in order that all direct costs and a portion of overhead costs may be recovered. Sometimes products are sold at prices too low to recover all costs in an effort to maintain a competitive product line and to prevent new competition from entering the market. The policy question can become one of determining when "a half a loaf is better than none."

Competition. Product cost and profit contribution are considerations internal to the firm; competitive factors are external to the firm and must be considered in establishing pricing policies. A company that establishes the reputation of consistently selling below competitive prices

---

[2] *Pricing: The Critical Decision.* (New York: American Management Association, 1962), Management Report No. 66, p. 96. This report presents a series of articles selected from papers presented at the American Management Association Special Conference on Pricing held in New York City in 1961. Included are discussions on the role of pricing in the American business system and the influence of competitive and economic factors in pricing.

reflects a marketing philosophy which implies that price is the most important factor in motivating the customer. Average or above average prices make it possible for a company to emphasize quality and excellence of service.

The actions of competitors in either raising or lowering prices are another phase of competitive pricing. Lowering of prices implies that the demand for the product is *elastic*; that is, for every one percent decrease in price there is an increase in sales greater than one percent. Before deciding to meet competitor prices that have been lowered, it is well to try to determine the elasticity of demand and project the profit that may be expected at a new level of sales. Knowledge of price elasticity is important in determining whether to follow a competitor's lead in increasing prices. If demand is inelastic in relation to price, a significant reduction in sales volume does not follow a price increase; however, if demand is price-elastic, the company that retains the lower prices may experience a substantial gain in sales volume at the expense of competitors who raised prices.

Pricing New Products Production costs are usually at their highest level when a new product is first introduced. Thus, the pricing decision is one of determining whether the initial price should reflect actual costs or whether the price should anticipate lower future costs associated with volume production and improved manufacturing techniques. The prices of existing items in the company's product line also influence the price of any new product. If the new product is smaller or simpler in its construction than similar items presently in use, the price should be recognizably lower; but if the product is of better design and uses more expensive materials, the price should be sufficient to recover these additional costs without creating a barrier that prevents the customer from moving up to the new product. The price of a compact car, $150 to $200 less than a similarly equipped standard model, offers a price differential attractive to some buyers. As both compacts and standard models acquire added accessories, the price increases; but at no time does the addition of any single accessory create a price barrier. Finally, when pricing a new product, consideration must be given to competing products, some of which—for example, household appliances—are similar in design and construction. Or, as is true in the packaging industry, the competing products may utilize different materials and designs, yet perform the same function.

Terms of Sale. The preceding discussion of factors influencing pricing policies—product cost, competition, and pricing new products—

outlines the effects that might be expected as the result of changes in price under varying conditions and implies that price is an absolute monetary value. However, some of the effects of price changes may be obtained without any change in the monetary price of a product or service by altering the terms of sale. Credit, lease-purchase agreements, and cash discounts are ways of altering the terms of sale and may have a marked effect upon sales volume. The availability of credit is an important determinant of consumer buying power. The effect of a price increase in consumer durables may be offset by reducing the amount of the down payment or extending the period of time for repayment. One method of assuring the availability of credit is illustrated by establishing a subsidiary credit corporation, such as General Motors Acceptance Corporation, whose purpose is to supply credit to purchasers of consumer goods. A lease-purchase agreement, usually calling for no down payment and the payment of a monthly charge, with an option to purchase at a predetermined price at the end of a specified period of time, is another means of extending credit. Offering cash discounts for prompt payment, usually within a period of 10 days, has the advantage of reducing credit and collection costs, yet allowing the seller to maintain a firm price structure.

Channel of Distribution Policies

Policy statements outlining methods for distributing a company's product are decisions that determine who is the customer. Customers and consumers are not necessarily synonymous. For the restaurant owner, the customer who buys a meal is the consumer; yet as an owner, he is the customer of a wholesaler or a distributor, but he is not the consumer. The decision to sell either directly to the consumer or through a series of intermediaries to the consumer is the selection of a *channel of distribution. Market penetration,* closely related to and sometimes dependent upon the channel of distribution, is the portion of the potential of a given market, usually defined geographically, that is realized. Policies governing the distribution of products— selecting the channel of distribution and determining the extent of market penetration—are discussed below.

Channel of Distribution. There are certain functions inherent in the process of distribution that must be performed. Orders are received, the product is drawn from stock, shipments are sent to the customer, a statement of the amount due is prepared, and provisions for collecting payment from the customer are needed. Any of these functions may be transferred from one position in the distribution cycle to another, but the function itself is not eliminated. A company selling directly to the consumer performs all of these functions; however, if one or more intermediaries, called variously jobbers, distributors, or wholesalers, are introduced into the cycle, some of these functions may be transferred to the intermediary. In many instances the selection of the channel of distribution is determined by industry practices, which are in turn dependent upon the nature of the product as well as the precedent established within the industry. Even so, the selection of a market channel offers an opportunity for innovation. Electrolux, for example, sells vacuum cleaners successfully directly to the consumer through the efforts of its own field sales force, while their competitors distribute their products through wholesalers, to retail department stores, and then to the consumer. The factors to weigh in selecting one channel of distribution in preference to another, assuming that the nature of the product and industry practices permit such a choice, are (1) the costs incurred as the result of performing the functions of the distribution cycle and (2) the advantages gained by controlling the selling effort of the company's own sales force and direct contact with the consumer.

One of the problems to be resolved by Electroware, Case Problem 6-A, is that of deciding whether more than one channel of distribution should be utilized. The utilization of more than one channel of distribution may permit a company to realize the advantages gained by controlling the selling effort of its own sales force and at the same time receive the benefits of reduced distribution costs and risks usually associated with intermediaries. Manufacturers of rock bits used in the oil-drilling industry sell directly to the consumer, a drilling company, and indirectly through oil-field supply houses. The price of bits purchased through a supply house is usually 10 percent higher than the manufacturer's price, since the supply house stocks all brands of bits along with other needed oil tools and is ready to extend credit when needed. Though the manufacturer receives a lower price than the supply house, he avoids the cost of extending credit and is assured of maximum sales effort by using his own salesmen.

Market Penetration. Closely related to the choice of a channel of distribution are policies expressing a company's position in respect to market penetration. As stated earlier, the degree of market penetration is the extent to which a company attains the potential of a specified market. Usually markets are defined in geographic terms such as a city, a state, or a region; however, a market may be defined in terms of its demographic groups; e.g., rural, urban, or age groups. Market share, or market penetration, is expressed quantitatively by defining present sales as a percentage of potential sales.

Electroware is distributing its water heaters to 1,000 retail stores located throughout the Midwest and the East at the rate of four each month, and the store owners are dissatisfied since they are not receiving a quantity sufficient to meet demand. If the company decides to sell its stoves through the same channel of distribution, its penetration of the market will be less than it is at present. The close relationship between degree of penetration and channel of distribution becomes more evident when we examine one of the alternate methods available for the distribution of electric stoves. If Electroware chooses four distributors, with each one located in a major city, the penetration of each city market would be much greater than the penetration realized in the vast geographic territory served by retail outlets.

Slight penetration of a market usually results in higher distribution costs per unit, less return per dollar of advertising, and the risk of losing customer goodwill. However, deep market penetration usually results in a position of strength within a given area and an ability to withstand a substantial decline in sales volume. The desired extent of market penetration should be stated clearly as a primary sales objective.

Sales Promotion Policies

The areas of sales policies discussed thus far consider the product, the pricing of the product, and the method of distribution. The final question to be considered is how to choose an effective means of persuading the customer to buy the product. One method used frequently is *direct selling,* a method that utilizes salesmen to personally persuade the customer to buy the product. *Advertising* permits the seller to contact many people simultaneously through mass media and is another means of promoting the sale of the product. The use of *special promotional devices* to supplement direct selling efforts and advertising is the third method employed to encourage customers to buy. Each of these methods of sales promotion—direct selling, advertising, and special promotional devices—is discussed in turn.

Direct Selling. The process of persuading a customer to buy a product is commonly called *selling.* Two dimensions of selling are particularly relevant in formulating sales promotion policies. The first is determining the importance of the role of sales personnel in persuading the customer to buy a given product. At one extreme are those persons—such as those employed by variety chains and supermarkets—who function as salesclerks and whose only contribution to the selling process is at the request of the customer. At the other end of the broad spectrum of the selling activity are the agents of life insurance companies who often seek and locate a prospect, create a felt need for the product, and finally persuade the prospect to buy an intangible item that may never offer a tangible reward to the buyer himself. If it is concluded that the role of a salesman is of minor importance to a specific selling process, the company may direct its efforts to those factors that are of greater importance, such as advertising, packaging, or point-of-sale displays. However, if it appears that the salesman plays a key part in the sales process, attention must be directed toward the selection and training of sales personnel. Thus, an analysis of the contribution of sales personnel to the selling process enables a company to direct its sales promotion efforts more effectively.

The second dimension of direct selling is that of establishing the optimum degree of control necessary to realize the greatest results from the sales personnel. A close degree of control is usually possible when those who sell the product are employees of the company making the product. Many industrial products, such as machine tools, are sold in this manner, but relatively few consumer products are sold by a sales force employed by the manufacturer. Typically, most consumer products—clothing, food, and appliances—are sold through the efforts of employees of the retailer. There is a direct relationship between the degree of control exercised over a sales force and the significance of the role of sales personnel in the selling process. If the efforts of sales personnel are incidental to the selling process, such personnel are usually not employed or controlled by the producer of the product; emphasis is placed upon advertising and special promotional devices. However, if salesmen are the decisive factor in persuading the customer to buy, the company making the product employs and exercises close control over its sales force; the emphasis upon advertising and other promotional devices is relatively less.

Advertising. The ultimate objective of advertising, a means of informing a large number of people, is to persuade potential customers to buy a company's product or service. Immediate objectives may be to establish an awareness of a particular brand name, to state the price and describe other attributes of the product, or to create a need for the product. The sale of many consumer products, particularly those that are displayed in conjunction with competing products in supermarkets and drugstores, depends to a large extent upon the kind and amount of advertising used. Earlier decisions concerning the desired market or customers exert an influence upon the selection of the media for advertising. Typical media used in advertising are television, radio, newspapers, outdoor posters, magazines, and direct-mail pieces such as catalogs and circulars. A method of evaluating the economic effectiveness of advertising is discussed in the next part of this chapter, "Application of Principles."

Special Promotional Devices. Special promotional devices are used as a means of augmenting the selling effort of salesmen and advertising. One such familiar device is the point-of-sale demonstration used in department stores and other retail outlets. Personnel for these demonstrations are usually trained by the manufacturer to demonstrate the outstanding features and proper use of the product to prospective customers. Another promotional device is the distribution of free samples as a way of introducing a product. Trial offers with money-back guarantees, coupons redeemable in cash or merchandise, testimonial letters, and advertising novelties such as pens and pencils, are other kinds of promotional devices. In summary, special promotional devices are attention-getting actions to induce the customer to make the initial purchase or trial with the expectation that the knowledge of the product thus gained will lead to repeat sales.

APPLICATION OF PRINCIPLES

Three principles of management—the Principle of the Objective, the Principle of Planning, and the Principle of Economic Effectiveness—are readily applied to planning a company's sales program. The application of the Principle of the Objective is revealed by reviewing the stated objectives of the company. Application of the Principle of Planning is partially achieved through the use of market research. Special analytical techniques, not unlike those used in planning for profit, are available to insure that sales plans are economically effective and fulfill the requirements of the Principle of Economic Effectiveness. Each of these principles as applied to the planning of a sales program is reviewed below.

Principle of the Objective

The Principle of the Objective states that *before initiating any course of action, the objectives in view must be clearly determined, understood, and stated.* In discussing the application of the

Principle of the Objective to planning for profit (Chapter 5), it is emphasized that profit objectives are but one of several groups of objectives. The objectives of the sales program must also be placed in proper perspective so they may be coordinated with the objectives of the other major functional areas of the business. An example of the interdependence of profit and sales objectives is a sales objective of stabilizing a sales volume through a program of product diversification. Achieving such stabilization has its effect upon the profitability of the firm expressed as a return on sales, a return on invested capital, and on the total dollar volume of profit.

Objectives of the sales program are most frequently directed toward achievement in each of the four major areas for which policy statements are prepared. Objectives may be stated in regard to (1) the product (including diversification, style, quality, and standardization); (2) price (particularly when price is viewed as a competitive factor); (3) the distribution of company products (primarily the effectiveness of the method of distribution and the degree of expected market penetration); and (4) the specific sales promotion methods selected by the company. A brief review of Continental Emsco Company's objectives on page 57 serves to illustrate how sales objectives may be stated and, when compared with profit goals, the interrelationship between profit and sales objectives is clarified.

Four of the 22 company objectives stated by Continental Emsco are specifically directed toward the attainment of goals that are primarily the function of the sales department. These objectives are Nos. 2, 4, 6, and 7, two of which deal with the product, one with pricing, and one with the establishment of new markets. The two that outline achievements in respect to the product are No. 2, which states that an objective is to "further the diversification of company operations," and No. 4, which is related to the type of product to be manufactured and distributed. Number 4 is concerned not only with the improvement of existing products but also aims toward the development of "proprietor" type products—items that can be identified by the buying public as coming from Continental Emsco—either as the result of research and development or as the result of acquisition. The objective directed toward pricing is No. 6, and emphasis is placed on the sale of quality products competitively priced. Objective No. 7 refers to market selection and urges new markets for existing product lines and services. The wording of No. 7 stresses the interdependence between sales and profit objectives, for it specifies that the new markets must be profitable market.

Principle of Planning

The Principle of Planning states that *effective planning results in plans that are objective, structured, and flexible, and the extent to which resultant plans possess these characteristics is a measure of their probable success.* Greater effectiveness in planning a sales program is possible through an analysis of those factors that influence the sale of a given product. The various techniques that have been developed to analyze market factors and predict probable sales success are known as *market research.* There are many techniques available for market research that are applications of the scientific method to the solution of specific sales problems. Each technique defines the problem under consideration, collects and utilizes data that are as objective as possible, and draws tentative conclusions. In some instances it is possible to test resultant hypotheses by conducting trial marketing programs and, if successful, a final full-scale sales plan is developed and put into effect. Let us examine more closely some of the techniques of market research in order to have a better understanding of effective planning for the sales program. First, the sources of information used in market research are considered, and second, the scope of market research is discussed.

Sources of Market Research Information. There are two sources of information frequently used in market research. One source, called *primary,* is obtained directly from those persons concerned with the marketing or use of the product or service in question. Such persons include customers, potential customers, and all who participate in the distribution system, including the wholesaler and the retailer. In using these sources, the method employed is generally one of asking specific questions regarding the product and observing reactions to the product. It is a polling technique similar to that employed by the political pollsters. The other source of information is *secondary* in nature and draws upon broad social and economic factors of significance to marketing. Case Problem 4-B, "How Much Planning Went into the Edsel?", is illustrative of the use of secondary sources. The nature of the problem being researched determines the relative use and importance of each source.[3]

---

[3] Robert N. Carpenter, *Guidelist for Marketing Research and Economic Forecasting* (New York: American Management Association, 1961), Research Study 50, pp. 1-94. This research study offers a useful listing of publications pertinent to marketing. Emphasis is placed upon bibliographies and directories of use in market research and economic forecasting.

Scope of Market Research. Since the primary purpose of market research is to analyze those factors that affect a company's sales so that an accurate forecast may be made regarding the probable success or failure of a given sales plan, the study of any situation or group of factors which might affect sales is within the province of market research. The areas susceptible to market research are the same areas for which sales policies are formulated. Remember, sales policies are broad plans, and market research is the collection and interpretation of data so that sound plans may be formulated; hence, the areas of application of market research are the same as those for which sales policies are developed. Market research may be applied to the product, to price and its effect on sales, to determining the most effective means of distribution, and to assessing the effectiveness of promotional methods. In practice, most market research efforts touch upon several areas of study as shown in the following example.[4]

Colgate-Palmolive Company developed a face soap, Choice, that was sufficiently different in its concept that it had to be treated as a new product. Three different chemical formulas are used in the manufacture of Choice, with each formulation being designed for a particular type of skin. Further, the customer is able to tell which formulation she is buying because the formulas are color-coded—the pink bar is designed for those who have dry skin, the white bar is for those with normal skin, and the aqua bar is for those with oily skin. Colgate was interested in determining not only the acceptance of this new concept in face soaps as a new product but also the effect of price on sales volume and the best promotional device to use in introducing the product.

Colgate selected test cities, a technique widely used in market research, to try the various introductions of the product. In effect, to the extent that the nature of the problem permitted, an experimental situation was created so that each of the independent variables, in this case the promotional method and price, could be varied. The test markets selected were Fort Wayne, Indiana; Richmond, Virginia; Wichita Falls, Texas; and Fresno, California. Each of these cities presents a typical economic cross section of the national market.

Four different methods of introducing the sale of the product were used; and, though Colgate will not reveal which method was used in which city, the four promotional devices were as follows: (1) an average amount of advertising, plus the distribution of free samples on a door-to-door basis,

---

[4] Anthony C. Collings, "Product Tryouts," *The Wall Street Journal* (New York: August 10, 1962), p. 1. In this feature story Mr. Collings tells why certain cities have become favorite test market areas and presents in detail the story of the market research that went into the introduction of Colgate's new soap, Choice.

(2) heavy advertising in conjunction with samples distributed in the same manner, (3) average advertising containing a redeemable coupon that entitled the holder to a single bar of soap, and (4) average advertising with no special introductory offer. The distribution of free samples did not work because the representative of the company had to give each housewife all three sample bars since there was a reluctance to ask whether she had oily, dry, or normal skin, with the result that she had two bars of soap that did not suit her needs, thus creating dissatisfaction with the product. The best promotional device was the use of average advertising and redeemable coupons since the customer could specify the type of soap desired.

At the same time, Colgate also studied the effect of price. It determined the elasticity of demand at a given price; that is, the effect of variations in price upon the demand for the product. Colgate found that in order to secure the profit desired and necessary from this product, it had to sell two of the regular bars at 33 cents and two of the bath-size bars at 45 cents. Lower prices did not increase sales volume sufficiently to create the desired profits. These studies were conducted for a period of two years in the test cities; then, as a further check, Choice was marketed in two of Colgate's regular marketing districts, northern Ohio and New York State, with the exception of New York City. Finally, the company decided to market Choice nationally.

From the account above, it can be seen that market research may be expensive in respect to both time and money; however, marketing a product that fails to sell is also expensive; for example, the Edsel. The use of test markets, as demonstrated by Colgate, provides more reliable information than that obtained from questionnaires, for differences have been noted between people's statements of what they will buy and what they actually buy when the product is on the market. Further, the use of test markets enables a company to determine the repurchase rate as well as the number of customers that might be expected on a continuing basis. Test marketing offers a means of planning a sales program objectively so that the final plan may more nearly meet the criteria set forth in the Principle of Planning.

Principle of Economic Effectiveness

In Chapter 4, planning is discussed as a managerial function, and it is stated that a plan may meet all the criteria of the Principle of Planning by being objective, flexible, and structured, yet it may not be the appropriate plan for a given situation. Appropriateness is best measured by determining the degree of economic effectiveness of the plan in question. The Principle of Economic Effectiveness states: *Economic effectiveness in planning results in plans that maximize achievement of company objectives through the most efficient utilization of company resources.* To determine the efficiency of a given plan, it is necessary to compare the incremental gains in output with the result of each additional unit of input. In discussing the application of this principal to planning for profit (Chapter 5), an example is cited of a company desiring a long-term investment of $1 million with an expected return of 15 percent on invested capital; but further analysis indicates that by investing $2 million, the return would reach 22 percent, and if the amount invested were $3 million, the rate of return would drop to 10 percent. In this instance, the most efficient utilization of resources is a capital investment of $2 million.

The same concept of incremental analysis may be applied to determine the economic effectiveness of sales effort. The cost of sales effort—advertising, direct sales force, or special promotional devices—is regarded as a factor of input, and the desired output is increased sales and profits. Figure 6-1 is a graphic model which illustrates a relationship that sometimes exists between advertising costs and resultant sales and profits. Note that the sales curve rises rapidly when advertising expenditures begin, then gradually slows its rate of increase, and finally illustrates the diminishing returns that result from additional advertising expenditures. The gross profit curve has a similar shape, though it flattens out much sooner than the sales curve. Since it is assumed that

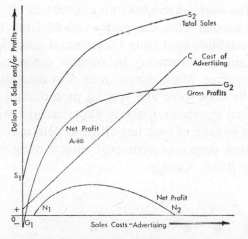

Figure 6-1

MODEL ILLUSTRATING THE ECONOMIC
EFFECTIVENESS OF ADVERTISING

Source: Milton H. Spencer and Louis
Siegelman, *Managerial Economics* (Homewood, Illinois: Richard D. Irwin, Inc.,
1959), Adapted from Figure 5-8, p. 156.

all other costs remain constant as a fixed percentage of sales, the area between the gross profit curve and the straight line of advertising costs is the net profit area. When net profits are plotted separately against advertising costs, a decline in the amount of net profits appears even though gross profits and total sales are increasing. If the criterion for deciding whether to expend additional units for advertising is total net profit, then advertising will be continued only until the net profit curve reaches its highest point. However, if the criterion is the economic utilization of resources, the incremental gains in net profit are compared with each additional increase in advertising costs. Thus, if advertising outlay is measured in $250,000 units, the expenditure of the last $250,-000 should result in a greater increase in profit than that obtained from the previous $250,000 unit. For example, if the second unit of advertising (making a total of $500,000), increases profits by $100,000 and the third unit (a total of $750,000) increases profits an additional $125,000, the expenditure of the fourth unit of advertising must increase profits more than $125,000 in order for it to be judged as economically effective.

The application of the model above offers management a means of determining the economic effectiveness of its sales effort. Specifically, management may determine the effectiveness of its advertising budget in respect to the total amount expended and media used. If Figure 6-1 represents the costs of advertising in a metropolitan newspaper and the expenditure of the fourth $250,000 unit results in an incremental gain in profit that is smaller than the gain realized from the third unit, it is possible to reestablish increasing incremental gains in profit by placing the fourth unit of advertising in another media such as television or a national magazine. Management may also determine the economic effectiveness of its sales force and special promotional devices by using the same analytical approach. Colgate experimented with different promotional devices in each of four test cities to determine the method that offered the greatest degree of economic effectiveness in promoting the sale of its new product, Choice.

• • • • • • • • •

Case Problem 6-B, "Changing Sales Policies," illustrates one company's experience with advertising and shows the need for a continuing measurement of the economic effectiveness of advertising. The case also demonstrates the close interrelationship existing between various sales policies and the need for reexamination and restatement of these policies when the maximum economic effectiveness of advertising and other forms of sales effort is reached.

Questions for Study and Discussion

1. Why do manufacturers of consumer durable goods expend large sums of money in advertising despite the statement that the efforts of a single company manufacturing consumer durable goods cannot significantly change the demand for those goods?

2. Why must a manufacturer of consumer nondurables consider all three economic determinants—buying power, demography, and price—when planning a marketing program?

3. How does a company define the demand for its products?

4. Is there a relationship between the rate of consumption of consumer durable goods and the demand for capital goods? If so, how is this relationship modified by other factors that influence the demand for capital goods?

5. How can the advertising of capital goods in a medium read by the general public, such as *Time* or *Newsweek,* be justified?

6. Assume that a company has established a policy of making major engineering changes in its product every five or six years. Shortly after one of these major product changes has been made, the engineering department develops a major breakthrough that would make all former models obsolete. What are the arguments for and against introducing the revolutionary model ahead of schedule?

7. What are the dangers inherent in producing or selling a product line consisting of several distinct levels of quality?

8. In addition to developmental and initial production costs, what factors must be considered in pricing a new product?

9. As a special research project, determine the comparative costs of financing an automobile through a bank, a credit union, a finance company, and the plan offered by the dealer. Exclude the cost of insurance but note the variations in total interest charges for 12-, 18-, 24-, and 36-month contracts.

10. Is there a relationship between the amount of money a salesman is paid and the importance of his role in the marketing process?

11. Critics of test marketing, as illustrated by Colgate's test for its product, Choice, state that extensive trial programs should not be used because it is possible for competing companies to audit the results of such a

program. Evaluate this statement and list the factors that must be considered in determining whether or not a test market program is appropriate.

12. In general, what are the characteristics of cities that are selected as test markets?

• • • • • • • • •

Cosmetone, a Chicago-based cosmetics company, manufactures a line of facial lotions, creams, and powders that are sold in accordance with a policy decision to the consumer through retail drug outlets. Another company policy, to obtain maximum market penetration in a given geographic area, has resulted in Cosmetone products being distributed in the Chicago area, northern Indiana, and Milwaukee, Wisconsin.

Case Problem 6-B

Changing Sales Policies

The advertising budget is allotted entirely to television, and consists primarily of spot announcements and occasional sponsoring of local beauty contest programs.

The company's growth in sales and profits has been consistent and quite satisfactory, with the exception of a small loss sustained during the first year of operation. Since the loss was attributed to a lack of public knowledge of the product and the newness of the brand name, special promotional devices—point-of-sale displays, in-store demonstrations, and free-trial offers— were used during the second and third years of operation. The costs of these special promotional efforts amounted to 5 percent of total costs each year, excluding the cost of advertising. The following table summarizes the company's annual sales; total costs of operation, excluding the cost of advertising, but including special promotional efforts for the second and third years; and the cost of advertising for each of the first six years of the company's operation.

SUMMARY STATEMENT OF OPERATIONS

Cosmetone

Year of operation	Annual sales	Total costs (excluding advertising)	Advertising costs
1	$ 1,500,000	$ 525,000	$1,000,000
2	5,000,000	2,000,000	2,000,000
3	8,500,000	3,400,000	3,000,000
4	11,500,000	4,025,000	4,000,000
5	13,500,000	4,725,000	5,000,000
6	15,000,000	5,250,000	6,000,000

After analyzing the data above, the president of the company concluded that advertising expenditures were no longer producing the desired level of sales or net profits. Several suggestions are now being considered so that the company may continue its rate of growth in sales and net profits. These suggestions are:

(A) The advertising agency recommends that Cosmetone market its products nationally or at least move into another major metropolitan area such as New York or Los Angeles.

(B) The vice-president, sales, is against national distribution and favors the introduction of new related cosmetic products. He argues that the distribution of new products in the present market area would permit the company to capitalize on its past advertising and its excellent established reputation.

(C) The company's advertising manager feels that the television media has been exhausted and that the company should reduce its television expenditures to $4 million and place $2 million of the current budget into other media —newspapers or radio—in the same geographic area.

(D) The field sales force manager argues that even though the last $2 million of sales might not be as profitable as it should be, it does represent a margin of safety that the company cannot afford to give up since the additional sales would enable the company to withstand a considerable loss in dollar volume without affecting profit significantly.

Problems

1. Plot in graphic form the data presented in Cosmetone's summary statement of operations. (Use Figure 6-1 as a guide.)

2. What is the net profit and the incremental gain in net profit for each year of operation?

3. Evaluate each of the four suggestions now being considered by Cosmetone's management.

4. What additional suggestions may be offered as a solution to this company's problem?

CHAPTER 7

Planning for Production

Tim Jones, owner-manager of Kwickie Kar Klean, sat in his office mulling over the results of his first year's operations. Before entering the automatic car wash business, Tim had investigated carefully the claims of several manufacturers of automatic car wash equipment and found, much to his surprise, considerable variation in what was considered to be the optimum amount of automatic equipment necessary for a successful business. One manufacturer suggested an installation that would cost over $50,000, exclusive of land and buildings, and pointed out that the savings in labor costs would soon pay for the equipment. At the other extreme, there was a unit that cost $12,000 but required almost twice as much labor on high-volume days. Tim chose the latter course; however, the equipment was designed to permit the addition of fully automatic units at a later date.

He considered himself fortunate in being able to rent a building for $500 a month on a busy through street in the center of a large residential area. Thus, his only capital outlay was for equipment capable of washing at least 600 cars a week. A summary statement of the average monthly expenses for Kwickie Kar Klean during its first year's operations appears below.

Tim regarded most of these expenses as fixed since there was little he could do toward controlling the first five items. However, he considered the cost of labor another matter and decided to direct his attention not only to controlling the amount of money spent for labor but also improving output per man-hour.

The conveyor that pulls the cars through the washing process is 80 feet in length. At

---

Case Problem 7-A
Kwickie Kar Klean

Expense	Average per month
Heat, light, and power	$ 80
Water	100
Supplies (towels, detergents, etc.).	50
Depreciation and repairs	125
Building and land rent	500
Labor	1,800
Total expenses	$2,655

the beginning, or front, of this line there is a portable vacuum cleaner used in cleaning the interior of the car. Next, there is a steam cleaning unit used to steam the wheels, bumpers, and grill; and following this station is the mitting area where one man on each side of the line washes the entire car with detergent as it is pulled through by the conveyor chain. The next three operations are automatic; first, the side and top brush unit (including automatic pre-rinse) washes the top and sides of the car; then there is an automatic rinsing unit that removes the detergent and loosened dirt left by the washing unit; and third, there is an automatic drying unit. The car is then moved forward to the front of the building where it is wiped and finished manually by the wipers.

Tim carefully studied the time required for each operation and concluded that the production bottleneck was at the end of the line where the cars are manually wiped. He discovered that two men could wipe one car in three minutes and concluded that his total daily production should be 20 cars per hour, or a total of 200 cars per day since the auto laundry remained open 10 hours each day. However, such was not the case because customers did not appear on a regular schedule. He decided to record the total number of cars washed during a 10-hour day for varying crew sizes. Here is a summary of the production records:

Number of men	Total cars washed in 10 hours
3	90
4	120
5	155
6	180
8	230
10	270
12	350

When using three men, one man at the front of the line operated the vacuum cleaner and the steam cleaner, while the other two men worked in the mitting area, one on each side of the car, and washed the car. Then, as the car moved through the automatic units of the line—the side and top brush unit, the rinsing unit, and the drying station—the two mitters moved to the end of the line and served as wipers after Tim drove the car from the conveyor to the front of the building. When the crew consisted of four men, the additional man was placed on the end of the line to help the mitters in wiping the car. The addition of a fifth man meant that there was still one man at the front of the line, two mitters now remaining in the mitting area, and two men functioning solely as wipers. Though this arrangement of manning yielded the highest average per man for a 10-hour day, it was found that there were times during the day, for example, during the lunch period, when the effective crew was actually four men. Also, if one of the men was absent, the result was a definite undermanning, and if it were a good day for business, Tim felt that he lost customers when they drove by and saw a line of cars waiting to be washed. Consequently, he decided that for the weekdays, Monday through Friday, he would man the crew regularly with six men, which almost always assured him of an effective crew of five, thus allowing him to handle peak periods on these days with ease. With a crew of six, one man vacuumed, one operated the steam cleaner, two were in the mitting area, and two wiped.

During the first year Kwickie Kar Klean washed, on the average, 500 cars a week, but the number washed was not distributed evenly throughout the six working days. Usually by Friday evening only 40 to 60 percent of the week's total had been completed, which meant that in order to reach the weekly average of 500, it was necessary sometimes to wash as many as 350 cars on Saturday. The addition of two more wipers, making eight, could handle 250 cars, but this was not enough for the busy days. And increasing the total crew to 10 men, with six of them wiping, enabled Tim to turn out only 20 more cars per man in a 10-hour day. After analyzing the production of a 10-man crew, Tim decided that the cars were not being prepared fast enough for the conveyor line, so he decided to put two men on the vacuum cleaning, two on the steam cleaning, and, of course, two in the mitting area. These six on the front of the line seemed to be able to keep the six wipers supplied with cars even during rush periods.

Problems

1. Evaluate Tim's original decision to man with a crew of six men during weekdays.
2. If the price charged for washing a car is $1.50, how many cars must be washed during a month in order for Kwickie Kar Klean to break even?

3. There were many weeks during the year when the total output, Monday through Friday, was 300 cars with the standard manning of six men. It is possible for these six men to wash approximately 200 cars on Saturday, thus bringing the weekly total to 500. Yet, Tim called in six additional men on Saturday to raise the possible output to 350, or 650 for the week. How much is it costing Tim to be prepared for the additional 150 cars? Would you recommend that this practice be continued? Why?
4. Under what circumstances would you recommend that fully automatic equipment be purchased, assuming that the purchase of such equipment would eliminate four men— the two in the mitting area and the two in the steam cleaning area?
5. Using Figure 7-4, page 184, as a guide, prepare a graph of the production output of Kwickie Kar Klean for each of the several crew sizes. Why is the production curve of the car wash operation different from the one portrayed in Figure 7-4? What probable effect would the addition of two more wipers, making a crew of 14, have on production output?

• • • • • • • • •

As a nation we are noted for both effectiveness and efficiency in our production processes. The effectiveness of production, that is, the providing of those goods and services desired by consumers, is the result of a close liaison between the demand side of the business, sales, and the supply side of the business, production. The efficiency of our industrial enterprise is the result of the production manager continually seeking answers to the following two questions: (1) What is the maximum attainable output with a given set of inputs? (2) What are the minimum inputs required to achieve a stated level of output? These questions form the framework within which policy decisions are made in regard to the production function. Before examining the scope of production policies, it is necessary to review the nature of the production function, then develop the areas of production policy, and finally, evaluate major policy decisions in the light of established principles of management. The following major topics are discussed in sequence in this chapter: (1) the production function, (2) scope of production policies, and (3) application of principles.

THE PRODUCTION FUNCTION

The production function is present in all business enterprises. It is easy to recognize the production function in those businesses that manufacture a product. The factors of input in manufacturing are the physical facilities, which include both plant and equipment used in making the product; the raw materials that are converted into a final form; and the human resources needed to produce the product. The output of the manufacturing firm is a tangible product with physical characteristics of size, weight, color, and form. Kwickie Kar Klean, Case Problem 7-A, is a service organization and, as a service organization, has as its function the production of clean cars. In this instance the customer supplies the product, an automobile, but the company changes the form or appearance of that product by cleaning it. A firm of certified public accountants works with data supplied by its clients and offers as an end result an interpretation of that information based upon its members' professional training and judgment. An airline has as its function the moving of passengers from one city to another, an operation that requires the utilization of airport facilities, ground crews, aircraft, and a flight crew—all factors of input necessary to transport the customer to a desired new location within a specified period of time. Finally, the wholesale distributing organization, typically considered a part of the marketing process, performs a function similar to that of the airlines in that the products to be distributed must arrive at a specified place at a given time.

The discussion above serves to emphasize the variety of activities that may be defined as production and raises a question concerning the classification of these various activities into a meaningful arrangement. A second question to be considered is whether or not there is a predictable relationship between factors of input and the resultant output; and, if there is such a relationship, how may it best be described.

Each of these questions is considered in turn and, in addition, a systems model is presented to show clearly the relationship between finance, sales, and production so that the planning function for each of these major functional areas of management may be better understood.

Types of Production

One might reasonably ask what is to be gained by developing a classification system for the production function. First, there is a definite relationship between the type of production and the characteristics of the inputs required. Classifying a given production process enables one to draw certain inferences concerning the nature of the physical facilities, the raw materials, and the human resources required for that specific production function. Second, knowledge of the type of production affords insight into the degree of planning required for the production process with particular reference to the planning required in establishing and controlling inventories. Production is classified within a two-dimensional frame of reference, one reference point being the quantity produced, and the other point of reference, the immediacy of customer demand.[1]

Reference to Quantity. The classification of production with reference to the quantity of product produced results in the categories of jobbing, continuous, and intermittent. Production classified as *jobbing* is usually in small quantities, ranging in number from the unique product, such as a bridge, to a lot size that rarely exceeds 50 in number. In addition to the small quantity produced, another characteristic of production classified as jobbing is that the product specifications often vary with the demands of each customer. Typical of the job-shop operation is the printing firm that produces a limited quantity of business forms for a customer. *Continuous production* implies that the product is being produced in large quantities meeting one set of unchanging specifications. The production of steel, chemicals, and paper often falls into this category. *Intermittent production,* as the name implies, lies somewhere in between the extremes of jobbing and continuous production, both in respect to the rigidity of product specifications and the quantity produced. The production of soft drink cans is an example of intermittent production; the quantity is large—usually several hundred

---

[1] Howard L. Timms, *The Production Function in Business* (Homewood, Illinois: Richard D. Irwin, Inc., 1962), Chap. 7, "Types of Production," pp. 91-127. In this chapter Professor Timms discusses the classification of the production function in the following types of businesses: manufacturing, marketing, financial, transportation, professional service, and miscellaneous service.

thousand—and the structural specifications of the can remain constant; yet the external lithographed label varies for each customer.

There is a definite relationship between each of the above types of production output and the nature of the required inputs. Jobbing production utilizes raw materials that may vary with each other, facilities must be flexible so that a wide range of product specifications may be met, and production personnel are usually highly skilled and versatile. In continuous production the facilities permit only a limited variation in product specification, as evidenced by a steel mill or a paper mill; raw materials usually meet rigid specifications; and the majority of the workmen are trained to perform specific jobs that are usually highly repetitive in nature. Again, intermittent production is between these two extremes. There is a greater variation in the raw materials utilized in intermittent production than in continuous production since the demands of several customers must be met. Physical facilities are also more flexible, and there are many highly skilled workmen whose function is to adjust and adapt the manufacturing equipment so that it can produce the required variations in the product.

Reference to Immediacy of Customer Needs. The types of production classified with reference to the immediacy of customer needs are: (1) production to order and (2) production to stock. These classifications enable one to infer the characteristics of product specification and the probable importance of planning inventory requirements. In addition, further insight is gained in regard to the kind of raw materials, production facilities, and human resources required by the business. Jobbing, continuous, or intermittent production may be produced either in direct response to a customer's order or it may be produced and placed in stock in anticipation of future orders.

An important factor in determining whether or not goods should be produced for stock is the degree of variation in product specification. When product specifications are unchanging from one customer to another, it is feasible to build a stock of finished goods inventory from which the orders of many customers may be drawn; however, when the specifications of the product vary with the demands of each customer, goods are usually produced to order. As a result, the establishment of finished goods inventories with the attendant problems of planning and controlling the size of inventories is usually connected with production for stock. Producing goods for stock usually implies that the quantity produced is greater than the amount produced for a single order, thereby making possible reduced costs associated with longer production runs. Also, when the quantity produced and placed into inventory is sufficient to meet the demands of future customer orders, the production facilities, provided they are flexible, may be used to produce other products—a capability that requires more highly trained human resources and a broader range of raw materials.

Production—Part of a Servo System

The ability to classify a given production process with reference to the quantity produced and the immediacy of customer needs is of value in drawing inferences concerning the nature of the inputs required and the characteristics of the product or service produced. However, a greater understanding of the production function and the previously discussed functions of finance and sales is gained when these functions and the personnel function are viewed as subsystems of a larger servo system.

In Chapter 1, page 12, the systems concept is introduced and the thermostatically controlled household heating system is mentioned as an example of a servo system. Also, the management processes of planning, directing, organizing, and controlling are discussed as parts of a system. Figure 7-1 shows the major functional areas of business operations— finance, personnel, production, and sales—as a servo system. Financial inputs supply the raw materials and the physical facilities necessary to produce the product. Personnel inputs furnish the required skills, knowledge, and judgment. The sales function is charged with the responsibility of selling the product to the customer. At this point, a feedback of information occurs which is interpreted by the sales department and

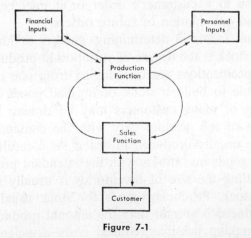

Figure 7-1

PRODUCTION—PART OF A SERVO SYSTEM

then relayed to production. If the customer buys the product in sufficient quantity, the cycle continues, and production signals for a continuation of financial and personnel inputs. If the demand is greater than the quantity being produced, production requests additional inputs. When the customer does not buy, the signal sent by production calls for a reduction of inputs. Figure 7-1 should be studied carefully for two reasons: first, it is the essence of a current concept in production termed *automation,* which will be discussed later in this chapter, and second, it is within this servo system that production policies are formed.

PLANNING PRODUCTION POLICIES

The analysis of the scope of sales policies, presented in Chapter 6, shows that policies are developed to guide management in making decisions in regard to the channel of distribution, pricing, the method of sales promotion, and the product. Figure 7-1 shows sales and production as interrelated functions forming a continuous cycle of producing and selling a product. Decisions concerning the product are also responsibilities of the production function as well as of the sales function since production is charged with producing the required product or service. Therefore, formulating policies concerning the product is a logical part of production policies. The guides used in determining the appropriate physical facilities are another phase of production policy, and the selection of sources of supply, or vendors, is the third area of production policy. Each group of policies is discussed in turn.

Product Policies

In the preceding chapter, we found that sales policies concerning the product encompass product diversification, obsolescence and style, quality, and standardization. Production policies cover these aspects of the product, with the exception of policy statements on obsolescence and style—an area usually reserved for the sales department because of its close contact with the needs of the market. In addition to considering the policies for product diversification, quality, and standardization, the production function is interested in establishing policies governing the control of inventories. The full range of production policies in regard to the product, discussed below, is product diversification, quality, standardization, and inventory.

Diversification. We have seen in Chapter 6 that sales policies relating to questions of product diversification confine the meaning of the word, diversification, to the acquisition of new products. Production policies relating to product diversification also utilize this meaning and, in addition, extend the meaning of diversification so that it includes the problem of integration and the question of whether to make or to buy a component part of the end product. The implication of each meaning —new products, integration, and make or buy—is examined below.

NEW PRODUCTS. Production policies relating to the acquisition of new products must be closely coordinated with the efforts of the sales department in establishing guidelines for acquiring new products so that the end result is a cohesive set of company policies. In addition, there are questions peculiar to the production process itself that must be considered. Will the new product utilize present production facilities or will it require new or additional facilities? Will the same raw materials be used and the same human skills be required in its production? Will the knowledge gained, as the result of research and development work on the new product, benefit existing products? Almost every business has the opportunity to acquire new products or offer additional services that conform with existing sales and production capabilities.[2] For instance, the automatic car wash service described in Case Problem 7-A can offer to its customers the additional service of polishing and waxing their automobiles.

INTEGRATION. The combining of a sequence of distinct production processes, sometimes existing in the form of separate companies, is referred to as *vertical integration*. As an example, a Wisconsin company manufacturing glassine paper bags used for packaging potato chips formerly purchased the paper from a nearby mill that produced only glassine paper. When the mill owner died, his heirs decided to sell, and the Wisconsin company bought the mill in order that the company might be assured an uninterrupted source of raw materials. As a result of the acquisition, the bag manufacturer had a new product, glassine paper, some of which was utilized as raw material in manufacturing its bags and the remainder was sold to other users of glassine paper. This example illustrates the acquisition of earlier stages of production, but the same process is applicable when moving in the other direction; that is, continuing the production process so that present products, currently utilized by other manufacturers as raw materials, can be converted into finished consumer goods. Some steel companies have inte-

---

[2] Joel Dean, "Product-Line Policy," *Journal of Business*, Vol. XXIII, No. 4 (October, 1950), pp. 248-58. This article presents a synthesis of sales, production, and financial criteria to be utilized in selecting new products.

grated in both directions. These companies have acquired raw material sources, iron ore mines, and have also directed the expansion of their operations so that they are able to convert their basic product, steel, into finished consumer goods such as steel pails and even prefabricated houses. The result is a single company with vertically integrated production processes that mine ore, produce steel, and fabricate the finished consumer products.

MAKE OR BUY. The make-or-buy decision is a miniature of the integration decision. When the make-or-buy question is raised, it usually refers to whether or not a company should make or buy a specific component part that is used in its product. Ball bearings are a typical example of a part that may be purchased from an independent source of supply or manufactured by the user. In formulating a policy that outlines the course of action to follow, the questions to be answered are the same as those raised when considering whether or not a company should adopt a policy of integration. The following questions are a useful checklist in formulating policies concerned with whether or not a company should integrate other related production operations into its present structure and in resolving the make-or-buy decision:

1. Can present facilities be used, or are new facilities required?
2. What new technical skills and knowledges are required?
3. Is the present source of supply satisfactory in respect to quantity, quality, cost, and reliability of service?
4. Will making the new product result in an excess quantity that must be sold by the sales department?

Quality. In addition to formulating policies concerning product diversification, the production function (along with the sales function) is concerned with the formulation of policies concerning the quality of the product. Production policies concerning quality emphasize the cost of quality rather than the sales potential associated with the level of quality. Figure 7-2 is a model showing the relationship of the three variables to be considered in formulating policies that define the desired level of quality for a given product or service. The general term, "corrective action," is used since the model is a statement of the factors that must be considered when taking any action designed to improve performance. The vertical axis is a measure of cost, and the horizontal axis indicates units of corrective action. Assume that the quality of a given product can be improved when additional inspectors are added to an assembly line. The cost of additional inspection is shown by line A, the rising diagonal line— the cost of corrective action inputs.

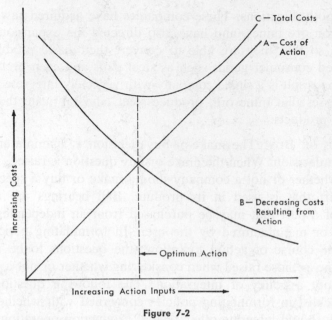

Figure 7-2

MODEL SHOWING THE EFFECT OF MANAGEMENT ACTION

Line *B,* a downward sloping curve, shows the decreasing costs resulting from the corrective action (in this case, the use of additional inspectors). Total costs, line *C,* form a U-shaped curve. When there is no inspection, the cost of that function is zero, but the cost resulting from poor quality due to excessive scrap, replacement of defective parts, and loss of sales is high; consequently, the total cost of producing the product is also high. As additional inspection is added, the cost of such inspection increases, but this rising cost is being offset by the decreasing costs attributable to poor quality, with the result that total costs decline until an optimum point is reached. Beyond that point, total costs again rise since the cost of inspection is greater than the decreasing costs resulting from improved quality.

The cost of additional inspection has been used as an example; however, the same reasoning applies when considering the purchase of new precision equipment as a means of improving quality or the utilization of more uniform or expensive raw materials. One must continually balance the cost of corrective action against the cost of not taking that action to determine the total cost of the plan being considered.

Standardization. There is need for close coordination between the sales department and the production department in the formulation of policies that determine the degree of product standardization. From the viewpoint of sales, the addition of models that vary in size, color, function, or quality means that a greater share of the potential market may be gained; yet each variation in the product increases the complexity of the production function with an attendant increase in production costs. Nonetheless, it is possible to achieve a relatively high degree of standardization in some instances without seriously compromising sales volume and yet maintain relatively low production costs. The standardization of parts and subassemblies that make up the finished product offers such an opportunity. For example, a manufacturer of refrigerators may standardize the insulating materials, compressors, hinges, door latches, and quality of steel plate used in its product in order to increase production efficiency and still continue to produce a variety of sizes and colors in order to maximize its share of the market.

Inventory. Inventory policies determine the practices that a company follows in carrying raw materials, parts in process, or finished goods in order to fill customer orders. The model presented in Figure 7-2 may be applied to the general problem of determining an optimum inventory level. Since establishing a given inventory level is the result of management action, let the horizontal axis represent increasing amounts of inventory and the rising diagonal, line *A*, the increasing cost of carrying an inventory. The downward sloping curve, line *B*, shows the decreasing costs that might be expected as the result of fewer stock-outs. When stock-outs are frequent, total costs, line *C*, are also high since stock-outs may mean either a loss in sales volume as the result of not being able to fill customer orders, or increased production costs as the result of frantic efforts to fill a succession of small orders. As the amount of inventory increases, so does the cost of carrying that inventory increase, line *A*; but the cost of inventory is offset by the decreasing number of stock-outs which enables the company to fill customer orders promptly and increase the efficiency of the production process through longer production runs. The optimum level of inventory, as measured by total cost, is reached when the total cost curve, line *C*, reaches its lowest point. Beyond this point the cost of carrying additional inventory is greater than any advantage gained as the result of further reduction in the number of stock-outs, and total costs again begin to rise.

Though it is impossible to carry a stock of finished goods on hand in a service business, a similar decision is made in determining the total quantity of service to be offered. Kwickie Kar Klean's manager, Tim Jones, makes such a decision when he decides to carry a reserve of manpower on Saturdays in order to meet the peaks of customer demand, thereby minimizing stock-outs; i.e., customers driving away because the waiting line is too long.

Facility Policies

The physical facilities of production include the land, buildings, and all equipment used in the production process. The nature of some processes—for example, paper making—offers relatively few degrees of freedom to the manager in selecting either equipment or location; and some production, such as steel-making, is so technical that only those persons who are highly trained in the industry can appreciate the problems involved. For these reasons a discussion of the selection of specific facilities for a given industry is beyond the scope of this book. Nonetheless, these are three aspects of facility policies that are broad in scope and applicable to most business firms. These are policies that aid management in determining the best location for production facilities, the proper capacity of such facilities, and the subsequent plan for maintaining plant and equipment.

Location. For many businesses the location decision has been made and usually little can be done about it; but for those that are contemplating expansion or establishing a new business, the decision may be crucial, particularly when choosing the location of a new retail or service establishment. The location of Kwickie Kar Klean, Case Problem 7-A, on a busy thoroughfare surrounded by a large residential area, illustrates the importance of two factors that are significant in choosing a location. The factors are availability of raw materials and ready access to market; in this instance, as is true in many service businesses, the customer also supplies the raw material. Other factors that must be considered in choosing a location are availability and cost of space, cost of construction, and the cost of services such as heat, light, and power. Another consideration of significance in determining the effectiveness and cost of subsequent operations is the availability and cost of labor.

Capacity. Again, Kwickie Kar Klean illustrates the essential features of the problem present in determining proper size, or capacity, of production facilities. If facilities are too large, waste is evident; if too small, loss in sales volume and inefficiencies in the production process may result. Tim Jones compensates for the normal capacity of his car wash by doubling the size of the labor force on Saturdays, and though the results may not be the most efficient or profitable, his policy does offer a means of satisfying and retaining customers. The alternative is the installation of fully automatic equipment, thereby permanently increasing capital outlay and depreciation charges (fixed costs) in order to meet periods of peak demand more efficiently. Policies relating to capacity for production should provide for maximum flexibility so that variations in output may be handled in the most efficient manner possible.

Maintenance of Facilities. Figure 7-2 provides the basis for determining the policy to be followed in the proper maintenance of production facilities. In this application the management action is a predetermined scheduled maintenance program, known as *preventive maintenance,* designed to minimize lost production time as the result of equipment failure. The reduction of losses due to breakdown is shown by the downward sloping curve of line *B*. As action inputs, sound preventive maintenance, increase, the cost of such maintenance also increases (shown by line *A*). But this cost is offset by the decreasing costs of production failures that are reduced by the maintenance program. Consequently, total costs are also declining as shown by the U-shaped curve of total costs, line *C*. When total costs are at the lowest point, the optimum degree of preventive maintenance is attained. When total costs rise excessively as the result of an extensive maintenance program that becomes necessary to keep worn equipment in operation, consideration should be given to replacing existing facilities with new equipment requiring less maintenance.

Selection of Vendors

Policies relating to the selection of vendors are developed to insure an uninterrupted flow of materials and supplies vital to the production process. Usually the factors of quality, service, and price are of prime importance in selecting a vendor; however, attention must be given to the number of vendors, and in some instances it is necessary to consider the question of reciprocity.

Number of Vendors. Many companies attach great importance to those policies that govern the number of vendors selected to provide needed products or services. Frequently, vendors are pitted against each other by the purchaser as a means of improving the quality of the item purchased and insuring prompt service if the need arises. Multiple sources of supply are also used as a means of providing a continuing source of materials in the event that one supplier is unable to make delivery due to difficulties arising from strikes or mechanical failure.

On the other hand, small companies frequently find it advantageous to patronize a single source of supply. The reason is that the volume purchased by a small company is such that if it were divided among several suppliers, the amount of business for each supplier would not be large enough to warrant special attention and service. In addition, the vendor may offer credit, provided he receives the entire account. In formulating policies concerning the number of vendors, a company must be able to view itself as a customer as well as analyze its own needs as a purchaser.

Reciprocity. Reciprocal agreements are possible when the purchaser of a given item produces a product or service that can, in turn, be used by the vendor. For example, the ABC company, a printer of office forms and stationery, may agree to purchase the services of an industrial catering company to operate its plant cafeteria provided the caterer agrees to purchase its office forms and stationery from the ABC company. The existence of reciprocity between purchaser and vendor does not mean nor imply collusion or unethical conduct. There is no reason to develop a policy statement barring reciprocity provided such agreements are evaluated in respect to quality, service, price, and strategic position.

APPLICATION OF PRINCIPLES

In applying principles of management so that planning of the production function may be improved, it is necessary to introduce several new concepts. In order to understand the full implication of the application of the Principle of the Objective to the production process, the concept of *suboptimization of objectives* is introduced. The Gantt chart, which utilizes time as a unit of measurement in determining the effectiveness of the production process, is presented in discussing the application of the Principle of Planning, and an understanding of the meaning of automation is necessary for an appreciation of the application of the Principle of Economic Effectiveness.

Principle of the Objective—Suboptimization

The Principle of the Objective, which states that *before initiating any course of action, the objective in view must be determined, understood, and stated,* is a general statement applicable to all levels of the organization and to all objectives. The principle is also applicable in formulating objectives for each of the major functional areas of the business organization—finance, sales, production, and personnel. Within any one of these functional areas—for example, production—each succeeding lower level of the production organization has objectives of its own that must be fulfilled so that the overall production objectives may be realized, which in turn makes possible the optimization, or maximum realization, of broad company objectives. The process of company objectives being optimized by each succeeding lower level of the organization is known as *suboptimization*.[3]

A review of company objectives as stated by Continental-Emsco Company (Chapter 3, page 57) illustrates the parallelism that exists between the hierarchy of company objectives and the hierarchy of the organization. Objective No. 1 states that it is a goal of Continental-Emsco "to be a growth organization to the degree that is permitted by the profitableness of our current operations." Objectives Nos. 21 and 22 state broad profit objectives, with No. 21 indicating a desire to return to the owners a reasonable profit on their investment, and No. 22, "to maintain and increase the value of our owners' investment in the company." Objective No. 5, "to manufacture quality products at the lowest possible cost, utilizing modern manufacturing practices, facilities, tools, and equipment," is a specific objective of the production function of the organization that must be fulfilled in order that the overall objectives, Nos. 1, 21, and 22, might be optimized.

After developing company objectives, Continental-Emsco encouraged each plant to develop objectives of its own. The Houston, Texas, plant, one of several manufacturing facilities, has as its specific goal the achievement of company Objective No. 5. In order that this might be accomplished, the management of the Houston plant developed a list of 23 objectives to guide its operations. Four of these objectives detail the goals of the production function within the plant organization and are as follows:

1. To manufacture quality products at the lowest possible cost which will sell at a profit.
2. To maintain a national reputation as a metal fabricator for industry.
3. To introduce and implement operations with the latest knowledge, techniques, methods, and systems and procedures to improve company products and plant efficiency.
4. To continuously review and improve economy of operations in all phases of engineering and manufacturing.

---

[3] Charles Hitch, "Sub-optimization in Operations Problems," *Journal of Operations Research Society*, Vol. I (May, 1953), pp. 87-99. This article is one of the first discussions of suboptimization. Mr. Hitch discusses the concept in reference to the optimization of naval operations and then relates the concept to fundamental economic theory.

Note that the first of these plant objectives is a restatement of company Objective No. 5. The second plant objective is also broad but pertains to achievement as the result of excellence in the production function. The third and fourth objectives become more specific; No. 3 stresses methodology and efficiency, and No. 4 stresses economy of operations. Thus, we see a narrowing of the scope of operations and responsibility as we move downward from the broad company organization and objectives to plant objectives for a specific function, production. The next lower step in the organizational hierarchy is the production department, and its objectives must, of necessity, be worded in terms of efficiency of operations. Thus, an understanding of the concept of suboptimization enables us to appreciate more fully why the production process, as we know it in our society, emphasizes efficiency. It must be efficient so that overall company objectives may be optimized.

Principle of Planning—the Gantt Chart

The Principle of Planning states that *effective planning results in plans that are objective, structured, and flexible, and the extent to which resultant plans possess these characteristics is a measure of their probable success.* H. L. Gantt, a pioneer in the field of management and close associate of Frederick W. Taylor, developed a means of showing, in graphic form schedules, or plans, for the completion of the production process. However, the unique contribution of Gantt in developing a more effective planning technique is not the utilization of a chart that now bears his name, but rather the utilization of *time* as a common denominator for the scheduling of production.

Figure 7-3 is an example of a Gantt chart used in production planning. The chart shows the work scheduled for the month of February for each of four operating departments—milling, lathe, grinding, and assembly. When a customer's order is received, it is assigned a shop order number and an estimate is made of the length of time required to complete each operation. The result of this estimate, expressed in days, is then entered in the form of a light line opposite the name of the department scheduled to perform the operation. Above the light line is the order number. Furthermore, the entry is made for the specific days and week for which the work is scheduled. For example, during the first week the milling department is scheduled to work Job No. 45 on Monday and Tuesday and Job No. 51 on Wednesday and Thursday. The heavy line appearing opposite the name of each department represents the cumulative total (again expressed in days) of work scheduled for that department for the entire month. Therefore, it can be seen

Figure 7-3

A GANTT CHART FOR PRODUCTION PLANNING

that the milling department has scheduled 15 of 20 possible work days, while the lathe department has only 9 days of scheduled work. As a result of recording production schedules in chart form, it is possible to tell at a glance the scheduled progress for each order, the total elapsed time needed for the completion of each order, and the total work load that has been scheduled for each department.

The extent to which production plans are objective is dependent upon the accuracy of the estimated time for the completion of a given order. Also, the posting of scheduled production time and the subsequent comparison of scheduled time with the actual time used to complete the work offer a means of revising and making production estimates more accurate. Using the Gantt chart contributes to the development of more highly structured plans in that the sequence of successive operations is clearly shown, and the work for each department is planned on a daily basis. Immediate flexibility in planning is possible to some extent by utilizing nonscheduled workdays where the need arises as the result of an unforeseen emergency such as a machine breakdown. Long-range flexibility is achieved through a better balance of production facilities. In Figure 7-3 the schedule for the lathe department is relatively light in comparison to other departments; perhaps personnel from the lathe department could be assigned to the milling department.

Though the example presented in Figure 7-3 is descriptive of a metal working operation, the same technique of visual charting of production plans is possible for other industries. A trucking firm or an airline could list the name and size of its equipment on the left side of the chart and then project the scheduled use of that particular piece of equipment for the time period under consideration. A firm of certified public accountants might list the names of its staff members and develop the number of work days scheduled for each member. In all applications of the Gantt chart, the capabilities and projected utilization of the production unit, whether it be a machine, a truck, an aircraft, or an accountant, are expressed in terms of the common denominator of production—time.

Principle of Economic Effectiveness—Automation

Economic effectiveness in planning results in plans that maximize achievement of company objectives through the most efficient utilization of available resources. For some companies the application of the concept of automation offers the "most efficient utilization of available resources." In order to evaluate the economic effectiveness of plans that call for the automation of production processes, it is necessary to establish, first, the meaning of the concept, "automation"; second, the essential characteristics of the production function that may lead to automation; and third, the factors that must be considered before embarking upon a plan calling for automation.

The Concept of Automation. There are two distinct but closely related meanings of the word, *automation,* as it is currently used in describing a production process. One of these meanings relates to the technical specifications of the equipment used in the production process; the other meaning refers to a way of organizing work into an integrated system which may or may not contain equipment that is automated in the sense of meeting certain technical specifications. Automated equipment, when defined in terms of technical specifications, must function as a servo system. The discussion of Figure 7-1, which presents the major functions of a business organization—production, sales, finance, and personnel—as components of a servo system, states that a servo system is capable of correcting its own actions. In a business firm, management receives and interprets information from both internal and external sources and designates the corrective action necessary for the firm's continuous and successful operation.

Automated machines usually employ electronic devices to perform the self-correcting action, hence, the use of the term, "electronic brain." The "brain" used in automated equipment may range from the relatively simple photoelectric cell to a giant computer. An application of the photoelectric cell, which is sensitive to light, is found on printing presses that print on materials which come in roll form. The next time that you open a bag of potato chips or take the cellophane wrap from a food package, look for the "eye spot," a dark blue or black rectangle about ⅜ x ⅝ of an inch in size, that appears on the edge of the printed material. These eye spots keep the fast-moving material drawn from the roll in perfect alignment as it moves through the presses. If the material weaves to one side or the other, the eye spot interrupts a beam of light focused on a photoelectric cell, which in turn activates a mechanism that moves the roll back into the proper position. A more complex application of electronic devices that function in a self-correcting capacity is the guidance systems of missiles. These systems send electronic impulses to computers that analyze and relate the various impulses thus received and then produce a feedback impulse that corrects the course of the missile.

But there is more to automation than the creation of servo systems; in fact, the term, automation, was first used in 1947 to describe a production process that did not contain a servo system. Delmar S. Harder, then a vice-president of the Ford Motor Company, applied the term to a new system of production that views manufacturing as a continuous, integrated process from start to finish.[4] The key to the concept of automation that does not employ servo systems is the viewing of the production function as an integrated process and then making every effort to create a continuous process through the use of automatic machinery, including the mechanization of the materials-handling function. The process described by Mr. Harder as "automated" called for the precise automatic machining of each part and then the transfer of that part to the next machining operation by use of automatic transfer devices. The result of organizing the work of manufacturing in this manner is the elimination of an accumulation of partially completed parts waiting to be transferred by hand to the next operation and then manually loaded, one at a time, into the next machine.

Either form of automation, whether it be the one utilizing a servo system or the integration of production into a continuous automatic process with heavy reliance upon automatic material handling usually results in a drastic reduction of required manpower for that particular operation. Either form of automation seems to epitomize the slogan, "Untouched by human hands."

Characteristics of the Production Function. In the development of the Principle of Economic Effectiveness in Chapter 4, a set of production records, presented in Table 4-1 (page 97), was used to illustrate

---

[4] "Auto-building Prodigies," *Business Week* (October 27, 1962), pp. 150-54. This article discusses the limitations of the original "Detroit automation" and tells of the changes that are being made to make the production process more flexible.

the relationship that exists between varying units of input, total product, average product, and marginal product. When the figures from Table 4-1 are charted in graph form in Figure 7-4, the varying rates of change for each measure of product output can be visualized. Notice that total product produced continues to rise, though at a decelerating rate, through the addition of the eighth man; and when the ninth man is added, the total amount produced declines. Average product per man moves in a much narrower range than total product, with the highest average per man being 13 when three men are used, and 7 when nine men are used. Marginal product, the incremental gain attributable to each additional man, ranges from 15 to -1, a percentage variation that is greater than that shown by total product or average product. It is also important to note that the decline in the marginal product curve appears when the fourth man is added. Therefore, the most efficient utilization of *current* resources is the employment of three men. Does this mean

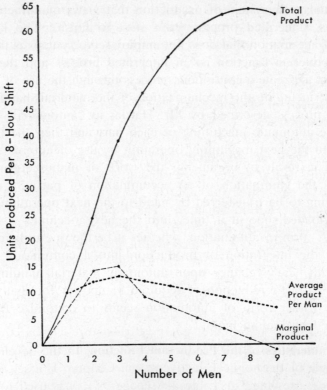

Figure 7-4

THE RELATIONSHIP BETWEEN TOTAL PRODUCT, AVERAGE
PRODUCT PER MAN, AND MARGINAL PRODUCT

that it is poor management to employ more than three men and that the production process is doomed to a continual decline in efficiency if it produces beyond the capabilities of three men?

Your answer to Problem 3, raised as one of several in connection with Kwickie Kar Klean, should provide a basis for answering the first part of the question above, which when restated in general terms is as follows: Is it poor management to employ a given input (in this instance manpower) beyond the point of maximum efficiency as determined by the marginal product curve? Obviously when Tim Jones calls in six extra men on Saturday so that a total of 350 cars can be washed, rather than approximately 200 produced by the normal crew of six men, he is not planning with maximum economic effectiveness as defined by the marginal product curve. However, it is sound business in that it satisfies customers, many of whom will return on weekdays when the demand for the product is at a minimum. By providing Saturday service, Tim is meeting one of the objectives of his business, satisfying the needs of customers. Now let us turn to the second part of the question raised in the paragraph above, again stated in general form: Is the production process doomed to a continual decline in efficiency if it produces beyond the point of maximum efficiency as determined by the marginal product curve of current inputs?

Evaluation of Automation. For Kwickie Kar Klean, the answer to the question above is "No." There are several automated car wash units that integrate the washing of cars into a continuous process and require only eight men for a daily output of 350 cars. Two men vacuum the car and attach it to the conveyor line; steam cleaning of the wheels and chrome is performed automatically; and the two mitters are replaced by an automatic mitting machine. The wiping operation still requires six men for an average daily output of 350 cars. However, the availability of an automated method of production does not necessarily mean that it is economically effective, even though it does result in a reduction of required manpower. There are other economic factors which must be considered in determining the economic feasibility of automating a given production process. In addition, the social and psychological impact of automation must be recognized. Consequently, an evaluation of automation must consider (1) economic factors and (2) social implications.

ECONOMIC FACTORS. In 1832, when discussing an American process of making pins by machine, Charles Babbage (Chapter 2) raised five questions that he considered important in determining whether or not the process should be adopted:

1. To what defect pins so made (i.e., by machine) are liable?
2. What advantages they possess over those made in the usual way?
3. What is the prime cost of a machine for making them?
4. What is the expense of keeping it in repair?
5. What is the expense of moving it and attending to it? [5]

In addition to these questions raised by Babbage, which are concerned primarily with the quality and cost of the product, consideration should also be given to the effect of automation upon the flexibility of the production process. For those companies that have continuous production, either to stock or to order, less flexibility in production may pose no problem; however, the job shop producing a small quantity to customer order needs flexibility in its operations if it is to survive. The availability and cost of labor are also important factors in deciding whether to automate. If labor is plentiful and its cost moderate, automation may prove too expensive; however, if labor becomes scarce or expensive, then the cost of further mechanization becomes relatively less. The Gantt chart schedules production in units of time, and when time is of great importance, it may determine the need for automation. Men can perform the mathematical wizardry of computers, but not in the same length of time as computers; so when near instantaneous interpretation and feedback of data are required, computers become essential. Time saved in production may also improve customer service.

A checklist of factors to consider in determining the economic effectiveness of automation is as follows:

1. Quality of product.
2. Unit cost of product—including original cost of equipment, depreciation and maintenance costs, and cost of labor.
3. The effect of automation upon the flexibility of the production process.
4. The availability and cost of labor.
5. The importance of time.

SOCIAL IMPLICATIONS. Management must consider the social and psychological effects of automation as well as the above-mentioned economic factors. The first reaction of workers to a discussion of automation is that of fear. It is a fear resulting not only from facing the unknown, but also a fear of being displaced from one's job. There is a solid basis for this apprehension, because machines have gradually dis-

---

[5] Charles Babbage, *On the Economy of Machinery and Manufactures* (Philadelphia: Carey and Lee, 1832), Chap. 17, pp. 121-40, "On the Division of Labour" reprinted in H. F. Merrill (ed.), *Classics in Management* (New York: American Management Association, 1960), pp. 29-44.

placed men in one job after another since the beginning of the industrial revolution. Management must recognize the validity of these fears and take every possible step to alleviate them if maximum benefits are to be gained from automation. Second, changes in job content occur, not only in those jobs filled by production workers who are directly affected by automation, but also throughout the entire organization. Closer liaison is usually required between production and sales as the result of organizing work into a continuous, integrated process. The production planning function becomes more precise and, in turn, usually requests more extensive and detailed information from the accounting department. The third effect of automation is that there is usually a change in the type of personnel required for the successful operation of the company. At the production level the unskilled and semiskilled jobs of machine operators and material handlers become minimal in number and are replaced by highly skilled maintenance personnel. However, there is no reservoir of skilled craftsmen for these jobs, nor is there an established apprentice program for training such personnel. Each company that automates must shoulder the responsibility of training its own personnel. If automation requires the use of electronic data processing equipment and computers in the accounting and production control functions, personnel in those departments must also acquire new skills.

In addition to the problems of fear, organizational change, and the need for more highly specialized personnel which must be solved by each company planning to automate production, consideration must be given to the effect of automation on the national economy. For years we have had in our vocabulary a phrase, "technological unemployment," to describe the plight of those who have been displaced from their jobs by new and improved methods. Unfortunately, we lack definitive data concerning the exact number of those unemployed as the result of automation, but it does seem that the continuing trend toward automation lessens the demand for unskilled and semiskilled workers. Management must be aware of the broad sociological changes attributed to automation so that it may fully evaluate the worth of plans calling for automation and assess its responsibility in minimizing the dislocation of employees that might result from the adoption of such a plan.

● ● ● ● ● ● ● ● ●

Case Problem 7-B, Social Aspects of Automation, emphasizes the noneconomic factors to be evaluated when automating the production process.

Questions for Study and Discussion

1. What is the production function? What are some of the production problems encountered in each of the following types of companies: a bank, an insurance company, a public utility, and a restaurant?

2. Would you classify the production of aircraft as jobbing, continuous, or intermittent? Why?

3. Compare the meanings of the phrase "product diversification" when used in reference to sales policies and when used in reference to production policies. Which meaning is broader?

4. Show the application of Figure 7-2, The Effect of Management Action, to areas other than quality control (for example, the cost of advertising or the optimum number of salesman for a company).

5. Prepare a chart showing the relationship between financial, sales, and production policies.

6. What is meant by suboptimization? Develop an example showing the application of the concept of suboptimization to sales objectives.

7. Do you consider the automation of production processes to be an application of the Principle of Economic Effectiveness? Why?

8. What are the two meanings of the term automation as presented in the text? Is the difference between the meanings one of degree or one of kind? Support your position by citing several examples.

9. Why is time rather than the number of units produced used as a basis for planning production schedules?

10. Prepare a Gantt chart showing your activities for a period of one week.

11. What types of industries are generally unable to utilize automatic or automated devices?

12. As a manager, would you place greater emphasis upon the social factors of automation or the economic factors of automation? Why?

Automotive Parts Company, a manufacturer of automobile hubcaps, wheel covers, and mufflers, is one of the five remaining manufacturing firms located in a small town about 50 miles from Detroit. Prior to 1950, there had been two additional manufacturers, each employing over 1,000 persons; however, they are no longer in existence as the result of a gradual relocation of the automobile industry and the trend of auto manufacturers to make their own parts rather than buy them from outside suppliers.

Case Problem 7-B
Social Aspects of Automation

Les Brown, president of Automotive Parts, returned to his office late one afternoon after a three-hour meeting as a member of the mayor's planning group, a committee that had been organized by the local chamber of commerce to attract new industries to the area and thereby reduce the number of unemployed. On his desk was a report from the chief industrial engineer entitled "Feasibility Study—Automating Muffler Line." Mr. Brown turned to the summary and recommendation section of the report and read:

"1. It is possible to construct a completely automatic material handling and assembly operation to replace the present manual assembly of mufflers. The cost of such equipment completely installed is approximately $200,000 for the first unit, and it can be expected to be in operation 10 months after the order for the equipment has been placed.

"2. After reviewing automated operations in plants of several of our competitors, there is no doubt concerning the higher quality level of the products produced on the automated line in comparison to those produced manually.

"3. It is expected that the output of the automated line will exceed by 50 percent the present output on the manual lines with a personnel reduction of six men per line. Currently we now have three lines, each operating two shifts, with approximately 30 men on each line—a total of about 180 men. The automated line will be manned with no more than 24 men who will place light parts into the automatic assembly units. In addition to this saving, it will be possible to eliminate one shift on one of the manual lines since the automated line operating on a two-shift basis will produce the same quantity now produced by three shifts. The estimated savings in manpower as the result of automating one line is approximately 42 men. When the second line is installed, the number of employees in the muffler department should be reduced by approximately 80 men. Saving in labor cost alone will pay for the project in one year's time.

"4. It is recommended that the incentive plan be discontinued for those employees on the automated line; however, it is recognized that the incentive plan must be continued for those employees in the department on manual lines.

"5. Current employees in the tool room will be trained by the manufacturer of the automated equipment to maintain such equipment."

As Mr. Brown was reading the feasibility report, James Stone, a machinist in the tool room and president of the local union, was preparing for a meeting with the other members of the union's contract negotiation committee. The union was aware that Automotive Parts was conducting a study in regard to automating the muffler lines and that automation had been accomplished in several competing companies. Mr. Stone knew that his own position was secure since he was a machinist and would be needed for maintenance work. He also recognized the competitive pressures facing the independent automotive parts suppliers; nonetheless, he believed that as an elected representative of the workers, he had an obligation to secure the best possible terms and conditions of employment for his fellow employees. He was also aware that very few of the men on the assembly line had the educational background necessary as a prerequisite for training in maintenance work. It seemed certain that the membership of the union would authorize a strike if the negotiating committee did not achieve its objectives. Several proposals had been suggested as demands to be presented to the company. Among them were: (1) severance pay equal to one year's earnings as a minimum for employees with one year or more of service, (2) a 30-hour week with triple time for overtime, and (3) negotiating into the contract a clause that would require union approval before any change in manning or present production methods could be put into effect.

Problems

1. Outline the course of action that you would follow as president of the Automotive Parts Company.
2. Outline the course of action that you would follow as president of the local union.

CHAPTER 8

Management Information Systems

Once upon a time the president of a large chain of short-order restaurants attended a lecture on "Human Relations in Business and Industry." He attended the lecture in the hope he would learn something useful. His years of experience had led him to believe that if human relations problems ever plagued any business, then they certainly plagued the restaurant business.

The speaker discussed the many pressures which create human relations problems. He spoke of psychological pressures, sociological pressures, conflicts in values, conflicts in power structure, and so on. The president did not understand all that was said, but he did go home with one idea. If there were so many different sources of pressure, maybe it was expecting too much of his managers to think they would see them all, let alone cope with them all. The thought occurred to him that maybe he should bring in a team of consultants from several different academic disciplines and have each contribute his part to the solution of the human relations problems.

And so it came to pass that the president of the restaurant chain and his top-management staff met one morn-

ing with a sociologist, a psychologist, and an anthropologist. The president outlined the problem to the men of science and spoke of his hope that they might come up with an interdisciplinary answer to the human relations problems. The personnel manager presented exit-interview findings which he interpreted as indicating that most people quit their restaurant jobs because of too much sense of pressure caused by the inefficiencies and ill tempers of coworkers.

This was the mission which the scientists were assigned: find out why the waitresses break down in tears; find out why the cooks walk off the job; find out why the managers get so upset that they summarily fire employees on the spot. Find out the cause of the problems, and find out what to do about them.

<hr>

[1] Elias H. Porter, "The Parable of the Spindle," *Harvard Business Review*, Vol. 40 (May-June, 1962), pp. 58-65.* The parable presented in this article, pages 58-61, is attributed to Professor William Foote Whyte of Cornell University. The remainder of the arcle, pages 61-65, discusses the spindle in the light of current systems theory. Mr. Porter is a member of the research staff of System Development Corporation, Santa Monica, California.

Case Problem 8-A

The Parable of the Spindle [1]

Later, in one of the plush conference rooms, the scientists sat down to plan their attack. It soon became clear that they might just as well be three blind men, and the problem might just as well be the proverbial elephant. Their training and experience had taught them to look at events in different ways. And so they decided that inasmuch as they couldn't speak each other's languages, they might as well pursue their tasks separately. Each went to a different city and began his observations in his own way.

First to return was the sociologist. In his report to top management he said:

"I think I have discovered something that is pretty fundamental. In one sense it is so obvious that it has probably been completely overlooked before. It is during the rush hours that your human relations problems arise. That is when the waitresses break out in tears. That is when the cooks grow temperamental and walk off the job. That is when your managers lose their tempers and dismiss employees summarily."

After elaborating on this theme and showing several charts with sloping lines and bar graphs to back up his assertions, he came to his diagnosis of the situation. "In brief, gentlemen," he stated, "you have a sociological problem on your hands." He walked to the blackboard and began to write. As he wrote, he spoke:

"You have a stress pattern during the rush hours. There is stress between the customer and the waitress. . . .

"There is stress between the waitress and the cook. . . .

"And up here is the manager. There is stress between the waitress and the manager. . . .

"And between the manager and the cook. . . .

"And the manager is buffeted by complaints from the customer.

"We can see one thing which, sociologically speaking, doesn't seem right. The manager has the highest status in the restaurant. The cook has the next highest status. The waitresses, however, are always 'local hire' and have the lowest status. Of course, they have higher status than bus boys and dish washers but certainly lower status than the cook, and yet they give orders to the cook.

"It doesn't seem right for a lower status person to give orders to a higher status person. We've got to find a way to break up the face-to-face relationship between the waitresses and the cook. We've got to fix it so that they don't have to talk with one another. Now my idea is to put a 'spindle' on the order counter. The 'spindle,' as I choose to call it, is a wheel on a shaft. The wheel has clips on it so the girls can simply put their orders on the wheel rather than calling out orders to the cook."

When the sociologist left the meeting, the president and his staff talked of what had been said. It made some sense. However, they decided to wait to hear from the other scientists before taking any action.

Next to return from his studies was the psychologist. He reported to top management:

"I think I have discovered something that is pretty fundamental. In one sense it is so obvious that it has probably been completely overlooked before. It is during the rush hours that your human relations problems arise. That is when the waitresses break out in tears. That is when the cooks grow temperamental and walk off the job. That is when your managers lose their tempers and dismiss employees summarily."

Then the psychologist sketched on the blackboard the identical pattern of stress between customer, waitress, cook, and management. But his interpretation was somewhat different:

"Psychologically speaking," he said, "we can see that the manager is the father figure, the cook is the son, and the waitress is the daughter. Now we know that in our culture you can't have daughters giving orders to the sons. It louses up their ego structure.

"What we've got to do is to find a way to break up the face-to-face relationship between them. Now one idea I've thought up is to put what I call a 'spindle' on the order counter. It's kind of a wheel on a shaft with little clips on it so that the waitresses can put their orders on it rather than calling out orders to the cook."

What the psychologist said made sense, too, in a way. Some of the staff favored the status-conflict interpretation while others thought the sex-conflict interpretation to be the right one; the president kept his own counsel.

The next scientist to report was the anthropologist. He reported:

"I think I have discovered something that is pretty fundamental. In one sense it is so obvious that it has probably been completely overlooked before. It is during the rush hours that your human relations problems arise. That is when the waitresses break out in tears. That is when the cooks grow temperamental and walk off the job. That is when your managers lose their tempers and dismiss employees summarily."

After elaborating for a few moments he came to his diagnosis of the situation. "In brief, gentlemen," he stated, "you have an anthropological problem on your hands." He walked to the blackboard and began to sketch. Once again there appeared the stress pattern between customer, waitress, cook, and management.

"We anthropologists know that man behaves according to his value systems. Now, the manager holds as a central value the continued growth and development of the restaurant organization. The cooks tend to share this central value system, for as the organization prospers, so do they. But the waitresses are a different story. The only reason most of them are working is to help supplement the family income. They couldn't care less whether the organization thrives or not as long as it's a decent place to work. Now, you can't have a noncentral value system giving orders to a central value system.

"What we've got to do is to find some way of breaking up the face-to-face contact between the waitresses and the cook. One way that has occurred to me is to place on the order counter an adaptation of the old-fashioned spindle. By having a wheel at the top of the shaft and putting clips every few inches apart, the waitresses can put their orders on the wheel and not have to call out orders to the cook. Here is a model of what I mean."

When the anthropologist had left, there was much discussion of which scientist was right. The president finally spoke. "Gentlemen, it's clear that these men don't agree on the reason for conflict, but all have come up with the same basic idea about the spindle. Let's take a chance and try it out."

And it came to pass that the spindle was introduced throughout the chain of restaurants. It did more to reduce the human relations problems in the restaurant industry than any other innovation of which the restaurant people knew. Soon it was copied. Like wildfire the spindle spread from coast to coast and from border to border.

Problems

1. In your opinion, which of the three scientists offered the most plausible explanation of the restaurant's problems?

2. Are the personnel problems observed by the owner "problems" or are they "symptoms"? Defend your answer.

3. In recommending the spindle, the scientists are tacitly admitting that the restaurant is a form of system. Name the kind of system they are thinking of and show how the restaurant meets the requirements of a system.

4. Prepare a chart showing the flow of information in the restaurant and designate the major steps in this process.

•   •   •   •   •   •   •   •   •

Figure 7-1 of Chapter 7, "Planning for Production," depicts the business firm as a servo system. In the discussion of this figure, it is stated that management receives and interprets information from both internal and external sources and designates the corrective action necessary for the firm's continuing and successful operation. Since management must receive, interpret, and transmit information in order to accomplish its stated objectives, the planning of an effective communication system is an important management task. Also discussed in Chapter 7 are two closely related meanings of automation—one that describes automation as a servo system, and the other that refers to the integration of production into a continuous automatic process with heavy reliance upon automatic material-handling devices. The production of information may also utilize servo systems and rely heavily upon the automatic collection and transmission of data.

This chapter extends the concept of automation from the production of a manufactured item to the design and operation of information systems. First, it is necessary to establish the meaning of the phrase, information system, and to determine the major functions of such a system. Second, electronic data processing techniques of handling information are reviewed in connection with the design and evaluation of integrated data processing information systems.

FUNCTIONS OF AN INFORMATION SYSTEM

The concept of a *system* implies a dynamic relationship between the component parts of a larger whole and at the same time permits the recognition of each part as a separate *subsystem* which makes its own unique contribution to the functioning of the whole. The human organism is an excellent example of a system composed of many subsystems. There is a gastro-intestinal system with its function of converting food into energy so that the larger whole may survive. The circulatory system carries the nutrients thus provided to every part of the body, supplies needed oxygen to the tissues, and removes waste materials. The nervous system, a communications network, is composed of several subsystems. The autonomic nervous system monitors and controls the gastro-intestinal and circulatory systems. The peripheral nervous system receives stimuli, such as heat or cold, from the external environment and warns of impending danger by transmitting a signal of pain. The central nervous system performs an integrative function by coordinating the many subsystems of the body.

In many respects an *information system* is analogous to the human nervous system. Patterns of information flowing from production and sales may be likened to the impulses transmitted by the autonomic nervous system in controlling the vital functions of the body. Messages from the sales force, field engineers, and buyers are similar to the stimuli transmitted by the peripheral nervous system in that they represent contacts with an environment external to the organism. Management, like the central nervous system, must interpret the data received and transmit directions so that corrective action may be taken. Unlike the human organism, however, a company is not created with a complete information (nervous) system; therefore, management must design its own system so the firm may function properly. What are the components of such a system, and how does each part contribute to the operation of the complete system?

Components of an Information System

Information systems range in degree of complexity from the very simple as described in Case Problem 8-A, "The Parable of the Spindle," to the extremely complex system utilized by Westinghouse, which is described in Case Problem 8-B. Regardless of the simplicity of the system, an effective information system has the following five parts: (1) *input device*—a means of placing information into the system, (2) *storage unit*—provides for the accumulation of information (performs a memory function), (3) *control unit*—selects the proper information from the storage unit and controls the operations of the (4) *processing unit*—the part that handles and interprets the data, and the (5) *output device*—presents the original information in usable form after it has been processed.

Contribution of Each Part

Before discussing the contribution of each part of an information system to the functioning of the total system, it is well to recognize that all organizations have some form of information system. When the system functions imperfectly, as illustrated in Case Problem 8-A, the symptoms of such malfunction may become so acute that they appear to be the problem. Each of the three scientists consulted by the restaurant owner determined that the problem arose during rush hours; however, each presented a different interpretation of the causes. The sociologist described the situation in terms of stress patterns coupled with the concept of status; the psychologist saw ego involvement arising from a disregard of classic familial authority relationships; and the anthropologist couched his explanation of the problem in terms of values. Fortunately, all agreed on one solution—an improved information system—though none of the three defined the basic problem as one resulting from the imperfect functioning of an inadequate information system. Let us determine the contribution of each part of the recommended system.

Input Device. The input device recommended as the first step of the new information system is a ticket on which the waitress writes a description of the desired order. Formerly the waitresses called their orders to the cook, a method that invites error and confusion. In addition to decreasing the possibility of misunderstanding, a written record provides a means of checking the accuracy of the eventual output and serves as a basis for correcting errors should they occur. When written records are used, it is possible to designate the point of origin; in this instance the initials of the waitress serve that purpose. Further, an input record may serve more than one purpose. When the ticket is returned with the prepared order, it may be used as a bill to be presented to the customer and then retained by the manager as a permanent record of the day's activities. Thus, written inputs minimize the introduction of error, provide a basis for correcting errors when they do occur, indicate the origin of the input, and serve as a permanent record.

Storage Unit. The main contribution of the spindle to the flow of information is the effect it has upon the cook's work. With orders of the waitresses attached to the revolving spindle, it is no longer necessary for the cook to remember each order. The spindle is performing a function formerly performed by the cook's memory; consequently, a storage unit is frequently referred to as a *memory unit*.

Rarely does information enter a system at a uniform rate; instead, the flow of information during a normal business day forms a chart with many peaks and valleys. The introduction of a storage unit into an information system makes it possible to control the rate of flow to subsequent units. The spindle storage unit has another important feature in that data may be drawn from it without reference to the sequence followed in putting information into the system. Storage units that permit the withdrawal of information without regard to the sequence of input are called *random access* units. If the tickets had been placed in a box rather than on a spindle, the cook would be relieved of remembering each order and could control the rate of flow of information from the box by selecting one or two tickets at a time. However, he would see only the top ticket; consequently, he could not combine several orders so they might be filled more efficiently. The visual display of the spindle allows random access without regard to the sequence in which the orders are received. At a single glance, the cook has access to all written tickets and can determine the number of steak dinners on order, thus enabling him to prepare similar orders simultaneously. The spindle adequately performs the functions of a storage unit in that it stores, or remembers, the information; regulates the flow of information to subsequent units in the system; and permits random access to the stored information.

Control Unit. In an information system the influence of the control unit is felt throughout the entire system. Though the unit cannot control the rate at which information enters the system, it can reject those items not suitable to the system or that are incapable of interpretation. The cook, who functions simultaneously as a control and a processing unit, may reject an order that is not on the menu; i.e., not suitable for the system, or ask that a ticket be rewritten because it is illegible. However, he cannot control the rate at which waitresses enter the orders. Also, in exercising his power of control the cook may determine the sequence in which orders are selected from the random access memory unit. The control unit also determines the method to be used in processing the order and checks the final results to make sure that the original input request is fulfilled. In addition, the output of the processing unit is monitored in respect to quality, quantity, and rate of output. In complex systems employing electronic data processing equipment, the control unit and the processing unit are separate pieces of electronic equipment; yet the control function remains the same—checking the flow of information into the system, determining the sequence in which material will be drawn from the memory unit, setting up the methods to be used in processing, and controlling output in respect to quality, quantity, and rate of output.

Processing Unit. The chief task of the processing unit is one of interpreting information so that the output of the system conforms to requirements laid down by the control unit. Since the cook is performing the processing function as well as the control function, it is his task to interpret the symbols on the tickets and translate these symbols into action that produces the specified output—orders of food. Simple arithmetic computations are necessary to determine the number of orders on each ticket, and on occasion the cook may compute the total number of identical orders capable of being prepared at the same time, thereby increasing efficiency of output. In more sophisticated systems, such as the one used by Westinghouse in Case Problem 8-B, advance-design computers form the processing unit. However, the function remains the same—the interpretation and manipulation of symbolic data to produce the desired output.

Output Device. The output of an information system is the final step in the sequence of input, storage, control, and processing of information. Frequently the output of the processing unit is additional information, usually directions requiring action on the part of subsequent elements in the system. The cook could, for example, interpret the information stored on the spindle and give directions to his assistants, indicating the work that each is to perform. Or immediately after interpretation, the information may be converted into action that fulfills the objectives of the system, in this instance, the preparation of food. In any event, the end result of the system, either additional information or action that fulfills the objectives of the system, should be capable of being checked against the original input so that the reliability of the entire process is insured. In our present example the original ticket may be placed with the prepared food, which enables both the cook and the waitress who placed the original information (order) into the system to check the accuracy of the final result.

In addition to providing a basis for discussing the major parts of an information system, "The Parable of the Spindle" points up the value of viewing business problems as occurring within a system rather than isolated problems to be analyzed and solved as separate entities.

Suppose that none of the scientists had recommended the installation of a spindle, but that one had recommended a more tolerant cook; another, a more stable manager; and the third, the selection of waitresses with a higher degree of emotional stability. Such recommendations represent an approach that emphasizes the strength of each element rather than the design of the system itself. The solution that was adopted, the installation of a spindle, illustrates the systems approach to the management process. Seymour Tilles has suggested that the manager's job is essentially one of managing systems and that a manager should define the company as a system, establish objectives for the system, create formal subsystems, and then integrate all such systems.[2] The chief advantage to be derived from regarding the manager's job as one of managing systems is the recognition of the interdependence and contribution of each part to the whole system and the realization that failure to meet objectives may be due to an improper design of the system itself rather than the result of shortcomings attributable to the individual components of the system.

INTEGRATED DATA PROCESSING

"The Parable of the Spindle" serves a useful purpose since it provides a means of illustrating the components of an information system and the importance of recognizing the management of systems as an important element of the manager's job. Obviously, the number of business situations in which a spindle may be used as a storage unit is limited; also, most business situations are so complex that an information system that relies solely upon human capabilities for the functions of control, interpretation, and output of data would be extremely limited in its effectiveness. Fortunately, there are techniques available for the design of effective communication systems for those situations too complex for the spindle and the powers of human memory and reasoning. An increasing number of modern communication, or information, systems rely upon the use of electronic data processing (EDP) equipment which may be combined into an integrated data processing (IDP) system. In discussing integrated data processing,

---

[2] Seymour Tilles, "The Manager's Job—A Systems Approach," *Harvard Business Review*, Vol. 41 (January-February, 1963), pp. 73-81.

R. A. Johnson, F. E. Kast, and J. E. Rosensweig, *The Theory and Management of Systems* (New York: McGraw-Hill Book Company, 1963), pp. viii, 350.

Both of these works emphasize the business organization as a complex of systems and the manager's job as a manager of systems. *The Theory and Management of Systems* relates the systems concept to the management functions of planning, organizing, controlling, and communication.

we will touch upon the development of electronic data processing, the steps in the design of an integrated data processing system, and an evaluation of integrated data processing.

Before discussing the development of electronic data processing, it is necessary to define some commonly used terms. *Data processing* refers to the act of handling information or data, either *manually* or *automatically*. Typical of the manual methods of handling data is the work of clerical employees such as bookkeepers, accountants, billing clerks, and payroll clerks. *Automatic data processing (ADP)* is the handling of information by machines rather than by human beings. The punch card equipment, discussed below, is an example of automatic data processing. The phrase, *electronic data processing (EDP)*, means that the data are processed at high speed by electronic equipment. When the word electronic was first used to describe data processing equipment, it designated equipment that utilized the vacuum tube rather than the earlier electromechanical devices. The term electronic is still used to describe data processing units that are completely transistorized and no longer use vacuum tubes. Since the computer is the best known example of an electronic data processing unit, the phrase EDP also implies that a computer is part of the electronic data processing system. *Integrated data processing (IDP)* refers to the integrated collection, transmission, handling, and use of all data needed for the operation of a business. It is an integrated management information system. It must be recognized that there are varying degrees of integration and that technically IDP is not dependent upon any form of automatic equipment. For example, "The Parable of the Spindle" described an integrated flow of information that is manually operated. However, as the term IDP is now used, it almost always means that EDP is being utilized, but the emphasis is upon the integrative aspects of management information rather than upon the means of processing the data.

Development of EDP

The origin of automatic data processing may be traced to Charles Babbage, who in 1823 conceived the idea of a "Difference Engine" to compute and print mathematical tables.[3] Though he worked on this project for 10 years, it was never completed due to difficulties encountered primarily in its manufacture. The next major step in automatic data processing occurred in 1890 when Dr. Herman Hollerith developed the now familiar punch card as an aid in tabulating the results

---

[3] See Chapter 2, page 31.

of the 1890 census. Information was coded by means of holes punched in the cards, and an electrical contact completed through the holes activated mechanical counters. The first computer, started in 1937 by Professor Howard Aiken of Harvard University in conjunction with the International Business Machines Corporation, was placed in operation in 1944 and is still in use. The computer, the Automatic Sequence Controlled Calculator—Mark I, operated on electromechanical principles with the counters controlled by electrical relays. The first electronic computer, completed at the University of Pennsylvania's Moore School of Engineering in 1946, was called the Electronic Numerical Integrator and Calculator (ENIAC). This computer replaced the relays and counters of Mark I with 18,000 vacuum tubes. By 1950 there were approximately 20 different types of computers in use and in 1960 this number had reached at least 300.[4]

Computers are only one part of the present-day electronic data processing equipment used in electronic data processing systems. The components of an electronic data processing system are the same as the components of the information system described in "The Parable of the Spindle." Inputs into the system are in the form of electrical impulses placed in the system by means of punched cards, punched paper tape, magnetic tape, or magnetic ink characters such as those used by banks in the processing of checks. Paper tapes may be prepared as a by-product of conventional typing and may be fed into the system at speeds in excess of 500 characters per second. The information is usually stored in the "memory unit" of the computer as an electronic charge on a magnetic core, a magnetic drum, or magnetic discs. Most modern systems permit random access to any bit of information, and storage capacities of two or three million alphanumeric characters are not at all unusual. The computer is the arithmetic processing unit and performs all arithmetic operations—addition, subtraction, multiplication, and division—at extremely high rates of speed by using the binary system, which expresses all numbers and letters in various combinations of either 0 or 1. The control unit, equipped with a console, offers a means whereby the operator communicates with the computer and enables the computer to inform the operator of any errors that may be encountered or mechanical breakdowns that may occur. The control unit directs the

---

[4] It is beyond the scope of this chapter to present a detailed analysis of the construction of electronic data processing equipment. The student is referred to the following reference as a broad source of information concerning the principles of electronic data processing equipment and its application to the behavioral sciences.

Harold Borko (ed.), *Computer Application in the Behavioral Sciences* (Englewood Cliffs, New Jersey: Prentice-Hall, Inc., 1962).

operation of the arithmetic processing unit by means of a predetermined program that sets forth each step to be performed and the sequence of that step in relation to other operations. Also, the control unit decodes incoming information, places it in proper form in the storage unit, and regulates the form and rate of output. Due to the tremendous speed of the arithmetic processing unit, original output is placed on magnetic tape which may be transcribed onto punched paper tape and then fed through a typewriter or a printer, or transferred to punched cards which are processed through a printer. Or, high-speed electronic printers, capable of printing up to 5,000 lines per minute, may be used.

Designing an IDP Information System

Electronic data processing is a powerful tool capable of handling large quantities of information in very short periods of time. Integrated data processing usually employs electronic data processing techniques and combines the various applications of EDP into an integrated flow of information to and from all levels of the organization so that management has relevant and timely information for decision making. The following discussion outlines five major steps in designing an IDP information system, reviews some of the problems encountered in each step, and offers suggested ways of overcoming these problems.[5]

State Objectives. Normally company-wide objectives are expressed in terms of accomplishments in specific functional areas and do not specify the information needed to achieve these goals. Objectives should be reexamined and expressed as information needed for their achievement. For example, the sales department might specify the need for additional economic information in order to improve the accuracy of sales forecasts. A way of gathering the information required to meet objectives is to ask each department manager to develop the information needs required to improve the performance of his department. This approach, in addition to aiding in restating objectives, serves to acquaint the organization with the benefits to be derived from IDP and helps to allay fears associated with the introduction of automatic, high-speed processes. Stating information objectives carefully also avoids the tendency of indiscriminately collecting and processing large masses of information simply because the equipment is capable of handling a

---

[5] M. K. Evans and L. R. Hague, "Master Plan for Information System," *Harvard Business Review*, Vol. XL (January-February, 1962), pp. 92-103. A similar analysis of five steps is presented in this article.

huge volume of work. Remember, the ultimate purpose of IDP is to aid in decision making; the preparation of irrelevant information confuses the issue and hinders the manager in making a decision. Too, the accumulation of unnecessary information is wasteful.

Designate Authority. When the information needs of the company have been stated and it has been decided to install an IDP information system, it is necessary to designate authority for the planning of the system and its later administration. Usually it is best to choose one person to be responsible for both planning and administration since the knowledge gained of the organization and its information needs during the planning phase of the program is invaluable in administering the program. If possible, the person chosen should have a thorough knowledge of the company and a reputation that merits the confidence of the company's top officials. In small and medium-size firms the person usually designated is the controller, since he generally has a broad knowledge of the company and usually administers a large part of the present information system. In large companies—those having several plants, a diverse product line, and several sales offices—it is best to create an information function independent of the controller's office. Frequently the manager of IDP carries the title of vice-president, administrative services. Regardless of title, the person in charge of planning and administering IDP should report to the chief operating head of the company, who is usually the president.

Analyze Present Systems. There are two divergent theories concerning the extent to which present information systems should be examined in order to develop a new IDP system.[6] One of these theories holds that there should be a detailed analysis of present systems even though the information gained is not completely relevant. Most companies have established procedures to describe a series of related tasks, such as payroll procedures, employment procedures, or accounting procedures. Procedures are usually implemented by methods, a descriptive statement of the precise way to perform a given job, such as detailing the steps to be completed in preparing an invoice. Procedures and methods are examples of the flow of information; however, it is information flowing primarily in one direction since the major emphasis in developing procedures and methods is that of describing the manner

---

[6] James D. Gallagher, *Management Information Systems and the Computer* (New York: American Management Association, 1961), Research Study No. 51, p. 127. Mr. Gallagher's research study surveys the problems generally associated with information systems and contains two case studies of information systems of special interest: the American Airline Sabre System and the system used by Sylvania Electric Products, Inc.

in which a given task or job is to be accomplished.[7, 8] Since the purpose of procedures and methods is to accomplish work, rather than develop information for an integrated system, a detailed analysis of an existing system is of questionable value. A danger of the detailed analysis of present systems is the building of mountains of data that obscure real information needs.

The second theory holds that only information pertinent to the meeting of company information objectives should be analyzed and recorded. Selecting only pertinent data not only reduces the amount of work but also avoids one of the dangers inherent in the first theory— unconsciously trying to fit powerful electronic data processing techniques to existing procedures and methods that were originally designed to direct manual operations rather than to create information. In practice, a middle ground is usually chosen. Thorough knowledge of present information is required, but the collection of voluminous data is avoided since the purpose and techniques of IDP differ from those of the existing system.

Install Short-Range Improvements. There are those who say that a complete system must be developed before making any changes in present procedures; yet there is much to be gained by installing short-range improvements provided such steps mesh with the goals of a total IDP information system. Critics of short-range improvements state that until the entire systems analysis is complete, there is no way of knowing ultimate equipment requirements; however, modern EDP equipment is of modular design, and units acquired at a later date are usually compatible with existing units. Further, the early experience with IDP influences the design of subsequent systems and affords an early demonstration of benefits resulting from an integrated approach to information handling. In some instances it is possible to realize an immediate reduction in costs. Applications of IDP to inventory control procedures, payroll procedures, or the processing of sales orders are examples of short-range applications that may result in immediate cost reduction. The Westinghouse installation of EDP, Case Problem 8-B, illustrates the realization of immediate gains that are at the same time a part of an overall IDP information system.

Each of the following two references presents sound discussions of business procedures:

[7] Ralph C. Davis, *The Fundamentals of Top Management* (New York: Harper & Brothers, Publishers, 1951), Chap. 20, "Business Procedure," pp. 744-84.

[8] William H. Newman and James P. Logan, *Business Policies and Management* (4th ed.; Cincinnati: South-Western Publishing Company, 1959), Chap. 24, "Operating Methods and Procedures," pp. 637-665.

Prepare for Organizational Change. Despite the many technical problems encountered in the installation of a company-wide information system, the greatest difficulties experienced by many firms are the effects of IDP upon the organizational structure of the company. George Fleming of the Boeing Company states that installation problems are more people oriented than machine oriented.[9] One factor contributing to Fleming's statement is the obvious fear and resistance on the part of employees who might be displaced by electronic data processing equipment. Yet, in many respects, the major problems with people come from middle and top management. Organizational structures usually conform to and are derived from the work patterns of the organization. People doing similar work are grouped into units that may develop into departments. For example, those persons engaged in scheduling the product through production form the production control department, and those who keep financial records make up the accounting department. Supervisors of departments tend to develop a proprietary interest in the work performed in their departments and the people performing this work. An IDP system, by automating manual operations, frequently eliminates the need for entire departments and their respective supervisors. Consider the plight and attitude of the employees and the supervisor of a payroll department when it is learned that an IDP system will record the hours worked for each production worker, accumulate the total number of hours for each worker during the pay period, and at the close of the period compute all necessary extensions and deductions and print individual checks for the net amount due.

As yet, very few companies are organized to take full advantage of an IDP information system; but it appears certain that if maximum advantage is realized, it will occur in those companies that are organized to conform with the capabilities of the system rather than in those companies that have planned the system to fit current organization structure.

Evaluation of EDP

Few companies have completely integrated data processing systems. However, most EDP installations are hopefully a first step toward an integrated management information system. A question that normally arises whenever the design and installation of EDP is being

---

[9] *Advances in EDP and Information Systems* (New York: American Management Association, 1961), Management Report No. 62, George J. Fleming, "Developing a Practical Data Collection System at Boeing," pp. 82-87. The article by Mr. Fleming is one of 21 reports based on material originally presented at AMA's Seventh Annual Data Processing Conference held in March, 1961.

considered is the matter of cost. It is extremely difficult to develop meaningful figures because each company presents its own unique information needs. Also, rental charges for equipment, depending upon the kind selected and the number of units required, range from a low of $1,000 per month to approximately $200,000 per month. Should the user decide to purchase the equipment, the sales price is roughly equivalent to the rental charges for a four-year period.

There have been isolated instances where the installation of EDP resulted in marked reductions in the number of clerical personnel, as illustrated by the Treasury Department's installation of a computer, programmed to reconcile the government payroll and print the checks, which resulted in a reduction of clerical workers from 755 to 270. In addition, Federal Reserve banks were able to eliminate some 400 employees as the result of this move.[10] However, the personnel reductions experienced by the government are not typical of industry's experience since personnel reductions of this magnitude occur only when an extremely large volume of repetitive clerical work is mechanized. For most companies the number of clerical workers remains the same and many firms have been forced to increase their clerical staff. The reasons for this paradox are not due to the inefficiencies of EDP but are attributable to normal expansion of and the accumulation and use of data not readily available when manual information systems are used.

Although there is a wide variation in information needs among companies and in charges for EDP equipment, there is a fairly stable, predictable pattern of costs.[11] Prior to ordering any electronic equipment a feasibility study, which normally takes about six months to complete, is usually made. At the end of this time, equipment may be ordered, with delivery usually promised in one year. During this year between 15- and 30-man years, at a cost of $10,000 to $12,000 per man-year, may be spent in systems analysis, training, and programming. Also occurring during this period is the necessary remodeling or building of physical facilities to house the EDP installation. The cost of physical facilities may range from $50,000 to $250,000. When the equipment arrives, rental charges begin and for a few months there is little produced, and duplicate manual and electronic systems work side by side.

---

[10] *Use of Electronic Data Processing Equipment,* Hearing before the Subcommittee on Post Office and Civil Service, House of Representatives, 80th Congress, 1st Session (Washington, D. C.: U. S. Government Printing Office, 1959) Appendix A, pp. 34-40.

[11] E. W. Martin, Jr., "Practical Problems of Introducing a Computer," *Business Horizons,* Vol. III (Fall, 1960), pp. 4, 6, 8, 10, 12, 14-16, 84-86. The illustration of cost patterns that appears in the text is taken from this article and is typical of what might be expected to occur as the result of a large installation.

With a machine rental of $30,000 a month, it is possible to have a total of $780,000 invested in feasibility studies, training personnel, programming, physical facilities, magnetic tapes, and the overlap period when both electronic and manual operations are in use. Assuming that the installation is expected to earn $30,000 a month, or $360,000 a year, it is at least a year and a half after the initial study before the break-even point is reached. Another two years beyond the break-even point are required to recover the $780,000 spent prior to the equipment's effective use. Thus, the total recovery point may be at least three and one-half years after the initial feasibility study. The example above is typical of a large installation and it must be recognized that though the dollar amount varies from one installation to another, there is a period of approximately one and one-half years before an installation can be expected to reach the break-even point in respect to current operations, and another two to three years before the total costs are recovered. Thus, it is usually three to four years before any profit may be realized as the result of installing an EDP information system.

In addition to potential earnings resulting directly from a well-planned EDP information system, the major value to be derived from such an installation is the improved effectiveness of the business organization as an information-decision system. Peter Drucker expresses the value of an improved information-decision system as follows: [12]

> The new organization, whether an army or a business, is above all an information and decision system. Information, ideas, questions, flow from the outside environment as well as from people within. They not only have to be perceived and transmitted; the relevant has to be separated from the merely interesting. Then somebody has to make a decision which in turn has to flow back to the places where it can become effective action. Information and decision systems are around us everywhere; every living being is one, and so is every machine. But the organization is probably the most complex.

•   •   •   •   •   •   •   •   •

As you read "The Short-Order Economy," Case Problem 8-B, try to trace the information decision flow in Westinghouse.

---

[12] Peter Drucker, *Landmarks of Tomorrow* (New York: Harper & Brothers, Publishers, 1959), p. 92.

Questions for Study and Discussion

1. Is it possible for an information system to function with one or more of the five components missing? If so, which components could be omitted? If not, why not?
2. Does EDP eliminate the possibility of human error? If not, where is human error most likely to occur?
3. What is meant by "random access" and why is it a desirable feature of a management information system?
4. What is meant by the statement that failure to meet objectives is more often due to an improper design of the system rather than to the shortcomings of the separate components of the system?
5. State what is meant by and give an example of each of the following abbreviations: ADP, EDP, and IDP.
6. When are the meanings of EDP and IDP synonymous?
7. How does EDP aid the manager in making decisions? Does this necessarily mean that the manager's decisions are easier to make?
8. What is meant by the statement that the major problems of installing an information system are people oriented rather than machine oriented?
9. Comment on the statement: Most companies experience a sharp reduction in the number of clerical personnel as the result of an EDP installation.

●   ●   ●   ●   ●   ●   ●   ●   ●

On the outskirts of Pittsburgh, in an old warehouse that once housed transformers, switchgear, and hundreds of other products made by Westinghouse Electric Corp., sits a little machine with a fabulous memory. It is an I.B.M. 1401 computer hooked up to a random-access memory bank that holds some 20 million bits of information. To the observer, the bank is merely a stack of flat disks about the size of long-playing phonograph records. At one side of the

---

Case Problem 8-B
The Short-Order Economy [13]

---

stack, working up and down on a spindle, is a long stylus that flicks in and out among the disks faster than the eye can follow. That little machine is busier than a couple of hundred salesmen, order clerks, stenographers, traffic men, and switchboard operators.

It knows more about the territory—indeed, about scores of territories—than the oldest salesman. It has more information about sales than the smartest sales manager. It remembers far more ac-

---

[13] Carl Rieser, "The Short-Order Economy," *Fortune,* Vol. LXVI (August, 1962), pp. 90-94. Reprinted from the August, 1962, issue of *Fortune* Magazine by Special Permission; © 1962 *Time,* Inc. In addition to the detailed account of Westinghouse's application of electronic data processing, the article presents other applications of data processing.

curately than the stock clerks where the nuts and bolts can be found in any warehouse. It is a wondrous combination of traveling salesman, mathematical genius, and the Sears, Roebuck catalogue. With affectionate pride, the people who work with it call it their "monster." It is revolutionizing distribution at the producers' level, just as the discount merchants discussed earlier in this Fortune series have revolutionized retailing. The distribution of goods has finally begun to get the full benefit of the accumulated technology of the Western world, which for two centuries has been miraculously transforming the production of goods.

What the monster is doing to old Westinghouse is awe-inspiring. It knows all the pertinent facts about some 15,000 customers who buy Westinghouse industrial products directly from the company, including about 500 distributors who in turn supply many thousands of smaller customers. The computer knows each major customer's address, what normal trade discounts he is entitled to. The memory bank stores data about some 60,000 finished industrial products, from large electric motors and line transformers to tiny replacement parts— prices, shipping weights, discount structures, production schedules, and the number of units presently in stock in each of twenty-six field warehouses and nineteen factory warehouses across the U.S. The equipment handles an average of 1,800 orders a day, and on busy days the total may go up to 2,400.

From the moment a salesman in, say, the Seattle office gets an order for an integral horsepower motor and hands it to a clerk, the whole order process is almost completely mechanical. The clerk looks up the number for the motor in a code book thick as a small telephone directory, supplies the customer's code number and the necessary details about the order, and teletypes it to Pittsburgh. From there on the computer takes over. Aside from some handling of data-processing cards, no human hands touch the order until the motor is shipped.

When the order comes in from Seattle, the monster first searches its memory to find the warehouse nearest the customer that has the item in stock. It then adjusts the inventory record. If the stock has now fallen to a predetermined danger point, the electric-motor factory in Buffalo gets the word to put the model back into production. Next the computer reaches into the memory bank for the customer's normal trade discount, figures out the state sales tax, shipping charges, and so forth, and types out an invoice. Finally the computer transmits the order to the proper warehouse, where it emerges a few seconds later from the teletype machine complete with bill of lading, addressed labels for the carton, and instructions telling the order picker what bin to go to.

All this takes no more than fifteen minutes on the average. By startling contrast, before Westinghouse installed the system in 1959, it used to take an average of five days to fill a similar order, five days that were often filled with worry and confusion. First the salesman had to waste precious time checking around to see where the item was in stock. (Now all he has to do is put a query on the teletype and the computer will have word back to him within ten minutes.) If the order was mailed to the warehouse or factory, that took a couple of days, and two or three days more were spent by the clerks figuring out the prices and processing the paper work. In the course of this, likely as not, the impatient salesman got on the phone or the teletype to see if the order had been shipped, and all that accomplished was to help jam up Westinghouse's communications system.

"We were always dealing with history," says David C. McAlister, who is manager of distribution, accounting, and procedures and the chief architect of the computerized ordering system. No one ever quite knew the state of inventories on a national basis because both sales and inventory figures were weeks behind time. Then tendency therefore was to keep large "protective" inventories on hand in order to guard against the danger of running out of stock, which is anathema to a sales manager. Because the whole system was so slow, sales managers also pressed the company to maintain a large network of warehouses so as to be near as many customers as possible. Even so, Westinghouse found itself out of stock on a quarter of the orders received.

The speedy little monster has drastically altered all this. Westinghouse can now ship its orders from any point no matter how far away—even from the factory itself—and still get the goods to the customer faster than it once did. In many instances it can assure overnight delivery. The company has been able to close five of its field warehouses—one of them has been converted into a home for the computer —and some of the remaining twenty-six are scheduled to go. It has also slashed overall inventories, and has cut

stocks of one line of products from $5 million to $1,700,000. Yet Westinghouse now is out of stock on only one out of every twenty orders.

The treasurer's office has been made happy by all kinds of savings. Cash flow has been speeded up by five days because the invoices are mailed out to the customers the day the orders are received. Since the monster does all the bookkeeping, costs have been cut sharply; one factory has reduced its operating costs by more than $200,000 a year. And there has been at least one unexpected financial boon. Westinghouse, like any large industrial company, has a melange of normal trade discount structures for its thousands of products. ("You name it; we've got it," says McAlister.) It is also changing prices constantly. In precomputer days, there was always a lag between the time a price change was announced and the time the news got to the 100-odd Westinghouse sales branches. Now the computer gets the news immediately and applies the new price at once. As a result, Westinghouse realizes an average of about one-half of one percent more on the price of each item.

The sales force has mixed feelings about the new system. McAlister contends that "the salesmen never had it so good." They can assure faster service, and as one sales manager puts it, "We are able to ship when we say we are going to ship." On the other hand, the monster has automated the whole process of selling to a degree that is unsettling to many an older salesman. It used to be that the customer had several days' leeway if he placed an order, then decided to cancel. Now, with lead time down to fifteen minutes, the order has been invoiced and shipped by the time he changes his mind. The salesman then has the unhappy choice of reconvincing the customer that he needs the product—which may be difficult—or of having the goods returned.

McAlister has recently bypassed some salesmen altogether by putting teletype machines right into the offices of a few of Westinghouse's larger industrial customers, enabling them to order directly through the Pittsburgh computer center. "I give 'em a catalog and let 'em buy," says McAlister. "I tell the salesmen that in the future all they will have to do is to carry an oilcan and keep those sending machines well oiled."

For major appliances (washing machines, refrigerators, etc.), Westinghouse has a second ordering system, located at a central shipping point in Columbus, Ohio. The problems here are different, and there is a somewhat lesser degree of automation. One of the important logistical considerations is to save freight costs by assembling full rail carloads of various appliances for pooled shipments to several dealers. Human brainwork is still required for putting together the mix. But the system has achieved enormous gains, similar to those for the industrial goods. The computer has speeded up the time needed to process an order from seven days to three days, has cut overall inventories by 25 percent, and has leveled out seasonal peaks and valleys on the production lines.

Sometime late this fall Westinghouse will cap four years of work by opening a glittering new Tele-Computer Center a few miles from Pittsburgh, built around one wonderfully versatile computer that will handle the work now done by both the Columbus and the present Pittsburgh ordering systems. This newest monster, a Univac 490 Real-Time computer, will be the brain for Westinghouse's entire teletype communication system, linking some 265 offices, factories, warehouses, and sales branches throughout the U.S. and Canada. More than 15,000 messages of all kinds each day will flow directly into Univac, which will sort out the 2,000 to 3,000 specially coded orders for industrial goods and appliances and put them through an even more highly automated process than now exists. (It will eliminate the need for using data processing cards for the industrial goods.) And as a sideshow, the Univac will also be turning out sales, financial, and engineering data for corporate and divisional staffs. "My worst nightmare," says McAlister, "is that someday the machine is going to goof and I'm going to deliver a carload of line transformers to a corner drugstore."

Westinghouse was one of the first corporations to experiment with the application of the computer to the day-to-day problems of distribution, and in four years it has advanced so far with its system that it has become a mecca for U.S. and foreign businessmen who are fascinated by the new possibilities of the electronic era. But many other companies have installed similar systems—General Foods, Armstrong Cork, Clark Equipment, Scott Paper, Chemstrand, and Pittsburgh Plate Glass, just to name a few. Throughout a broad segment of industry, engineers like Westinghouse's McAlister are shaking up sales and order-filling procedures, inventory handling, and production scheduling.

Problems

1. Is the computer thinking or making decisions when it notifies a factory to start production when the stock of a given item has fallen below a specified point? Defend your answer.

2. What are the major advantages realized by cutting the time required to fill an order from 5 days to 15 minutes? Are there any disadvantages?

3. Do you believe that the Westinghouse installation has paid for itself? Why?

4. What organizational problems and changes do you foresee resulting from the use of the "monster"?

CHAPTER 9

Decision Making

John Anderson, a design engineer for Apex Valve Company, believes that he has a secure future with his present employer and expects to continue until his retirement when he hopes to spend more time in his home shop and perhaps develop some patentable ideas. John is 45 years old and has had 15 years of service with Apex. Although there is little chance of his being promoted to chief engineer, he is next in line for the job of chief of the design section, a promotion that would raise his annual salary from $10,000 to $12,000. He likes his present position and has turned down several job offers in defense industries that would have paid more money because, in his opinion, the positions offered were not permanent.

Recently John inherited Anderson's Clothing Store, a men's specialty shop formerly owned by his uncle. The store has a good downtown location, a parking lot next door, and no outstanding major debts. After reviewing his uncle's records, John believes that the store is as profitable as the average for that industry. For the past three years average sales volume has been $100,000; average value of inventory, $25,000; and a net profit of $3,500 a year be-

fore taxes. Currently a temporary manager is employed at $500 a month. Prior to his death, the uncle had drawn a salary of $6,500 a year, which is typical for stores of this size.

In some respects John would like to operate the store as manager; however, he is reluctant to do so as it would mean quitting his present position. He realizes that in order to increase the dollar volume of sales, it is necessary to increase inventory, a step that would necessitate expanding the present building. Expansion is possible because the uncle owned both the store and the parking lot, and the local bank has indicated that the present building can be mortgaged to finance the new construction. But as a matter of good business policy, the bank prefers that any additional inventory be handled on a cash basis. If John leaves Apex Valve Company to manage the store, he can withdraw approximately $7,500 from the retirement fund; the cash value of his life insurance and savings amounts to another $10,000.

Although John has made no attempt to sell the store, he believes that the building, the property including the parking lot, inventory, and goodwill are worth at least $75,000.

Case Problem 9-A

A Personal Choice

Problems

1. What decision do you recommend for Mr. Anderson?

2. What courses of action are available for Mr. Anderson to follow?

3. How do Mr. Anderson's personal goals affect the ultimate decision?

4. Develop a means-end analysis for your recommended solution.

• • • • • • • • •

Chapter 8, "Management Information Systems," concluded with Peter Drucker's observation that organizations are information and decision-making systems. We have examined in some detail the nature of information systems. Now it is necessary to study the decision-making phase of the information and decision-making cycle. In this chapter we analyze the decision-making process, examine the contributions of operations research as an aid to decision making, and conclude with some suggestions to enhance the creative aspect of decisions.

THE DECISION-MAKING PROCESS

Decision making is frequently defined as the selection of one course of action from two or more alternate courses of action. This definition has the advantage of brevity, is easy to remember, and focuses attention upon the essential element of decision making— making a choice. There are also disadvantages in this definition, for it does not emphasize the making of a decision as only one of several steps that occur in sequence as part of an intellectual process. Nor does it indicate that business decisions, if they are to be effective, must be executed or translated into a course of action. However, the definition is satisfactory provided we understand that making a decision is part of a process which includes the following four steps: Definition of Problem, Analysis, Development of Alternate Solutions, and Selection of Decision. A fifth step—although technically not a part of the decision-making process itself—must be included if management decisions are to be effective in meeting company objectives. That step is Execution.[1, 2]

---

[1] Most present-day analyses of problem solving, or decision making as it is called in management literature, are based upon John Dewey's analysis of thinking which includes the following five steps: a felt difficulty, its location and definition, suggestion of possible solution, development by reasoning of the bearings of the suggestion, and further ŏbservation and experiment leading to its acceptance or rejection. These steps are discussed in detail in the following work: John Dewey, *How We Think* (Boston: D. C. Heath & Co., 1910), pp. 68-78.

[2] Peter Drucker, *The Practice of Management* (New York: Harper & Brothers, Publishers, 1954).

Definition of Problem

The intellectual process that culminates in making a decision is referred to as *problem solving* or *reasoning*. It is an activity undertaken by an individual to resolve tensions created by a situation that thwarts his normal course of activity. Problems are personal in their nature in that they thwart the activity of an individual. Herein lies an explanation of the difficulty frequently encountered by managers in securing employee participation in solving company problems—there is no problem for the employee unless the situation creates tensions which may be resolved through problem-solving activity. Employee suggestion systems are an attempt to elicit problem-solving activity through the creation of a problem—how can I get the money?—and offering a suggested means of attaining the goal—suggesting an improvement in company operations. Suggestion plans are successful only to the extent that they create within employees tensions that are capable of resolution as the result of problem-solving activity.

No amount of care and effort in the subsequent steps of analysis and development will yield a decision capable of reaching desired objectives unless the problem is properly defined. It is a common error in the diagnosis of problem situations to confuse obvious symptoms, usually those characteristics that attract attention, with the problem itself. Poor decisions are many times correct solutions to the wrong problem and are considered poor because they do not contribute to stated goals. We have seen in "The Parable of the Spindle," Case Problem 8-A, how an inadequate information system may result in poor human relations. Excessively high manufacturing costs may be attributable to too many people; yet an excess number of workers is a symptom, not a cause. The cause may be due to poor product design, poor scheduling, or excessive equipment breakdown. Likewise, unsatisfactory sales volume may be the result of factors such as incompetent salesmen, an excessively high sales price, an improper channel of distribution, or poor quality of product. It is not easy to differentiate between symptoms and problems. A good way of getting behind the symptom and to the problem itself is to ask *why*: Why are the people upset? Why are manufacturing costs too high? Why is sales volume too low? This approach usually involves listing all the possible causes and consumes considerable time and effort; nonetheless, it is better than solving the wrong problem.

Also, it is helpful to ask the following question: Would the solution to the problem as diagnosed provide an effective means to the desired end or goal? This question is stated diagrammatically as follows:

Problem ⟶ Solution = Means ⟶ End

When enlisting the help of others in solving a problem, it may be necessary to restate the problem in terms understandable to those asked to participate. A sales manager would be well advised to restate the problem of attaining a desired percentage of the market in terms that present a challenge to each salesman. This may be done by having the individual salesman define the problem in his territory and develop a plan that will result in increased sales volume from existing customers and the acquisition of new customers.

Analysis

When the problem has been satisfactorily defined and there is reasonable assurance that its satisfactory solution provides a means to a desired end, the next step is the analysis of available information. At first glance, it may seem that this step implies the gathering and analysis of facts not presently at hand, an assumption which is correct in most instances; however, there are at least two classes of problems that require no additional information for their correct solution. First, there are those problems that clearly fall within the scope of existing policies. One of the major purposes of a policy statement is to provide a predetermined course of action, in effect, a solution to a multitude of similar problems. A personnel director, when asked to decide whether or not an employee's request for early retirement should be granted, has a ready answer after the question is properly defined and it is determined that it falls within the province of the company's retirement policy. The second class of problems not requiring the acquisition of additional information consists of those problems that fall within the decision maker's range of experience. He may possess, as the result of prior experience and training, the factual information and conceptualizations necessary to resolve the question and make a decision. Man's ability to synthesize past experiences so that they form a cohesive network of information that can be used in solving current problems is one of the primary reasons for the emphasis placed upon past experience as a factor in the selection of managers.

For those situations that do not fall within the range of existing policies or within the decision maker's experience background, it is necessary to acquire additional information, a process of "getting the facts." One step that has been taken to assure proper information for analysis is the building of information systems such as the one used by Westinghouse (Case Problem 8-B). When information systems provide a timely flow of relevant information to management, they become information-decision-making systems. Such systems are of particular value in providing the information necessary for decisions concerning production schedules or optimum inventory levels, for they provide up-to-date and accurate information. Even so, there is need for judgment. Too much information may be gathered, with resultant masses of data, not relevant facts. Judgment is also required in determining when it is advisable to make a decision even though all necessary facts have not been acquired or analyzed.

Development of Alternate Solutions

Having defined the problem and analyzed the available information, the decision maker is now ready for the third step, the development of alternate courses of action. Logicians refer to this step as the formulation of hypotheses—tentative explanations or conclusions. Alternate solutions come as the result of weighing the concepts derived from the analysis of data in the preceding step. Concepts are weighed and interpreted in the light of past experience; and continuing effort should be made to rearrange the information of Step 2, Analysis, so that new concepts emerge and, in turn, may be examined and evaluated. Both inductive and deductive reasoning processes are used, and the validity of the tentative conclusions may be tested against the rules of logic.[3] The development of alternatives is usually regarded as the central step of the decision-making process, for it is during this step that creative, or original, solutions to problems come into being. Suggestions for the encouragement of creative solutions to problems are discussed later in this chapter. Operations research techniques and other applications of the computer have been developed as special aids in the development of alternate courses of action. These, too, are discussed later in the chapter.

Selection of Decision

The selection of a decision is the process of making a choice between two or more alternatives. The number and quality of choices available are dependent upon the degree of productiveness and originality employed in the third, or developmental, stage. It is unusual for a manager to have only two alternatives from which he must make his selection; rather, his problem is that of selecting one from many.

---

[3] Robert W. Morell, *Managerial Decision-Making* (Milwaukee: The Bruce Publishing Company, 1960). The student is referred particularly to Chapters 4 through 9, which discuss in considerable detail the rules and application of logic to the solution of business problems.

In addition to the choices that represent new courses of action, there is always one alternative—to do nothing. Volkswagen's decision not to change body styles is in every sense of the word as much a decision as Detroit's annual selection of one body style, from among many, to be adopted for the coming year.

Making the correct choice is not easy. Seldom is there only one correct choice with all others classed as incorrect. Instead, business decisions are neither black nor white; for the most part they are grey. Part of the difficulty in making the final or correct decision stems from the element of risk. It is difficult to assess the probable success or failure of a projected plan since the environment in which business operates is continually changing. In addition to the element of change, incomplete and unavailable data often limit the number and quality of concepts developed during the third stage of the decision-making process. Because of the difficulties encountered in selecting the best decision, the development of criteria for determining the worth of decisions is very important. The following three questions form a basis for judging decisions:

Does the decision contribute toward the attainment of stated objectives? Implied in this question is recognition that a course of action is but a means to an end, and if a proposed solution to the problem does not further the stated objectives, it should not be adopted.

Does the decision represent the maximum degree of economic effectiveness? The decision selected should represent the maximum utilization of all available resources; anything less than this would not contribute toward maximum economic effectiveness.

Is the decision capable of execution? Here we are asking whether or not it is possible to develop a plan to make the decision effective.

The use of the above questions to judge the worth of a decision is another application of the Principle of the Objective, the Principle of Economic Effectiveness, and the Principle of Planning. These principles are also used as criteria in the formulation of policies, and they are useful in evaluating any projected course of action. The act of deciding does not stand for long by itself as a single act; it rapidly merges into a series of actions designed to implement the decision.

Before discussing the fifth and final step of the decision-making process, execution, let us examine some of the difficulties arising in the selection of a decision that are due to the personality characteristics of the decision maker. Prejudice and bias frequently have a marked influence in making the final selection. It is possible for prejudice to be so pronounced that it limits the amount and kind of information acquired in Step 2, Analysis. Persons making decisions should be constantly on guard against the tendency to select one choice over another because it fits in with preconceived notions. Frequently, inability to make decisions is attributable to personal indecisiveness rather than to the intellectual difficulties encountered in selecting the proper choice. Indecisiveness may result from feelings of personal inadequacy and insecurity. Persons with these characteristics are fearful of criticism and tend to magnify the uncertainty of the outcome. We all know that decisions involve risk, but to the insecure person the risks are insurmountable; hence the safest course is to do nothing. Pressure from superiors in the organization merely heightens their feelings of insecurity and reinforces the tendency to put off making a decision. Impulsiveness is the other extreme; a predisposition to jump headlong into a situation without weighing all factors. For these individuals the problem is not one of making decisions; the problem is one of making the correct decision. The executive should be continually aware of the influence that personality exerts in determining choice and the role that it may play in delaying or blocking a decision, for decision making is a rational process only when the influence of personality is recognized and controlled.

Execution

The fifth and final step of the decision-making process, Execution, converts the selected decision into action. Unlike the problem solver who has completed his task when he has found the correct solution to a problem, the manager must follow through to make his choice effective. When measured in terms of contribution to company objectives, there is no difference between no decision at all and an ineffective decision that is not feasible. A decision has been made possible as the result of utilizing the flow of information from both within and without the firm; now the information-decision-making cycle must be completed with information flowing to those persons in the organization who will translate the decision into action. It must be recognized that the current decision is but one of a series and when translated into action, additional problems will arise that will demand solutions and subsequent decisions. The decision to build a new plant in Chicago provides an answer to two questions, whether or not a plant should be built and where it should be located; but it also opens the door to a flood of new questions related to the construction of the plant.

When communicating a decision, every effort must be made to use clear, concise terms understandable by those who will translate the decision into action. Perhaps it will be necessary to point out the logic of the decision and state the reasons for making it. The extent to which such persuasion, or selling, is necessary serves as a measure of the probable success of the decision, since it reveals the degree of participation on the part of those directly affected by the decision. Group participation in both decision making and creative thinking is discussed in the last section of this chapter.

AIDS IN DECISION MAKING

In our discussion of the second step in the decision-making process, Analysis, we mentioned that policies may serve as an aid to decision making provided the problem under consideration falls within the scope of the existing policy. For this reason, policies have sometimes been called *standing plans,* and as such provide the means for making these decisions effective. However, policies and other standing plans are of assistance only in the solution of recurring problems. During World War II, certain mathematical techniques were developed to aid in the resolution of complex military problems and in recent years have been applied to aid managers in their decision making. A general term used to describe these rather sophisticated mathematical techniques is "operations research." The following discussion defines operations research, reviews some of its major techniques and applications, and suggests limitations.

Definition of Operations Research

Operations research (OR), like automation, is a term that apparently means different things to different people. It is, above all else, an application of the scientific method to problem situations; however, the scientific method is not the distinguishing characteristic of OR. Frederick W. Taylor advocated the use of the scientific method as a fundamental approach to management problems, yet we do not consider him a forerunner of operations research. Nor is the decision maker who faithfully follows the five steps of the decision-making process, an application of the scientific method, using operations research techniques. In OR the scientific method is applied to the analysis of the operations of a system rather than to the solution of a specific problem.

The phrase, operations of a system, implies that the problems undertaken by OR are much broader than those susceptible to solution by other decision-making techniques. Examples of operating systems that have been analyzed by operations research are weapons systems, man-machine systems such as aircraft, and business organizations. Further, the research on the system being studied is directed toward an understanding of the functioning of the entire system and ultimate improvement of the degree of control over the operation of the system. The specific techniques of OR demand that the system be represented as a mathematical model; that the solution to the problem be obtained by solving the mathematical equations representing the system (i.e., the model); and in addition, that the obtained solution be tested and recommendations made for its application.

Operations research may be defined as: *(1) an application of the scientific method to (2) problems arising in the operations of a system which may be represented by means of a mathematical model and (3) the solving of these problems by resolving the equations representing the system.*[4]

The following examples are illustrative of applications of operations research to industrial problems.[5]

Locating Warehouses.

A company with a number of products made at three different locations was concerned about the items to be produced at each location and the points at which the items would be warehoused. Freight costs constituted a substantial part of the delivered cost of the material. Operations research showed that what appeared to be a complex and involved problem could be broken into a series of rather simple components. Adaptations of linear programming methods were used to find the warehousing schedule which would minimize freight costs. The study is now being extended to determine the best distribution of products among manufacturing plants and warehouse locations in order to minimize net delivered cost in relation to return on investment.

Allocating Advertising Budget.

A manufacturer of chemical products, with a wide and varied line, sought more rational or logical bases than the customary percentage of sales for distributing his limited advertising budget among products, some of which were growing, some stable, and others declining. An operations research study showed that advertising effectiveness was related to three simple characteristics, each of which could be estimated from existing sales data with

[4] C. West Churchman, Russell L. Ackoff, and E. Leonard Arnoff, *Introduction to Operations Research* (New York: John Wiley & Sons, Inc., 1957), p. 18.

[5] C. C. Herrmann and J. F. Magee, "'Operations Research' for Management," *Harvard Business Review*, Vol. XXXI, No. 4 (July-August, 1953), p. 102. This article presents a complete discussion of the application of OR to management problems.*

satisfactory reliability: (a) the total market potential; (b) the rate of growth of sales; (c) the customer loss rate. A mathematical formulation of these three characteristics provided a rational basis for distributing advertising and promotional effort.

Determining Value of Missionary Sales Effort.

In a company making a line of light machines, the executive board questioned the amount of money spent for missionary salesmen calling on customers. Studies yielded explicit mathematical statements of (a) the relation between the number of accounts called on and the resulting sales volume and (b) the relation between sales costs and manufacturing and distribution costs. These were combined by the methods of differential calculus to set up simple tables for picking the level of promotion in each area which would maximize company net profits. The results showed that nearly a 50% increase in promotional activity was economically feasible and would yield substantial profits.

Setting Time Standards.

An industrial products manufacturer wanted to set time standards as a basis for costs and labor efficiency controls. The operations research group studied several complex operations; expressed the effect of the physical characteristics of products and equipment and the time required to produce a given amount of output in the form of mathematical equations; and then, without further extensive time study or special data collection, set up tables of production time standards according to product characteristics, equipment used, and worker efficiency, which could be applied to any or all of the production operations.

Setting Inventory Levels.

A company carrying an inventory of a large number of finished items had trouble maintaining sound and balanced stock levels. Despite careful attention and continued modification of reorder points in the light of experience, the stock of many individual items turned out to be either too high for sales or inadequate to meet demand. The problem was solved by a physical chemist who first collected data on the variables, such as size and frequency of order, length of production and delivery time, etc.; then set up an assumed system, which he tried out against extreme sales situations, continually changing its characteristics slightly until it met the necessary conditions—all on paper (a technique well known to physical scientists); and thus was able to determine a workable system without cost of installation and risk of possible failure.

Each of the above applications of operations research to industrial problems requires an analysis of the functioning of a system, the construction of a mathematical model, and a solution—obtained by solving the mathematical equations representing the system—which results in greater control over the operations of the system.

OR—Techniques and Applications

The following review of operations research techniques and applications indicates a few major applications of OR and touches briefly upon some of the underlying mathematical techniques.

Linear Programming—Allocation Problems. *Linear programming* techniques are most useful in those situations requiring an optimum allocation of resources. As the name implies, linear programming is concerned primarily in analyzing those relationships capable of being expressed mathematically as linear functions, and in most instances there are several such linear functions operating simultaneously.

One of the classic applications of linear programming is of assistance in determining the location of an additional plant within an existing complex of plants and warehouses. Assume that a company has existing plants in Milwaukee and Philadelphia and that the single product of these plants is being distributed to warehouses in Chicago, St. Louis, New York, and Atlanta. Further, preliminary studies have narrowed the choice of possible new plant sites to Memphis and Indianapolis. If optimum allocation of resources is defined as least cost, including both manufacturing costs and the cost of transporting the finished product from plant to warehouse, a partial statement of the problem is determining which location offers the lower cost. However, the introduction of a new plant into the existing system of plants and warehouses necessitates revision of the allocation of the output of present plants to warehouses; therefore, the problem stated in its entirety is determining which of the two proposed systems offers the lower cost.

In addition to providing solutions to location problems, linear programming also aids in determining the most profitable product mix, whether to make or buy, and economic inventory levels. *Quadratic programming*, like linear programming, is an algebraic technique developed for analyzing those systems whose functions are nonlinear in nature.

Queuing Theory—Intermittent Servicing Problems. *Queuing theory*, sometimes called *waiting-line theory*, is of value in determining the correct balance of factors necessary for the most efficient handling of intermittent service. There are costs involved in having a waiting line, whether it be customers waiting for service in a restaurant or machines waiting to be repaired and returned to production. Time lost in waiting, particularly the downtime of machines needing repair, is also a factor of cost; and if the line is one of impatient customers, sales volume is reduced. In order to eliminate the line or decrease its length, thereby reducing waiting-line costs, it is necessary to increase servicing capacity. In turn, there is an increase in the cost of physical facilities and labor necessary to perform the desired service. The restaurant has to enlarge its seating capacity and hire more waitresses, cooks, and bus boys to reduce its line of waiting customers; the industrial plant needs more maintenance men and a larger stock of repair parts to minimize production losses resulting from idle machines waiting for repair.

Another important factor in determining the optimum size of servicing facilities is time of arrival. Occasionally, actual observations may be made and a tally kept of the exact number of units requiring service during each hour of the workday. In many instances, such observations cannot be carried on for a long enough period of time to produce a stable pattern of work load. The *Monte Carlo* technique is used to produce a sample of random arrivals for those situations where actual observation is impracticable or impossible. Essentially, the Monte Carlo technique provides a large sample of random numbers that may be generated by a computer. From the large Monte Carlo sample, rather precise determinations may be made in regard to the expected servicing load for each hour of the day. Queuing theory is of value in reaching decisions concerning the optimum balance between the cost of service and the cost of having a waiting line; and when combined with the Monte Carlo technique, projections may be made for those situations where the work load varies in a random fashion.

Game Theory—Simulation of System Operation. "War games" have been used for many years as a means of training personnel and testing plans and equipment under field conditions. The process of obtaining the essential qualities of reality without reality itself is known as *simultation*. "Management games" have been developed to provide training in decision making by providing laboratory situations that simulate as nearly as possible real-life operations. The development of management games is incredibly complex, particularly if it is a game involving a situation in which there is a competitor aware of changing conditions—an increase in price or volume of goods produced—and responds with counter moves. At the moment, the application of game theory to business problems has been used primarily for training purposes rather than for solving competitive problems because of the complexities in analyzing and programming the many variables as they exist in real life.

Another example of simulation is the analysis of an actual system through the use of a simulated system programmed into a computer. United Air Lines has simulated the operations of aircraft at New York's LaGuardia Field by running a program of a "station model" on an IBM 704 computer. The elements included in this program are time of day, week, and year; weather conditions; maintenance required; type and length of repair job; availability of spare aircraft; delays in landing or take-off; absenteeism of personnel; and number of maintenance personnel. By varying any one or a combination of factors, the functioning of the system may be observed under changed operating conditions, and subsequent analysis reveals operating efficiencies and cost.[6] Though game theory and simultation have not been developed extensively at present, their future appears to be progressing as a means of training managers and analyzing operations of a system under changing conditions.

Probability Theory—Determining Degree of Risk. Statistical techniques in their simplest form provide a descriptive statement of the characteristics of a group. For example, a wage survey may show that the average wage for tool and die makers in an area is $3.75 an hour. Further analysis, an application of *probability theory,* results in a measure of the reliability or accuracy of the obtained average. A probable error of ±5 cents an hour is interpreted to mean that the chances are 50-50 that the true average wage of all tool and die makers in the area falls between $3.70 and $3.80 an hour. A probable error of ±3 cents an hour indicates that the chances are 50-50 that the true average wage lies between $3.72 and $3.78. Thus, the smaller the probable error, the greater the degree of confidence that can be placed in the average obtained. Measures of probable error are significant when dealing with a sample, or a portion, of an entire population by not only showing the reliability of the obtained data but also by revealing whether or not additional time and money should be spent in securing more information.

Predictions concerning the probable outcome of future events are inferences based upon careful statistical analysis of existing data. Life

[6] Elizabeth Marting (ed.), *Top Management Decision Simulation* (New York: American Management Association, 1957), pp. 50-51. In addition to United Air Line's "station model," a simulated distribution and inventory control model used by Imperial Oil Limited of Canada is presented. There is also a description of the development of the AMA game.

expectancy tables used by insurance companies in setting their rates are statements of the probable death rate expected for each age group of the entire population during the present year. Statistical quality control is another application of the theory of probability. The volume of goods produced in high-speed manufacturing is so great that the cost of inspecting each item produced would be prohibitive. But a detailed inspection of a small sample, say one out of every thousand, and periodic checking of the production equipment make it possible for a quality control supervisor to predict with a high degree of accuracy the number of defective products that may be expected in every thousand produced.

Limitations of OR

Operations research is a direct aid to the decision-making process through its contribution to the steps of analysis and development, and, indirectly, OR forces a clearer statement of the problem. It does not, however, make the final choice nor translate the decision into action. The effectiveness of OR is limited to the analysis and comparison of relationships that may be expressed quantitatively and transformed into a mathematical model. Even so, there are times when the subjective judgment of the decision maker must override the recommendations of OR. Operations research may set the economic level of raw material inventory for an auto manufacturer, but in the face of an impending steel strike, the judgment of the individual executive should control. As yet, OR techniques are not adaptable to the prediction of customer reactions to a given style or color, nor do they clarify alternatives in human relations problems.

CREATIVITY IN DECISION MAKING

In spite of the saying, "There is nothing new under the sun," we all recognize the results of creative thinking. Creativity may range in content and quality from the musicians' "jam" sessions to Einstein's theory of relativity. Whatever the line of endeavor, creativeness is measured by the end result—a new idea, a new product, a new way of doing something, or a new application of existing ideas and products—something new and different.

Creativity is a much sought after talent in the business world, for there is continual need for fresh and original solutions to existing problems. The nature of business problems continually changes, and when a competitor discovers a new and better way of solving these problems, present solutions become obsolete. The environment of any given industry is essentially the same for all companies within that industry. Therefore, in order to gain a competitive edge, it is necessary to develop a better way of doing those everyday things which must be done, or develop something new to do—manufacture a new product. The constantly changing environment resulting in new and different problems and the continual pressure of competition form the basis for the demand for creative decision making.

In considering creativity in decision making we will first relate the steps of creative thinking to those of the decision-making process and include suggestions to improve creativity. Second, we will discuss group participation as a means of stimulating creative thinking.

Steps in the Creative Process

Creative thinking is closely related to the decision-making process; indeed, there is a distinct advantage in considering creative thinking as a special part of the decision-making process. Though slightly different terminology is used to describe the creative process, the number and sequence of steps are the same as those of decision making; however, each process emphasizes a different aspect of the same type of thought processes. Decision making emphasizes the choice, the act of making the decision and its subsequent execution so that there is a commitment of resources and ensuing action. The creative process, on the other hand, emphasizes the uniqueness of the solution, its newness, and to a certain extent, the step immediately preceding the solution, Illumination, thereby stressing the highly individual and personal nature of creativity. When decision making and creative thinking are considered as variations of the same underlying thought processes, we increase the opportunity for truly creative decisions. The following tabular arrangement of the steps of these two processes demonstrates their similarities: [7]

Creative Thinking	*Decision Making*
1. Personal need	1. Definition of problem
2. Preparation	2. Analysis
3. Incubation	3. Development of alternate solutions
4. Illumination	4. Selection of decision
5. Verification	5. Execution

---

[7] Graham Wallis, *The Art of Thought* (New York: Harcourt, Brace, and Company, Inc., 1926). Mr. Wallis identifies the four steps of the creative process as Preparation, Incubation, Illumination, and Verification. The first step, Personal need, has been added since creative thinking is the resolution of a problem.

Personal Need. The adjective, "personal," stresses the individual aspect of the creative thinking process; and, as in the case in decision making, there must be a motivating force to initiate the creative thought process. The motivation of the poet, the artist, or the essayist may be an obscure inner urge, an urge similar to the motivation of the hobbyist who spends countless hours at his bench creating furniture, or the gardener who raises orchids under adverse conditions. The hobbyist and the gardener are mentioned to illustrate that creativity is latent within all of us; the problem, from an industrial point of view, is one of stimulating the innate urge to be creative and channeling creativity into areas of value to the organization. The question arises concerning the ability of an individual to be creative on request, and fortunately the answer is in the affirmative. Advertising agencies produce their creative work on assignment, industrial research departments have been very productive, and many of the outstanding works of literature and art have been produced to meet the demands of externally imposed goals. The decision maker does not seek a solution until confronted with a problem; nor does creative thinking appear until the individual is motivated, either by the need of self-expression or as the result of an externally imposed problem situation.

Preparation. Preparation and the last step, Verification, may properly be called the *work* stages of the creative process. Contrary to popular belief, creative ideas do not come as a "bolt out of the blue." Instead they emerge from an intensive period of preparation. Einstein's theory was developed by Einstein the physicist, not by a musician or a novelist. The Salk vaccine was developed by a physician, not by an architect; and though Coleridge's *Kubla Khan* is said to have appeared to him in a dream, it was preceded by 25 years of study and travel. Preparation is not only a period during which one becomes saturated with information, it is also a period of trying to perceive new and meaningful relationships so that an original solution to the problem may be obtained. The originality of the ultimate solution is dependent to a large extent upon the number of avenues explored and the extent to which all possible interrelationships and solutions have been examined. Taking notes on materials read and keeping a file of clippings may prove helpful in providing source materials for constant review so that all possible combinations may be developed. Perhaps emphasis upon the need for creativity is due to the fact that most decisions are the result of only cursory preparation and examination, with the result that there are only a few commonplace solutions available. Aside from technical libraries for engineering and research groups, few companies maintain libraries so that an executive may saturate himself with the literature of marketing, production control, or quality control prior to undertaking a major decision in one of these fields. If only obvious bits of information are analyzed superficially, it is difficult to visualize a truly creative solution.

Incubation. The intellectual processes that occur during the third step of the creative process, Incubation, mark the difference between a good decision and an original or creative decision. The difference is inferred to a certain extent by the descriptive terms used to describe the third step of the processes of creative thinking and decision making. The word, "development," as applied to the decision-making process, implies the logical sequences of either inductive or deductive thought processes and emphasizes the perception of logical relationships. Seemingly there is an "either or" quality to the choices that must be made, a concept substantiated by the mathematical approach of OR, a process of finding the one best solution and eliminating all other alternatives by measuring each against an objective criterion such as cost. The logical aspects of evaluation provide an accurate and adequate description of the development stage when measurable criteria are available; but when considering an original or creative solution, there are no preconceived objective criteria against which the solution may be tested. In fact, there is no solution in the sense of making one choice from among several apparent choices. Instead, it is a process of finding a new solution, a new arrangement and interpretation of information acquired during the period of preparation. True, it is possible for an original solution to be found immediately or as the result of a relatively brief analysis of information, but this is rare. There is a definite need for the concept of incubation, a period of mulling the problem over, sometimes consciously and sometimes totally unaware of the thinking process. It is during this period of incubation when the creative person may be described as absent-minded; note that the adjective *absent* is used, not *empty*-minded. His mind is absent from the mundane affairs of the world, but present and working on the problem. Some writers ascribe an important role to the "unconscious mind" during the period of incubation. Whatever the nature of the process, it is clear that the period of incubation is a period of gestation and may result in a fully developed creation, or illumination, that solves the problem.

When should one set a problem aside and allow it to incubate? Usually after intensive periods of study and reflection, the phenomenon of *perseveration* appears. Perseveration is easily recognizable because thoughts seem to go around in circles, with no new ideas or interpretations occurring, an indication of fatigue. This is the time when the subject should be dropped momentarily and attention turned to something else, thus permitting incubation to take place. However, it is wise to set a deadline; and if the solution does not appear within a matter of days, review the problem once again and reexamine the notes and other materials acquired during preparation.

Illumination. One of the earliest and most famous illuminations is attributed to Archimedes. We have all heard the story that Archimedes, a Greek mathematician of the third century B.C., shouted, "Eureka" (I've found it), while sitting in his bath and discovering that his body displaced its own volume in water. But how many of us remember the problem that had been occupying his mind during the period of incubation? Archimedes had been assigned a problem by King Hiero of Syracuse who had received a new crown and had reason to believe that not all the gold delivered to the goldsmith had been used in the crown. But how does one determine the volume of an object with the irregular shape of a crown? Archimedes' illumination solves the problem; if gold is adulterated by a lighter metal, the bulk of the crown must be increased to equal the original weight of the gold, and as a result displaces a greater amount of water than an equivalent weight in gold.[8] The story of Archimedes illustrates the suddenness that characterizes creative solutions to problems. There is a period of insight, and the answer appears in a flash. The story also supports two statements made earlier. First, the solution came to one well prepared; the king went to Archimedes, the mathematician and scientist, not to a leading poet of the time; second, truly original and creative solutions are possible when working on an assigned project. When solutions appear, it is suggested that they be jotted down immediately so that every detail may be remembered.

Verification. For most creative thinking, verification represents the second of the "hard-work" stages, the first being Preparation. It is rare that the final solution, even though appearing suddenly and apparently complete, is sufficiently polished to be adopted without further change and modification. For the writer, verification may be a period of vacillation between one mode of expression and another, and changes made may seem to be the result of trial-and-error behavior not unlike that of the laboratory rat seeking its way through a maze. For the inventor, verification is a period of refinement and elimination of minor defects that may mar an otherwise ideal invention. This last stage of creative thinking transforms the insight of illumination into finished form,

---

[8] The goldsmith had alloyed the gold with baser metals and was executed.

whether it be an artistic effort, a new product, or a better way of performing everyday tasks. Charles Babbage's Difference Engine is conceptually the same as the computer, but it remained only an idea, for he was unable to transform it into an operative machine.

Verification implies a willingness to experiment, to modify, and to improve. A good antidote for pride of authorship, which may cause resistance to suggested changes, is to assume the role of the devil's advocate by trying to anticipate and answer potential criticism. We should also recognize that ideas, like mechanical devices, evolve over a period of time and that the solution adopted today may be improved in years to come. How many times have you said to yourself, "Why, I had that idea two years ago"? The difference between the idea and the implemented creative thought is verification, a period of change, improvement, and sometimes compromise to make the idea acceptable. In the last analysis, creativity is judged by quality and quantity of completed work.

Group Participation in Creative Thinking

Thus far, our discussion presents creative thinking as an individual undertaking; certainly illumination is experienced only by the creator of an idea. However, man is a social animal and one of the characteristics of his gregariousness is the influence exerted on him by a group and the effect that he, in turn, has upon other members of the group. Each of us is acquainted with someone who in private conversation is rather quiet and reserved, yet when present at a social gathering blossoms forth and becomes the life of the party. The capacity to be stimulated by a group, and at the same time contribute to shaping the group's behavior is called *social interaction* and forms the basis for successful group participation in creative thinking.

Several techniques have been developed as group aids to creativity and their success is dependent upon the following two basic psychological phenomena:

1. Free association of ideas is a process of producing reactions in the form of ideas in rapid succession with a minimum of inhibiting or restraining action. The original stimulus word is presented by the group leader and immediately the free associations thus produced function as additional stimuli for the group.

2. Social interaction, as defined above, increases the productivity of each individual and his increased productivity further stimulates other members of the group.

A summary of the rules and suggestions for conducting two different types of group sessions in creativity is presented in Table 9-1.[9] Each one of these types, Osborn's brainstorming and the Gordon technique, is discussed below.

Brainstorming. Brainstorming was developed by Alex F. Osborn as an aid in producing ideas for an advertising agency; however, since that time the technique has been applied in many other situations where there is a need for the production of a large number of new solutions in answer to a specific problem. In order to develop the desired quantity of ideas, an atmosphere conducive to the free flow of ideas is created. The group leader informs the participating members of the desired objective, quantity of new ideas, and cautions them against being critical of their ideas. He encourages "free wheeling," and usually all criticism of ideas is barred. Occasionally checklists and suggestions for developing new ideas are distributed to the group. One such list, developed by Osborn, is as follows: [10]

1. Put to other uses
2. Adapt
3. Modify
4. Magnify
5. Minify
6. Substitute
7. Rearrange
8. Reverse
9. Combine

One of the major criticisms of brainstorming is that, by its very nature, it tends to produce rather superficial ideas since the problem is worded in specific terms and thus limits the development of broad free association. Also, the technique may be very time-consuming; for in addition to the man-hours spent in the session itself, time is required to evaluate the ideas produced. Nonetheless, it is a valuable group aid to encourage creative thinking, particularly in those situations where a specific answer is desired such as a name for a new product or an advertising slogan. Above all else, it tends to create an atmosphere within the organization that encourages individual creative thinking long after the session has ended.

Gordon Technique. William J. J. Gordon developed a technique to meet the needs of Arthur D. Little, Inc., a consulting group specializing in industrial research and other technical problems. The participants of a Gordon session, unlike those of a brainstorming group, are

---

[9] Charles S. Whiting, "Operational Techniques of Creative Thinking," *Advanced Management* (October, 1955), pp. 24-30.* In addition to the Osborn and Gordon techniques, Mr. Whiting discusses several forced-relationship methods.

[10] Alex F. Osborn, *Applied Imagination* (New York: Charles Scribner's Sons, 1953), p. 284.

Table 9-1

SUMMARY OF RULES AND SUGGESTIONS FOR GROUP SESSIONS

Osborn Brainstorming

Rules:

1. Judicial thinking or evaluation is ruled out.
2. Free wheeling is welcomed.
3. Quantity is wanted.
4. Combinations and improvements are sought.

Suggestions for the Osborn technique:

1. Length: 40 minutes to one hour, sessions of 10 to 15 minutes can be effective if time is short.
2. Do not reveal the problem before the session. An information sheet or suggested reference material on a selected subject should be used if prior knowledge of a general field is needed.
3. Problem should be clearly stated and not too broad.
4. Use a small conference table which allows people to communicate with each other easily.
5. If a product is being discussed, samples may be useful as a point of reference.

Gordon Technique

Rules:

1. Only the group leader knows the problem.
2. Free association is used.
3. Subject for discussion must be carefully chosen.

Suggestions for the Gordon technique:

1. Length of session. two to three hours are necessary.
2. Group leader must be exceptionally gifted and thoroughly trained in the use of the technique.

General Suggestions That Apply to Both Techniques

1. Selection of personnel: a group from diverse backgrounds helps. Try to get a balance of highly active and quiet members.
2. Mixed groups of men and women are often more effective, especially for consumer problems.
3. Although physical atmosphere is not too important, a relaxed pleasant atmosphere is desirable.
4. Group size: groups of from four to twelve can be effective. We recommend six to nine.
5. Newcomers may be introduced without disturbing the group, but they must be properly briefed in the theory of creative thinking and the use of the particular technique.
6. A secretary or recording machine should be used to record the ideas produced. Otherwise they may not be remembered later. Gordon always uses a blackboard so that ideas can be visualized.
7. Hold sessions in the morning if people are going to continue to work on the same problem after the session has ended; otherwise hold them late in the afternoon. (The excitement of a session continues for several hours after it is completed, and can affect an employee's routine tasks.)
8. Usually it is advisable not to have people from widely differing ranks within the organization in the same session.

Source: Charles S. Whiting, "Operational Techniques of Creative Thinking," *Advanced Management* (October, 1955), p. 28.

not aware of the specific problem under consideration. For example, if the desired result is an improved method of dehydrating food, the key word selected might be preservation, a stimulus which would elicit suggestions for the preservation of many items other than food. Also, it must be remembered that the Gordon technique was developed for the highly trained designers of the Arthur D. Little organization. Proponents of Gordon's approach claim that the technique results in a higher quality of ideas since the generic key word does not tend to limit ideas, nor is there the likelihood of a member developing pride of authorship as he has no information concerning the application of his idea. Further, many of the ideas produced may be of value in later projects. If the leader is highly skilled and the participants have both depth and breadth of knowledge in the field in question, the Gordon method is an excellent means of generating new ideas.

Continuing Conditions for Creativity

The real lesson to be learned from brainstorming and the Gordon technique is that ordinary people under proper circumstances may create new ideas. The free association device employed by both techniques is applicable to individual problem-solving situations; the only factor absent is the stimulation of a group. Companies can contribute a great deal to continuing creativity by developing an atmosphere that encourages new ideas. Organizations that discourage new ideas with the comment, "We tried that 20 years ago and it didn't work," are in effect telling their employees not to think. In the next major part of this book, "The Organizing Function," some of the benefits derived from group participation in creative thinking and other forms of decision making are discussed.

●　●　●　●　●　●　●　●　●

Case Problem 9-B offers an interesting opportunity for a group to use either the Osborn or the Gordon technique in finding a creative solution to a business problem.[11]

---

[11] Theodore Levitt, "M-R Snake Dance," *Harvard Business Review*, Vol. XXXVIII, No. 6 (November-December, 1960), pp. 76-84. Mr. Levitt presents an interesting analysis of the sameness that appears in much advertising. "M-R Snake Dance" provides a good background for Case Problem 9-B.

Questions for Study and Discussion

1. Why is the fifth step, Execution, included as part of the decision-making process even though it may be argued that execution is not a part of decision making?

2. In defining a problem, how does one distinguish between the symptoms resulting from the problem and the problem itself?

3. Give an example of a correct decision to an improperly defined problem.

4. Give several examples of the need for restating problems in terms that are understandable to those who are asked to help in solving the problem.

5. What is the relationship between established policies and decision making? Give an example of a recurrent business decision that could be eliminated by establishing a policy.

6. Why is experience valuable in making decisions? What are some of the dangers in relying too heavily on experience in decision making?

7. What is meant by the term operations research? What is the relationship between OR and the scientific method?

8. Discuss the following statement: Most modern applications of OR would be impossible without the aid of the computer.

9. What are the similarities and differences that exist between the creative-thinking process and the decision-making process? Give the arguments for and against the thesis that creative thinking is a special case of the decision-making process.

10. Give an instance from your own experience when you have said, "I thought of that." Was your failure to complete the creative process the result of not verifying your solution or the lack of adequate preparation?

11. Comment on general suggestion No. 8 in Table 9-1.

● ● ● ● ● ● ● ● ●

For many years, Dordon, Dobson, and Duke, Inc., a large and well-known advertising agency, has retained the Sea Captain Tobacco account. Sea Captain is manufactured and distributed by the Carolina Tobacco Company, and its slogan, "The Captain's Choice," is well known to pipe smokers throughout the world. In addition to its pipe tobacco, Carolina manufactures and distributes an established brand of snuff.

> *Case Problem 9-B*
> *Another Mentholated*
> *Cigarette*

As part of a planned expansion program, now two years old, the company is ready to introduce a mentholated cigarette. In a recent conference with Mr. Dordon, senior partner and founder of the advertising agency, Mr. Walter Davis, the president of Carolina Tobacco Company, made the following remarks:

"It seems to me that when people buy cigarettes, or for that matter any other item at a drugstore counter, they are buying on impulse until they firmly decide upon a particular brand. This is one of the reasons why we want to enter the mentholated cigarette market; as yet, with the exception of Kools, all the brands are relatively new and none are as firmly established as, say, Camels are in the nonmentholated field.

"I can't make any special claims for our cigarette; it is no better, nor is it any worse than any of the others. We have no secret process in making it, and we can hardly claim that it is good for anyone's health. We do think that people will enjoy it as much as they do any other cigarette of the same type.

"Yesterday when I stopped at a drug-store counter, I was overwhelmed by the number of mentholated cigarettes on display. All the packages seem to be green or blue, with ice or waterfalls, and with beautiful young girls on the point-of-sale display smiling as though they were refugees from a toothpaste advertisement. I don't think we have the money to buck that kind of advertising; anyway, we don't want to be just one more green-packaged waterfall. Frankly, one of the reasons for the success of our Sea Captain is that it is packaged in an octagonal can, while every other can on the market is square or round. People can recognize our product for what it is. Also, as you know, our snuff is packaged in a triangular shaped tin which makes it distinctive. And, thanks to you people, our copy for these products has been different."

Problems

1. Working within the framework suggested by Mr. Davis, develop a name, a package design, and the initial advertising copy for Carolina Tobacco Company's mentholated cigarette.

2. Do you agree with Mr. Davis' desire to develop a new and different approach for advertising mentholated cigarettes? (The article mentioned in footnote 11 will be of help in formulating your answer to this question.)

3. How much originality is evident in the advertising of competitive products within the same price range; e.g., Cadillac, Lincoln, and Imperial?

● **CHAPTER 10**

Organization Theory

"Good morning, gentlemen." Robert Billings, vice-president for manufacturing of Centroid Corporation, paused and briefly surveyed the group of five management trainees reporting to the manufacturing division for a two-month training period. "I note here that your previous assignment was in the personnel department," he continued as he shuffled a sheaf of personnel folders. "Now, let me tell you how personnel really works in the manufacturing division of this company."

"First, each of you men will be assigned to a general foreman who is in charge of one of the major areas of the shop. You will report directly to the general foreman. If, for any reason, you want to see me you must first go to the general foreman and ask his permission; he will, in turn, send you to the plant manager, and if he can't answer your question, arrangements

---

Case Problem 10-A
What Kind of Organization?

---

will then be made for you to see me on Saturday mornings or after 5 o'clock on weekdays.

"This is a large plant, about 1,500 employees, and we have a problem with absenteeism. We also have a provision for sick pay in our union contract. When a man calls in and says that he is sick, I want you to get in touch with the industrial relations department immediately and have them send one of the industrial nurses out to the man's home.

"The third point I want to make with you fellows is in regard to shop rules. We're known around here as 'tough but fair' and I want it kept that way. If you see any workman breaking one of the rules, give him a verbal warning if it is the first time—and be sure and make a written record of the fact that you gave him a verbal warning. If it is his second offense, issue a written reprimand; and if it is the third time, suspend him for five working days. The fourth offense usually means discharge. Turn these cases over to your general foreman.

"Grievances are next. We have a lot of them, and we go by the book in the way we handle them. According to our labor contract a foreman has 24 hours before he has to answer a grievance. I expect you to take the full 24 hours. The plant manager has three days in which to give his answer, and I have one week after that before writing my answer. We intend to take all of the time allotted to us in handling grievances; that way it discourages the filing of petty complaints.

"Fourth, you are going to have to watch quality. Quality is very important to us, so the first thing you should do every morning is find out whether or not the quality control inspector is in your area. If any questions arise during the day, turn the problem over to him. He knows how the machines should be set and he will tell the operators what to do.

"We have a suggestion system here in the plant. If any of your men come up with a suggestion, have him put it in writing on the proper forms. Sign these forms, then forward them to the industrial engineering department. They will check them out and write a letter to the worker telling him whether or not his suggestion is accepted. Usually it takes from 60 to 90 days to get an answer from them. Incidentally, foremen do not participate in the suggestion program; it's part of your job to have new ideas so you don't get paid extra for them. One or two foremen, who are no longer with us, gave their ideas to men working for them and then split the award. Don't try it.

"Number 6 on my list of things to cover with you concerns job openings. Keep your eyes open for good, hard workers; these are the men we want to promote. We notify the man chosen for promotion when an opening occurs; and if the union thinks that we have not followed seniority, they file a grievance. We don't allow people to transfer from one department to another, so if a man starts in the shipping department, where the rates aren't too high, that's his tough luck. In this company you live and die in the department you start in.

"Finally, I want to say that we have openings on our manufacturing team for two or three of you fellows. Those of you who demonstrate true leadership ability and originality will be kept on permanently. Good luck!"

Problems

1. Does the manufacturing division of Centroid Corporation subscribe to the tenets of Theory X, Theory Y, or Theory Z?
2. Which assumptions regarding the nature of work and/or the nature of human beings underlie each of the seven points made by Mr. Billings?
3. How would you, as a management trainee, demonstrate originality and leadership in this situation?
4. How can an hourly production worker develop personally in his job at Centroid Corporation?

It is a truism that organizations are a major force in determining the course of our lives; yet few of us recognize the extent to which organizations shape our behavior. We are born in hospitals and immediately the process of adapting to formal organization begins; for the hospital, an organization, imposes a schedule of eating, sleeping, and bathing. There is a brief respite from formal organizations during the next five years; then at the age of six, when school begins, we are members of a succession of formal organizations—grade and high school, college, and the places where we work. Retirement from active employment does not mean retirement from organizations, for usually membership in social clubs, civic organizations, and churches continues.

The word, organization, has two distinct meanings, one of which refers to *an* organization as an *entity* in itself, and the other one which refers to organization as a *process*. Some of the more common organizations, as entities, are mentioned above—schools, places of employment (including industrial organizations, governmental agencies, or private institutions), social clubs, civic service organizations, and churches. There are three characteristics common to each of the organizations above: first, each is composed of people; second, each has a distinct purpose or goal to achieve, thus offering a reason for its existence; and third, each has a degree of formality in the structure of the organization that results in a definition and limitation of the behavior of its members. *Thus, as an entity, an organization is a group of people bound together in a formal relationship to achieve organizational goals.*

The second meaning of organization is that it is a *process of structuring, or arranging, the parts of the organization;* a meaning exemplified by the phrase, "what this place needs is more organization." The question arises, what is being organized? There are three possible answers to this question; first, *work* is being organized; second, *people* are being organized; and third, *systems* are being organized. The answer you choose as being most descriptive of the process of organization is dependent upon certain fundamental assumptions in regard to the nature of work and the behavior of human beings in a work situation. These assumptions, known as theories of organization, are important for they determine the structure of an organization and the methods used in administering the organization. The theoretical framework leading to the conclusion that organization is a process of organizing *work* is known as *Theory X*; those assumptions concluding in the belief that *people* are the central theme of organization form *Theory Y*; and an approach that emphasizes the organization of a *system* is designated as *Theory Z*.

THEORY X—A WORK-CENTERED APPROACH

Underlying every management action is a set of assumptions concerning the nature of work and the nature of human beings. Theory X is a group of assumptions that results in what is referred to as the traditional, or classical, approach to organization.[1] In discussing Theory X, let us first examine the basic assumptions concerning work and the nature of human beings in a work situation.

Assumptions of Theory X

Theory X is the traditional, or classical, approach to organization and rests upon four basic assumptions. The first of these assumptions is concerned with the nature of work, and the remaining three describe the behavior of human beings in a work situation.

1. *Work, if not downright distasteful, is an onerous chore to be performed in order to survive.*
2. *The average human being has an inherent dislike of work and will avoid it if he can.*
3. *Because of this human characteristic of dislike of work, most people must be coerced, controlled, directed, threatened with punishment, to get them to put forth adequate effort toward the achievement of organizational objectives.*
4. *The average human being prefers to be directed, wishes to avoid responsibility, has relatively little ambition, wants security above all.*[2]

Briefly, Theory X states that there is no intrinsic satisfaction in work, that humans avoid it as much as possible, that positive direction is needed to achieve organizational goals, and that workers possess little ambition or originality. Let us assume that Theory X is an accurate statement of conditions as they exist today. How do these assumptions affect the structure and processes of an organization?

---

[1] Douglas McGregor, *The Human Side of Enterprise* (New York: McGraw-Hill Book Company, 1960), pp. viii, 246. Professor McGregor summarizes the assumptions of traditional management under the heading, Theory X, and presents those assumptions which result in a human relations approach to management under the heading of Theory Y. The theoretical assumptions of both theories are presented in Part I of the book; Part II is a discussion of Theory Y in practice; and Part III is a discussion of the development of management talent.

[2] Douglas McGregor, *ibid.,* pp. 33-34. Assumptions 2, 3, and 4 are quoted directly from McGregor. Assumption 1 has been added as an explicit statement of the nature of the work to which humans are reacting. For a good treatment of work theory, see Dale Yoder, *Personnel Management and Industrial Relations* (5th ed.; Englewood Cliffs, N. J.: Prentice-Hall, Inc., 1962), Chap. 5, "Theories in Management: Work Theory," pp. 56-77.

Effect of Organization

Adherence to Theory X results in a *work-centered* organization. As noted earlier, one of the characteristics of an organization is that it has a goal—a *raison d'étre*. It is normal to be concerned about the work of an organization, and when work is distasteful, something to be avoided like the plague, firm steps must be taken to assure its accomplishment. An external force is needed to accomplish organizational objectives under the conditions prescribed in Theory X. This force is dependent upon the traditional concept of authority; indeed, it is so dependent upon authority that organizations which subscribe to Theory X are frequently referred to as *authoritarian* organizations. Once the foundation of an organization has been laid upon the cornerstone of authority, the location of the decision-making process is determined, the organizational structure acquires certain characteristics, and the roles of the supervisor and the individual member of the organization are sharply defined.

Authority. Authority has been succinctly defined as *the right to command and the power to exact obedience,* a definition that raises two questions: (1) the source of the *right* and (2) the method of *power*. One source of authority, used by the early European monarchies, is expressed by the phrase, the divine right of kings. A corresponding point of view applied to the management of industrial enterprises regards authority as emanating from the right to own property and the attendant obligation to manage that property. The power of the monarchist in enforcing obedience is absolute, for he can exact the supreme penalty, death, if need be. In the industrial situation the supreme penalty for disobedience is discharge, a penalty that prohibits an employee from fulfilling his economic needs. It is interesting to note that many arbitrators, when writing decisions concerning the discharge of an employee, equate the death penalty to discharge by an employer. We will see when we discuss Theory Y that there is another concept of authority, but Theory X rests upon an assumption of complete authority as the motivating force directing the course of the organization.

Location of Decision Making. The analogy of a political monarchy and a highly authoritarian industrial organization continues as an effective means of describing the location of the decision-making process. In the monarchy, decision making is highly centralized and located at the apex of the organization, the king, since it is the king who has the divine right to command. For the authoritarian industrial organization, the nominal head of the organization is the locus of the decision-making process; again this is a logical location when the right to manage is derived from ownership. Centralized decision making requires a certain form of organizational structure if the decisions are to be carried out effectively.

Organization Structure. When authority to make decisions is centralized at the top of the organization and its primary purpose is the accomplishment of work, a structure must be designed that permits (1) the ready exercise of authority at all levels of the organization, and (2) maximum effectiveness in the accomplishment of work.

Figure 10-1 is a model showing the structure of the traditional work-centered, or authoritarian, organization. Note that authority to manage flows from the owners through the board of directors to the president who is appointed by the board. Reporting to the president are several vice-presidents, each of whom is in charge of a specific phase of the work of the organization. Figure 10-1 is an exploded diagram of the organization reporting to the vice-president, manufacturing; similar pyramidal structures could be developed for each of the other vice-presidents. Reporting to the manufacturing vice-president is the manager in charge of a specific manufacturing unit, a plant. The major operations of the plant—receiving, machining, assembly, and shipping—are assigned to four general foremen who report to the plant manager. The general foremen direct the efforts of foremen who are in charge of the operating departments within each of the four major functions. Four assistant foremen, each of whom directs the work of a specific area, report to each foreman; and, finally, production employees report to their respective assistant foreman.

Figure 10-1 refers to production workers as *rank and file* employees, a phrase borrowed from the military expression used to describe the rows and columns of the infantry platoon. Another military phrase, *chain of command*, is used to describe the means of transmitting the president's authority so that ultimately production employees produce the desired work. Authority is transmitted through a chain of command, the successive levels of management, between the president and the production worker. When Figure 10-1 is read from top to bottom, the chain of command, which permits the ready exercise of authority at all levels in the organization, is easily followed; and when viewed from left to right, the division of the organization into units of work is apparent.

Role of Supervisor. The pyramidal structure of the organization determines the role, or function, assumed by the supervisor. First, he is an integral part of the chain of command, and as such it is his func-

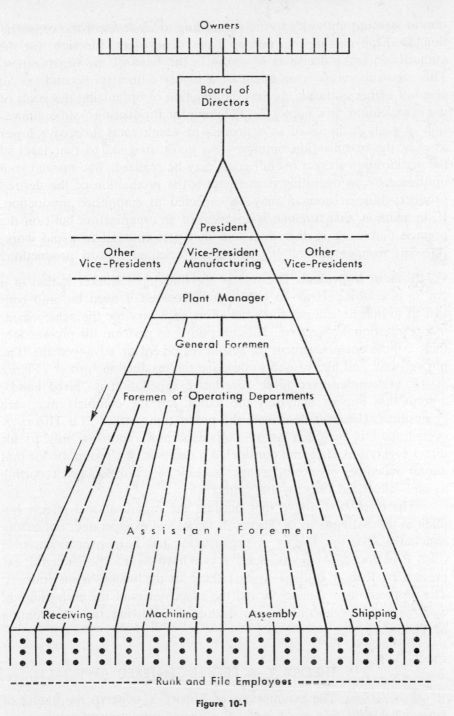

Figure 10-1

PYRAMIDAL STRUCTURE OF TRADITIONAL ORGANIZATION

tion to transmit authority to the succeeding lower level of the organization. Decision making is a minor, if not nonexistent, function, for the authority to make decisions is vested in the head of the organization. Thus, the supervisor is an agent of a higher authority. Second, as an agent of higher authority, he has the function of optimizing the goals of the organization. In Chapter 7, "Planning for Production," suboptimization of goals is discussed as a process in which each successive lower level of the organization optimizes the goals assigned to that level of the organization so that overall goals may be realized. The normal goal optimized by an operating department is the production of the desired product; thus, a foreman may be expected to emphasize production. If, in addition, that foreman is an agent of an organization built on the premise that work is distasteful and that persons tend to avoid work, is it any wonder that all his efforts are oriented toward production?

Role of Individual. The role of the individual worker is that of a cog in a machine. He is to be directed, coerced if need be, and controlled so that he will put forth the effort necessary for the achievement of organizational objectives. His function is to perform his present job; there is little encouragement for self-development or advancement. The phrase, rank and file, is used to describe the production worker (Figure 10-1); perhaps an even more descriptive appellation is "hired hand," a term that implies that only the hands, not the complete man, are being hired. However described, the production worker in a Theory X organization is regarded as an individual unit reporting only to his direct supervisor. He is not considered a member of a group, or for that matter a member of several groups; instead, he stands isolated reporting to and influenced only by his supervisor.

The discussion above that outlines the organizational effects implicit in the assumptions of Theory X may seem exaggerated, but before concluding that the Theory X organization has been overdrawn, read Case Problem 10-A again. Surely, you have heard the thoughts expressed by Robert Billings when talking to the management trainees. The propositions of Theory X and the effectiveness of the authoritarian, work-centered organizations are evaluated following the presentation of Theory Y.

THEORY Y—A PEOPLE-CENTERED APPROACH

The assumptions of Theory Y concern the nature of human behavior that are based upon an interpretation of modern behavioral sciences. The same format used in the presentation of Theory

X is used in presenting Theory Y; first, the assumptions of the theory are stated and, second, the consequent effects of these assumptions upon the organization are reviewed.

Assumptions of Theory Y

The assumptions of Theory Y are the antitheses of the point of view stated by Theory X. The six assumptions of Theory Y are as follows:

1. *The expenditure of physical and mental effort in work is as normal as play or rest.* The average human being does not inherently dislike work. Depending upon controllable conditions, work may be a source of satisfaction (and will be voluntarily performed) or a source of punishment (and will be avoided if possible).
2. *External control and the threat of punishment are not the only means for bringing about effort toward organizational objectives. Man will exercise self-direction and self-control in the service of objectives to which he is committed.*
3. *Commitment to objectives is a function of the rewards associated with their achievement.* The most significant of such rewards, e.g., the satisfaction of ego und self-actualization needs, can be direct products of effort directed toward organizational objectives.
4. *The average human learns, under proper conditions, not only to accept but to seek responsibility.* Avoidance of responsibility, lack of ambition, and emphasis on security are general consequences of experience, not inherent human characteristics.
5. *The capacity to exercise a relatively high degree of imagination, ingenuity, and creativity in the solution of organizational problems is widely, not narrowly, distributed in the population.*
6. *Under the conditions of modern industrial life, the intellectual potentialities of the average human being are only partially utilized.*[3]

Effect of Organization

Adherence to Theory X results in work-centered, authoritative organizations. Theory Y is an approach to organizational problems that emphasizes human relations and results in an organization characterized as *participative*. The two forms of organization, authoritative and participative, are the extreme points of a continuum. Between these poles are many gradations and shades of organizational behavior. One writer distinguishes the following steps: (1) exploitive authoritative, (2) benevolent authoritative, (3) consultative, and (4)

---

[3] Douglas McGregor, *ibid.*, pp. 47-48.

participative group.[4] Thus, when discussing the effect of the propositions of Theory Y on organizational structure and processes, it is well to remember that we are dealing with the other end of the continuum in order to present in clear, sharp lines the differences existing between the two approaches.

Authority. Authority, as presented when discussing Theory X, is the right to command and the power to enforce obedience. However, there is more to authority than right and power as illustrated by the following brief story:

> An agent for the Textile Workers Union of America likes to tell the story of the occasion when a new manager appeared in the mill where he was working. The manager came into the weave room the day he arrived. He walked directly over to the agent and said, "Are you Belloc?" The agent acknowledged that he was. The manager said, "I am the new manager here. When I manage a mill, I run it. Do you understand?" The agent nodded, and then waved his hand. The workers, intently watching this encounter, shut down every loom in the room immediately. The agent turned to the manager and said, "All right, go ahead and run it." [5]

Unquestionably the manager has the right to run a plant, and it is possible, under certain circumstances, for him to exercise his power and discharge all workers for engaging in an unauthorized work stoppage. Then he can start anew with a different group of workers, but this seems the hard way to manage a plant. Theory Y presents man as a rational being who is willing to work; in fact, he must work if he is to satisfy deep-seated psychological needs (propositions 1 and 3). Also, he has intelligence and is capable of making his own decisions. Among the decisions that man makes is that of deciding *which* leadership he will accept. The above incident does not portray a situation in which there is no authority; on the contrary, there was a great deal of authority—in the hands of the agent for the union. The workers in the mill had decided to accept one source of authority and reject another source. Thus, *acceptance* of authority, rather than right of authority, is one of the major differences between Theory Y and Theory X.

If authority based upon the concept of the right to command is displaced by authority which must be accepted to be effective, what

---

4 Rensis Likert, *New Patterns of Management* (New York: McGraw-Hill Book Company, 1961), Chap. 14, "A Comparative View of Organization," pp. 222-236. This book is recommended as a summary of research in organizational behavior and leadership.

5 Douglas McGregor, *op. cit.,* p. 23.

happens to power? Power, too, is displaced. Look at proposition 2 of Theory Y, which states that "man will exercise self-direction and self-control in the service of objectives to which he is committed." One tool available to management as a replacement for power in gaining an employee's commitment to organizational objectives is *persuasion*; another means of assuring commitment is to afford an opportunity for *participation* in the setting of objectives.

Location of Decision Making. Setting objectives is one form of decision making and, according to Theory X, is retained by the nominal head of the organization. Proposition 5 of Theory Y states that "the capacity to exercise a relatively high degree of imagination, ingenuity, and creativity in the solution of organizational problems is widely, not narrowly, distributed in the population." Under these circumstances it is no longer necessary to retain decision making in the hands of a few. As a result, decision making in the Theory Y organization is widespread and diffuse, and it may occur at any level of the organization. Herein lies the meaning of participation; it is participation in decision making, including the determination of objectives.

Organization Structure. Figure 10-1 shows the pyramidal structure of the typical traditional organization with successive layers of supervision and the development of work functions for each supervisor. The relationships between superior and subordinate at any level of the organization appear in the usual organization chart as shown below.

Figure 10-2 emphasizes the work-centered aspects of the organization. Each subordinate is in charge of a specific function. It is an organization constructed primarily for the downward flow of authority in order to accomplish work. Communications between superior and subordinates are illustrated in Figure 10-3.

Figure 10-2

THE TYPICAL RELATIONSHIP BETWEEN SUPERIOR
AND SUBORDINATES

Figure 10-3

INTERPERSONAL RELATIONSHIPS IN THEORY X
ORGANIZATION

Figure 10-3 implies that interpersonal face-to-face relationships occur only between a superior and each subordinate in succession. The individual is the basic unit of the organization, and at best there can be no more than two-way communication between superior and subordinate. Earlier in this chapter an organization was defined as a *group* of people bound together in a formal relationship to achieve organizational goals. Theory Y emphasizes that organization has to do with groups and that when an individual accepts organizational goals, he does so as a member of a group. Thus, the group, not the individual, becomes the basic unit of organization. The reasons for recognizing the group as the basic unit are found in proposition 3 of Theory Y. Since the degree of commitment to organizational objectives is a function of the rewards derived from satisfying ego and self-actualization needs, which include participation in and recognition by a group, it is logical that superior and subordinates be considered a functional group. The large triangle of Figure 10-4, enclosing superior and subordinates, is one way of representing the group as the primary organizational unit. Figure 10.4 also illustrates the free communication of ideas between every member of the group.

Role of Supervisor. Under the conditions of Theory X, the supervisor, a vital link in the chain of command, is an agent of higher authority. As such, it is his role to optimize the goals of the organization by directing the efforts of the individuals who report to him. But Theory Y replaces authority with the concept of acceptance and replaces power with persuasion and participation. Also, the supervisor is no longer dealing with individuals; he is now working with a group and in addi-

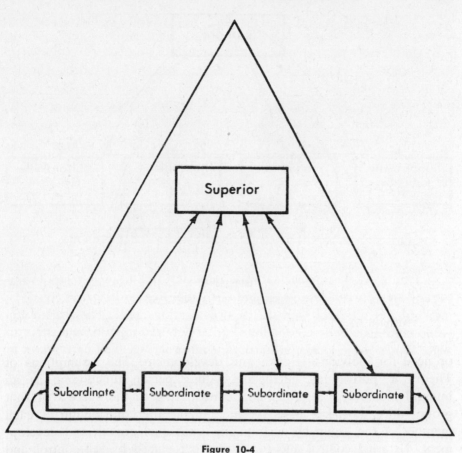

Figure 10-4

SUPERIOR-SUBORDINATE FUNCTIONING AS A GROUP

tion he is a member of that group. Thus, he has an *intragroup* function of leading his own group. At the same time he is a member of a supervisory group which means that he has an *intergroup* function to perform —coordinating the efforts of the two groups to which he belongs. Likert refers to this coordinative function as the "linking pin" function.[6] Note the arrows in the heavily shaded areas of Figure 10-5; these are the linking pins which denote that the supervisor has an intergroup and an intragroup coordinative function.

Role of Individual. Theory X regards the individual as an isolated worker whose function is that of a cog in a machine. His responsibility is limited to quality and quantity of production, control of his work is ever present and from external sources, and there is little opportunity

─────────

[6] Rensis Likert, *op. cit.,* pp. 113-115.

Figure 10-5

THE "LINKING PIN" FUNCTION *

* Adapted from Likert, *ibid.*, p. 113.

or need for individual growth and development. The assumptions of Theory Y portray an intelligent, willing person functioning as an integral member of a group and contributing to the success of that group; thus, the need arises for maximizing the contribution of each member of the group by encouraging individual growth and development. External control and coercion are replaced by self-control and motivation derived from satisfying ego and self-actualization needs. The individual is creative and should participate in determining the objectives of his group, for it is through the act of participation that the goals of the organization and the goals of the individual become congruent. It must be remembered that although Theory Y encourages individual growth and development, the employee is not an isolated individual; rather, he is a participating member of a group and the group is the smallest functioning unit of the organization.

Evaluation of Theories X and Y

Before presenting a third approach to organization, Theory Z, a summary statement of the positions of Theory X and Theory Y and an evaluation of the two theories are in order. One such summary, perhaps an oversimplification, asserts that Theory X describes "organizations without people," while Theory Y presents "people without organizations." [7] The characterization of Theory X as organizations without people comes from the observation, supported in many but not all instances by sound research, that the traditional *organization* experiences low production, not as the result of an inability to perform but rather as the result of deliberate restriction of output, and any attempt to increase output merely aggravates the situation. Conflict arises between the various subunits of the organization and between individual workers and their supervisors. Under such conditions worker morale is low, there is little job satisfaction, and workers withhold any creative ideas they might have. Thus, measured either from the standpoint of productive output or in terms of worker satisfaction, the traditional organization makes a poor showing. Theory Y attempts to correct these shortcomings by emphasizing the importance of psychological needs and stressing democratic processes as a means of fulfilling these needs. It is implied that work will take care of itself. Again, there is significant research to support the emphasis on human relations and the satisfaction of individual needs as the basis for designing organizational structure and determining administrative practices; but the evidence is not conclusive for there are some instances where Theory Y organizations, measured either in terms of worker satisfaction or productive output, are not as effective as the traditional organization.

Both theories suffer from too much generalization in that sweeping statements are made concerning work and human behavior in a manner that implies that all work and all behavior are thus and so. A study of the findings of both sociology and psychology tells us that such generalizations are not a correct statement of conditions as they actually exist. There are marked variations in the demands placed on persons as the result of work, and what is considered as pleasant work by one individual is boredom and drudgery for another. Likewise, the behavioral characteristics suggested by each theory represent the extremes of the distribution of personality traits in the population. Few people consistently demonstrate the characteristics postulated by either theory.

A second criticism that also applies equally to each theory is that neither Theory X nor Theory Y is consistently in accord with current research findings. Either theory leads one to assume that there might be a consistent relationship between job satisfaction and productivity, between the type of supervision received and productivity, and between the degree of participation in decision making and productivity. Let us examine a few studies which report the relationships existing between these three sets of variables.

---

[7] W. G. Bennis, "Leadership Theory and Administrative Behavior," *Administrative Science Quarterly*, Vol. IV (December, 1959), pp. 259-301.

Job Satisfaction and Productivity. The relationship between the degree of job satisfaction and productivity appears to be a function of the level of skill required by the job. For jobs that are highly routine with a low level of skill, there is an inverse relationship between satisfaction and productivity; i.e., the high producers are less satisfied with their jobs than the low producers; but in professional occupations where the level of skill is high, productivity on the job is positively related to a liking for the job.[8] The study by Walker and Guest of the automotive assembly line supports the conclusion that high productivity is entirely possible without intrinsic job satisfaction.[9] However, it has also been shown that when jobs are excessively monotonous and routine, production may drop significantly. *Job enlargement,* a process that increases the variety and complexity of tasks to be performed, usually results in increased job satisfaction and frequently is accompanied by increases in production.[10] Apparently there are situations, even among low-skill jobs, when job satisfaction is positively related to productivity.

Supervision and Productivity. Since Theory Y is offered as a means of correcting some of the shortcomings attributed to the traditional organization, one might expect a democratic approach to supervision— in contrast to an authoritarian approach—to result in greater productivity. Such is the case. The Survey Research Center of the University of Michigan, on the basis of research conducted at the Prudential Insurance Company, reports that high productivity occurs when supervisors are "employee-oriented." In this instance, six of the nine groups classified as high producers were led by employee-oriented supervisors and seven out of eight groups classified as low producers were managed by supervisors classified as "production-oriented." [11] The clerical workers supervised by the employee-oriented supervisors also reported more favorable attitudes toward their supervisors than did those supervised by the work-oriented supervisors. But a study of railroad section gang workers indicates that close supervision and attention to work on the part of the supervisor are needed to push the work along at a faster rate.[12] Authoritarian patterns of leadership are not limited in their effec-

---

[8] Rensis Likert, *op. cit.,* pp. 15-16.

[9] C. R. Walker and R. H. Guest, *The Man on the Assembly Line* (Cambridge, Massachusetts: Harvard University Press, 1952).

[10] F. C. Mann and L. R. Hoffman, *Automation and the Worker: A Study of Social Change in Power Plants* (New York: Holt, Rinehart, and Winston, Inc., 1960).

[11] Daniel Katz, Nathan Maccoby, and Nancy C. Morse, *Productivity, Supervision and Morale in an Office Situation* (Ann Arbor, Michigan: Survey Research Center, 1950).

[12] Daniel Katz, Nathan Maccoby, Gerald Gurin, and Lucretia Floor, *Productivity, Supervision, and Morale Among Railroad Workers* (Ann Arbor, Michigan: Survey Research Center, 1951).

tiveness to railroad workers; they are also associated with a high degree of job satisfaction and productivity among research workers.[13]

These studies demonstrate that there is no single consistent relationship existing between the type of supervision received and either productivity or job satisfaction. Another investigation conducted at General Electric shows that job satisfaction is higher when the supervisor is either very autocratic or very democratic; supervision midway on the autocratic-democratic scale resulted in average job satisfaction.[14]

Participation and Productivity. Theory Y suggests that participation in decision making integrates the goals of the employee with those of the organization and should result in increased output. An interesting experiment conducted by Coch and French in a garment factory supports the view that participation increases productivity.[15] In this study the workers were divided into four groups, one control and three experimental. The control group was notified as usual when the production department modified a job and set new piece rates on the job. This notification consisted of a statement that the change was necessary due to competitive conditions, and a careful explanation of the new piece rates. One of the experimental groups had representatives, selected from among their members, who participated in designing the job changes. All the members of the other two experimental groups participated in making the job changes. All experimental groups showed greater productivity after the changes than that showed by the control group; however, the productivity of the two groups in which every member participated in making the change was considerably higher than the production of the experimental group with only selected representatives participating in the change.

Yet another experiment conducted in an office situation shows entirely different results.[16] This study involved 500 office workers who were members of four divisions within one company. All divisions were organized in the same way and all performed the same kind of clerical work. Management felt that there should be greater productivity and a consequent reduction in costs. In two of the divisions, referred to as

13 I. R. Wechsler, M. Kahane, and R. Tannenbaum, "Job Satisfaction, Productivity, and Morale: A Case Study," *Occupational Psychology,* Vol. XXVI (January, 1952), pp. 1-14.

14 Public and Employee Relations Research Service, *Leadership Style and Employee Morale* (New York: General Electric Company, 1958).

15 I. Coch and J. R. P. French, Jr, "Overcoming Resistance to Change," *Human Relations,* Vol. I, No. 4 (1948), pp. 512-532.

16 Nancy Morse and E. Reimer, "The Experimental Change of a Major Organizational Variable," *Journal of Abnormal and Social Psychology,* Vol. LII (January, 1956), pp. 120-129.

"hierarchically controlled," decision making was moved upward in the chain of command and the supervision exercised was close—a typical authoritarian pattern. In the other two divisions the decision-making level was pushed downward as far as possible and the supervisors were trained in participative methods of supervision. Both groups increased production substantially. The two groups with lower level decision making and participative supervision increased production; i.e., reduced costs, by 20 percent, but the authoritarian groups which were hierarchically controlled increased their production by 25 percent. However, the additional 5 percent gain in productivity by the hierarchically controlled group resulted in losses in other directions because the employees of these two groups felt less responsible for their work, felt more antagonism toward high producers, and had a less favorable attitude toward their managers than did the employees of the participative groups.

To recapitulate, both Theories X and Y utilize as premises broad, sweeping generalizations concerning work and the characteristics of human beings which are not found in either all work or all human beings. Second, each theory implies a direct causal relationship between a specific change in organization structure or process and the resultant output, productivity or attitudes and feelings on the part of workers. The research studies cited above show that given a specific change in organization structure or process, neither theory is capable of predicting the resultant outcome.

THEORY Z—A SYSTEMS APPROACH

Fortunately there is an approach to organization theory that holds promise that eventually we will be able to predict with considerable accuracy the effects of organizational changes. It is an approach that considers an organization as a system. The systems concept is first introduced in Chapter 1 as an approach to the study of the management process, and in Chapter 7 production and the other major business functions are discussed as parts of a servo system. The concept is presented again in Chapter 8 in connection with information systems and expanded in Chapter 9 into information-decision-making systems. We know that a system is a recirculating type of process and is capable of some degree of corrective action, either as the result of internal changes within the system or in answer to external environmental changes. A system is usually made up of one or more subsystems, and the capabilities of the entire system are dependent upon the capabilities of each subsystem; in turn, any change in the function or capacity of the larger system requires corresponding changes in the subsystems. Inputs into the total system may originate from outside the system or come from internal subsystems; the same is true of outputs—they may be placed outside the system or fed back into any one of the subsystems.

Assumptions of Theory Z

The main problem in developing a systems approach to organization theory is determining the parameters of the system; in other words, what are the factors (either component parts of the larger system or subsystems) that make up the total system? March and Simon in their book, *Organizations,* consider 206 variables as parameters of organization.[17] Many of the variables presented and considered by March and Simon are new and as yet have not been tested by research; in addition, it is almost impossible to comprehend 206 variables and all the possible interrelationships that might arise. Their work stresses the belief that organizational effectiveness is dependent upon recognizing and adapting to many variable and interdependent situational factors, and that what is considered effective organization for one situation may be woefully inadequate for another. The following six interacting, situational variables are presented as factors that determine the appropriateness of any given organizational structure or process: (1) size of organization, (2) degree of interaction, (3) personality of members, (4) congruence of goals, (5) level of decision making, and (6) state of the the system.[18] The following propositions are derived from each of these variables; and though worded in terms of organizations, each proposition is equally applicable to every work group within a larger organization.

---

[17] James G. March and Herbert A. Simon, *Organizations* (New York: John Wiley & Sons, Inc., 1958), pp. xi, 262. *Organizations* is primarily a systems approach to the study of organizations. The list of 206 variables is contained in the appendix, pp. 249-253. The book is recommended to the advanced student interested in organization theory.

[18] Raymond A. Katzell, "Contrasting Systems of Work Organization," *American Psychologist* (Washington, D. C.: American Psychological Association, February, 1962), Vol. XVII, pp. 102-108. In this paper, Professor Katzell's presidential address to the Division of Industrial Psychology, American Psychological Association, five situational parameters are presented. They are: size, degree of interaction and interdependence of organization members, personality of organization members, the degree of congruence or disparity between the goals of the organization and that of its employees, and who in the organization has the necessary ability and motivation to take action that will further its objectives. Professor Katzell has suggested the name, Theory Alpha and Omega, for the theoretical approach based upon these variable constructs; however, the designation, Theory Z, is used since it is consistent with the alphabetical names of the two theories presented earlier in the chapter. Several of Professor Katzell's factors are rephrased and a sixth, state of the system, is added by the writer.

Size of Organization. *As size (defined as number of people) increases, organization structure becomes more formal and complex, with the result that the appropriate processes of motivating employees toward the achievement of organizational goals become more authoritarian—rather than participative—in nature.*

Degree of Interaction. *As the need for interaction between members of an organization increases in order to accomplish the prescribed work, the organization structure should permit a free flow of information and ideas, and the accompanying processes of motivation should become more participative and informal in nature.*

Personality of Members. *Effective organizational structure and processes conform to the personality and the expectations of subordinates. Subordinates who do not expect participation and who are dependent upon others for motivation react best to authoritarian patterns of structure and motivation, while those who expect participation and are motivated largely from within react best to participative organizational processes and less formality in organizational structure.*

Congruence of Goals. *When the goals of the organization and those of its members are congruent, participative processes and a less formal structure are appropriate; but when organizational goals and members' goals are divergent, greater reliance must be placed upon authoritative processes and formal structure so that adequate control is assured.*

Level of Decision Making. *When decision-making functions are retained within a work group of an organization, participative processes and informal structure are effective; as the decision-making processes move upward in the organization and away from the work group affected by those decisions, formal structure and authoritative processes are more effective.*

State of the System. *When the performance of an organization is relatively poor in achieving organizational goals, authoritative processes of motivation and structure may be necessary to initiate corrective action; however, as the organization achieves expected goals, participative patterns of organization become more effective and are expected by the members of the organization.*

The propositions listed above form the framework of Theory Z, a systems approach to the study of organizations. These propositions are not broad generalizations concerning the nature of work and the characteristics of human beings, nor do they prescribe "the one best way." Instead, the variable propositions of Theory Z offer a means of analyzing each organizational situation as it arises so that the most appropriate organizational structure and process may be designed to fit the needs of that particular situation. One might well preface each statement with the phrase, "other things being equal," for the parameters expressed in Theory Z function as a system and a change in the value of one factor modifies the significance of the remaining five variables.

The propositions of Theory Z have been presented in a manner that reflects only one facet of organization theory—style of leadership. Yet, there are structural aspects of organizations that are as important as the process of leadership in determining the effectiveness of an organization. Organization theory to be complete should provide a basis for determining the appropriateness of organization structure as well as evaluating the style of leadership. In Chapter 11, "Organization Structure," the propositions of Theory Z are rephrased so that they apply to two of the structural problems encountered in organizations. These two problem areas are: (1) determining the basis for dividing the work of an organization, a process known as *departmentation,* and (2) the arrangement of departments in a way that permits effective administration, a structural characteristic referred to as *span of management.* In Chapter 13, "Organizational Processes—Delegation and Decentralization of Authority," Theory Z is used as a guide to determine the optimum degree of *decentralization of authority* to make decisions to the various units of an organization. The applications of Theory Z as a means of evaluating organization structure and processes are summarized in Chapter 15, "Preparing for Organizational Change—Organizational Analysis."

●   ●   ●   ●   ●   ●   ●   ●   ●

Case Problem 10-B, Plant Shutdown for Vacation, provides another opportunity to evaluate a type of leadership. It also raises to some extent the question of where in the organization certain types of decisions should be made.

Questions for Study and Discussion

1. Give examples from your experience that illustrate the two meanings of the term, organization. Are these meanings mutually exclusive or is there a degree of overlap between the two meanings? Discuss.
2. After reviewing the assumptions of Theory X, describe a work situation that reflects these assumptions as nearly as possible.

3. Describe a work situation that reflects the assumptions of Theory Y.
4. In your opinion, in our industrial society do most work situations conform more closely to the assumptions of Theory X or of Theory Y?
5. Compare a Theory X organization and a Theory Y organization with respect to the type of authority, the location of the decision-making process, the characteristics of the organizational structure, and the roles of the supervisor and the individual members of the organization.
6. Is it possible to have an organization that conforms to Theory X in some respects and to Theory Y in other respects? Give an example.
7. Describe in your own terms what is meant by a systems approach to organization theory.
8. Theory Z presents six assumptions concerning the characteristics of organizations. If you were to reduce the number of assumptions to three, which three would you present? If the number of assumptions for a systems approach to organization theory were to be increased, which ones would you add?

• • • • • • • •

General Manufacturing Company produces a line of small power tools for home workshops which are distributed nationally through department and hardware stores. The company has grown steadily since its founding, and at the present time there are approximately 500 employees, 400 of whom are directly connected with manufacturing, and about 100 employed in the office, which is located in the same building. Mr. Ransom, founder and president, often refers to the company as "one big happy family."

However, as June 1 approaches each year, the manager of manufacturing raises a perennial question concerning the possibility of closing the plant for two weeks during the summer and having all employees take their vacation at that time. He offers the following reasons for his position:

Case Problem 10-B
Plant Shutdown for Vacation

1. At present, in the plant alone, there are 100 employees entitled to three weeks' vacation, 200 entitled to two weeks, 50 entitled to one week, and 50 who have not earned any vacation. The grand total is 750 man weeks of vacation during a 13- or 14-week period from June 1 to September 1—an average of 50 people on vacation each week during the summer. The result is increased overtime, which is costly, and unskilled summer replacements which increase scrap costs and quality complaints.

2. A plant shutdown affords an opportunity to perform much needed machine repair that otherwise has to be done on an overtime basis and usually results in lost production.

3. A plant shutdown would permit the supervisors to have their vacations during the summer months. Under the

present system, they are working either short-handed or have so many new employees as replacements that it is impossible to let them have vacations during the June-to-September period.

Mr. Ransom considers these reasons valid but desires that the employees participate in making the decision. Here is his statement during a recent management meeting:

"As you know, we pride ourselves in our good human relations, and—in my opinion—one of the reasons our relationships are so good is that we encourage our employees to make as many decisions for themselves as possible. For example, each year they elect their own officers and administer the entire employee activity fund, including the determination of how much money is to be allotted to each activity. I suggest that they be permitted to vote on whether or not the plant should be closed for two weeks and all vacations taken at that time."

"Voting is all right for some things," replied John Havers, the manager of manufacturing, "but I'm not sure that they should vote on something that is as important and costly as this is to the company. We have increased our inventory and rented additional warehouse space so that we can close for a two-week period. Also, if your plan is used, how many should be allowed to vote? I feel certain that most of the girls in the office will vote against closing the plant since most are married and want to take their vacations with their husbands. Then, too, we want the 25 men in the various maintenance departments to stay on. Should they be allowed to vote even though it has

been decided that they have to work? And what about the new men who are not entitled to vacation? It's hard to imagine their voting themselves out of two weeks' pay. It seems to me that we might even get a majority vote against closing the plant that actually wouldn't be representative of the majority of those involved. I'm for preparing an announcement that the plant will close on such and such a date for a period of two weeks and that vacations will be taken at that time with certain exceptions."

Mr. Riley, director of personnel, added: "This situation is somewhat similar to one that I experienced several years ago in another company. We let the office employees vote on whether or not office hours should be changed for the summer months from the normal eight to five with an hour off for lunch to 7:30 to 4:00 with a half hour for lunch. The margin in favor of changing was only three votes out of the 110 voting, and there was nothing but trouble throughout the entire summer because of the exceptions that had to be made. One thing that stands out is that voting seems to solidify the losing side, with the result that during the summer they always said, 'Well, I didn't vote for it.' Another point to remember is that this situation isn't going to get better; as time goes on, we will have more and more employees entitled to three weeks' vacation, which means that under our present policy each summer is going to become more costly."

The other members of the management committee agreed with Riley and Havers.

Problems

1. What is your recommendation to Mr. Ransom as the proper course of action?

2. Would there be any inconsistency in Mr. Ransom's behavior if he overruled his management committee and insisted that the employees vote on this question? Discuss.

3. Comment on the following statement: Minorities should be protected from the action of the majority.

CHAPTER 11

Organization Structure

Excelsior Products, originally a sales organization owned and operated by a manufacturer's representative, is now a wholly owned subsidiary of Triumph Chemical Company, a relatively large concern in its industry and engaged in the development, manufacture, and distribution of industrial maintenance chemicals. Excelsior, like the parent company, sells direct to the industrial consumer and counts among its best selling items degreasers, waxes, detergents, insecticides, weed killers, special paints, and liquid fertilizers. All told, there are 85 products currently in the line; new products are added at a rate of about ten a year and usually the five poorest selling items are dropped from the line.

The sales force is composed of commission salesmen who are among the highest paid of any industry. Although the commission rate varies from a low of 20 percent on some items to a high of 35 percent on a very few items, the average rate paid—based on current sales analysis—is 25 percent of total sales volume. Salesmen earn an average gross income of $14,000 a year, and out of this amount they pay their own expenses. However, many sales-

Case Problem 11-A

Span of Management

men who have been with the company for more than a year earn at least $25,000.

The sales expense of Excelsior Products includes the 25 percent direct selling cost paid to salesmen as commissions and 8 percent allocated to advertising in trade journals, printed specification sheets carried by all salesmen and distributed to customers, semi-annual national sales meetings, and other miscellaneous sales expenses. Thus, from the $56,000 sales volume generated by each salesman, the total sales expense is $18,480, or 33 percent.

During the first complete year of operations following the acquisition by Triumph, all five of the salesmen employed by the former owner of Excelsior remained; true to expectation, they produced a total sales volume of $280,000. During this year no effort was made to expand the sales force by Mr. Thomas Jackson, a former district sales manager for Triumph and the new general manager of Excelsior. In the second year Mr. Jackson hired and trained ten new salesmen, but by the year's end only five of the new men remained; however, sales for that year totaled $375,000. At the beginning of the third year, Mr. Jackson had ten good men, each capable of producing a sales volume of $56,000. The plans for the third year called for hiring and training two new men each month. Actually this goal was not realized, but he did hire 20 men, 12 of whom were still with the company at the end of the third year. Fortunately, none of the ten salesmen working at the beginning of the year quit, and as a group they produced $570,000. This amount, combined with the volume of the new men—none of whom sold for a full year—totaled $810,000. Mr. Jackson is convinced that the 22 men presently employed are capable of producing a sales volume of $1 million in a full calendar year. These 22 men are located in the following areas: Los Angeles, 2; San Francisco, 2; St. Louis, the home office, 5; Dallas, 2; Houston, 2; Florida, 1; New York City, 3; Chicago, 3; Detroit, 1; and Colorado, 1.

Now Mr. Jackson is planning for the coming year and realizes that the growth of Excelsior Products is dependent primarily upon the number of salesmen hired. Most of the men live in relatively large cities and sell not only to customers in that city but also to customers in the small towns in that section of the state. He recognizes that he has only one salesman in the southeastern part of the United States and none in the Northwest or New England.

Mr. Jackson spends most of his time in recruiting and training new salesmen. Some of the new men are referred to the company by present salesmen, but most are recruited through newspaper advertising. Usually a new man is sent out on the road for a period of one week with an experienced salesman; then Mr. Jackson spends a week with the new man in the territory assigned to him. He realizes that the training received under these circumstances is probably inadequate, but it is all that time allows. In addition to recruiting and training new salesmen, Mr. Jackson conducts two national sales meetings a year in order to introduce new products, and these meetings afford an opportunity to brush up on sales techniques. Although the laboratories of the parent company develop new products, it is the general manager's responsibility to choose the product name, approve the package design, and prepare the layout and copy of the specification sheets that describe the product and are carried by all salesmen. In the home office there are three clerical employees who process sales orders as they are received from the field. The billing of customers, the computation of commissions, and the payment of salesmen are performed by personnel of the parent company. Jackson realizes that if Excelsior Products is to continue to grow, he needs more managerial help, but he feels obligated to stay within the 33 percent selling cost imposed by the parent corporation.

Problems

1. Develop an organization structure for Excelsior Products that will permit the company to attain a sales volume of $5 million annually. Will this structure be effective when sales reach $15 million?

2. Of what significance are the findings of Graicunas in understanding the problems of Mr. Jackson?

3. Is it possible to change the organization structure of Excelsior Products and still remain within the 33 per cent overall selling cost? State the reasons for your answer. How does the answer to this question affect the recommendations made concerning organization structure in your answer to Problem No. 1?

● ● ● ● ● ● ● ● ●

Three theories of organization are presented in Chapter 10, each of which emphasizes a different aspect of organizing. Theory X presents organization as centered around the work to be performed, Theory Y stresses the people of the organization, while Theory Z views organization as a system that integrates the requirements of work and the desires and capabilities of the people who make up the organization. The alert student has probably said to himself that the three theories talk more of people than organizations, an observation which has considerable merit, for it is through people that the work of an organization is accomplished. Nonetheless, the structure of the organization—the arrangement of the component parts, people and work—is a major determinant in shaping the behavior of people, and, in turn, determines the extent to which organization goals are realized. One writer makes the following statement about the relationship between organization and people:

> People have about the same relationship to the organization as the driver and passengers in an automobile have to the automobile itself. If we want to improve the effectiveness of the automobile in reaching its objectives, that is, improve it as a means of rapid, safe, and comfortable transportation, we can do a number of things. We can improve the design of the automobile to better adapt it to the people who will probably use it. We can modify it to better conform to the characteristics of the roads it will travel. We can alter the furnishings of the automobile or adjust certain of its mechanical features to human needs. Such flexibility is inherent in good design. The design of the automobile must always be predicated upon the characteristics of the people who will use it and the environment in which it is to be used. The automobile is neither the people nor the environment, but it is inextricably linked with both.[1]

---

[1] Louis A. Allen, *Management and Organization* (New York: McGraw-Hill Book Company, 1958), p. 353. This book is a presentation of organization which emphasizes an orientation toward the work to be accomplished. It should be read as a supplement to the concepts of organization presented by Rensis Likert in *New Patterns of Management* and Douglas McGregor in *The Human Side of Enterprise.*

We all know something about the design of an automobile in relation to its purpose and the people who use it. If the automobile is to carry 50 people, it becomes a bus; if it is to enter the Indianapolis 500, there is room only for the driver; and Ford learned as the result of a survey, which surprises no one who has given the matter much thought, that engaged couples do not like bucket seats. We all know something about the structure and design of organizations, even though an organization is not a tangible entity like an automobile. When organizing a group, such as a fraternity, for a social outing, one of the first items to be considered is the part that each person is to play in preparing for and conducting the event. Five members may be chosen to arrange transportation, three more to assume responsibility for providing food and beverages, and a third group to select and make advance arrangements for the site. Each group has a chairman who works closely with the person in charge of special social events, usually a designated officer in a fraternity, so that the efforts of all groups will be coordinated.

The example of a fraternity preparing for an outing illustrates two characteristics of organization structure. First, the work to be accomplished is divided and then arranged into manageable portions. The word used to describe the process of analyzing, dividing, and arranging work into manageable portions is *departmentation*. Second, the leader of each group works closely with the permanent social chairman so that the efforts of each group may be coordinated. The number of work groups reporting to the chairman is a structural characteristic resulting from the manner in which the work is organized. To the chairman, these are the number of groups that must be coordinated, or managed; hence, the expression, *span of management*. This chapter discusses the two major characteristics of organization structure—departmentation and span of management—and then applies the six variables of Theory Z as guides for selecting the most effective structure.

DEPARTMENTATION

A reservation concerning the use of the term, organization, must be made. For the most part, organization is actually *reorganization*. Seldom is an entire organization projected from scratch; instead, it is a process of changing and refining present structure and personnel. Problem No. 1 of Case Problem 11-A requests that you develop an organization structure for Excelsior Products and reflects a common use of the word, organization, in management literature. A more precise, though cumbersome, wording would request a reorganization. We will continue to use the expression, organization, as it appears in most management writings, but it is well to remember that in practically all instances we are discussing reorganization.

The need for departmentation, defined as the grouping of work and/or individuals into manageable units, is easily understood, and usually the process of creating manageable units is the first step in building an organization structure. It is conceivable that one man can perform all the work of an enterprise provided he has the necessary skills, knowledge, and time. A one-man hamburger stand is illustrative of a business whose *functions* are managed by one person. As the business prospers, the owner finds that he does not have the time to perform the work of preparing food and serving customers. Thus, as a first step in organization, he divides the work into units that can be completed by one man. Perhaps a cook who performs all functions associated with the preparation of food is hired, and the owner retains those functions connected with serving customers and managing the business. If the hamburger stand continues to grow and becomes a restaurant capable of seating 100 customers, the work of the cook is further subdivided. A chef is now in charge of the preparation of food and is responsible for all work performed in the kitchen. He supervises the work of several assistants, each of whom is skilled in the preparation of a certain type food. A supervisor of the dining room directs the waitresses who serve the customers. The owner is performing the managerial function of coordinating the efforts of all personnel. Should a chain of restaurants develop, each restaurant may be regarded as a manageable unit. Thus, departmentation, the grouping of work and people, occurs at all levels of an organization. What are the bases most commonly used in determining departmental structure?

Bases of Departmentation

Certain well-recognized and accepted bases for departmentation have developed over a period of years. These bases, which are common to all types of organizations, appear with such frequency and consistency that they may be regarded as common denominators of organization. The units created through the process of departmentation combine to form the total structure of the organization, and are work-centered in their origin and application since the primary goal is an effective division of work. The most frequently used bases of departmentation are: (1) function, (2) product, (3) customer, (4) geography, (5) process, and (6) sequence. Each basis for dividing work is discussed below.

Function. *Function* denotes related activity. It is a relationship that is apparent because of the similarity of the skills required to perform a given kind of work, or a relationship that binds together a group of tasks in the accomplishment of a common goal. The fundamental appeal of function as a basis for dividing work is its logical simplicity. What is more natural than grouping together all work requiring the skills necessary to operate machine tools and placing persons with those skills under the direction of one supervisor? By the same token, all persons having the required skills to assemble the product form the assembly department. These and other seemingly unrelated skills may be grouped together on a functional basis because the application of each skill results in the accomplishment of a specific task; and when these tasks are combined, a logical relationship may be perceived, for machining and assembling are activities (functions) necessary to accomplish a common goal—the production of the product.

The functions usually identified in the top echelon of business organizations are production, finance, and sales. These functions have been described as primary, vital, or organic; the implication is that the absence of any one of the three functions would result in the death of the organization. The terminology used to describe these functions and the significance of these and other functions varies from one type of enterprise to another. Manufacturing firms use the terms production (or manufacturing), finance, and sales; wholesalers recognize the functions of finance and sales, but production takes the form of buying, warehousing, and distribution; and airlines use the word, operations, to describe their production function—the movement of passengers. For some organizations one or more of the functions may be vestigial in nature; for example, hospitals and banks have no sales function per se; rather, these organizations refer to the function of public relations. On the other hand, it is difficult to imagine a function more vital to pharmaceutical firms than research, because over half of their current sales volume results from products which were unknown ten years ago.

In addition to the primary functions, which vary in respect to the terminology used to describe them and their significance and number for different types of enterprises, there are auxiliary functions that must be performed. Traditionally, auxiliary functions—frequently called staff functions—are considered supportive in nature and supplement the primary functions of the organization. Delicate interpersonal relationships between persons performing primary functions and those carrying out auxiliary functions often arise and are discussed in considerable detail in the next chapter.

Product. Companies with diversified product lines frequently create managerial units based upon the product. Three forms of product departmentation are shown in Figure 11-1. Chart 1 shows the division of both the sales and the manufacturing functions into product departments, while Chart 2 shows product departmentation applied to the sales function only. In Chart 3 the manufacturing function is departmentalized according to product, and sales remains as a single unit. Figure 11-1 also illustrates that the process of creating departments quite properly employs more than one basis. In this instance, the bases of function and product are used.

Customer. Retail stores may organize their sales force to meet the needs of a specific class of customer by forming special departments to cater to teenagers, collegians, or brides. An industrial firm manufacturing valves might divide its sales force so that one part of it sells to original equipment manufacturers (OEM) and the other part sells to the replacement market.

Geography. At one time, poor communications was the reason advanced in most instances to justify departmentation based on territorial or geographic units. While this reason may still have some validity for those companies with foreign operations, the quality of communications is usually no longer a valid reason for geographic departmentation within the United States. When the number of people to be supervised is large and dispersed over a wide area, territorial units afford a logical means of developing manageable units. The creation of regional units offers a possible solution to the organization problem confronting Excelsior Products, Case Problem 11-A.

Process. The process or equipment used in producing a product may be the basis for determining departmental lines at the plant level of the organization. The grouping of all milling machines into one department and the placing of lathes in another department is illustrative of departmentation by equipment. In other industries the process serves as the basis for determining effective departmentation. Thus, in a chemical plant a process, such as distillation, becomes the operating unit.

Sequence. Departments sometime conform to alphanumeric or time sequences. The bookkeeping machine section of a large department store may be subdivided into two units, one of which posts accounts for all customers whose last names begin with the letters A through M; the other unit posts for those customers whose names begin with the letters N through Z. Numerical sequence is often the basis for dividing un-

Figure 11-1

THREE POSSIBLE ARRANGEMENTS OF DEPARTMENTATION
BASED UPON PRODUCT

differentiated labor gangs into controllable units; i.e., every 30 men are placed under the direction of a straw boss. Plants operating 16 or 24 hours a day establish separate shifts, and each shift—designated first, second, or third, according to hours worked—is a distinct administrative unit.

Creating Manageable Departments

The above bases of dividing work are an extension of the definition of departmentation and a description of the building blocks that make up the organization structure. Creating manageable departments is not an end in itself; instead, it is a means of facilitating the achievement of organizational objectives. There is no set of rules that prescribes the one best pattern of organization structure; however, there are guides, discussed in the last section of this chapter, which are useful in selecting the most appropriate structure.

SPAN OF MANAGEMENT

Once the bases of departmentation are determined—whether by function, product, customer, geography, process, sequence, or any combination thereof—another problem in organization structure immediately arises: How many departments are to be placed under the direction of one person? This problem is frequently referred to as *span of control*; however, the phrase, *span of management*, describes the question more accurately since an executive performs the functions of planning, organizing, and leading, as well as the function of control. The span of management has a direct bearing upon the number of hierarchical levels in an organization which, in turn, is a measure of the length of that organization's *lines of communications*.

For example, Thomas Jackson of Excelsior Products, Case Problem 11-A, has 22 salesmen and three clerks in the home office reporting to him, a span of management of 25 persons. Let us assume that he names a chief clerk and appoints four regional sales supervisors; his span of management is reduced from 25 to five, but there is now one level of supervision through which communications between him and the salesmen and clerks must pass. Suppose that he appoints an eastern division sales manager and a western division sales manager, each of whom supervises three regional sales managers. Mr. Jackson's span of management is reduced to three persons. While there is one supervisor between him and the clerks, he must now communicate to his salesmen through two levels of supervision, the divisional and the regional managers.

From the discussion above, it is apparent that if the span of management is decreased, the lines of communications are lengthened; and, conversely, if the lines of communication are shortened, the manager's span is increased. Yet, there are instances in the literature of management that advise the chief executive to simultaneously reduce his span of management and shorten the organization's communication lines. Let us review the reasons frequently advanced in support of a limited span of management and then examine the experience of several companies that have deliberately increased the manager's span.

Reasons for a Limited Span

One of the earliest recommendations in support of a limited span of management is found in Jethro's advice to Moses that he establish "rulers of thousands, and rulers of hundreds, and rulers of fifties, and rulers of tens." [2] In modern literature the development of the concept that supports a limited span of management is attributed to the work of three men. First, there is the statement of Sir General Ian Hamilton; second, the work of A. V. Graicunas; and third, the formal statement of a principle by Lyndall F. Urwick.

Hamilton's Recommendations. General Hamilton's conclusions are drawn from his experiences as a military officer. He begins his line of reasoning with the statement that the average human brain finds its optimum work level when handling three to six other brains. His observation that a noncommissioned officer is not fully occupied when directing only three soldiers and that a lieutenant general finds it difficult to direct the activities of six divisional generals is recognition that the number of persons under the direction of one supervisor should be greater at the lower levels of the organization than the number supervised at the top of the organization. General Hamilton recommended that "the nearer we approach the supreme head of the whole organization, the more we ought to work toward groups of six." [3]

The Theory of Graicunas. An important consideration in establishing an appropriate span of management is the number of potential interactions that might occur between a manager and his subordinates.

[2] See Chapter 2, "The Development of Management Concepts," page 24, for a more complete analysis of Jethro's recommendations which are contained in Exodus 18: 13-26.

[3] Sir Ian Hamilton, *The Soul and Body of the Army* (London: Edward Arnold Publishers, Ltd., 1921), p. 221.

A. V. Graicunas, a Lithuanian management consultant, developed a formula for determining some, but not all, of the relationships inherent in a given span.[4]

If, for example, one supervisor, S has two subordinates, A and B, reporting to him, a *direct relationship* may occur between the supervisor S and A, and the supervisor S and B. But there are times when S talks to A with B present or to B with A present; thus, two *group relationships* are possible. Further, *cross relationships* may exist between A and B and between B and A. As shown in Figure 11-2, these three sets of relationships—direct, group, and cross—combine to form six possible interactions between one supervisor and two subordinates.

Figure 11-2

DIRECT, GROUP, AND CROSS RELATIONSHIPS THAT MIGHT OCCUR BETWEEN A SUPERIOR AND TWO SUBORDINATES

[4] A. V. Graicunas, "Relationship in Organization," *Papers on the Science of Administration,* ed. L. Gulick and L. Urwick (New York: Columbia University, 1947), pp. 183-87.

When a third subordinate, *C*, reports to *S*, one additional direct relationship is established between *S* and *C*; but seven additional group relationships (*AC, CA, BC, CB, ABC, CBA,* and *BAC*) are possible. Also, four more cross relationships (*A*♦*C, B*♦*C, C*♦*A,* and *C*♦*B*) are added, thus bringing the potential number of interactions to 18. A fourth subordinate raises the theoretical interactions to 44, the fifth results in an even 100 relationships, and the executive with eight subordinates is the center of a web of 1,080 potential relationships.[5]

Graicunas's mathematical analysis of the potential relationships in a given span of management is significant for two reasons. First, his theory emphasizes the complex social processes that occur between a superior and his subordinates and between the subordinates themselves. Second, the application of his formula stresses the alarming rate at which the complexity of these social processes increases with each additional subordinate. The addition of the fifth subordinate raises potential interactions from 44 to 100, the eighth subordinate moves the potential from 490 to 1,080, and the fourteenth subordinate finds the total relationships soaring to 114,872 from 53,404 with 13 subordinates. Fortunately, the relationships envisioned by Graicunas do not occur on a daily basis, or for that matter may not occur at all; but the warning is clear—somewhere there is one additional subordinate who proves to be the straw that breaks the managerial camel's back.

Urwick's Principle. Lyndall F. Urwick, a noted management consultant who credits Sir General Ian Hamilton as the first to call attention to the concept of a limited span of management, encouraged Graicunas in developing his mathematical analysis of relationships. Urwick offers as a reason to support a limited span the observed psychological phenomenon that man has a limited "span of attention"—a limit to the number of items that may be attended to simultaneously. Other limitations in human spans, such as the amount of energy available to a supervisor in the performance of his job, may be advanced. Further, time may be a limiting factor. Admittedly, not all the relationships recognized by Graicunas develop during the course of a single day, but if only a small fraction of the 1,080 potential relationships that might

---

[5] The number of relationships, *r*, may be determined by the following formula, in which *n* represents the number of subordinates:

$$r = n \left(2^{n-1} + n - 1 \right)$$

As mentioned in the text, Graicunas does not take into account all possible relationships. Any one of the subordinates could conceivably initiate action, which in effect doubles the number of potential direct relationships; in addition, the supervisor could participate as a member of each group, with successive members of that group assuming the dominant role.

arise with eight subordinates occurs with any degree of regularity, an executive's span is limited by the amount of time that may be allocated to each personal contact. Graicunas recognizes that the number of cross relationships between subordinates, a major factor in determining the complexity of a supervisor's job, is dependent upon the nature of the work being performed. Colonel Urwick recognizes the variable complexity of a supervisor's job as a function of the work being performed in the following statement of principle:

"No superior can supervise directly the work of more than five or, at the most, six subordinates whose work interlocks." [6]

Span of Management in Practice

Lyndall Urwick's recommended limitations on the span of management—"five or, the most, six subordinates"—is rather specific; but it must be noted that the suggested limitations are modified by the qualifying phrase, "whose work interlocks." How valid is this precept? One way of determining the validity of the concept of a limited span of management is to examine current industrial practice in this respect. If there are differences between practice and recommendation, why do the differences exist? A research study conducted by the American Management Association (AMA) presents a good picture of current practice in respect to existing spans of management.

The American Management Association's study presents the results of a survey of current practices in respect to the span of management of the presidents of 141 companies that are "all known to have good organizational practices." [7] The results of the survey are presented separately for large companies (over 1,000 employees) and for medium-size companies (500 to 1,000 employees). The first two columns of Table 11-1 show the number of executives reporting to the presidents of the 100 large companies participating in the survey. The third column

---

[6] Lyndall F. Urwick, "The Manager's Span of Control," *Harvard Business Review,* Vol. XXXV (May-June, 1956), pp. 39-47. Colonel Urwick's article is an excellent discussion in support of the concept of a limited span of management. The principle stated above first appeared in Lyndall F. Urwick, *Scientific Principles and Organization* (New York: American Management Association, 1938), Institute of Management Series No. 19, p. 8.

[7] Ernest Dale, *Planning and Developing the Company Organization Structure* (New York: American Management Association, 1952), Research Report No. 20, p. 56. This research report is divided into two parts. Part I discusses the dynamics of organization in respect to determining objectives, delegating responsibility, span of control, the staff assistant, the staff specialist, group decision making, and decentralization. Part II presents established procedures in the mechanics of organization, including the development of charts and manuals. Many persons consider this work a "handbook" of organization.

Table 11-1

NUMBER OF EXECUTIVES REPORTING TO PRESIDENT IN 100 LARGE
COMPANIES AND COMPUTED POTENTIAL RELATIONSHIPS

No. of Executives Reporting to President *	No. of Companies *	Potential Relationships ** (Graicunas Formula)
1	6	1
2	—	6
3	1	18
4	3	44
5	7	100
6	9	222
7	11	490
8	8	1,080
	◀ Median	
9	8	2,376
10	6	5,210
11	7	11,374
12	10	24,708
13	8	53,404
14	4	114,872
15	1	245,974
16	5	524,534
17	—	1,114,392
18	1	2,359,612
19	—	4,981,090
20	1	10,486,154
21	1	22,020,532
22	—	46,137,824
23	2	96,469,518
24	1	201,327,166
	100	

* Columns 1 and 2 are from Ernest Dale, *Planning and Developing the Company Organization Structure* (New York: American Management Association, 1952), Research Report No. 20, p. 57.
** Column 3 is from Walno V. Suojanen, "The Span of Control—Fact or Fable?" *Advanced Management*, Vol. XX (November, 1955), p. 6.

of Table 11-1 shows the number of potential relationships according to the formula developed by Graicunas.[8] Note that the medium number of executives reporting to the president is between eight and nine, which is considerably above the limits recommended by Colonel Urwick. Also, there are ten companies whose chief executive has 12 subordinates and one company whose president supervises 24 subordinates. The results tabulated for the medium-size companies are essentially the same;

[8] Walno V. Suojanen, "The Span of Control—Fact or Fable?" *Advanced Management*, Vol. XX (November, 1955), pp. 5-13. The third column of Table 11-1 utilizes the figures computed by Professor Soujanen. Professor Soujanen's paper is an interesting criticism of the concept of a limited span of management and should be read in conjunction with the article written by Lyndall F. Urwick, which is cited in footnote No. 6.

however, the median number of persons reporting to the president drops from eight to between six and seven, and the range in the number reporting to the chief executive is reduced from a high of 24 for the large companies to 17.

It is evident that more than half of the companies in each group do not adhere to the recommendation that "five, or at the most, six" subordinates report to each superior. Nor does it seem possible that the deviation from the recommended five or six is due to work of subordinates that does *not* interlock. Again, there is marked similarity between the two groups of companies with respect to the functions performed by the subordinates reporting to the president. Among those functions most frequently mentioned by both groups that are supervised by the president are production, sales, industrial relations, legal counsel, controller, treasurer, finance, purchasing, research, plant management, and engineering. The nature of these functions is such that there is usually a high degree of interrelationship between them.

Clearly, these companies, "all known to have good organizational practices," are not following Urwick's principle. A systems approach to organizational structure explains to some extent why the AMA survey reports such a marked variation in the number of persons reporting directly to company presidents.

A SYSTEMS APPROACH TO ORGANIZATION STRUCTURE

In Chapter 10, "Organization Theory," the six propositions of Theory Z are couched in terms that aid in selecting the most effective pattern of leadership. Leadership is an important process of organization, a means of coordinating and giving direction to the efforts of the members of the organization, but it is not the structure of the organization. Our concern with organization structure is twofold: first, the creation of manageable work units—the process of departmentation—and second, the corollary stemming from departmentation—the grouping of people and work into effective spans of management. The bases most commonly used for departmentation—function, product, customer, geography, process, and sequence—have been examined. Also, we have reviewed the recommendation of Urwick, based upon the work of Graicunas, and the findings of the AMA study which show that more than half of the firms surveyed exceed the recommended span of management. What are the guides to be followed in determining effective departmentation and efficient spans of management? Each of the six assumptions of Theory Z—size of organization, degree of interaction, personality of members, congruence of goals, level of decision making, and state of the system—is applied as a guide for establishing departments and determining effective spans of management.

Size of Organization

Departmentation. There is a direct relationship between the size of an organization, when defined as number of people, and the structure of the organization. As size increases, the need for departmentation, the grouping of people, becomes evident. Consider a small machine shop engaged in the building and repair of metal parts. The owner-manager may be able to effectively direct the work of ten to fifteen journeymen machinists and, in addition, perform the functions of design, cost estimating, scheduling production, and selling the services of his shop. During this period he may develop a strategic, long-range plan to increase the size of his organization, perhaps the manufacture and distribution of a patentable product in large quantities. If successful, the size of the organization may increase to 200 people; and in order for the organization to maintain a high degree of economic effectiveness, the structure of the organization must change to accommodate the enlarged size.[9] One of the characteristics of organizational change is the creation of departments to perform the functions of design, estimating, scheduling, and selling. The sales function may be further departmentalized according to geographic areas or on the basis of product sold. Whatever the basis selected for the creation of departments, whether it be function, geography, product, or any other unifying characteristic, an increase in the size of an organization operates as a major force in creating the need for departmentation.

Span of Management. The size of an organization, again defined as the number of people, is also operative in determining the span of management. Table 11-1, showing the number of persons reporting to the presidents of 100 large corporations (over 1,000 employees), reveals that the median number of executives reporting to the president is between eight and nine and the range in the number reporting is from one to 24. The same analysis for 41 medium-size companies (500 to

---

9 Alfred D. Chandler, Jr., *Strategy and Structure* (Cambridge, Massachusetts: The M. I. T. Press, 1962), pp. 1-17. In this section, "Introduction—Strategy and Structure," Mr. Chandler develops the thesis that organizational form results from growth, and that the growth of an organization is the result of strategic planning. Detailed analyses of DuPont, General Motors, Standard Oil Company (New Jersey), and Sears, Roebuck and Company are presented.

1,000 employees) shows that the median number of executives reporting to the president is between six and seven and the range in the
number reporting is from one to 17. Ernest Dale, who conducted the
study, attributes the reduction in the median and the range of the span
of management to size in the following statement: "The reduced median
and range reflect the lesser volume of important problems faced by the
smaller companies and the smaller number of people required to assist
the president in coordination and control." [10] To be sure, factors other
than size determine the span of management; nonetheless, the size of the
organization is important in determining the manager's span.

Degree of Interaction

Departmentation. An important guide in determining effective
departmentation is the need for interaction between members of
an organization in order to achieve organizational goals. The need
for interaction arises when several persons are solving a common problem, developing and using the same information, or when there is need
to communicate with each other. The following example illustrates the
effect of interaction upon organization structure: Prior to reorganization,
a manufacturer of twist drills, had four separate departments working
on various phases of quality control. There was the field engineering
department, whose function is to answer customer complaints, aid in
solving technical problems, and prepare postmortem reports analyzing
the causes of product failure. Field engineering reported to the vice-
president, sales. Reporting to the director of quality control was the
plant quality control department, which inspects the product during the
manufacturing process. Under the direction of the chief metallurgist was
a department responsible for metallurgical specifications, and the supervision of the heat-treating process, an important step in manufacturing.
Finally, there was a product design department supervised by the vice-
president, engineering. The members of these departments were all
highly skilled technicians, many having engineering degrees; all were
interested in the quality of the product and might have benefited from
a free exchange of ideas and information; yet they were located in
physically separated departments with little opportunity for interaction
or communication. Recognizing the problem, the company located all
four departments in one geographic area under the direction of the
vice-president, engineering, a move which not only permits interaction
between the members of the four departments but also facilitates
coordination of effort.

---

[10] Ernest Dale, *op. cit.,* p. 59.

Span of Management. The degree of interaction between persons supervised by one superior may be a factor in determining the limits of an effective span of management. The geometrically progressive increase in the number of relationships described by Graicunas is a function of the cross relationships between those being supervised, a function recognized by Urwick in the qualifying phrase, "whose work interlocks." However, there is evidence that there are factors which counterbalance interaction and thus make possible the effective use of an increased span of management. James C. Worthy reports the effects of an increased span of management in his study of two groups of Sears, Roebuck and Company stores, each having approximately 150 to 175 employees.[11] The structure of one group of stores followed the conventional limited span of management with a level of supervision between the store manager and the heads of the more than 30 merchandising departments. In the other group of stores, the manager had an assistant manager and the more than 30 merchandising managers reported directly to him. When compared in respect to employee morale, sales volume, and profit, the stores having a large span of management resulting in a relatively "flat" structure were superior to those stores with the smaller span of management and a level of supervision between the manager and the department heads. There is evidence that the flat structure encouraged the department heads to develop into strong managers capable of operating with a minimum of supervision, thereby making a large span of management effective.

Personality of Members

Departmentation. The personality of the members of an organization (defining personality as the sum total of the skills, abilities, interests, and personal characteristics) is an important guide in determining departmental lines. Admittedly, the structure of the organization is not the people, but like the well-designed automobile that conforms to the characteristics of the persons using it, so should the well-designed organization structure adapt to the personalities of the members of the organization. Work is often departmentalized according to the skills employed, an arrangement which encourages specialization and the maximum development of individual skills and abilities. Specialized knowledge concerning a specific product or function may well

---

[11] James C. Worthy, "Organization Structure and Employee Morale," *American Sociological Review,* Vol. XV (April, 1950), pp. 169-79.

serve as the basis for defining a department. However, there are dangers inherent in overspecialization. The members of a highly specialized department and their supervisors may become so narrow and engrossed in one limited aspect of a problem that they fail to recognize broader organizational goals. Also, jobs may become so limited in scope that boredom and monotony are the result. It is essential to maintain a balance between specialization, which often facilitates training and results in a high level of skill, and the enlargement of jobs and departments so that there is maximum utilization of the capabilities of members.

Span of Management. The personality of the members of an organization is an important consideration in determining the extent of an effective span of management. First, consider the personality of the manager. It is axiomatic that there are wide variations in the capabilities of managers in respect to range of interests, breadth and depth of knowledge, and the amount of energy expended on the job. In addition to these characteristics, which are usually recognized without too much difficulty, there is that relatively rare quality—the ability to inspire others. Managers who inspire subordinates to "play over their heads" should have larger spans so that their dynamic qualities of leadership are felt by as many as possible.

Second, the personality characteristics of subordinates contribute to the manager's span. It is apparent that if subordinates are well trained, interested in their jobs, and capable of making their own decisions, less supervisory effort is required, thereby making it possible for a superior to increase his span of management. It is suggested by critics of an extended span of management that one of the chief reasons for the large spans in the Sears' stores (discussed above) is the lack of interaction between the merchandising department heads, with the result that there are very few cross relationships. Though this appraisal may be valid to some extent, the primary reason for the success of the large span of management in the Sears retail stores is the effect that a large span has on the members of the organization. The store manager, knowing that he can devote only a limited amount of time to each subordinate, exercises greater care in the selection and training of each department manager. Of equal importance is the effect a large span of management has upon the development of the subordinate. Since he receives less supervision, the subordinate is forced to make his own decisions in the operation of his department, and this experience in managing without close supervision makes it possible for him to develop into a capable departmental manager.

Congruence of Goals

Departmentation. Congruence of goals may serve as a guide in drawing departmental lines when the immediate objectives of several diverse activities are similar. Plant maintenance departments usually include personnel who possess the diverse skills of millwrights, electricians, plumbers, steamfitters, and machinists—a variety which at first glance may seem to have little in common. However, all are concerned with the immediate objective of keeping plant facilities in a good state of repair, and the combining of many crafts into a single administrative unit improves the coordination of the many skills necessary for plant maintenance. The placement of salesmen and service personnel under the direction of the sales manager is another example of combining into a single department apparently unrelated activities. In this case, the common objective is customer satisfaction. The chief advantage resulting from the application of congruence of goals as a guide in grouping diverse activities is a structure that permits a high degree of coordination.

Span of Managment. Congruence of goals as a guide for departmentation relates primarily to the similarity of objectives that exist between persons who perform apparently unrelated activities. When applied as a guide in determining an effective span of management, congruence of goals refers not only to the similarity of goals of various work groups, but also includes the degree of congruence between the immediate goals of the individual and those of the organization. An illustration of congruence in the goals of several work groups is found in our example of the need for interaction as a guide for determining departmental lines. In this case the need for interaction is resolved by placing the four quality control departments under the direction of the engineering vice-president, a solution that increases his span of management. Yet, it is a tenable arrangement since the four departments all have a common goal—the improvement of product quality. An argument often presented in support of the establishment of incentive plans, which relate the pay of an individual to his productivity, is that the installation of such plans is a means of making the goals of the individual congruent with those of the organization. In general, as the immediate goals of subordinates become congruent with the goals of other subordinates and with the goals of the organization, the span of management may be increased.

Level of Decision Making

Departmentation. In some organizations the power to make important decisions is retained by the chief executive and his immediate subordinates, while in other firms decision making occurs at all levels of the management hierarchy. The retention of decision making by the topmost level of the organization may be due to the need for a high degree of coordination or may result from the fact that only the top level of the organization possesses all information needed for sound decisions. Both of these reasons are valid under certain circumstances; for example, purchasing and production planning decisions may be retained by the top echelons of the organization in multiplant companies where there is a need to coordinate the purchase of raw materials from several different sources and the scheduling of production among many plants. However, there are occasions when the creation of managerial units is guided by the need for moving the level of decision making downward in the organization. Departments may be created for the specific purpose of placing decision making at the level where it will be most effective. The creation of geographic units is an example of the downward movement of decision making. The reasons most frequently advanced for such a move is the need for timeliness, a better coordination of activities in that particular region, and the ability to meet and take full advantage of local factors such as the actions of competitors. The determination of the most effective level of decision making is a major consideration in the organizational process known as *decentralization* which, in effect, is the decentralization of authority to make decisions—a topic discussed in full in Chapter 13.

Span of Management. The level at which decisions are made in an organization has a direct bearing upon the breadth of an executive's span of management. The executive who retains the responsibility for making decisions usually reduces his span of management; however, if he permits his subordinates to make decisions, his span of management may be increased. One of the reasons for the success of the extended span of management in the retail stores of Sears, Roebuck and Company is attributable to the development of decision-making capabilities on the part of the departmental managers.

State of the System

Departmentation. The state of the organization in respect to the achievement of organizational goals—in effect, the state

of the system—is an important consideration in developing departmental units. The reduction of costs, a continuing goal for most organizations, is frequently achieved by avoiding duplication of effort. A plant
manager may desire to have fully autonomous purchasing and payroll
departments as a part of his organization; however, if these functions
are being performed adequately at a higher level of the company, the
creation of duplicate departments at lower levels is not justified. The
personnel function and the public relations function may be conducted
by separate departments at the corporate level of an organization, and
at the plant level these functions may be combined within the personnel
department as a means of reducing expenses. Occasionally, the needs
of the organization are such that it becomes necessary to emphasize a
particular function by creating a separate department which reports to
the chief executive. For example, a firm manufacturing electronic equipment may create a separate sales department, reporting to the president,
to secure government contracts. The desire to reduce costs or to emphasize a particular function is an example of the organization, viewed as
a system, responding to the pressures of its environment.

Span of Management. The extent to which the goals of an organization are stabilized and the degree to which an organization is
achieving these goals serve as a guide in determining an effective span
of management. The recommendation that the span of management be
limited is based upon observations of military organizations. Hence, it
is well to note two characteristics of military types in order to estimate
the applicability of these to business situations. First, the military organization is operating in a situation of continuing emergency during war.
Though the long-range goal, the defeat of the enemy, may not change,
the pressure and demands of day-to-day tactics combined with shifts
in broad strategy make necessary an organization capable of adjusting
rapidly to environmental changes. Narrowing the span of management
is a means of structuring an organization so that it may be compre-
hended and controlled by one man, thereby permitting relatively rapid
adaptations to changing organizational goals. Second, during periods
of war the military is managed by a nucleus of highly skilled regulars,
but the vast majority of the organization is composed of relatively
unskilled, or at best newly trained, civilians. Because of inexperience,
the number that may be supervised effectively declines somewhat; hence,
a narrow span is more appropriate than an extended span.

These two characteristics of the military, a continuing state of
emergency during war with resulting changes in goals and the relative

inexperience of organizational members, are not typical of the average business organization. Though the goals of a business venture change, they do not change with the rapidity of military goals; also, a business grows over an extended period of time, with the result that the proportion of new and inexperienced members is small. The relatively stable goals of business and the high proportion of experienced members contribute toward the effectiveness of extended spans of management.

• ● ● ● ● ● ● ● ●

Case Problem 11-B, "Needed—A Plan for Organization," provides an opportunity to apply the bases for departmentation and the guides for determining an effective span of management to a real situation. Like many companies, the Flexopak Company just grew; there is little evidence of organization planning, and the resultant structure is the result of adding a bit here and a bit there over a period of years. When change occurs, occasioned by the retirement of the chief executive and founder, the company may enter a period of reorganization so that the new president can effectively guide the organization.

Questions for Study and Discussion

1. The quotation from Louis A. Allen on page 263 presents an analogy that compares the design of an organization to the design of an automobile. What is the lesson to be learned from this analogy? What other similar analogies can you develop? What are the limitations of such analogies?

2. What is meant by the statement that most of what is called organization is actually reorganization?

3. What is meant by the term departmentation? Give an example of each of the six bases of departmentation.

4. Comment on each of the following statements: (a) The characteristics of people should be given prime consideration in the creation of departments. (b) The characteristics of the work performed should be given prime consideration in the creation of departments.

5. Why is the phrase, span of management, used in the text rather than the phrase, span of control? Which phrase do you prefer? Why?

6. Comment on the advisability of shortening the lines of communication and at the same time decreasing an executive's span of management.

7. Evaluate the reasons presented by Hamilton, Graicunas, and Urwick for a limited span of management.

8. What phrase in Urwick's principle makes possible the justification of increased spans of management? Does this seem a valid reason for increasing the span of management?

9. Summarize in your own words the results of the AMA survey (Table 11-1) and advance several reasons why these companies "all known to have good organizational practices" do not follow Hamilton's recommendations or Urwick's principle.

10. Summarize in your own words how the propositions of Theory Z can be applied as a means of evaluating the bases used for departmentation and for determining the probable effectiveness of a given span of management.

• • • • • • • • •

Flexopak, founded in 1910 in Madison, Wisconsin, as a printing job shop, soon began to specialize in the printing of flexible packaging materials sold primarily to food processors. During the years immediately after its founding, growth was steady but not particularly rapid; however, with the advent of the modern supermarket and the phenomenal growth of chain stores, the company grew quite rapidly. Flexopak celebrated its 50th anniversary as the largest company in its field, with annual sales in excess of $60 million and with approximately 2,600 employees. Shortly thereafter the president and founder, Thomas Samuels—then in his 70's—decided to step down and turn the active management of the company over to one of the present officers of the company. Recognizing that there had been little organization planning and that a new president, even one from within the company, would find the present structure confusing and unwieldy, he decided as a first step in reorganization to analyze the top management of the company. Figure 11-3 shows the present top management of Flexopak.

Case Problem 11-B
Needed—A Plan for
Organization

Reporting directly to President Samuels as an "assistant to" is Thomas, Jr., his 30-year old son. The younger Samuels works primarily on special projects assigned to him by his father as part of a long-range program designed to groom him for the presidency. At the moment, because of his youth and inexperience, he is not being considered as a replacement for his father. The treasurer, who has 25 years' service, is slated to replace Mr. Samuels as president. There are several reasons for his selection. First, he is thoroughly acquainted with the financial affairs of the company and has personally arranged all long-term financing. Second, there is the possibility that Flexopak will either "go public" or merge with a larger company seeking diversification. In either case, the major strategic moves of the company seem to lie in the financial field, hence the desire to have a chief executive thoroughly familiar with the company's finances.

The controller of the company actually functions as chief accountant and does not have the necessary breadth to assume the duties of treasurer. There

Figure 11-3

TOP MANAGEMENT—THE FLEXOPAK COMPANY

is the vice-president, product development, formerly an outstanding salesman, who directs the work of a small research group. The chief chemist, reporting directly to the president, is responsible for the development, production, and distribution of vinyl film, which is produced in a small Wisconsin plant. The development laboratory is located in the plant and is supervised by the chemist.

The plant managers of the Phoenix plant and the Green Bay plant report directly to Mr. Samuels. The plants in Phoenix and Green Bay are of special interest to Mr. Samuels and, at the time they were founded, he told the managers of these plants that they were his personal representatives in the communities in which the plants are located. It should be noted that the manager of the lithograph department also reports to the president. The lithograph department, in reality a complete operation within the main plant in Madison, is operated on a profit-sharing basis by an old friend of Mr. Samuels. The vice-president, manufacturing, supervises the works manager of the Madison plant; however, his chief function is machine design.

The executive vice-president, also located in Madison, supervises the company's one subsidiary, a paper mill, and has reporting to him, in addition to the president of the paper company, the corporate director of industrial relations. The director of purchases, who joined the company two years ago, performs the purchasing function for the Madison plant only, but hopes in time to purchase for the entire company.

There are four men who have the title, vice-president, sales. Actually, the eastern division and the western division vice-presidents function as general managers. In the eastern division there is an assistant manager who supervises the activities of the 20 salesmen in the eastern states. In addition to the assistant manager, the sales vice-president of the eastern division, whose offices are in New York, has reporting to him the managers of plants located in Philadelphia, Lancaster, and Brooklyn. The western division vice-president, with offices in Madison, has Mr. Samuels' younger son as his assistant sales manager. The assistant manager directs the work of 15 salesmen who are located in the southwestern and southeastern states. The vice-president of the western division also supervises the managers of the Los Angeles and San Francisco plants and the ten salesmen who are located in the western states. The vice-president of the midwestern division is not responsible for any plants. He, too, has an assistant manager who supervises the 15 salesmen of the midwestern region who do not live in Chicago. From his Chicago office the vice-president works closely with the 11 salesmen assigned to the Chicago area. The fourth vice-president, sales, is located in the home office in Madison and has reporting to him four product sales managers, three city salesmen located in Madison, the director of advertising, and the director of the creative art department, a group that designs packages as a customer service.

Problems

1. Recommend a plan of reorganization for Flexopak. Present the new organization in chart form and justify your solution.

2. Comment on Mr. Samuels' span of management. How can this span be justified?

CHAPTER 12

Organization Relationships

The Muskegon Machine Works is a Delaware corporation that operates two plants. One is located in Muskegon, Michigan, and employs 700 people; the other is located in Nashville, Tennessee, and employs 300 persons. The Machine Works, as it is known locally, is proud of its relations with its stockholders and their active participation in annual meetings. At the last meeting the present board of directors was reelected and, in turn, the board reappointed the present officers of the company. A meeting of the board of directors of the Machine Works is now in progress.

"Gentlemen," John Johansen, president of the company and a member of the board, began. "I have asked for a meeting so that we might review our current labor negotiations. We have been negotiating with the local union for the past 60 days in an effort to reach an agreement satisfactory to both parties. Two months ago we met in this same room and authorized our negotiating team to hold the line with a seven cent an hour increase, some slight improvement in the pension plan, and a modification of our group insurance to bring the benefits in line with the daily room charges of the local hos-

pitals. Mr. Lusker, chairman of our negotiating committee, tells me that the union is adamant in its demands: a 12 cent an hour wage increase, one additional holiday which brings the total to nine, and four weeks' vacation for all employees with 10 years' service.

The seven cents an hour represents an increase in labor costs of $145,000 a year for the company since we give the same increase to the Nashville plant that we settle for here. The 12 cents that the union is demanding would add another $100,000 to the $145,000. You are well aware that our average hourly rate in Muskegon is 20 cents an hour above the average for the industry and 30 cents more than our average in the Nashville plant. Also, I am told that the union is meeting tonight to take a strike vote on our final offer presented to them this morning and in line with the instructions we gave our committee at the start of these negotiations. We have a meeting scheduled with the union tomorrow, the expiration date of our current labor agreement; if we don't reach an agreement then, the union is free to strike. Shall we stand firm in the face of what promises to be a long and costly strike?"

287

All issues are discussed thoroughly and the board votes unanimously in support of the company's final offer and instructs the negotiating team not to change its present position.

* * * *

In another part of town a special meeting of the local union is in progress. Norvell Slater, a 39-year old electrician with 20 years' seniority is speaking to the membership. He has been an active member of the union since its certification as the bargaining agent of the employees of the Muskegon Machine Works by the National Labor Relations Board more than 15 years ago.

"I am reporting to you as president of the local and chairman of your bargaining committee. For the past two months we have been meeting with company representatives in an effort to reach agreement on a new contract. So far, not much has been accomplished. We have gained some slight improvement in our pension plan, and the daily room allowance of the hospitalization insurance has been increased so that it now covers the full cost of a hospital room. The real problem seems to be wages. When we started negotiations, we decided that we wouldn't take less than 12 cents an hour. The company says that they won't give more than seven cents. They say that we are getting 20 cents an hour more than the rest of the industry and 30 cents more than Nashville. I don't know about that. All I know is that we are getting 10 cents an hour less than other workers here in Muskegon for the same kind of work and we live here, not in Nashville." At this point there is a roar of approval from the floor.

"The other things we can't get together on are holidays and vacations. Don Toms, our international representative, tells us that it would be a feather in our cap if we could lead the parade for once and get something first in this town. Getting that ninth holiday would put us out in front for a change. And about the four weeks' vacation for you fellows with 10 years' service; you should get that now and not have to wait for 20 years for that fourth week like I did. Anyway, that fourth week doesn't seem like much to me when you compare it to the three-month vactions that some companies are giving. Any questions?"

Again all issues are discussed thoroughly and the vote to strike is unanimous unless the company meets the union's demands for wages, the fourth week of vacation at the end of 10 years, and the ninth holiday.

* * * *

At nine o'clock the following morning both negotiating teams meet in a downtown hotel. The meeting finally ends at 6 p.m. with no agreement. As the meeting closes, Norvell Slater makes the following comment: "You know that our contract expires at midnight tonight. We have a strike vote backing us up, and since we can't get together we have no choice but to strike. Pickets will be placed around the plant tomorrow morning."

The next morning pickets are at every gate and none of the hourly employees, all members of the union, make any effort to cross the picket line.

Problems

1. What is the source of authority granted to the board of directors of the Muskegon Machine Works? Did the board exceed that authority in authorizing the company negotiating committee to stand fast in the face of a certain strike?

2. What is the source of authority that permits the local union to enforce its contract demands by striking? Has the union exceeded its authority in the above case?

3. Does the action taken by the union; i.e., an economic strike, negate or cancel in any way the authority of the management to operate the plant? If so, how?

4. What are the obligations of the employees of the Machine Works to (a) the company and (b) the union?

● ● ● ● ● ● ● ● ●

When discussing theories X and Y in Chapter 10, brief statements were made concerning the *source* of authority. It was mentioned that Theory X assumes that the source of authority is related to the right to own property and the attendant obligation to manage property, while Theory Y states that in order for authority to exist, it must first be accepted by those who are being subjected to that authority. These two positions concerning the source of authority are diametrically opposed; one regards authority as being granted by a source external to the organization and the other views authority as being granted internally by the members of the organization through their acceptance of the exercise of authority. The first purpose of this chapter is to discuss the nature of authority and to reconcile these opposing points of view concerning the *source* of authority. In addition to understanding the sources of authority, it is necessary to appreciate the relationships between two types of authority that are exercised in most formal organizations. These different types of authority are usually called *line* authority and *staff* authority. The second part of the chapter discusses the important organizational relationship of line-and-staff authority.

AUTHORITY

One way of developing an understanding of the differences concerning the source of authority is to present statements representative of each point of view. However, before presenting and analyzing these statements, let us examine various familiar meanings of the word, authority.

Meanings of Authority

There are many different meanings to authority. A board or a commission empowered to act in a specific area may be termed an authority; for example, the port authority. We recognize government as an authority in the phrase, the authority of the state. An individual may be recognized as competent in a given field of learning or as possessing technical qualifications that enable him to speak with authority. Technical writers and expert witnesses are examples of this kind of authority. When we refer to the authority of the president, we are associating authority with an office or a position.

Authority is an abstract concept and, as shown by the above examples, it is a concept applicable to many situations. When used in management literature, the term authority has yet another meaning. Managerial authority may be defined as *the right to act or to direct the action of others in the attainment of organizational goals*. This definition states explicitly two characteristics of authority: (1) authority is a *right* and (2) as a result of possessing this right, one is entitled to *act,* either directly through his own actions or indirectly through the actions of others. Implied, but not stated explicitly, is a third characteristic of authority—(3) the *power* to employ penalties or rewards so that the desired action is completed. Power remains implicit, for there is a great deal of variation in the amount of power associated with managerial authority; in fact, there is one form of authority, staff authority, that may be purely advisory in nature with no power whatsoever. In addition, there are situations in which two or more conflicting or overlapping authorities are entitled to act and the power assigned to one authority may outweigh the power of the others; yet, the authority of those with lesser power remains.

Sources of Authority

Theory X, the work-centered approach, relates the source of authority to the right to own property. The right to own property and the association of authority with that right are dependent upon the organization of the society in which we live. Relating the source of authority to the right to own property and the subsequent management of that property may be termed an *institutional* source of authority since it is dependent upon the institution of organized society. Theory Y, the people-centered approach, regards authority as a situational phenomenon. Authority exists only when the subordinates of a situation accept another individual as having the authority to direct them. Therefore, this source of authority may be designated as *subordinate-acceptance*.

Institutional Source. To state that authority is derived from the right to own private property is a narrow view of the source of authority and not entirely correct since there are instances of managerial authority not dependent upon the ownership of property. To discover the source of authority one must first determine why it is possible to own private property. Our constitutional form of government in the United States rests upon the concept that government represents the will of the people, a will expressed through the action of elected representatives, Congress, and enforced by a judicial system. One aspect of our legal system is that it permits the ownership of private property and the management of that property in accordance with established law. Thus, the real source of managerial authority lies not in the right to own property, but rather in the laws that permit the ownership of property. Case Problem 12-A states that the Muskegon Machine Works is a Delaware Corporation, a statement which indicates that the company is created by law and, as such, possesses the authority necessary for its operation. If further evidence is needed to emphasize that authority is derived from law and not the ownership of property, consider the Tennessee Valley Authority. The managerial authority exercised by the managers of TVA, a publicly owned and operated utility, is derived from an action of Congress, which created the Tennessee Valley Authority. The authority of the management of TVA can come from no other source than law since the ownership of private property is not involved.[1]

Subordinate-Acceptance Source. Do you remember the following story that appears in Chapter 10?

> An agent for the Textile Workers Union of America likes to tell the story of the occasion when a new manager appeared in the mill where he was working. The manager came into a weave room the day he arrived. He walked directly over to the agent and said, "Are you Belloc?" The agent acknowledged that he was. The manager said, "I am the new manager here. When I manage a mill, I run it. Do you understand?" The agent nodded and then waved his hand. The workers, intently watching this maneuver, shut down every loom in the room immediately. The agent turned to the manager and said, "All right, go ahead and run it." [2]

---

[1] Cyril J. O'Donnell, "The Source of Managerial Authority," *Political Science Quarterly,* Vol. XLVII (December, 1952), pp. 573-88. Professor O'Donnell's article is a skillful presentation of authority derived from institutional sources.

[2] Douglas McGregor, *The Human Side of Enterprise* (New York: McGraw-Hill Book Company, 1960), p. 23.

The story illustrates, according to the subordinate-acceptance approach, that the manager has no authority because the subordinates, the men in the mill room, refuse to accept his authority.

Among the first to dissent from the institutional concept of authority was Chester I. Barnard, a successful business executive, who, in the words of Professor Mandeville, "writes with authority about authority." [3] The following quotations from Barnard present his definition of authority and the related concept that the source of authority is its acceptance by a subordinate.

> Authority is the character of a communication (order) in a formal organization by virtue of which it is accepted by a contributor to or "member" of the organization as governing the action he contributes, that is, as governing or determining what he does or is not to do so far as the organization is concerned. [4]

Barnard's statement concerning the source of authority is as follows:

> If a directive communication is accepted by one to whom it is addressed, its authority for him is confirmed or established. It is admitted as the basis of action. Disobedience of such a communication is a denial of its authority for him. Therefore, under this definition the decision as to whether an order has authority or not lies with the person to whom it is addressed, and does not reside in 'persons of authority' or those who issue these orders. [5]

We now have before us two conflicting views of authority. One, the institutional approach, says that authority is derived from the laws of the society in which we live; the other view of authority, the subordinate-acceptance approach, says that there is no authority unless the person who is the object of that authority accepts the order or directive as authoritative. Thus, it is the subordinate's acceptance, not the laws of society, that is the source of authority.

---

[3] Morton J. Mandeville, "Organizational Authority," *Journal of the Academy of Management,* Vol. III (August, 1960), pp. 107-18. An adaptation of Professor Mandeville's article appears in Paul M. Dauten (ed.), *Current Issues and Emerging Concepts in Management* (Boston: Houghton Mifflin Company, 1962), pp. 199-207. Professor Mandeville presents the entire range of opinion concerning the definition of authority. Immediately following Mandeville's "Organizational Authority," in *Current Issues and Emerging Concepts in Management,* is a reply by C. Edward Weber entitled "The Nature of Authority: Comment" and Mandeville's reply to Weber's comment, pp. 208-12. The original citation for Professor Weber's article is as follows:

C. Edward Weber, "The Nature of Authority: Comment," *Journal of the Academy of Management,* Vol. IV (April, 1961), pp. 62-66.

The student who reads both of these articles will gain insight into a current management issue that is far from settled.

[4] Chester I. Barnard, *The Function of the Executive* (Cambridge: Harvard University Press, 1938), p. 163.

[5] *Ibid.*

Effectiveness of Authority

Effective management requires a manager to have a clear understanding of the nature of authority. Managerial authority is not absolute; however, a manager cannot permit himself to be reduced to a state of indecision resulting from self-questioning concerning whether or not he has the right to manage. On the other hand, he cannot blithely assume that his every action or directive will result in the fulfillment of organizational goals. There are three factors that limit the effectiveness of managerial authority—(1) superior authority, (2) overlapping authority, and (3) subordinate acceptance of authority. Note that subordinate acceptance as stated above does not negate or cancel managerial authority; *it merely limits the effectiveness of that authority.* Let us examine each of the three limitations on authority.

Superior Authority. The actions of the officers of a corporation are subject to review and limitations imposed by the board of directors. In Case Problem 12-A, the president of the company calls for a meeting of the board to review current labor negotiations. In so doing he is recognizing the higher authority of the board and seeking a course of action that meets with their approval. The board, in turn, is subject to the legal authority of the owners, the state and the federal governments. Companies impose limitations on the authority of managers by establishing policies and procedures; for example, a plant manager may be authorized to make capital expenditures up to $1,000 without prior approval, but required to submit for approval the expenditure of any amount in excess of $1,000. Each of these instances illustrates that authority is not absolute; rather, it is always subject to limitation by higher authority.

Overlapping Authority. Problem No. 3 of Case Problem 12-A asks whether or not the action of the union, i.e., the calling of a strike, negates or cancels the authority of management. If the source of authority lies in the acceptance of that authority by subordinates, then the answer to Problem No. 3 is affirmative. Now, analyze the situation carefully. The company, a corporation created by law, is exercising proper authority in determining what it believes to be best for its economic welfare. The union, too, is created by law and is certified by the National Labor Relations Board as the official bargaining agent for the employees of the Muskegon Machine Works. Also, the union is exercising properly the authority granted by law in enforcing its economic demands by striking. Thus, here is a situation in which both parties are exercising legally constituted authority to determine the wage rates of the employees of the company. Clearly, there is overlapping and dual authority, with each authority having the same source, law, and each authority being properly exercised. The rejection of the company's offer by the union and the subsequent strike do not negate the authority of management; it simply means that at this point in time the power of the union is sufficient to prevent the management from exercising its authority to operate the plant. Later, as the strike progresses, the company may accede partially or fully to the union's demands, or the union may agree to the original offer made by the company. Authority is not cancelled by power conflicts, which arise frequently when authority overlaps; it is only held in abeyance until the forces of power are resolved.

Subordinate Acceptance. Some proponents of the subordinate-acceptance concept of authority leave the impression that disobedience and the rejection of authority are the normal behavior for members of an organization. Nothing could be further from the truth. The institutions of society, including authority, serve a purpose desired by the majority of that society; however, occasions do arise when subordinates refuse to accept the direction of authority. Most authority carries with it rewards and penalties that may be used to encourage compliance. Robert Tannenbaum, who recognizes authority as derived from the acceptance of subordinates, also recognizes that the weighing of rewards and penalties by subordinates is an important factor in their determining whether or not to accept authority.[6] The weighing of rewards and penalties is in effect a recognition of authority. Disobedience does not cancel authority, but it does render it ineffective for that particular situation unless the attendant reward and/or punishment is sufficient to exact compliance.

LINE-AND-STAFF RELATIONSHIPS

The preceding discussion emphasizes superior-subordinate relationships—the relationships between the managers and the workers of an organization. There is another authority relationship that is equally important—the relationship between two different types of authority exercised by the managers of an organization. These two forms of authority are called *line authority* and *staff authority*, designations of authority that result in the corresponding expressions of *line organiza-*

---

[6] Robert Tannenbaum, "Managerial Decision Making," *Journal of Business,* Vol. XXIII (January, 1950), pp. 22-39.

tion and *staff organization,* phrases which classify the entire organization according to the predominant type of authority exercised. In discussing line-and-staff authority relationships, we will seek answers to the following four questions:

1. What is line authority and what are its functions?
2. What is staff authority and what are its functions?
3. What are the problems inherent in line-and-staff relationships?
4. Is the line-and-staff concept of authority obsolete?

Line Authority

The concept of line-and-staff authority recognizes that within an organization there are two types of managerial authority. There are also two aspects to the definition of line authority. First, line authority may be defined as a relatively simple authority relationship that exists between a superior and a subordinate. Second, line authority may be defined in terms of the organizational function supervised by a manager. When line authority is defined in respect to organizational function, the critical characteristic of the function that determines whether it is line or staff is the degree to which the function in question contributes to the direct achievement of organizational objectives. Let us examine each aspect of line authority.

An Authority Relationship. When defined as an authority relationship, *line authority entitles a superior to direct the work of a subordinate; in essence, this is a command relationship.* It is a command relationship extending from the top of the organization to the lowest echelon and is aptly described as the *chain of command.* As a link in the chain of command, a manager has the authority to direct the work of his subordinates, and, in turn, he is subject to the direction of his superior. He reports "in line" to his superior and is a part of the line organization. Figure 12-1 shows the authority relationships that form the chain of command.

Contribution to Organizational Objectives. The second definition of line authority does not contradict the above view which holds that line authority is a command relationship between superior and subordinate. It does, however, shift the emphasis of the definition from one of relationship between superior and subordinate to organizational function. This shift in emphasis results in the following definitions.

Figure 12-1

LINE AUTHORITY RELATIONSHIP
AS A CHAIN OF COMMAND

"Line refers to those positions and elements of the organization which have responsibility and authority and are accountable for accomplishment of primary objectives." [7]

and,

"Line positions in an organization are those concerned directly with the creation and distribution of salable utilities or with the management of such activity." [8]

The key to distinguishing between line and staff is not the function itself, but rather it is the degree to which the function contributes directly to the achievement of organizational objectives. In an army, the infantry, the artillery, and armored units are known as "line" since they contribute directly to organizational objectives—engaging the enemy in battle; the supporting services—ordnance, medical, engineering, and supply—are regarded as auxiliary in nature and referred to as "staff." In manufacturing organizations, production and sales are regarded as line functions, while purchasing (supplies) is usually classified as staff. Yet, in a department store, the purchasing function, called buying, and sales make up the line organization. Most firms regard finance as a staff function, but for a loan company the acquisition and management of capital is part of the line organization. In each of these examples, the basis for designating a function as line is the contribution of that function to the direct achievement of organizational objectives.

[7] Louis A. Allen, *Management and Organization* (New York: McGraw-Hill Book Company, 1958), p. 206.
[8] William McNair Fox, *The Management Process* (Homewood, Illinois: Richard D. Irwin, Inc., 1963), pp. 78-79.

Staff Authority

Staff authority is advisory in nature. *A member of management possessing staff authority has the right to advise or to provide a service for line managers.* An organization may function quite effectively without any designated staff managers, and in small organizations such is the case.

In Case Problem 11-A, Thomas Jackson, the general manager of Excelsior Products, is effectively managing an organization of 22 salesmen and three clerks. Assume that, as a first step in developing an organization structure capable of extended growth, Mr. Jackson appoints five regional sales managers, each of whom is responsible for the sales in his geographic area. These managers are line managers since they report directly to Mr. Jackson. They have the authority to direct the work of the salesmen and are fully responsible for and contribute directly to the achievement of the organization's primary goal of selling its product. The first step in the development of staff might occur when Mr. Jackson employs Tom Richards as a *personal* assistant. At first, the duties of Tom Richards are not specified, but in a letter to the sales managers, Mr. Jackson states that Tom Richards is to function as his personal assistant. Perhaps Tom's first assignment is to make all arrangements for the next sales meeting. Then he completes a statistical analysis of the dollar volume of sales for each of the many products that Excelsior sells. Eventually, Mr. Jackson may assign Tom Richards to the specific job of training new salesmen and discover that training is a function which demands the full time of a specialist. As a next step, he may hire a man whose sole function is the training of new salesmen. Thus, the undifferentiated work of the personal assistant may develop into a specialized staff role.

This example illustrates that the need for staff services arises partially as the result of increasing size in an organization with an attendant increase in the work load of the chief executive. Consequently, one of the functions of staff is to ease the load of top management.[9] The personal assistant is frequently engaged as a means of easing the work load. As size increases, operations usually become more complex and the need for specialized services arises and results in the creation of a specialized staff. These two forms of staff, which are termed *personal staff* and *specialized staff,* are discussed briefly.

---

[9] Ernest Dale and Lyndall F. Urwick, *Staff in Organization* (New York: McGraw-Hill Book Company, 1960), pp. 1-14. The first chapter of the book, entitled "The Load on Top Management," serves to introduce the various applications of staff in management.

Personal Staff. There is need to define clearly the difference between an *assistant-to* a manager and an *assistant* manager. The former, the assistant-to, is a personal assistant to his chief. His duties vary widely from one organization to another and they also vary considerably from time to time within the same company. He receives the necessary authority to perform his duties from his chief and usually the authority is granted on a limited basis; that is, it is extended for a specific job and for a relatively short period of time. The duties of an assistant-to may range from the routine task of opening the chief executive's mail to negotiating a purchase agreement for a new plant site as a personal representative of the chief. Note that the assistant-to usually has no specific function to perform; his duties vary with the assignment at hand. Second, there is no authority associated specifically with the position; it is authority granted only for each individual assignment. Third, the assistant-to does not act in his own behalf; instead, he is acting as a personal representative of his superior.

The assistant manager is not regarded as staff; rather, he is part of the line. As shown in Figure 12-2 (A), the operating executive reports through the assistant general manager to the general manager. In the absence of the general manager, the assistant manager acts in his stead. The assistant-to, Figure 12-2 (B), usually does not have the authority to act as general manager when the latter is absent. If the general manager desires, he may assign certain specific functions to the assistant manager. For example, all activities related to manufacturing may report to the assistant manager, while the general manager supervises those activities associated with sales. Another possible arrangement is for the general manager to oversee the line functions of the organization, while all staff services report to the assistant manager. In each of these possibilities we note that (1) subordinates report directly to the assistant manager, (2) the assistant manager has fairly constant, well-defined responsibilities assigned to him, and (3) in the absence of the general manager, the assistant manager assumes the full authority of the general manager's position.

Specialized Staff. As an organization grows in size and complexity, the undifferentiated role of the personal assistant develops into specialized staff assignments. There is no unanimity concerning the functions that may be performed by specialized staff personnel, nor is there complete agreement concerning the type of authority that may be exercised by staff managers. Nonetheless, the following three types of specialized staff authority appear in business organizations with great frequency:

(A)
The assistant manager

(B)
The assistant–to

Figure 12-2

ORGANIZATIONAL POSITION OF THE ASSISTANT GENERAL MANAGER
AND THE ASSISTANT TO GENERAL MANAGER

1. A staff specialist may have the authority to provide a specific *service* for the line organization and thus exercise *service authority*.
2. Not all staff positions are created for the purpose of providing service; some have as their sole function the offering of advice in respect to a special group of problems. Staff men in these positions exercise *advisory authority*.
3. Another type of specialized staff authority is *functional authority,* an authority that provides the staff specialist with considerable latitude and freedom to make decisions in his own functional area.

It must be understood that these three forms of staff authority are not clear cut; there is considerable overlap, and many positions utilize all three forms of staff authority.

Figure 12-3 shows a typical staff organization at the plant level of a manufacturing firm. The supervisor of production planning and control is responsible for planning and controlling the flow of production; the supervisor of purchasing serves by making necessary purchases; and the plant engineer is responsible for maintaining physical facilities. The supervision of each of these functions exercises *service authority* in providing a service for the line organization. The authority of the supervisor

Figure 12-3

TYPICAL STAFF ORGANIZATION AT THE PLANT LEVEL

of personnel may be either service authority or advisory authority. When performing the employment function of recruiting and screening applicants, the personnel supervisor is clearly rendering a service for the line; however, his duties may also include the administration and analysis of morale surveys with the purpose of advising the line in regard to actions necessary to improve employee morale. The staff supervisor, when offering advice to the line, is drawing upon advisory authority. The industrial engineer, the quality control supervisor, and the head of the accounting department have as their primary function the offering of advice in specialized areas; and though there is a strong element of service in the work that each performs, it is best to regard their authority as *advisory* in nature.

Functional authority broadens the concept of service and advisory authority so that a staff manager may exercise effective direction and control of his functional specialty. There are two ways of exercising functional authority. First, staff managers may be granted functional authority over their counterparts who are in lower levels of the organization; and second, the particular functional specialty in question may be separated from the line manager's job and assigned to the appropriate staff specialist. Figure 12-4 shows both forms of functional authority. Note that the plant supervisor of each staff function reports functionally (usually indicated by a dotted line) to his staff counterpart at the next higher level. In large organizations this next higher level may be a geographic division, and the managers at the divisional level report to their counterparts on the corporate staff. In addition, the plant staff supervisor performs that portion of the production foreman's job which falls within his specialty. Thus, there are cost clerks in the production department who report to the supervisor of cost accounting and prepare all production costs. The plant industrial engineer supervises time studies and institutes changes in methods, and the quality control supervisor

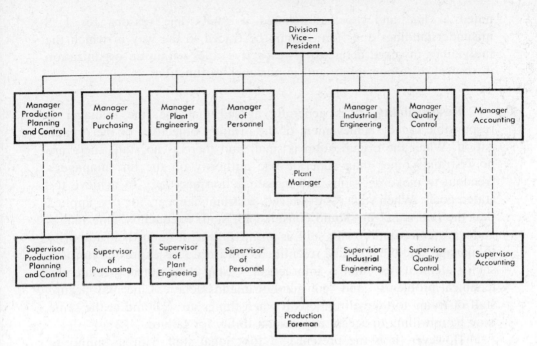

Figure 12-4

THE EXERCISE OF FUNCTIONAL AUTHORITY

Staff department supervisors report functionally to the next higher level, and the specialized portions of the production foreman's job are assigned to the appropriate staff specialist.

directs the work of inspectors who accept or reject the finished product. Although functional staff authority is limited to a specific function, it may sometimes be quite absolute within that particular function, with the result that the auhority of the line manager may be severely restricted.

Problems in Line/Staff (L/S) Relationships

The duality of the line-staff (L/S) concept inherently creates problems of interpersonal relationships. Two authorities exist within an organization—line authority with its right to command, and staff authority, with its right to advise. There is a duality of function—the line function is associated with the achievement of primary company objectives and the staff function supports the line. It is a duality that results in referring to an organization as though it were two separate units—the line organization and the staff organization. The concepts of dual authorities, functions, and organizations set the stage for some rather serious misunderstandings between those persons who are designated as line and those designated as staff. The reasons for L/S misunderstandings and friction may be traced to the way in which the individuals involved define their respective roles within an organization in respect to responsibility and importance of function.

Responsibility. It is generally agreed that the line manager is responsible for the achievement of the primary objectives of the organization. When the organization is small and there is no staff, there are no restraints other than superior line authority on the line manager's freedom to make decisions and initiate action necessary to achieve the stated goals. When staff is introduced, restraints appear, for it is implied that the line manager should consult with staff. Frequently, line managers view consultation with staff as an infringement upon their authority to manage, and the resulting resentment toward staff is expressed through such statements as "staff is impractical," "staff does not appreciate the technical problems," and "consultation means delay." Line may accuse staff of trying to take all the credit when things go well and at the same time be unwilling to accept any responsibility for failure.

However, it is the presence of functional staff with its authority to administer its own particular function that presents the severest test of interpersonal L/S relationships. For example, the president of a subsidiary company that is one of several subsidiaries of a large corporation is responsible for the profits of his company; and as a means of emphasizing this responsibility, a part of his incentive pay is based upon the profitability of his company. At the same time the corporate industrial relations staff, empowered by functional authority, is expected to negotiate the labor agreements for all subsidiary companies to prevent the various unions from playing one company against another. Thus, the president is told that he is responsible for profits, but one of the major cost factors—wages and work rules—is determined to a large extent by staff personnel who do not report to the responsible executive. Is it any wonder that resentment toward staff arises? It is only normal that friction builds up in a situation in which one feels that he has lost a significant part of the decision making and control necessary to operate effectively, and the resulting tensions are expressed as a specific resentment toward staff. The same situation holds for the line managers in lower levels of the organization. The production foreman may be told that he is responsible for the costs of his department, yet the requirements of staff may force him to hire additional clerks. To summarize, one of the main sources of friction between line and staff is the manner in which the line manager defines his responsibilities. When the line manager defines responsibility, or when it is defined for him, as *total* responsibility, it is only normal for him to resent any intrusion of authority that tends to weaken his control of the situation.

Importance of Function. Staff's infringement upon the line manager's authority to manage is the major cause of L/S conflict from the point of view of line, but the idea that staff functions are supportive, with the attendant implication that they are secondary and somehow less important, is the main source of L/S conflict as viewed by staff managers. To understand staff's position, it is necessary to state briefly the personal characteristics of staff personnel. As a rule, staff men are highly ambitious and eager to advance, and they are somewhat younger and have a higher level of formal education than their line counterparts.[10] The staff manager is also aware that the reason for his employment is his specialized knowledge, and since he is ambitious and desires to advance, it is only natural that he advance by the avenue which seems most logical to him—advancing his ideas. When his ideas are restricted by line, he is told that it is the function of line to decide and that his role is supportive in nature. To the staff man the statement that line makes the decision is a distortion of what happens in practice, if not pure fiction. The following example supports staff's contention that it is staff, not line, who makes critical decisions or, at the very least, makes it possible for the line manager to decide.

In a typical manufacturing organization, the manager of manufacturing is charged with the responsibility of producing the product and the sales manager has as his area of responsibility the distribution of the product. Both are line managers whose activities are coordinated by a higher line authority, a president or a general manager. Who determines how much of each product is to be manufactured and the sequence in which these items are to be produced and subsequently sold? As a result of analyzing market trends and customer needs, the staff manager of the market research department recommends the optimum product mix. The manager of production planning and inventory control, another staff department, interprets and translates the findings of market research into production schedules that specify the quantity and the sequence in which each product is to be manufactured. Though the sales manager approves the recommendations of the market research group and the production manager approves the schedules developed by the production

---

10 Melville Dalton, "Conflicts Between Staff and Line Managerial Officers," *American Sociological Review*, Vol. XV (June, 1950), pp. 342-51.

planning and inventory control department, it is understandable why the staff managers of market research and production planning consider that it is they who in effect make the decisions. It is difficult to relegate either staff function to a supportive role when the very nature of these functions influences so greatly the success of the company in fulfilling its primary objectives—the manufacture and the distribution of a product.

Is Line-Staff Obsolete?

Conflict between line and staff has long been recognized as a major deterrent to organizational effectiveness, with the result that many students of management have offered suggestions to minimize such conflict. One such set of recommendations states that line has the final responsibility for the successful operation of the company and consequently should have the authority to make operating decisions. Staff functions are carefully defined as providing either service or advice to the line; an advice or service that should be presented when requested by line and also when, in the opinion of staff, it is considered necessary. It is stated that whether or not staff's advice or service is accepted is dependent entirely upon the judgment of line, and line is urged to seriously consider the recommendations of staff. The last recommendation suggests that both line and staff should have the right of appeal to a higher authority.[11]

The recommendations presented above are helpful in some cases; however, such recommendations are of limited value primarily because they rest upon assumptions that are of questionable validity. These assumptions are: (1) line managers will accept the advice and recommendations of staff and (2) staff is able and willing to accept a supportive role in the organization and continue to put forth its best effort when in fact its recommendations are generally ignored.[12] Also, recommendations for improving line-staff relationships implicitly assume that the line-staff concept is necessary for organizational effectiveness. There are two alternatives to the line-staff concept that deserve careful consideration.

[11] Louis A. Allen, "The Line-Staff Relationship," *Management Record,* Vol. XVII (September, 1955), pp. 346-49. In this article Mr. Allen presents an excellent analysis of L/S relationships. The recommendations cited in the text are based upon Mr. Allen's suggestions for improving L/S relationships. Also see the set of recommendations found in Ernest Dale, *Planning and Developing the Company Organization Structure* (New York: American Management Association, 1952), Research Report No. 20, pp. 76-83.

[12] Rocco Carzo, Jr., "Organizational Realities," *Business Horizons,* Vol. IV (Spring, 1961), pp. 95-104. See pages 99-100 for Mr. Carzo's analysis of line and staff.

Functional-Teamwork.[13] Functional-teamwork is an organizational concept presented by Gerald Fisch, a management consultant, as an alternate to the line-staff concept. It is suggested that three functional areas be defined and each area represent a function significant to the well-being of the organization. In addition to defining the functional areas that are grouped under *time, resources,* and *human interrelations,* the task of top management is carefully defined. Let us see how the many activities of a business organization that are classed as either line or staff are treated under the functional-teamwork concept.

PROCESS FUNCTIONS. All functions within the business that must be controlled with *time* as a major element are classed as *process functions.* Included as process functions are product design, purchasing, manufacturing, advertising, physical distribution (sales), and billing. Note that in this arrangement the usual line functions of sales and manufacturing are grouped with functions normally regarded as staff to form a functional unit concerned with the movement of the product from its inception in product design, through manufacturing, the distribution system, and the final billing—all related activities accomplished under the pressure of time; hence, they are process functions.

RESOURCES FUNCTION. All resources—physical, monetary, and human—are considered as part of the resources of a company, and it is the function of the resources manager to acquire, maintain, and utilize these resources in the most efficient manner possible. Physical facilities, capital invested in the business, the skills of employees, and patents on products or processes are all considered as resources that should be carefully controlled and utilized.

RELATIONS FUNCTION. The relations function can be summed up in one word, communications, and it includes both internal and external communications. Business in our society has an acute communications problem; and, in most companies, little is being done to present a consistent, coherent picture of the company and its problems to employee groups, shareholders, the community, various government agencies, and to the customer. These are the relations that would be supervised by the director of the relations function.

---

[13] Gerald G. Fisch, "Line-Staff Is Obsolete," *Harvard Business Review,* Vol. XXXIX (September-October, 1961), pp. 67-79. This section is based upon Mr. Fisch's article which states the author's belief that the line-staff concept is obsolete. In place of the line-staff (L/S) concept, Mr. Fisch suggests *functional-teamwork* (F/T). The first part of the article presents a careful analysis of the line-staff concept and the second part presents in detail the functional-teamwork concept.

GENERAL MANAGEMENT. Though not a function in the same sense as the above three functions, general management deserves particular attention under the functional-teamwork concept. With the day-to-day work allocated to the three functional managers, the top management of the organization is free to establish corporate goals and objectives, to offer leadership when needed, to coordinate and realign the functions when necessary, and to control the entire operation.

There are several characteristics of the functional-teamwork concept that differentiate it from the line-staff concept of organization. First, there is only one authority, managerial authority, that is exercised by each of the managers of the process, resources, or relations function within his own functional area. Second, once the goals of the organization are established and the resources determined to be adequate for the project at hand, the decisions concerning the production of the company's product or services fall within a logical framework. Third, a structure encouraging teamwork is stressed so when the actions of one function touch upon those of another function, the problem is one of resolving the question on a teamwork basis rather than determining which party has the superior authority. Also, top management is free to encourage a teamwork solution to problems as they arise.

Task Force Organization. The functional-teamwork concept implies a fundamental redesign of the organization structure. An approach similar to functional-teamwork, though generally much more limited in its scope, is often called *task force organization* or *task force management*. Like functional-teamwork, a task force is essentially a team effort. There are several distinctive characteristics of a task force. First, it is a tightly organized unit under the direction of a manager who usually has broad powers of authority. Second, a task force is organized to accomplish a specific task or goal such as the introduction of a new product or building and placing into operation a new physical facility. A task force is working against a time deadline since its objectives must be accomplished by a certain date. Third, the personnel who comprise the task force possess a diverse range of skills and abilities, thus making it possible for each member of the group to make a unique contribution to the solution of the problem.

A good example of the application of the task force concept of organization to the solution of a specific problem is Minneapolis-Honeywell's Polaris Missile task force headed by a manager of the team with a production manager, an account manager, a subcontract manager, and a procurement manager reporting to him. The task force organization is also successfully used in such diverse activities as construction, advertising, military fighting units, and motion picture film production. Whenever there is a need for *concerted* team effort to accomplish a specific goal within a relatively short period of time, the creation of a task force may offer a means of creating an organization capable of accomplishing the desired goals.[14]

●　●　●　●　●　●　●　●　●

There is no universal answer to the question raised at the beginning of this section—is line-staff obsolete? The line-staff concept serves many companies very well, particularly those companies operating in an environment of minimal change. However, when stress situations appear with the accompanying need for prompt action in order to survive, many companies turn to the functional-teamwork concept of organization by creating a task force to solve the immediate problem. Since the application of the concept of functional-teamwork is effective in a crisis situation, it is only logical to consider the possibility of applying the functional-teamwork approach to organization as a continuing form of organizational structure to insure the maximum utilization of resources in meeting the daily challenges of competition. In addition to stress situations with their accompanying need for prompt action, the introduction of integrated information-decision-making systems also calls for a reexamination of the line-staff concept. Such systems cut across traditional departmental lines and functions with a resultant change in the locus of the decision-making function. Modern information systems also result in the creation of large functional units composed of several traditional line-staff departments. Further, when the need for interaction between the members of an organization is high, the functional-teamwork concept offers a structure that makes possible highly effective communications.

Questions for Study and Discussion

1. Comment on the following statement: Authority emanates from the office or the position that a person holds and not from the person himself.
2. How is the concept of power related to the concept of authority? Is it possible to exercise authority without power? Give an example.
3. What is meant by the statement that managerial authority has its source in law rather than as the result of a right to own property?

---

[14] A. K. Wicksberg and T. C. Cronin, "Management by Task Force," *Harvard Business Review*, Vol. XL (November-December, 1962), pp. 111-18. In this article the authors stress team effort in task force management and offer practical suggestions for the reassignment of personnel after the completion of a specific project. "Management by Task Force" is the primary basis for the discussion of task force organization.

4. Under what condition does the quotation on page 291 that describes the relationship between a union agent and a plant manager illustrate the loss or the absence of authority? Is the plant manager still managing the plant even though it is not in operation?

5. In your opinion is the quotation on page 291 illustrative of the absence of authority or the lack of effectiveness of authority? If your answer is lack of effectiveness, why is the manager's authority ineffective?

6. Develop examples that illustrate each of the conditions that limit the effectiveness of authority.

7. Identify, by occupation and function performed, the line organization of the following types of organizations: a manufacturing firm, a bank, a retail store, a hospital, and a university. Why do certain occupations such as accountants and physicians shift from line to staff positions in different types of organizations?

8. Is there a chain of command within a staff department? If so, give an example.

9. Differentiate in your own words between an "assistant-to" and an "assistant" manager. Give an example of each. Which assistant is staff?

10. On what grounds can the concepts of line and staff as applied to industrial organizations be criticized? What are the advantages resulting from utilizing the L/S concept in industrial groups?

11. Under what conditions is the functional-teamwork or the task force type of organization feasible?

12. Is the functional-teamwork or the task force type of organization a play on words, or is it actually a different type of organization? Support your answer.

● ● ● ● ● ● ● ● ●

The Glass Container Company, with headquarters in Chicago, is a large manufacturer of glass containers that operates 18 plants located throughout the United States. The company has three geographic divisions—Eastern, Central, and Pacific—each of which is headed by a vice-president and general manager who is responsible for the sales and manufacturing functions within his division. The Central Division's general manager is a young, aggressive executive who seems destined to become the president of the company. Under his direction the profits and sales volume of the division have grown each year, a growth due in large part to the successful operations of the Minneapolis plant. The manager of the Minneapolis plant, a graduate engineer, was brought into the company as a plant manager as part of a planned program to strengthen the management of the company. Plans are now being made to transfer the Minneapolis manager to the corporate headquarters in New York, thus making it necessary to select a new manager for Minneapolis.

In Chicago, there is a director of organizational planning who is a member of the corporate staff and reports directly to the president of the company. At the suggestion of the director of organizational planning, the Minneapolis plant manager was recruited from outside the company since a survey of key personnel indicated a need for technically trained managers. Normally the director of organizational planning works directly with the division

---

Case Problem 12-B
Line/Staff Relationships

---

vice-presidents in an advisory capacity; and when he and the vice-president agree upon a proposed move of key personnel, the move is made without consulting the president of the company. However, when there is disagreement, the matter is usually referred to the president, who makes the final decision.

There is still a need for graduate engineers capable of filling top managerial positions that are presently available and those expected to develop within the next five years as the result of expansion and the retirement of present personnel. It is believed by all concerned that sound preparation for top management should include two or three years of experience as a plant manager as a means of learning the technical aspects of the glass container industry.

In regard to the Minneapolis position, there are three possible choices. First, another man can be recruited from outside the company and be assigned to the Minneapolis plant as manager, thus providing a period of training with subsequent assignment to a more responsible position in the corporation. Second, there are several young assistant plant managers who would profit from experience as manager of a large plant; and although it would probably take longer for any of them to develop, they too could be promoted to more responsible positions. The third possibility is to promote the present assistant plant manager, a man who is 50 years old with 25 years' service with the company. The assistant plant manager is responsible to a large extent for the success of the plant since he directly supervises the operating departments and is thoroughly familiar with the technical aspects of glass making. However, he has indicated an unwillingness to move from the Minneapolis area and has expressed a desire to retire upon the completion of 30 years' service at age 55, which is permissible under the terms of the company's pension plan.

In discussing these three possibilities with the general manager of the Central Division, the director of organizational planning recommended either of the first two choices and pointed out that if the third choice were adopted, it would mean the blocking of a valuable training position for at least a five-year period. He also stated that should the assistant plant manager elect to work until normal retirement at age 65, it would mean an even longer period of time before the plant could be used as a training position. However, the division vice-president insists upon promoting the present assistant plant manager. He readily admits that the promotion of the assistant plant manager will effectively block the use of that position as a training position; but he does not want to see any of the younger assistant plant managers in the Minneapolis position, nor will he approve the recruitment of a man from outside the company. To him, either of the first two choices means putting an unknown quantity into an important operating position that markedly affects the profitability of his division. In summing up his position, he makes the following statement to the director of organizational planning:

"I'm charged with the responsibility of maintaining profitable operations in the plants under my direction, and the extent to which I meet this responsibility determines to a large extent my future in this company. For me to accept either a new man from outside or a younger man from within the company whom I don't know personally is to run the risk of being responsible for a less profitable plant. I realize that you are responsible for planning for corporate organizational needs, but I'm responsible for the operating success of this division."

Since the matter could not be resolved with the vice-president of the division, the director of organizational planning decided to refer the question to the president of the company.

Problems

1. As president of the company, how would you decide the matter?
2. Should the director of organizational planning be given the authority to overrule the division vice-president in the functional area of organizational planning?
3. Is the concept of functional-team-work applicable in this situation? If so, how?

CHAPTER 13

Organizational Processes — Delegation and Decentralization of Authority

Thomas Dayton, now 41 years old, is one of several candidates who are being considered for the position of general manager of manufacturing for Engineered Products, a firm with seven manufacturing plants. A review of Tom's personnel file indicates that he joined the firm as a design engineer immediately after receiving his degree in mechanical engineering from the state university. His first assignment was on the board as a draftsman, and a notation by the supervisor of the drafting department indicates that Tom did this job willingly and well. The notation reads in parts:

"Mr. Dayton is now in his sixth month as a member of the design department. There have been several occasions when he has come in voluntarily on weekends to rework drawings so that they meet the most exacting specifications. It is unheard of for Mr. Dayton to turn in work that is smudged or messy in any way."

At the end of 18 months Tom was promoted to section chief and placed in charge of ten draftsmen. As might be expected, the work from his section

Case Problem 13-A
A Need for Delegation

was almost perfect. One reason for the high level of accuracy was that Tom actually performed the work of the section checker and personally reviewed all drawings thoroughly and carefully before passing them on to the head of the department. On more than one occasion Tom reworked the drawings of his subordinates in order to meet specified deadlines.

Following these early years in the design section, Tom's rise was steady and sure. During the time that he served as assistant manager of the research laboratory there were several important product modifications, primarily the result of his own work and effort. After several years in research, he was transferred to one of the larger plants as assistant manager in charge of all production departments so that he could supervise the introduction to manufacturing of one of the products which he had developed. He remained in this position for over five years and during most of this time the production costs for the manufacturing departments under Tom's supervision were the lowest in the company. Upon the retirement of the plant manager, Tom was moved up to manager with the honest congratulations of all concerned. There were no reservations concerning his ability to work long and hard in order to get the job done; nor was his loyalty to the company questioned.

It did not take long to realize the success predicted for Tom as plant manager; that is, success measured by the operating statement. Operating efficiency increased slightly, and when combined with the substantial reduction in administrative expenses, the result was a marked increase in the profitability of the plant. However, all was not well with Tom's administration. The chief industrial engineer of the plant resigned and told Tom his reason for resigning was that he had been offered a similar position in another company at considerably more money. Yet, in a conversation with the corporate general manager of industrial engineering, the following remarks were made:

"We no longer have any weekly staff meetings at the plant. These were stopped about a month after Tom became plant manager. He told us then that they were a waste of time and that if we had any special ideas about improving operations we should see him personally. Also, he now approves all changes in pay. As a department manager, I used to be able to approve pay changes for the engineers in my department as long as they were within the provisions of the corporate salary plan; but not now, because he approves all changes in pay, regardless of the amount or whether they are within the terms of the salary plan. As for overtime, he approves all overtime in advance, not only in the general administrative departments but also within the production departments, a responsibility that normally lies within the control of the assistant plant manager. And the cost control program results in his actually running all departments. We are supposed to run our departments within the limitations set by the annual budgets, but not any more. Tom wants all expense accounts sent directly to him; as department managers, we no longer see them. The switchboard operator sends him a daily tally of all long-distance telephone calls with the name of the party called, the name of the person making the call, and the amount of the call. But what really irritates me is that he plans the work of my department and calls my men into his office to check on the accuracy of their work. If he wants to run the industrial engineering department, he is welcome to do so, but he doesn't need a department manager for the job—he needs a chief clerk."

Mr. Thompson, the present general manager of manufacturing, is slated to move to the presidency of the corporation. He is a staunch supporter of Tom Dayton and points to Tom's outstanding record of success in the company. The general manager of manufacturing coordinates the production of all seven plants and is accountable to the president of the company for the performance of the plants. Traditionally there is a substantial degree of delegation of authority to the individual plant managers for day-to-day operations. Such a policy of delegation results, on occasion, in some rather expensive mistakes on the part of plant managers and the attendant temptation to step in and correct things immediately; but the net result is the development of strong plant managers and a highly efficient manufacturing organization. Mr. Thompson realizes that Tom Dayton is not a good delegator, but he believes that as president of the company, he can develop Tom into a good manufacturing manager and teach him how to delegate.

Problems

1. What are the underlying causes of Tom's failure to delegate?
2. Do you agree with Mr. Thompson that Tom can be taught how to delegate?
3. Why should a manager be criticized for his failure to delegate?

•　•　•　•　•　•　•　•　•

In Chapter 12 the sources of authority were examined and the interpersonal relationships that exist between those persons performing line functions and those who are engaged in staff work were discussed. Fundamental to the exercise of managerial authority, either as line authority or staff authority, is an organizational process that permits the transmission of authority from one member of management to another— a process called the *delegation of authority*. It is this process of delegating authority from one member of management to another that makes it possible for organizations to grow. The extent to which organizations consistently delegate authority downward to lower levels of management is described as the process of *decentralization of authority*. In this chapter we shall first discuss the nature of the process of delegation of authority with particular emphasis upon the factors that make it difficult for an executive to delegate effectively. The second part of the chapter applies the concepts of Theory Z in determining the optimum degree of decentralization of authority within an organization and examines the potential effect of modern information-decision-making systems upon the extent of decentralization.

THE PROCESS OF DELEGATION

Delegation of authority is an organizational process that permits the transfer of authority from superior to subordinate. There is general agreement that the process of delegation is made up of three distinct steps; however, there is considerable variation in the terminology used to describe each of the three steps. The following three quotations illustrate the variation in terminology and emphasize the need for a careful definition of terms so that the process of delegation may be understood.

Professors Koontz and O'Donnell describe delegation as follows:

> The entire process of delegation involves the *assignment* of tasks, the *delegation* of authority for accomplishing these tasks, and the *exaction* of responsibility for their accomplishment.[1]

Professor Newman describes the delegation process as follows:

The process of delegation has three aspects:

1. The assignment by an executive of *duties* (planning and doing of specified activities) to his immediate subordinate.
2. The granting of *permission* (authority) to make commitments, use resources, and take other actions necessary to perform the duties.
3. The creation of an *obligation* (responsibility) on the part of each subordinate to the executive for the satisfactory performance of the duties.[2]

The third quotation from Louis Allen, a management consultant, defines responsibility as work rather than an obligation and introduces the concept of accountability.

> We have now described the three essential aspects of delegation: the entrustment of *work*, or *responsibility*, to another for performance; the entrustment of *powers and rights*, or *authority*, to be exercised; and the creation of an *obligation*, or *accountability*, on the part of the person accepting the delegation to perform in terms of the standards established.[3]

Aspects of Delegation

Although each of the definitions above recognizes three major steps in the process of delegation, there is considerable difference in the terms used to describe each step. In this textbook, the following terms will be used to describe the three aspects of the process of delegation:

1. The assignment of responsibility.
2. The delegation of authority.
3. The creation of accountability.

---

[1] H. Koontz and C. O'Donnell, *Principles of Management* (3d ed.; New York: McGraw-Hill Book Company, 1964), p. 57. Chapter 4, "Authority and Responsibility," pp. 49-68, discusses the process of delegation in considerable detail.

[2] W. H. Newman, *Administrative Action* (2d ed.; Englewood Cliffs, New Jersey: Prentice-Hall, Inc., 1963), pp. 185-86.

[3] L. A. Allen, *Management and Organization* (New York: McGraw-Hill Book Company, 1958), p. 116. On pages 116-17, footnote 3, there is a brief discussion of the various terms used to describe the process of delegation.

Assignment of Responsibility. The term, *responsibility,* has been used to refer to either the work that is being assigned or to the obligation created by the assignment of such work. In the first two quotations cited above, responsibility is used to denote an obligation; yet the third statement by Louis Allen defines responsibility as work to be performed. There are several reasons for limiting the meaning of responsibility to duties, or work, to be performed in fulfilling an assignment. In our everyday speech we frequently equate responsibility and duties by referring to the responsibilities of a parent or the responsibilities of a student. Also, many companies in their descriptions of managerial positions state the responsibilities of a given position as duties to be performed. Another reason for limiting the meaning of the word responsibility to assigned duties is that there is a specific term, *accountability,* which is used to describe the obligation created by the assignment of responsibilities.

Thus, responsibility is defined as *all of the duties that must be performed in order to complete a given task.*

Delegation of Authority. Delegation has a precise meaning. One who delegates to another person *empowers that person to act for him.* Two facets of this definition deserve careful attention. First, the delegator *empowers* the delegatee. In Chapter 12, authority is defined as the right to act or to direct others to act. Since responsibilities—or duties— are assigned as the first step in the process of delegation, it is necessary that the person to whom responsibility is assigned either act or direct others to act in the performance of those duties. Authority empowers such action; hence the expression, the delegation of authority, with the result that the delegatee is empowered to act or to direct others to act.

The second facet of the definition deserving careful attention is the phrase, *for him.* A person possessing delegated authority is acting for, or representing, the person who delegated the authority. The implications of acting for another are significant as an organizational process because it means that even though authority is delegated to subordinates so that they may successfully fulfill their assigned duties, the delegator still retains full control over the delegated authority and may recall that authority as the occasion demands. Delegation in no way implies abdication. When a king abdicates, he divests himself of all responsibility and authority; however, an executive who delegates remains responsible for the accomplishment of assigned duties and retains full control over delegated authority.

Creation of Accountability. The moment one accepts a loan from a bank he incurs an obligation to repay the money that he has borrowed. Likewise, when a subordinate accepts responsibility and the authority necessary to carry out those responsibilities, he incurs an obligation—a duty to perform the assigned work and to properly utilize the authority delegated to him. The creation of such an obligation on the part of a subordinate, when viewed as an organizational process, is defined as the creation of *accountability*. The subordinate is *accountable* to his superior for the proper exercise of authority and the performance of assigned responsibilities. An easy way to differentiate between the concepts of responsibility and accountability is to remember that a subordinate is *responsible for* the completion of work assigned to him and is *accountable to* his superior for the satisfactory performance of that work.

Principles of Effective Delegation

The preceding analysis of delegation presents a process that is relatively easy to understand and seemingly simple in its nature; however, in actual practice a great deal of difficulty is experienced in achieving effective delegation. There is general agreement among students of management and management practitioners that three fundamental principles must be observed for the process of delegation to be most effective. These principles are:

1. Principle of parity of authority and responsibility.
2. Principle of absoluteness of accountability.
3. Principle of unity of command.

Each principle is discussed briefly below.

Principle of Parity of Authority and Responsibility. *For effective delegation, the authority granted to a subordinate must be equal to the responsibility assigned to him.*

When a subordinate undertakes assigned duties, it is logical and fair that he be delegated the authority necessary to enable him to act, or direct others to act, so that the assignment may be completed. The principle of parity of authority and responsibility recognizes the need for delegated authority and emphasizes that delegated authority should be of sufficient scope so that the assigned responsibility may be accomplished. Too little authority usually manifests itself by a manager having to consult his superior before making relatively routine decisions. A manager of manufacturing, charged with the responsibility of producing the company's product within specified cost and quality limits, should be able to make decisions pertaining to purchasing raw materials, maintenance of equipment, selection and training of personnel, and the determination of the most efficient methods of manufacturing. In short, the authority granted should be of sufficient scope so that all related activities may be accomplished.

Although the granting of too little authority is a frequent reason for ineffective delegation, failure to fully understand and recognize the limitations normally inherent to managerial authority causes most of the difficulty in the application and interpretation of the principle of parity of authority and responsibility. One limitation, not always understood or appreciated, is that managerial authority seldom carries with it the power necessary for the literal achievement of assigned responsibilities.

For example, a sales manager cannot force customers to buy, nor can a personnel director force a union to cooperate with management; yet, it is not uncommon to say that the sales manager is "responsible" for the sales in his territory and that the personnel director is "responsible" for establishing cooperative relations with the union. Another limitation on managerial authority results from restrictions imposed by the organization itself. Authority is not absolute; instead, it is circumscribed by statements of company policy and procedure that have the effect of defining the limits of authority for each level of the organization. A regional sales manager may have a substantial advertising budget and the authority to select the media appropriate for his geographic area, yet the total spent may not exceed the budgeted amount without prior approval from his superior. Restrictions set by higher authority exist for every position within a company.

We have described three conditions that may result in an imbalance between authority and responsibility. First, there may be too little authority granted for the task at hand; second, there are situations in which a manager has little or no power to direct the actions of others; and third, organizational policies and procedures often limit the extent of a manager's authority. With such restrictions on authority, one might reasonably ask whether or not a principle of parity of authority and responsibility is practical. The answer is yes, because knowledge of the difficulties encountered in creating coextensive authority and responsibility should help in developing effective techniques of delegation and in realistically assessing the extent to which an executive should be held responsible for the accomplishment of assigned duties.

Principle of Absoluteness of Accountability. *Although responsibility and authority may be delegated to subordinates, accountability to one's superior cannot be delegated.*

When the process of delegation is defined as the assignment of responsibilities, the delegation of authority, and the creation of accountability, it is evident that both responsibility and authority may be delegated. Indeed, the continuing redelegation of authority and responsibility makes organizations possible. Departmentation, the dividing of work into manageable units, is an example of the delegation of responsibility. When major departments are created, the chief executive is dividing his responsibility—his work load—so that others may more effectively accomplish the tasks necessary for the achieving of organizational goals. At the same time that responsibilities are delegated, commensurate authority is also delegated so that managers of the newly created work units may effectively act or direct others to act. In turn, the major departmental units are further subdivided, with the managers of the subunits receiving delegated responsibilities and authority. But accountability, the obligation to report to one's superior, cannot be delegated. The president of a company, although delegating to a sales vice-president the responsibility and authority necessary to carry out the sales function, remains accountable to his superior authority, the board of directors, for the achievement of sales objectives. Also, the sales vice-president, though redelegating authority and responsibility to division sales managers, remains accountable to his superior, the president, for the successful discharge of the sales function. In theory the concept of accountability is absolute and cannot be redelegated. However, in practice it is recognized that delegated responsibilities are performed by subordinates whose work may fall short of expected standards of performance. For example, the sales vice-president considers the number of new and inexperienced salesmen when evaluating the performance of a division sales manager; and the president, in turn, considers these facts when appraising the work of the vice-president.

Principle of Unity of Command. *Each subordinate should be accountable to one, and only one, superior.*

The unity of command principle states something we all know well—no man can serve two masters well. The expression, unity of command, stresses that the sources of command should be unified so that a subordinate receives assigned duties and authority from one superior and is accountable only to that superior. The following four examples are representative of the many situations that result in a subordinate having more than one master and serving none well.

UNDIFFERENTIATED ORGANIZATIONS. Occasionally in small organizations there are work groups that are undifferentiated in respect to rank or job assignments. Frequently the head of such a group characterizes his work force as "one big happy family." An employee who is a member of an undifferentiated work group is not certain what is expected of him nor is he sure of the relative powers of the several persons who direct him. As a result, he is forced to select from several job assignments those that he believes to be most effective in placating his several supervisors. Even though an employee may succeed in keeping his job by "greasing the wheel which squeaks the loudest," it is doubtful that organizational objectives are being met effectively. Objectives may be attained much more efficiently when an organization structure is established so that each supervisor knows clearly the subordinates accountable to him and each subordinate knows the supervisor to whom he reports.

INTENTIONAL DISREGARD OF UNITY OF COMMAND. Frequently organizations that have progressed beyond the undifferentiated workgroup stage and have established well-defined superior-subordinate relationships intentionally assign one subordinate to two or more supervisors. Such assignments are justified on the grounds that the work load is light and that it is necessary for an employee to work in several departments in order to keep fully occupied. However, it must be recognized that disputes may arise when one supervisor demands more than his share of time. These difficulties can be avoided or minimized by designating in advance a higher authority to determine which department has precedence.

BYPASSING INTERMEDIATE SUPERVISION. A third violation of the unity of command principle arises as the result of leapfrogging or bypassing one or more levels of intermediate supervision. For example, a plant manager who ignores his superintendent and directs a foreman to change a production schedule is bypassing an intermediate level of supervision. Such action is unfair to the foreman who is put into the position of serving two masters and carrying out two sets of conflicting directions. It is also unfair to the superintendent who remains accountable to the plant manager for the performance of his subordinates even though he has lost effective control over their actions. The remedy for the difficulties and misunderstandings which appear as the result of bypassing is not found in recommending that each supervisor have contact only with his immediate superior and his immediate subordinate; rather, it is found in clearly defining the nature of these personal contacts. It is desirable and necessary for an executive to be aware, as the result of personal observation and contact, of the activities of all levels of the organization; however, the actual direction of subordinates should remain the specific responsibility of that subordinate's designated supervisor.

STAFF RELATIONSHIPS. Figure 12-4 on page 301 illustrates the concept of functional staff authority and shows the relationship that may exist between two or more levels of staff personnel and between line-and-staff personnel at the plant level. The exercise of strong functional authority may result in situations that violate the unity of command principle.

Dual command arises when the supervisor of quality control at the plant level receives instructions concerning the establishment of acceptable levels of quality from his functional superior, the division manager of quality control, that conflict with those standards established by the plant manager who is his direct line superior. In the same manner, a production foreman may be placed in the position of receiving orders from more than one source of authority when the plant quality control supervisor sets quality standards in conflict with those previously stated by the plant manager. The potential difficulties resulting from the dual authority sources of line and staff are minimized when the functional authority of staff is clearly defined and it is emphasized that even though staff properly has authority within a given functional area, any direct orders are to be issued only by the immediate line superior.

Practical Suggestions for Successful Delegation

The principles of delegation discussed above provide a basis for understanding more fully the process of delegation and recognizing the conditions that may result in ineffective delegation. Admittedly, a delegation of sorts can occur even though all three principles are violated simultaneously, yet few deny that observance of the principles of delegation results in more effective delegation. The following practical suggestions for successful delegation are offered as a means of putting into practice the principles of delegation.[4]

1. Determine Objectives. Remember the principle of the objective: *Before initiating any course of action, the objectives in view must be clearly determined, understood, and stated.* The process of delegation affords an excellent opportunity for the application of the principle of the objective. As a first step, it is necessary to determine the goals expected as the result of a specific work assignment. A statement of goals is important to the process of delegation for two reasons: First, the duties and responsibilities of a job are derived from and directed toward

---

[4] L. A. Allen, *ibid.,* Chap. 7, "Better Methods of Delegation," pp. 134-55. Chapter 7 presents an extensive discussion of specific methods that may be used for more effective delegation.

the achievement of stated objectives. Second, the person to whom work is assigned is accountable to his superior for the successful completion of assigned duties; consequently, unless the work performed is pertinent to achieving stated goals, the entire concept of accountability becomes exceedingly vague.

2. Assign Duties and Delegate Commensurate Authority. Determine all the duties that must be performed to complete the task at hand; then assign the whole job—not just parts of it. There are too many instances where supervisors assign only the minor or routine details of a job and retain the key decision-making aspects of the job for themselves. Such assignments are not delegation in the true sense of the word since there is little need for the delegation of authority. Defining the whole job at the very start of a project brings into proper perspective the amount of authority needed to insure parity of responsibility and authority. Also, subordinates are more likely to be better motivated by assignments that encompass the whole job.

3. Select Subordinate. Select the man for the job in the light of what is expected. Assigned responsibilities are in effect the duties of a job; and duties, if they are to be completed successfully, require certain skills and knowledge. In addition to possessing the necessary skills and knowledge, the best candidate for the job is the man who is willing to accept full responsibility for achieving stated objectives. Among the many reasons for a subordinate's unwillingness to accept responsibility are lack of understanding of what is expected, fear of failure or criticism, and insufficient motivation. Whatever the reason, if a choice must be made between two subordinates with one possessing the necessary skills and experience but unwilling to assume responsibility, and the other short on experience but willing to assume responsibility, it is probably better to choose the one who is willing to accept responsibility.

4. Establish Necessary Controls. In the discussion of the second step of the process of delegation, the delegation of authority, it is stated explicitly that delegation is not synonymous with abdication. Instead, the delegator retains the right to recall delegated authority and remains accountable to his superior for those responsibilities assigned to others. Thus, it is necessary for the delegator to establish and exercise necessary control over the actions of his subordinates so that he may fulfill his obligations. Essential to proper control is the maintenance of clear channels of communication between superior and subordinate so that a complete interchange of information is possible. Controls also imply that corrective action may be taken if needed to insure the fulfillment of stated objectives. Resentment toward controls on the part of subordinates is minimal when the subordinate participates in establishing the controls to be used.

Personality and Delegation

Thus far, our discussion of delegation includes an analysis of the three steps in the process of delegation, a statement of three principles that should be observed for most effective delegation, and specific practical suggestions for successful delegation. Frankly, there has been nothing said about the process of delegation that is not perfectly straightforward and relatively easy to understand. Yet, if this were all of delegation, or even a major portion of the process of delegation, there would be little reason for discussing delegation so extensively in management literature. The real problems of delegation lie not in the observance of the principles of delegation nor in following the practical suggestions for successful delegation, but rather they are found in the personality of the person doing the delegating.[5]

Usually it is easy to recognize the superior who finds it difficult to delegate. His behavior is characterized by an excessive attention to details, coupled with a marked distrust and questioning of the ability of subordinates. There are many reasons for these two characteristics, which for purposes of discussion, may be grouped into four broad categories. First, there are those persons who seemingly have always been interested in activities and studies that require precision and exactness. These persons seem to often follow vocations requiring and emphasizing precise action. Second, there are those persons who immerse themselves in details as a means of avoiding the central problems of a situation. Third, there are those who refuse to relinquish any part of their job to others because of a deep-seated fear of failure. The fourth group who refuse to delegate and must retain all of a job for themselves are those who have a paranoid (fear of persecution) distrust of others. Let us examine each of these groups separately, realizing that there is considerable overlapping between each group and that most failures to delegate can be traced to one or more of the four categories.

---

[5] Ernest Dale, *Planning and Developing the Company Organization Structure* (New York: The American Management Association, 1952), Research Report No. 20, pp. 38-48. Professor Dale presents a discussion of the impact of the chief executive's personality upon the process of delegation.

Vocational Choice. Any discussion of personality factors and vocational choice may evolve into the proverbial question of which comes first, the chicken or the egg. In other words, does one enter a given vocation because of certain underlying personality traits or does the specific vocational training received mold the personality? Admittedly, both processes operate simultaneously. There is much in our culture that emphasizes the importance of doing a job well and following it through to completion. Some people have been brought up with the admonition, "If you want a job done well, do it yourself." Whatever the sources of desire for personal accomplishment, we are taught to respect those persons capable of hard and effective work.

There are specific forms of vocational training that tend to reinforce and make even more permanent the normal inclinations of attending to detail. Accounting and engineering are good examples of such vocational training in that both courses of study require a meticulous attention to detail, a liking for exactness expressed in the form of numbers to the third decimal place, and considerable hard work and drudgery to complete the course. Upon graduation, the engineer may find himself in the position of doing exacting work on a drafting board and the accountant may be performing the work necessary for a detailed audit. It is the ability to do this first assignment—close attention to detail—and to do it well that results in promotion. Is it any wonder that a man with a normal liking for detail, reinforced by four years of college training in precise work and subsequently reinforced en route to success and promotions, should find it difficult to let go of the detail part of his job and turn it over to others?

Some of these highly trained persons, and Thomas Dayton of Case Problem 13-A is one of them, are frequently very competent in their field of work, a competency often expressed by the phrase, "I can do it better myself." Although they may not be able to do it better, they usually can perform the work as well. Another characteristic is the 12- to 16-hour day, which with few exceptions is the result of an inability to delegate, rather than due to the press of important affairs. It is difficult to change persons such as Thomas Dayton and make them successful delegators. Basic to the difficulty is their liking for work and their ability to do it well. Admonitions concerning health may fail to encourage them to delegate. Even after the occurrence of physical breakdown, some are still unable to slow down and delegate their work to others.

Avoidance of Major Issues. Attention to detail sometimes offers a security and comfort not possible when one's attention is directed toward the major problems at hand. In extreme cases the ability to attend to detail rather than to the central issue is important for life itself, for were one to face the real problem, he would be overwhelmed and unable to carry on. An example of the extreme is illustrated in the following brief quotation describing the plight of a refugee:

> The refugee was a peasant woman from down San Carlos way. She was complaining of the haste with which she and her family had had to flee. The burden of her complaint was that her husband's new suit and his Sunday gloves had had to be left behind. I had heard exactly the same kind of protest years ago in China; I was to hear it later in Austria and Czechoslovakia. The mind of the refugee, dazed and uprooted, concentrates upon the small, specific losses that it can cling to with understanding. To be homeless and without food or shelter as a result of the "policy" of foreign dictators and prime ministers—that is a state so terrible that it cannot be taken in all at once. The new suit, the Sunday gloves, these are the losses one can still comprehend.[6]

Although managers may not be faced with problems of such personal magnitude as those confronting the war refugee, there are instances where some managers simply cannot cope with the central issues of their environment and as a result direct their attention to peripheral details that are related to, but are not the real problem. The sales manager who personally reviews each salesman's expense account and then tallies the amount spent on telephone calls may be avoiding the real problem of increasing the number of new customers. The president of a company who reviews every change in salary may hold down payroll costs and then complain that he does not have time for the major task of coordinating the development of new products.

Fear of Failure. Feelings of personal insecurity with the attendant fear of failure may be the cause of inability to delegate. These are not the feelings of insecurity and unsureness associated with lack of knowledge and experience that are normal when one undertakes a new job; rather, it is the unsureness derived from a feeling of personal inadequacy. For some, fear of failure may be very real and imminent, for they may be on the brink of failure and realize that one more mistake can cost them their job or, at the very least, an opportunity for promotion. For others, failure may not be near, but there is the constant fear of what might happen if failure does occur. In either case, whether failure

---

[6] Vincent Sheehan, *Not Peace but a Sword* (New York: Doubleday Doran, and Company, Inc., 1939), p. 86. Reprinted by permission of Doubleday & Company, Inc.

is imminent or imagined, the underlying thought processes are somewhat as follows: This is a very difficult job to be done. It is full of problems and pitfalls; it requires a great deal of attention, hard work, and skill. It is going to tax my abilities to the limit. Since it is such a hard job for me to do, how can anyone else possibly do this job?

Whatever the cause of personal inadequacy, the result tends to be the same—a refusal to delegate, with the firm belief that the job is so taxing that it is inconceivable that anyone else can possibly handle it. As expected, it is extremely difficult to persuade these individuals to let go, because the motivating force is a fear of personal failure. It is a fear that immobilizes action since there is a complete inability to take a risk.

Distrust of Others. A fourth reason for not assigning duties and delegating authority to subordinates may be the result of a paranoid distrust of the motives of others. The word paranoid is used to describe a person who has delusions or false beliefs of persecution. The phrase, paranoid distrust, as used here refers to a distrust of others based upon the false belief that a subordinate's drive for success is founded upon a desire to displace or discredit his boss. The supervisor who distrusts his subordinates and fears that they intend to displace him refuses to delegate authority to them as a means of countering their threat. Such refusal is a weakening of organizational processes. There is also a long-range effect on the organization, for when a supervisor tormented by fears of distrust has the opportunity to select subordinates, there is understandably a strong tendency to select only those persons who are so weak that they are incapable of threatening any superior's position.

To summarize, whatever the reasons for failure to delegate, whether it be the highly trained technician with a liking for detail work, a defense against having to face the central issues of a problem, the fear of failure, or the desire to maintain one's own security through the process of weakening competition, the results are essentially the same. First, the refusal to delegate and let subordinates carry projects through to their normal completion results in the elimination of valuable training experiences. If the reason for reluctance to delegate lies in a well-founded belief that subordinates are not trained or capable, the sad fact remains that by not delegating, subordinates never become trained or capable since the opportunity to learn through the experience is denied. Second, refusal to delegate has the effect of stifling initiative, with the result that it is not long until suggestions and new ideas cease entirely. The subordinate is saying to himself, "Why should I say anything? I'm not allowed to do anything around here anyway." The third effect of refusing to delegate is that the better people, defining better people as those who need to develop and accept more responsibility, leave the company at the earliest opportunity. The industrial engineer of Case Problem 13-A is a case in point. The net result is not a pretty picture—a frustrated superior incapable of delegating and surrounded ultimately by subordinates incapable of accepting responsibility, even if it were offered.

DECENTRALIZATION OF AUTHORITY

Delegation of authority is described in the first part of this chapter as a process that transfers authority from superior to subordinate in an organization. The extent to which authority is delegated within an organization is a measure of the degree of decentralization of authority within that organization. The concept of decentralization of authority is relative in its nature; an organization is never completely centralized nor is it completely decentralized. Complete centralization of authority would require one man with no subordinates —hardly an organization—while complete decentralization implies that there is no longer a central authority, again a situation resulting in no organization.

In discussing decentralization of authority, it is first necessary to define decentralization and to establish guides for determining the extent to which a company is decentralized. Second, criteria are developed in the light of Theory Z to determine the optimum degree of decentralization for an organization. Third, the probable effects of the application of integrated information-decision-making systems upon the extent of decentralization within an organization are examined.

Definition of Decentralization

Before defining decentralization, it is well to differentiate between decentralization and two other processes often confused with it. These two processes are departmentation and geographic dispersion. In Chapter 11, "Organization Structure," *departmentation* is defined as the grouping of work and people into manageable units, and the bases most frequently used in the creation of departments are discussed. These bases are departmentation by function, product, customer, geography, process, and sequence. However, the mere creation of separate departmental units does not constitute decentralization. For example, the vice-president of sales who appoints five sales managers, each in charge of a different product, is further departmentalizing the sales function along product lines, but he is not necessarily decentralizing the sales function. The division of one large manufacturing plant into six widely separated smaller plants certainly results in *geographic dispersion,* but not necessarily in decentralization. The key to whether the appointment of product sales managers or the building of geographically separate plants is decentralization, or merely further departmentation, is revealed by analyzing the effect of such changes upon the decision-making process within the organization.

Decentralization is the delegation of authority to make decisions to the managers of lower echelon organizational units. The decentralization of the decision-making function is relative, and the degree of decentralization is dependent upon the following three characteristics of the decisions made at lower levels of the organization: (1) frequency of the decisions, (2) breadth of the decisions, and (3) the extent of the controls exercised over lower level decisions. Let us examine briefly each characteristic.

Frequency of Decisions. The greater the frequency or number of decisions made at lower levels of an organization, the greater is the degree of decentralization in that organization.

Breadth of Decisions. The broader the scope of decisions made at lower levels of an organization, the greater is the degree of decentralization. The breadth of decision making is determined by the number of functions affected by the decisions. A plant whose manager is limited to making only those decisions directly affecting production is less decentralized than the plant whose manager's scope of decision making includes, in addition, the negotiation of labor agreements with a union.

Extent of Controls over Decisions. The extent of controls exercised over the decisions made at lower levels of an organization is an important measure of the degree of decentralization. Decisions are frequently classified in terms of the number of dollars involved, with dollar limitations placed upon decisions that may be made without prior approval. Thus, an organization that permits a sales manager to approve customer credit up to $5,000 is more decentralized, other things being equal, than the organization that permits approval by the sales manager of only $1,000 credit. Timeliness of approval is also a factor. There is less decentralization when approval is required before the decision is made than when a superior is notified after the decision is made or when higher authority is not even informed. The number of approvals required prior to the making of a decision is also an index of the degree of decentralization. Generally, the fewer the number of persons who must be contacted for approval, the greater is the degree of decentralization.

Theory Z—Application to Decentralization

The preceding discussion of the varying degrees of decision making that may exist at lower levels of an organization emphasizes the relative nature of the concept of decentralization of authority. Decentralization is dependent upon the process of delegation of authority, for without delegation there can be no decentralization. Yet decentralization, as an organizational style, is much more than delegation; it is an expression of a basic management philosophy of operation. With such a philosophy of management, the maximum degree of decentralization is achieved when the authority to make decisions is delegated to the lowest possible level of the organization yet consistent with the needs of the organization, the ability and knowledge of the manager in question to make the decision, and the extent to which information necessary for a sound decision is available at that level of the organization. To implement an approach toward decentralized decision making in an organization, it is necessary to examine some of the factors that influence the extent of decentralization.

In Chapter 10, "Organization Theory," the six propositions of Theory Z are presented as an aid in selecting the most effective pattern of leadership. In Chapter 11, "Organization Structure," the propositions of Theory Z are interpreted as guides for determining effective departmentation and efficient spans of management. Let us now examine the six variable propositions of Theory Z—size, interaction between members, personality of members, congruence of goals, level of decision making, and state of the system—and apply these concepts as guides in determining the optimum degree of decentralization for a given organization.

Size. There is a direct relationship between the size of an organization, when defined as the number of people, and the number of decisions that must be made. In addition to an increase in the number of decisions resulting from increased size, there is also a tendency for decisions to become more complex. The increased volume of decisions and the additional time required for the analysis of more complex problems may result in an overburdening of top management and may be accompanied by serious delays in the decision-making process. Thus, one of the major goals of decentralization of authority is the creation of effectively sized decision-making units. Among the advantages claimed for the smaller decentralized units is that the total number of decisions to be made is less, with the result that more time can be devoted to each problem. Also, the decision-making authority is closer to the point of operations, which results in a shortening of the lines of communications and a consequent reduction in the amount of time taken to make each decision. Further, the manager close to the point of operations should be thoroughly familiar with local conditions and able to take these factors into consideration when making decisions.

Interaction Between Members. In Chapter 11, when discussing the need for interaction between members of an organization as a guide for determining departmental lines, it is pointed out that the need for interaction arises when several persons are working on the solution of a common problem, developing and using the same information, or when there is any other need for communications with each other. Similarly, the need for interaction between members can be used as a guide in determining the optimum degree of decentralization. If the quality of the decision-making process is improved as the result of interaction between members of a given level or unit of an organization, it is wise to decentralize the authority to make decisions at that level. Much of the decentralization that appears in sales departments is recognition of the need for close interaction between the customer, the salesmen, and the local manager in reaching satisfactory solutions to a common problem.

However, there are some decisions requiring the interaction between members of several different organizational units or different levels of the same organization. In these instances it is wise to centralize the decision-making function at a sufficiently high level of the organization so that information may be obtained from all sources. The vice-president, manufacturing, who retains the final authority over the production schedule of plants under his jurisdiction may be doing so as the result of a need to coordinate the schedules of all plants so that customer needs, as defined by the sales vice-president, are met.

Personality of Members. The personality of the members of an organization (defining personality as the sum total of the skills, abilities, interests, and personal characteristics) is an important consideration in determining the appropriate degree of decentralization. The personality of the chief executive is highly significant as a predictor of the extent and effectiveness of decentralization within an organization since the first step toward decentralization is taken when he delegates authority to his subordinates. If he is insecure personally, or for any other reason is unable to delegate, the concept of decentralization of authority to make decisions is neither encouraged nor understood. If, on the other hand, the chief executive is capable of delegating authority and circumstances permit him to delegate, the first step toward decentralization is assured, for his understanding of the process of delegation enables him to encourage his subordinates to delegate as fully as possible.

Despite the willingness of top management to decentralize authority, there are instances when the degree of decentralization is severely limited by the availability of competent managers at lower levels of the organization. It is interesting to note that the highly centralized company, upon realizing the gains that might be obtained from decentralization, frequently finds its capabilities to decentralize limited by the availability of competent managers. Often it is necessary to recruit personnel from outside the company as a means of filling the need for managers capable of fulfilling the responsibilities of decentralized operations. Decentralization in itself offers the soundest basis for providing a supply of capable managers. Usually decentralized companies provide more middle management positions that serve to challenge and motivate personnel. The positions are challenging because the areas of responsibility are relatively large and well defined. Middle managers are motivated because there is a greater likelihood that achievement will be recognized and that opportunity exists for advancement to even more responsible positions.

Congruence of Goals. The extent to which the goals of the members of an organization are congruent is an important factor in determining the most effective type of leadership and in establishing departmental lines. Usually decentralized units are much broader than departments and often are referred to as operating divisions. The need for congruency of the goals of the various parts of a decentralized unit is every bit as important as the need for similarity of objectives of the members of a smaller departmental unit. The result is the same as in the case of the department, for when all parts of a decentralized unit are working toward the same objectives—by definition, a high degree of congruency of goals—it is much easier to coordinate the efforts and activities of the various parts. One way of helping to assure congruent objectives among the various decentralized units of a company, and within each separate decentralized unit, is through the establishment of clearly stated company objectives and policies intended to implement these objectives. Continuing two-way communications between the highest and lowest levels of an organization is of importance in maintaining consistent goals for all levels of the organization.

Another method frequently used to assure a high degree of congruence of goals between the corporate managers of a company and the managers of decentralized operating units is through the application of the concept of a *profit center* as the basis for defining the extent of and the goals of a decentralized unit. When profit centers are used as the basis for establishing decentralized units, the process is often described as *profit decentralization*. Either expression, profit center or profit decentralization, emphasizes the use of profit as a basis for establishing decentralized units, an emphasis having several marked effects upon the organization. When the responsibilities, or job duties, of the manager of a decentralized unit are defined in terms of profit, the goal established is congruent with the objectives of the top management of the corporation. Also, when a manager is held responsible for the profits of his division, two additional steps must be taken. First, the unit must be carefully defined so that all segments that contribute to profit come under the jurisdiction of the manager; and second, necessary authority must be granted (the Principle of Parity of Authority and Responsibility) so that the manager may be held fully accountable to his superior for the profits of his unit. The very concept of profit decentralization has a tendency to further the process of decentralization since both the structure of the organization and the responsibilities of the manager are more sharply defined. However, there are limitations to the extent that the concept of profit decentralization may be applied. Generally, the concept is more readily applied to companies having clearly differentiated product lines that may be combined into logical units, relatively independent of each other, and with each unit capable of producing a measurable profit. General Motors with its highly decentralized Chevrolet, Buick, Oldsmobile, Pontiac, and Cadillac divisions is an example of decentralized product divisions, with each manager responsible for the profits of his division.

Level of Decision Making. When discussing the level of decision making as a guide to the optimum degree of decentralization, we are referring to the level in the organizational hierarchy at which a decision should be made in order to most effectively fulfill the needs of the organization. The appropriate level of decision making changes with respect to each of the major business functions—manufacturing, sales, finance, and personnel.

Typically, manufacturing and sales are among the first functions to show some degree of decentralization, since the purpose of the organization is often served best by decentralizing these functions. In manufacturing, the plant is usually considered as an organization unit and is relatively self-sufficient and capable of performing all functions necessary for its successful operation. Also, separate plants imply geographic dispersion and tend to encourage decentralization. The same factors that lead to the decentralization of manufacturing are also present as forces in the decentralization of the sales function. Many times on-the-spot decisions demanding special knowledge of a particular customer have to be made. The best decisions from the standpoint of correctness and timeliness come from the local level; hence, the tendency to decentralize the authority to make these decisions.

Finance remains a highly centralized function in most companies. There are several reasons why financial decisions remain centralized in the highest echelon of the organization. Problems relating to the procurement of capital and the distribution of earnings as capital expenditures are properly the functions of the highest level of the organization. These functions, upon which the very existence of the corporation depends, cannot very well be delegated to decentralized units.

Although many of the decisions made in the area of personnel may be decentralized to the operational units of manufacturing and sales, there is a growing tendency to make the key decisions of the personnel function at a centralized level in the organization. For example, operating units usually have the authority to hire employees at the local level; yet the range of salaries paid, and the amount and type of pensions, vacations, and other so-called fringe benefits are determined by corporate personnel policy established by top management. The existence of a master labor agreement, i.e., a single contract between an international union and the several plants of a multiplant company, is the key factor in determining whether or not the previously mentioned areas of personnel decision making are centralized at the corporate level of the company rather than being decided at the local plant level.

In general, those decisions that are best made at a high level of the organization are more costly in their nature, affect a larger number of employees, and are more significant in determining the course of the business than those decisions delegated to lower levels of the organization.

State of the System. The state of the system is an important consideration in determining the optimum degree of decentralization. In addition to including the extent to which organization goals are being achieved, the concept of the state of the system includes the stage of growth of the company, the nature of the company's business, and the availability of controls. As a company succeeds in achieving its financial objectives, it is possible to exercise a more participative, permissive form of leadership. In a large measure such a form of leadership tends to encourage and further the process of decentralization. Although permissive and participative leadership patterns are not synonymous with decentralization, there is considerable relationship since decentralization is the delegation of authority to make decisions, a move that means that subordinates are participating in the shaping of decisions.

The stage of a company's growth cycle is a phase of the state of the system that influences the extent to which decentralization is operative. As a general rule, most companies retain a high degree of centralized authority during their early years. Centralization at this stage of growth is particularly characteristic of closely held businesses where the major stockholder is also the founder of the firm and its chief executive. The Ford Motor Company, while still under the direction of its founder, Henry Ford, provides an example of highly centralized management during a company's early years.

Another aspect of a company's growth cycle is the manner in which growth occurs. Some companies grow as the result of a gradual expansion from within, while others grow by purchasing existing firms. When growth occurs as the result of gradual expansion, there may be relatively little need for further decentralization of managerial authority because additional products and processes are usually homogeneous in nature and readily assimilated into existing methods of operation. On the other hand, growth resulting primarily from acquisition frequently means dissimiliar products and processes. Also, an acquired firm may have its own management and, if management is capable, it may be left intact to operate in a highly decentralized fashion.

The nature of a company's business may force a high degree of centralization even though other factors such as size and the stage of development of the firm point toward a more decentralized form of management. Of specific concern are such factors as the needs of the customer, the source and kind of raw materials, and the location and type of manufacturing facilities. When the industrial customer produces his products in diverse locations; when raw materials are purchased from several sources; and when the supplying company has many plants, all producing the same product, there is a need for coordinating the decision-making process at a high level in all three organizations. For these reasons a firm such as Continental Can Company that purchases its raw material from several steel mills in order to service the many refineries of a company like Humble Oil Company (ENCO) tends to be more centralized in many phases of its decision making than a firm manufacturing a diverse line of products sold to many small localized customers.

Finally, the availability of controls, an index of the state of development of a system, is of great importance in determining the potential success of decentralization. In discussing delegation, we state that delegation is not abdication; nor is decentralization abdication. A manager cannot be expected to decentralize decision making to a lower level of the organization without adequate controls. Adequate controls are the feedback loop of the system, for they provide the information necessary to determine the extent and kind of corrective action which may be needed.

Integrated Data Processing and Decentralization

The preceding discussion of the applications of Theory Z to determine the optimum degree of decentralization serves to emphasize that decentralization is not a concept which calls for one being either for it or against it. The proper degree of decentralization is determined by carefully considering all factors in relation to the objectives of the organization. One factor that causes a great deal of interesting speculation in regard to its effect on decentralization is the introduction of high-speed, integrated data processing equipment. Review Case Problem 8-B, The Short-Order Economy, an account of the application of an IBM 1401 to the information-handling problems of Westinghouse. The 1401, storing 20 million bits of information in its "memory," receives an order for an electric motor from a customer on the West Coast, selects the warehouse nearest the customer, and prepares for the warehouse in printed form the customer's name, address, and pertinent credit information. If the order results in the level of inventory being reduced below a predetermined point, the manufacturing plant is notified and the motor is scheduled for production. There are even instances of large customers placing their orders direct to the 1401 from teletype equipment in their own offices, thereby bypassing the local sales office.

When considering that customers can order directly through the 1401, it is easy to point to the sales office and conclude that the decision-making role of middle management is weakened with the introduction of integrated data processing. With the undermining of middle management's decision making and the centralization of information handling, one can develop the argument that modern information systems are more conducive to a centralized rather than a decentralized style of management. Whether or not this argument is valid is dependent upon the definition of middle management decision making and the basic philosophy of the company in regard to decentralization. If middle management's decisions are defined as the processing of orders, the checking of inventories, and the performance of other routine functions, then in all probability these functions are better handled by electronic equipment. Also, if the basic philosophy of the company is one of centralization—the desire to place as many decisions as possible in the hands of a few top executives—modern information-decision-making systems tend to strengthen that philosophy. But if the underlying philosophy of the company is one of decentralization, it is possible to direct the flow of information to subordinate managers so that they may make better decisions, thereby increasing their contribution to the organization and making their positions more secure. Companies which are frequently centralized because needed information is complex and must be laboriously handled in a central location may find that modern data processing eases the burden of handling such information, thereby making it possible to decentralize. Thus, whether or not integrated data processing strengthens or weakens the trend toward decentralization depends upon the definition of decision making on the part of middle managers and the basic philosophy of the company in regard to decentralization.

SUMMARY OF PRINCIPLES

As a basis for understanding more fully the process of delegation and recognizing the conditions that may result in ineffective delegation, the following three principles of delegation have been presented in this chapter:

Principle of Parity of Authority and Responsibility	For effective delegation, the authority granted to a subordinate must be equal to the responsibility assigned to him.
Principle of Absoluteness of Accountability	Although responsibility and authority may be delegated to subordinates, accountability to one's superior cannot be delegated.
Principle of Unity of Command	Each subordinate should be accountable to one, and only one, superior.

Questions for Study and Discussion

1. Several descriptive statements of the process of delegation are given in the text. How do these statements differ from each other and in what respects are they the same?

2. Why is it necessary to define the term *to delegate* precisely? How does such a definition contribute to an understanding of the control exercised by the person who does the delegating?

3. Why is it necessary to have three principles covering the process of delegation? Explain what would happen if accountability were not considered absolute.

4. Should the president of a company be held accountable for the following action of subordinates?

    (a) Price fixing in violation of federal laws and stated company policy.

    (b) Failure to meet stated company sales objectives.

    (c) Loss of competitive position in the development of new products.

5. Why is it possible for the process of delegation to work even though one or more of the Principles of Delegation is violated?

6. How valid is the concept that an executive should be held accountable for the performance of his department even though he has no power to control the actions of others? (for example, the sales manager who cannot force customers to buy.)

7. Give an example of each of the four situations that results in a violation of the Principle of Unity of Command.

8. If delegation includes the granting of authority and empowers a subordinate to act, why is it necessary to establish controls to see that the subordinate performs as expected?

9. What is meant by the statement that the real problems of delegation lie not in a violation of the principles of delegation but rather are found in the personality of the person doing the delegating?

10. How is the concept of decentralization of authority related to the concept of delegation? In what respects do these two concepts differ? In what respects are they the same?

11. Differentiate between decentralization and geographic dispersion. Develop an example of geographic dispersion and show how it can be transformed into decentralization of authority.

12. Discuss each of the criteria used in determining the extent of decentralization.

13. Discuss the following statement: The development of integrated data processing systems tends to centralize authority and limit the decision-making powers of the middle manager.

Dynamic Industries, a diversified manufacturer of automotive replacement parts, is a company that is growing rapidly as the result of an aggressive policy of acquisition. Board chairman John Rafferty believes that the growth of his company is sound and that the main reason for the extremely rapid growth is due to the operation of the company on a highly decentralized basis. Since growth is the result of acquiring companies that are going concerns, Rafferty encourages the managements of the subsidiary companies to carry on as they had prior to joining Dynamic Industries. At present, discussions regarding merger are being held with Central Electronics, a company that manufactures a broad line of electronic components, many of which have applications in the defense and space industries. Central Electronics is interested in Dynamic Industries because Dynamic could supply the much-needed capital to complete the final stages of the development of a high-performance transformer and the building of a plant in which to manufacture the new product. However, George Owens, the founder and president of Central, realizes the potential dangers of merging with another company in that he might lose control of his own firm and be placed in the position of being an employee for a larger corporation.

But Rafferty continually assures Owens that Dynamic Industries operates on a highly decentralized basis and describes their concept of decentralization as follows:

"We expect you, as the president of a subsidiary company, to manage as

---

Case Problem 13-B
Decentralization—Fact or Fiction?

---

you have in the past. You are successful with your own company and there is no reason why you shouldn't continue to be a success operating as a part of Dynamic. The major functions of sales, manufacturing, engineering, and product development are all yours to do with as you see fit. In a sense we are sort of the banker; that is, we supply the money that you need for capital improvements and expansion. Even though the profits of each subsidiary company go into the corporate till, it is still like having your own company because your pay for the year is a combination of a guaranteed salary and a percentage of the net profits of your company."

Thus assured, Owens decided to merge with Dynamic Industries.

During the first six months all went well and Owens saw very little of anyone from corporate headquarters. At the beginning of the seventh month, the corporate controller paid Owens a visit and explained to him in detail the company's requirements for profit planning and requested that Owens develop a profit plan, a detailed forecast of Central's revenues and operating expenses, for the coming year. Though very pleasant, the controller made it quite plain that should the performance of the company deviate significantly from the forecast, a team of cost analysts and industrial engineers would arrive from headquarters to determine the cause of the deviation and to recommend necessary changes.

Shortly after this experience with the controller, the industrial relations vice-president of Dynamic Industries called on Owens and informed him that a member of the corporate industrial relations staff would be on hand to conduct the coming negotiations with the union representing Central's employees. Owens protested, saying that he had been negotiating his own labor contracts for years; however, it was explained to him that because of company-wide employee benefit plans, such as pensions and insurance, and to prevent the unions from pitting one subsidiary company against another in the area of wages, centralized control over negotiations was very necessary. At the time of this visit, the provisions of the company's salary plan were outlined to Owens and arrangements were made for the installation of the corporate clerical and supervisory salary plans by a member of the headquarters industrial relations staff.

The following month Owens called Rafferty and asked what steps should be taken to secure capital for the new building intended for the manufacture of the high-performance transformer.

Rafferty answered by saying, "I'll have someone from the treasurer's office call on you and show you how to fill out the forms used in requesting funds for capital expansion. It's quite a process, but remember you are only one of 15 subsidiaries and they all seem to want money at the same time. Whether or not you get it this year depends not only upon your needs but also upon the needs of the other 14 companies."

Problems

1. Has Dynamic Industries decentralized its operations as much as possible?
2. As George Owens, president of Central Electronics, would you regard the management policies of the parent corporation as primarily centralized or primarily decentralized?
3. Is Dynamic Industries exerting too much control over Central Electronics? Why or why not?
4. Recommend the optimum degree of decentralization for the situation described in this case.

CHAPTER 14

Group Functions in Organization — The Committee

Ray Talbert, the president and founder of Electric Manufacturing Corporation (Emcorp), is wondering how he can follow the advice of his doctor, who told him to take it easy after last year's coronary attack. Emcorp manufactures a full line of fractional horsepower electric motors sold to both original equipment manufacturers (OEM) and distributors throughout the country.

At the present time, the company employs approximately 1,000 persons.

Talbert, an engineer, has maintained tight control over all major functions throughout the years; and though each of the heads of the engineering, manufacturing, sales, finance, and personnel departments has the title of vice-president, they come to Talbert for approval before making any changes in procedure. Usually, each of these men sees Talbert several times a day. The personnel director once suggested a weekly meeting, but Talbert vetoed the idea as too time consuming. Now, worried about his health as well as the problems of the company, Talbert is beginning to feel the need for some relief from the constant pressure.

Case Problem 14-A

A Problem in Coordination

The manufacturing department shows a picture of rising costs, consistent failure to meet delivery schedules, and an increasing number of quality complaints. John Stroud, vice-president of manufacturing, admits to poor performance, but says that the cost figures from accounting are pure history and of no use since they do not reach manufacturing until the 15th of the month following the month in which the work is completed. He states that his failure to meet delivery schedules is due almost entirely to the fact that the sales department makes unrealistic promises and does not bother to check manufacturing schedules. Stroud attributes most of the quality problems to the incessant flow of engineering changes that come without warning and with no time to work out the production problems present in all new products. Talbert admits to himself that he forgot to tell Stroud that he had approved the last set of engineering changes and that he had asked Frank Smyth, vice-president of engineering, to put all of the approved changes into production immediately.

The vice-president and general manager of sales, Jack Linder, recognizes that he has no knowledge of the manufacturing schedules and realizes that he, too, is being criticized by Talbert for the many broken promises in regard to delivery dates. However, Linder's chief complaint at the present time is the result of having sold a large order of standard motors to a distributor having a supply of replacement parts in stock and then discovering that engineering had changed specifications—a change that made all replacement parts in the field obsolete. Another irritant for Linder is the tightened credit requirements instituted by the finance department without prior consultation with the sales department. Again Talbert admits privately that it is the same engineering change which caused so much trouble in manufacturing that is causing trouble for the sales depart-

ment and obsoleting the existing stock of replacement parts. He also realizes that at his request, due to an unusually short cash position, the finance department tightened up on credit requirements.

Problems

1. Define the major problem facing Emcorp's management.
2. Would the formation of a committee be of any value in this situation? If a committee is needed, assign a title to the committee and indicate who should be members of the committee. Is there a need for an outside member on the committee?
3. Would an *ad hoc* committee be of any value?
4. In the event that Talbert decides to retire, would the presence of a committee make it easier or more difficult for Talbert's successor? Discuss.

●   ●   ●   ●   ●   ●   ●   ●   ●

Up to this point in our discussion of organizational processes and organizational structure, the relationships between individuals are emphasized. In the preceding chapter, the process of delegation is treated as a superior-subordinate relationship, a relationship between individuals. However, there are many instances when functions are assigned to a group rather than to an individual. Frequently a group that has been assigned managerial functions is called a committee since specific functions have been committed, or entrusted, to the group. This chapter is divided into two parts: first, there is a general discussion of committees and, second, there is a discussion of the keynote committee of the corporate organization, the board of directors.

COMMITTEES

Usually a committee is assigned functions that are homogeneous in nature, and the scope of its activities and powers is defined. There is also a chairman, or leader, of the group who may be elected by the committee itself or appointed by the party who creates the committee. Another characteristic of committees is that in most organizations, membership on a committee is a part-time activity. A committee member typically has other organizational functions to perform, and an individual often serves as a member of several committees simultaneously.

Committees are a major part of organizational structure, and most students of management sooner or later serve as a member or chairman of a committee. A study of committees is necessary for a full understanding of the process of organizing and the potential assignment as a committee member. First, let us examine some of the underlying assumptions that are implied when a managerial task is assigned to a committee rather than to an individual, and also evaluate committees to determine those situations that lend themselves best to committee action. Second, the committee is analyzed as it functions in business organizations; and lastly, the concept of the *plural executive* is discussed.

Evaluation of Committees

Before discussing the advantages and disadvantages of the use of committees, it is helpful to examine the underlying assumptions whenever a committee is created as part of an organizational structure. At least one of the following two assumptions is implicit in the creation of any committee. The first of these assumptions is that somehow, as a result of interaction between the members of a committee functioning as a group, the results produced by the committee should be better than the results achieved by an individual. The benefits of interaction between the members of a group may take one of several forms. If ideas are sought from the group, interaction will hopefully increase either the quantity or quality of ideas produced; and if action is desired as a result of committee deliberation, the fact that all members of the committee have participated in determining the course of action is likely to improve the quality and forcefulness of such action. The assumption that the interaction of the members of a group is beneficial is best described as a *participative belief*—a belief in the efficacy of participation *per se*.[1]

---

[1] Harold J. Leavitt, "Unhuman Organizations," *Harvard Business Review*, Vol. XL (July-August, 1962), pp. 90-98. The paper by Professor Leavitt examines carefully some assumptions concerning organizations that he terms "participative beliefs." Although mentioned only in passing in this chapter, the concept of participative beliefs is reviewed in detail in Chapter 16, "Leadership Patterns."

The second assumption implicit in the creation of a committee is that as an organization increases in complexity, primarily as the result of the increased number of delegated functions and the complexity of the individual functions, it becomes necessary to have the managers of these various functions meet periodically to exchange information.[2] The need for an exchange of information between the managers of the major functions of an organization is illustrated in Case Problem 14-A. Committees formed as the result of a need to exchange information perform not only a message-center function, thereby improving the quality of communications, but they also perform a coordinative function as the result of channeling information.

Advantages of Committees. Advantages resulting from the use of committees are discussed under the following four headings: (1) advantages resulting from group judgment, (2) advantages resulting from improved motivation, (3) advantages resulting from committees operating as a check on authority, and (4) advantages that are the result of improved coordination. The first three of these advantages are attributable to the interaction of the members of a committee functioning as a group, while the fourth advantage is attributable to the committee performing a coordinative function made possible by the exchange of information.

GROUP JUDGMENT. The idea that the judgment of a group is superior to that of an individual is expressed in the phrase, "two heads are better than one." We all know that two heads are not necessarily better than one; however, there are certain situations in which the judgment of a group tends to be better than that of a single individual. A problem requiring diverse knowledge and varied experience for optimum solution is ideally suited for group consideration, since it is more likely that a group is able to contribute knowledge and experience broader than the knowledge and experience of an individual. The final determination of whether a given product should be placed in a company's product line is a good example of a situation requiring diverse information from production, finance, and sales. A word of caution is in order, however. Even with problems requiring information drawn from each of the major functions of the company, it is not always necessary that the managers of these functions act as a group to obtain the values derived from such diverse backgrounds. The president of

---

[2] Ernest Dale, *Planning and Developing the Company Organization Structure* (New York: American Management Association, 1952) Research Report Number 20, pp. 83-93. The above concept is stated by Professor Dale on page 83.

the company can talk to the heads of each department separately and acquire from each manager the breadth of information required for a sound decision. Staff specialists who conduct a survey by interviewing many department heads are gaining the values associated with broad experiences without the necessity of meeting as a group.

In addition to values attributable to breadth of knowledge and experience, group judgments are sometimes improved by the internal self-criticism developed within the group as the result of interaction between its members. Self-criticism may result in a compromise solution containing the best aspects of several solutions proposed by individuals. Impulsive decisions and actions are minimized by the self-criticism generated by the group. A further benefit possible from interaction when meetings are conducted as "brainstorming" sessions, as described in Chapter 9, is an increase in the quantity of ideas produced by the group.

Another valuable characteristic of group judgment occurs when the membership of the group is carefully selected so that all interested parties are represented, thereby increasing the likelihood that the final decision takes into consideration the needs and interests of each member of the group. The daily production meeting of a manufacturing plant usually includes representatives from each production department, shipping, production control, and quality control so that any action taken considers the needs of all participating departments.

IMPROVED MOTIVATION. Although the values received from the pooled knowledge and experience of committee members are often cited as the major contribution of a committee, there is much to indicate that one of the underlying reasons for committees, if not the dominant reason, is to assure cooperation in the execution of any plan developed by the committee. Cooperation, or improved motivation, in the execution of the plan may result from having participated in the work of the committee, for one of the benefits directly traceable to participation is increased knowledge, and, consequently, greater understanding of concepts that were formerly unknown and rejected. Another advantage resulting directly from participation is best described as pride of authorship. It is difficult not to support the execution of a plan developed, at least in part, by one's own efforts. An example of a committee owing its success to the positive values derived from participation is a salary or compensation committee that describes and evaluates all jobs and then develops and administers a plan of compensation.

An additional characteristic of committee participation that contributes toward better motivation is obtained by using membership on a committee as a means of "selling" or persuading a lukewarm member to go along with the majority. Such persuasion may range from the benefits gained by a better understanding acquired through participation to the implied pressure created by the stamp of approval that comes as the result of being a member of the committee.

A CHECK ON AUTHORITY. One of the functions of a committee that may be considered an advantage is its operation as a check on authority. The use of committees in business organizations to limit authority is not frequent, yet committees are used for this purpose in other forms of organizations—governmental, religious, social, and educational—to such an extent that a brief discussion of the subject is warranted. The Supreme Court of the United States is, in effect, a nine-man committee that serves to check the authority of all agencies of the government; and the two houses of Congress serve, not only as a check on the powers of the chief executive, but also as a check and balance upon the powers of each other. Most religious and social organizations such as fraternal groups are governed by boards that effectively restrain the powers of designated officials. In universities we find good examples of restraint through the action of committees. The president of a university is usually restrained not only by the committee that appoints him, often called a board of regents, but also by committees of the faculty that may have authority ranging in scope from determining the curriculum to administering faculty pay increases and determining tenure policy.

The use of a committee as a restraining agent is not quite so clear cut in business organizations. Perhaps it is because many businesses have their origin as a result of the efforts of a single individual, or it may be the recognition that there are inefficiencies inherent in committee organization. Even so, the board of directors, a committee elected by the stockholders, serves as an effective check on the powers and actions of the president.[3]

IMPROVED COORDINATION. The three advantages of committees described above—group judgment, improved motivation, and a check on authority—are advantages that are believed to be derived from the participation of a group. Improved coordination resulting from committee action is not so much the result of participation *per se*; instead, it is the result of receiving, interpreting, and channeling information.

---

[3] Harold Koontz and Cyril O'Donnell, *Principles of Management* (3d ed.; New York: McGraw-Hill Book Company, 1964). For a more complete discussion of the function of a committee as a check on authority, see pages 343 and 344.

Committees whose purpose is to transmit information and coordinate the activities of the various functions of the organization are formed at the upper levels of an organization and may be called an executive committee or an operating or management committee. Usually these groups are composed of the managers of functional areas such as sales, manufacturing, engineering, and finance. The person-to-person contact afforded by regularly scheduled meetings permits all interested parties to receive and exchange information with considerable savings in time and an improved degree of understanding.

A further strength of committees whose purpose is one of coordination is that such committees may be granted an authority greater than that possessed by any of the individual members. For example, a new products committee, composed of the heads of sales, manufacturing, engineering, and finance, may be granted the authority to accept or reject a given product, thereby exercising an authority greater than that of any of its members. By granting superior authority to the committee, rather than to an individual, the coordinative purpose of the committee is emphasized.

In Case Problem 14-A, the Electric Manufacturing Corporation can achieve improved coordination by creating an executive or management committee whose function is primarily the exchange of information. Such a group, meeting on a regularly scheduled basis, would serve to channel information to Ray Talbert so that he could better coordinate the various management functions. Also, if Talbert's health problems persist, the committee could be delegated sufficient authority to coordinate and administer the affairs of the company.

Disadvantages of Committees. The disadvantages and criticisms leveled at committees often result from the misuse of committees as well as from weaknesses inherent in the committee system itself. The criticism most frequently charged to the committee system is that the cost is greater than the value received. Committees are also charged with not being able to produce good decisions since their very nature tends to develop a compromise decision rather than the one solution that is best for the situation; and lastly, the composition of a committee with its several members and semblance of democratic action makes it difficult to establish accountability. Each of these criticisms is discussed below.

Cost. The costliness of committees comes not only from the direct cost of each man-hour spent in committee service but also from the losses incurred when timeliness is a factor in determining the worth of the decision. Committees are very time consuming, since one of the premises upon which they operate is that the committee serves as a forum in which all members have a right to express a point of view no matter how trivial or inconsequential. If there is an important item under discussion, it is highly unlikely that any action will be taken without a review of the written minutes of the meeting by each individual member, an action that results in further delay and expense.

Though it is difficult to determine the cost of committees, particularly when measured against value received, an approach suggested by Ernest Dale forces, at the very least, a critical review of the worth of a committee. First, determine the number of man-hours spent per year in meetings by multiplying the total number of meetings, times the average length of each meeting, times the average number of executives in attendance. Add to this figure the cost of the secretary of the committee and other clerical and staff work; then assign an average dollar cost to the total time spent (remember that the cost of a $25,000 a year executive is about $15 an hour). Review the work of the committee for the past year and place a monetary value on its accomplishments. Balance this value of work accomplished against total cost; then determine whether the work of the committee could be carried on as effectively if the committee were dissolved.[4]

COMPROMISE DECISIONS. Although the value of group judgment derived from varied backgrounds and experiences of the members of a committee is listed as one of its chief values, it is a value realized only under relatively limited conditions. For too often the decision of a committee may result in a compromise at what appears to be the level of the lowest common denominator. The reasons for poor quality in committee decisions are not hard to find. Committees often develop a belief that they should reflect a unanimity of opinion, and unless a unanimous decision can be achieved, there is a tendency to delay any decision. The desire for unanimity, even though it means compromise, is understandable when there is a decision requiring execution because a recalcitrant member can sabotage the entire action of the committee by refusing to aid in carrying out the plan. Another reason for compromise is that committees within a company are made up of men who must work together in many different capacities, with the result that there is opportunity for a degree of political trading and a reluctance to force unpleasant situations—conditions that encourage compromise.

Still another factor affecting the quality of committee decisions is the control of a committee by a minority, a control particularly effective when there is a tradition of unanimous action. Such control may be

---

[4] Ernest Dale, *op. cit.*, p. 88.

exercised by the power of veto, or as illustrated in national politics by the power of the filibuster. Although the filibuster is not operative as a formal institution in business, there are times when a subject is avoided rather than invite what everyone knows is going to be a protracted discussion of an issue.

If decisions are not compromised, either in an attempt to secure unanimity or as the result of minority control, the other extreme may occur, a single dominant person hiding behind the screen of a committee composed of a group of "Yes men." If such is the case, the following question should be raised: Why have a committee in the first place?

LACK OF ACCOUNTABILITY. In discussing the process of delegation in the last chapter, the three steps of the process are set forth: (1) the assignment of duties or responsibilities, (2) the delegation of authority, and (3) the creation of an accountability on the part of a subordinate to his superior. Committees, like individuals, may be assigned responsibilities and may be granted delegated authority. However, the establishment of accountability is very difficult. Theoretically, all members of a committee may be held accountable for the action of the committee, yet this is not a practical point of view when the final position of the committee is a compromise reached as the result of many hours of discussion. One might wish to hold the chairman accountable, but he may have no effective control over the individual members of the committee. The inability to establish accountability clearly and to take any necessary subsequent corrective action makes committees particularly ineffective as an organizational structure when the responsibility assigned is one of action or execution.

Committees in Use

The use of the committee as a part of the organization structure of top management is relatively recent, the first notable example being the top management committee established in 1921 by E. I. du Pont de Nemours & Company.[5] Since 1921 the use of committees has grown extensively; however, before discussing the extent to which committees are used, it is helpful to develop a means of classification because committees vary widely in respect to functions assigned and the degree of authority granted to them.

---

[5] M. R. Lohman, *Top Management Committees* (New York: American Management Association, 1961) AMA Research Study 48, p. 5. Research Study 48 of the American Management Association presents information gathered from 93 firms that have a total of 319 management committees of all types and discusses the current status of committees in American industry today.

One method of classification results in committees being grouped by function as either *general management* committees or as *restricted* committees. The major function of a general management committee is policy making and the effect of its work is usually company-wide in scope. Those committees not engaged in general management activities are classified as restricted committees and their scope is limited to one function or, at the most, to a group of related functions. Typically, restricted committees are concerned with such functions as marketing, production, or personnel. Both of these broad categories, general management committees and restricted committees, may be further subdivided in respect to the degree of delegated authority possessed by the committee. If the committee has the power to make decisions and an effective means of carrying out these decisions, it is regarded as an *authoritative* committee. If the committee is not capable of carrying out its recommendations, or if it is organized solely for the purpose of study and advice, the committee is classified as *nonauthoritative*.[6]

Functions of Committees. There are two studies of the extent to which committees are used and the functions assigned to them. M. R. Lohman's survey of 319 top management committees in 93 different companies reveals that 78 of the 93 companies have general management committees. Of these general management committees, two thirds of them receive their authority from the president of the company and the other one third is appointed by and receives its authority directly from the board of directors. Twenty-five percent of these general management committees are classified as authoritative and 25 percent are classified as nonauthoritative. The remaining 50 percent have some degree of authority in specific areas of operations, but the authority is not of sufficient breadth to warrant their classification as authoritative. It is interesting to note that of those general management committees appointed by the board of directors—one third of the total—83 percent are classed as authoritative, while only 20 percent of the committees reporting to and drawing their authority from the president of the company are regarded as authoritative. Seemingly, the degree of authority granted top management committees is dependent upon and related to the source of authority. Only 12 of the 78 firms reporting the presence of a general management committee are limited to that one committee; 66 of the 78 firms have at least one restricted committee in addition to the general management committee. All the firms surveyed reported some form of top management committee.[7]

---

6 *Ibid.*, pp. 13-21.
7 *Ibid.*, pp. 10-11.

The other study, conducted by Rollie Tillman, Jr., is a survey of 1,200 executives in regard to the functioning and extent of committees in their companies. The presence of a regular, or a "standing" committee, is to some extent related to the size of the company defined in terms of total number of employees. Of those firms with less than 250 employees, only 63.5 percent have one or more regular standing committees, while 93.8 percent of those firms with more than 10,000 employees report one or more standing committees. The average for all firms represented by the 1,200 executives who participated in the study shows that 81.5 percent have one or more standing committees.[8] One aspect of Tillman's study is that it presents in concise form the major functions assigned to each of the various types of standing committees. The distinction between standing or regular committees and those that are temporary in nature is that the temporary committee is usually organized for a specific purpose and dissolved when that purpose is satisfied. Temporary committees are generally called *ad hoc* committees. The results of Tillman's study are presented in Table 14-1.

Table 14-1

COMMITTEES—WHAT ARE THEIR FUNCTIONS?

Type of Committee	Percent of Executives Serving on Each Type of Committee Who Report This Function				
	Advisory	Operating Decisions	Review	Planning	Policy
General Management	43%	58%	43%	64%	67%
Finance & Control	30	47	39	55	42
Marketing	42	44	76	43	10
Production	34	54	42	63	25
Labor & Personnel	41	43	38	39	39
R & D and New Products	40	38	48	73	38
Public Relations	53	33	31	50	39
Other	45	46	35	52	36

Note: The rows of figures in this table add to more than 100% because respondents report their committee as having more than one purpose and function.

Source: Rollie Tillman, Jr., "Committees on Trial," *Harvard Business Review,* Vol. XXXVIII (May-June, 1960), p. 162.

The committees listed by Tillman conform to the classification developed by Lohman. Sixty-seven percent of the executives serving on

---

[8] Rollie Tillman, Jr., "Committees on Trial," *Harvard Business Review,* Vol. XXXVIII (May-June, 1960), pp. 6-8, 11, 12, 162-164, 166, 168, 171-173.

general management committees report the primary function of the committee as one of setting policy, and the functions of planning and making operating decisions are second and third in importance. The remaining types of committees—finance and control, marketing, production, labor and personnel, research and development and new products, public relations, and the miscellaneous classification of other—correspond to Lohman's classification of restricted committees.

It is interesting to note the variation in the major function assigned to each of the restricted committees. The committees of finance and control, production, and research and development are engaged primarily in the function of planning, while marketing mainly performs a review function. Very few of those serving on marketing committees report a policy function for this committee; apparently the policies of marketing are determined by general management committees. The function most frequently performed by the labor and personnel committee is that of making operating decisions and is probably due to the necessity for these committees to interpret labor agreements as they affect company operations. The committees on public relations most frequently serve in an advisory capacity. Although Tillman's study shows definite trends in the functions assigned to various management committees, it is unwise to generalize concerning the purpose of a given committee since there is substantial variation in the functions assigned to general management committees and to each of the restricted committees. Nonetheless, the study is of value in that it shows succinctly the wide range of activities that may be delegated to various committees.

Du Pont and Committees. In 1921 E. I. du Pont de Nemours & Company, Inc., became the first company to establish committees as a permanent part of its top management structure. A recent organization chart of Du Pont, Figure 14-1, shows that there are four major committees—bonus and salary committee, executive committee, finance committee, and the committee on audit—reporting directly to the board of directors.[9] As a direct result of having these four committees report directly to the board of directors, virtually every function within the company ultimately reports to a committee.

One of the difficulties that arises as a result of Du Pont's committee structure is that of designating, in chart form, the proper position and function of the president of the company. The organization chart shows the president reporting to the executive committee, the finance com-

---

[9] K. K. White, *Understanding the Company Organization Chart* (New York: American Management Association, 1963) Research Study No. 56, p. 161. This study includes a discussion of the committees in Du Pont on pages 159, 162-163.

Figure 14-1

ORGANIZATION CHART OF E. I. DU PONT DE NEMOURS AND COMPANY

Source: E. I. du Pont de Nemours and Company.

mittee, and the board of directors; but in practice, he is a member of all committees including the board of directors and is not, as shown on the chart, accountable to each committee. The executive committee is composed of the president, who functions as its chairman, and eight vice-presidents, who, unlike their counterparts in most companies, have no other duty than that of serving on the executive committee. Since these officers are not responsible for the functions of an operating department, there is less likelihood for bias and prejudice in their decisions. Reporting to the executive committee are the general managers of the 12 industrial (line) departments and the directors of all auxiliary (staff) departments. The treasurer reports to the finance committee.

How well has the committee system worked for Du Pont? According to Mylander, who asked this and other questions of the 12 top executives of the company, the system has worked well for Du Pont.[10] The advantages of the committee system are listed as giving the strength and security that arise from group decisions, an improved objectivity in decision making, continuity in administration, and opportunity for the maximum development of personnel. There are no major disadvantages attributable to the committee system; however, several of the top 12 executives did mention an occasional feeling of frustration resulting from inability to direct others because, by tradition, individual members of the committee do not give orders—they only make suggestions and serve as advisors to the general managers of the industrial departments and directors of the auxiliary departments. Mylander summarizes his findings as follows:

> In conclusion, the 12 top executives stressed that (1) they are not urging other companies to adopt their committee-line system, (2) they believe unanimously it has been successful for Du Pont, and (3) they feel it should work for any other large producer of diversified lines.[11]

The Plural Executive

When committees assume the responsibilities of an executive, they are referred to as a *plural executive*; and, as the phrase implies, the group functions as a single executive. The executive com-

---

[10] William H. Mylander, "Management by Executive Committee," *Harvard Business Review,* Vol. XXXIII (May-June, 1955), pp. 51-58. Mr. Mylander's article affords excellent insight into the workings of Du Pont's executive committee. Included is an agenda for one of the regular Wednesday meetings, which shows the full range of committee action.

[11] *Ibid.,* p. 58.

mitte of Du Pont operates as a plural executive, for with one voice it performs the duties normally assigned to the chief executive. Specifically, the Du Pont executive committee is charged with the responsibilities of determining the broad policies that govern the company's operations, the selection of personnel to execute those policies, and the exercise of a continuing control function to insure the meeting of company objectives.

Let us examine in greater detail a committee that almost invariably functions as a plural executive, the board of directors. At the same time, it must be remembered that not all committees are regarded as a plural executive. Among those not considered as a plural executive are committes whose function is advisory in nature or whose function is that of research and study.

THE BOARD OF DIRECTORS

The corporation is a legal entity created under the provisions of the laws of the various states. Although the laws of each state differ, there are certain provisions common to all. The law states that the board of directors, usually with a minimum of three members, be elected by the stockholders of the corporation, and that the board is charged with the responsibility of directing the affairs of the corporation as representatives of the stockholders, who are the legal owners. The law, in effect, designates the board as a plural executive, for an action must come from the board as a group and not from the action of any single board member. The line of authority flows from the individual stockholders to the elected board of directors and thence to the officers of the company who are appointed by the board. There is no clear delineation between the activities normally associated with directing the affairs of the corporation and those activities assigned to the officers of the corporation who are responsible for the day-to-day management of the company. In some companies, it is not unusual for the chairman of the board to hold the dual title of chairman of the board and chief executive officer, an example of the overlap that may exist between directing and managing. Despite the lack of separation between functions normally associated with directing and those assigned to the officers of the company, there are certain responsibilities traditionally reserved for the board. In our discussion of the board of directors, we shall examine those functions normally associated with boards of directors, some of the problems that must be considered in determining the most effective composition of the membership of boards, and lastly, the value of boards of directors in small companies.

Functions of the Board of Directors

Before considering the specific functions of the board of directors, it is well to recognize that, in practice, the authority of boards varies considerably. Such authority may range from *making decisions* that affect the life of the corporation, and subsequently assigning the execution of these decisions to the management of the company, to a situation in which the board merely acts as a *rubber stamp* by perfunctory approval of the actions of management. Between these extremes are the exercise of authority that amounts to *confirmation* of action taken by management, *influence* exerted by individual members of the board through counseling with management, and formal *review* of management's handling of the affairs of the company with the implication that such review may lead to criticism and suggestions for improved performance.

A listing of the functions of the board of directors would include the selection of officers and directors; determination of basic policies in finance, production, sales, and personnel; allocation of the earnings of the company; and the determination of financial structure. However, the many items that come before the board for consideration and action may be grouped under four major headings; (1) determination of objectives, (2) selection of management, (3) financial well-being of the company, and (4) review and stimulation. Each major area of responsibility is discussed below.

Determination of Objectives. Fundamental to the concept of the corporation is that, as a legal entity, the corporation exists in perpetuity; that is, it exists until formal action to dissolve the corporation through liquidation of assets or by merger with another company. The board of directors acts as a steward or trustee of the assets that belong to the owners of the company. Because of the responsibility of stewardship, the major duty of the board is to determine the objectives of the company. Underlying all decisions concerning objectives is the ultimate welfare of the stockholders. Usually the interest of stockholders is considered in terms of long-range potential as well as concern for immediate earnings, and consideration must also be given to the public welfare. An example of the interrelationship between long- and short-range earnings and the public welfare is afforded by the action of the Du Pont board of directors when considering whether to expand existing facilities for the production of neoprene rubber or whether to build a new plant. It was decided that since Du Pont was the sole supplier of neoprene for the free world and that there existed a possibility of the destruction of a single plant through enemy attack, it would be wiser for both the public and the stockholders to build an additional plant even though immediate costs would be greater.

Another duty related to the statement of objectives is the translation of objectives into policies governing sales, finance, production, and personnel to insure the fulfillment of stated goals.

Selection of Management. Closely associated with the function of policy making is the selection of the management necessary for the execution of policy. There are degrees of the extent to which boards participate in determining the choice of executives. Usually the selection of the president is the sole responsibility of the board of directors; however, the extent to which the board participates in the selection of other officers and key officials varies widely. Since it is recognized that the success of the president of a company is dependent in large measure upon the capabilities of the other officers, it is not unusual for the president to nominate, subject to the approval of the board, his associates. Along with the selection of the president and the confirmation of other officers, is the determination of salaries and bonuses of top executives.

In addition, the board of directors plays a prominent role in choosing replacements or additions to the board itself. Again, practice varies. The president, almost always a member of the board, may submit nominations and, if such is the case, the nominees are inclined to be friendly toward management. The same is true if the nominees are presented by other members of the board; they, too, are inclined to be friendly. In either event, the final selection to membership is made by the board. Though it is true that there are occasional proxy battles for control, they are relatively rare and represent the interests of large financial holdings rather than the desires of many small stockholders. Thus, there is a self-perpetuating characteristic of boards and managements.

Financial Well-Being of the Company. The financial well-being of a company is one of the major responsibilities of the board, a responsibility that in most cases is not delegated; and whenever it is delegated, there are tight controls and prescribed limits within which the officers of the company must perform. Figure 14-1 showing the top management of Du Pont stresses the importance of this function, for it shows that the finance committee reports directly to the board. Further evidence of the importance of financial position, including capital budgets, appears in Case Problem 14-B in which the executive committee of

Jersey Standard, also members of the board, sets the limits of expenditures for a new refinery. The directors of a company are also responsible for approving or initiating any changes in the capital structure of the organization, and not the least of their responsibility in the financial area is determining the distribution of earnings—the portion that should go to the stockholders, the amount to be retained for cash reserves, and the amount to be ploughed back into the business for replacement of present facilities and expansion to meet new objectives.

Review and Stimulation. In order to assure that objectives are met and policies properly executed, it is necessary that the performance of management be reviewed periodically. Discerning questions at this time may do much toward stimulating management and suggesting possible avenues of improvement. A management that must account to a discerning board is more apt to check its own performance than one reporting to a rubber-stamp board. In addition to the formal review of management's work during scheduled meetings, there is much that can be gained by individual counsel between board members and executives of the company. Although the board's formal action is that of a plural executive, advice and counsel may be given by individual members. Of course, the worth of such advice is dependent upon the qualifications and persuasiveness of the individual board member.

Composition of the Board

In an earlier discussion in this chapter, four advantages are cited that may result from the proper use of committees. They are advantages that come from group judgment, improved motivation, a check on authority, and improved coordination. Since the board of directors is a committee, a board with properly chosen membership reflects the advantages normally ascribed to effective committee action. The pertinent question to be answered in determining the proper composition of the membership is whether the board should be an *inside* board, composed of employees of the company, or whether it should be an *outside* board, with the majority of its members chosen from outside the company. There are advantages to both types, and no hard-and-fast rule can be stated that favors either form.

Outside Boards. The advantages attributed to outside boards appear only when the members are able men with truly diverse backgrounds and have the time and interest to acquaint themselves carefully with the problems of the company. The reasons most frequently cited for wanting to serve on a board are prestige, a sense of obligation to the business community, and an opportunity to make additional business contacts. The pay for services as a board member is nominal, on the average about $100 per meeting. Thus, the medium-size or small company, unable to offer sufficient prestige or business contacts, may find it difficult to attract the caliber of men it should have in order to realize the benefits that come from a well-chosen membership from outside the company.

Inside Boards. The value of group judgments from committee action is dependent upon the knowledge of each member, the time available for preparation, and the diversity of backgrounds of the members. The value is not dependent upon whether or not the board member is an employee of the company. A superficial examination of the problem may lead one to conclude that an external board is more objective in its judgments, but of what use is objectivity if the real requirement for sound judgment is an intimate knowledge of the company and the time necessary to evaluate the mass of information necessary for a decision? Thus, some companies, in order to avoid the problems that arise from having board members who can devote only a small portion of their time to the company and who do not have an intimate knowledge of the company's processes and problems, have turned to inside boards. Du Pont, for example, has a full-time board whose members have formerly served as members of management and when serving on the board have no responsibility other than that of a board member. Jersey Standard has a 15-man board, seven of whom serve as members of the executive committee that oversees the day-to-day operations of the company. Dow Chemical and Bethlehem Steel have inside boards with members who serve both as officers of the company and as directors.

It is worthwhile to examine the conditions that make the functioning of an inside board effective. First, the company must be large enough so that there is a sufficient number of executives to permit a choice from many qualified men. Second, there should be a tradition of promotion from within and, when combined with a large organization, there is opportunity for an executive to mature over a period of years and acquire a diverse background in company operations. Third, there is a tendency for inside boards to appear in companies where the operations are technical in nature and where technical knowledge is a requisite for sound judgments. And lastly, the company must be able to afford and need the services of an inside board that devotes full time to the affairs of the company.

Boards in Small Companies

The selection of a board of directors for a small owner-managed corporation or a medium-size publicly held corporation with professional management poses several problems. In the small owner-managed company, the board of directors in many instances merely meets the legal requirement that there be a board, and frequently it is composed of members of the owner's family. Family boards may be due in part to a fear of having outsiders participate in the management of the company or it may be due to an honest belief that outside help is not necessary.

The small to medium-size publicly held company faces a dilemma in securing the advantages of an effective board. The small company is unable to offer prestige, one of the main reasons for serving on a board, with the result that those whom it does attract from outside the company may not be fully qualified. Outside boards, even with the best of personnel, suffer from the shortcomings of part-time activity. Nor are inside boards the answer. In all probability, there is no need for the services of a full-time inside board of directors. Inside boards performing the dual role of officer and director may not have the breadth of experience and diversified knowledge necessary for corporate growth in a competitive economy.

The best solution for the small to medium-size corporation often is the selection of an outside board. True, an outside board presents the part-time problem, but the question of individual competence can be overcome to a large extent through the selection of men well qualified in their respective fields of work. Bankers, attorneys, educators, consultants, and executives from other companies are likely candidates and, when combined with the key officers of the company, the resulting board should provide the stimulation and guidance necessary for survival and growth.

● ● ● ● ● ● ● ● ●

Case Problem 14-B, How Rathbone Runs Jersey Standard, is an interesting account of a meeting of the executive committee of the Standard Oil Company (New Jersey). A brief background of Jersey's chief executive officer is presented and some of the problems encountered in reorganizing the board of a large company are described. The members of Jersey's executive committee are also members of the board of directors.

Questions for Study and Discussion

1. What assumptions are implied whenever a committee is formed? Which assumption is more applicable to the formation of a general management committee? Which is more applicable to the formation of an *ad hoc* or restricted committee?

2. Under what conditions is the judgment of a group likely to be superior to that of an individual? Is the information presented in Chapter 9 concerning brainstorming applicable to the improvement of the judgment of a group? How?

3. Why are committees not used as a check on authority more frequently in business organizations?

4. What problems concerning accountability arise when a committee is granted the authority to make decisions? How can the chairman of a committee be held accountable for the action of the group?

5. Lohman's study indicates that committees appointed by the board of directors are more authoritative than committees appointed by the president of the company. Why is this true?

6. Is there any conflict that might arise as the result of individual board members influencing members of management and the concept of the board as a plural executive? Discuss.

7. In his article, Mylander refers to the committee system of Du Pont as a "committee-line system." What do you think is meant by this phrase?

8. What conditions make it advisable for a company to have a full-time board whose membership is limited to those who have had prior experience with the company?

9. What are the hazards of having an inside board for a small company? Do these same hazards apply to an inside board for a larger company with a sales volume of approximately $500 million a year?

10. How can the shortcomings of an outside board be minimized?

•   •   •   •   •   •   •   •   •

Little knots of waiting men are standing in the paneled boardroom. They are dressed in sober blue or dark gray; here an assertive little flower is pinned to a lapel; there a cuff link, half hidden by a well-tailored sleeve, gleams in the soft fluorescent light. The men are executives of the Standard Oil Co. (New Jersey) and they are waiting for a meeting to begin—or, more precisely, they are waiting for another man, whose appearance will mark the beginning of a meeting. The man they are waiting for is Monroe Jackson Rathbone, the president of Jersey Standard and its chief executive officer.

Most of the men now waiting for Rathbone once had their well-tailored sleeves plunged to the elbows in crude oil. They have spent many years with Jersey or one or another of Jersey's 100-odd affiliates that pump crude from the ground, transport, refine, or market it. But now the whole group belongs to Jersey, which strictly speaking is not an oil company at all, but a holding company that invests in the oil business— a kind of Roman Empire of the modern business world. Paramount in the minds of the men now gathered together— on the twenty-ninth floor of Jersey's New York offices at Rockefeller Center, around the boardroom's oval table, beneath a pensive portrait of John D. Rockefeller, Sr.—is the aggregate prosperity of a great and sprawling mosaic of investment. An affiliate may importune from the heat of competitive struggle or the environment of a foreign country, but (as with the Roman Empire) Jersey can never accede to a major request from a family member without considering what the reverberations through the provinces will mean to the larger interest—that of the Jersey company itself.

How Jersey executives manage the affairs of empire make a case study in American management. Over its eighty years, Jersey has developed a highly refined managerial philosophy, which puts primary emphasis on the committee system. Thorough staff work digs out and distills the mountains of facts needed by Jersey's committees. Decisions that reach beyond one committee's scope are passed up to another level of committee management. At the top of the chain sits a seven-man executive committee whose members also serve on Jersey's fifteen-men board of directors. Meeting every day, this committee looks to the general good of Jersey by two major means. First, it governs the finances of affiliates by a detailed review of budgets and contemplated new investments. Second, bearing a different formal designation, the executive committee passes on the selection and promotion of the top officers who run Jersey's companies around the world. On this day, the executive committee is about to hold discussions in both these broad areas of responsibility.

Case Problem 14-B
How Rathbone Runs
Jersey Standard [12]

---

[12] Walter Guzzardi, Jr., "How Rathbone Runs Jersey Standard," *Fortune*, Vol. LXVII (January, 1963), pp. 85-87, 89, 171, 172. The student is urged to read the entire article, which presents in great detail the problems faced by the chief executive of a large corporation.

Now the side door opens, and Rathbone, a man with the husky frame of a roustabout and the craggy features of an amiable pugilist, steps from his office into the boardroom. As always, he sits in a chair close to his office door, in the middle of the oval's broad curve. Other chairs are pulled up around the table, beneath the pensive Rockefeller portrait. There is no gavel-rapping. At a nod from Rathbone, the meeting begins. Every executive officer has his style of running things. Let's watch the carefully modulated style of the man who presides over a corporation with assets of almost $11 billion.

REFINEMENTS IN BUILDING A REFINERY

The first matter to come up for decision is a proposal for the construction of a refinery in France. Once the executive committee's controls were so tight that it had to pass on many small purchases contemplated by affiliates. Controls were loosened as Jersey grew. Then, when Rathbone became Jersey's chief executive, he and the board delegated a great deal of financial authority to another Jersey committee, the board advisory committee on investments, headed by company director Marion Boyer; now the executive committee considers only those expenditures over $1 million.

This refinery at Marseille, if Rathbone and the committee approve it, will cost Jersey in the neighborhood of $35 million. Three times before, the committee has been informed of the progress of the plans for the refinery; this time the proposal, to be explained in detail by staff officers, comes to the committee for formal action. Following his usual technique, Rathbone first hears the proposal all the way through, with only an infrequent interruption to clarify a point. He tests the staff work by calling attention to staff studies showing that the excess refining capacity in France will diminish over the next ten years, and asking sharply: "What about the fact that the decrease in that excess capacity depends partly on export markets? Are we sure those markets will still be there in 1966, when the refinery will be finished?" Satisfied with the reply, Jersey's president lets the presentation of details about the refinery run on to its end.

Then he moves in heavily on a matter always foremost in his mind—costs. "What about the estimates of the cost of the refinery—how good are they?" Told that while they were not yet detailed, they seemed good enough so that the cost would probably come within the 10 percent latitude that Jersey allows in such cases, the president bears down: "We allow that 10 percent to take care of emergencies or unforeseen situations. But we don't want to start a project of this size with the idea that cost can be allowed to go up $3 million or $4 million. It's bad psychology to start with the idea that you have that kind of leeway. We've had some horrible overruns on these refineries, and I don't want that to happen in this case. If there is an overrun, the size of the refinery may have to be reconsidered. What we are approving is this: a $35-million refinery at Marseille. If it comes to more, you come back to us. The proposal is approved on that basis."

Chairs are pushed back. The staff men who presented the refinery proposal depart. Presently the executive committee, now sitting in its capacity as the compensation and executive-development committee, turns its attention to the careers and next assignments of top officers. Rathbone has spent forty-one years working for Jersey; he appears to know everyone who comes up for discussion, and listens carefully. Occasionally he drops in a comment. Upon hearing of the good performance of a man on a new assignment, he remarks: "It has taken a long time, but it looks like he has finally found his niche in this company. It's nice to have him in the right place at last."

A Jersey affiliate abroad needs a top manager, and one of the executive-committee members knows just the right man. But the man cannot move into the job for a year. One officer comments: "We'll send him next year. He's the man we want." Nodding of heads. The president (sharply): "But what about leaving that job vacant for a whole year? Can we afford to do it?" There is a small shock, and more discussion; it is decided to keep the job open for the man. But Rathbone has left hanging in the air just a suspicion that so long a delay borders on being unwise.

There is a discussion of a slate of three names for another job. "Don't forget that this spot is a breeding ground for the board of directors," says Rathbone. "When we look over these names, let's keep that in mind. Let's look down the road a way. Which of these men is going to be best for the board?"

Rathbone (on still another Jersey man): "I know he's got three children. But they have a fine nurse who's just like a mother to those kids. The children

will get along fine out there. He's making $25,000 a year now—below the minimum for his class. Even after this raise, he'll still be below the minimum. But we can leave him at that level for a while. He's been moved along very well."

The meeting breaks up. A few people drift off. One or two stay behind for a word with Jersey's president. Answering questions or giving curbstone opinions, Rathbone seems consciously to eschew the attributes popularly assigned to the boss: he has no tough bearing, he generates no tension, he affects no elegance. He gives the impression of a willingness to talk every problem through, no matter how long it takes. His language is not incisive; instead he often clothes his positive views in negative syntax: "I'm not sure I'd buy that," or "That may not be the best basis to put it on." Such replies seem to satisfy his interrogators, who hurry away. Rathbone steps back into his own office. His schedule has run late on this particular day and the afternoon is almost over. Rathbone flips through a few documents his secretary brings him. He remembers to give to her the $5.64 that he owes her from the day before. Around 5:30 p.m., with his correspondence signed and his desk cleared, Rathbone goes home. He takes a thick tan briefcase with him.

A SPECIAL STRAIN OF MANAGER

Whether in board meeting, in the privacy of his office, or even at home, Rathbone has come almost automatically to think of Jersey first. Like Frederick Kappel of A.T.&T., Lawrence Litchfield, Jr., of Alcoa, and Frederic Donner of General Motors, Rathbone belongs to a distinct managerial strain—men who mature in one company with the conviction that they or someone else going through the same maturation process eventually will be in charge of it. Rathbone was brought up in the Jersey system, shaped by it and at the same time shaping it. Virtually every Jersey board member has spent most of his working life with Jersey. None has worked for any other oil company. On an average, each board member has served thirty-one years with Jersey or its affiliates. The total time spent in the company by present members of the board comes to over four hundred and fifty years. The company believes that the place to learn the oil business is inside Jersey's family—a belief supported by the performance of system-made men like Rathbone.

The son of a Jersey Standard man, Rathbone studied chemical engineering at Lehigh, and joined Standard Oil Co. of Louisiana after graduation in 1921. He went to work in the big refinery at Baton Rouge. "Rathbone was the first man of a new wave," recalls Henry Voorheis, general manager of the refinery. "Refining oil was a combination of guesswork and art in those days. Jack was the first of a group of educated men who made refining into a science." Rathbone worked "in that old hellhole, the acid plant." Then he went into thermal cracking. "The first time I saw Jack, he was climbing up the ladder of one of the first big cracking units," recollects David Shepard, now an executive vice president of Jersey. "He seemed to be practically running up the ladder. I'll never forget the sight—there went Rathbone, climbing, climbing."

As Jersey measures time, the climb was quick. Rathbone became general superintendent of the refinery at thirty-one, and five years later was president of Standard Oil of Louisiana, the Jersey affiliate whose chief asset was the refinery. In an early test of his diplomacy, Rathbone staved off predatory attacks by Huey Long, who "customarily ran for office against Standard Oil of Louisiana." Then, in 1944, Rathbone took a big step. He left Baton Rouge, to which he now occasionally returns for a vacation at his camp on the Amite River. Taking with him a whiff of the bayous in his accent, Rathbone moved to New York to become president of Esso Standard. Five years later, he became a member of Jersey's board of directors. That took him another long stride forward—out of an operational oil company, and into the broader business of management of the empire. Five years afterward, Rathbone became the president of Jersey. Then, in May, 1960, he succeeded the late Eugene Holman as Jersey's chief executive. By then Rathbone was sixty years old.

Rathbone's accession meant many changes for Jersey. As a colleague says: "Rathbone and Holman worked closely and in harmony for many years. But it was natural that Jack should change some things—he would have been less than human if he hadn't." The first important change lay deep in the psyches of the two men. A friend who knew them both recollects that "Gene was shy and reserved. Jack is outgoing and enthusiastic. Holman solved tough problems by making the partners to the dispute work them out —he kept them coming back to him until they arrived at a compromise.

Rathbone's procedure is different. He looks the situation over, figures out what's best, and proposes his solution to both parties. He may adjust it to meet their objections, and like Holman he may end up with everyone satisfied. But the solution comes initially from Rathbone." Another friend who once worked for Jersey adds: "Holman was a softer and a gentler man. He did well at stockholders' meetings, but I think they were an ordeal for him. Jack actually seems to enjoy them."

THE REORGANIZATION MAN

Since becoming chief executive, Rathbone has changed Jersey's organization in various ways. Like his predecessors, he believes in the wisdom of an inside board of directors, all of whose members are full-time executives of the company. As it did before, the board still delegates most of its executive functions to the smaller executive committee. But soon after he became chief executive, Rathbone changed the board's organization and direction. Before his accession, executive responsibilities were parceled out along functional lines. One director, for example, was charged with overseeing marketing, or refining, or transportation. As a collateral responsibility, the same man would oversee a group of affiliates, usually the ones whose principal activity lay within his functional province. But the system had serious deficiencies. At the joints, where the various functions dovetailed—as they did with the big integrated affiliates—Jersey's top-level responsibility tended to blur. Some directors were carrying enormously heavy loads. Others, to relieve the burden, took responsibilities for some affiliates

on the basis of expediency; the transportation director, for example, supervised the Scandinavian affiliates. Further, no one was looking at areas broadly enough: people thought about Brazil or Argentina, but no one was encouraged to consider the total problem of Latin America. To give a director experience in more than one function, says a Jersey man, "every couple of years we threw all the papers in the air and sat different men down at different piles. The result of it all was a dilution of the abilities and time of our top executives."

The time of dilution corresponded with a time of deluge. For Jersey was then being caught up in the flood tide of international oil surpluses, which threatened to bring down the whole fancy price structure of international oil. And, abroad, Jersey had never faced bigger or more difficult political complications. In seeking to meet those challenges, Jersey had to move swiftly in two areas. It had to search out and exploit new markets. And it had to bear down hard to reduce the per-barrel cost of oil everywhere in the world. But just when it needed most to move swiftly, Jersey found itself hamstrung by its old organizational patterns.

After he took over in May of 1960, Rathbone made some quick repairs. Atop Jersey's functional groupings Rathbone superimposed a regional grouping—"like an overlay of diagonal streets imposed upon a grid." In addition to their functional assignments, Rathbone gave some board members responsibilities as contact directors of geographic regions. While two or more functions dovetailed, the new regional contact director now took responsibility for their coordination. The problems of new or difficult areas, like the Common Market or Latin America, could be considered as a whole. By thus breaking up the old compartmentalized approach, Rathbone did a good deal to prepare Jersey for combat in its new and tougher world. "After reorganization," explains David Shepard, "we couldn't point to a new chair or a new job title and say 'There's the answer to our need for new markets or for new economies.' It wasn't that simple. But the emphasis on regional thinking in fact enabled us to do just that."

Problems

1. How would you classify the executive committee of Standard of New Jersey?
2. In your opinion, why do you believe the executive committee was given the responsibility of overseeing the financial affairs of affiliates and the compensation and selection of the top officers of the company? Would it have been better to have given the latter function, compensation and selection, to another committee? Discuss.
3. Of what significance is it that the executive committee considered the assignment of a $25,000-a-year-man? Should this problem be delegated to a lesser committee?
4. Could outside board members make a significant contribution to the management of Jersey Standard? Support your answer.
5. Are there dangers of inbreeding that might result from having an inside board in a company the size of Jersey Standard? What about the dangers of inbreeding in a smaller company?

CHAPTER 15

Preparing for Organizational Change
— Organizational Analysis

Twenty-five years ago Stanley Johnson founded the Johnson Valve Company, which has grown and prospered over the years. Mr. Johnson, now 62 years old, realizes that he cannot continue as president indefinitely, but there are no well-formulated plans for management succession. The stock in the company is closely held by Mr. Johnson and members of his immediate family, with only ten percent held by an outsider, the attorney who serves as the only outside member of the board and as general counsel for the corporation. The attorney has suggested that the position of executive vice-president be created and a man brought in from another company with the intention of moving him up to the presidency, if he performs satisfactorily, upon Mr. Johnson's expected retirement at age 65. Currently the organization is as follows.

Reporting directly to Mr. Johnson as an "assistant-to" is a man in his early thirties who has a master's degree in marketing. Although his title is "assistant-to," his primary function is to conduct market research studies

Case Problem 15-A

Charting an Organization

in the valve industry and to prepare detailed analyses of current sales. Johnson often refers to his assistant as "my forward planning unit." Also reporting to the president are the treasurer, the vice-president of sales, the purchasing director, the production vice-president, the chief engineer, and the plant manager. The plant manager, now nearing retirement, has been ill most of the past year, so in effect the plant superintendent reports directly to the president.

The treasurer, who for several years was the firm's only accountant, has been with the company since its founding. Reporting directly to the treasurer is the office manager who not only manages the office but also performs the personnel function for all salaried and clerical personnel. The controller, responsible for the cost accounting section, and the supervisor of general ledgers also reports to the treasurer. The vice-president in charge of sales has been an officer of the company for the past five years; however, for many years he was in charge of the field sales force and the entire sales function with the title of sales manager. Although there is now a sales manager reporting to him, the vice-president actually directs the sales force and the sales manager spends most of his time in the office handling the paper work generated by the salesmen. The supervisor of the sales order department also reports to the sales manager.

The purchasing director, with a staff of two buyers and a clerk, reports directly to the president as a result of Mr. Johnson's desire to control the cost of raw materials. Formerly, the director of purchases reported to the production manager, who is a vice-president and Mr. Johnson's brother-in-law, but the only person now reporting to the production manager is the head of the production scheduling department. The chief engineer, also an officer of the company, knows the product well and supervises the section chief of the drafting department, the chief metallurgist, and the director of the research laboratories.

Most of Johnson Valve Company's current problems center in the production area. The plant manager's staff consists of the maintenance foreman, the plant personnel and employment manager, and the foreman of the tool room; but for the past year, as the result of his illness and absence, the plant staff has been reporting directly to the plant superintendent, who also reports on paper to the plant manager. Normally reporting to the plant superintendent are the shipping and receiving foreman, the machining foreman, the quality control manager, the factory stores supervisor, the assembly foreman, and the supervisor of the experimental shop, which is engaged primarily in carrying out projects assigned by the chief engineer.

Problem

Prepare an organization chart showing the present structure of Johnson Valve Company.

• ● ● ● ● ● ● ● ●

Organizations are not static structures; instead, organizations are made up of dynamic interrelationships existing between people performing those functions necessary for the achievement of organizational goals. As either goals or people change, the need for modification of organization structure and function arises. Symptoms calling for organizational change, such as those described below, may appear as inadequacies or inefficiencies in any part of the organization.

1. *Decision making.* Decision making may be too slow to gain full advantage of the situation, or there may be errors in decisions that are being made. Perhaps the difficulty in decision making may be traced to the placement of the responsibility for decisions at a level of the organization not having access to necessary information.
2. *Poor Communications.* Case Problem 14-A, A Problem in Coordination, illustrates poor communications between one man, the presi-

dent, and his executive group. The Parable of the Spindle, Case Problem 8-A, is illustrative of the complete breakdown of an information system with its resultant personnel problems.

3. *Failure in Functional Areas.* There may be failure or inefficiency in any one of the major functional areas. Production may not meet schedules or it may show excessive costs and quality defects. Sales may show a steady loss of customers and failure to achieve expected market penetration, while finance may reveal an inability to provide for long-range corporate demands. In the area of personnel, the need for organizational change may arise as the result of personnel not meeting the requirements of changing positions, with poor performance as a result; or the need for change may be highlighted by excessive personality clashes between employees (again, the Parable of the Spindle).

4. *Lack of Innovation.* There may be a dearth of new ideas, either in the form of new products or new and better ways of performing present functions. When innovation ceases, growth ceases also.

Change is the one constant if the organization is to survive. The challenge is to plan for organizational change so that any proposed reorganization may have reasonable expectations of success. The purpose of this chapter is threefold: First, to present some of the common tools used in organizational analysis. While this portion of the chapter may be of some interest to top management, it is of vital importance to the department manager who uses these techniques in the analysis of his own department. Second, to discuss the principles and concepts of organization as they function in a dynamic system. Third, it is intended, as a result of studying the techniques and concepts of organization, that the student of management be better qualified to evaluate the organizational effectiveness of a potential employer. The first part of the chapter analyzes some of the tools commonly used in organizational analysis, and the second part develops a means of evaluating organizational effectiveness in the light of the systems approach to organization theory that is presented in Chapter 10 as Theory Z.

ORGANIZATIONAL ANALYSIS

When conducting organizational analyses, one is, in effect, planning for the future of the organization, and as in the case of planning for profit, sales, or production, it is helpful to follow a procedure based upon the scientific method. After the procedures for organizational analysis are developed, the specific tools of analysis are used in securing information and presenting the recommended results.

However, not all companies favor a formal organizational analysis, so it is necessary to evaluate the advantages and disadvantages of formal analysis. In this section, we shall discuss the procedures of organizational analysis, the specific tools of organizational analysis—the organization questionnaire, the position description, the organization chart, and the organization manual—and evaluate the advantages and disadvantages of formal organizational analysis.

Procedures for Organizational Analysis

The procedures for sound organizational analysis are an application of the scientific method. They are: (1) assign responsibility, (2) collect data, (3) prepare alternate plans of organization, and (4) install the best plan and follow up.

Assign Responsibility. There are three questions to be answered in the assignment of responsibility for organizational analysis. The first of these questions is, who is to initiate the study; the second, who is to collect the necessary data and develop recommended changes; and third, who is to approve the recommended changes and place them into effect? A study by K. K. White of 118 companies sheds some light on what is actually done by industrial firms in one phase of organizational analysis, preparing the organization chart.[1] White's study shows that the company president initiates the charting of the organization in 42 percent of the companies surveyed; a company vice-president in 22 percent of the companies; and the personnel executive in 12 percent of the companies. In most instances, 25 percent of the companies surveyed, the personnel executive compiles the necessary data and prepares the chart. The president of the company does the charting in 17 percent of the cases, a company vice-president in 14 percent, or an outside consultant in 13 percent of the companies. Final approval for any organizational change must come from top management itself. It goes without saying that the chief executive, usually the president, must approve any changes and, to insure maximum cooperation, approval of other members of top management is much desired.

Collect Data. Once the responsibility for analysis and preparation of proposed changes is established, it is necessary to collect all pertinent information so that any proposed change is founded on fact, not upon supposition. The availability and type of information sought varies

---

[1] K. K. White, *Understanding the Company Organization Chart* (New York: American Management Association, 1963), Research Study Number 56, pp. 16-17.

from one situation to another. Certain historical records are of interest, particularly those that show the growth of the company in respect to the number of people, their titles, their duties, and their personal backgrounds and qualifications. The pattern of growth of the company as reflected by gross sales is of value, especially when these figures can be correlated with the need for personnel. In this manner, definite trends may be established, and personnel needs for expected future levels of sales may be projected. The analysis of current reports and forms, for example, the monthly distribution of manufacturing costs, shows the flow of information within the company. Activity charts showing the distribution of an employee's time for each day or week may be prepared for key jobs or for all the jobs within a department. When interpreted in the light of information gained from an analysis of existing reports, the activity chart indicates whether or not the information is needed.[2] Information gained from the organization questionnaire (which is discussed below) is of value in defining authority relationships, the nature of assigned responsibilities, and the extent of authority delegated to carry out these responsibilities. The gathering of data for an organizational analysis is often a long and tedious task, but it is an important step for it establishes the factual basis for any proposed change.

Prepare Alternate Plans. Ultimately, any proposed change in organization must be sold to key personnel and alternate plans should be prepared as a form of insurance. Among these plans, there should be an "ideal" structure that is theoretically desirable, but not necessarily attainable. Using the ideal as a starting point, modifications in the plan may be developed that consider the economic and competitive position of the company. If only a single plan is presented, it may be rejected by one displeased executive; an alternate is necessary since organizational change is a situation in which "half a loaf is better than none" and the adoption of the alternate is at least a step in the right direction.

Install the Best Plan and Follow Up. The criteria for determining the best plan are discussed in the last section of this chapter. When the plan is approved, it should be installed and there should be provisions for continuing study and analysis so that any necessary modifications can be made. This task is usually assigned to the group that proposes the initial change. Proper follow-up and modifications of the plan, when

---

[2] C. L. Littlefield and Frank Rachel, *Office and Administrative Management* (2d ed.; Englewood Cliffs, N. J.: Prentice-Hall, Inc., 1964) Chapter 5, "Techniques of Organizational Analysis," pp. 59-79, includes a discussion of work distribution and activity charts. The organization questionnaire on page 372 may be used as a means of securing information for the preparation of activity charts.

needed, emphasize the continuing nature of organizational change. In a literal sense, organizational analysis is a process of reorganization, for most organization studies are undertaken to reorganize an existing structure.

Tools of Organizational Analysis

There are many tools available for use in organizational analysis. Among those most commonly used are the organization questionnaire, the position description, the organization chart, and the organization manual. Each of these techniques used in studying organizations is discussed briefly.

The Organization Questionnaire. One of the first steps in describing the present organization is to determine the functions and positions of present personnel. Figure 15-1 is an Organization Questionnaire to Executives that has been found useful in securing information from executives, supervisors, and department heads concerning their positions in the organization. The first five items of the questionnaire are for the purposes of identification. The answer given to item 4, title or name of your position, may provide one of the first clues pointing toward the need for clarifying the organization structure. Discrepancies may appear in designating the organizational unit. For example, one department head may describe himself as a section supervisor, cost accounting, while another department head describes himself as supervisor, general accounting; yet both units are at the same level of the organization and report to the same supervisor.

Questions 6 through 10 reveal the nature and extent to which responsibilities have been delegated, the authority granted to meet these responsibilities, and the clarity of the lines of accountability. Note that questions 6 and 8 may be refined to determine the specific degree of authority by specifying those actions that must be reported prior to their occurrence, after the action has occurred, or not reported at all. Question 9 requires a listing of all responsibilities and duties and offers the opportunity for describing the relationships, both internal and external, that must be maintained.

The three questions, 11 through 13, form the basis for an activity analysis and the preparation of flow charts to show the movement and utilization of existing reports and forms. These questions may be modified for use in production departments to trace the movement of the product and the contribution of each production department.

ABC COMPANY
ORGANIZATION QUESTIONNAIRE TO EXECUTIVES
Outline for Describing Your Position

1. Your name.

2. Your department.

3. Your division.

4. Title or name of your position.

5. Your location.

6. To whom do you report?

7. Title or name of the position of the immediate supervisor.

8. Give the names and titles (or names of positions) of those who report to you. In (6) and (8), a distinction might be made of the types of actions which must be reported: (a) actions reported before they take place; (b) after they take place; and (c) those which need not be reported at all.

9. Describe fully the responsibilities of your position as you understand them to be at present. (As part of this description, you should also include your existing responsibilities and relationships with other units within your division and with affiliates and with any outside service agencies.)

10. What is the nature of your authority?

    (a) For establishing policy?
    (b) For incurring expense?
    (c) For personnel changes including selection, promotion, termination, and compensation?
    (d) For establishing methods and procedures?

11. Indicate any committees in the Company or trade groups of which you are a member. If you are chairman, include a description of the purpose, scope of activities and accomplishments of your committee.

12. List by name or title the regular reports which (a) you receive and (b) you prepare, and indicate whether daily, weekly, monthly, etc.

13. List the basic records you are responsible for keeping.

14. Mention anything else of interest in understanding your responsibilities and activities, including any special problems needing attention, any suggestions for improvements or general comments on the overall Company organizational structure.

Source: Ernest Dale, *Planning and Developing the Company Organization Structure* (New York: American Management Association, 1952), Research Report No. 20, p. 135.

Figure 15-1
ORGANIZATION QUESTIONNAIRE

The last question, 14, calls for suggestions concerning the improvement of the organization and serves as a means of insuring two-way communications in organizational analysis.

There are two methods of securing the information called for by the questionnaire. One method is to have the incumbent in the position fill out the questionnaire and return it to the person conducting the study; the other method is to secure the information through interview. While the latter method is more costly and time consuming, it is generally agreed that the interview yields much more information and understanding of the organization as a result of aside remarks and nuances of meaning implied in the way in which answers are given. Once the questionnaires have been completed, they are usually reviewed with the next higher level of authority. It is at this stage that significant discrepancies in the opinions of superior and subordinate with respect to the nature of assigned duties, the nature and extent of delegated authority, and the lines of accountability may become apparent.

The Position Description. The data obtained from the questionnaire is the primary source of information for preparing the *position description*, a written statement that describes a specific position in the organization. Whether a written position description merely sketches the major duties of the job or whether it goes into minute detail depends upon the uses to which it will be put. If the purpose is to define the major positions in the organization and show their relationships to each other, the description may be relatively brief; if however, the primary purpose of the description is for training, the job duties may be detailed so that they approach the completeness of a procedural manual.

Most position descriptions usually include the following information. There is a section that *identifies* the job and may range from a statement of the title only, as in Figure 15-2, to the inclusion of statements indicating the title of the immediate superior, the date of preparation of the description with dates of revision, and the number and types of employees supervised. Generally, the name of the incumbent is not included since a change in personnel would necessitate a revision of the description. Next, there is a statement of the major responsibility or *primary functions* of the job, a capsule description of the purpose of the position. A statement of *responsibilities* presents the major tasks that must be performed in order to fulfill the functions of the job. It is this portion of the description, when developed in great detail, that may serve as a useful training device; but for the most part, executive and supervisory descriptions are limited to a statement of between six and ten major responsibilities. The *authority* delegated to the position

---

MANAGEMENT GUIDE

SUPERVISOR ACCOUNTING SECTION, MANUFACTURING DIVISION

I. FUNCTIONS

Furnishes functional guidance to the Plant Superintendents on, and provides services in connection with accounting, auditing, budgets, inventory and stock control, payroll, and tax activities.

II. RESPONSIBILITIES AND AUTHORITY

The responsibilities and authority stated below are subject to established policies.

1. Administers approved policies and procedures pertaining to accounting, auditing, budget, payroll, and tax activities, making such recommendations as he deems necessary to the Comptroller through channels.
2. Administers approved policies and procedures pertaining to inventory and stock control activities, making such recommendations as he deems necessary to the Manager of the Supply and Transportation Department through channels.
3. Consolidates the financial, accounting, budget, inventory and stock control, payroll, and tax reports and statements of the plants, and prepares such reports and statements for the Division.
4. Establishes and maintains necessary accounting records for the Division.
5. Establishes and maintains necessary cost control records for the Division.
6. Maintains necessary inventory and stock control records for the Division.
7. Maintains necessary production records for the Division.
8. Maintains necessary records of receipts and disbursements and has custody of funds on hand for the Division office.
9. Maintains necessary payroll records and accounts; prepares and pays Division office payrolls and confidential payrolls of the Division.
10. Conducts all tax activities for the Division.

III. RELATIONSHIPS

A. General Manager, Manufacturing Division
   Reports to the General Manager.
B. Plant Superintendents and Section Supervisors
   As directed, or as requested by the Plant Superintendents and Section Supervisors, advises and assists them in the accomplishment of their respective functions in all matters within his province.
C. Outside Auditors
   Cooperates with independent auditors.
D. Others
   Conducts such other relationships as are necessary to the accomplishment of his function.

Source: George Lawrence Hall, *The Management Guide* (2d ed.; San Francisco: Standard Oil Company of California, 1956), p. 63.

Figure 15-2

A TYPICAL POSITION DESCRIPTION

in order to perform the required functions may appear as a separate section of the position description or, as in Figure 15-2, it may be combined with the statement of primary responsibilities. The last section of most descriptions is a statement of *relationships*. The reason for stating relationships is twofold. First, it shows the position in its proper relationship to other positions within the company and relationships to persons outside the company such as vendors, auditors, or public relations contacts. Second, a statement of relationships tends to answer criticism often made of position descriptions that descriptions force a man into a narrow role and make him oblivious to other events and persons in the company.

As a general rule, position descriptions do not include a statement of the specifications and qualifications required of incumbents. If such specifications are prepared, they are on a separate sheet and include requirements in respect to age, education, experience, and other personal characteristics. Specifications are of value as an aid in evaluating and selecting potential replacements.

The Organization Chart. An organization chart presents in graphic form the major functions and the lines of authority of an organization as of a given moment in time. Charts range in complexity from the simple chart shown in Figure 15-3 to complex charts that utilize color and the photographs of the incumbents in key positions. However, for purposes of organizational analysis and reference, it is best to keep charts as simple as possible.

The mechanics of constructing an organization chart are not difficult. Figure 15-4 presents in tabular form ten suggestions for preparing organization charts. These are not hard-and-fast rules and they should be modified when the occasion demands. By far the most common form of organizational charting is the *vertical* chart, (Figure 15-3) which shows the organizational hierarchy ranked from top to bottom. A variation of the vertical chart is the *horizontal* chart, which is read from left to right rather than from top to bottom. A more complex form of charting is the *circular* organization chart, which places the chief executive in the center of the circle with the horizontal lines of the vertical chart forming a series of concentric circles around the chief executive. Proponents of the horizontal form of charting contend that we normally read from left to right and that a horizontal chart follows this natural tendency. Those who favor the circular chart claim that dynamic relationships are better portrayed through a series of concentric circles. However, precedent and ease of construction and interpretation favor the continued use of the vertical chart.

ORGANIZATION CHART-XYZ CORPORATION

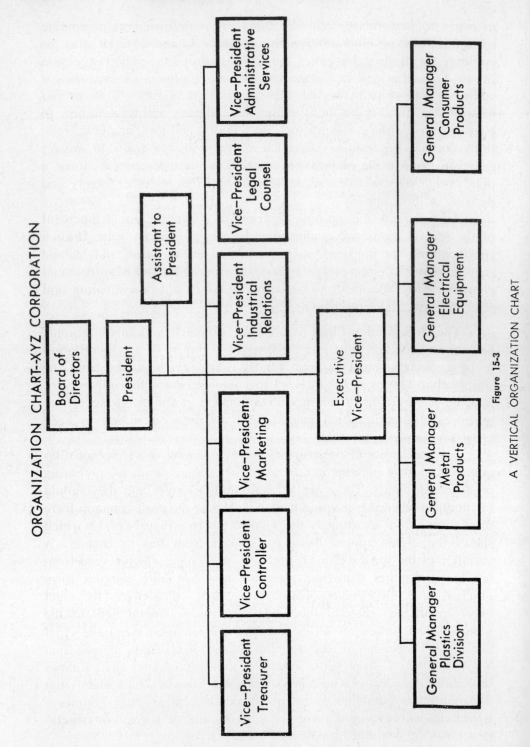

Figure 15-3

A VERTICAL ORGANIZATION CHART

SUGGESTIONS FOR PREPARING AN ORGANIZATION CHART

1. Identify the chart fully showing the name of the company, date of preparation, and title of person or name of department responsible for preparation. If the chart is for one division of the company only, include such information as part of the title.

2. Use rectangular boxes to show either an organizational unit or a person. Plural executives and other committees occupy one box. (See Figure 14-1.)

3. The vertical placement of the boxes shows relative positions in the organizational hierarchy; however, due to space limitations, line units are frequently shown one level below staff units. (See Figure 15-3.)

4. Any given horizontal row of boxes should be of the same size and should include only those positions having the same organizational rank.

5. Vertical and horizontal solid lines are used to show the flow of line authority.

6. If necessary, use dotted or broken lines to show the flow of functional authority. (See Figure 12-4.)

7. Lines of authority enter at the top center of a box and leave at the bottom center; they do not run through the box. Exception: the line of authority to a staff assistant or an "assistant-to" may enter the side of the box. (See Figure 15-3.)

8. The title of each position should be placed in the box. The title should be descriptive and show function. For example, vice-president is not sufficient as it does not show function. The functional area; e.g., manufacturing, should be included even though it is not a part of the official title. Titles should be consistent; if necessary, revise titles so they are both consistent and descriptive.

9. Include the name of the person currently holding the position unless personnel turnover is so great that revision of the chart becomes burdensome.

10. Keep the chart as simple as possible; include a legend if necessary to explain any special notations. When preparing a separate chart for an organizational unit, include the superior to whom the unit reports.

Figure 15-4

SUGGESTIONS FOR PREPARING AN ORGANIZATION CHART

The Organization Manual. An *organization manual* is a compilation of descriptive statements usually bound in manual form concerning the organization of a specific company.[3] The content of organization manuals varies widely; however, two of the tools of organizational analysis are included in almost all manuals—position descriptions and

---

[3] George Lawrence Hall, *The Management Guide* (2d ed.; San Francisco: Standard Oil Company of California, 1956) p. 74. The Standard Oil Management Guide is one of the best known organization manuals and is available in most libraries.

organization charts. The combination of these two instruments shows the lines of authority and accountability, the major functions of each position, the responsibilities and authority for each position, and the primary interrelationships between key positions. In addition, organization manuals may include a statement of company objectives and statements of company policy. In large companies, it is not uncommon to find organization manuals consisting of several volumes, one for each of the major functional areas of the company. In such cases, each volume includes a statement of company objectives, policies, and the organization charts and position descriptions for that specific functional area.

Evaluation of Formal Organizational Analysis

Not all companies believe in using the formal tools of organizational analysis. The extent to which formal tools of analysis are used is related to the size of the company as shown in Table 15-1. To be sure, White's study deals only with the use of organization charts; however, it is safe to assume that a company without organization charts has not prepared position descriptions or an organization manual. Note that even in the large companies, 5,000 employees and over, four of the 15 companies in this category do not have organization charts. The absence of charts in small companies may be due to a belief that they are not needed, a lack of available personnel to prepare charts, or any of a number of similar reasons. However, large companies without charts have not prepared them because it is felt that the disadvantages of charting the organization outweigh the advantages. Let us examine the advantages and disadvantages usually attributed to the use of formal tools of organizational analysis.

Table 15-1

RELATIONSHIP BETWEEN COMPANY SIZE AND PRESENCE OF ORGANIZATION CHARTS

No. of Employees	No. of Companies with Charts	No. of Companies without Charts	Total Companies	Percent of Companies with Charts
1–249	34	41	75	45
250–499	27	4	31	87
500–999	15	7	22	68
1,000–4,999	28	9	37	76
5,000 and over	11	4	15	73

Source: K. K. White, *Understanding the Company Organization Chart*, (New York: American Management Association, 1963), Research Study No. 56, p. 19.

Advantages of Formal Organizational Analysis. The advantage most frequently cited in support of preparing a formal analysis of an organization is that the process of analysis itself forces the key executives of the company into critical thinking that is directed toward organizational problems. The process of analysis leads to a reexamination of present structure and functions and makes possible the correction of obvious organizational defects. Second, charts and manuals are of use in training replacements for present personnel. True, the man holding the position at present may not benefit greatly, but new people coming into the organization or a man moving into a position new to him find charts and manuals helpful during their period of orientation. The third reason advanced for formalizing the organization structure is that charts and position descriptions offer an authoritative source which describes the major functions and responsibilities for each position and thus become a means of settling disputes that may arise concerning lines of authority and accountability.

Disadvantages of Formal Organizational Analysis. Those who prefer not to use formal analysis claim that the formalization of organization structure by means of charts and position descriptions leads to rigidity and inflexibility in organization structure and function. They point out that a new man coming into a position complete with chart and position description is bound by precedent and does not have the full opportunity to express himself and show how much he can really contribute to the organization. In a sense, these critics of charting are saying "Put a man into a square and you have one." In addition to organizational inflexibility and the stultifying effects that charting may have on individuals, opponents of formal analysis state that formal charting ignores completely the informal organization—the many interpersonal relationships, lines of communications, and influence—which exists among people who work together every day and is often quite different from the formal relationships shown on the chart.[4]

There is a need for balance. Charting is not intended to stultify or limit the achievement of individuals. It is intended to show in broad strokes major functions and relationships. Nor is charting intended to promote organizational inflexibility; on the other hand, an organization with relationships that change from day to day or with every crisis cannot properly be called an organization.

---

[4] Frank J. Jasinski, "Adapting Organization to New Technology," *Harvard Business Review,* Vol. XXXVII (January-February, 1959), pp. 79-86.* Mr. Jasinski's article contains an extensive discussion of horizontal relationships.

EVALUATING ORGANIZATIONAL EFFECTIVENESS

The application of the tools of organizational analysis —the organization questionnaire, the position description, and the charting of the present organization—is the second step in the process of organizational analysis. In order to complete the third step of analysis, to prepare alternate plans of organization, and move on to the fourth step of selecting the best plan for a given situation, it is necessary to establish a basis for evaluating present organizational effectiveness. Due to the dynamic nature of organizations resulting from patterns of leadership, the structure of the organization, the types of organizational authority, the efficiency of organizational processes such as delegation, and the utilization of groups to perform organizational functions, any concept of measuring effectiveness must recognize these variables and interpret them in terms of the needs of each specific organization. Figure 15-5, Checklist of Organizational Effectiveness, is presented as a systematic means of checking each of the major factors contributing to organizational effectiveness. Let us examine Figure 15-5, remembering that the concept of organization is not an area of absolutes where every characteristic is either black or white.

Overall Planning

The extent of overall planning lends direction and purpose to an organization and is basic to the effectiveness of any enterprise. In the collection of data for organizational analysis, the examination of company records may determine the extent of overall planning. Two questions are asked in this regard: Is there a written statement of company objectives, and Is there a written statement of company policy? Objectives define the goals of the organization, while policy statements indicate the broad framework within which each of the functional areas of the firm should operate in achieving the objectives. Chapter 3, "Objectives and Ethics," includes a statement of company objectives for Continental Emsco, a company that has similar statements for each of its plant organizational units. The breadth and purpose of company policy statements are discussed in Chapter 4, "Planning," and as an absolute minimum, there should be policy guides for each of the major functional areas of finance, production, sales, and personnel. There is a reluctance, especially among smaller companies, to state in writing their company objectives and the policies intended to implement those objectives. If objectives and policies are not clearly stated, the

CHECKLIST OF ORGANIZATIONAL EFFECTIVENESS

1. Overall Planning

Written Statements of
Company Objectives _____
Company Policies
Sales _____
Finance _____
Production _____
Personnel _____
Other _____

2. Patterns of Leadership

Primarily
Authoritative
Participative _____
Appropriate _____

3. Organization Structure

Departmentation

Function _____
Product _____
Customer _____
Geography _____
Process _____
Sequence _____

Span of Management

One over One _____
Two or Three _____
Three to Seven _____
Eight or More _____

Overall Impression

Proper Balance _____
Proper Emphasis _____

4. Authority Relationships

Factors Limiting Effectiveness
of Authority

Overlapping Authority _____
Superior Authority _____
Provisions for Subordi-
nate Acceptance _____

Line-and-Staff Relationships

Use of "Assistant-to" _____
Limits of Line Authority _____
Limits of Staff Authority _____
Task Force Organization _____

5. Delegation

Parity of Authority and
Responsibility _____
Absoluteness of
Accountability _____
Unity of Command _____
Personality Factors _____

6. Decentralization

Definition of Decen-
tralized Unit _____
Scope, Type, and Fre-
quency of Decisions _____
Availability of Controls _____
Statement of Goals for
Unit _____
Degree of Decentrali-
zation
Optimum _____
Too Little _____
Too Much _____

7. Use of Committees

Committees

Ad Hoc _____
Advisory _____
Management _____
Composition _____
Benefits _____

Board of Directors

Outside Members _____
Inside Members _____
Contribution _____

8. Provisions for Control

Definition of Standards _____
Units of Measurement _____
Reporting of Exceptions _____
Timeliness of Controls _____
Strategic Placement of
Controls _____
Control Information for
Line Managers _____

Figure 15-5

CHECKLIST OF ORGANIZATIONAL EFFECTIVENESS

organization has little sense of direction and moves from one crisis to another. Under these circumstances, there is little hope for establishing effective organizational structure and processes.

Patterns of Leadership

Chapter 10, "Organization Theory," discusses Theory *X,* which is a work-centered approach to organizational leadership, and Theory *Y,* which is a people-centered or human relations approach to leadership. When an extreme position is taken in support of Theory *X,* the result may be characterized as an organization without people, while a similarly extreme position in support of Theory *Y* may be termed people without organization. Theory *Z,* a systems approach to organization theory, holds that the most effective leadership pattern, whether it be predominantly authoritative or participative, is dependent upon the characteristic of the organization and its members. As the organization grows in size, defining size as number of people, there is a tendency for leadership patterns to become more authoritative. The same tendency exists when there is little need for interaction between members, when members of the organization are submissive and dependent, when the goals of individuals and the organization are divergent, when decision making occurs at a high level of the organization, and when the organization is under pressure to survive and meet stated objectives. The converse of the above situation—a small organization or unit, need for interaction, independent members, congruent goals, decision making at all levels in an organization achieving its objectives—calls for a participative form of leadership. Although a judgment concerning the effectiveness of leadership is highly subjective in nature and its worth dependent upon the skill of the person performing the organizational analysis, such a judgment should be made in evaluating an organization.

Organization Structure

When evaluating the structure of an organization, three structural characteristics are considered: departmentation, span of management, and an overall impression of balance and emphasis. It is necessary to review the bases used in determining *departmentation*. The most frequently used bases for departmentation are function, product, customer, geography, process, sequence, and any combination of these. The basis chosen for forming a department varies from one level of the organization to another and there is also variation in the bases for departmentation even among units of the same level. The test of proper departmentation is whether or not the result is a grouping of activities that is capable of functioning effectively.

Span of management is the number of departments or functions under the direction of one manager. The checklist in Figure 15-5 provides a basis for grouping the range of the span of management into four broad categories. When a one-over-one arrangement is found, it deserves careful examination. A situation in which a one-over-one arrangement is probably effective and necessary is that of an executive vice-president as the sole person reporting to the president. In this instance, the president's other duties, such as relations with the board of directors and with groups outside the company, may make it mandatory that only one person report to him. However, one-over-one relationships at lower levels of the organization should be regarded with suspicion. The designation of an assistant manager, a line relationship showing only one subordinate, may be justified if there is a clear understanding of those functions to be performed by the manager and those functions to be performed by the assistant manager.

An overall impression of the effectiveness of an organizational structure includes evaluating the structure; *i.e.*, departmentation and span of management, in respect to the *balance* and *emphasis* accorded those functions and activities most closely related to the objectives of the organization. It is helpful to view the structure as components of a system, and the propositions of Theory *Z*, as discussed in Chapter 11, are helpful as a basis for determining whether the departmentation, span of management, and the degree of balance and emphasis represent the optimum for organizational effectiveness.

Authority Relationships

In reviewing authority relationships within an organization, our concern is directed toward those factors that limit authority, the clarity of established line-and-staff relationships, and ultimately a consideration of the feasibility of a task force form of organization. When determining the effectiveness of lines of authority, it is necessary to determine the extent to which there is overlapping authority between managerial functions. The source of this information is the questionnaire and the position description. Occasionally authority may be ineffective because provisions for subordinate acceptance of authority are inadequate, which may result in ineffective performance, lack of cooperation, and on occasion, refusal to follow directions. The pattern of leadership is an important item to consider when assessing provisions for subordinate acceptance.

When checking line-and-staff relationships, review any position entitled "assistant-to" and question the possibility of designating a specific staff title more descriptive of the functions performed. In small organizations or in the case of new positions, descriptive titles may not be possible. When determining the authority relationships of established line-and-staff positions, attention is directed toward the degree to which authority relationships are defined—the stating of definite limits of authority for each, and the extent to which each authority understands the role of the other. In some organizations, characterized by changing projects, with well-defined objectives and limiting time tables, it is well to consider the possibility of using a task force organization designed for the specific task at hand. It is necessary that responsibility for the entire project be stated and that provisions are made for the reassignment of personnel upon the completion of the project. Authority relationships are discussed in Chapter 12.

Delegation

Violation of any of the three principles of delegation —the Principle of Parity of Authority and Responsibility, the Principle of Absoluteness of Accountability, or the Principle of Unity of Command—may result in ineffective delegation. Admittedly, these principles are ignored on many occasions; but when ignored and when the resultant delegation seems effective, it is effective in spite of the fact that the principles have been disregarded. Also, failure to delegate may be due to personality characteristics of either the superior or the subordinate which make the process of delegation ineffective. The principles of delegation and the personality factors that limit the effectiveness of delegation are discussed in Chapter 13.

Decentralization

The measure of the effectiveness of decentralization of authority is whether it meets the needs of the organization. The tenets of Theory Z, discussed in Chapter 13, form a useful set of questions concerning the appropriateness of the degree of decentralization. Additional questions may be raised concerning the definition of the decentralized unit, the scope and type of decisions made within the unit, provisions for adequate control, and the statement of goals for the unit. An overall determination of effective decentralization expresses the degree of decentralization as optimum, too little, or too much.

Use of Committees

When properly used, committees may perform quite effectively the managerial functions assigned to them. In rating the effectiveness of committees, it is necessary to determine the extent to which the duties assigned to the committee are in keeping with the functions normally assigned to a given type of committee. *Ad hoc* committees are temporary in nature and are formed to consider a specific question. They are disbanded upon the completion of their assignment. *Ad hoc* groups may appear at any level of the organization and the functions assigned may range from making recommendations to making decisions and taking action necessary for the completion of the assignment. Advisory committees are, as the name indicates, assigned advisory functions with the right to take action reserved for another, usually the person to whom the committee reports. The management committee, whose members are from the top level of the company, offers a means of coordinating the work of individual functional areas and may operate as a plural executive. Benefits derived from the proper use of committees, discussed in Chapter 14, are the value of pooled judgments coming from the diverse knowledge of the individual members, the creation of a favorable training situation, and improved cooperation on the part of individual members as the result of having participated in the work of the group.

Boards of directors, also discussed in Chapter 14, are necessary to meet the legal requirements of corporate organization. In determining the contribution of the board, review the backgrounds of individual members, not only in respect to their status as employees of the corporation which determines whether they are inside or outside members, but also in respect to the amount of time each member is able to devote to the company. The contributions of a board are dependent upon the manner in which they perform their directive functions of setting corporate objectives, selecting management, and subsequently reviewing and guiding management's efforts.

Provisions for Control

Even though the control process is not discussed fully until Part V of this textbook, items concerning the control function are included in the checklist for organizational effectiveness for the sake of completeness. In evaluating control provisions, it is necessary to determine the extent to which standards of performance are clearly defined—particularly for the production and sales functions. The units of measurement employed to measure performance against standard should be appropriate and as objective as possible. Consideration is also given to the degree that controls report the exceptional deviation from standard, to their timeliness, and to their strategic placement. Since the last step of the control process may require corrective action, controls should provide necessary information for the responsible manager so that he may take appropriate corrective action.

●　●　●　●　●　●　●　●　●

Case Problem 15-A describes the organization structure of the Johnson Valve Company and requires the development of an organization chart showing the present structure. Additional information concerning this company is presented in Case Problem 15-B and offers an opportunity to develop a chart of the proposed organization structure and to use the Checklist of Organizational Effectiveness in making final recommendations concerning the reorganization of the firm.

Questions for Study and Discussion

1. Why is organizational analysis considered a form of planning?
2. What basic similarity exists between organizational analysis and planning for production and sales?
3. Discuss briefly the tools commonly used in organizational analysis.
4. Using Figure 15-1 as a basis for arranging the necessary information, prepare a position description of an industrial job that you have held.
5. Rearrange Figure 15-3 so that it appears as a horizontal chart and as a circular chart. What are the advantages attributed to each form of charting—vertical, horizontal, and circular?
6. Discuss the strengths and weaknesses of formal organizational analysis. When would the disadvantages of formal analysis outweigh the advantages?
7. Why is it important to evaluate organizational effectiveness? Should this be done prior to the introduction of any organizational change or after the change has been introduced?
8. What is meant by the statement that most organizational studies are actually reorganizational studies?

●　●　●　●　●　●　●　●　●

Assume that you have been employed by the Johnson Valve Company, Case Problem 15-A, as executive vice-president as recommended by the company's legal counsel. You have completed six months as executive vice-president and are preparing recommendations for a special meet- ing of the board— a meeting that has been scheduled so that you can present your views concern- ing the organiza- tional changes you

<hr>

Case Problem 15-B
An Organizational Audit

<hr>

would introduce if elected president. The following account is a summary of your impressions concerning the organ- ization based upon your first six months with the company.

There is no concise written statement of objectives, particularly in respect to market position. Yet, the assistant to the president, who has performed the market analysis function, has data showing that the company has con- sistently ranked fifth among the ten major manufacturers of the industry as measured by sales volume. Despite the absence of written overall company objectives, it can be inferred that the financial policies of the company have been consistent and conservative. The same observation applies to the sales function, since the administration and achievement of the sales department have followed a rather consistent pat- tern. The chief engineer has written objectives for his department and has followed them well, but manufacturing and personnel seem to blow with the wind and follow whatever course seems most appropriate at the time.

Due to the continued illness of the plant manager it is impossible to assess accurately his contribution to the func- tioning and structure of the manufac- turing department. Apparently, when he was on the job he was easy going and quite permissive in the manner in which he operated the plant. Evidence of his permissiveness is inferred by the action of Mr. Johnson, the presi- dent, in removing purchasing from manufacturing and having it report di- rectly to him so that it could be better controlled. Standards of performance do not exist for any of the production departments. Each foreman determines the work load for his department. The accounting for direct labor costs is of questionable validity since direct labor costs are summarized on a weekly basis and are not allocated to the in- dividual orders processed by the plant. However, the operating procedures be- tween the various manufacturing de- partments seem well established and result from the efforts of the plant superintendent. Yet, there is a marked degree of laxness in the enforcement of these procedures since the super- intendent is carrying the dual responsi- bilities of superintendent and plant manager. The entire scheduling process is uncertain at best. The superintendent says that the performance of the plant could be improved significantly if the scheduling supervisor reported to him rather than to the production manager, Mr. Johnson's brother-in-law, who has no contact with, or responsibility for, manufacturing. The scheduling super- visor claims that he is caught in the middle; he realizes that he reports to the production manager on paper, yet all his daily contacts are with the plant superintendent. As a result, he feels as though he has two bosses.

The personnel function is not unified. The office manager maintains the salaried and office clerical personnel records, but the plant personnel manager has the records for all hourly rated production employees and for clerical personnel employed in the plant. In many instances there are marked discrepancies in rates of pay between clerical personnel in the office and in the plant who are performing the same kind of work. At no time has the personnel function been considered a major functional area of responsibility in the company's organization. There are no organizational charts, nor is there an evaluation plan or stated salary ranges for either exempt or non-exempt salaried personnel. Mr. Johnson has consistently frowned on position descriptions since he believes that they tend to limit the efforts of employees. Although rate ranges do exist for hourly rated production personnel since they are members of a union, there are neither formal job descriptions nor a job evaluation plan despite continued complaints concerning job-rate inequities.

The overall impression is one of lack of direction and coordination. The two strongest functions, as measured by performance, are engineering and sales. Yet, there is a marked lack of coordination between these two functions. Some of this lack of coordination could be corrected by establishing a management committee, a step never taken by Mr. Johnson since he preferred to work with each member of his management team on an individual basis.

Problems

1. Prepare a written report, containing in chart form the proposed reorganization and the supporting reasons, to be presented to the board of directors. In preparing the proposed reorganization, develop a set of consistent, descriptive titles.

2. What items on the Checklist of Organizational Effectiveness, Figure 15-5, are not applicable to this case?

3. Would recommendations concerning a proposed reorganization of necessity include all items shown on the checklist? Discuss.

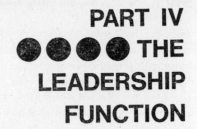

PART IV
THE LEADERSHIP FUNCTION

● CHAPTER 16

Leadership Patterns

You are in a position to participate in the selection of a president for a company in which you have a large financial interest. The search has narrowed to two men, one of whom is named Sanders and the other named Selden. Before you are descriptive statements of the two men prepared by a consulting psychologist.

Case Problem 16-A

Selecting a President

Sanders

"He is a persistent pusher and an enthusiastic team leader. Energetic, frank, and direct, he does not hesitate to speak his mind to prevent what he feels are mistakes or to suggest a better way of doing things. He does not mind a difference of opinion or a fight, but also gladly and easily helps and protects members of his staff when he thinks they need it. He has the reputation of being generous. He encourages and invites others to behave in the same straightforward way. He seems to like to be first, but first among equals. He is most attentive to others, tries to make them very comfortable, and provides them with every aid so that they may perform their work under the most favorable conditions.

"Sanders' method of directing his corporation includes periodic and thorough discussions of all important matters with his close top staff members. He takes a very active part in the discussions, both as a critic and as an initiator and promoter of new projects or changes of old procedures. While he is very independent in reaching his conclusions and making his decisions, he also likes to have the benefit of other people's experience and judgment and wants to learn about all possible objections before a matter is decided one way or another. Sanders has the ability to make people think out loud and contribute constructive criticisms and positive ideas. He judges

389

people by their personal qualities rather than by the positions they occupy. He leads a very alert and tense life, but he thrives on it. He initiates rather than reacts, modifies undesirable situations rather than adapt to them.

"Sanders enjoys the power he exercises, but he genuinely likes people. . . . One of his striking characteristics is great liveliness, both physical and mental." [1]

Selden

"He is a very quiet and thoughtful person, with subdued overt motor activity. He controls his organization closely but does it in quiet and unobtrusive ways. He tries to create the impression that his role is mainly that of an advisor. He is also available for aid in overcoming obstacles and seeing that things are done according to schedule and plan, but he likes to give his subordinates the feeling of independence and allows them a great deal of personal initiative. He encourages each individual to try his best.

"Selden does not limit this behavior to his own corporation. He is active in many cultural community affairs in which his accomplishment is very positive, outstanding, and lasting. His name is known throughout his state. A strong belief in the importance of adequate communication is one of his outstanding characteristics as head executive. He has frequent conferences with each

of his top associates and tries to make the men feel that decisions were arrived at jointly, each man's views having been listened to and weighed carefully. However, Selden does not like group meetings and prefers to confer with one person at a time, which not only enables him to establish a deeper and warmer rapport with each of his associates, but also to influence and control them better. The impression which Selden makes is that of a superior, experienced, benevolent gentleman who is there to set an example and to help rather than to boss. The most noticeable feature of Selden's type of leadership is that things happen in a calm and apparently unhurried way." [2]

Problems

1. Assume that the company seeking a new president is in a highly competitive field such as electronics. Which man would you select? Why?
2. Would you select the same man if the company were well established in its field and engaged in the manufacture of a stable product with few changes from year to year? Why should the situation affect the type of leader needed?
3. It is quite possible that the reason Sanders and Selden are available for a new position is due to the fact that one of them might have failed in a previous position as president of a company. Which man, in your opinion, might have failed as president? Why?

---

[1] Zygmunt A. Piotrowski and Milton R. Rock, *The Perceptanalytic Executive Scale* (New York: Grune and Stratton, Inc., 1963) pp. 92-93, by permission.

[2] *Ibid.*, pp. 101-102.

Our concern with leadership is its function in an organization. We are not concerned with leaders in the arts, such as painters, sculptors, or musicians, who through their own exceptional accomplishment inspire others to strive to reach the same pinnacle of success. *Leadership as it functions in organizations is the accomplishment of organizational objectives as the result of interpersonal relationships with other members of the group.* Managerial leadership is present at all levels of an organization: the president, by stimulating, directing, and coordinating functions assigned to his line and staff officers, sets in motion the wheels of organizational accomplishment. In turn, each of these key executives, serves in the dual role of subordinate and supervisor as the result of personal interaction with subordinates, contributes his share to the attainment of stated goals. At the lower levels of the management hierarchy, the production foreman or the supervisor in the accounting department meets departmental goals by personally coordinating and directing the efforts of workers who have *no* supervisory responsibilities. It would seem highly unlikely that one method or pattern of leadership would be equally effective for all types of organizations or for different levels of the same organization. However, there is a strong tendency for a given pattern of leadership to permeate an entire organization.

In our discussion we will review the major theories of leadership and then examine the components of effective leadership. Finally, we will review the factors that determine an effective pattern of leadership. However, before discussing the theories of leadership it is necessary to establish a frame of reference by recounting the myth of Ken.

The ancient Egyptians used the word *ken* to mean strong-weak. With this word they expressed the quality that characterizes many of the attributes of man. Later the two meanings of *ken* were separated. When the intended meaning was strong, a picture of an upright, armed man followed the symbol for ken; but when the word weak was desired, the pictogram portrayed a man tired and bent over in a crouching position.[3] The story of the meaning of ken has significance in our study of leadership for two reasons; first, it establishes the concept of duality as a frame of reference for a discussion of leadership. A leader must be decisive, yet listen to others; he must be firm, yet know when to retreat; and he must exercise authority, but it is an authority circumscribed with many restrictions. In brief, the leader must know when to zig and when to zag. The second reason for our interest in ken is that recent psycho-

---

[3] Eugene E. Jennings, *The Executive* (New York: Harper & Row, Publishers, 1962), pp. 30-31. Professor Jennings attributes the Myth of Ken to Sigmund Freud, "The Antithetical Sense of Primal Words," Collected Papers, Vol. 4, Basic Books, 1959, pp. 184-190.

logical studies of the executive personality show that a proper blending of "strong-weak" has much to do with successful leadership. These research findings are discussed in the section entitled "Components of Leadership."

THEORIES OF LEADERSHIP

The first application of ken, the concept of duality, appears in defining the objectives of leadership and the task of the leader. Duality appears in the form of an abstract organization on the one hand and a very real individual on the other. The leader is confronted with a series of seemingly imponderable choices. Is he to fulfill the objectives of the organization regardless of the goals and aspirations of its members? Is he to preserve the organization at all costs even if it means reducing its members to a series of numbers or cogs in a machine? Or is there a way that will permit both the organization and the individual to reach their respective goals? Attemps to answer these questions form the substance of theories of leadership. Three theories of leadership—scientific management, human relations, and the revisionists' approach—are discussed below.[4]

Scientific Management—A Work-Centered Approach

Scientific management is discussed in Chapter 2, "The Development of Management Concepts," and some of its implied assumptions concerning the nature of human behavior are presented as Theory X in Chapter 10, "Organization Theory." The role of the leader is determined as a result of these assumptions concerning human behavior. Since men are assumed to be slothful and prone to make errors, such behavior must be corrected so that the organization may survive. Scientific management offers as a means of correction the strengthening of the organization. This may be accomplished in two ways—by improving the structure and definition of the organization, and by improving the methodology of the organization. Improvements in structure and definition are directed toward management itself. Policies, procedures, and standard practices are established to minimize the chance for error resulting from human frailty. The manager is taught to respect and revere the organization at all times. Thus, the bureaucrat, the organiza-

---

[4] Warren G. Bennis, "Revisionist Theory of Leadership," *Harvard Business Review*, Vol. 39, No. 1, (January-February, 1961), pp. 26-36, 146-150. The discussion of theories of leadership is based largely upon the excellent review of the revisionists' work in organization theory written by Mr. Bennis.

tion man, emerges. The reward for subservience to the organization is economic security in the form of continued employment, advancement through a well-defined path of promotions, and the acquisition of status symbols to denote rank to others in the organization.

Improvements in methodology are directed toward controlling the behavior of lower echelons. If problems of quality control appear, the answer lies in engineering the product so that errors in production are reduced to an absolute minimum, not in training the worker to perform with greater skill. Quantity of production is controlled by measurement, not motivation. Under these conditions the duality of the problems of leadership disappears. All questions are resolved in favor of the organization. What is best for the organization is, by definition, best for the individual, for is he not a member of the organization and dependent upon its welfare for his own survival?

Human Relations—A People-Centered Approach

The human-relations approach to leadership emphasizes the potential strength and contribution of each member of the organization rather than the organization's structure and methodology. Instead of tinkering with the organization, management motivates the members of the organization to reach their full potential. Man is viewed as an individual with basic psychological needs that not only must satisfy, but can also be satisfied within the framework of an industrial organization. Man needs recognition, the feeling of belonging to a group, and the opportunity to develop his capacities so that he may realize his full potential. The role of the manager-leader changes with these assumptions of human behavior. He must recognize that there is both a formal and an informal organization and deal with both, but his prime task is one of developing and guiding the members of the organization in order that they may reach their full potential. The leader's function is that of a catalyst. Questions are resolved in favor of the individual, since individual needs must be satisfied in order that he may reach his full potential and maximum contribution as a leader.

The Revisionists—Expressions of Doubt

Admittedly, the above descriptions of the work-centered approach and the people-centered approach to the role of leadership are overdrawn. There has probably never been a successful organization either entirely work centered or completely people centered, but the exaggerated statements representing the scientific-management and the human-relations views of leadership serve a useful purpose. They bring into sharp focus a question confronting all managers—balancing the needs of the organization with the needs and desires of its individual members. Expressions of doubt have arisen concerning the validity of either point of view. Research produces conflicting evidence. There is seemingly no consistent relationship between morale and productivity; high productivity appears in conjunction with low morale; and in some groups with high morale, productivity may be very low. An interesting expression of doubt comes from Douglas McGregor, one of the first exponents of the human-relations approach, after six years as a college president:

> I believed, for example, that a leader could operate successfully as a kind of adviser to his organization. I thought I could avoid being a "boss." Unconsciously, I suspect, I hoped to duck the unpleasant necessity of making difficult decisions, of taking the responsibility for one course of action among many uncertain alternatives, of making mistakes and taking the consequences. I thought that maybe I could operate so that everyone would like me—that good "human relations" would eliminate all discord and disagreement.
>
> I couldn't have been more wrong. It took a couple of years, but I finally began to realize that a leader cannot avoid the exercise of authority any more than he can avoid responsibility for what happens to his organization.[5]

The revisionists, unlike the early proponents of either of the polar approaches described above, realize that there are distinct needs for the organization and for the individual. Three of the revisionists, Robert N. McMurry, Chris Argyris, and Douglas McGregor, deserve attention, for each recognizes organizational needs and the needs of individual members. Their differences lie in their assessment of human needs and capabilities. McMurry's position results in a call for the organization to become a "benevolent autocracy" and for its head to be a "great man." He has no quarrel with participative management and the development of the individual to his fullest capacities. He simply believes, based upon many years of experience as a consulting psychologist working in an industrial setting, that the capacity for most humans to participate and contribute significantly to the organization is rather limited. The basic human need postulated by McMurry is a need for security and direction, a need that is readily met by the well-structured organization. Members

---

[5] Douglas M. McGregor, "On Leadership," *Antioch Notes* (May, 1954), pp. 2-3.

of middle management need well-defined positions of authority derived from structure, since they are, for the most part, incapable of personal leadership. At the top of the pyramid there is room for a mere handful of dynamic individuals to direct the workings of the organization. Though this view is strikingly similar to the scientific-management approach there is a major difference; McMurry's "benevolent autocracy" not only satisfies the needs of the organization, it also satisfies the dependency needs of the individual members of the organization.[6]

Another revisionist, Chris Argyris, expresses a more optimistic view in his book, *Personality and Organization*.[7] To a degree Argyris is answering McMurry by saying "yes, but." He agrees that at present most workers are dependent, but they do not need to remain in a continued state of dependency. He disagrees entirely with McMurry as to the effect of the formal organization upon the individual. McMurry sees the organization as a means of answering dependency needs; for Argyris, the goals of the typical organization are in basic conflict with the needs and goals of the individual. By fragmenting jobs into discrete activities such as the assembly line and emphasizing the formal relationship, the organization creates dependency and restrains the development of the individual to his fullest capacities. But Argyris sees hope for the future through the enlargement of jobs, employee-centered leadership, and a reality leadership that recognizes the needs of the organization and the individual.

The position of the third revisionist, Douglas McGregor, is not so glum as that expressed by McMurry, nor is it so optimistic as the expression of Argyris. In his book, *The Human Side of Enterprise*, McGregor outlines four steps as a possible solution to the problems confronting the leaders of organizations.[8] He suggests, first, that goals be determined jointly, a step that facilitates the second phase of his recommendations, which is collaboration between superior and subordinate. The third step, the development of self-control, is based upon the belief that people are capable of learning and exercising self-control. The last step is the integration of the goals of the individual and the organization, a bit of give and take on both sides, toward the solution of a mutual problem. McGregor does not claim that his approach will work; he only says that it *may* work.

---

[6] Robert N. McMurry, "The Case for Benevolent Autocracy," *Harvard Business Review*, Vol. 36, No. 1 (January-February, 1958), pp. 82-90.

[7] Chris Argyris, *Personality and Organization* (New York: Harper & Row, Publishers, 1957). The appendix, "Some Basic Categories of a Theory of Organization," pp. 239-250, summarizes Argyris' position.

[8] Douglas McGregor, *The Human Side of Enterprise* (New York: McGraw-Hill Book Company, Inc., 1960).

The discussion above of the various approaches to a theory of leadership shows clearly that there is no single definition of what constitutes effective leadership. Instead, several serious questions are raised: What are the characteristics of a leader and what does he do? Are these characteristics and functions of leadership constant or do they vary with the situation and the nature of the people being led?

COMPONENTS OF LEADERSHIP

From this analysis of the preceding theories of leadership one may conclude that the behavior and role of the leader vary considerably, ranging from the dominant position of the autocrat through the dependent characteristics of the bureaucrat, to the participative leader capable of interacting freely with the members of his group. Despite variations in the kinds of leadership and in the situations in which leadership is exercised, research findings present a rather remarkable agreement in respect to the personality characteristics required for effective leadership.

The following discussion is limited to those studies pertaining to managerial leadership. Excluded are the leaders of social movements and political and military leaders.

The Trait Approach to Leadership

There are many studies dealing with the traits required for successful leadership. Generally, the traits listed include such attributes as objectivity, judgment, initiative, dependability, drive, a liking for and understanding of people, and decisiveness. Also mentioned frequently are emotional stability and maturity, a strong desire to achieve, the ability to cooperate with others, and a high degree of personal integrity. After surveying the literature, R. M. Stogdill concludes that leadership is associated with the following personal factors: (1) factors of intelligence including judgment and verbal facility, (2) a record of past achievement in scholarship and athletics, (3) emotional maturity and stability expressed in dependability, persistence, and a drive for continuing achievement, (4) the ability to participate socially and to adapt to various groups, and (5) a desire for status and socioeconomic position.[9]

---

[9] Robert M. Stogdill, "Personal Factors Associated with Leadership: A Survey of the Literature," *Journal of Psychology*, Vol. XXV (January, 1948), pp. 35-64.

Another summary expresses the dual strong-weak concept of the word ken in the following characteristics of a successful executive: "(1) the ability to meet people from all walks of life and talk with pleasure on a wide range of subjects, (2) the ability at all times to work at 'a mad pace' and sometimes with the 'reflectiveness and slow tempo of a Buddhist priest,' (3) an interest in world affairs and events in the personal lives of those around him, (4) pleasure in talking and the confidence required for isolation and pondering, (5) the ability to drive people hard when necessary, yet be subtle and tactful at other times, (6) the ability to take a witty or serious approach, as circumstances may require, (7) the capacity to deal with both concrete and abstract problems, (8) the capacity for originality and willingness to follow precedent, (9) the willingness to be conservative but at other times to take risks no gambler would dare to take (that is, the executive must know when to take risks and when to seek security), (10) assurance in decision making and humility in advice seeking." [10]

There are several shortcomings in the trait approach as a means of analyzing and understanding leadership: (1) Trait studies, as a general rule, do not assign weightings to each of the traits so that the relative importance of each trait as it contributes to leadership can be determined. (2) There is considerable overlap between the various traits mentioned. Seldom are they mutually exclusive. Also, there are many instances of conflicting or incompatible traits, such as the ten traits listed above. (3) An analysis of personality traits makes no differentiation between those traits of value in acquiring leadership positions and those traits necessary to hold or maintain leadership. (4) Trait analysis is based upon the rather shaky assumption that personality is a composite of discrete traits, rather than viewing personality as an integrated functioning whole with a continually shifting pattern of characteristics both in respect to their significance and to their strength. (5) The trait approach to leadership ignores situational factors in the environment that influence the effectiveness of leadership. Let us discuss briefly how situational factors influence leadership.

Situational Factors in Leadership

Experienced executive recruiters are frequently confronted with the problem of determining whether an applicant is available for a new position because personality factors created an inability to function as an effective leader in his former position, or

---

[10] Zygmunt A. Piotrowski and Milton R. Rock, *op. cit.,* p. 4.

whether environmental factors beyond the applicant's control limited the expression of his leadership abilities. The following experiment conducted by Alex Bavelas shows the importance of situational factors as determinants of leadership.[11]

Each experimental group consisting of five subjects was arranged in the positional patterns shown in Figure 16-1. Each member of a group had a card on which there were printed five symbols from a total set of six; however, there was only one symbol that appeared on all five cards. The problem was completed when, as the result of passing information back and forth to each other, the group correctly determined the full set of six symbols. At the end of 15 trials each group was asked whether or not it had a recognized leader. The number of votes received by each member of each group is shown in the circles representing the individual members of each group. Note that in Group A every member receives at least one vote, yet no one member emerges clearly as the leader of the group; however, in Groups B, C, and D, there is definite recognition of one member of the group as the leader.

In order to solve the stated problem it is necessary for the members of each group to pass information; in other words, to function as a part of an information system. The positions of the members determine the pattern of the informational network, and, as the pattern changes, the strategic value of each position also changes. In Group A, arranged in the form of a circle, every member receives at least one vote, but there is no one person emerging without question as the leader. In Group B, arranged as a straight line, neither of the individuals on each end of the line receives a single vote. Each of the persons on either side of the middle member of the group receives several votes, while the central figure receives 12 votes as the recognized leader. In Group C the person at the juncture of the Y receives the greatest number of votes, and in Group D, the person at the hub of the wheel is the only member receiving any votes as the recognized leader.

In Group B each of the members at the end of the straight line can communicate directly with only one other member of the group. The ones next to the end position can communicate directly with two members, but the one in the center communicates with two members directly and has only one intermediary when he desires to communicate with those on the end positions. Likewise, the person at the juncture of the Y communicates directly with three members of the group and is only one removed from the person at the end of the stem of the Y.

—————
[11] Alex Bavelas, "Communications Patterns in Task-Oriented Groups," in D. Lerner and H. D. Lasswell (Eds.), *The Policy Sciences* (Palo Alto, California: Stanford University Press, 1951), pp. 193-202.

Group
A

Group
B

Group
C

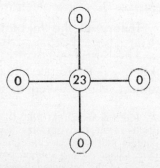

Group
D

Figure 16-1

THE EFFECT OF POSITION AS A DETERMINANT OF LEADERSHIP

The number within each circle is the number of votes each person received as recognized leader of the group. (From Bavelas, "Communications Patterns in Task-Oriented Groups," op. cit.)

The person at the hub of the wheel can communicate directly with each of the other members and there is no need to pass information through an intermediary. Thus, the one in the center receives all the votes. The positioning of each member of the group was determined by chance, with no consideration given to personality factors; therefore, the conclusion of this study is inescapable: recognition as a leader is dependent upon the strategic value of one's position in a communication network—a situational factor—and not upon personality characteristics.

PERSONALITY DYNAMICS IN LEADERSHIP

In our criticism of the trait approach to assessing personality, it is stated that trait analysis is based upon the rather shaky assumption that personality is a composite of discrete traits, instead of viewing personality as an integrated functioning whole with a continually shifting pattern of characteristics of significance and strength. There is, however, another method of analyzing personality that offers considerable promise as a means of understanding the successful—and also the failing—executive as a person. This method utilizes the *Rorschach Inkblot Test* and applies the *Perceptanalytic Executive Scale* as a means of predicting the success or failure of an executive. First, we shall examine some elementary aspects of the theory of the Inkblot Test, then review the validity of the method when applied to 110 top-level executives, and last, develop a dynamic personality portrait showing the outstanding characteristics of the successful executive.[12]

Theory of the Inkblot Test

The Rorschach Inkblot Test consists of 10 bilaterally symmetrical "inkblots" that are presented in a definite sequence, one at a time, to the subject who is asked to interpret the blot and tell what

---

[12] Zygmunt A. Piotrowski and Milton R. Rock, *op. cit.* Chapter 3, pp. 34-79, presents the main results of the study and the development of the perceptanalytic scale. Chapters 5 and 6 contain individual case presentations of the successful executive and of the failing executive. Chapter 7 is a summary of the successful executive as a person. For an earlier discussion of the perceptanalytic approach, see Zygmunt A. Piotrowski, *Perceptanalysis: A Fundamentally Reworked, Expanded, and Systematized Rorschach Method* (New York: The MacMillan Company, 1957). Dr. Hermann Rorschach's original publication is as follows: Hermann Rorschach, *Psychodiagnostics: A Diagnostic Test Based on Perception* (Berne, Switzerland: Verlag Hans Humber, 1921, English translation, 1942, and New York: Grune and Stratton, Inc., 1942).

The discussion of the Perceptanalytic Executive Scales is based upon Piotrowski and Rock's *The Perceptanalytic Executive Scale*, which is cited, in full in footnote 1.

Figure 16-2

AN INKBLOT SIMILAR TO THOSE OF THE
RORSCHACH TEST

he sees or what he is reminded of by the blot. Why should a series of indeterminant inkblots, similar to the one shown in Figure 16-2, offer an effective means of understanding the dynamics of personality? The task presented draws upon visual perception and visual imagery, the basis for much of the knowledge we acquire and one of the main determinants of overt behavior. To perceive a single visual image in an inkblot means that the one image has been selected from among many. The process of selection, which one to see and accept and which one to reject, is a function of the total personality—emotions, past experience, intelligence, desire, and physiological makeup. Also, we are to an extent creatures of habit and past experience. When confronted with a new situation we select from our repertory of responses a pattern of behavior that has proven useful in the past in dealing with new experiences. For most persons the interpretation of an inkblot is a new experience; hence, established patterns of analysis (a form of behavior) appear. The Rorschach test is frequently called a *projective technique* in contrast to the questionnaire method associated with the trait approach of personality assessment. To psychologists the term *projection* has a specific meaning; it is the projection, or assigning, of one's own characteristics to an external object, whether that object be another person, a group, or an inkblot. The inkblots of the Rorschach are intrinsically indeterminate in respect to meaning. Thus, any attributes assigned to the inkblot are the result of the subject's *projecting* his personality, through the processes of selective visual perception and imagery, to the blot.

Further insight into the usefulness of the Rorschach method is gained by examining the major scoring categories of the test. Each response is scored in respect to location; i.e., the portion of the blot eliciting the response; the factors that determine the response—color, movement, form, shading or any combination thereof. The content of each response is classified into broad categories such as human, human detail, animal, animal detail, art, nature, geography, and sex. In addition, it is determined whether or not the response is popular (seen quite frequently), or whether it is an original response. Further, the total number of responses is computed along with the amount of time used to make the initial response to each card and the total time taken in responding to each card. Analysis of the record reveals much concerning the functional level of intelligence and the way in which a person typically approaches problem situations. We can determine whether or not the subject is capable of synthesis, of viewing an entire situation, or becoming lost in a maze of detail, and the extent to which he sees only the banal and obvious. Also, the strength of intellectual control is estimated, particularly in relation to the strength of emotional reactions. The nature of basic drives and tensions is also revealed.

Perceptanalytic Executive Scale

Piotrowski's Perceptanalytic Executive Scale consists of 32 signs—specific responses—that are assigned either positive or negative weights, ranging from a plus 4 to a minus 3. High positive total scores are associated with successful executive action, while low positive and negative scores are associated with failure. In general, the positive signs are responses that show human content revealing self-confident, strong postures; the presence of motor skills in games or on the stage; people engaged in positive social involvement; and warm-blooded animals in pursuit of prey, food, an enemy, or engaged in combat. Positive weights are also assigned to responses that show an ability to construct meaningful wholes, for originality, and evidences of emotional stability and strong intellectual control. Negative values are assigned when the humans or animals seen are in supine positions, subservient, frustrated, or submitting meekly to environmental factors.

Also assigned negative weights are those responses showing an inability to synthesize meaningful wholes, poor emotional control, insecurity, and a stereotyped perceptual ability that sees only the obvious.

The group of 110 executives studied by Piotrowski and Rock consists of presidents; vice-presidents of manufacturing, research, and marketing; controllers and treasurers. Of this group 52 were classified as successful, 42 failed in the very top positions of responsibility, and 16 were neither clear-cut successes or failures. (It must be remembered that success is relative—all of these men were successful enough to be included in the study.) The ages of these men ranged from 34 to 62 years, and all were in the top ten percent of the general population in respect to intelligence. Success is defined as continuing to perform assigned duties for a period of at least one year after the initial testing or advancing in the organization. Failures are those who were demoted, asked to resign, or had their duties decreased. The indeterminant group had records of success, to a degree, or they would not have been in top positions. They are not failures as defined above, but, on the other hand, they were bypassed for promotions. The results of the study are shown in Table 16-1.

Table 16-1

DISTRIBUTION OF FINAL PERCEPTANALYTIC EXECUTIVE SCALE SCORES OF 110 TOP EXECUTIVES OF THREE DEGREES OF SUCCESS

(In Absolute and Relative Numbers)

Scale Scores	Successful		Intermediate		Failing		Total	
	No.	%	No.	%	No.	%	No.	%
Over +7	36	69	—	—	—	—	36	33
7 to +2	10	19	4	25	—	—	14	13
+1 to 0	6	12	4	25	3	7	13	12
—1 to —4	—	—	7	44	15	36	22	20
—5 to —8	—	—	1	6	9	21	10	9
Below —8	—	—	—	—	15	36	15	13
Total	52	100	16	100	42	100	110	100

Source: Zygmunt A. Piotrowski and Milton R. Rock, *The Perceptanalytic Executive Scale* (New York: Grune and Stratton, Inc., 1963), p. 81.

The scores on the Perceptanalytic Scale range from a +27 to a —13. The range in scores for the successful group is from +27 to 0; none of this group have negative total scores. For the intermediate or indeterminate group, the range in scores is from +7 to a —8. It is interesting to note that virtually all of the intermediate group with negative scores are in these top-level positions as the result of either family ties or close social contacts. Scores for the failing group range from $+1$ to -13. Note that none of the failing executives score higher than $+1$ and that only 12 percent of the successful group score as low as 0 or $+1$.[13]

A Dynamic Personality Portrait

It has been said that all human endeavor is directed toward three goals: affection, power, and wisdom.[14] The goal of the executive is power, the desire to control and shape the environment in which he is working. The desire for power is congruent with the function of top management, which is to establish goals, shape the environment in which people perform their work, and coordinate the activities of employees so that stated goals are attained. Underlying and buttressing the executive's desire for power is an abundant supply of energy and stamina that can be channeled to meet each need as it arises. Desires for power in order to control the situation, and a high level of directed energy emerge as two distinguishing characteristics of the successful executive.

To accept the responsibilities of power one must anticipate the challenge of his position. The Perceptanalytic Scale differentiates between one who merely waits for the problem to come to him or to solve itself, and one who actively anticipates the challenge of the situation. The latter shows considerable foresight, the ability to perceive the entire situation, not only as it is, but also as it may develop in the future. The active constructive mentality required for synthesis of the parts of a situation into meaningful wholes is a hallmark of the executive's mental processes. Once the problem is assessed, the anticipation of challenge leads to risk-taking. But it is not the gambler's bet on the roll of the dice; it is risk weighed in terms of perceptive skill and analysis and directed toward the achievement of a goal.

Although he does not realize it, the top-level successful executive is an example of the precepts of mental hygiene. One of the requisites for sound mental hygiene is the pursuit of a predominant interest—for the executive the interest is power. Another indication of mental health is self-confidence, a quality lacking in the failing executive. A leader is above all an active, not a reactive, agent; he must make his decision and move on to the next with no time to examine and reexamine his

---

13 William H. Whyte, Jr., "The Fallacies of 'Personality' Testing," *Fortune,* Vol. LX (September, 1954), pp. 117-120, 204-208. Mr. Whyte presents a rather spirited but superficial criticism of personality testing directed for the most part toward the questionnaire type of personality test. The reader can judge for himself how applicable Whyte's criticisms are when applied to the study conducted by Piotrowski.

14 Zygmunt A. Piotrowski and Milton R. Rock, *op. cit.,* p. 6.

position to assure himself of its correctness. Self-confidence is impossible when goals are incompatible. At high levels of intensity the three goals of human endeavor—affection, power, and wisdom—are incompatible; but for the successful leader this poses no problem. He has but one goal, power, and he is confident that it is the right goal. The failing executive is unsure of himself and his purpose, with resulting overt behavior that is erratic and unpredictable. In addition, he is prone to project his lack of self-confidence to his subordinates.

Deep and strong emotional responses are present in the successful manager, but they are emotions under control. He is capable of working well under pressure with no diminution of either quality or quantity of intellectual output. The effective leader, at least in our society, must communicate to subordinates and peers, and imbue them with a desire to achieve organizational objectives. There is an understanding of people and a willingness to trust them to the limits of their abilities. His perceptual skill in evaluating the human aspects of the organization is no less than his perceptual skill in assessing situational factors. Though cooperative and understanding, the effective manager displays at the same time the socially dominant characteristics of leadership required for power. His innate self-confidence reflects a competitive spirit, but it is the competition of athletics, which is bounded by stated rules. His dominance is by no means the destructive force of uncontrolled aggression. In summary, the successful top executive is a person whose energies, intelligence, emotions, and desires combine to form an integrated whole directed toward high levels of personal and organizational achievement.[15]

SELECTING A LEADERSHIP PATTERN

In the discussion at the beginning of this chapter, two theories of leadership that are poles apart are presented: scientific management, a work-centered approach, and human relations, a people-centered approach. Most classifications of leadership patterns utilize similar dichotomies, although the terminology assigned to each classification varies. The human relations approach to leadership is frequently described as a *democratic* or *participative* style of leadership, while the scientific-management approach is termed an *autocratic* method of leadership. One of the weaknesses of dichotomizing the types of leadership into distinct categories is that we build up stereotypes of each style

[15] For another description of leadership, the student should read "Leadership Pattern in the Plant." Chris Argyris, "Leadership Pattern in the Plant," *Harvard Business Review,* Vol. 32 (January-February, 1954), pp. 64-75.*

of leadership—the inflexible "autocrat" making decisions without regard to human values and the "democrat," flexible, permissive, and getting the most out of satisfied subordinates. Further, we run the risk of assuming that all leadership that is called "democratic" is more desirable than other forms of leadership since we have a strong *national* bias in favor of a democratic form of government.

Leadership, a Continuum

Managerial leadership involves much more than the kind of interpersonal relationship between superior and subordinate. The situation must be appraised by the manager in respect to available resources and the possible actions of external forces, such as the action of competitors or governmental agencies. There is also need to assess the capabilities of the personnel of the organization. The nature of the decision or the problem to be solved has to be evaluated, and lastly, the capabilities and personality of the manager influence the type of leadership. With so many factors determining successful executive action, it seems highly unlikely that the interpersonal relationships between superior and subordinate can be neatly classified into one of two categories—autocratic or democratic. Instead, the relationships between superior and subordinate follow a continuum as shown in Figure 16-3.[16] Let us describe briefly each of the seven gradations of leadership behavior.

Manager Makes Decision and Announces It. This form of leadership represents the most autocratic form: i.e., there is no chance for the subordinate to express his thoughts either in the formulation or the solution of the problem. The superior formulates the problem, solves it, and announces his decision. Coercion, to assure the execution of the decision, is not necessarily implied since subordinates may be willing to follow such directions.

Manager "Sells" Decision. At this stage the manager recognizes the feelings of subordinates and the possibility that there might be resistance to his decision. Consequently, he attempts to persuade them to recognize the merits of his decision. However, the manager is still in control of all phases of the decision-making process.

---

16 Robert Tannenbaum and Warren H. Schmidt, "How to Choose a Leadership Pattern," *Harvard Business Review,* Vol. 34 (March-April, 1958), pp. 95-101.* In addition to the discussion concerning the seven leadership patterns that form a continuum, the authors discuss the factors which determine the pattern of leadership: forces in the manager, forces in the subordinates, and forces in the situation.

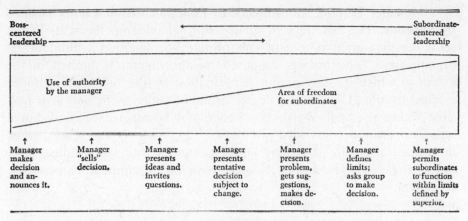

Figure 16-3

CONTINUUM OF LEADERSHIP BEHAVIOR

Source: Robert Tannenbaum and Warren H. Schmidt, "How to Choose a Leadership Pattern," *Harvard Business Review,* Vol. XXXIV (March-April, 1958), p. 96.

Manager Presents Ideas and Invites Questions. The third form of managerial behavior marks the beginning of a degree of participation on the part of subordinates—at least they are being asked to express their ideas. However, the manager has in his own mind made the decision. Nonetheless, the presentation of his ideas to subordinates with the opportunity of their expressing themselves opens up the possibility that the decision may be modified.

Manager Presents a Tentative Decision Subject to Change. Here, at the midpoint of the range of leadership styles, there is definite participation on the part of subordinates in shaping a final decision. Although the manager's decision is tentative, he still defines the problem and works out the initial solution.

Manager Presents Problem, Gets Suggestions, Makes Decision. This is the first time the manager comes to the group without having at least a tentative solution to the problem; however, he still defines the problem in general terms. Consultation with the group prior to making a tentative decision increases the number of possible solutions.

Manager Defines Limits, Asks Group to Make Decision. Up to this point the decision is made by the manager with varying degrees of participation on the part of subordinates in influencing his decision; but this is the first time that the group makes the decision. However, the manager still states the problem and the limits within which the decision must be made. Usually these limits are expressed in terms of either cost or time, or both.

Manager Permits Subordinates to Function within Limits Defined by Superior. The last stage of managerial behavior on the scale represents the maximum degree of subordinate participation within formal organizations. The manager, himself a subordinate, is limited in the extent to which he may permit participation by the limits of authority granted to him. The greatest degree of subordinate participation is possible within the framework of a Functional-Teamwork or Task-Force type of operation (described in Chapter 12); even so, the objectives of the organization are stated by higher authority, but subordinates may define and solve problems consistent with the attainment of company objectives.

Determinants of Effective Leadership

The discussion above of patterns of leadership shows the varying degrees of understanding and participation on the part of subordinates in the decision-making process. The process ranges from the completely authoritarian situation with no subordinate participation to the maximum degree of democratic leadership that enables the subordinate to participate in all phases of the decision-making process. The problem now is that of determining how to select an effective pattern of leadership. Tannenbaum and Schmidt suggest that there are forces in the manager, in subordinates, and in the situation that must be weighed in order to select the most effective form of leadership.[17] In Chapter 10, Theory Z, a systems approach to organization, is presented and in subsequent chapters it is applied to the organizational problems of departmentation, span of management, and determining the optimum degree of decentralization. Let us examine the forces in the manager, in subordinates, and in the situation within the framework of Theory Z as a means of understanding those factors that determine an effective pattern of leadership.

Size of Organization. As size, defined as number of people, increases, organization structure becomes more formal and complex. The result is that the appropriate processes of motivating employees toward the achievement of organizational goals become more authoritarian— rather than participative—in nature.

There is a positive relationship between the size of organizations and the formalization of organization structure and relationships as evidenced by the presence of organizational charts and position descriptions. Also, as organizations grow, there is greater dependence upon

---

[17] *Ibid.*

written rather than oral communications, a development that tends to restrict the degrees of freedom of subordinates. As relationships in an organization become more formalized, there is a clearer definition of areas of responsibilities and lines of accountability, with the result that a supervisor may find his authority to delegate decision-making functions to his subordinates severely limited. For example, in a small company with a single plant it is quite possible for a foreman to invite employee participation in the location of a piece of production equipment. However, in a large company with many plants it is likely that the layout of production facilities for all plants would be determined by a central production engineering department.

Degree of Interaction. As the need for interaction between members of an organization increases in order to accomplish the prescribed work, the organization structure should permit a free flow of information and ideas, and the accompanying process of motivation should become more participative and informal in nature.

The degree of interaction between the members of a group may be a function of the specialized knowledge that each member is capable of contributing toward the solution of a problem, or interaction may be a function of structural or situational factors in the problem-solving situation. In instances where subordinates have little or no knowledge of the problem, the need for participation is slight and the leadership exercised in these instances tends to be authoritative. Research and development teams composed of highly skilled technicians frequently are most productive when the manager participates as a member of the group in solving their common problem. Even so, if the problem is extremely complex, decision making may be reserved for the manager since he is the only one with complete knowledge of all phases of the work.

The need for interaction arising from structural characteristics of the problem-solving situation poses a rather interesting question: Should the situation be redesigned so that the need for interaction is minimized? In another experiment similar to the one conducted by Alex Bavelas (see Figure 16-1), it was found that people arranged in the pattern of Group D, four persons communicating with the fifth who forms the hub of a wheel, offered the most efficient problem-solving arrangement.[18]

---

[18] Harold J. Leavitt, "Unhuman Organizations," *Harvard Business Review*, Vol. 40 (July-August, 1962), pp. 90-98. Professor Leavitt describes another experiment similar to the one conducted by Alex Bavelas. The original reference for the study is: L. Christie, D. Luce, and J. Macy, "Communication and Learning in Task Oriented Groups," Research Lab of Electronics, MIT (Tech Report No. 231, May, 1962). Professor Leavitt emphasizes organizations as systems that may be dependent upon humans or they may be "unhuman."

Next in efficiency were those arranged as Group B, with one man in the center and two on either side; while the least efficient group was structured similar to Group A, which forms a circle. Remember, when selecting a leader, Group D unanimously selected the person in the center; the leader for Group B was selected by a substantial margin; and in Group A, the circle, there was no clear choice of a leader. However, we find that a structure similar to Group A, although the least efficient, results in a group whose members are "happier" than the members of either Group D or B. Of greater significance is the fact that Group A was able to incorporate new ideas for the solution of the problem much more readily than either of the other groups and was also able to solve modified or new problems more readily.

What is the criteria for organizational effectiveness? Is it happiness and the ability to solve new problems, or is it efficiency in solving routine problems? Or, putting the question another way, how much interaction among members is needed? Apparently, if the problems to be solved are routine, similar to those found in the daily operations of most business firms, little interaction is needed. But if the problems are continually changing and dependent upon new ideas for their solution, the need for interaction—and a corresponding shift in leadership patterns—is critical.

Personality of Members. Effective organizational structure and processes conform to the personality and the expectations of subordinates. Subordinates who do not expect participation and who are dependent upon others for motivation react best to authoritarian patterns of structure and motivation, while those who expect participation and are motivated largely from within react best to participative organizational processes and less formality in organizational structure.

In the first section of this chapter, "Theories of Leadership," the position of several revisionists is stated. If McMurry is correct in assuming that the organization answers the dependency needs of people, the leadership pattern of a benevolent autocrat is appropriate; however, if one adopts Argyris' view that man is capable of development and self-direction, a participative or democratic style of leadership is desirable. In either case, emphasis is placed upon the personality and capabilities of subordinates as the determining factors in choosing a pattern of leadership.

Of equal, if not greater, importance is the personality of the top executive and his staff in determining an effective pattern of leadership. Piotrowski's work shows that the successful executive is a strong, dominant person motivated primarily by a desire to control his environment (power) in such a manner that both personal and organizational goals are met. Both Sanders and Selden (Case Problem 16-A) are cut from the same cloth, and, despite the differences in their methods of working with people, both men maintain tight control over their organizations. In real life, Sanders is president of a large manufacturing corporation in a highly competitive field with a gross income of over $400 million a year, and Selden is president of a $200 million-a-year corporation in a somewhat less competitive field. Imagine either of these men participating as a member of one of the group described in the experimental work of Bavelas and told that it is his job to pattern the group into the most efficient problem-solving arrangement. Each man would probably consult with other members of the group for a clearer definition of the problem, but each would undoubtedly choose as the final form of organization the wheel arrangement with himself in the key center position.

Congruence of Goals. When the goals of the organization and those of its members are congruent, participative processes and a less formal structure are appropriate; but when organizational goals and members' goals are divergent, greater reliance must be placed upon authoritative processes and formal structure so that adequate control is assured.

There is little question concerning the validity of the assumption above, yet the implications of this assumption that call for a variety of leadership patterns within the same company are often overlooked. The degree to which the goals of members and of the organization are congruent is a function of organization level. Among the members of top management, the president and his staff, the goals are usually congruent and result in an informal relationship with a high degree of participation. (Review "How Rathbone Runs Jersey Standard, Case Problem 14-B.) For lower levels of management there are committees, staff meetings, and training programs, all of which contribute to an understanding of the goals of the organization and the member's role in achieving these goals. However, most industrial organizations routinize jobs at the clerical and hourly levels, thereby widening the gap between organizational and individual goals. Consequently, leadership at these levels tends to be more authoritative and a greater reliance is placed upon formal controls. Thus, within a single organization there should be a differentiation in the pattern of leadership from one level of the organization to another, dependent upon the degree of congruency between organizational and members' goals.

Level of Decision Making. When decision-making functions are retained within a work group of an organization, participative processes and informal structure are effective; as the decision-making processes move upward in the organization and away from the work group affected by those decisions, formal structure and authoritative processes are more effective.

The level of decision making within an organization is in part a function of the organization's information system and in part the result of organizational policy. Information necessary for decision making may be available within the work group; for example, the knowledge needed to solve a quality control problem occurring in a production department. In such cases, participation in the decision-making process by the group may be the most effective means of solving the problem. But, as the result of a policy statement, a higher level of authority such as a company-wide quality control office may be established. Directives from this office are authoritative in nature and, in turn, effect the pattern of leadership at lower levels of production by removing a possible area of participative decision making. In many companies decision making at high levels is not the direct result of a policy statement; instead, it is due to the complexity and nature of the information needed to make decisions. A multiplant manufacturer supplying materials to customers with many plants must make decisions concerning production scheduling and purchasing on a companywide basis. Leadership in such an organization tends to be directive rather than participative in nature.

In judging the extent of participative decision making and the degree of participative leadership, the importance and scope of the decisions made should be given more weight than the sheer number of decisions.

State of the System. When the performance of an organization is relatively poor in achieving organizational goals, authoritative processes of motivation and structure may be necessary to initiate corrective action; however, as the organization achieves expected goals, participative patterns of organization become more effective and are expected by the members of the organization.

An extreme example of an organization failing to meet its goals is a company showing a loss, rather than a profit, at the close of the fiscal year. Under these circumstances the pattern of leadership of the president tends to be authoritative. Although he may have long-range plans for improving the company's profit position, his immediate reaction is to reduce variable costs, and the greatest potential of variable cost reduction is achieved by reducing payroll costs.[19] To ask subordinates to participate in eliminating their positions is unrealistic; consequently, such decisions are made without participation, and the means of communicating the decision is directive in nature.

Organizations in a continual state of crises, either real or imaginary, often cite the limitations of time as the reason for directive leadership. Admittedly, participative processes of decision making are more time consuming than the decision of a single individual, but there are instances when increased cooperation in the execution of the decision amply offsets the additional time taken in reaching the decision.

The above discussion emphasizes that there is no one successful pattern of leadership. Many factors contribute to the effectiveness of leadership. The personality and expectation of subordinates are important. Also, important are the situational or environmental factors that so clearly demonstrate the experimental work of Alex Bavelas. However, of greatest importance is the personality of the leader himself, for he brings to his position a definite concept of the role of the leader, and he should be able to assess accurately the potentials of the situation and the capabilities and needs of subordinates.

•   •   •   •   •   •   •   •

Case Problem 16-B is a case history similar to those presented in Case Problem 16-A, but this man failed in the top spot as president of his company. Your task is to find out why—was his failure due to factors in the situation, in his subordinates, or was it due to weaknesses in his own personality?

Questions for Study and Discussion

1. Do you believe that there has ever been a successful organization that was entirely work centered or entirely people centered? Why?
2. Much of the literature of management equates management with leadership. Do you believe that managing is necessarily leading? Discuss.
3. From your own experience describe a manager (or a teacher) whom you would characterize as typifying the scientific management approach to leadership. Describe one who typifies the human relations approach. Which one was more effective? Why?
4. How would you describe the revisionists' approaches to leadership?

---

[19] See Chapter 5, "Planning for Profit," for a review of the significance of variable and fixed costs.

5. What are some of the characteristics of leadership as revealed by the trait approach to the study of leadership? What are the shortcomings of this approach?
6. Describe a business situation that supports the situational aspects of leadership.
7. Certain positions in an organization, such as the presidency, carry with them a traditional prestige. Could this be considered similar to a situational factor? How?
8. What are some of the basic assumptions of the Rorschach test? Why is this test considered a projective technique? Can you give another example of projection?
9. Why is there a need for flexibility in leadership patterns?
10. Discuss in your own words the application of Theory Z to the choice of an appropriate leadership pattern.

● ● ● ● ● ● ● ● ●

The following is a narrative report submitted to you, the president of the company, describing a candidate for a second spot in your firm. You know that he failed as president of a competing company in the same industry, but you are not looking for another president—the need is for a good man reporting to one of your senior vice-presidents.

Case Problem 16-B

A Leader Who Failed [20]

Felling

"Felling's managerial career started well, he was very successful at first. One of the main reasons seems to have been his good graduate university training in two very different fields, in a professional specialty and in business administration. He was a very good student, received excellent grades, and excelled particularly in the speed and accuracy of his reading. In mathematics, problem solving, and scientific procedures other than those used in his specialty, his achievement was average for a graduate university student. Felling was attracted to political science, politics, sociology, and economics. These subjects fascinated him much more than those within his specialty.

"From the very beginning of his professional career, Felling has been interested almost exclusively in the administrative and business aspects of his profession. He sought and found administrative professional positions and never attempted to function as a professional or technical specialist. He never showed any active interest in specific technical procedures of his profession. His main aim has been to direct technical services rendered by a large group of professionals to large

---

[20] Zygmunt A. Piotrowski and Milton R. Rock, *op. cit.*, pp. 154-155.

numbers of clients. As he himself said, three aspects of the work fascinated him particularly: the possibility of influencing promotions, the assignment of duties, and ultimate responsibility for settling financial claims in this large insurance-like organization. He liked most to perform the functions of a judge and supervisor of people.

"Felling seemed supremely self-sufficient and created the impression of unconditional self-confidence. He impressed practically everyone with his apparent ability to act in an effective and independent manner in handling administrative problems. However, there was little room in his plans for the ideas of others. He always seemed to have a view of his own which he defended with persuasive forcefulness and he showed an enthusiastic willingness to tackle the most complicated and difficult problems himself. Some of his critics felt that Felling was rather impulsive and would rush into situations that required considerable forethought and caution if they were to be handled well. For years he was not in a position to act with complete independence and on his own initiative because, while his position was high, there were two men above him who exercised general control and direction of all the activities of this large organization. However, he enjoyed their confidence and had their support because he displayed imagination about some aspects of the future development of the organization. He also was known to have a sense of humor, which softened the impression of authoritarianism his subordinates felt he displayed too frequently.

"Felling moves about vigorously, is gregarious, and enjoys being with people. He is affable, pleasant and attractive. He seems to have had an inexhaustible amount of energy and endurance. He was demanding that his responsibilities be increased and that he have a greater share in the decision-making processes of his organization."

Problems

1. Do you detect any specific signs of weakness in Felling as a president? If so, what are they?
2. What form of leadership would you adopt if Felling were your assistant?
3. Would you hire Felling as an assistant to a vice-president? Why?

CHAPTER 17

Communications

John Thurman, president of the Thurman Manufacturing Company, recognizes the importance of keeping employees informed in respect to the economic problems of the company. He realizes that his company is entering a difficult competitive period resulting from a steady decline in prices. Thurman knows that he must lower prices in order to retain his share of the market.

He believes that his monthly letter, entitled *From The President's Desk*, which is sent to all employees, is adequate as a means of transmitting information. However, when a major crisis arises, he summons all department heads to the austere oak-paneled board room, an action which, in his opinion, assures them that they are a part of management and participating in major decisions. The established protocol for these meetings requires that all attending personnel be seated prior to the scheduled time and that they arise when Mr. Thurman enters the room and remain standing until asked to be seated again. John Thurman has made his entrance and has indicated by a curt nod of his hand that all may be seated.

Case Problem 17-A
A Message for Management

"I have called you together to explain our dire economic situation. We are face to face with competitive wolves who are snapping at our heels. They are making us sell at prices which are too low and delivery schedules that are utterly impossible to meet. If this great company of ours—one of the bulwarks of free enterprise—is to survive, we must all pitch in and pull together. Let me tell you what I mean."

Following his opening remarks, John Thurman glared at everyone in the room as though he were daring them to speak. No one spoke, since all knew that any expression of opinion would be classified as negative thinking by Mr. Thurman.

"First, what we need here is imagineering. We need positive thinkers and everyone has to play on the same team. We have to optimize production and nothing can be left out of account when we are considering cost reduction. To implement this crash program of cost reduction, I have gone outside the company and hired a top-drawer production manager.

"The second thing we have to do is maximize quality. Quality means everything in this business. Every machine has to be inspected on a regular schedule by the foreman of the department and when that machine starts up in production, it means that he has given it his stamp of approval. Nothing is too small to overlook when we are thinking of quality.

"Third on my list of items deserving serious consideration is beefing up our sales force. Customers are the lifeblood of this business, and even though they are not always right, they still must be handled with kid gloves. Our salesmen have to learn how to put themselves across and make every call count. Our method of compensating salesmen is eminently fair, but even so, we're going to try to sweeten the pot by upping the commission rates on slow-moving items. We would do it across the board, but we have to hold the line on costs.

"The last thing on my list is team-work. This we need more than anything else. Unless we all pull together, we can't make it. Leadership is team-work, and teamwork is striving and straining for the same goal. You are the representatives of management, you are the leaders, and you know what our goals are. Now let's all put our shoulders to the wheel and wrap up the whole ball of wax immediately. Remember, we're one big happy family."

As John Thurman concluded, all arose and stood by their chairs while he gathered his papers and left the board room through the connecting door to his office.

Problems

1. What was the purpose of this meeting?
2. What is John Thurman trying to say? Rewrite his remarks in simple, direct language. Do you think his analysis was correct?
3. What factors other than language cause a communication barrier in this case problem?
4. How would you arrange the above meeting so that two-way communication is assured?

•　•　•　•　•　•　•　•　•

THE MEANING OF MEANING

Communication is defined in its broadest sense as *the transmission of meaning to others.* However, the definition as it now stands does not mean or signify much, since two words used in the definition—*transmission* and *meaning*—need further elaboration. The word, *transmission,* used in the definition is broad and does not limit the methods of communication to the use of language in either spoken or written form. The word, *meaning,* is also broad. It includes information consisting not only of facts and descriptive statements of objects and other people but also attitudes and feelings that may be conveyed to others. For purposeful communications, such as those in a business organization, it is necessary to restrict our definition further by stating that communication is the transmission of *intended* meaning to others. The above restriction implies that the sender of the communication has a clear concept of the meaning that he wishes to convey; and in order for the communication to be purposeful, the receiver must interpret the message in such a manner that he receives the intended meaning.

The scientific study of meaning is known as *semantics,* a word derived from the Greek term, *semantikos,* which means significant. Semantics is concerned with the relationship between (1) objects and/or events, (2) the thought processes involved in interpreting these objects and/or events, and (3) the signs and/or symbols used to express a given thought or to describe a specific object or event. First, let us discuss these three aspects of semantics and then apply the lessons learned in analyzing Case Problem 17-A.

The Triangle of Meaning

The relationship between objects and events, their interpretation, and the development of signs and symbols are shown in Figure 17-1, The Triangle of Meaning.[1] Objects and events are known as the *referent*; thoughts, interpretations, and emotions are called the *reference*; and the devices used to express the reference are referred to as *signs* or *symbols.*

The following example shows the relationship between a referent, a reference, and the way in which meaning is attached to a sign or a symbol. The object in question is taken from the ocean; it is elliptical in shape, three inches long, and inch and one half in width, an inch thick. The surface is a rough, brown, shell-like substance. Three persons are observing (thinking about) this object. One of them, a scientist, recognizes the object immediately and labels it a bivalve mollusk of the genus *Ostrea.* The second observer "sees" a dozen such objects on the

---

[1] C. K. Ogden and I. A. Richards, *The Meaning of Meaning* (8th ed.; New York: Harcourt, Brace & Company, Inc., 1956). *The Meaning of Meaning,* first published in 1923, still stands as one of the basic works in the field of semantics. The triangle shown in Figure 17-1 is adapted from a figure in the first chapter (page 11) entitled Thoughts, Words, and Things. *The Meaning of Meaning* is a good reference for the serious study of semantics.

Stuart Chase, *The Tyranny of Words* (New York: Harcourt, Brace & Company, Inc., 1938). Mr. Chase's book is based largely upon the writings of Ogden and Richards and the work of Korzybski (listed below) and is an excellent popularization of the field of semantics.

Alfred Korzybski, *Science and Sanity: An Introduction to Non-Aristotelian Systems and General Semantics* (Lancaster, Pa.: The Science Press Printing Company, Distributors for The International Non-Aristotelian Library Publishing Company, 1933). Count Alfred Korzybski, a mathematician, develops in this massive volume, 798 pages, the applications of general semantics to all fields of science as they existed in 1933. *Science and Sanity* is recommended only for the advanced student.

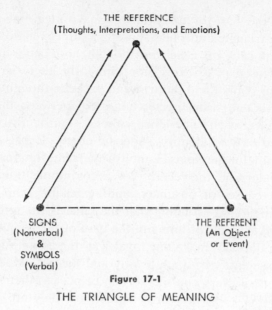

Figure 17-1

THE TRIANGLE OF MEANING

half shell ringing a platter full of ice; to him it is an object to be eaten, an oyster. The third person takes one look, grimaces, turns pale, and leaves the room. All have seen the same object, yet three distinct meanings are reflected in their labeling of the object. The scientist uses the symbol, bivalve mollusk of the genus *Ostrea*, to label the object; to him it is one more form of marine life to be classified in relation to other forms of life. To the person who calls it an oyster, the object is food and a source of delight. However, the third person does not use a symbol (word) to label the object; instead, he eloquently expresses his interpretation of the object by the signs of grimacing, becoming pale, and leaving the room—the object is a source of disgust.

Let us examine each element of the triangle in greater detail.

Signs and Symbols. Signs and symbols, the left-hand base of the triangle (Figure 17-1), are the labels used to initiate a particular thought, or reference, in regard to a specific referent. The two terms, signs (nonverbal) and symbols (verbal), are used to emphasize that communication is not dependent upon language. There is no intrinsic meaning in the color red, yet a red light as part of a traffic signal means that one must stop; but when used as a running light on a boat, red indicates the port side. Likewise, silence on the part of a supervisor may express disapproval as effectively as a dozen words. Status in an organization is conveyed almost entirely by signs; for example, a carpeted office, special parking privileges, punching a time clock, and the hour at which one reports for work all designate status.

Note that the base of the triangle is a dotted line and that the two sides of the triangle are solid. There is a direct relationship between the referent that calls up a certain thought and between the thought and the symbol used in its expression. Similarly, there is a direct relationship between symbol and thought and between thought and referent. There is, however, no such direct relationship between the label (symbol) and the object itself. The label, either a sign or a word, is *not* the object; it is used only to identify a specific object. Labels are arbitrary, and to be meaningful they must establish the same reference (thought) in both the sender and the receiver of a communication. Yet, one of the commonest causes of misunderstanding results from filling in the base of the triangle and assuming that the label is the referent. Loyalty oaths are a good example of filling in the base of the triangle. The act of signing an oath does not make one loyal; yet, the assumption underlying such oaths is an identity between loyalty and the act of signing an oath.

Verbal symbols vary considerably in respect to their value as tools for communication. All words are abstractions; they are not the object or event itself. As words become more abstract; i.e., further removed from the specific object or event, their meanings become more difficult to transmit and their value as instruments for communication decreases. Words as names of things may be classified as follows:

1. *Names for objects* are a table, a chair, a milling machine, a lathe, an automobile, a truck, a machinist, and a clerk. When naming an object, we are at a relatively low level of abstraction, and there should not be too much misunderstanding since the referent may be seen and touched, and its characteristics detailed with accuracy.

2. *Events* are more complex in their nature since action and time, in addition to an object, are implied. A table turning over, a milling machine cutting metal, a moving automobile, and a machinist reporting late for work are all statements of events—something happening to a specific object at a specified time.

3. Labels may be used to designate *clusters, groups,* or *collections of objects or events* composed of elements that have varying degrees of similarity. We refer to furniture, machine tools, motor vehicles, and employees.

4. At the highest level of abstraction, the referent may not be an object or event at all; instead, the referent is an *essence* or *value judgment* of an object or event. The furniture is described as beautiful, machine tools are valuable, motor vehicles are either necessities or luxuries, and the employee is lazy (the machinist reported late for work). Also in this category of high-order abstractions are such labels as democracy, free enterprise, truth, and honesty.

Reference and Referent. There are at least two persons involved in communication—a sender and a receiver. Symbols should create within the receiver a thought process (call it a mental image, if you wish) that leads him down the right-hand side of the triangle to the desired referent. Conversation has been described as the art of saying something when there is nothing to be said. In contrast, communication is saying something when there is something to be said and saying it clearly. The purpose of communication is to influence the behavior of another person. Behavioral changes may consist of additional knowledge, a change in attitude, or action on the part of the receiver. Conversation takes place almost entirely on the left side of the triangle, from symbol to thought and back to another symbol again. There is no need for a common meaning between sender and receiver because the purpose of conversation is merely to occupy time. In communication, however, there is a purpose; and in order for the intended meaning to reach the receiver, both sender and receiver must travel the same route around the triangle from symbol, to reference, to referent.

A Semantic Analysis

A great deal can be told about how much meaning is transmitted through a given communication by answering these questions:

1. What is the purpose of the communication?
2. Do the symbols used by the sender have a precise meaning understandable to the receiver?

Let us ask these two questions in our semantic analysis of Case Problem 17-A, A Message for Management. At the same time we must keep in mind the triangle of meaning—symbol, reference, and referent.

What Is the Purpose of the Communication? Before there can be any communication, the sender must determine the purpose of the communication. Why has John Thurman called his department heads together? In the first paragraph of his talk, he states that he has called them together to explain "our dire economic situation." He closes his opening remarks with the statement that he is going to explain what he means. Apparently, Thurman is trying to state four things that the company needs in order to survive the dire economic situation. These needs are imagineering, which he does not define; instead, he talks about cost reduction. The second need is quality, the third is beefing up the sales force, and the last is teamwork. The conclusion is inescapable;

Thurman is not sure of what he wants to say or why he wants to explain an economic condition to his department heads.

The purpose of the meeting is not to explain; instead, it is to change the behavior of the department heads—to direct their actions so that the company may make a profit and at the same time lower the prices of its product to the level established by competition. Information concerning the actions of competitors and the development of attitudes resulting in teamwork and effective leadership are necessary if management is to do its job well. The purpose of the meeting is to change behavior.

Do the Symbols Have a Precise Meaning for the Receiver? Look at the first paragraph of Thurman's speech again. It is filled with abstractions having no precise meaning. He starts with a high-order abstraction, "dire economic situation," and does not bother to define what he means. Somehow he manages to drag into his remarks "the bulwarks of free enterprise," again without definition. Further, his use of metaphors indicates that he is not thinking clearly. How can he be "face to face with wolves snapping at his heels?" Prices are too low, but what does too low mean? If the delivery schedules are utterly impossible, how does the company manage to stay in business? The remainder of his talk is nothing but a collection of worn-out, meaningless words and phrases. What is "imagineering"? What is "positive thinking"? Are they going to play on the same team or are they working for the same company? What does he mean by "beefing up" the sales force? Does he want the salesmen to gain weight? Is leadership teamwork? If so, leadership is striving and straining for the same goals. How does one simultaneously "put his shoulder to the wheel" and "wrap up a ball of wax"?

John Thurman is having a wonderful time running up and down the left-hand side of the triangle—from symbol to reference and back to symbol without once attempting to go down the right-hand side of the triangle to a common referent. To some of you, Thurman's *Message for Management* may seem overdrawn and exaggerated. It is not. It is hoped that you will not have to sit through many such meetings as a member of management and that you *never* conduct a meeting as John Thurman did. Remember this case as an example of how *not* to communicate.

PRINCIPLE OF COMMUNICATION

The above analysis of A Message for Management answers two questions. When the questions are recast as statements, they form the Principle of Communication:

For effective communication the sender must determine the purpose of the communication and use symbols having the same meaning for sender and receiver.

The following guides are presented to aid the application of the Principle of Communication:

1. Determine and state the purpose of the communication.
2. Develop a plan of presentation. Consider the information to be transmitted and the interests and abilities of the receiver.
3. Eliminate unnecessary words.
4. Use words known to the receiver. Establish the meaning of abstractions by referring to objects and events within the experience range of the receiver.[2]

PROBLEMS IN COMMUNICATION

The transmission of intended meaning is the central problem in communication; however, there are problems other than lack of agreement on intended meaning that contribute to communication breakdowns. One problem is determining the amount and kind of information needed for the managerial functions of planning and control. Another source of difficulty is that managers are not always aware of the media available for communication. Superior-subordinate relationships, the vertical flow of information from superior to subordinate and back to superior again, present certain barriers to communication. Related to the need for vertical information flow is the establishment of pathways for the horizontal flow of information. Communication networks develop within an organization due to structural factors of the

---

[2] It is beyond the scope of this book to develop a manual of style. The following references are presented for the student who wants additional help in improving his ability to express his thoughts clearly:

George Orwell, "Politics and English Language," from *Shooting an Elephant and Other Essays* (New York: Harcourt, Brace, and World, Inc., 1950). Reprinted in N. R. F. Maier, L. R. Hoffman, J. J. Hooven, and W. H. Read, *Superior-Subordinate Communication in Management* (New York: American Management Association, 1961), AMA Research Study 52, pp. 78-88. Mr. Orwell's essay is one of six presented in the AMA research study. Orwell presents six rules for clarity of expression and although his essay is concerned primarily with the language of politics, it is applicable to all subject matter. The annotations of George H. Hass provide many examples of hackneyed expressions used in business communications.

William Strunk, Jr., and E. B. White, *The Elements of Style* (New York: The MacMillan Company, 1959), pp. xiv and 71. This book should be in the personal library of every student of management. The Elements of Style deals with English usage and style. Professor Strunk had the book privately printed and for many years used it in his English classes at Cornell University. The 1959 edition, revised by E. B. White includes a chapter on how to write. *The Elements of Style*, dubbed "the little book" by Professor Strunk, reduces English rhetoric to 18 rules with examples of correct and incorrect usage to illustrate each rule.

situation and the personality of participants. Finally, there are informal channels of communication known as the grapevine, an efficient means of transmission when speed is the main determinant of efficiency. Each of these problem areas is discussed under the following headings: (1) communication and information systems, (2) communication media, (3) superior-subordinate communication (4) horizontal communication, and (5) the grapevine.

Communication and Information Systems

In Chapter 8, "Management Information Systems," the functions and characteristics of information systems are discussed. Case Problem 8-A, The Parable of the Spindle, describes an information system used in a restaurant and shows the positive relationship between system design and effective communication. Prior to the introduction of the spindle there was a complete breakdown in communications. Steps in the design of an integrated data processing (IDP) system and the functioning of an IDP system are illustrated by the experience of Westinghouse in Case Problem 8-B, The Short-Order Economy. Although the emphasis in Chapter 8 is upon the concept and design of information systems, such systems must be considered as part of the communication process since their function is to transmit meaning. Of particular importance to management is securing and transmitting information for the functions of planning and control. The type of information needed for these functions is shown in Figure 17-2, Anatomy of Management Information.[3]

Planning Information. As shown in Figure 17-2, planning information comes from the environment, from competitors, and from internal sources. Environmental data include information about population level, trends, and the demographic characteristics of age, sex, and economic status. General economic factors such as price trends and predicted levels of consumer and capital goods expenditures are also reported. Although most environmental information is readily available, an interpretation of its meaning is necessary before the data can be used for management planning. In addition to determining the validity and reli-

---

[3] D. Ronald Daniel, "Management Information Crisis," *Harvard Business Review*, Vol. 39 (September-October, 1961), pp. 111-121. Figure 17-2 appears as Exhibit I on page 114. Mr. Daniel's discussion of information required for planning and control emphasizes the need for multiple sources and types of information. He presents the flow of information within the framework of a systems concept.

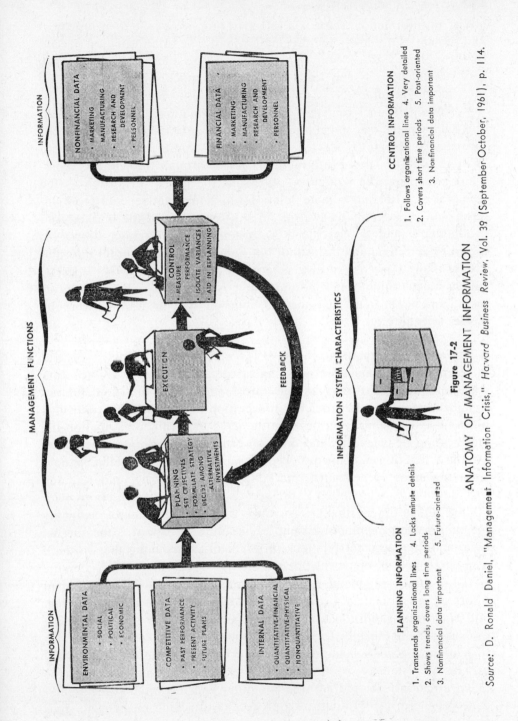

PLANNING INFORMATION

1. Transcends organizational lines
2. Shows trends; covers long time periods
3. Nonfinancial data important
4. Lacks minute details
5. Future-oriented

CONTROL INFORMATION

1. Follows organizational lines
2. Covers short time periods
3. Nonfinancial data important
4. Very detailed
5. Post-oriented

INFORMATION SYSTEM CHARACTERISTICS

MANAGEMENT FUNCTIONS

INFORMATION

INFORMATION

NONFINANCIAL DATA
• MARKETING
• MANUFACTURING
• RESEARCH AND DEVELOPMENT
• PERSONNEL

FINANCIAL DATA
• MARKETING
• MANUFACTURING
• RESEARCH AND DEVELOPMENT
• PERSONNEL

ENVIRONMENTAL DATA
• SOCIAL
• POLITICAL
• ECONOMIC

COMPETITIVE DATA
• PAST PERFORMANCE
• PRESENT ACTIVITY
• FUTURE PLANS

INTERNAL DATA
• QUANTITATIVE-FINANCIAL
• QUANTITATIVE-PHYSICAL
• NONQUANTITATIVE

CONTROL
• MEASURE PERFORMANCE
• ISOLATE VARIANCES
• AID IN REPLANNING

EXECUTION

PLANNING
• SET OBJECTIVES
• FORMULATE STRATEGY
• DECIDE AMONG ALTERNATIVE INVESTMENTS

FEEDBACK

Figure 17-2

ANATOMY OF MANAGEMENT INFORMATION

Source: D. Ronald Daniel, "Management Information Crisis," *Harvard Business Review,* Vol. 39 (September-October, 1961), p. 114.

ability of information, there is a selective process, a matter of judgment and semantics, to determine the amount and type of information needed by the company. The wrong information or false interpretations fed into a communication system leads to failure as quickly and surely as no information at all.

Sales personnel frequently furnish information about the present and future plans of competitors. The information may be presented in formal written reports, during sales meetings, or in conversation with an immediate superior. Information passed through the chain of command, whether it be written or oral, runs the risk of distortion as the result of superior-subordinate relationship. Quantitative data from internal sources relating to level of sales, costs, share of the market, and productivity may be developed for planning with a high degree of accuracy and minimum distortion; but nonquantitative internal information runs the same risk of distortion when passing through the superior-subordinate relationship. The subordinate may tell only what he believes his superior wants to hear, or the superior may hear only what he wishes to believe.

Control Information. Figure 17-2 classifies the types of control information as financial or nonfinancial data. In general, control data are more detailed than planning information, and this flow follows organizational lines. In order for information to be of use for control, it must be timely and accurate, requirements that call not only for the clarification of organizational lines of communication but also for the establishment of well-defined procedures and methods. Nonfinancial data from the areas of personnel, marketing, manufacturing, and research and development are often expressed as high-order abstractions with all the difficulties normally associated with the problem of assigning meaning to these symbols. Examples are the evaluation of the success of a labor-management relations program or determining the worth of a research and development project.

In small- and medium-size companies, the flow of management information is a manual process—a subordinate collecting, interpreting, and transmitting information to his superior and the superior asking his subordinate directly for information. Even when management information systems become as highly automated as the integrated data processing system of Westinghouse, determining the amount and type of information to be fed into the computer and determining the significance of the printed output are a process of attaching meaning to signs and symbols—a problem in communication.

Communication Media

Communication media within a company may be classified either in respect to the method used to transmit information or according to the directional flow of the communication. Using the means of transmission as a basis for classifying media, communications are either *written* or *oral*. When the directional flow is the basis for classification, defining direction in terms of the organizational hierarchy, communications flow *downward, upward, horizontally,* and *diagonally*. Examples of written and oral communications are discussed briefly below.

Written Communications. Letters, memos, and reports are examples of written communications used to transmit information either downward, upward, or horizontally within an organization. Formal statements of policies, procedures, and methods are designed primarily for downward communications. Bulletin boards, house organs, annual reports, and handbooks are also directed downward. Written grievances, suggestion systems, and union publications serve as a means of upward communication. The information gained from attitude and morale surveys provides another means of directing information to higher levels of the organization. Letters and memos between department heads are examples of the horizontal or diagonal flow of communications. The distribution of carbon copies of written materials to all interested parties may be used as a means of directing information in several directions at one time.

Oral Communications. Even though a business may consume tons of paper during the course of a year in written communications, by far the greater percentage of information is transmitted by informal oral communications, either face to face or by telephone. Oral communications may involve as few as two people or as many as hundreds attending a training session or conference. All oral communication offers the potential of a two-way information flow; and, dependent upon the relative organizational positions of the participants, the communication may be directed either vertically or horizontally. Most members of an organization prefer oral to written communications because they seem quicker and offer an immediate feedback in the form of questions and expressions of approval or disapproval. The advantages of speed and feedback may be more imagined than real, since oral messages are notoriously subject to misinterpretation and to the effects of barriers arising from interpersonal relationships.

Superior-Subordinate Communication

It is generally assumed that superior-subordinate communication operates as a two-way information system permitting a free flow of information in an upward direction as well as downward. Yet, there are barriers in the superior-subordinate relationship that markedly interfere with the free two-way flow of information. Before discussing these barriers, it is well to determine the effectiveness of superior-subordinate communications in a relatively objective and limited area—in relation to a subordinate's job.

Superior-Subordinate Understanding. The American Management Association conducted a statistical research project to determine the extent of agreement between superior and subordinate concerning the subordinate's specific job duties.[4] Fifty-eight superior-subordinate combinations from the upper management levels of five different companies were selected for this study, and the information from both members of each pair was obtained by patterned depth interviews. The following specific areas of the subordinate's job were discussed:

1. Job duties—a descriptive statement of what the subordinate does in the performance of his job.
2. Job requirements—a statement of the skills, background, experience, formal training, and personal characteristics needed for the job.
3. Future changes in job duties—anticipated changes in either job duties or requirements that might be anticipated in the next several years.
4. Obstacles in the performance of the job—problems that interfere with getting the job done, as seen by the subordinate and as viewed by the superior.

The results of the study are presented in Table 17-1. An analysis of Table 17-1 shows that 85 percent of the pairs interviewed agree on one half or more of the subordinate's job duties (Columns 2, 3, 4), but the extent of the agreement in respect to subordinate qualifications drops to 63.7 percent. Only 53.3 percent of superiors and subordinates agree upon anticipated changes in the subordinate's job within the next few years. In interpreting the obstacles in the way of subordinate success, 68.2 percent showed either no agreement or agreement on less than half of the obstacles. The following is a narrative summary of the study by the authors:

---

[4] Norman R. F. Maier, L. Richard Hoffman, John J. Hooven, and William H. Reed, *Superior-Subordinate Communication in Management* (New York: American Management Association, 1961), AMA Research Study 52. In addition to the presentation and interpretation of the statistical results of the study, there are six interpretative comments on the project and its findings in Part 2 of the report.

Table 17-1

COMPARATIVE AGREEMENT BETWEEN SUPERIOR-SUBORDINATE PAIRS ON FOUR
BASIC AREAS OF THE SUBORDINATE'S JOB

	0 Almost No Agreement on Topics	1 Agreement on Less than Half the Topics	2 Agreement on About Half the Topics	3 Agreement on More Than Half the Topics	4 Agreement on All or Almost All Topics
Job Duties	3.4%	11.6%	39.1%	37.8%	8.1%
Job Requirement (Subordinate's Qualifications)	7.0%	29.3%	40.9%	20.5%	2.3%
Future Changes in Subordinate's Job	35.4%	14.3%	18.3%	16.3%	18.7%
Obstacles in the Way of Sub- ordinate's Performance	38.4%	29.8%	23.6%	6.4%	1.7%

Source: Norman R. F. Maier, L. Richard Hoffman, John J. Hooven, and William H. Reed, *Superior-Subordinate Communication in Management* (New York: American Management Association, 1961), AMA Research Study, p. 10.

If a single answer can be drawn from this detailed research study into superior-subordinate communication on the managerial level in business, it is this: If one is speaking of the subordinate's specific job—his duties, the requirements he must fulfill in order to do his work well, his intelligent anticipation of future changes in his work, and the obstacles which prevent him from doing as good a job as is possible—the answer is that he and his boss do not agree, or differ more than they agree, in almost every area. Also, superior and subordinate very often disagree about priorities—they simply don't see eye to eye on which are the most important and the least important tasks for the subordinate.[5]

Barriers to Communication. The effect of communication barriers, whether they arise from semantic problems or from one of the specific superior-subordinate relationships discussed below, results in either a distortion of meaning resulting from embellishment or a filtering of information by suppression or withholding. Semantic barriers usually result in a distortion of meaning. Distortion also occurs as the result of introducing errors into a message. Filtering information results in only a part of the message getting through. Filtering of communications by either the sender or the receiver of the message may be intentional or unintentional. The following barriers are frequently found in superior-subordinate communications; nonetheless, it must be remembered that these same barriers may occur in any two-way personal communication.

---

[5] *Ibid.*, p. 9.

SEMANTIC PROBLEMS. One barrier to communication, not limited to superior-subordinate relationships, is a semantic problem—determining a common referent and meaning for the symbols used in communication. In the research study described above, descriptions of the subordinate's job, of necessity, require the use of high-order abstractions. These are middle management jobs and, unlike operative jobs, they cannot be described as movements to be completed in a given sequence. Judgment, the interpretation of data, anticipation of future events, and skill in interpersonal relations are the important requisites for managerial jobs, and all of these characteristics are abstractions. Rudolf Flesch, in his comment on the study, believes that the problem of superior-subordinate communication as presented in Table 17-1 presents a somewhat exaggerated view of the inability of superior and subordinate to communicate effectively.[6] According to Flesch, who interpreted the same data, the lack of agreement is no greater than what might be expected when the subject is abstract and viewed from two entirely different positions; i.e., superior and subordinate. In brief, Flesch is saying that to some extent the results of the study are due to the methodology used in the study.

STATUS. One of the barriers arises from the relative positions of the superior and subordinate in the organization. There is a strong tendency in formal organizations to express hierarchical rank through the use of signs known as status symbols. Status symbols within an organization, such as a better type of office furniture, may be deliberate as an attempt to reinforce the superior's position of authority. However, too much emphasis upon status may increase a subordinate's perception of organizational distance and consequently widen the communication gap between him and his superior.

PRESSURE OF TIME. In business organizations the pressure of time plays an important role as a communications barrier. The busy superior with many subordinates simply does not have the time to see all of them as frequently or to talk with them as fully as might be desired. Also, a busy subordinate does not have the time nor the inclination to report every detail of every problem to his superior. Supporting the subordinate's position is the concept of delegation. He has been assigned responsibilities, and the authority to fulfill these responsibilities has been delegated. In addition, he is accountable to his superior. One might argue quite properly that as the effectiveness of the process of delegation increases, the need for detailed communication between superior and

---

[6] *Ibid., Is the Problem Exaggerated?* pp. 60-67. Mr. Flesch discusses the results of the study as a semantic problem.

subordinate decreases. The pressure of time and the presence of an effective delegation process may decrease the amount and frequency of superior-subordinate communication; but even so, communication may be more than adequate because information necessary for the operation of the business is being transmitted.

VALUE JUDGMENTS. Making value judgments of a message prior to receiving the entire communication interferes with receiving the intended meaning of the message. A value judgment is the assignment of overall worth to a message and may be based upon its origin, its reliability, or its anticipated meaning. When value judgments are made too hastily, the receiver hears only that part of the message that he wishes to hear. Closely related to hearing only selected parts of a message is the lack of sensitivity to the emotional content of the communication, which is often reflected by the mannerisms and tone of voice of the sender. In many instances the real message is conveyed not by the words of the sender, but by the emotions and feelings accompanying his expression of the message.

SUBORDINATE'S MOBILITY. One of the specific characteristics of the superior-subordinate relationship is the dependency of the subordinate upon his superior for advancement within the organization, either more pay for his present job or attaining a higher position. A study by Read supports the hypothesis that the more a subordinate desires to advance in an organization, the more he tends to filter by selecting the information he sends upward to his boss.[7] If he desires to advance, he passes upward only the good news and the positive aspects of his achievement and suppresses (filters) the problem-oriented aspects of his work. However, Read does report that the amount and nature of the information transmitted upward, even by the subordinate strongly desiring advancement, is influenced greatly by the degree of trust that he has in his superior and the extent to which he perceives the influence of his superior. As trust in the judgment and understanding of his superior increases, and as the perceived influence of the superior on the subordinate's advancement becomes greater, the amount of problem-oriented information communicated upward increases.

Horizontal Communication

Traditional organization theory with its concepts of line authority and the chain of command emphasizes vertical lines of

---

[7] William H. Read, "Upward Communication in Industrial Hierarchies," *Human Relations*, Vol. XV (February, 1962), pp. 3-15.

communication between superior and subordinate. Figure 17-3 shows in schematic form the transmission of a message from D_1, foreman of production department 1, to D_2, foreman of production department 2, using the chain of command as a channel of communication. The advantage claimed for this formalized line of communication is that A, who is responsible for both production departments, is better able to coordinate the functioning of the two departments when he is fully informed of the activities of each department. The obvious disadvantages of following these formal lines of communication are the amount of time taken to transmit a message, the increased risk of error and distortion, and the loss of flexibility necessary to meet emergencies. The extent

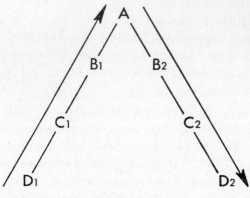

Figure 17-3

TRADITIONAL VERTICAL COMMUNICATION

to which an organization insists that its lines of communication conform to the organizational lines of authority is dependent to a large extent upon the technology of that organization. Failure to recognize communication needs arising from and dependent upon technology often results in poor communications.[8] There are several empirical studies that show the need for horizontal and diagonal communications between first-line supervisors as a function of the technology, or method, of production. In a study of an automobile assembly line, Blau finds that the role of the foreman is one of problem solving and expediting material flow. The line itself determines the pace of production, and the jobs on the line are well defined. Under these circumstances there is

---

[8] Frank J. Jasinski, "Adapting Organizations to New Technology," *Harvard Business Review*, Vol. 37 (January-February, 1959), pp. 79-86. Although Mr. Jasinski's article is concerned primarily with the adaptation of organizations to technology, much of what he writes is also applicable to the need for adapting communications to technology.

relatively little need for the traditional vertical communications of giving orders to subordinates and there are not many orders received from one's superior. The result is that the bulk of the foreman's communications is with other foremen on the assembly line and with other departments such as material handling and maintenance.[9] All of these relationships are either horizontal or diagonal. However, Faunce in a study of a highly automated automobile factory finds, in an apparent contradiction, that there is a marked need for vertical communications through the traditional chain of command.[10] Simpson, in a study of the spinning department of a textile mill, obtains results similar to those of Blau; namely, a decrease in the need for vertical communications between superior and subordinate and an increase in the need for communications between supervisors on the same level.[11] In Simpson's study, the primary direct communication between the general foreman of the department and his subordinate foremen consists of a written message stating the type and amount of material to be produced on each machine for each shift.

Simpson also resolves the apparent discrepancy between his findings, similar to those of Blau, and the findings of Faunce. He describes three broad types of technology used in production and suggests that the relative need for vertical or horizontal communication is determined by the technology. First, in unmechanized operations there is a relatively greater need for vertical communications than there is for horizontal communications. In this situation the various production departments are relatively independent, and the amount of work produced is determined by the effectiveness of the supervisor of the department. The manager responsible for coordinating the work of all departments needs detailed information from each supervisor. Second, when technology is characterized by mechanization, such as a textile mill or an automobile assembly line, separate departments are bound together by that technology. The success of the foreman of an assembly line is dependent upon the right part arriving at a certain place in the line at a scheduled time and upon the reliable functioning of the tools used in production. Providing the necessary parts for assembly is the function of the production control and material handling departments, and the proper operation of the tools for production is the function of the maintenance

---

[9] Peter M. Blau, "Formal Organization: Dimension of Analysis," *American Journal of Sociology*, Vol. LXII (July, 1957), pp. 58-59.

[10] William A. Faunce, "Automation in the Automobile Industry," *American Sociological Review*, Vol. 23 (August, 1958), pp. 401-407.

[11] Richard L. Simpson, "Vertical and Horizontal Communication in Formal Organizations," *Administrative Science Quarterly*, Vol. IV (December, 1959), pp. 188-196.

department. Rate of output is determined by the speed of the assembly line or other automatic equipment. Under these circumstances the need for horizontal communications among the foremen of the various departments increases. Third, in highly automated plants where the breakdown of a single machine may result in the shutdown of all production facilities, the need for control becomes greater and the need for vertical communications also increases.

In summary, no mechanization or a low degree of mechanization emphasizes vertical communications; moderate mechanization (such as the assembly line) requires a greater emphasis upon horizontal communications; and highly automated production facilities reestablish the need for vertical communications.

The Grapevine

Our discussion of the problems of communication has been directed toward formal channels and methods of communication. It is necessary for management to recognize that there are also informal methods of communication that may be far more effective in some respects than the formal means of transmitting information. An informal system of communication is generally referred to as the *grapevine*. As the name suggests, the grapevine is entwined throughout the entire organization with branches going in all directions, thereby short-circuiting formal vertical and horizontal channels.

Two characteristics of communications via the grapevine are noted by those who have studied it. First, the grapevine is often an exceedingly rapid form of communication; and second, the information transmitted is frequently subjected to a great deal of distortion. Formal channels of communication, particularly those following the vertical chain of command, usually pass information from one person to another—a time-consuming process. In contrast, the grapevine transmits information along a pathway described as a *cluster chain*.[12] Instead of passing information from one person to another, as in superior-subordinate communication, information is passed to a group of three or four persons, and from this initial link in the cluster chain, one or two individuals inform other groups. Thus, there is an ever-increasing rate in the flow of information. In part, this is due to the makeup of the grapevine;

---

[12] Keith Davis, "Communication Within Management," *Personnel*, Vol. XXXI (November, 1954), pp. 212-217.* In this article Professor Davis discusses a method of communication analysis and applies the method to the communications of one company. He also discusses the characteristics of the grapevine in management communications.

people who work near each other or whose work regularly brings them in contact with others are frequently on the same grapevine. The grapevine that includes the mail clerk, the switchboard operator, or any other person whose work requires contact with several groups transmits information much more quickly than formal channels of communication. Another factor encouraging rapid communication is that the information carried by the grapevine reflects the interests and personal concerns of its members; for example, news of an impending layoff, an increase in pay, or news about other people.

The grapevine is notorious for distorting information, so much so that information received from this source is often referred to as rumors. In the discussion of superior-subordinate communications, the filtering of information—passing on only certain parts of a message—is mentioned as one of the causes of distortion. The grapevine information at its source is often fragmentary and incomplete, with the result that there is a strong tendency to fill in the missing parts. Since the grapevine is informal, there are no formal lines of accountability. Consequently, a member of the grapevine does not have to answer to his superior for any misstatement of facts. Further, the elaboration of a fragment of news into a full-blown story offers to some people an opportunity to express feelings of self-importance and to compensate for feelings of insecurity.

The characteristics of the grapevine are summarized by Davis as follows:

1. People talk most when the news is recent.
2. People talk about things that affect their work.
3. People talk about people they know.
4. People working near each other are likely to be on the same grapevine.
5. People who contact each other in the chain of procedure tend to be on the same grapevine.[13]

IMPROVING COMMUNICATIONS

There are two approaches available for the improvement of communications. The first of these approaches is from the point of view of the sender of the message. Recognize the purpose of the communication, the significance of the symbols used, the organizational lines through which the communication travels, and its possible effect on the receiver. These and other ways of improving one's ability

---

[13] *Ibid.*, p. 212.

to communicate clearly as a sender of messages are discussed below as ten general rules for improving communications. The last of these rules states that in order to achieve effective communication it is necessary to learn how to listen. It is a listening to the feelings and emotional content of messages expressed by others as well as being able to understand the factual information that is being presented. The process of learning how to detect the emotional content of communications is discussed under the heading, *empathetic listening*.

Rules for Improving Communications

The American Management Association refers to the following rules as the Ten Commandments of Good Communication:

1. Seek to clarify your ideas before communicating.

   The more systematically we analyze the problem or idea to be communicated, the clearer it becomes. This is the first step toward effective communication. Many communications fail because of inadequate planning. Good planning must consider the goals and attitudes of those who will receive the communications and those who will be affected by it.

2. Examine the true purpose of each communication.

   Before you communicate, ask yourself what you really want to accomplish with your message—obtain information, initiate action, change another person's attitude? Identify your most important goal and then adapt your language, tone, and total approach to serve that specific objective. Don't try to accomplish too much with each communication. The sharper the focus of your message the greater its chances of success.

3. Consider the total physical and human setting whenever you communicate.

   Meaning and intent are conveyed by more than words alone. Many other factors influence the overall impact of a communication, and the manager must be sensitive to the total setting in which he communicates. Consider, for example, your sense of timing—i.e., the circumstances under which you make an announcement or render a decision; the physical setting—whether you communicate in private, for example, or otherwise; the social climate that pervades work relationships within the company or a department and sets the tone of its communications; custom and past practice— the degree to which your communication conforms to, or departs from, the expectations of your audience. Be constantly aware of the total setting in which you communicate. Like all living things, communication must be capable of adapting to its environment.

4. Consult with others, where appropriate, in planning communications.

   Frequently it is desirable or necessary to seek the participation of others in planning a communication or developing the facts on which to base it. Such consultation often helps to lend additional insight and objectivity to your message. Moreover, those who have helped you plan your communication will give it their support.

5. Be mindful, while you communicate, of the overtones as well as the basic content of your message.

   Your tone of voice, your expression, your apparent receptiveness to the responses of others—all have tremendous impact on those you wish to reach. Frequently overlooked, these subtleties of communication often affect a listener's reaction to a message even more than its basic content. Similarly, your choice of language—particularly your awareness of the fine shades of meaning and emotion in the words you use—predetermines in large part the reactions of your listeners.

6. Take the opportunity, when it arises, to convey something of help or value to the receiver.

   Consideration of the other person's interests and needs—the habit of trying to look at things from his point of view—will frequently point up opportunities to convey something of immediate benefit or long-range value to him. People on the job are most responsive to the manager whose messages take their own interests into account.

7. Follow up your communication.

   Our best efforts at communication may be wasted, and we may never know whether we have succeeded in expressing our true meaning and intent, if we do not follow up to see how well we have put our message across. This you can do by asking questions, by encouraging the receiver to express his reactions, by follow-up contacts, by subsequent review of performance. Make certain that every important communication has a "feed-back" so that complete understanding and appropriate action result.

8. Communicate for tomorrow as well as today.

   While communications may be aimed primarily at meeting the demands of an immediate situation, they must be planned with the past in mind if they are to maintain consistency in the receiver's view; but, most important of all, they must be consistent with long-range interests and goals. For example, it is not easy to communicate frankly on such matters as poor performance or the shortcomings of a loyal subordinate—but postponing disagreeable communications makes them more difficult in the long run and is actually unfair to your subordinates and your company.

9. Be sure your actions support your communications.

In the final analysis, the most persuasive kind of communication is not what you say but what you do. When a man's actions or attitudes contradict his words, we tend to discount what he has said. For every manager this means that good supervisory practices—such as clear assignment of responsibility and authority, fair rewards for effort, and sound policy enforcement—serve to communicate more than all the gifts of oratory.

10. Last, but by no means least: Seek not only to be understood but to understand—be a good listener.

When we start talking we often cease to listen—in that larger sense of being attuned to the other person's unspoken reactions and attitudes. Even more serious is the fact that we are all guilty, at times, of inattentiveness when others are attempting to communicate to us. Listening is one of the most important, most difficult—and most neglected—skills in communication. It demands that we concentrate not only on the explicit meanings another person is expressing, but on the implicit meanings, unspoken words, and undertones that may be far more significant. Thus we must learn to listen with the inner ear if we are to know the inner man.[14]

Empathetic Listening

The tenth rule admonishes us to listen to others—listen to the explicit meaning and also the implicit meaning. Explicit meaning is conveyed by the meaning of the words used by the sender; and in order to understand, it is necessary that we pay careful attention to what is being said.[15] However, we must also listen with the "inner ear" if we are to hear the "inner man." Hearing the inner man, the implicit meanings of the message, calls for *empathy*—the ability to put oneself in the other person's place, to assume his role, his viewpoint, and his emotions. *Empathetic listening* is hearing and understanding the emotional content, the feelings, and the mood of the other person. Empathetic listening requires a special technique of listening.

Case Problem 17-B, A Case of Misunderstanding, should be read now, for it is the basis of our discussion of empathetic listening. As stated in the third paragraph of the case, we do not know exactly what Hart, the foreman, said to Bing, the workman. We do know what each

---

14 "Ten Commandments of Good Communication," (New York: American Management Association, Copyright, 1955).

15 Ralph G. Nichols, "Listening Is Good Business," *Management of Personnel Quarterly,* Vol. I (Winter, 1962), pp. 2-9.* Professor Nichols discusses ten bad habits of listening and suggests the positive steps that should be taken to overcome these bad habits. He also touches slightly upon the problem of emphatic listening.

said to the personnel representative. With this information, let us reconstruct the conversation between Hart and Bing.

Hart: "Bing, I want to talk to you."

Bing: "Yeah?"

Hart: "Listen, why don't you try to get along here like other people do for a change?"

Bing: "How?"

Hart: "Well, for one thing, stop deliberately upsetting this department by going to lunch early and asking others to go with you."

Bing: "I haven't been to lunch early for a week."

Hart: "You have, too. And another thing, I want you to stop carrying three panels at one time over to your bench for inspection— you know the rules on that."

Bing: "That's what I want to talk to you about. I've got an idea . . ."

Hart: "Never mind your ideas, just follow the rules and you'll get along better."

Bing: "I want a transfer."

Hart: "We'll see about that. In the meantime, stop singing around here. What do you think this is, a nightclub, and you're Frank Sinatra?"

The above conversation and the comments made by Hart and Bing to the personnel representative show quite clearly that Hart is not listening to Bing. It appears that he is more interested in telling Bing off than he is in trying to determine the reasons for Bing's behavior. Hart is *not* using the techniques of empathetic listening. Without empathetic listening there cannot be two-way communication.

Listen with Understanding. Empathetic listening as a part of two-way personal communications is a concept borrowed from the methods of nondirective psychotherapy that have been highly developed by Dr. Carl Rogers.[16] In this form of psychotherapy the role of the therapist is one of encouraging not only good communications between himself and the patient, but also good communications within the patient himself. The patient must learn how to express himself and have the oppor-

---

16 Carl R. Rogers and F. J. Roethlisberger, "Barrier and Gateways to Communications," *Harvard Business Review*, Vol. 30 (July-August, 1952), pp. 46-52. The first part of the article is written by Dr. Rogers, who suggests that the major barrier to communication is the tendency to evaluate and that the main gateway to communication is listening with understanding. In the second part of the article, Dr. Roethlisberger analyzes a communications situation and suggests positive steps that may be taken to improve communications.

For a full discussion of Dr. Roger's views on therapy, see: Carl R. Rogers, *Client-Centered Therapy* (Boston: Houghton Mifflin Company, 1953).

tunity for that expression. Although a foreman and other members of management are not therapists, if they are to have successful two-way communications with another, that other person must have the opportunity to express himself. In order to encourage such expression, nondirective techniques are employed. The one conducting the interview encourages the expression of the feelings, emotions, and desires behind the words of the other person. In order to do this he listens—he does not talk. In the conversation above, Hart does most of the talking, not Bing. If he were listening with understanding, his comments would have been designed to encourage Bing to talk and the following conversation might have occurred:

Hart: "Bing, I want to talk to you."
Bing: "Yeah?"
Hart: "I've noticed that you have been carrying three panels over to your bench for inspection. Do you have a new idea for a methods change?"
Bing: "Well, maybe."
Hart: "Um-hum."
Bing: "Well, maybe it won't work all the time, but with these smaller panels there is no reason why three of them can't be carried at once."

With this approach to communication, Hart is encouraging Bing to talk, not to defend himself. The problems caused by his leaving for lunch early and his singing may be explored in the same easy manner.

Guides for Listening. The following guides for empathetic listening have been found to be as effective in industrial settings as in their original clinical setting.

1. *Avoid Making Value Judgments.* Value judgments are global in nature and made from the point of view of the listener, not from the frame of reference of the person doing the talking. Such judgments place a single value—good or bad, desirable or undesirable, true or false—on a series of complex statements, each of which varies considerably in respect to any given characteristic. In addition, the origin of value judgments is often derived from an earlier judgment of the source of the statement. How can Bing say anything worthwhile to Hart when he is prejudged by Hart as being mentally deficient and a sow's ear? Once the value judgment is made, the mind is closed and it becomes impossible to understand the other's point of view.

2. *Listen to the Full Story.* In the first interview, Bing started to say that he has an idea, but is stopped abruptly by Hart. In order to

understand, listen to the whole story. Time is a critical factor in empathetic listening, and arrangements must be made for adequate time and a place where there will be no interruptions. Ask the other person to be seated; if he smokes, offer him a cigarette. Do everything you can to put the other person at ease.

3. *Recognize Feelings and Emotions.* Remember, empathetic listening is putting yourself in the position of the other person. Try to pinpoint the meaning of the feelings and emotions behind the statements being made, rather than the meaning of the words being said. Look for signs of eagerness, hesitancy, hostility, anxiety, or depression. At the same time watch for evasions, the things left unsaid, or areas of discussion consistently avoided.

4. *Restate the Other's Position.* As a test of your understanding, restate the other person's statement from his point of view, not yours. For example, Hart might say, "You believe that I'm watching you like a hawk, treating you like a naughty kid, and as a result you feel like a marked man." Imagine the change in Hart's behavior if he can make the statement above with the same feeling that Bing would put into it.

5. *Question with Care.* The simplest way to keep the conversation going is to use the noncommittal "um-hum." If this is insufficient, phrases such as "and then what happened" or "what did you do" may start the story again. Occasionally restatements such as the one mentioned in (4) may be rephrased as questions. Avoid argumentative statements such as "that isn't true" or "I don't believe you." These statements not only cause you to lose your objectivity and become emotionally involved, but also put the other person on the defensive, thus making it impossible for him to express his true feelings.

SUMMARY OF PRINCIPLE

The principle underlying the content of this chapter is reviewed to impress upon the reader the necessity for purposeful and meaningful communications.

Principle of Communication	For effective communication the sender must determine the purpose of the communication and use symbols having the same meaning for sender and receiver.

●   ●   ●   ●   ●   ●   ●   ●   ●

The Principle of Communication and the guides for empathetic listening are relatively easy to remember; however, their application requires a skill that may take years to develop. As a manager you will have to develop these skills to achieve two-way communications. Solving the problems for Case Problem 17-B is the first step in learning the techniques of empathetic listening and effective communicating.

Questions for Study and Discussion

1. Explain in your own words the triangle of meaning. Why is it important that the triangle have a dotted line for its base?
2. What are some of the things transmitted by an oral face-to-face message other than facts descriptive of a situation? Can these other things be transmitted as effectively in written form? Discuss.
3. Does highly effective and efficient communication between people eliminate conflict between them? If not, why not?
4. Why is conversation not necessarily communication?
5. Why are superior-subordinate communications more susceptible to certain types of communication problems than communication between two persons on the same organizational level?
6. Differentiate between embellishment and filtering. Are communications directed downward in an organization likely to be filtered or embellished? Explain.
7. Develop an argument that supports the thesis that sound processes of delegation minimize the need for face-to-face communication between superior and subordinate.
8. What are the major differences between planning information and control information? Is a discussion of this type of information properly a subject for communications? Why?
9. Develop several examples showing how the technology of the organization influences the need for and the type of formal communications.
10. How can the grapevine be used effectively as a communications device?
11. Since communication is primarily the sending of a message, why is it necessary to be able to listen empathetically?
12. What is meant by a value judgment? Why are value judgments often barriers to effective communication?

In a department of a large industrial organization, there were seven workers (four men and three women) engaged in testing and inspecting panels of electronic equipment. In this department one of the workers, Bing, was having trouble with his immediate superior, Hart, who had formerly been a worker in the department.

Had we been observers in this department we would have seen Bing carrying two or three panels at a time from the racks where they were stored to the bench where he inspected them together. For this activity we would have seen him charging double or triple setup time. We would have heard him occasionally singing at work. Also, we would have seen him usually leaving his work position a few minutes early to go to lunch, and noticed that other employees sometimes accompanied him. And had we been present at one specific occasion, we would have heard Hart telling Bing that he disapproved of these activities and that he wanted Bing to stop doing them.

However, not being present to hear the actual verbal exchange that took place in this interaction, let us note what Bing and Hart each said to a personnel representative.

What Bing Said

In talking about his practice of charging double or triple setup time for panels which he inspected all at one time, Bing said:

"This is a perfectly legal thing to do. We've always been doing it. Mr. Hart,

---

Case Problem 17-B
A Case of Misunderstanding [17]

---

the supervisor, has other ideas about it, though; he claims it's cheating the company. He came over to the bench a day or two ago and let me know just how he felt about the matter. Boy, did we go at it! It wasn't so much the fact that he called me down on it, but more the way in which he did it. . . . I've never seen anyone like him. He's not content just to say in a manlike way what's on his mind, but he prefers to do it in a way that makes you want to crawl inside a crack on the floor. What a guy! I don't mind being called down by a supervisor, but I like to be treated like a man, and not humiliated like a school teacher does a naughty kid. He's been pulling this stuff ever since he's been . . . promoted, he's lost his friendly way and seems to be having some difficulty in knowing how to manage us employees. He's a changed man over what he used to be like when he was a worker on the bench with us several years ago.

"When he pulled this kind of stuff on me the other day, I got so damn mad I called in the union representative. I knew that the thing I was doing was permitted by the contract, but I was intent on making some trouble for Mr. Hart, just because he persists in this sarcastic way of handling me. I am about fed up with the whole

---

[17] F. J. Roethlisberger, "The Administrator's Skill: Communication," *Harvard Business Review*, Vol. 31 (November-December, 1953), pp. 55-57. Reproduced by permission of the *Harvard Business Review*. This case (names and places disguised) is adapted from a case in the files of the Harvard Graduate School of Business Administration.

damn situation. I'm trying every means I can to get myself transferred out of his group . . . He's not going to pull this kind of kid stuff any longer on me. When the union representative questioned him on the case, he finally had to back down, because according to the contract an employee can use any time-saving method or device in order to speed up the process as long as the quality standards of the job are met.

"You see, he knows that I do professional singing on the outside. He hears me singing here on the job, and he hears the people talking about my career in music. I guess he figures I can be so cocky because I have another means of earning some money. Actually, the employees here enjoy having me sing while we work, but he thinks I'm disturbing them and causing them to 'goof off' from their work. Occasionally, I leave the job a few minutes early and go down to the washroom to wash up before lunch. Sometimes several others in the group will accompany me, and so Mr. Hart automatically thinks I'm the leader and usually bawls me out for the whole thing.

"So, you can see, I'm a marked man around here. He keeps watching me like a hawk. Naturally, this makes me very uncomfortable. That's why I'm sure a transfer would be the best thing. I've asked him for it, but he didn't give me any satisfaction at the time. While I remain here, I'm going to keep my nose clean, but whenever I get the chance, I'm going to slip it to him, but good."

What Hart Said

Here, on the other hand, is what Hart told the personnel representative:

"Say, I think you should be in on this. My dear little friend, Bing, is heading himself into a showdown with me. Recently it was brought to my attention that Bing has been taking double and triple setup time for panels which he is actually inspecting at one time. In effect, that's cheating, and I've called him down on it several times before. A few days ago it was brought to my attention again, and so this time I really let him have it in no uncertain terms. He's been getting away with this for too long and I'm going to put an end to it once and for all. I know he didn't like my calling him on it because a few hours later he had the union representative breathing down my back. Well, anyway, I let them both know I'll not tolerate the practice any longer, and I let Bing know that if he continues to do this kind of thing, I'm going to take official action with my boss to have the guy fired or penalized somehow. This kind of thing has to be curbed. Actually, I'm inclined to think the guy's mentally deficient, because talking to him has actually no meaning to him whatsoever. I've tried several different times to talk some sense into that guy's head, and I've just about given it up as a bad deal.

"I don't know what it is about the guy, but I think he's harboring some deep feelings against me. For what, I don't know, because I've tried to handle that bird with kid gloves. But his whole attitude around here on the job is one of indifference, and he certainly isn't a good influence on the rest of my group. Frankly, I think he purposely tries to agitate them against me at times, too. It seems to me he may be suffering from illusions of grandeur, because all he does all day long is sit over there and croon his fool head off. Thinks he's a Frank Sinatra! No kidding! I understand he takes singing lessons and he's working with some of the local bands in the city. All of which is o.k. by me; but when his outside interests start interfering with his efficiency on the job, then I've got to start paying closer attention to the situation. For this reason I've been keeping my eye on that bird and if he steps out of line any more, he and I are going to part ways.

"You know there's an old saying, 'You can't make a purse out of a sow's ear.' The guy is simply unscrupulous. He feels no obligation to do a real day's work. Yet I know the guy can do a good job, because for a long time he did. But in recent months he's slipped, for some reason, and his whole attitude on the job has changed. Why, it's even getting to the point now where I think he's inducing other employees to 'goof off' a few minutes before the lunch whistle and go down

to the washroom and clean up on company time. I've called him on it several times, but words just don't seem to make any lasting impression on him. Well, if he keeps it up much longer, he's going to find himself on the way out. He's asked me for a transfer, so I know he wants to go. But I didn't give him an answer when he asked me, because I was steaming mad at the time, and I may have told him to go somewhere else."

Problems

1. Based upon Hart's (and Bing's) report to the personnel supervisor, what are the factors that would make empathetic listening difficult for Hart to achieve?
2. Reconstruct in full the conversation as it probably occurred.
3. Reconstruct in full an interview between Bing and Hart utilizing the techniques of empathetic listening.
4. Discuss Bing's responsibility to listen empathetically to Hart.

CHAPTER 18

Motivating Employees

Acme Manufacturing Company, located in an eastern metropolitan area, produces a complete line of small household electrical appliances such as toasters, blenders, coffee percolators, and electric can openers. The products are of good quality and are distributed through department stores and mail-order houses under private labels. The small fractional horsepower motors and heating elements used in the products are purchased; however, the company does its own stamping, machining, plating, painting, and assembly. Two hundred hourly paid workers perform these operations.

The personnel policies of Acme Manufacturing are not stated in writing, nor is there an employee handbook. The company conducts an annual wage survey and maintains its wage level at the average of the area for similar jobs. There has not been the same effort to maintain fringe benefits at a competitive level. Surveys concerning employee benefits are not conducted on a regular basis, the last survey having been completed about five years ago. The company never conducted an attitude or morale survey.

> *Case Problem 18-A*
> *Part I: An Employee*
> *Benefit Program*

John Rider, the general manager, is somewhat puzzled by one aspect of the monthly personnel department activity report. For the second successive month there are 10 production jobs to be filled. To the best of his knowledge there have been no changes in production schedules, nor has he authorized any additional factory personnel. Consequently, Rider wonders why the 10 openings exist. He has called the personnel manager to determine the reasons for the vacancies.

As the personnel manager, Frank Stevens, entered his office, Mr. Rider said, "Frank, I notice that for the second straight month we have 10 vacancies in our plant labor force. If this rate of turnover continues, we will be replacing over half of our labor force within a year. What is the reason for our hiring so many new employees?"

"Part of the reason is that we still have four vacancies to be filled from the preceding month, and the other six are vacancies created by employees with less than six months' service who quit last month," Frank answered.

"About the four jobs remaining from last month, why haven't we filled them?"

"Well, these are all skilled jobs. Even so, we managed to hire two people, but they didn't report for work. Both called and said that they had taken better jobs somewhere else."

"Do you know where they went to work?" Rider asked.

"Yes, and neither company has a higher wage rate than we have." Anticipating the next question, Stevens continued, "The only reason for their going to these other companies is that they offer better employee benefits than we do; and in a tight labor market like the one we have now, that kind of difference is significant."

"I also notice from your report that our absentee rate is running about eight to ten percent a day—about twice what it was this time last year. Is that part of the same pattern?"

"I believe it is," Frank answered.

"In that case I suggest that we take a good look at our fringe benefits. After you have determined what is happening in the area, summarize the results and recommend the level that we should adopt for our company. I know that we have more or less paid the average in regard to wages, but in view of our increasing quality problems and our productivity rate per manhour, I'm willing to pay more for fringe benefits if they will help quality and production. Let me have the summary of the survey and your recommendations as soon as possible," Rider concluded.

Frank returned to his office and took from his files a partial list of fringe benefits. The list is shown in Exhibit I.

Problems

1. Would you include all the items listed in Exhibit I in your survey of fringe benefits for Acme Manufacturing Company? If all items are not included in the survey, which should be included?

2. What is your recommendation in regard to the level of fringe benefits that should be paid; i.e., below average, average, or in the upper quartile?

3. What can Acme expect as the result of a competitive employee benefit program in regard to turnover, absenteeism, productivity, and product quality?

4. How can a company measure the effectiveness of its employee benefit program?

5. Is there any justification for using the phrase, fringe benefits, to describe employee benefit programs?

I. For Added Leisure and Income

Call-back pay
Call-in pay
Clean-up time
Clothes-change time
Coffee breaks
Cost-of-living bonus
Downtime pay
Family allowances
Holidays
Hour limits
Jury duty pay
Leave, for illness
Leave, death of relative
Leave, for grievances
Leave, for negotiation
Leave, for voting
Lonely pay
Military bonus
Overtime pay
Portal-to-portal pay
Reporting pay
Rest pauses
Room and board allowance
Setup time
Shift differentials
Standby pay
Supper money
Travel pay
Vacations
Voting time

II. For Personal Identification and Participation

Anniversary awards
Athletic activities
Attendance bonus
Beauty parlor service
Cafeteria
Canteen
Car wash service
Charm school
Christmas bonus
Counseling
Credit union
Dietetic advice
Discounts
Educational aids
Financial advice
Food service
Home financing
Housing
Income tax aid
Information racks
Laundry service
Legal aid

Loan association
Moving aid
Music with work
Orchestra
Parking space
Quality bonus
Recreational programs
Savings bond aid
Safety clothes
Scholarships
Suggestion bonus
Thrift plans
Transportation aids
Year-end bonus

III. For Employment Security

Death benefits
Layoff pay
Leave for maternity
Retraining plans
Technological adjustment pay
Severance pay
Supplementary unemployment benefits
Unemployment insurance

IV. For Health Protection

Accident insurance
Dental care
Disability insurance
Health insurance
Hospitalization
Illness insurance
Life insurance
Medical care plan
Medical examinations
Optical services
Plant nursing service
Sickness insurance
Sick benefits
Sick leave
Surgical care plan
Temporary disability insurance
Visiting nurse service
Workmen's compensation

V. For Old Age and Retirement

Deferred income plans
Old age assistance
Old age counseling
OASDI
Private pension plans
Profit sharing plans
Rest homes
Retirement counseling
Stock ownership plans

Source: Dale Yoder, *Personnel Management and Industrial Relations* (5th ed.; Englewood Cliffs, New Jersey: Prentice-Hall, Inc., 1962), p. 494.

Exhibit I

A PARTIAL LIST OF EMPLOYEE BENEFITS AND SERVICES

• • • • • • • • •

One of the most difficult tasks of an organization is that of motivating its employees—managerial and nonmanagerial alike—to perform the work assigned to them in a manner that meets or surpasses expected standards of performance. Many methods are used to encourage employees to put forth their best effort. Among those commonly found in industrial firms are a variety of formulas intended to relate pay to performance, provisions for security on the job and during the later years of retirement, praise and reproof, and recognition in the form of special awards or promotion. The existence of so many different approaches to motivation suggests the complexity of the problem. Many factors are capable of motivating employees. Some of these factors are a normal part of the industrial situation and can be controlled in some measure by the company; other factors have their origin in the individual employee, in his home, or in his community, and are beyond the company's control. Also, those forces that motivate a person today may be of little value as motivators next month or next year. Fundamental to the success of any plan for motivating employees is the extent to which the intended motivators meet the needs of the individual employees for whom they are designed.

In this chapter we discuss first the basis of motivation as a means of developing certain concepts that will enable us to better understand the worth of intended motivators. Next, specific problems of motivation in an industrial situation are presented. In the last part of the chapter the concept of morale is developed and the relationship between job satisfaction and productivity is reviewed.

THE BASIS OF MOTIVATION

The study of motivation attempts to answer the *why* of human behavior. Why do people behave as they do? Why does John Jones consistently complete his work on time while Pete Smith has to be urged to meet the minimum requirements of his job? When we speak of motivation or, in more precise terms, motivated behavior, we are referring to behavior having three distinguishing characteristics. First, motivated behavior is sustained; that is, it persists for relatively long periods of time. Second, motivated behavior is directed toward the achievement of a goal; and third, it is behavior resulting from a felt need. The third characteristic, behavior resulting from a felt need, introduces a concept requiring further explanation.

Various terms have been used to describe the motivating forces of human behavior. Some of the terms are need, drive, aspiration, and desire. Although each term has a precise meaning in psychological theory, they may be grouped together for our purpose, since each is felt and recognized by the individual as a motivating force. As a result of perceiving a need, a tension or imbalance is created within the individual that leads to activities intended to reduce the tension thus created. The process may be diagrammed as follows:

A Perceived ⎯⎯→ Tension ⎯⎯⎯→ Activity ⎯⎯→ Reduction of Tension
Need   (Motivating   (Achievement of Goal)
                Force)

The importance of the discussion above is this: if the efforts of organizations to motivate employees are to be successful, management must either create felt needs within the individual or offer a means of satisfying needs already in existence within the individual. Thus, in order to motivate employees, we must know something about the fundamental needs of man.

A Hierarchy of Needs

Numerous systems have been developed for the classification of human needs, ranging from those that attempt to explain all human motivation as the result of satisfying one basic need or drive to classifications that list 25 or more separate needs. Among those who have sought to explain behavior in terms of a single need is Freud, who stressed the libido—a broad concept of the sex drive—as the basic motivator of man. Two of his students, Adler and Jung, also postulated single motives; the former designated the desire for power as the primary motivator, while the latter believed that a desire for individuality served as the basic source of motivation. The economists also have had a hand in trying to describe human motivation as evidenced by Marx's description of economic determinism as a primary motivator. However, one of the most useful and widely quoted classifications of human needs is that developed by Maslow who recognizes the following five basic needs. These are: [1]

---

[1] A. H. Maslow, "A Theory of Human Motivation," *Psychological Review*, Vol. L., (July, 1943), pp. 370-396. The theory of motivation, first presented in 1943 as a journal article, is treated in greater detail in *Motivation and Personality* (New York: Harper and Brothers, 1954).

1. Physiological needs.
2. Safety needs.
3. Affection needs.
4. Esteem needs.
5. Self-actualization needs.

Each of these needs is discussed briefly below.

Physiological Needs. Hunger and thirst are considered classic examples of physiological drives. Also included in this category are the tissue needs such as maintenance of the proper water content of the blood; maintenance of proper amounts of salt, sugar, protein, fat, calcium, oxygen, and acid-base balance; and the maintenance of the proper temperature for the tissues and the blood stream.[2] Satisfaction of the physiological needs is necessary for the preservation of life, and in most industrial economies these needs are satisfied relatively easily. Once satisfied, they cease to operate as the primary motivators of behavior and are replaced by motivational forces of a higher order.

Safety Needs. When considered as a goal of motivated behavior, the meaning of the term, safety, is broad because it includes the desire for psychological security as well as the need for physical security. Factors such as clothing, shelter, and protection from attack contribute to physical safety, thereby preserving and reinforcing the satisfaction of physiological drives. Much of the effort of organized society at the community level, such as police and fire departments, is directed toward the maintenance of security needs.

The desire for psychological security is of particular interest to management since the safety needs may become the predominant motivators when the physiological needs are fulfilled. Psychological safety takes the form of ordering the environment into a predictable pattern and attempts to cope with anticipated difficulties of the future. Demands for supplemental unemployment benefits, pension plans, termination pay, and other forms of economic insurance stress the need for predictability and security. The desire for the familiar and the predictable goes a long way toward explaining the resistance to change found in many organizations. It is not the direction or nature of the change being resisted; it is the fact that change implies something new and unfamiliar —a psychological threat.

---

[2] W. B. Cannon, *Wisdom of the Body* (New York: W. W. Norton and Company, 1932.) W. B. Cannon describes the functioning of the human body as a homostatic system.

Affection Needs. Some writers combine physiological needs and safety needs into one category and call them the primary needs. They then refer to the needs for affection, esteem, and self-actualization as secondary needs. Such a classification is misleading because in our society the needs for survival and safety may be satisfied to a large extent. Consequently, the predominant needs are those of affection, esteem, and self-actualization. Need for affection and love is best described as the need to belong, not only as a wanted member of a family unit but also as a member of other relatively small groups such as work groups. Loyalty to small work groups and the need to belong to that group often outweigh the financial incentives and the logical appeals of management.

Esteem Needs. The esteem needs, like the needs for affection and group belonging, are particularly significant as motivators in the industrial setting. Esteem needs may be summarized as the need for self-respect, for accomplishment, and for achievement. An important corollary to the need for esteem and achievement, perhaps as important as the need itself, is that the achievement must be recognized and appreciated by someone else. Few people are able to continue a pattern of achievement and success without the added encouragement and additional motivation provided by recognition of success by others. The desire for prestige and status (in reality, a form of recognition by others) is an important aspect of the drive for achievement. Attaining goals leads to feelings of self-respect, strength, and confidence. On the other hand, continued failure, frustration, and defeat can result in feelings of inadequacy and a withdrawal from competitive situations.

Self-Actualization Needs. Self-actualization, the capstone of the hierarchy of needs, is self-fulfillment. Maslow's original statement—"what a man can be, he must be"—may be paraphrased to state that *what a man can do, he must do.* Self-actualization takes many forms. We usually think of the creative works of painters, musicians, composers, and authors as expressions of self-fulfillment; however, the realization of one's full potential is not limited to expression in the creative arts. The woman who desires to be the ideal mother, the professional athlete, and the dedicated teacher are all doing what each must do. Complete self-actualization is rare, perhaps because all the other needs—physiological, safety, affection, and esteem—must reach a level of minimal satisfaction before the self-fulfillment needs become the dominant motivation in one's life.

Variations in the Hierarchy

The discussion of Maslow's hierarchy of needs serves a useful purpose, provided we recognize that the concept of a hierarchy is used only as a model and is not intended to imply that the emergence and the strength of needs follow a rigid pattern. There are many reversals and substitutions of needs. For some persons the sole goal in life seems to center upon the esteem needs, the acquisition of prestige, wealth, and status, to the exclusion of the needs for love and affection. Closer examination often reveals a thwarting of the love needs early in life, with a permanent dampening and suppression of those needs; thus, the drive for self-esteem may serve as a substitute for the need for love. There is also evidence that the needs for esteem and self-actualization may be blocked to such an extent that seemingly they disappear and do not emerge. Those who have faced a life of unemployment, or at best marginal economic adjustment, are often motivated predominantly by the desire for safety and security as a means of protecting at a minimal level the basic physiological needs.

There is probably no universal motivator for all mankind, nor is there a single motivating force for any one individual. Needs are relative in their strength, and it is not necessary to satisfy a "lower" need fully before a "higher" need may emerge and operate as a motivator. Assume that 90 percent of a person's physiological needs are satisfied, that 80 percent of his safety needs are fulfilled, and that 55 percent of his needs for love and affection are being met. This does not mean that there are no needs for esteem or self-actualization. Needs are felt gradually and may become motivators along with the other needs, even though the earlier needs are not completely satisfied. The complexity of the problem of motivation can be fully grasped when it is realized that the hypothetical percentages stated above vary from one person to another, that the significance of each need also varies, and that within the same person the relative degree of satisfaction and the significance of each need also vary from time to time. In addition, there are factors other than the variable characteristics of the basic needs that influence motivation. Among those factors are a person's evaluation of himself and his interpretation of his environment.

Concepts of Self and Environment

A person's concept of himself and his interpretation of his environment provide a source of consistency to behavior throughout his entire life and determine to a large extent those motives that

454 • The Leadership Function • Part IV

influence him the most. The image of self is formed relatively early in life and is reflected to the outer world by the manner of dress, speech, posture, and actions. The reflection remains fairly constant throughout life, thereby enabling others to predict with considerable accuracy one's behavior under a given set of circumstances. In this sense it is true that clothes do not make the man; indeed, clothes (along with actions, posture, and speech) are the man.

There are many dimensions to the self-image. Of particular concern in respect to the problems of motivation in industry is a person's estimate of his degree of competence and his ability to achieve. Biographical studies show that patterns of achievement appear early in life. Initial successes lead to later successes and reinforce one's estimate of his competence and ability to achieve. By the same token, failures, either imagined or real, deflate one's self-image of competence and achievement. Achievement, or the lack of it, shapes the environment in which man lives. Those who achieve develop a sense of *power* over their environment, for they are able to cope with that environment and seemingly control it to their advantage. A person who exercises power and control over his environment learns to expect a high degree of *reward* from that environment, and when received, the reward tends to make him feel that he is master of his own destiny. On the other hand, persistent lack of reward leads to an environmental image that is hostile and unrewarding. There are also the possible combinations of the person who believes that he has a low degree of power to control his environment, yet has expectations of relatively high rewards, and the person who feels that he can control his environment but expects little reward in return for his effort.

Let us examine the expected behavior patterns of each of these possible combinations of the extent of power over the environment and expectations of reward from that environment, as described by Gellerman.[3] At the same time, we must remember that there are many possible shadings and combinations of these two factors between the hypothetical extremes presented below.

High Reward Expectation and High Control over Environment. First, consider someone who has learned to have both high expectations of reward and a high sense of power to influence his environment. He will probably feel that life is full of exciting possibilities for him and

---

[3] Saul W. Gellerman, *Motivation and Productivity* (New York: American Management Association, Inc., 1963) pp. 194-197. *Motivation and Productivity* presents in very readable form a summation of the outstanding research in the field of motivation and its applications to the industrial setting. A complete bibliography is included.

that he can very likely get whatever he wants if he puts his mind to it. His dominant motive will probably be an achievement drive. The thought that he may fail at something is no doubt rather foreign to him, and should he fail he may be baffled for a time, although he will recover soon enough and have another try at it.

He is likely to be a thoroughgoing optimist, so much so that he takes his optimism for granted and maintains a calm, unsurprised attitude toward his successes. Probably he seldom experiences much anxiety, except in the heat of a difficult situation, and even then it will be more of an exhilarating tingle than a sickening feeling of foreboding. He may be somewhat lacking in understanding of people who are more fearful or passive than he is, not out of snobbishness but merely because he hasn't much awareness of how crippling deep fear can be. He is probably the product of a fortunate childhood in a fortunate society.

High Reward Expectation and Low Control over Environment. Second, take a person who also has high reward expectations but who feels that he has only a low degree of influence on the happenings of his environment. His will be a rather privileged life, and much of his thinking will revolve around attempts to justify and preserve these privileges. Since bettering his position seems unlikely, or at any rate out of his hands, he concentrates on protecting what he has. He may gamble for diversion but not to enhance his estate; economic risks will not attract him because the outcome will seem capricious and unreliable. He is more concerned with failures than with successes, partly because he needs no successes and partly because failures will seem like an ever-present possibility to be guarded against.

Since his station in life will usually have been won for him by his forebears, he will be conscious of his heritage and fearful that he may not be equal to it. However, he is less likely to emulate the acquisitive ways of his predecessors than to demonstrate that he knows how to spend money in a sophisticated way. In a sense what Thorstein Veblen labeled "conspicuous consumption" is this person's way of proving that he has the taste and breeding to qualify for wealth. He is likely to be proud, gay, and insouciant when all is going well but easily alarmed by bad news.

In many ways he can be compared to a general who has to defend a plush area with untrained troops against a powerful and resourceful enemy. His life is sweet but it is also precarious; he is well acquainted with fear although he can usually control it well enough. He is not likely to be very sympathetic toward others, largely because he is too absorbed in his own problems to be particularly aware of other people's problems. He is likely to be the pampered product of a well-to-do background.

Low Reward Expectation and High Control over Environment.
Third, take the case of someone who has low reward expectations but
feels a high degree of power over his environment. He may very well
decide that the environment can be reshaped to become more rewarding
if he will work at it hard enough and accumulate enough money. Consequently, he is likely to be primarily money-motivated and to pursue
wealth with relentless vigor—perhaps even with a dash of un-
scupulousness at times. Successes will seem to be entirely possible, but
so will failures. Yet the game will be eminently worth the candle, and
failures can be tolerated if the successes are big enough. Determination,
grit, and stubborn unwillingness to quit will be the strategy most likely
to pay off for him. Accordingly he will come back more energetically
than ever after a setback and will not rest on his laurels after a success.
He will feel a certain guarded optimism, never sure enough of success
to become complacent but never really doubting that he can win in the
long run.

He will be socially mobile, struggling upward—possibly with the
gaudy pretensions of the *parvenu* or just as possibly with a single-minded
severity that leaves little room for anything but his business. The people
with whom he works will note him as a comer, a fireball, a man to
watch. He will be under a perpetual strain, unable to settle for what
he has already acquired and uncertain that he can acquire more soon
enough. Therefore, he will be inwardly tense and may reveal this in
occasional eruptions of temper. While he demands more of himself
than he does of anyone else, he may be quite intolerant of errors by
people whose assistance he needs. However, he knows what it means
to be an underdog, and in his calmer moments he can be very generous
and sympathetic toward his subordinates.

He is likely to be the product of a society that is in transition
from poverty to greater wealth. It was men like him who became
the first capitalists in the early days of the Industrial Revolution and
who are emerging today as business or political leaders in economically
awakening areas. The pattern has been particularly notable among
slumdwellers in big American cities, which indicates that economic
deprivation can release a terrific flow of enterprise if there are enough
opportunities for personal gain to create a sense of power over the
environment.

Low Reward Expectation and Low Control over Environment.
Finally, consider a person who has low reward expectations and who
also feels a low degree of power over his environment. For him life will
be a vale of tears. While he may acquire a peasant's wisdom that enables
him to appreciate simple things and to laugh occasionally, the imminence
of death and the indifference of the world will seldom be far from his
thoughts. His primary motive will be to secure at least a bare subsistence

for himself and his family, and if he ever succeeds in insuring even a meager income for himself—for example, by getting a salary or a pension—he may regard himself as unusually fortunate.

He more or less expects to fail in projects undertaken at his own initiative; therefore, he seldom acts except out of habit or in obedience to someone else's instructions. He is passive and pessimistic but probably not particularly disturbed at his lot. It is only when people like himself begin acquiring some safety and comfort that the possibility of improvement becomes meaningful to him, and only then can he be stirred out of his apathy by job opportunities or by demagogues.

Ordinarily, he spends much of his life waiting, or working listlessly, or socializing amiably with people like himself. He is under relatively little tension. Life holds no surprises for him since he expects no more than he gets, and it holds no terrors for him because he expects no mercy. He can be whipped into mass hysterias, because a leader who seems to understand his incomprehensible world is worth following blindly, but he is not likely to get particularly agitated about anything by himself. He is capable of a deep and genuine sympathy for other people—even those who abuse him a little more than he earns—but even his debts will not be enough to enrich a lender because of his limited capacity to repay them.

Such resigned, ineffectual people have made up the majority of mankind until a few hundred years ago, and in countries which have not yet been industrialized they are probably still a majority. Nor are they uncommon in industrialized countries. What Mayo called anomie is precisely the reaction of people with little hope to a bewildering, overpowering environment."

MOTIVATION IN INDUSTRY

The preceding discussion of needs and the way in which they are influenced by the concepts of self and the environment is presented in general terms with little specific reference to the application of these concepts to the day-to-day motivation of employees in an industrial situation. At the beginning of this chapter it is stated that in order to motivate employees, management must either create felt needs within the individual or must offer a means of satisfying those needs already in existence within the individual. Undoubtedly the most widely used incentive to motivate employees is money, yet the evidence is overwhelming that more money does not necessarily mean greater productivity. The factors limiting the usefulness of money as a tool for motivating employees and the research findings concerning employee motivation are discussed below.

Money and Motivation

Money has no intrinsic value, yet we recognize the economic worth of money in that it can be exchanged for goods and services. There is also a psychological emotionally toned worth attached to money. The economic worth of money enables it to serve as a means of satisfying the basic physiological and safety needs. Its psychological value is that for many persons money may symbolize achievement, success, prestige, or power—a way of fulfilling the higher social needs.

Control over Environment. Not all people are capable of regarding money as an incentive. Refer to the four combinations of expected rewards and perceived power over one's environment as described by Gellerman—(1) a high reward expectation and a high degree of perceived power to control the environment; (2) high expectation, but low power to control the environment; (3) low expectation, but high power to control; (4) low in both reward expectation and perceived control. Those persons best characterized by either the first or third category are the ones who are capable of responding to money as an incentive. These are the people who perceive themselves as having a high degree of power in shaping their environment; the magnitude of the expected reward is relatively unimportant. In the first group—high reward and high power—are those who are highly trained in either technical or professional fields, a training that by its very nature represents a pattern of success. To these people money very readily becomes a symbol of success and achievement and can be exchanged for desired goods and services. Those in the third category, who expect little but believe that they can effectively control their environment, are likely to amass money, not for its own sake, but as a means of further controlling and shaping the environment. Entrepreneurs (including successful managers) often belong to the third group. People who perceive little chance of changing their environment are not motivated by money in excess of that amount required to satisfy their minimal needs.

Conflicting Needs. The belief that money is and should be a strong motivator is deeply rooted, and not without foundation, as evidenced by those who believe that they can control their environment. For the most part these people respond well to monetary incentive plans in sales and managerial jobs, but similar plans for hourly production workers experience questionable success at best. Whyte estimates that only 10 percent of the hourly production workers in the United States respond to a financial incentive plan by producing to capacity, thereby increasing their earnings.[4] What about the other 90 percent? Why don't they produce more, particularly when greater productivity means more money? Zaleznik and his coworkers at Harvard University offer some sound answers to this question; albeit the answers are not encouraging for management.[5]

Before discussing Zaleznik's work we must take another look at groups one and three mentioned above. These are the people—the physician, the lawyer, the accountant, the salesman, or the entrepreneur—capable of responding to financial incentives, people who believe that they can shape their environment and control it to a large extent. To them the world is not a foreboding place in which to live since there are more successes than there are failures. Further, success is the result largely of individual effort. Although any one of these people may work as a member or a leader of a group, each is usually recognized as an individual having a unique contribution to make to the group. Admittedly, membership in a small work group is necessary and highly prized, but it is not the key to success. Instead, success is attributable largely to individual effort. Members of groups one and three usually satisfy to a considerable extent their need for belonging; but even more important, the esteem needs—prestige, achievement, power, and recognition—also have a measure of satisfaction. Many are realizing a degree of self-actualization in that they are doing and being what they must do and be.

The environment of the production worker, as described by Whyte and Zaleznik, is one of sharp contrast to the environment described above. First, let us consider the production worker as an individual, then a group of production workers, and finally the statistical exceptions—Whyte's 10 percent who respond as individuals to incentives.

THE PRODUCTION WORKER. It is often said that all generalizations are false, including this one. Nonetheless, the following generalizations help to place in perspective some of the problems of motivation in an industrial society. For some reason, or perhaps a combination of reasons, the production worker (think of the man on the assembly line) has not become highly skilled. His lack of progress may be due to a lack of ability, lack of physiological drive and stamina, poor environmental

---

[4] William F. Whyte, *Money and Motivation* (New York: Harper and Row, Publishers, Inc., 1955).

[5] Abraham Zaleznik, C. R. Christensen, and F. Roethlisberger, *The Motivation, Productivity, and Satisfaction of Workers: A Prediction Study* (Boston: Harvard Business School, 1958). Both the Harvard study and Whyte's work emphasize the limitations of money as a means of motivating production workers and stress the importance of the work group as a motivating force.

factors, inability to acquire training in his youth due to economic conditions, or any one of a host of other reasons. Whatever the cause, the environment has not surrendered much over the years, with the resultant feelings of frustration and the conviction that the world is hostile and unyielding. Expectations of reward may have been high in his youth, but early socio-economic forces may have permanently limited his expectations to a minimal level. If expectations were high, the years of frustration and lack of anticipated rewards serve to emphasize the hopelessness of ever achieving original goals.

The basic physiological and safety needs of the worker described above are, in all probability, fairly well satisfied. But what about the higher needs? It is difficult for most of us to imagine self-actualization or self-fulfillment on an assembly line. Punching a clock, being identified by number, and performing a routine task are not conducive to feelings of status, prestige, or high esteem in the eyes of others. Since these esteem needs are not satisfied, the next step in descending order of the hierarchy of needs is the need for belonging—for belonging to a group.

THE GROUP. Imagine our hypothetical worker accepting a new job and a new clock number with a different employer. The new job is not much different than several previous jobs, nor are the opportunities for advancement appreciably different, at least as the worker sees the situation. Since the job is the same, the possibilities for satisfying the esteem and self-actualization needs are effectively blocked, but the opportunity is present to become a member of a group. The informal group is established and composed of men with similar backgrounds and concepts of self and control over the environment. At this point in time our new employee is not a "regular" member of the group (he may never become a member of the inner circle), but he aligns himself with the group as a means of satisfying a basic need—the need to belong. Zaleznik refers to these groups as "frozen groups"; Gellerman calls them "sick." Frozen or sick, these are the groups that set patterns of behavior and shape the attitudes of workers in the plant.

Conformity in respect to both overt behavior and attitudes is the price of membership in the group. One of the most noticeable aspects of the group's behavior is the restriction of output, in reality a reflection of attitudes toward management. Management is viewed with suspicion, and any change is regarded as ultimately resulting in an increase in the amount of work required from each member of the group or a reduction in the size of the work force. The objective of the group is to maintain a *status quo* since expectations of high reward and the belief that the environment can be shaped no longer exist. At least, present conditions assure the satisfaction of the physiological and safety needs, and membership in the group satisfies the need for belonging. For the new worker, joining or not joining the group may be a difficult choice in terms of satisfying his needs. Conformity to the group's standards of behavior and attitudes usually means giving up satisfying the esteem and self-actualization needs while on the job; but his prior experience shows that the satisfaction of these needs is difficult and in the distant future. To pursue the higher needs could mean rejection by the group, with the resulting frustration of the belonging needs. For many workers the dilemma exists only in theory; the choice is made early in life to belong to the group, thus satisfying the belonging needs and foregoing the higher esteem and self-actualization needs. Yet for some, the rate buster for example, needs other than belonging to the group are more important.

THE RATE BUSTER. A small percentage, Whyte's estimate is 10 percent, rejects the group's demand for conformity and responds to money as an incentive. These people are known as *rate busters*. Conceivably they could be responding to management's plan to reduce costs and improve productivity, but it is seldom that such is the case. For the rate buster who sought membership in the group and was rejected by the group, his behavior may be a form of revenge, a means of showing up the group by outproducing them. Others who excel in production do so as the result of their socio-economic background rather than as the result of responding to the merits of a specific incentive plan. Socially the rate buster tends to be a "loner" both inside and outside the industrial organization. Further, he generally comes from a home that stresses the virtues of individual achievement and economic independence. He still believes that as the result of his own efforts he can shape his environment and improve his lot in life. Either reason, revenge against the group or socio-economic background, points up the irony of incentive plans. The 10 percent who respond to incentives are not responding to the plan itself; instead, they are motivated by forces seldom recognized by and far beyond the control of management.

When Money Works. The above discussion shows the shortcomings of monetary incentives as a means of motivating the vast majority of production workers. Nonetheless, many companies are satisfied with incentive plans and attribute a reduction in cost and an increase in productivity to these plans. Admittedly, many such plans work, but they are not working as the result of the effectiveness of money as an incentive. There are several reasons why incentive plans often attain management's desired results. First, the presence of a realistic standard tends to motivate employees since it defines a goal to be reached within a specified period of time. In this respect a standard is the same as par in golf or a 200 game in bowling. Second, without stated standards, supervisors do not know what is expected of them and often reflect their unrest through aggressive attitudes toward production workers. When standards are in effect, the production worker who meets these goals assures himself of a more pleasant working relationship with his supervisor. A third reason is that prior to the installation of production standards there is usually a period of intensive methods analysis which improves the mechanics of actually performing the job, with the result that more work can be done with less effort and fatigue. Fourth, the introduction of standards forces management to improve the production control function so that the flow of work is at a more even pace with fewer periods of idleness due to waiting for materials.

Job Satisfaction and Motivation

The discussion of money and motivation should not lead us to the conclusion that money is unimportant in the total process of motivating employees; it is important, but money is a *hygienic* factor, not a *motivator*. The differentiation between hygienic factors and motivators is the result of research conducted by Dr. Frederick Herzberg and his associates of the Psychological Service of Pittsburgh.[6] Several hundred engineers and accountants were interviewed and asked to recall incidents related to their work and to indicate the effect of these incidents upon their productivity and attitudes toward their jobs. The subjects of the Pittsburgh studies were also asked to indicate the duration of the feelings aroused by each incident.

Herzberg found that experiences which create positive attitudes toward work arise from the job itself and function as *motivators*. These incidents are associated with feelings of self-improvement, achievement, and the desire for and the acceptance of greater responsibility. The feelings thus generated are of a relatively long duration and result in increased productivity. Since the subjects of the Pittsburgh studies were engineers and accountants, the change in productivity was more qualitative than quantitative in nature. The second set of factors related to productivity on the job are conditions peripheral to the job itself. Pay, working conditions (such as heating, lighting, and ventilation), company policy, and the quality of supervision are all part of the environment of

---

[6] Frederick Herzberg, Bernard Mausner, and B. Snydeman, *The Motivation to Work*, 2d ed., (New York: John Wiley & Sons, Inc., 1959).

work but peripheral to the tasks of the job itself. When these factors are inadequate; i.e., when one believes that these conditions are not up to par, they function as *dissatisfiers;* but when present, they do not motivate employees to greater productivity. Instead, they are *hygienic* in character in that their presence makes it possible for the motivators to function. Positive feelings aroused by these peripheral conditions of work, such as a word of encouragement from a supervisor or an increase in pay, are relatively brief in duration. Another finding of the Pittsburgh study is significant. When employees are highly motivated and find their jobs interesting and challenging, they are able to tolerate considerable dissatisfaction arising from the peripheral factors of work, but the reverse is not true. A full measure of all hygienic factors does not make the job interesting.

One obvious limitation of Herzberg's work is that his subjects were engineers and accountants, people who have had the motivation to acquire professional training, who believe that they can shape their environment, and who expect considerable reward from that environment. Does the same hold true for the nonprofessional worker?

Hygienic and Motivating Factors at Work

Dr. M. Scott Myers, Manager of Personnel Research for Texas Instruments Incorporated, using essentially the same technique employed by Herzberg, raises and answers the three following questions concerning employee motivation.

What motivates employees to work effectively?
A challenging job which allows a feeling of achievement, responsibility, growth, advancement, enjoyment of work itself, and earned recognition.

What dissatisfies workers?
Mostly factors which are peripheral to the job—work rules, lighting, coffee breaks, titles, seniority rights, wages, fringe benefits, and the like.

When do workers become dissatisfied?
When opportunities for meaningful achievement are eliminated and they become sensitized to their environment and begin to find fault.[7]

---

[7] M. Scott Myers, "Who Are Your Motivated Workers?," *Harvard Business Review,* Vol. XXXXII (January-February, 1964), p. 73. Dr. Myers' report, pp. 73-88, presents in detail the findings of his research conducted at Texas Instruments. The article contains many pictorial presentations well worth careful study.

Myers' study is not limited to the analysis of the professionally trained, since it is a representative sample of 282 employees from five different job classifications, three of which are salaried and two are hourly classifications. The salaried classifications included are scientists, engineers, and manufacturing supervisors; the hourly classifications include technicians (male) and assemblers (female). Although the answers to the three questions raised above apply to all job classifications, the differences in the importance ascribed to various motivational factors other than achievement are significant enough to warrant a brief analysis of the responses of each group.

Scientists. For scientists, 50 percent of the favorable incidents reported are related to achievement on the job. The most intense feelings of satisfaction; i.e., those feelings that endure for at least two months, are related to "work itself." The most frequently mentioned source of dissatisfaction stems from company policy and administration, an implication that rules and regulations sometimes interfere with the achievement of scientific goals. However, the most intense feelings of dissatisfaction come from a feeling that their work lacks full responsibility.

Engineers. Engineers show a motivational pattern much like that shown by the scientists in respect to the importance of achievement and the satisfaction derived from work itself. Yet they differ from scientists in that advancement and pay are also predominant sources of feelings of intense satisfaction. In addition to reporting a lack of responsibility and poor company policy as causes of dissatisfaction, the engineers report that incompetence and lack of friendliness on the part of supervision and inadequate pay (in their estimation) create dissatisfaction.

Manufacturing Supervisors. Although achievement is mentioned most frequently as a source of satisfaction, manufacturing supervisors—a nonprofessionally trained group—show a pattern distinctly different from that of the scientists and engineers. Advancement, recognition, and the possibility of growth create the intense feelings of satisfaction, with advancement being by far the greatest single source of intense satisfaction. Lack of responsibility, inadequate pay, and failure to advance are causes of dissatisfaction among manufacturing supervisors. The designation of advancement as the major source of satisfaction is not surprising since supervisors are frequently promoted from hourly classifications and seek such promotions because of their strong desire to achieve through advancement within the organization.

Hourly Technicians. Hourly electronic technicians, like manufacturing supervisors, do not mention work itself as either a frequent or intense source of satisfaction; to them, work itself is the greatest dissatisfier. Increased responsibility is by far the strongest motivator of technicians and is followed by advancement. It is quite possible that enlarged responsibilities and successfully achieving these responsibilities are considered a means of advancing.

Female Assemblers. The preceding groups—scientists, engineers, manufacturing supervisors, and hourly technicians—are all characterized by Myers as motivation seekers or, at the very least, potential motivation seekers. These people can be motivated by factors within the job itself, but the female assemblers are described as *maintenance seekers* in that factors peripheral to the work itself are dominant in creating either strong positive feelings of satisfaction or negative feelings of dissatisfaction. Although achievement is mentioned most frequently as a source of satisfaction, the competence and friendliness of supervision along with pay offer the most intense feelings of satisfaction. By the same token, lack of recognition by supervision and lack of security (the threat of layoff) are the chief causes of dissatisfaction. Increased responsibility and advancement are not motivators; instead, recognition and understanding by the immediate supervisor motivate the female assembler.

Management's Choice

The results of Dr. Myers' study are presented in pictorial form in Figure 18-1, Employee Needs. Note that the inner circle—motivational needs—contains those factors directly related to the job, while the outer circle is composed of maintenance needs. Employees seek satisfaction in the area of maintenance needs—those factors peripheral to the job itself—when the motivational needs of growth, achievement, responsibility, and recognition are not satisfied. The relative importance of maintenance needs diminishes when motivational needs are satisfied. Thus, management has two broad alternatives: (1) directing its efforts toward the satisfaction of motivational needs by designing jobs having the capability of fulfilling those needs, or (2) directing its efforts toward the satisfaction of those needs peripheral to the job itself. Acme Manufacturing Company, Case Problem 18-A, has apparently decided to choose the second alternative and satisfy the peripheral needs. Let us discuss this alternative and the results that might reasonably be expected from this approach to employee motivation.

Figure 18-1

EMPLOYEE NEEDS—MAINTENANCE AND MOTIVATIONAL

Source: M. Scott Myer, "Who Are Your Motivated Workers?," *Harvard Business Review*, Vol. XXXXII (January-February, 1964), p. 86.

Employee Benefit Programs. In all probability no company has a vice-president in charge of fun and games, yet most companies of any size have several highly paid administrators in their personnel departments in charge of various phases of employee welfare and benefit programs. These programs are concerned with those items shown in the outer circle of Figure 18-1. Such activities are costly, not only in terms of dollars spent but more importantly because of their inefficiency as motivators. The dollar cost of maintaining these extrinsic factors at competitive levels is rising in a never-ending spiral. Unions have traditionally directed their bargaining efforts toward improvement of the physical and economic factors shown in the outer circle. Managements have, perhaps unwittingly, aided unions in their efforts to raise the level of employee benefits. Most companies take considerable pride in their benefit and welfare programs and in most instances are forced to keep them at competitive levels in order to attract needed personnel.

In addition to the ever-mounting total cost of these programs, a hidden cost lies in their inefficiency as motivators. When hygienic factors are absent, or not present in sufficient quantity, they function as dissatisfiers and can actually interfere with productivity. However, when present, they do not motivate personnel to greater productivity. They merely form a floor or base and represent the minimum acceptable conditions of employment. Employees who are best described as maintenance seekers are an insatiable group; maintenance needs are never fully satisfied. There is always a greener pasture offering more employee benefits. The designation of various employee benefits as fringe benefits is peculiarly apt, since they are on the fringe of the real benefits that should be derived from the job itself.

Job Design. If we are to tap the motivators of achievement, growth, responsibility, and recognition, we must examine closely the design of the job itself, for these factors are intrinsic. In some jobs, such as that of the scientist, the engineer, or the accountant, minor changes in company policy and administration might permit the potential motivators to operate effectively. However, there are many jobs in industry characterized by highly repetitive, monotonous activities offering few opportunities for growth, additional responsibility, or recognition. The obvious question arises: Can these jobs be designed in a manner that will offer a greater measure of motivation from factors inherently a part of the job? In answering this question, let us look first at current practices in job design and then examine two alternatives for increasing job satisfaction.

CURRENT JOB DESIGN. Fundamental to present practices in job design are specialization, the nature of the production process, and the goal of lowest unit cost.[8] The concept of specialization is applied not only to the design of machinery used in the production process but also to the jobs performed by the workers. Jobs are composed of a sequence of individual tasks or operations that are grouped and then assigned to a single individual. Usually a particular method for performing each of the separate tasks of a job is specified. In many instances the tasks performed by the worker are determined by the characteristics of the machine; for example, the bag catcher who removes and boxes bags made by a machine designed to produce a single product.

When there is a choice in determining which tasks should be combined into a single job, the criterion of lowest unit cost is applied. Since cost is to be minimized, it seems only logical to design tasks and combine them in such a fashion that the lowest level of skill is required. The application of this procedure usually results in a highly repetitive operation, composed of relatively simple movements requiring little skill, and

---

[8] Louis E. Davis, "Job Design and Productivity: A New Approach," *Personnel*, Vol. XXXIII (March, 1957), pp. 418-430. Dr. Davis' article presents an excellent analysis of specialization and job design. It also contains a detailed review of the study conducted by Marks that is cited in reference no. 10.

capable of being learned by a large number of workers in a comparatively short period of time. Thus, training costs are at a minimum and an adequate potential of labor is assured. Assembly operations are typical of jobs composed of repetitive, unskilled tasks capable of being learned by most industrial workers.

How valid are these assumptions? Judging by this nation's level of productivity, consumption, and pay, the assumptions underlying the design of production processes and fitting jobs to these processes are quite effective. Yet it remains to be answered whether or not current practices of job design utilize the best available means of designing jobs since there are relatively few instances in which jobs have been designed to be more complex and challenging to the worker.

JOB ENLARGEMENT. *Job enlargement* is the process of making industrial jobs more challenging and interesting by increasing the variety of the tasks required for a given job. One of the main reasons for enlarging jobs is found in the results of the work conducted by Walker and Guest of the Institute of Human Relations at Yale University.[9] Their studies reveal a very low level of job satisfaction on the part of assembly-line workers; in fact, the workers despise their jobs even though most of them indicate that pay, supervision, and working conditions are more than satisfactory. The reasons for the intense dislike of the work is reported to be due to the anonymity of the worker himself and the complete depersonalization of the job. Feelings of anonymity and depersonalization arise because the pace is determined mechanically by the speed of the line, the low level of skills required, the highly repetitive nature of the tasks performed, the lack of choice or control over methods and tools to be used, and the lack of social interaction resulting from an isolated and fixed position on the line.

An experimental approach to enlarging the job content of an assembly operation is described in a study completed by A. R. N. Marks.[10] The total number of employees in the department was 35, of which 29 were female assemblers engaged in assembling a hospital appliance, and six performed supporting jobs of inspecting and supplying materials. Each assembler performed one of nine operations at a station on a

---

[9] C. R. Walker and R. H. Guest, *The Man on the Assembly Line* (Cambridge, Mass.: Harvard University Press, 1952). C. R. Walker and R. H. Guest, "The Man on the Assembly Line," *Harvard Business Review,* Vol. XXX (May-June, 1952), pp. 71-83. *The Harvard Business Review* article presents a summary of the feelings and attitudes of automobile assembly-plant workers as revealed by carefully conducted depth interviews.

[10] A. R. N. Marks, "An Investigation of Modifications of Job Design in an Industrial Situation and Their Effect on Some Measures of Economic Productivity," Ph. D. dissertation, University of California, 1954.

conveyor-paced assembly line. Every two hours positions on the line were rotated to lessen fatigue and break the monotony. The speed of the conveyor determined the output for the group, and since positions on the line were rotated, there was no individual responsibility for quality. The experiment consisted of four stages:

1. Line Job Design—The normal method of assembling, performed on a conveyor-paced line with six workers supporting the 29 assemblers.

2. Group Job Design—The conveyor is eliminated but other conditions remain the same. In effect, the pace of the operation and consequently the output are determined by the worker.

3. Individual Job Design No. 1—Each worker performs all nine operations at her own station and is responsible for procuring her own parts, the inspection of the parts, and the quality of the final assembly. This stage of the experiment was conducted in a room near the main production area to provide training in the new method. Each worker spent two days in this phase of the study. The conveyor is eliminated.

4. Individual Job Design No. 2—Following the two-day training period, each worker performs the assembly operation using the method of individual job design No. 1 in the main production area for six days. (In discussing the results of the experiment, individual job designs Nos. 1 and 2 are treated as a single method since design No. 1 served as a training period for design No. 2. The method is the same; the only variable is the location in which the work is performed.)

With the group job design method, which lasted only two days, productivity was considerably lower than the normal production of the line job design. Individual job design No. 1 resulted in a higher level of productivity than that attained from the group job design, and the level of production of individual job design No. 2 continued to rise, with the average for the group being about 95 percent of the amount produced using the original line job design. These results are quite remarkable considering that the total number of days' experience in using the individual job design methods is only eight, while the average length of time on the line job design is over four years.

A detailed analysis of the production records of the individual job design method shows that production increased each consecutive day, and on the sixth day the average production for the group exceeded the average for the line design method. Further, as a result of each assembler operating independently of the others, individual differences in productivity were noted, with some of the women producing 30 to 40 percent more than the average for the line job design. In addition, the level of quality improved considerably—a 75 percent reduction in kinked (wiring) assemblies—and the six supporting workers who normally inspected final assemblies and procured parts were eliminated. Marks also found that those who participated in the experimental individual job design developed a more favorable attitude toward their jobs in that they desired more responsibility and were willing to put forth more effort, and when returned to the line job design method at the end of the experiment, they disliked the loss of personal responsibility inherent in a conveyor-paced assembly operation.

The experiment in job enlargement described above raises some provocative questions. The level of production on the sixth day of individual job design No. 2 exceeded the average of the line production method, thus challenging the assumption that the highly engineered assembly-line operation is the *optimum* arrangement for producing at the lowest unit cost. We do not know whether or not the individual job design method would result in productivity equal to that of the line job for a sustained period of time; in other words, did the high production of the assemblers on the sixth day result from the job design itself, or did it result from their awareness that they were participating in an experiment? How applicable are these results to other industries? Assume that individual job design does yield a higher degree of productivity; what is the capital investment required for individual job design as compared with line job design in assembling a complex product such as an automobile? Can the same procedures be applied to the routine, repetitive clerical jobs of a bank or an insurance company? And finally, how important are feelings of job satisfaction and productivity?

JOB SATISFACTION AND PRODUCTIVITY

In our discussion of Myers' work on employee motivation at Texas Instruments Incorporated, the brief comments on Walker and Guest's *The Man on the Assembly Line,* and Marks' experimental study of job enlargement of an assembly operation, we may have overemphasized the importance of job satisfaction *per se.* As a first step in placing the importance of job satisfaction in perspective, let us define morale—a function of needs as well as job satisfaction, then determine the statistical incidence of job *dissatisfaction,* and finally examine the relationship between job satisfaction and productivity.

Morale

Morale is a word with many meanings. Definitions include statements that morale is the absence of conflict, a feeling of happiness, good personal adjustment, those attitudes pertaining to work, and the extent of ego-involvement in one's job. Some definitions would limit the concept of morale to only those persons working in a group by defining morale as the extent of cohesiveness or "we feeling" of a group or the extent to which there is personal acceptance of the goals of the group. Dr. Robert Guion offers a definition of morale that includes most, if not all, of the attributes previously mentioned. *"Morale is the extent to which an individual's needs are satisfied and the extent to which the individual perceives that satisfaction as stemming from his total job situation."* [11] Guion's definition is of value since it stresses the importance of need satisfaction and applies equally to individuals as well as to those who are members of groups. It also emphasizes the complexity of the sources of morale by referring to the total job situation rather than to job satisfaction alone. Intrinsic job satisfaction is only one factor of the total job situation. An analysis of the job attitudes of 6,000 industrial workers in a midwestern tractor factory shows that there are four relatively independent factors contributing to satisfaction derived from the total job situation. They are: intrinsic job satisfaction, satisfaction with the company, satisfaction with supervision, and satisfaction with rewards and the opportunity for mobility. [12] Another study using the technique of multiple-factor analysis—a statistical tool for determining independent factors—investigated the needs to be satisfied by the total job situation. There is a general factor of morale resulting from overall satisfaction as a result of need fulfillment, the need for social recognition of status, and the need for self-respect. [13] Thus, the recognition of morale as a function of satisfying both individual needs and total job situation forces intrinsic job satisfaction into the position of one of several factors and not necessarily the most important.

---

[11] Robert M. Guion, "Industrial Morale (A Symposium) 1. The Problem of Terminology," *Personnel Psychology*, Vol. XI (Spring, 1958), p. 62. This symposium was presented at the 1957 meetings of the Midwestern Psychological Association in Chicago. Dr. Guion's article, pp. 59-61, summarizes varying concepts of morale.

[12] Robert L. Kahn, "Productivity and Job Satisfaction," *Personnel Psychology* Vol. XV (Autumn, 1960), pp. 275-287. In addition to reporting the results of a multiple-factor analysis of employee attitudes, Kahn summarizes the major findings of the Survey Research Center of the University of Michigan in their studies of job satisfaction and productivity.

[13] Oakley J. Gordon, "A Factor Analysis of Human Needs and Industrial Morale," *Personnel Psychology*, Vol. VIII (Spring, 1955), pp. 1-18. This work complements the study of Kahn. Gordon's analysis is concerned with needs, while Kahn's is concerned with the job situation. Note that the definition of morale offered by Guion ties these two aspects of morale together.

Job Dissatisfaction

Another way of placing the importance of job satisfaction in perspective is to examine the other side of the coin—determine the incidence of job dissatisfaction. One survey, conducted by Robinson in 1958, examines 406 estimates of the percentage of dissatisfied workers in the United States, Great Britain, the Netherlands, and Germany for a 24-year period.[14] He found, first, that on the whole only 13 percent of the dissatisfied workers are generally dissatisfied with their jobs, and second, that the percentage of dissatisfied workers has remained fairly constant in recent years. In a study of almost 1,000 men in two automobile assembly plants and one metal mill, Walker and Marriott place the number of assemblers who express dissatisfaction arising from the boredom of their jobs at 35 percent and 36 percent for the two automobile plants and at only 8 percent for the workers of the metal plant.[15] A comparison of the workers in the two assembly plants shows significant differences in the extent of dissatisfaction, with a higher frequency of dissatisfaction among those working on highly mechanized, conveyor-paced operations than among workers on non-mechanized, off-the-line jobs. Presumably the difference in dissatisfaction is due to the repetitiveness of the mechanized jobs. The results of these two studies are not in conflict; Robinson's survey covers all types of industrial jobs, while Walker and Marriott's percentages of dissatisfied workers apply to the epitome of repetitive work—the assembly line.

Although Walker and Marriott place the incidence of dissatisfaction among assembly-line workers considerably above that for industry as a whole, their study does not define the number of assembly workers in the entire automobile industry. Blauner estimates the percentage of assembly-line workers at less than 5 percent of the total number employed in the automobile industry. His reasoning is as follows:

If we consider total employment in the industrial groupings involved in the manufacture, sales, repair, and servicing of automobiles, we find that assembly-line workers make up less than 5% of all workers in this complex. There are approximately 120,000 automobile workers who are line assemblers, yet the number of skilled repair mechanics in all branches of the industry, a job which in many ways resembles the craft ideal, exceeds 500,000. In addition, the 120,000 assemblers are

[14] H. Robinson, "Job Satisfaction Research of 1958," *Personnel and Guidance Journal*, Vol. XXXVII (May, 1959), pp. 669-673.

[15] C. R. Walker and R. Marriott, "A Study of Some Attitudes to Factory Work," *Occupational Psychology*, Vol. XXV (July, 1951), pp. 181-191.

outnumbered by 400,000 managers who own or operate gas stations, garages, new and used car lots, and wrecking yards, and by 200,000 skilled workers in automobile plants.[16]

It is clear from the above that only a minority of industrial workers are dissatisfied with their jobs. True, there are those who base their case on human values and contend that all jobs should be made as interesting as possible. The study conducted by Marks indicates that perhaps this can be done in some instances. Yet there is evidence that job enlargement, a means of reducing monotony and boredom, has no significant effect upon the attitudes of workers.[17] Kennedy and O'Neill, using a carefully constructed attitude survey to measure attitudes toward 14 different aspects of work and the work situation, compared the responses of men on the assembly line of an automobile plant with those of the utility men working in the same department. Since the utility man's job is varied, requires a higher level of skill, and is not controlled by the pace of the conveyor, it is logical to expect that his attitudes might be more favorable toward the work situation than the attitudes of the on-the-line worker. Such was not the case; there were no statistically significant differences between the two groups of employees.

It should be noted that the studies of Herzberg, Myers, Walker and Guest, and Walker and Marriott utilize an interview technique as a means of gaining their information. However, Kennedy and O'Neill used a printed attitude survey. Thus, the question arises: Are the results obtained an artifact of the methodology? Do workers find the interview an opportunity to "get things off their chests" in the presence of a sympathetic ear, or is the nature of the interview such that it probes only the areas of dissatisfaction? On the other hand, is the printed attitude survey, usually a questionnaire or a checklist, sensitive enough to probe areas of dissatisfaction? The answer is not clear, since we may be dealing with an artifact arising from the method employed in gaining information.

We have seen that job satisfaction is only one of several factors in morale, that the incidence of job dissatisfaction is relatively small, and

---

[16] Robert Blauner, "Work Satisfaction and Industrial Trends in Modern Society." From Walter Galenson and Seymour M. Lipset, (Eds.), *Labor and Trade Unionism* (New York: John Wiley and Sons, Inc., 1960) p. 360. Blauner's estimate of 5 percent is based upon the 1950 census figures which show a total of 2.5 million employed in automobile manufacturing, automobile sales, automobile garage and repair shops, and gasoline service stations. The number of assembly workers is taken from the U. S. Department of Labor's *Occupational Outlook Handbook,* 1957.

[17] J. E. Kennedy and H. E. O'Neill, "Job Content and Workers' Opinions," *Journal of Applied Psychology,* Vol. XLII (December, 1958), pp. 372-375.

perhaps is unrelated to attitudes toward the total work situation. As a third step in placing job satisfaction in perspective, let us examine the relationship between satisfaction and productivity.

Productivity and Job Satisfaction

Psychologists have devoted a great deal of time and effort to studying the effects of reward and punishment upon human behavior. In general, it seems that situations that reward a person are satisfying and those situations that punish a person are dissatisfying. Further, people have a tendency to prolong or return to satisfying situations and to avoid those situations that are not satisfying. This line of reasoning is applied to the interpretation of morale as a factor in turnover and absenteeism. Thus, people with high morale (a high degree of perceived satisfaction of needs through the total job situation) can be expected to continue their job with a minimum amount of absenteeism, and those who quit or are chronically absent do so because the situation is not satisfying to them. Although this reasoning is plausible in explaining turnover and absenteeism, it does not follow that satisfaction with the job should or does result in a high level of productivity.

All individuals are simultaneously members of several social systems and the attainment of goals within each of these social systems serves to satisfy the needs of the individual. High productivity is seldom a goal, but high productivity may lead to the fulfillment of a goal, thereby creating a feeling of satisfaction. In this case, productivity is varying concomitantly with satisfaction (goal attainment); there is no causal relationship.

Katz and Kahn suggest that the industrial worker is a member of four social systems: (1) A system outside the plant and within the plant, (2) a system of relationships with other workers, (3) a system of the formal union structure, and (4) an organizational system of the company itself.[18] It might be argued that higher productivity is a means of achieving prestige, recognition, and higher status in the social system outside the plant. But evidence does not show that the majority of

---

[18] D. Katz and R. L. Kahn, "Some Recent Findings in Human Relations Research in Industry." From G. E. Swanson, T. M. Newcomb, and E. L. Hartley (Eds.), *Readings in Social Psychology,* (New York: Henry Holt and Company, 1952), pp. 650-665.

Arthur H. Brayfield and Walter H. Crockett, "Employee Attitudes and Employee Performance," *Psychological Bulletin,* Vol. LII (September, 1955), pp. 415-422. Brayfield and Crockett present an excellent survey of the literature on employee attitudes in relation to productivity and use the four social systems suggested by Katz and Kahn as a format for their presentation.

industrial workers are strongly motivated toward social achievement outside the plant.[19]

Further, many industrial workers are in Gellerman's classifications of those who perceive little chance of control over their environment. In analyzing the relationships of industrial workers among themselves, we must remember Zaleznik's "frozen groups," groups that have pegged production at minimal levels, and the desire to belong to the group—an impossibility with high levels of production. Workers who have aspirations of achieving rank and position within the formal structure of the union may do so without resorting to high production; in fact, high levels of productivity frequently serve as a detriment for advancement within the union. Seemingly the employee desirous of advancing within the company organization by receiving increased pay, a promotion, or a higher position in the hierarchy would be motivated to produce more. Yet, productivity is only one of several factors considered for advancement; quality, ability to get along with others, and dependability may outweigh productivity in determining advancement within the company.

The Michigan Studies

In 1947 the newly founded Survey Research Center of the University of Michigan undertook a series of investigations to determine the relationships between supervisory practices, employee satisfaction, and productivity.[20] In the first study of the relationships of these three variables, the setting is the home office of a large insurance company. As might be expected, most of the employees are young women new to the labor force. Three indexes of satisfaction are used in this study. They are satisfaction with the company as a whole, satisfaction with pay and job status, and satisfaction with the job itself. The results show that there is no significant relationship between any of these indexes of satisfaction and the productivity of the work group. However, members of high-producing work groups recognize their groups as high producers; but this may not be satisfaction. Rather, it is a perception of the situation as it exists.

The design of the second study is the same as the first; however, the setting is as different as night from day. The work situation is the right-of-way maintenance jobs of approximately 300 railroad laborers and

---

[19] W. L. Warner and P. S. Lunt, *The Social Life of a Modern Community* (New Haven, Conn.: Yale University Press, 1941).

[20] Robert L. Kahn, "Productivity and Job Satisfaction," *op. cit.* In this article Dr. Kahn also summarizes the results of the insurance study, the study of railroad workers, and the tractor study.

72 foremen. The tasks performed are manual labor, not clerical functions; and the subjects are men, not young girls. Yet, the results are the same. No consistent relationship is found between productivity and the three indexes of job satisfaction. Again, the members of high-producing work groups are able to perceive their groups as high producers, but this ability to perceive a situation as it exists is not necessarily job satisfaction.

The third study is different in several respects from the first two. Instead of using group measures of productivity, individual production records for 6,000 production workers of a midwestern tractor company were examined and compared against known time study standards for each job. Also, instead of assuming indexes of job satisfaction, a factor analysis of data obtained from a carefully constructed questionnaire was performed to determine the dimensions of job satisfaction. These dimensions—presented in the discussion of morale—are: intrinsic job satisfaction, satisfaction with the company, satisfaction with rewards and mobility. Again, none of these measures of satisfaction are related to productivity.

Job satisfaction is but one of several factors making up the complex of needs and the total job situation that contributes to morale; and, as yet, there is no demonstrable relationship between job satisfaction and productivity. Does this mean that management should ignore satisfaction derived from work itself as a potential motivating force? It does not seem likely that it is possible to achieve maximum organizational effectiveness over a long period of time with a low level of morale; i.e., a low degree of need satisfaction, and a low degree of satisfaction with the total job situation. Therefore, in designing motivational systems—the environment in which work is performed—a balance must be maintained between the goals and needs of the organization and the goals, needs, and capabilities of its members. To do otherwise could result in the depletion of one of the organization's most valuable resources—its people.

● ● ● ● ● ● ● ● ●

Case Problem 18-B describes the results experienced by Acme Manufacturing Company after having raised the level of its employee benefit program and poses another question to be resolved by the same management group: Should the company install a monetary incentive plan or should the company embark upon a program of job enlargement?

Questions for Study and Discussion

1. Why is it necessary for managers to know something about the fundamental needs of man in order to motivate employees successfully? From your own experience, describe an intended motivator that did not correspond to your own personal needs.

2. Of what significance are the physiological and safety needs in our economy today? Under what conditions would these needs become more significant?

3. What is meant by variations in the hierarchy of needs? Why is it necessary to recognize that such variations exist? In your opinion, which is the most important single variation in the hierarchy that can occur?

4. Evaluate the four categories of perception of one's self in relation to his environment as described by Gellerman. What is the probable outcome of using money as a means of motivation for each of Gellerman's four categories?

5. Give an example of conflicting needs in an industrial situation and show how this conflict affects employee motivation.

6. Why do monetary incentive plans achieve the desired goal of increased production in some companies if money is not a true motivator?

7. Differentiate between hygienic factors and motivators. Why is this distinction important?

8. What reasons can you advance to support the present practice of job design?

9. What is meant by job enlargement? What factors limit the opportunity for job enlargement?

10. Describe in your own words the meaning of the phrase "industrial morale."

11. Does it seem reasonable to you that whenever possible a company should strive to provide an industrial situation that will result in high morale on the part of its employees even though productivity is not increased? Discuss.

• • • • • • • • •

Approximately 18 months after the meeting described in Case Problem 18-A, Frank Stevens, the personnel manager, and Al Conrad, the manager of industrial engineering, are in the general manager's office discussing ways of improving productivity and product quality. Following the survey of fringe benefits, Acme changed its practices in regard to holidays, vacations, life insurance, hospitalization insurance, and sick leave. After making these changes the company now ranks in the upper quartile of companies in the area in respect to these particular benefits. The company decided not to initiate employee services such as legal aid, counseling, a credit union, and a recreation program because these benefits are offered by very few companies in the area. There has been no change in the policy of setting wage levels equal to the average of the area.

Since increasing the level of its fringe benefits, the company has been able to hire replacements without undue delay; turnover, which had been most noticeable among employees with less than six months' service, has declined to its previous level; and absenteeism has been reduced. However, there has been no change in productivity per man-hour, nor has there been any improvement in product quality. An analysis by the quality control department shows that about 80 percent of the quality problems can be traced to errors in assembly.

Because of the persistent quality problem and the lack of improvement

> ## Case Problem 18-B
> ## Part II: Incentives or
> ## Job Design?

in productivity, Mr. Rider, the general manager, requested two feasibility studies. One of these, prepared by industrial engineering, discusses the feasibility of an incentive plan for hourly employees; the other is a report by the personnel department concerning job enlargement. After reading these reports, Rider asked for a conference with the heads of the industrial engineering and the personnel departments.

Rider turned to Conrad and said, "Apparently your department questions the value of incentives as a means of increasing productivity. Would you summarize your position for Frank's benefit?"

"As you know," Conrad began, "we now have a measured day work plan; that is, we have time standards in most departments, but we do not have an incentive pay plan. The plant average is about 90 percent of standard for those departments that have standards. The press room, where we form the metal parts of our appliances, and the machining department average about 93 percent; the plating and painting departments run about 95 percent; the assembly department, about 85 percent; and in shipping and receiving the packers are the only ones on standards and they average about 85 percent also."

At this point Stevens commented, "It seems that assembly and the packers are the ones pulling the plant average down."

"That is right," Conrad continued. "Even so, a plant average near 90 percent is not too bad. Frankly, I question how much we would gain with an incentive. In the press room and the assembly departments, the big factor in determining the output is the engineering design of the equipment and the manner in which it is maintained. Also, chrome plating requires a specified length of time for a given thickness of plate, and the capacity of the drying ovens is the limiting factor in our paint department. Improvement in production in these departments would be relatively small and the net gain in terms of earnings might be even smaller."

"Why is that?" Rider asked.

"To maintain standards for an incentive pay plan, I would have to double the size of my department. We would have to set additional standards for jobs that are run only infrequently. Complaints about standards would have to be answered promptly. All of this takes more people—I estimate at least an additional $50,000 a year in salaries alone. Sooner or later we would be forced into the position of paying the plant average to all workers—maintenance men, janitors, shipping and receiving—because they will contend that they are having to do more work since more units are being produced; yet, actually their work load would change very little."

Looking at Frank Stevens, Mr. Rider said, "It seems to me that it is questionable whether we would actually gain very much from an incentive pay plan in view of what Conrad has said. What about your recommendation of job enlargement?"

"Since most of our difficulty is in the assembly department, I would suggest that we start there by eliminating the assembly lines and having each person

assemble the entire product and do his own packing. There have been several instances where this approach has worked. If we had each person assemble the entire unit, inspect that unit, then insert an inspection slip into the box after packing the unit, we would have a much better control over quality."

"But assembly accounts for only one department," Conrad said. "What about the other departments?"

"In the press room and the machining departments we could have the operators learn how to make their own setups and make minor repairs instead of having the tool room make the setups and the maintenance department making all repairs, even the minor ones."

"You do that and we will have to pay all the machine operators a much higher rate since they will be classed as skilled rather than semiskilled," Conrad interrupted. "Also, we would be undertaking a tremendous training program, and at present we don't have that kind of staff."

Rider realized that he was no nearer a solution after talking to Conrad and Stevens than he had been before the conference. He decided to meet with them again in a week.

Problems

1. As the general manager of Acme, would you accept the recommendations of the personnel department? Why?

2. What additional information would you need to make a decision?

3. Is the industrial engineering department correct in not recommending an incentive plan? Discuss.

CHAPTER 19

Management's First Line: The Supervisor

The managers of Apex Manufacturing, a company with approximately 750 employees, prided themselves in running what the company called a "tight ship." They are satisfied with the results of a recent attitude survey which shows that most employees believe that supervision is "strict, but fair." Like most of the other members of management, John Sweeney, has come up through the ranks and is currently assigned to Department #40, the lacquer department, where he supervises 35 hourly employees. He has been with the company for 20 years, and for the last 10 years he has been a foreman. John tries to be fair to the men working for him, and at the same time administer company policies in accordance with the wishes of the general superintendent who is very strict in his interpretation of company rules and regulations. John is waiting in his office for the arrival of Joe Adams, the union steward for Department #40.

"John, I'd like to talk to you about Jim Wilson, the man you discharged yesterday afternoon."

"Not much to talk about, Joe," John replied. "You know he was smoking in restricted areas."

Case Problem 19-A

No Smoking

"That's just the point, John. The rules don't say that you have to discharge him. All they say is that anyone who violates any of the Group One rules is *subject to* immediate discharge. That's a long way from saying that you *have* to discharge him."

"Look, Joe, I know that you have your job to do with the union and that you have a perfect right to question any action that I may take. But look at this case. Jim was with the company for over 12 years; certainly in that length of time he should know what the company rules mean. They are there for a reason. You know that this department could blow up the whole plant if there was a fire in here, what with this lacquer we have to work with. There are *No Smoking* signs all over the place and the men in the spray booths even wear rubber soles so there is no chance for sparks. Sorry, there's nothing I can do about it; one mistake here would blow us all to hell and back."

"You say that Jim has been with us 12 years. That's true, but he's only been in your department for three months. He just forgot, maybe worried or something."

"I can't help that. Maybe it was some guy down the street last month who was just worried, or new, or something, and you know what happened. That fire took the lives of three employees in that plant and cost millions of dollars, and none of them are back to work yet We don't want that happening here, and it won't if I have anything to do about it."

"John, you aren't leaving me much choice. I'm going to file a grievance, and I promise you this one will go all the way to arbitration. Twelve years of service without a single reprimand ought to mean something." With that remark, Joe Adams, the steward, left the foreman's office.

Problems

1. Do you agree with the action taken by John Sweeney, the foreman? Explain.
2. Has the steward presented his case well? Is he quibbling when he says that the words "subject to" do not mean that the foreman must discharge an employee?
3. The next step of the grievance procedure in Apex Manufacturing calls for a decision by the general superintendent. If he reverses Sweeney's stand, what effect will this have on Sweeney's relations with his men?
4. Of what significance are the "fire down the street" and the "12 years of service without a reprimand"?

● ● ● ● ● ● ● ● ●

Many statements have been made concerning the importance of the first-line supervisor because of the significance of his contribution to the achievement of the productivity goals of the organization and his unique position as the only member of management who directs the work of nonmanagerial employees. In the preceding chapter doubt is cast upon the value of monetary incentives for the majority of production workers as a means of increasing productivity. Nor do employee benefit programs motivate employees to greater productivity since they are hygienic in nature and do not function as motivators. The Michigan studies also show that there is no consistent relationship between productivity and morale. However, these studies do reveal a predictable relationship between supervisory practice and productivity; hence, the importance of the supervisor in the achievement of the production goals of the organization. The importance that arises from his unique position in the managerial hierarchy is that the supervisor is in a position to encourage the personal growth of his subordinates, to aid in their achievement, and to offer recognition for the work they perform. By so doing he contributes to the motivation of employees.

This chapter is intended to provide an insight into the problems encountered by a supervisor. Most of the examples of supervisory practices refer to the manufacturing supervisor; however, it should be recognized that the supervisor of an accounting section or an order processing group has essentially the same problems. In order to provide insight into supervisory practices the following topics are discussed: (1) The Supervisor's Job, (2) Selection and Training of Supervisors, and (3) Improving Supervisory Performance.

THE SUPERVISOR'S JOB

The terms *supervisor* and *foreman* are frequently used interchangeably; however, in this chapter the term supervisor is used since it is somewhat broader in its application and also implies one of the major functions of supervision—to supervise. The term foreman is usually limited to supervisors in manufacturing organizations or to those supervising semiskilled or unskilled workers. The title supervisor is applicable to those who direct the work of others in laboratories, offices, retail establishments, and sales organizations as well as to those directing the work of hourly paid employees in manufacturing concerns. By definition, a supervisor is a part of management. His position in management is unique—his is the only level of management charged with the responsibility of directing the work of nonmanagerial employees. Members of middle and top management perform various administrative tasks, and if they do direct the work of others it is the work of other managers.[1] The supervisor's position, between the upper levels of management and the hourly nonmanagerial employees has been described rather caustically, if not disparagingly, as the "man in the middle"[2] and the "marginal man of industry."[3] The supervisor has also been referred to as both "master and victim of double talk" as well as being "victim, not monarch, of all he surveys."[4] It is important to recognize that the supervisor is the man in the middle and because of his sometimes ambiguous position we have the key to the primary function of his job—"the linking-pin function."[5] Before developing the concept of the linking-pin function, let us review the legal definition of the supervisor's job.

---

[1] It is recognized that many members of middle and top management may have secretarial employees reporting to them, but the direction of these employees is incidental to their primary function which is usually administrative or the performance of a staff duty.

[2] B. B. Gardner, and W. F. Whyte, "The Man in the Middle: Postions and Problems of the Foreman," *Applied Anthropology,* Vol. IV (Winter, 1945), pp. 1-28.

[3] D. E. Wray, "Marginal Man of Industry: The Foreman," *American Journal of Sociology,* Vol. LIV (January, 1949), pp. 298-301.

[4] F. J. Roethlisberger, "The Foreman: Master and Victim of Double Talk," *Harvard Business Review,* Vol. XXIII (September, 1945), pp. 283-298.

[5] Rensis Likert, *New Patterns of Management* (New York: McGraw-Hill Book Company, Inc., 1961), p. 113. Chapter 8, "An Integrating Principle and an Overview," pp. 97-118, presents a detailed discussion of the linking-pin function of supervision.

Legal Definition

As defined by federal legislation, a supervisor is:

. . . any individual having authority, in the interest of the employer, to hire, transfer, suspend, lay off, recall, promote, discharge, assign, reward, or discipline other employees, or responsibility to direct them, or to adjust their grievances, or effectively to recommend such action, if in connection with the foregoing the exercise of such authority is not of a merely routine or clerical nature, but requires the use of independent judgment.[6]

Another federal law, the Fair Labor Standards Act of 1938 (as amended) is often called the minimum wage law and uses as one of its tests in determining whether or not a person is a supervisor the amount of time spent performing work that is the same as that performed by the people under his direction. Supervisors are expected to spend no more than 20 percent of their time doing the same kind of work that is performed by employees whom they are directing. In effect, the National Labor-Management Relations Act determines who is eligible to join an employees' union, and the Fair Labor Standards Act determines whether or not an employee is paid on an hourly basis (usually with overtime for hours in excess of a specified number) or whether he is to be paid a salary with no compensation required for overtime. Supervisors cannot join a union of production or clerical employees; however, they can form a union composed entirely of supervisors. With respect to pay, supervisors are paid a salary and are exempt from the provisions of the law requiring compensation for overtime. Hence, supervisors are commonly called "exempt" employees.

The net result of these two pieces of legislation is that the supervisor is by definition a part of management, but the supervisor does not always view himself as being the same as the other members of management.

How the Supervisor Sees Himself

We have mentioned that the supervisor's position is unique in that it requires him to interact with nonmanagerial employees as well as with management. There is also a personal history characteristic that tends to set the supervisor apart from other members of management. Typically the first-line supervisor is promoted from the hourly ranks, and it is not at all unusual for him to supervise men whom he has known for years and with whom he has worked as an equal. At

---

[6] National Labor-Management Relations Act (Taft-Hartley), 1947 (as amended), Section 101, Subsection 2 (11).

other levels of management, men usually start their careers as managers and are not in the position of having to change their attitudes toward former associates as they advance in the organization. With this difference in background, it is worthwhile to ask whether the supervisor sees himself in the same light as other members of management see themselves or whether he views himself as being more like the hourly group from which he was promoted.

Lyman W. Porter administered a self-description inventory consisting of 64 pairs of adjectives to 172 first-level supervisors, 291 upper-level management personnel, and 320 hourly production employees.[7] Each person was required to check one adjective of each pair that in his opinion offered the best self-description. The results of this study show that supervisors most frequently see themselves as planful, deliberate, calm, fair minded, steady, responsible, civilized, self-controlled, logical, judicial, and honest. Upper-level management personnel, a group including department heads, staff personnel, and vice-presidents, see themselves as resourceful, sharp witted, sincere, thoughtful, sociable, reliable, dignified, imaginative, adaptable, sympathetic, and generous. The hourly worker believes himself to be ambitious, industrious, sharp witted, efficient, thoughtful, sociable, pleasant, reliable, and adaptable.

Note that there is a clear differentiation between each of the three groups. The supervisor sees himself as a moderate, if not conservative, individual who acts as a stabilizing influence—an image not at all unsuited for "the man in the middle." The upper levels of management picture themselves as the successful entrepreneur who is imaginative, resourceful, and sharp witted; yet thoughtful, sympathetic, and dignified. The hourly worker is clearly on the way up. There does not seem to be any trend in self-image from the hourly ranks, through the supervisory group, to the upper levels of management. The supervisor's image of himself does not retain the elements of the hourly image, nor has it acquired the outgoing self-confident characteristic of the higher levels of management. A look at a typical day in the life of a supervisor shows us why a calm, judicial attitude is the safest role for him to assume.

A Typical Day

We know that the supervisor's primary function is to direct the efforts of hourly personnel reporting to him. The data pre-

---

[7] Lyman W. Porter, "Self-Perception of First-Level Supervisors Compared with Upper-Management Personnel and with Operative Line Workers," *Journal of Applied Psychology*, Vol. VIL (June, 1959), pp. 183-186.

sented below are a composite of many supervisors and many days in an automobile assembly plant; however, the results are typical of supervisory activities in most of the mass-production industries—cans, glass containers, appliances, etc. The method employed in the research study described is applicable to any industrial setting and should be used by any organization interested in improving the performance of its supervisors.

The Method. Walker, Guest, and Turner decided to follow up their work on the man on the assembly line by studying the foreman on the assembly line.[8] Fifty-six foremen were observed for a full eight-hour day. On the day before the actual observation, the observer spent approximately three hours with the foreman becoming acquainted with the layout of the department, the nature of the operation, and the names and duties of key personnel. Starting the next morning at the beginning of the shift each of the foreman's activities was recorded and classified as follows: *Time*—the time the incident occurred; *Topic*—what the incident concerned, what it was about; *Activity*—what the foreman did; *Place*—where the incident occurred; *Contact*—who was involved in the incident; and *Interaction*—what was the nature of the contact. At the end of the day the observations were dictated and transcribed, then the typewritten record (some 40 to 70 pages in length) was reviewed with the foreman for interpretation and corrections. The results of the 56 observations were tabulated and analyzed. A total of 32,652 incidents was recorded. The following is a sequence of 14 incidents during an 11½-minute interval for a foreman named Pat.

Time	*Description*
2:15 p.m.	Pat checks with scheduler, S. Looks at hourly report of number of cars coming through body shop.
2:16	Walks over to R (repair man) on pickup line and checks to see if earlier repair trouble was corrected.
2:17	Calls over inspection foreman to show him a hole missing in a piece. Inspection foreman acknowledges he will notify the trim department.
2:19	Pat tells the repair man to locate the hole by eye until it comes through all right.
2:19½	Pat has a drink of water.
2:20	Pat walks over to station 5 and asks his utility man how many men he still has to relieve.

---

[8] C. R. Walker, R. H. Guest, and A. N. Turner, *The Foreman on the Assembly Line* (Cambridge, Mass.: Harvard University Press), 1956.

2:20½   Moves along the line—stations 5, 6, 7—checking visually on the quality of work.

2:21   Checks a loose nut on a fixture at station 7. Speaks with operator.

2:22   Man at station 3 calls for materials.

2:22¼   Pat tells man at subassembly bench E to make up more material.

2:23   Walks over to MH (stock man). Tells stock man the line is getting low on hinges. They discuss the number short and agree there is enough for tomorrow.

2:25   Pat walks from MH to station 1 and makes visual inspection of the car body to check on the hole discussed earlier at the pickup line.

2:26   Pat sees foreman from preceding section and tells him about the missing hole.

2:26½   A hand signal from welder, W.[9]

The range in the number of incidents for each foreman during an 8-hour day is from a low of 237 to a high of 1,073. The average number of incidents is 583; thus during a 480-minute workday a foreman does something different every 48 seconds. It requires a great deal of flexibility to move from one problem to another at the rate of more than one every minute. The supervisor's perception of himself as a calm and moderate person is no accident—he must believe and act like a moderate; otherwise the pressures of his job could cause a complete psychological breakdown.

Let us now look more closely at the nature of the foreman's work, the topics; the actions he must take to accomplish the work, the activities, and the persons involved in these activities, the contacts.

Topics. Table 19-1, Average Amount of Time Spent by Foreman on Each Topic, shows that almost one third of his time, 31.4 percent, is directed toward the product—quality and progress of work. These figures are averages; there is a wide variation in the allocation of time between foremen, and for the same foreman from day to day. It is noted that when emergencies arise, the first activity to suffer is the amount of time spent on personnel relations, normally 10.2 percent, or about 50 minutes a day. When an emergency arises, whether it be a shortage of materials, a change in schedule, a defective jig or fixture, the problem must be solved and often solved immediately. Consequently, two or three hours may be directed to the topic needing attention. One conclusion is inescapable from reviewing the nature of the topics—the

---

[9] Robert H. Guest, "Of Time and the Foreman," *Personnel,* Vol. XXXII, (May, 1956), p. 480. This article, pp. 478-486, shows clearly the pressures of time on a supervisor and points up the difference between what he should do and what he can do.

Table 19-1

AVERAGE AMOUNT OF TIME SPENT BY FOREMEN ON EACH TOPIC

Topic	Percent of time
Quality	18.2
Work progress	13.2
Personnel administration	11.2
Personal relations and other nonjob-related topics	10.2
Foreman performance of an operation	8.1
Tools, jigs, and fixtures	8.1
Materials	8.0
Employee job performance	7.6
Production schedule	5.2
Grievances	2.0
Injury, illness	1.2
Housekeeping	.5
Work standards	.4
Safety	.2
Meeting	.1
Miscellaneous	2.4
Topic unknown	2.4

Source: Robert H. Guest, "Of Time and the Foreman," *Personnel,* Vol. XXXII (May, 1956), p. 481.

foreman has little control over where he is going to spend his time from day to day or from minute to minute. The amount of effective planning that a foreman can do is limited by the structure of the situation in which he works.

Activities. Table 19-2 reveals that almost half of the foreman's time is spent talking, thereby emphasizing the importance of communication. There is a lot of walking, between four and six miles a day, and very little sitting, less than a minute a day. The need for health and stamina is obvious. The high percentage of time spent in looking, 20.9 percent, is related to the first two topics of Table 19-1, quality and work progress. Looking, as it is used in Table 19-2, means interpreting the work situation. If showing is considered an instructional activity, there is very little time spent in instructing personnel. The small amount of time spent in reading and writing is significant in that it shows that practically all clerical work has been eliminated from the foreman's job, thus freeing his time to observe the operations under his direction.

Contacts. Over 57 percent of the foreman's time is spent in face-to-face contacts, as indicated in Table 19-3. The percentage of time spent in contacts is somewhat higher than the percentage of time spent talking since some of the contacts involve a sign or gesture as a means of communication. Remember, the average amount of time spent on each

Table 19-2

AVERAGE AMOUNT OF TIME SPENT BY EACH FOREMAN ON EACH ACTIVITY

Activity	Percent of time
Talks	46.6
Looks	20.9
Manipulates	9.6
Walks	6.9
Hands, carries	5.6
Reads	2.9
Telephones	2.4
Writes	2.1
Stands	1.0
Signals	.8
Listens	.6
Shows	.4
Sits	.2
	100.0

Source: Robert H. Guest, "Of Time and the Foreman," *Personnel,* Vol. XXXII (May, 1956), p. 482.

Table 19-3

AVERAGE AMOUNT OF TIME SPENT BY FOREMEN ON EACH CONTACT

Contact	Percent of time
Own operators	26.4
Other foremen	7.0
General foreman	4.6
Department superintendent	1.1
Other superiors	.4
Service personnel:	
Maintenance	2.5
Inspection	2.3
Material	2.6
Work standards	.4
Other operators	3.8
All Others	6.2
	57.3

Source: Robert H. Guest, "Of Time and the Foreman," *Personnel,* Vol. XXXII (May, 1956), p. 482.

topic is only 48 seconds; therefore, contacts and verbal exchanges with others are brief and sometimes fragmentary. Only a fourth of the foreman's day is spent in contact with his own operators. Yet training programs emphasize superior-subordinate relationship, even though most contacts are with other foremen, supportive personnel, and superiors.

In our discussion of the method used by Walker, Guest, and Turner in analyzing the foreman's job, it is stated that the incidents were also classified in respect to the place where the incident occurred and the type of interaction involved. Fourteen percent of the incidents normally occur outside the work area under the foreman's supervision, and 60.3 percent of the contacts are initiated by the foreman himself. Thirty-seven percent of the contacts were the result of someone else wanting to contact the foreman.

In conclusion, the study of the foreman on the assembly line shows the variety of tasks that go to make up a foreman's job and the extent to which the job is structured by the nature of the operation, the objectives, the plans, and the controls of top management, and the facilities provided to do the job. Although the supervisor is the one member of management in direct contact with operating employees, he spends relatively little time directly supervising subordinates.

Dimensions of Supervisory Performance

The preceding discussion illustrates the variety of tasks a supervisor must perform during the course of a typical day in a mass-production industry. It tells us little about the broad aspects of supervision or those factors that determine effective supervisory performance. Sandia Corporation of Albuquerque, New Mexico, wanted to know the independent dimensions, or factors, of administrative and general supervisory positions. Four hundred and fourteen supervisors were asked to write an essay describing the performance of the best supervisor that they knew at Sandia Corporation. The descriptive statements were tabulated and a questionnaire containing 303 items describing supervisory performance was constructed. Three hundred and seventy-two supervisors then applied this questionnaire as a checklist to develop a descriptive rating of the best and the worst supervisor they knew. These ratings were analyzed by means of multiple-factor analysis, and six independent dimensions of supervisory performance were obtained: [10]

1. Establishment of work climate.
2. Management ethics.
3. Self-development and subordinate development.
4. Personal maturity and sensitivity.
5. Knowledge and execution of corporate policies.
6. Technical job knowledge.

---

[10] Sherwood H. Peres, "Performance Dimensions of Supervisory Positions," *Personnel Psychology,* Vol. XV (Winter, 1962), pp. 405-410. Seven factors were isolated; however, the seventh factor is a bias factor resulting from the halo effect present in rating scales. It is not a true factor of supervisory performance.

Establishment of Work Climate. Descriptive statements characteristic of this factor are: expects a day's work, disciplines when necessary, and expects only the best. A supervisor rating high in this respect establishes and maintains high performance standards. He is goal oriented and if necessary will put the attainment of stated objectives above the likes and dislikes of subordinates.

Management Ethics. The essence of this dimension is ethical behavior on the part of a supervisor in his dealings with other supervisors and members of top management. The same ethical behavior is also shown in his relationships with subordinates. Statements characterizing this trait are: gives credit where due, honest in discussing development of subordinates, no under-the-table deals, and doesn't promise anything he can't do.

Self-Development and Subordinate Development. The effective supervisor is interested in personnel development—the growth of subordinates as well as his own. He attempts to make assignments interesting and challenging and tries to know his subordinates better so that he may direct their growth. He encourages outside study and pursues such activity himself. He tries to keep up with the professional aspects of management through reading and participation in outside groups.

Personal Maturity and Sensitivity. Two elements are closely related in this factor; one is personal maturity and emotional stability, and the other is empathy—a sensitivity to the feelings of others. Supervisors strong in this dimension of performance maintain an "open door" policy, they have a knack of saying the right thing at the right time, do not lose control under pressure, and seem to lighten serious situations with their sense of humor.

Knowledge and Execution of Corporate Policies. Note that knowledge of policy is not sufficient; there must also be execution of policy. Strong supervisors keep up with changes in policy and procedures and keep their subordinates informed of such changes. Those strong in this characteristic are orderly and tend to follow the "letter of the law." The result of this trait is that it gives a supervisor's behavior consistency and predictability.

Technical Job Knowledge. This dimension of supervision suggests not only technical knowledge but also the drive and willingness to get the job done. The supervisor has sufficient background and information to understand new problem quickly. He is technically competent and does more than is expected of him.

The "Linking-Pin" Function

The legal definition of a supervisor cited at the beginning of this chapter details only the relationships between a supervisor and his subordinates. If questioned, many managers would also answer that a supervisor's job is to direct the work of those who report to him. The breadth of contacts of the assembly-line foreman shows the narrowness and inadequacy of a definition that stresses the direction of subordinates. Only 26 percent of the assembly foreman's time is spent in contact with personnel under his direction; the balance of his time is in contact with superiors, service personnel, other foremen, and operators other than his own who contribute to the work of his department.

The analysis of supervisory positions at Sandia Corporation reveals that successful performance requires a person capable of much more than directing the efforts of others. Successful performance requires a structuring of the work situation; ethical behavior in personal relationships with superiors, peers, and subordinates; and effective execution of company policy. Further, the supervisor sees himself as a calm, moderate, judicial person.

The key to the supervisor's primary function is his unique position in the organization—the only member of management in direct contact with nonmanagerial personnel. He is the one member of management capable of linking management to operative personnel. For this reason his major function is best described as a *linking-pin* function.[11]

SELECTION AND TRAINING OF SUPERVISORS

Now that we have some insight into the nature of the supervisor's job, let us examine some of the problems associated with the selection and training of supervisors.

Selection of Supervisors

As the first step in the selection of personnel for any position in an organization, whether it be the job of janitor or president, it is necessary to know the job requirements for the position in question. One way of stating job requirements is by preparing a job description such as those shown in Chapter 15. However, the usual job description with its statement of responsibilities and duties to be performed leaves much to be desired as a measure of personal characteristics needed to

---

11 Rensis Likert, *op. cit.,* p. 113.

meet the demands of a given position. What is needed is a statement of job requirements using a terminology applicable to both the job and its incumbent. A *job complexity profile* performs both functions.[12]

Job Complexity Profile. Based upon several hundred interviews with supervisors at different levels of many organizations, psychologists have come to the conclusion that supervisory positions—and also executive jobs in the upper levels of management—require six different activities for their successful performance. These activities, arranged in approximate chronological sequence, are:

1. Planning an activity.
2. Deciding what to do or not to do.
3. Organizing a group of persons to carry out the plans.
4. Communicating the plan to the organization.
5. Leading a group to fulfill the plan.
6. Analyzing progress being made so that plans may be revised if necessary.

These are not discrete independent activities; instead, one leads into another and several may be performed at the same time. Their value is that they are readily understandable and can be used to describe both job requirements and the personal qualifications of any candidate being considered for the job. Each job is analyzed and graded on a 16-point scale for each of these activities in the same manner that jobs are rated in a job evaluation program.

When presented in profile form, the factors are rearranged and abbreviated so that they appear in the following order: plan, communicate, analyze, lead, delegate, and decide. The first three activities— planning, communicating, and analyzing—draw upon the intellectual capabilities of a person. Planning requires the ability to reason, to perceive relationships; communicating requires verbal skills and the ability to express ideas that range from the simple to the very complex; and analyzing, as the term is used here, is dependent upon the ability to understand mathematical relationships. There are very few managerial

---

[12] Harold F. Rothe, "Matching Men to Job Requirements," *Personnel Psychology,* Vol. IV (Autumn, 1951), pp. 291-301. A detailed statement of job complexity analysis may be obtained from Dr. Rothe, or the author, or Stevenson, Jordan, and Harrison, Inc., 205 W. Wacker Drive, Chicago. Similar approaches to the analysis of jobs have been prepared by L. R. Gaiennie and J. C. Flanagan.

L. R. Gaiennie, "An Approach to Supervisory Organization Control in Industry," *Personnel Psychology,* Vol. III (Spring, 1950), pp. 41-52.

J. C. Flanagan, "A New Approach to Evaluating Personnel," *Personnel Psychology,* Vol. XXVI (July, 1949), pp. 35-42.

jobs not requiring the ability to understand numerical concepts. The next three activities—lead, delegate, and decide—demand certain personality characteristics for their performance. Leadership is defined primarily in terms of the degree of social dominance or aggressiveness required and is dependent to a large extent upon the characteristics of the group being led. Delegation requires a sense of personal security and the willingness to accept responsibility for the work of others. The making of decisions is considered as dependent upon personality, not the intellectual ability of planning and arriving at a "correct" solution. To decide is to make a mature, responsible choice and be willing to follow that choice through to its conclusion. It is the characteristic of decisiveness.

Figure 19-1 shows the job profiles for the positions of section supervisor, general supervisor, and superintendent of a manufacturing firm. Note the requirements for leadership and delegation of the general superintendent position. The size of the group being led is large and heterogeneous, and leadership must be accomplished by working through several levels of supervision. The section foreman does very little delegating and his group is relatively homogeneous in character, conditions that require only an average ability to lead and to delegate. The personal qualifications of a candidate, also shown in Figure 19-1, may be matched against the requirements of the job as an aid in making the final choice in the selection process. One of the methods used in preparing the personal qualification profile of the candidate is discussed later in this chapter under the heading, "The Personnel Evaluation."

Sources of Supervision. Most companies fill vacancies in supervisory ranks by promoting personnel from hourly jobs; however, some supervisors are recruited from other companies, and there is a growing tendency to recruit college graduates for these positions. Promotion from within aids in building the morale of an organization since it satisfies employee needs for recognition and mobility. In addition, there is reasonable assurance that the candidate has the necessary technical knowledge and skills for the position. When supervisors are sought from other companies, it is usually because an organization is in a period of rapid expansion and does not have a sufficient number of trained hourly personnel.

Companies that promote from within may be able to identify the successful supervisor rather early in his career and establish a pool of potential supervisors through the use of peer (buddy) ratings. Weitz investigated the use of peer ratings as a means of identifying supervisors

Figure 19-1

COMPARISON OF QUALIFICATIONS OF ONE CANDIDATE WITH REQUIREMENTS OF THREE JOBS

Source: Harold F. Rothe, "Matching Men to Job Requirements," *Personnel Psychology,* Vol. IV (Autumn, 1951), p. 297.

prior to their promotion to supervisory positions.[13] The company in question was a large insurance company with 2,200 agents (salesmen) in 127 sales districts. Each district was headed by a district manager who had reporting to him several assistant managers. Each assistant manager supervised an average of four agents. Each agent rated the other agents with whom he worked by completing a questionnaire; total scores for each agent were then computed and for those promoted to assistant manager the scores were later compared with ratings obtained in supervisory positions. Weitz concludes that there are characteristics which differentiate between successful and unsuccessful supervisors and that these characteristics can be identified prior to promotion to a supervisory position by obtaining ratings from peers performing the same nonsupervisory job.

College graduates may be recruited and assigned supervisory positions in several different departments as part of a training program designed to acquaint them with the various phases of a company's operations. The graduate generally spends three to six months in a department as an assistant supervisor and is then assigned to another section. Upon completion of the training program, which usually takes two years, he may be assigned full supervisory responsibilities. The college-trained supervisor who has the personality characteristics necessary for supervision does surprisingly well despite his lack of technical knowledge. The reason for his success is probably due to his "influence" with upper levels of management.[14] Though presently in a supervisory position of the lowest level of management, he is hired with the expectations of advancing to the upper levels of the organization. His subordinates are aware of his potential in the company and, if they perceive his influence with his superiors and like him personally, they supply the necessary technical knowledge. Subordinates are also capable of making the trainee appear a dismal failure.

Selection Methods. The methods used in selecting supervisors range from an informal interview to the highly sophisticated personnel evaluation. Each of the tools used in selection is capable of contributing to the selection process, provided it is used with skill and there is a clear

---

[13] Joseph Weitz, "Selecting Supervisors with Peer Ratings," *Personnel Psychology*, Vol. XI (Spring, 1958), pp. 25-35. Weitz's article contains the questionnaire used by insurance agents in nominating their peers for supervisory positions and the rating form used by district managers which served as the criterion for the study.

[14] Donald C. Pelz, "Influence: A Key to Effective Leadership in the First-Line Supervisor," *Personnel*, Vol. XXIX (November, 1952), pp. 209-217. This study of employee attitudes of employees of the Detroit Edison Company shows the importance of influence as a factor in effective supervision.

concept of the requirements of the job. In our discussion of the methods used in selecting supervisors, it is assumed that the candidate is from within the organization; however, the same methods are applicable to the selection of personnel from outside the company.

THE INTERVIEW. In its simplest form, an interview is an informal discussion between the candidate and a general supervisor or a representative of the personnel department in which the candidate is informed that there is a supervisory position available and is asked whether or not he would like the job. With this form of interview there is little opportunity to learn more about the candidate, nor does he have much opportunity of becoming acquainted with the advantages and disadvantages of the job. The interview should provide a free exchange of information so that the candidate knows fully the requirements and opportunities of the position. At the same time, the interviewer should attempt to understand the motivation of the candidate in seeking the position and form an estimate of the personal characteristics of the candidate. A series of interviews conducted by present members of supervision and upper levels of management is often helpful when the impressions gained from the interviews are compared so that the best judgment of the group can be determined. Having the candidate appear before a group offers the possibility of observing his reactions to the pressures of an unfamiliar situation and inferences may be drawn concerning the way in which he might react under the stress of a supervisory job. The interview is a good means of assessing speech, gestures, personal appearance, persuasiveness, and the sincerity of a potential supervisor.

COMPANY RECORDS. Job titles of previous positions held in the company indicate the breadth of technical skills and knowledge that may have been acquired by the candidate. Previous jobs also show rate of progress, and from the pattern of progression certain inferences may be drawn in regard to the candidate's ability and interests. If the company has a merit rating plan, the record of merit reviews should also be examined and summarized. The application form completed at the time of employment usually provides information pertaining to age, education, prior experience, community activities, and other outside interests. Personal history items recorded in the application for employment should be supplemented with current information concerning outside activities and interests at the time of the interview.

TESTING PROGRAMS. Psychological tests may be used as part of the total program for selecting supervisors. When tests are used, the test battery usually includes a measure of intelligence, interests, personality, and mechanical or other special aptitudes. The usefulness of tests depends upon the skill of the interpreter and the extent to which the tests have been validated for the particular job in question. If the company has administered the test battery to its present supervisors and has found a clear relationship between performance on the job and performance on the tests, then the tests are considered valid; i.e., they measure what they purport to measure.[15] If a validating procedure has not been carried out, the use of tests borders on wishful thinking. All too frequently management looks to tests as a magic formula for improving supervisory performance, yet the real reason for inadequate performance is usually in the design of the supervisor's job, not the capabilities of the supervisor.[16]

THE PERSONNEL EVALUATION. The personnel evaluation—or as it is sometimes called, the psychological evaluation—is of special value in the selection process when a candidate is being considered for a position requiring skills and abilities he has not had the opportunity to demonstrate, or when a man is being recruited from another company. The personnel evaluation is an extensive analysis in depth conducted by a professional psychologist who has had training in both clinical and industrial psychology. The evaluation may begin with the development of a personal history that includes education, prior vocational experience, early life, aspirations, and views on current problems. A brief intelligence test may be administered to check the present level of intellectual functioning against work history items and educational background. Personality characteristics are usually evaluated by means of the Rorschach test (see Chapter 16, "Leadership Patterns") or the Murray Thematic Apperception Test.[17] From the information thus obtained, the psychologist is able to describe in dynamic, motivational terms the personality structure and function of the candidate. If the psychologist is familiar with the demands of the job in question, a combined job-man profile may be constructed as in Figure 19-1, page 494.

---

[15] Hubert Clay, "Experiences in Testing Foremen," *Personnel*, Vol. XXVIII (May, 1952), pp. 466-470. Dr. Clay presents a step-by-step approach to the introduction of a testing program for the selection of supervisors. He discusses the reaction of supervisors to tests and makes suggestions for the interpretation of test results.

[16] Mason Haire, "Use of Tests in Employee Selection," *Harvard Business Review*, Vol. 28 (January-February, 1950), pp. 42-51. Professor Haire discusses the difficulties of establishing a testing program and reviews many of the problems of performance that are not related to the capabilities of employees but which are the result of the structure of the situation in which they are working.

[17] Henry A. Murray, *Thematic Apperception Test Manual* (Cambridge, Mass.: Harvard University Press, 1943).

The worth of the personnel evaluation is dependent upon the clinical judgment and skill of the psychologist and management's insight into the demands of the job.[18]

A COMPOSITE APPROACH. The following suggested procedure combines each of the methods above into an integrated selection process.

1. Prepare a job complexity profile of the position to be filled. It is essential that the traditional job description be rephrased so that personal requirements and job requirements are clearly understood.
2. A trained representative of the personnel department should compile and summarize all available company records for each candidate.
3. Separate interviews with each candidate should be conducted by interested supervisors and personnel from other levels of management. The impressions gained from these interviews should be stated in written form.
4. An interview conducted by a group may be desirable as a check on the impressions gained from individual interviews and as a means of observing the candidate under moderate pressure.
5. If the personnel department is adequately staffed with professionally trained personnel, psychological tests may be utilized. If the personnel department is not adequately staffed, psychological tests should not be used in the selection of supervisors.
6. A personnel evaluation prepared by a professionally trained psychologist may be obtained for each candidate. The confidential report prepared by the psychologist should be sent to the personnel department or to a member of top management.
7. The personnel department should prepare a written record of all proceedings (including company records, test results, interview impressions, and the personnel evaluation) and forward the applicant's completed file to the appropriate line executive for final decision.

Training of Supervisors

"You could dispose of almost all the leadership training courses for supervision in American industry today without anyone knowing the difference." [19]

The above statement, made by Robert H. Guest, is not intended as a criticism of the content or methods of leadership training programs

---

[18] Charles D. McDermid, "The Psychological Evaluation," *Advanced Management-Office Executive,* Vol. I (November, 1962), pp. 22, 23-25. Dr. McDermid's article is one of the very few descriptive statements of the personnel evaluation written by a professional psychologist.

[19] Robert H. Guest, *op. cit.,* p. 478.

for supervisors; instead, it is intended to emphasize that the conditions of the supervisor's job—refer to Tables 19-1, 19-2, and 19-3—are often such that it is difficult, if not impossible, to exercise the type of leadership expected. Despite the very real limitations on supervisory leadership imposed by the structure of the job, much effort and money are spent on supervisory training. In addition to training in leadership, programs are designed to improve other skills necessary for effective supervision.

The content of supervisory training programs is geared to the needs of the supervisor. Thus, there is considerable variation in content and method from one organization to another and within the same organization from one level of supervision to another. Figure 19-2 shows a useful classification proposed by Georgopoulus and Mann of the skills needed for supervision.[20] Note that the range of supervisory positions

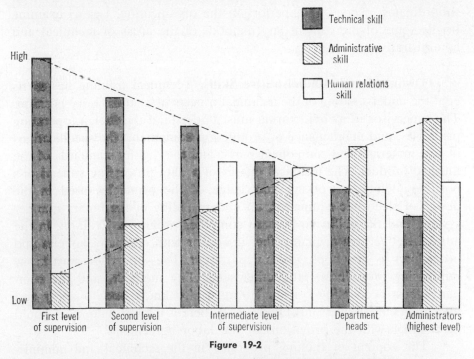

Figure 19-2

RELATIVE IMPORTANCE OF DIFFERENT SUPERVISORY SKILLS

Source: Basil S. Georgopoulus and Floyd C. Mann, *The Community General Hospital* (New York: The Macmillan Company, 1962), p. 431.

---

[20] Basil S. Georgopoulus and Floyd C. Mann, *The Community General Hospital* (New York: The Macmillan Company, 1962), Chapter 9. Reprinted in Robert A. Sutermeister, *People and Productivity* (New York: McGraw-Hill Book Company, Inc., 1963), pp. 381-385.

included in Figure 19-2 is from the first level of supervision, through department heads, and includes the highest level of administrators. With each step upward in the organizational hierarchy, the "mix" of supervisory skills changes. Technical skills are the skills and knowledge necessary for the performance of a given supervisory position in a specific industry. For the first-line supervisor, technical skills include the knowledge and skill required to perform jobs at the operational level. He must know the technology of his industry so that he can train the operators working for him. Administrative skills require a concept of the entire organizational system and the coordination of the component parts of the system. Planning, organizing, assigning work, and the establishment and exercise of necessary controls are administrative skills. For the first-line supervisor these skills are relatively less important than the technical and human relations skills. Human relations skills require a knowledge of the principles of behavior and an ability to work with subordinates, peers, and superiors in the organization. Let us examine briefly some of the content and methods of the areas of technical and administrative training.

Technical and Administrative Skills. Technical training has as its goal the understanding of the technical aspects of a supervisory position. The supervisor in manufacturing must understand the design, operating principles, and maintenance of production equipment; the specifications of raw materials and component parts; and the quality standards of the finished product. The technical phases of a data processing supervisor's position include a working knowledge of the principles used in the design of electronic equipment, an understanding of the binary number system, and the ability to prepare computer programs. Training in the administrative area acquaints the supervisor with company policies and procedures as they apply to his department. The supervisor must know purchasing procedures, production scheduling methods, and the company's cost accounting system. He must also know how to apply and interpret company personnel policies. If there is a labor union, he should be familiar with the provisions of the labor agreement.

The content of training programs in the technical and administrative areas is dependent upon the technology and administrative procedures of each individual company. As a result, most training programs are designed and conducted internally. There is little reliance upon outside agencies. The methods used are traditional in nature and rely heavily upon written materials such as technical manuals and statements of company policy and procedure. Formal classes are held at periodic intervals and may be supplemented by departmental meetings. In many large companies supervisors are furnished bound volumes of company policies and operating procedures to serve as a basis for technical and administrative decisions.

Training in Human Relations. Training in human relations poses problems not present in the development of skills in the technical and administrative fields. First, there is no concise definition of subject matter to be mastered. Second, there is typically a marked disparity between responses given in answer to written questions and the ability to transfer knowledge into effective supervisory patterns. Third, training in human relations requires the use of teaching methods quite different from those employed in the technical and administrative areas. Training programs in human relations stress: (1) communications, with particular emphasis placed on empathetic listening—the perception of the meaning and feeling of communications from subordinates, (2) the making of decisions involving people based upon the perceptions gained from empathetic listening, and (3) overcoming resistance to change, usually through the use of a participative leadership style.

Training Methods in Human Relations. In this section we present a brief overview of the methods used in human relations training and review experimental studies illustrative of specific problems in human relations encountered by all supervisors. The methods used in developing skills in human relations include the *case method,* the *incident process,* and *role playing.* Each of these methods is discussed briefly below.

CASE METHOD. The case method of leadership training utilizes case problems much like those contained in this book. The case problem usually sets forth a sequence of events in such a manner that a question calling for a solution is posed. Or, as in Case Problem 19-A, No Smoking, the solution is provided as part of the case and the learner is asked to evaluate the given solution. In order to solve a case problem it is necessary to acquaint the participant with the principles or procedures to be applied, a task usually accomplished by lectures or assigned readings. Case problems should describe a situation that is part of the learner's background or a situation that is understandable to all learners. The case method arouses greater interest than that created by answering questions not related to a specific situation. Also, a case problem offers a chance to apply the principles and methods to be learned. Thus, the case problem offers an opportunity to increase interest, to participate in discussion, and to illustrate the application of principles, policies, or methods to simulated or real situations.

INCIDENT PROCESS METHOD. The incident process method, a variation of the case method, is used in small discussion groups. If Case Problem 19-A were rewritten as an incident, the incident described could be the fact that the foreman discharged a worker for violating the no smoking regulations of the company. A bare statement of the facts—discharge for violation of a no smoking rule—cannot be evaluated without additional information. In the incident method, participants draw from the discussion leader all the information necessary to make a sound evaluation of the action taken and to recommend alternative courses that might have been available. Skill in questioning is developed by the incident method and experience is gained in gathering information needed for sound decisions in the area of human relations.[21]

ROLE PLAYING. The role playing method offers the advantages of the case method and, in addition, provides training in the perception of the attitudes and feelings of other persons. As the name suggests, role playing is the assignment of a definite role to each member of a training group. There is usually a brief explanation and discussion of the supervisory problem under study prior to the assignment of roles.

Case Problem 19-A may be adapted for role playing in the following manner. The supervisors of the plant in which the smoking incident occurred might attend a company training session concerned with the enforcement of company rules. The rules may be explained, the need for their enforcement stated, and the duties of the union steward described. Following this general session for all supervisors, groups of three or four meet separately and each member of the small groups is assigned a specific role. One is selected to be the supervisor, another the steward, and the remaining members assume the role of the employee in question who, in this instance, acts as an observer and evaluates the effectiveness of the steward in representing his case and the equity of the supervisor's decision. Each member is given a written statement describing the role to be assumed and is not aware of the details of the roles of the others in the group. The supervisor's statement may indicate that he *must* discharge the employee and cite as a reason the fire in a neighboring plant and the need to enforce company rules. He may or may not be informed of the employee's long service record. The steward's role emphasizes that one who violates the rule is only "subject to" discharge, and the long, faithful record of the employee may

---

[21] Paul Pigors and Faith Pigors, *Director's Manual: The Incident Process* (Washington, D. C.: The Bureau of National Affairs, 1955). For a brief article describing the incident method see James L. Centner, "The Incident Process," *Advanced Management*, Vol. XXI (December, 1956), pp. 15-20.

be outlined for the steward. Remaining members of the small group—no more than one or two—are asked to evaluate the behavior of the supervisor and the steward from the standpoint of an employee with a long seniority who has admittedly violated a rule. Roles may be rotated either within the same group or by forming new groups. Either way, each participant has the opportunity to assume the role of the supervisor, the steward, and to evaluate the incident as the employee. Role playing is particularly effective in developing empathy—the understanding of the other person's feelings and attitudes.[22]

Specific Problems in Leadership Training. Let us study in detail two specific problems in the area of leadership training. The first is concerned with discipline; the second, with the effectiveness of training in group decision making.

DISCIPLINE. Maintaining discipline is one of the perennial problems of supervision. In general, there are two approaches to disciplinary problems: (1) a *judicial* approach—determining the rightness or wrongness of an act as defined by a specific rule and applying the penalty prescribed, and (2) a *human relations* approach—an emphasis on problem solving with an ultimate goal of improving the employee's behavior.[23] A judicial approach may be forced upon a supervisor by his superior as intimated in Case Problem 19-A. Some supervisors by reason of personality may be rigid, insecure, and incapable of flexibility. These persons find in the rule and its prescribed penalty a ready-made justification for their own rigidity. Still others would prefer the human relations approach but are fearful of where it may lead—they envision an ultimate state of complete anarchy. The studies described below show how supervisors tend to enforce company rules and point up the need for training in human relations.

The subjects of the study were approximately 500 supervisors from a variety of industries attending the Foremen's Conferences held at the University of Michigan.[24] Following a lecture on attitudes and how to understand them, the supervisors were divided into workshop groups to

22 Norman R. F. Maier and Lester F. Zerfoss, "MRP: A Technique for Training Large Groups of Supervisors and Its Potential Use in Social Research," *Human Relations,* Vol. V (May, 1952), pp. 177-182. This article is a relatively brief statement of the multiple role playing technique. For a more detailed treatment of role playing, see Norman R. F. Maier, Allen R. Solem, and Ayesha A. Maier, *Supervisory and Executive Development, A Manual for Role Playing* (New York: John Wiley & Sons, Inc., 1957).

23 Norman R. F. Maier and Lee E. Danielson, "An Evaluation of Two Approaches to Discipline in Industry," *Journal of Applied Psychology* Vol. XL (October, 1956) pp. 319-323.

24 *Ibid.*

study a "No Smoking" case using the role playing method. Each of the 172 role playing units consisted of three men: the foreman, the steward, and the employee. The case was much like Case Problem 19-A, with one important exception—the penalty for violating the rule was a three-day layoff rather than a discharge. The roles assigned made it clear that a violation of the rule had occurred, the worker knew he had violated the rule, and he knew the penalty involved. The worker acted as an observer in the role playing situation, with the interaction occurring between the foreman and the steward who was instructed to press the worker's case. A 20-minute time limit was placed on the discussion between the foreman and the steward.

Maier and Danielson found that slightly over half of the foremen (52 percent) used the human relations approach and resolved the problem with an adjusted solution not calling for the three-day layoff penalty. Adjusted solutions ranged from no penalty, a warning or reprimand, or a one- or two-day layoff. Thirty-five percent of the foremen followed the judicial approach and found the worker guilty, invoked the penalty, and refused to change their positions. The problem was not settled in the allotted time by 13 percent of the foremen. The human relations approach resulted in greater satisfaction as judged by all three participants with the interviews being of a problem-solving type rather than argumentative, and the worker seemed more satisfied with the actions of the steward and less inclined to restrict future production. In another study the same authors found that only seven percent of the supervisors in a similar role playing situation laid off a worker who violated a safety rule.[25] In the safety case the situation was ambiguous: i.e., the foreman was not sure that the employee, a lineman for a utility company, was wearing his safety belt and the penalty was much more severe—a three-week layoff. Despite the fact that 45 percent of the participants who played the role of the lineman admitted violating the safety rule, only seven percent were laid off in accordance with the prescribed penalty.

These two studies indicate that foremen are inclined to use the human relations approach to discipline. Further, the formulation of strict rules with no latitude in their interpretation poses a dilemma for the supervisor. If he uses his judgment and modifies the penalty, he is not carrying out the wishes of a higher echelon; but if he enforces the letter of the law, he is demonstrating a lack of understanding and harshness toward his subordinates.

---

[25] Lee E. Danielson and Norman R. F. Maier, "Supervisory Problems in Decision Making," *Journal of Applied Psychology,* Vol. XL (October, 1956), pp. 319-323.

TRAINING FOR DECISION MAKING. In another study Maier investigated the effect of training in group decision making.[26] Forty-four role playing groups of supervisors were given an eight-hour presentation of the methods of group decision making. These experimental groups also participated in four hours of discussion that permitted them to ask questions and to express their attitudes toward the role playing problem which was introduced as part of the training. The 36 control groups were given no training in group decision methods, but were given one-half hour of instruction explaining the role playing situation. The problem is a proposed change in method—a change sure to arouse resistance—for a group of three workers who normally rotate three production jobs among themselves at the end of each hour during an eight-hour day. There is a variation in the length of time it takes each man to perform the duties of each position as shown in Table 19-4, Time Per Operation. A methods man has suggested that the work be assigned on a permanent basis as follows: Jack to the first position, Steve to the second position, and Walt to the third position. The reduction in time would amount to 2¼ minutes per cycle, a savings of 17 percent or 80 minutes per eight-hour day. In other words, when compared to the "optimum" solution, the men are now loafing 80 minutes a day.

Table 19-4

TIME PER OPERATION

	Position 1	Position 2	Position 3	Total
Jack	3 min.	4 min.	4½ min.	11½ min.
Walt	3½ min.	3½ min.	3 min.	10 min.
Steve	5 min.	3½ min.	4½ min.	13 min.
				34½ min.

Source: Norman R. F. Maier, "An Experimental Test of the Effect of Training on Discussion Leadership," *Human Relations Journal,* Vol. VI (May, 1953), p. 164. This table was originally published by John Wiley and Sons in Norman R. F. Maier's *Principles of Human Relations,* 1952.

In the role playing situation, the foreman desires to install the solution recommended by the methods man and is met with varying degrees of resistance on the part of each of the three men. The results of the role playing situations for trained and untrained supervisors, Table 19-5—

---

[26] Norman R. F. Maier, "An Experimental Test of the Effect of Training on Discussion Leadership," *Human Relations Journal,* Vol. VI (May, 1953), pp. 161-173.

Table 19-5

PERCENTAGE OF SUCCESSES, FAILURES, AND COMPROMISES OF
TRAINED AND UNTRAINED GROUPS

	Failures	Compromises	Successes
Trained leader	4.5	36.4	59.1
Untrained leader	50.0	0	50.0

Source: Norman R. F. Maier, "An Experimental Test of the Effect of Training on Discussion Leadership," *Human Relations Journal,* Vol. VI (May, 1953), p. 168. This table was originally published by John Wiley and Sons in Norman R. F. Maier's *Principles of Human Relations,* 1952.

Percentage of Successes, Failures, and Compromises of Trained and Untrained Groups, shows clearly the effect of training. Only 4½ percent of the trained foremen experience failure—with failure being defined as no solution, no change, or open rebellion against the foreman's imposed solution. On the other hand, 50 percent of the untrained leaders experienced failure. However, the striking result is that the untrained leaders did not produce a single compromise. It must be pointed out that many of the compromise solutions might in practice be the "optimum" or best solution, since the compromises contained varying plans for rotation of jobs in order to minimize the adverse effects of monotony and boredom on production.

IMPROVING SUPERVISORY PERFORMANCE

In Chapter 18, "Motivating Employees," it is stated that no consistent relationship is found between measures of employee morale and productivity. Fortunately there is a distinct positive relationship between supervisory practices and productivity. There are many characteristics of effective supervisory action; however, four stand out above all others. The first factor determining effective supervision, *organizational climate,* is largely beyond the control of the supervisor and determines how effectively he may exercise the other three characteristics of sound supervision. Good practices in *delegation,* the second factor, are necessary for effective supervision. The third requisite for an effective supervisor is an orientation toward his job, which is best described as a *systems* orientation with equal emphasis upon production and people. The fourth requirement is an ability to use *employee participation* skillfully as a means of introducing change. Each of these characteristics is discussed below.

Organizational Climate

The quotation from Guest's "Of Time and the Foreman," appearing at the beginning of the preceding section on training, dramatizes the limiting effects of organizational climate upon the efficacy of training. Fleishman also emphasizes the limitations of training unless the "leadership climate" is such that the supervisor can readily put to use his newly found skills.[27] Organizational or leadership climate is made up of the attitudes and practices of top management and is reflected by the extent that management practices delegation, the degree that they recognize the organization as a system, and their use of participation as a method of introducing change. Yet the chief advantage gained by a supervisor from the organizational climate created by his superiors is *influence* or power within his own department.

Pelz and others of the University of Michigan's Survey Research Center show that a supervisor's influence or power has a great deal to do with productivity and employee satisfaction.[28] In work groups having high production records, promotions recommended by supervisors were generally approved by higher management; or no recommendations were made at all. On the other hand, the supervisors of low-producing groups frequently made recommendations for promotion that were not approved by higher authority. Three factors seem to contribute most to a supervisor's influence: (1) the contribution that he makes to decisions made by his superior, (2) the freedom and autonomy that he possesses in the operation of his own department, and (3) his salary, interpreting salary as a measure of responsibility and status within the organization. Note that these conditions determining the amount of supervisory influence are not the direct result of a supervisor's actions within his own department or something that may be asked for and received; but rather, these traits of influence are a reflection of the supervisor's position and status in the organization—the result of organizational climate.

Improved Delegation

One of the keys to effective supervision, as measured by productivity and employee satisfaction, is the ability to delegate

---

[27] Edwin A. Fleishman, Edwin F. Harris, and Harold E. Burtt, "Leadership and Supervision in Industry." Reprinted in Robert A. Sutermeister, *People and Productivity* (New York: McGraw-Hill Book Company, Inc., 1963), pp. 410-425. This reading is a re-edited and up-to-date version of Chapter 9 of *Leadership and Supervision in Industry* (Columbus, Ohio: Bureau of Educational Research, Ohio State University, 1955) by the same authors.

[28] Donald C. Pelz, *op. cit.*

responsibility to subordinates and to allow as much leeway in the performance of assigned duties as the situation permits. Improvement in delegation requires that the supervisor have a clear perception of his role as leader and that he make a careful determination of how closely he should follow and oversee the work of subordinates. Let us discuss, first, the differentiation of the supervisor's role.

Differentiating the Supervisor's Role. Drs. Robert L. Kahn and Daniel Katz, in a summary of much of the work of the Survey Research Center of the University of Michigan, report that supervisors of groups with high production records assume a role that is more differentiated from the work of those supervised than the role assumed by the supervisors of low-producing work groups.[29] High-producing supervisors perform those tasks traditionally associated with the managerial functions of planning, organizing, directing, and controlling. The differentiation between the task of the worker and the supervisor begins with the supervisor's perception of himself as a member of management and an understanding of the functions of management; at the same time, subordinates have an unusually acute perception of what their supervisor is doing in comparison to what he should be doing. The supervisory task perceived most readily by subordinates is that of planning the work to be done. Members of high-producing railroad section gangs and departments in a tractor manufacturing company rate their supervisors as superior in planning work, providing materials, and watching or supervising the performance of the work. Supervisors with better than average production records also spend more time than their low-producing counterparts in solving the interpersonal problems arising in the work group. Low-producing supervisors are prone to get lost in paper work and spend too much of their time doing the same type of work performed by subordinates. Supervisory tasks include not only the planning function but also on-the-job training.

Closeness of Supervision. The supervisor who spends most of his time performing those tasks normally associated with supervision is delegating authority and assigning responsibility and, in the case of hourly workers, it is primarily the assignment of responsibility to perform work. However, the delegator still remains accountable to his superior for the performance of the assigned duties. Close supervision is associated with excessively detailed instructions, constant checking

---

29 Robert L. Kahn and Daniel Katz, "Leadership Practices in Relation to Productivity and Morale," from Derwin Cartwright and Alvin Zander (eds.), *Group Dynamics, Research and Theory* (New York: Harper and Row, Publishers, Incorporated, 1961), pp. 554-570.

on progress, and insistence that all decisions be approved before being put into effect. However, a careful engineering of the work to be performed and the establishment and exercise of necessary controls to assure proper progress are not considered excessively close supervision; instead, they are part of the normal supervisory function. Closeness of supervision refers primarily to the personal conduct of the supervisor, and when supervision becomes too close, it is a reflection of the supervisor's own insecurity and inability to delegate.

In studies of clerical workers in an insurance company and production workers manufacturing tractors, it is found that there is an inverse relationship between closeness of supervision and productivity; i.e., the closer the supervision, the lower the productivity. Also, the closeness of supervision has a great deal to do with the three factorial dimensions of employee morale. Employees not closely supervised are more likely to have a high degree of satisfaction with their jobs, their supervisors, and the company than those who are closely supervised. However, there is evidence that closeness of supervision is in many instances a reflection of the type of supervision received by the supervisor. If a superior fully delegates authority, the supervisor is likely to do the same; but when he is closely supervised, it is difficult for him to delegate as freely as he should. Thus, organizational climate exerts its influence on the supervisor's ability to delegate effectively.

A Systems Orientation

Much has been written about supervisors being either production-centered or employee-centered in respect to attitudes concerning the work of their departments and their subordinates. Early research in the area of job satisfaction and morale implicitly assumed that the orientation of the supervisor is best described in terms of a continuum with production-centered concepts at one pole and employee-centered concepts at the other extreme. However, later studies, particularly those conducted at the tractor company, cast doubt upon the usefulness of a continuum as a model for describing supervisory orientation. High-producing workers at the tractor company reported, as might be expected, that their supervisor took an interest in them, that they got along well with him, and that he was easy to talk to. Yet, they also stated that production was important to their supervisor and that he supervised them in such a manner that he saw to it that production standards were met—a situation quite impossible to describe on a continuum model.

Dr. Robert L. Kahn suggests that we use a four-celled table to describe the orientation of the supervisor.[30] In one cell are those supervisors who are high in their interest in production and at the same time have a high interest in the welfare of their employees. Another cell would best describe those with a high orientation toward production but low in employee-centered attitudes. The third square would fit those low in production but high in employee-centered interests. The fourth possibility consists of those supervisors with low interests in both production and employees. In effect, the four-celled table represents a systems orientation, with the most effective supervisor recognizing simultaneously the goals and needs of the organization and its members.

At first glance it may seem quite impossible to be production-centered and employee-centered at one and the same time, but such is not the case. Martin Patchen suggests that in order to achieve morale and at the same time a high level of productivity, the supervisor must do three things.[31] First, he must make it clear that he expects high but realistic and attainable standards of performance. By so doing he establishes the tenor of the operation. Second, he must have the power to deliver appropriate rewards or punishment if his statement of goals is to mean anything. Third, the supervisor must demonstrate to the satisfaction of his subordinates that he is capable of using this power effectively. One of the best ways of demonstrating a wise use of power and influence is a willingness to "go to bat" for a subordinate when the need arises. Obviously a supervisor does not stand alone in carrying out the suggestions of Patchen; he is part of a larger organization, and the management he represents must create the climate that will enable him to exercise effectively a systems orientation toward production and subordinates.

Participation and Change

Overcoming resistance to change is a problem confronting all levels of supervision. The proposed change in method or content may have little direct effect upon the worker's ability to perform his job, or the change may be of such a nature that the learning of new skills or the transfer of existing skills to a new work situation is required. Regardless of the amount or type of change, there are varying degrees of resistance that are manifested by an extremely long period of time to learn the new job, open expressions of hostility toward management,

[30] Robert L. Kahn, "Productivity and Job Satisfaction," *Personnel Psychology*, Vol. XIII (Autumn, 1960), pp. 275-287.
[31] Martin Patchen, "Supervisory Methods and Group Performance Norms," *Administrative Science Quarterly*, Vol. VII (December, 1962), pp. 275-293.

or an increase in the number of voluntary terminations of employment. One explanation that has been offered for resistance to change is that the rate of learning for the new job is inhibited because of its similarity to the old job. For example, an expert typist might experience greater difficulty initially in learning the finger movements required in playing a piano than one with no skill in typing. However, research indicates that resistance is caused by psychological factors and may be controlled by using participation when introducing change.[32]

The Coch and French experiments concerning resistance to change were conducted in the Marion, Virginia, plant of the Harwood Manufacturing Company, a garment manufacturer. Harwood's employees are paid on a piece-rate incentive system, with 60 units representing the standard production for one hour. Further, the company normally tries to cushion the effects of change by conducting orientation programs and by paying a special bonus to those affected by change. Despite these efforts, any change in production methods usually results in failure to meet production standards in the same length of time required by a new employee to learn the job, an increase in the number of resignations, and expressions of hostility toward the management of the company.

In the experiments, four groups of employees were studied. Group One, the control group, had the change introduced in the usual fashion, with no participation on the part of employees in the change. However, the reasons for the change were presented to them in a meeting. Group Two elected representatives who participated in developing the change and were trained as "special operators" to work out the details of the change prior to its being adopted by the entire group. In Groups Three and Four, the total participation groups, all employees participated from the very beginning in developing the need for the change and working out the details of how the changed jobs should be performed. Though the changes made in the jobs varied for each group, they were comparable and minor in nature. Group One, pajama pressers, formerly stacked their finished work in lots of one-half dozen on pieces of cardboard. The change required them to stack their finished work in one-half dozen lots in boxes. The change for Group Two consisted of an alteration in the method of folding pajama coats, while the change for Groups Three and Four, inspectors, required that only certain threads be cut from the garment and an inspection of all seams instead of cutting all loose threads and inspecting all seams.

---

[32] Lester Coch and John R. P. French, "Overcoming Resistance to Change," *Human Relations,* Vol. I (August, 1948), pp. 512-532. This study contains a discussion of the theoretical aspects of resistance to change as well as reporting in detail the results of the experiments.

Resistance developed in the control group immediately. There was conflict with the methods engineer, grievances were filed, and 17 percent of the group quit during the first 40 days after the change. As a group they did not reach the standard of 60 units an hour. Group Two, the one with elected representation, produced 61 units per hour at the end of 14 days; also, there was only one act of aggression against a supervisor and no layoffs during the first 40 days after the change. The two total participation groups recovered faster than the representation group. There was a slight drop in production on the first day of change, but production immediately rose to 14 percent above prechange levels. There were no acts of aggression, nor were there any quits during the first 40 days. At a later date, the remaining members of the control group were reassembled as a unit and a change was introduced in their work; but this time they participated in the change. As expected, the group performed in the same manner as the total participation group of the first experiment.

The results of these experiments are clear—participation reduces resistance to change. Yet, two limitations must be presented. The use of participative methods in the introduction of change is not a decision made by the supervisor; instead, it is an expression of organizational climate. The second limitation is that at the present time there is no record of the experience of a company that has used total participation as a means of introducing change over an extended period of time. Thus, the question arises as to how effective participation would be as a means of overcoming resistance to change if it were a normal operating procedure.

PRINCIPLE OF SUPERVISION

Underlying the effectiveness of supervision is the organizational climate in which the supervisor works. Chief among the benefits coming from the organization is the supervisor's influence, which is a function of his position in the management group. Effective supervision requires the supervisor to differentiate his role from that of subordinates and to perform those functions normally associated with the management process—planning, organizing, directing, and controlling. He must improve his ability to delegate and offer subordinates the maximum opportunity to exercise discretion and freedom in the performance of their jobs. His orientation toward production and people must be balanced with equal emphasis upon both. Finally, the use of participative methods when introducing change affords an opportunity to minimize resistance to change. Throughout the process of supervision the supervisor is a member of two groups. He is a member of management and at the same time the leading member of the work group. His is a "linking-pin" function. Best results, as defined by the level of employee morale and production, are obtained when the supervisor performs a supportive role and encourages employees so that the satisfaction of individual needs for growth, recognition, and achievement may serve as motivators.[33] The principle of supervision, an application of our knowledge of motivation and supervisory practices, is stated below.

Principle of Supervision { Effective supervision is recognized by subordinates as supportive in nature and results in the maximum satisfaction of employee needs in the attainment of individual and organizational goals.

Case Problem 19-B, The New Truck Problem, is different from the other cases you have analyzed in that its solution calls for role playing.[34] You may be asked to assume the role of the foreman or one of the repairmen. If you are not a participant, you will be asked to observe and evaluate the decision made by the foreman.

---

[33] Rensis Likert, *op. cit.* See Chapter 8, "An Integrating Principle and an Overview," pp. 97-118. Likert's integrating principle is stated as follows: "The leadership and other processes of the organization must be such as to ensure a maximum probability that in all interactions and all relationships with the organization each member will, in the light of his background, values, and expectations, view the experience as supportive and one which builds and maintains his sense of personal worth and importance." p. 103.

[34] *Note to Instructor:* Since role playing requires that the participants be unaware of the hidden motivations of other participants in the role playing situation, the roles of the members of the repair crew are not included in the case. They may be found in the instructor's manual and should be reproduced on separate sheets of paper and distributed to each member of the group prior to the role playing.

Questions for Study and Discussion

1. The supervisor has been described as being "the man in the middle." Is this characterization borne out by the two legal definitions of the supervisor? How?

2. What inferences could you make concerning the organizational climate of a company whose supervisors petitioned for a union of their own? As a member of middle or top management, what action would you recommend upon receiving notification of such petition?

3. What is the relationship between the results of Porter's study of how supervisors perceive themselves and the description of a typical day of a supervisor as provided by Walker, Turner, and Guest? Why does such a relationship exist?

4. Recognizing that most supervisors are promoted from the hourly ranks, why is there such a cleavage between the way in which the hourly worker describes himself and the manner in which the supervisor sees himself?

5. Discuss and give an example showing the significance of each of the dimensions of supervisory performance as described by Peres.

6. What is meant by the "linking-pin" function? How is this function related to the supervisor's position in the organization? Is it of significance in the motivation of employees? How?

7. Discuss the advantages and disadvantages of each of the several sources of supervision.

8. Describe and evaluate a composite approach to the selection of supervisors showing the contribution of each selection method that is utilized.

9. Comment on the following statement: "You could dispose of almost all of the leadership training courses for supervision in American industry today without anyone knowing the difference."

10. Describe and give an example illustrating the methods commonly used for training in human relations.

11. Define in your own terms the meaning of organizational climate.

12. Evaluate each of the factors that contributes to a supervisor's influence. Which do you believe to be the most important? Relate the concept of influence and the performance of college graduates in training positions.

13. What major factor limits the applicability of participation as a means of introducing change? What is the next step if the employees fail to see the need for change?

"General Instructions for Crew.

"You are repairmen for a large company and drive to various locations in the city to do your work. Each of you drives a small truck and you take pride in keeping it looking good. You have a possessive feeling about your trucks and like to keep them in good running order. Naturally, you like to have new trucks, too, because a new truck gives you a feeling of pride.

"Here are some of the facts about the trucks and the men in the crews who report to Walt Marshall, the supervisor of repairs.

"George—17 years with the company, has a 2-year-old Ford truck.

"Bill—11 years with the company, has a 5-year-old Dodge truck.

"John—10 years with the company, has a 4-year-old Ford truck.

Case Problem 19-B
The New Truck Problem [35]

"Charlie—5 years with the company, has a 3-year-old Ford truck.

"Hank—3 years with the company, has a 5-year-old Chevrolet truck.

"Most of you do all your driving in the city, but John and Charlie cover the jobs in the suburbs.

"In acting your part in role playing, accept the facts as given as well as assume the attitudes supplied in your specific role. From this point on let your feelings develop in accordance with the events that transpire in the role playing process. When facts or events arise which are not covered by the roles, make up things which are consistent with the way it might be in a real-life situation."

---

[35] Norman R. F. Maier and Lester F. Zerfess, *op. cit.,* pp. 180-181.

CHAPTER 20

Organization Development and Personnel Planning

William Evans, president of Toolco, Inc., looked up as Robert Kessler, the director of industrial relations, entered his office and asked, "What kind of progress are you making on the report I asked for last week?"

"Here are some notes I have prepared covering key executives in the company," Kessler answered as he handed Mr. Evans a copy of Exhibit I. "It appears that the compulsory retirement plan that went into effect the first of this year is going to create a real need for replacements within the next five years."

"We not only have a replacement problem," Evans rejoined, "we also have some problems coming up as the result of our decision to move into the industrial products area and create a new industrial products division. As you know, our existing product line is purchased by individuals through department and hardware stores; however, the new division means not only manufacturing new products, it also means a new method of distribution."

Case Problem 20-A
Organization Planning

"There is another factor other than replacement and expansion to be considered," Kessler stated.

"What is that?"

"The information I just handed you pertains only to replacements due to reaching the mandatory retirement age; thus far we have no information about the needs that might arise if we were to evaluate some of these people in terms of the quality of their performance. We both know that some of our managers are not doing the job that we would like to see done."

"Are you suggesting that we get into the area of performance appraisals?" Evans asked.

"We're going to have to get into it sooner or later; otherwise, how are we going to know who is promotable to these key positions when they open up as the result of retirement?"

"Bob, as you know, we have an executive committee meeting at the end of next week. I wonder if you could show our needs in some graphic form that would impress everyone at the meeting. There are still some doubting Thomases who believe that the cream will rise to the top—personally I don't think it will, and even if it does I doubt that we have that much time. When we have this meeting will you also recommend some definite name to designate this program we're going into? You and I have at various times called it executive development, management development, or organization development, and even organization planning. We ought to settle on a title that has meaning to everyone." Mr. Evans returned the notes Bob had given him and closed with, "See me again a day or two before the committee meeting so that I can review the recommendations you intend to present at the meeting."

Problems

1. Prepare an organization chart that shows clearly the replacement needs of Toolco for the next five years.
2. What title would you choose to designate the program being considered by Toolco? Why?
3. How many persons would you include initially as a part of any proposed development program?
4. Prepare a set of recommendations to be submitted to Mr. Evans prior to the committee meeting. Outline and justify each step in the proposed program.

President—Age 62, founder of company and the driving force behind the institution of the company's compulsory retirement plan a year ago.

Reporting to the President:

Director of Marketing—Age 40, has been in position only a little over one year, former director of economic research for an advertising agency. Performs economic research; has staff of two: a statistical typist and a statistician—both in early 30's. It was his recommendation that company enter industrial products field.

Legal Counsel—Age 45, functions primarily as liaison between engineering and outside firm of attorneys in patent matters. Occasionally handles real estate transactions; has one legal secretary.

Vice President and Treasurer—Age 50, a CPA who has been with the company 20 years; formerly head of the cost accounting section. Has heads of cost and general accounting sections reporting to him; responsible for all financial affairs of the company. As the company grew, it was his idea that the position of controller be established as a separate function reporting to the president.

Controller—Age 45, has been with the company only three years; has a small clerical staff; is in the process of establishing and refining budgets in the manufacturing plants. Though the chief of the cost section reports to the treasurer, the controller maintains a close working relationship with him.

Exhibit I

Director of Industrial Relations—Age 40, has been with the company five years; chief negotiator for the company; his staff consists of a secretary, a clerk, and a research assistant. Each plant has its own personnel director. Administers company-wide salary plan and employee benefits, including insurance and the new retirement plan. It will be his responsibility to administer any executive development program agreed upon.

Director of Purchasing—Age 60, formerly a purchasing agent in one of the plants. Serves in an advisory capacity to plant purchasing agents for the most part, although occasionally does purchase those items that can be used by all plants.

Executive Vice President—Age 62, formerly vice president in charge of manufacturing; over 20 years' service with the company; started as a plant manager in its number 2 plant.

Reporting to the Executive Vice President:

Vice President, Manufacturing—Age 55, has been with the company five years; came to company as vice president, manufacturing when the post of executive vice president was created. At that time it was believed that the plant manager of the number 2 plant, then 55 years old, was capable of filling the vice president position, but there was no suitable replacement for him in his plant. Since the number 2 plant is the largest plant in dollar volume and profit, he was kept in that position. Reporting to the vice president, manufacturing, in staff positions are: the Director of Industrial Engineering and the Director of Quality Control. These positions were created shortly after his taking the job. Both men are in their early 40's and well trained for their positions. Both have worked previously with the vice president, manufacturing, in another company.

The managers of the five manufacturing plants report to the manufacturing vice president. Each plant manager has managers of personnel, quality control, industrial engineering, purchasing, accounting, product engineering, and an assistant plant manager. Each staff department head has at least three exempt employees and several clerical employees reporting to him. The assistant plant manager supervises directly the plant engineer (building maintenance), the master mechanic who is responsible for the tool room and the machine shop, and the general foremen in charge of the production departments. The following summary shows the age of the plant manager, the number of hourly employees, and the number of general foremen and foremen for each plant.

Plant No.	Age of Plant Manager	Total Hourly Employees	General Foremen	Foremen
1 (outboard motors)	50	250	3	20
2 (engine plant)	60	700	4	32
3 (power hand tools)	45	400	3	18
4 (lawn mowers and edgers)	50	300	3	15
5 (power tools)	56	500	4	24

Exhibit I (Continued)

Vice President, Engineering—Age 48, has been with the company 22 years. He has been in his present position five years. There are five supervising design engineers who report to him, one for each of the product lines. There is also a chief metallurgist who directs the metallurgical laboratory.

Vice President, Sales—Age 61, has the advertising manager (age 50), the head of the sales order department (age 60), and the assistant general sales manager (age 58) reporting to him. Most of his efforts are devoted to the various advertising programs and promotional campaigns. The head of the sales order department acts as liaison between plants 1 and 4 since these plants purchase 50 percent of the output of the engine plant. The assistant general sales manager directs four regional sales managers. Each regional manager has a clerical staff of two and approximately 15 salesmen reporting to him. The manager of the Eastern region is 62 years old, the manager of the Central region is 58, the Southern regional manager is 50, and the manager of the Pacific region is 55.

Exhibit I (Concluded)

• • • • • • • • •

Case Problem 20-A poses a series of questions encountered sooner or later by all managements. There is an obvious need for the development of a planned approach to the replacement of key executives of a company who are due to retire within the next few years under the provisions of the company's mandatory retirement plan. Contemplated expansion increases the need for a planned program of executive development since the requirements of an expanded organization must be met as well as the needs arising as the result of attrition in the present organization. Case Problem 20-A also poses a problem of terminology; what are we to call the program designed to fill the management personnel needs of the company? Three terms are used, often interchangeably, to describe this process. These terms are: *executive development, management development,* and *organization development.* However, each descriptive term carries with it a slightly different connotation. "Executive development" emphasizes the development of the individual executive, "management development" indicates a plan for the development of all members of management, and "organization development" implies that the entire management structure is involved, not as individuals but as members of an organization, so that the organization functions in a different or improved manner.

In discussing organization development the following topics are considered. First, there is a review of several points of view now existing in organization development; second, a review of the elements of a formalized executive development program; and third, a brief discussion of some of the newer trends in the development of individual executives and the development of entire organizations. The discussion of new trends is included in this chapter because many students will participate in such programs as members of management. The last part of the chapter summarizes the scope of the personnel function and relates personnel policies to those established for the other major functions of finance, production, and sales.

EXECUTIVE DEVELOPMENT

The importance of developing managers is well illustrated by "The Great GM Mystery," a review of Alfred P. Sloan, Jr.'s *My Years with General Motors*.[1] GM has never been reticent about its techniques of management. On the contrary, there is probably no company exposed to public view as much as General Motors. In reviewing Sloan's book, Harold Wolff also summarizes much of the literature about GM and presents the following three concepts developed from the literature:

1. As far as most of the GM literature is concerned, decentralization and the related system of financial controls and profit responsibility are accorded much more credit than they merit. . . .

2. There is evidence in this book—and in other sources also—that what General Motors has achieved cannot be explained by any organizational cliches, but rather by some fundamental approaches that were conceived by Sloan and his group over 40 years ago, when they virtually gave birth to the concept of professional management—without ever calling it that. . . .

3. What is most remarkable about General Motors—and the most useful lesson to be learned from its record—is that long after 1946, when Sloan and his colleagues retired from active management of the company, GM not only maintained its industry leadership, but increased it. . . .[2]

---

[1] Harold A. Wolff, "The Great GM Mystery," *Harvard Business Review,* Vol. XXXXII (September, October, 1964), pp. 164-166, 168-172, 175-176, 192, 195-196, 200, 202. Mr. Wolff presents a critical analysis of the concept of decentralization. See also Alfred P. Sloan, Jr., *My Years with General Motors,* edited by John McDonald with Catherine Stevens, (Garden City, New York: Doubleday & Company, Inc., 1964).

[2] *Ibid.,* p. 166.

Wolff discusses each of the three points quoted above and in his analysis of the third point states that Sloan "created at GM a way of managing a business that perpetuates itself" and that the method of management is not dependent upon the capabilities of any one man or group of men. He concludes by stating "how this has been achieved is the real mystery of General Motors."[3]

GM's method of developing managers remains a mystery because nowhere in the vast literature of GM is there a definitive account of their plan for organizational development.[4] Nonetheless, the following conclusions may be drawn about General Motors' concept of management —a concept that is capable of serving as the basis for management development in any company.

1. Over a period of 40-odd years GM has devoted an inordinate amount of time and energy to getting across the fact that General Motors has a very specific concept of management. GM has taken great pains, moreover, to elaborate this concept in considerable detail. . . .
2. No one at GM has any doubts about the fact that the company regards these management concepts as extremely important. . . .
3. At GM everyone understands that developing managers is one of the prime responsibilities of management. . . .
4. It is part of the GM creed that management capability is communicable. . . .[5]

Approaches to Management Development

Douglas McGregor describes two extremes in the approaches to management development. The earliest approach to management development regards development as an automatic process requiring little attention on the part of management. This approach assumes that competent managers, like cream, will rise to the top and can be skimmed off when needed. There is much to be said for this view, provided conditions are such that the cream can rise to the top. For most companies the "hands-off" approach did not produce enough qualified managers, with the result that during the last 20 years another

---

[3] *Ibid.,* p. 166.

[4] One of the relatively few accounts of management development at General Motors is the plan developed by the Fisher Body Division of General Motors.

M. Joseph Dooher and Vivienne Marquis (Editors), *The Development of Executive Talent* (New York: American Management Association, 1952), pp. 457-462. *The Development of Executive Talent* is a handbook of management development techniques that presents both the theoretical basis for executive development and an analysis of the experiences of 18 companies with executive development programs. An extensive bibliography is also included in this work.

[5] Harold A. Wolff, *op. cit.,* pp. 196-202.

way of developing managers emerged. The second method may be called the "manufacturing" approach, in which the development of managers is looked upon as a production problem. When development programs are considered to be a problem of producing managers, people are "assigned the *engineering* task of *designing* a program and *building* the necessary *machinery,* toward the end of *producing* the needed *supply* of managerial talent." [6] The major criticism of the manufacturing approach to executive development is that all too frequently companies become so engrossed in the mechanics of the program that they lose sight of the original objectives of management development—the development of managers for the organization. Let us review briefly the current thinking in regard to management development that lies between the two extremes outlined by McGregor. First, the development of executives is recognized as a process of change; second, the role of the individual being developed or changed is considered; and third, the contributions of the organization are evaluated.

A Process of Change. When a company expresses a need for organizational development, it is in effect saying that change is desired so that the organization may become more effective. Change may be accomplished in several ways. Occasionally it may be necessary to remove an executive from his position by transferring him to another post or by terminating his services with the company.[7] The duties of the position may be modified so that the present incumbent's abilities are sufficient for the changed job requirements, or it may be necessary to undertake an extensive reorganization to align job requirements and personnel capabilities. The recruitment of executive talent from outside the company is frequently used as a means of introducing organizational change.[8] However, our concern is the development of management personnel—itself a process of change—as a means of changing organizations.

---

[6] Douglas McGregor, *The Human Side of Enterprise* (New York: McGraw-Hill Book Company, Inc., 1960), p. 191. Italics are McGregor's. Chapter 14, "Management Development Programs" and Chapter 15, "Acquiring Managerial Skills in the Classroom" pp. 190-226, provide a good general discussion of management development.

[7] Saul W. Gellerman, "When the Job Outgrows the Man," *The Management Review,* Vol. XXVII (June, 1960), pp. 4-8, 68-70. Dr. Gellerman presents the arguments for making a clean break; i.e., removing the executive from his job.

[8] Stephen Habbe, "What About Executive Recruiters?," *Management Record,* Vol. XVIII (February, 1956), pp. 42-44. The operations and services of executive search firms, sometimes called "flesh peddlers" and "body snatchers," are presented in simple question-and-answer form.

For a more detailed discussion of executive recruiting, the following article is recommended: Robert F. Moore, "The Executive Matchmakers," *Business Horizons,* Vol. IV (Fall, 1961), pp. 29-36.

A question arises concerning the objectives of management development programs—what is it about the executive that needs changing? It could be the acquisition of professional knowledge and skills such as those possessed by engineers or accountants. However, most managers have such skills at the time they are employed; and in those instances where additional knowledge or skill is required, either company or university training programs seem to meet this need satisfactorily. Development programs are aimed toward producing a set of attitudes that differentiate the competent, professional manager from the incompetent or immature manager. Part of the difficulty in achieving desired results in management development is due to an unsureness and inability to define the attitudes required, and part is due to our failure to apply consistently what is known about the process of changing an individual member of a social organization—a form of *influence*.[9] Edgar H. Schein, a psychologist at Massachusetts Institute of Technology, offers a model for change capable of being used in evaluating the potential effectiveness of management programs.[10] The model consists of the following three steps: (1) unfreezing, (2) changing, and (3) refreezing.

UNFREEZING. All learning, whether it be the acquisition of skills, knowledge, or changed attitudes, assumes that the learner is ready to learn. He is *set* for the experience and motivated. When attitudes are being changed, it is necessary to "unfreeze" present attitudes so they may be dropped and new ones acquired. Coercion may be used as an aid in unfreezing, as in the case of the "brainwashing" of the Chinese Communists; however, management development assumes that the manager is ready to learn. There is some evidence that such is not the case. One study shows that even top-level executives have ill-defined goals and merely wish "to get ahead" and that many middle- and lower-level managers fail to see the purpose of management development either in

---

[9] T. A. Mahoney, T. H. Jerdee, and S. J. Carroll, *Development of Managerial Performance, A Research Approach,* Monograph C-9 (Cincinnati: South-Western Publishing Company, 1963). This study directed toward a descriptive statement of the functional aspects of managerial performance illustrates the difficulty of specifying the attitudes necessary for such performance.

[10] Edgar H. Schein, "Management Development As a Process of Influence," *Industrial Management Review,* Vol. III (May, 1961), pp. 59-76. Dr. Schein's article is a well-reasoned statement of the application of current knowledge concerning social influence as a factor in changing attitudes. He applies the model he develops to the brainwashing of the Communists, the training of a nun, and the development of managers.

For a similar approach to the analysis of management development, see the following: Robert J. House, "Management Development Is a Game," *Harvard Business Review,* Vol. XXXXI (July-August, 1963), pp. 130-143.

terms of company needs or in respect to their own needs.[11] Other factors that aid in the unfreezing of old attitudes to make room for the new include a completely new environment, thus removing the individual from the sources of his old attitudes, a certain amount of punishment and humiliation for holding on to old attitudes, and a carefully planned series of rewards and punishments to emphasize the value of change. The hazing of fraternity pledges offers a good example of removal from an old environment, humiliation, and selected rewards and punishment.

In order to have successful management development programs, companies must communicate their organizational needs to prospective participants to insure an understanding of the aims of the program. The participants themselves must have clearly defined goals congruent with those of the organization and must perceive the need for change on their part. The use of environmental factors that aid in the unfreezing process poses a real problem in developing a planned company program of attitude change. The difficulty is not one of physically removing the executive from his old environment since there are many university training programs that meet this requirement; rather, it is the nature of the change process, the second step of the change model.

CHANGING. According to Schein's model, a change in attitudes is accomplished either as the result of *identification* or *internalization*. The opportunity to identify one's self with a person having the desired attitudes facilitates the acquisition of those attitudes. The executive who, in describing his early years with the company, refers to a superior with the words, "He treated me like a father," or "He treated me as though I were his son," is expressing identification with his former boss. Herein lies the problem of removing the trainee from his organizational environment—he is prevented from identifying with someone in the company. The same difficulty is present when executive development programs are conducted by staff men. Regardless of how competent staff personnel are, it is rare that a line executive will identify himself with a staff man.

Internalization is the process of trying, adopting, and using the new attitudes as a way of solving problems and learning how to live with them. Training programs away from home grounds usually offer an excellent opportunity for internalization since the environment is relatively controlled and other trainees are going through the same

---

[11] Reed M. Powell, "Growth Plans for Executives," *Business Horizons,* Vol. IV (Summer, 1961), pp. 41-50. This report is part of a study on the impact of university-sponsored development programs upon executives. For a more detailed treatment of the study, see the following article: Kenneth R. Andrews, "Reaction to University Development Programs," *Harvard Business Review,* Vol. XXXVII (May-June, 1961), pp. 116-134.

process of experimenting with the new attitudes. Further, rewards in the form of approval by the leader and other members of the group tend to encourage the adoption of the desired changes. It is difficult, it not impossible, to internalize attitudes if training is sandwiched in between the regular course of a day's work. Attitudes must be lived, studied, and experimented with in order that they may finally be accepted and integrated into one's personality.

REFREEZING. Refreezing is the final acceptance and integration of the desired attitudes so they become integrated as a permanent part of one's personality. Time and organizational support are needed for this phase of the process of change. In Chapter 19 the importance of organizational climate is discussed as a factor in the training of supervisors, and it is stated that unless the climate is favorable, training programs may be a complete waste of time and money. An organizational climate that encourages the executive to exercise his newly formed attitudes and rewards him for using them is essential to the process of refreezing.

The Individual and Change. The above discussion presents attitudinal change as a relationship between an individual undergoing the process of change and an organization inducing that change. Let us examine more closely the role of the individual, particularly in respect to those changes desired through the process of management development.

First, some evidence is presented that members of middle and lower management are not ready for change, as evidenced by their lack of understanding of the organization's goals for management development and their failure to perceive within themselves the need for change. Without proper motivation and readiness to learn, the desired change in attitude cannot be reasonably expected. Second, the opportunity for identification with another person seems to be an essential ingredient of attitudinal change. As part of psychological growth a son attempts an identification with his father, also a symbol of authority. If identification is not completed with the father, it may occur with a scoutmaster, a coach, a teacher, or some other adult figure. If the father is rejected as an object of identification, or if he discourages his son from identifying with him, psychological growth is stunted and at the same time the son rejects symbols of authority. One of the characteristics of organizations is that they are authoritarian to some degree. The son who has failed to form identifications with authority figures and who later becomes a manager in an organization has attitudes toward authority that are incompatible with the concept of authority as it operates in business organizations. He usually has difficulty in accepting authority, understanding it, submitting to authority, or using authority wisely when it is granted to him. The ability to identify and the related attitudes toward authority are well established before a man finishes college, yet management development programs are challenged to change these attitudes five or ten years after a manager has completed his professional training. The difficulty of the task is evident.[12] Third, there is also mounting evidence that success or failure as a manager is dependent to a considerable extent upon personality factors. Again we are dealing with behavioral patterns established early in life, and to change long-established patterns of personality is tedious and difficult.[13]

These three items—the readiness to learn new attitudes, the ability to identify with a person having the desired attitudes (along with the implications of former identifications), and the significance of personality as a determinant of managerial success—are characteristics of the individual manager who is the object of the desired change. It must be recognized that for one reason or another every manager is not subject to change; and for those who are capable of change, the direction and the degree of change vary with each individual.

The Organization and Change. The role of the organization in the process of change is of utmost importance in the unfreezing of the unwanted or old attitudes and the *refreezing* of the new or desired attitudes. In his analysis of management development as a process of influence, Dr. Schein describes the institution's total control over the environment in the shaping of attitudes. He cites the environmental control exerted by the Chinese Communists in their brain-washing technique and the rigid structure imposed by the convent in the training of nuns. Other less rigorous examples of institutional control over the individual

---

[12] Harry Levinson, "A Psychologist Looks at Executive Development," *Harvard Business Review,* Vol. XXXX (September-October, 1962), pp. 69-75. Dr. Levinson's article presents a point of view similar to that expressed in the text. He evaluates management development programs, particularly appraisals of performance and the opportunity for identification, as a means of encouraging psychological growth.

[13] Thomas W. Harrell, *Manager's Performance and Personality* (Cincinnati: South-Western Publishing Company, Editor's Series, 1961). This book presents a summary of the literature concerning personality and its relation to performance in the upper levels of business management. The following quotation from page 172 supports the concept that authority relationships are dependent upon identification with an adult figure early in life.

"Relations with one's parents seems to offer the best explanation for the development of a personality similar to that of successful managers. Who the parents are, especially what is the father's occupation, has already been discussed. Relations with parents regardless of their socio-economic status are also crucial. Many young presidents have been reported to be comparing with their fathers whom they respected but wanted to match or outdo. The mobile elite, who by definition did not have highly successful fathers, occupationally were still trying to prove themselves worthy of the acceptance they had not had from their fathers, and often had developed an identification with some other father figure who inspired them to great effort."

that result in the fixing of attitudes acceptable to that institution would include the internship and residency of a physician, and the various military and naval academies. To a lesser degree the college fraternity system accomplishes the same end. An important element in institutional control of environment is that the administrators of such institutions have been through the same process of influence and change—a condition that goes a long way toward explaining the rigidity of institutions. At the same time these administrators become acceptable objects for identification and thereby facilitate the acquisition of the new attitudes. Their presence, their behavior, and their attitudes serve to reinforce the new attitude during the process of *refreezing*.

Industrial organizations cannot and do not exert the same degree of control over the environment of their managers. However, the top management of some companies, for example, General Motors, has matured in the same organization, has similiar attitudes toward the functions and responsibilities of management, and is able to serve as objects for identification. Many companies have top managements with no common institutional background and the result is that there is no clear attitudinal pattern to transmit to managers, nor is there an acceptable image of managerial success as an object of identification.

The practice of *coaching;* i.e., individual counsel and guidance, is used frequently in management development, but its contribution to the development of managers is questionable. Lack of time is usually cited as the reason why coaching is not conducted on a systematic basis; however, the real reasons are a lack of understanding of the dependency needs of subordinates and the need for identification, an environment that tolerates precious few mistakes, and the fact that very few companies include development of subordinates as a major function of an executive's job.

The above outline of the knowledge we have available concerning the optimum conditions required for a change of attitudes shows the difference between industrial organizations and those organizations better suited for instilling a prescribed set of attitudes. Yet the development of managers and organizational planning is a necessity for the industrial firm. The following section describes the major steps in the administration of a management development program.

A Management Development Program

The steps necessary to establish a management development program are outlined in Figure 20-1. Three general comments in the form of warnings are in order so that the probable success

I. Analyze Present Organization

A. Preparation of Organizational Charts (Figure 15-1)
B. Preparation of Organizational Manuals
C. Completion of Organizational Checklist (Figure 15-5)

II. Determine Objectives of the Program

A. Management Manpower Requirements
  1. Replacement Needs
  2. Growth Needs
    a. Historic Growth
    b. Planned Expansion
  3. Improved Performance Needs
B. Management Personnel Inventory
  1. Inventory of Current Capabilities
  2. Appraisal of Current Performance
  3. Estimate of Potential Growth

III. Establish Opportunities for Development

A. Internal Sources
  1. Training Programs
  2. Job Rotation
  3. Committee Assignments
  4. Coaching
  5. Planned Promotional Sequence
B. External Sources
  1. University Programs
  2. Professional Meetings
  3. Industrial Conferences

IV. Evaluate Program

A. Continue Performance Appraisals
B. Opinion and Attitude Surveys
C. Feedback to I and II above

Figure 20-1

MANAGEMENT DEVELOPMENT PROGRAM

of any such program may be increased. First, it should be recognized that both the organization and the individual bear responsibility for management development. The organization can provide the proper climate and make available the tools and techniques for learning, but in the final analysis it is the individual executive who must accept the responsibility for developing himself. Second, note that Figure 20-1 does not designate specific administrative responsibility for the administration of a management development program. In some companies such programs are administered by the personnel department; in others, a staff assistant to the president or executive vice-president administers the program. In either case, administrative responsibility is assigned to staff personnel; yet the ultimate responsibility for the success or failure of any program belongs to the line personnel of the organization. The support and understanding of top management are a must for a successful program. Third, there is a danger of measuring the success of a program in terms of the completion of the administrative details and paper work suggested in Figure 20-1. The success of any program is measured by the number of needed executives supplied to the organization and an improvement in organizational effectiveness, not by the quantity of administrative details, such as the number of courses or appraisals completed within prescribed time limits. With these three limiting factors in mind, let us review briefly each of the major aspects of a management development program.

Analyze Present Organization. The present organization must be analyzed so that a clear concept of its structure and functioning may be obtained. As the result of this step, it may be decided that a reorganization is in order; if so, the development program should be defined in terms of the proposed organization rather than in respect to the present organization. The methods available for organizational analysis are described fully in Chapter 15. The extent of organizational analysis needed as a preparatory step in the establishment of a management development program varies with each company. However, the purpose of organizational analysis remains the same—to describe the structure and function of the present and the optimum organization so that executives may be developed in accordance with organizational needs.

Determine Objectives of the Program. After clarifying organizational goals by means of organization analysis, the determination of the specific objectives of a management development program entails two phases; one of which—*management manpower requirements*—may be regarded as quantitative in nature, and the other—*management personnel inventory*—as qualitative in nature. The quantitative aspects of a development program are relatively easy to determine. Needed replacements for the near future can be determined by comparing the ages of incumbents with the normal retirement age. Growth needs may be projected by developing data showing the relationship between varying levels of company sales and the number of management personnel employed at each level of sales. If planned expansion is contemplated, either through the acquisition of other companies, the addition of new products, or the building of new plant facilities, these needs should be added to those resulting from normal growth to reflect fully all needs attributable to growth. Planned expansion accelerates the need for management personnel and when combined with those needs projected as the result of normal historic growth, the results are often quite startling. In addition, the organizational analysis completed as part of Step 1 may show that some executives are not performing as effectively as desired; thus, there may be additional requirements for management personnel in order to improve organizational performance. The preparation of organization charts using a color code often dramatizes the replacement needs of a company. A square colored red may indicate retirement within three years, a green square may show an executive marked for promotion and the necessity to secure a replacement for him, and a yellow square may reveal that the incumbent is not performing satisfactorily and should be replaced. The problem becomes even more complex when an attempt is made to evaluate whether or not a qualified replacement is available.

A manpower inventory showing current skills and knowledge, ability as reflected through performance on the present job, and an estimate of growth potential expressed in terms of promotability is necessary to determine the needs of the individual executive. This information forms the qualitative part of the management development program, for it shows the substance or content of individual development needs. Though the form in which the inventory is kept varies, it usually consists of a separate file folder for each member of management.[14] The application for employment shows the education and experience at the time of hiring and serves as a starting point for building an inventory.

Provisions must be made to keep inventory records current so that additional experience and training acquired after becoming an employee of the company are shown. Appraisals of current performance and estimates of promotability are usually completed by the manager's immediate superior. Occasionally estimates of potential are made by consultants or by trained personnel with the company such as that used by the Bell System. The Bell System Assessment Centers process about 12 candidates a week. For a period of approximately 2½ days, each

---

[14] Lyle H. Fisher, "The Inventory System at Minnesota Mining and Manufacturing," in Jerome W. Blood (ed.), *The Personnel Job in a Changing World* (New York: American Management Association, 1964), pp. 214-224. This article discusses the inventory system of Minnesota Mining and Manufacturing and can be used as a guide in establishing an inventory system.

candidate undergoes extensive interviews, a series of paper-and-pencil tests of ability and knowledge, and other less usual assessment techniques. This latter group includes a simulated administrative (paper work) situation and certain business games.[15]

An analysis of the quantitative and qualitative objectives of a management development program reveals the extent that it is possible to secure replacements from within the company and the need for recruitment of personnel for entering and intermediate levels of management.

Establish Opportunities for Development. Large companies often have internally administered executive development programs similiar to those discussed in Chapter 19 for the first-line supervisor. All companies, regardless of size, can utilize to some degree job rotation, committee assignments, coaching, and a planned promotional sequence as a means of development. Participation in outside professional groups should also be encouraged. University executive development programs are available in most areas and the programs of various industrial groups, such as the American Management Association, may be used for individual development plans. The responsibility of the company is limited to the establishment of opportunities for development; the responsibility for growth and development is that of the individual executive.

Evaluate Program. The main purpose in evaluating the management development program is to provide a feedback so that the effectiveness of the program in respect to its contribution to the development of the entire organization may be determined. Evaluation of results is also necessary to revise manpower requirements and to bring up-to-date the information contained in the personnel inventory. Opinion and attitude surveys of those who have participated in the program are of value; however, there is evidence that the information elicited from such surveys may express at best only a general satisfaction with the "broadening effects" of management development rather than provide the specific data necessary for the improvement of such programs.[16] The most common device used to evaluate the development of managers is the *performance appraisal*. Since the performance appraisal is used not only

---

[15] Douglas W. Bray, "The Assessment Center Method of Appraising Management Personnel," in Jerome W. Blood, (Ed.), *The Personnel Job in the Changing World* (New York: American Management Association, 1964), pp. 225-234.

[16] Kenneth R. Andrews, "Reaction to University Development Programs," *Harvard Business Review*, Vol. XXXVIIII (May-June, 1961), pp. 116-134. The information contained in this article may serve as a guide for the development of a survey of the values received from a management development program.

as a means of evaluating a management development program but also as a means of supplying information for the management personnel inventory, there is considerable criticism concerning performance appraisals. The problems encountered in their use and methods suggested to improve their effectiveness are discussed.

PROBLEMS IN APPRAISING PERFORMANCE. Although a subordinate's performance is always appraised in some fashion by his superior, the introduction of formal performance appraisals into an organization is invariably met with resistance. Such resistance is usually evidenced by the inability to complete the required appraisals within the allotted time limits. Resistance is due in part to the lack of a clear statement of the purpose of appraisals, a definition of expected standards of performance, and an understanding of the objectives of the appraisal interview.

Purpose of Appraisals. There are two questions to be resolved in determining the purpose of performance appraisals. First, is the appraisal intended to measure current performance, or is it intended to measure the subordinate's potential for promotion? Second, is the appraisal to be used to determine advances in salary, or is it to be used as a basis for self-improvement?

It is difficult enough for a manager to appraise current performance without, as Douglas McGregor phrases it, "playing God" by being required to state his estimate of a subordinate's potential capabilities in the organization.[17] Admittedly, a manager makes such estimates and his estimate of potential is reflected each time a subordinate is selected for promotion, but having to state potential capabilities in writing and perhaps having to reveal and defend his estimate to the subordinate during the interview is one of the major causes of resistance to formal appraisal systems. An appraisal is not only a statement of a subordinate's performance but also a mirror of his superior's personality and concept of adequate performance. If the superior is unsure of himself and perhaps has lost hope of being promoted, it is possible he may reflect these attitudes in the appraisal of his subordinates. Further, few managers have a sound basis for determining the ability required for any position other than their own. Indeed, the question of capabilities and manager performance has only begun to be answered. Thus, it seems wise to limit appraisals to an evaluation of current performance.

---

[17] Douglas McGregor, "An Uneasy Look at Performance Appraisals," *Harvard Business Review,* Vol. XXXV (May-June, 1957), pp. 89-94.

Another critical summary of performance appraisals is found in: George S. Odiorne, *Personnel Policy: Issues and Practices* (Columbus, Ohio: Charles E. Merrill Books, Inc., 1963), pp. 304-329.

Having determined that the appraisal should be limited to an evaluation of current performance, the second question—whether the results of the appraisal should be used to determine salary or used as a basis for self-improvement—remains to be answered. When appraisals are used to determine whether or not a subordinate should receive an increase in salary, there is a tendency to distort the appraisal of current performance so that the decision in regard to salary may be justified. Performance is only one of several factors determining whether or not an increase in pay should be granted. Availability of funds, length of time on the job, salary ranges, and the subordinate's position within the range are a few of the other factors that must be considered. Since the goal of a management development program is the development of individual managers, appraisals of performance should serve as a basis for improving that performance in the future. Objective discussions of current performance are possible only when salary considerations are set aside and attention is directed toward the improvement of performance and the development of the individual. Decisions concerning salary should be made at a separate time and should include not only a review of current and past performance but also all other aspects of the company's salary policy.

Standards of Performance. Another problem encountered in the use of performance appraisals is that of developing criteria for measuring performance on the job. In many appraisal systems the manager is asked to rate his subordinate on a five-point scale in respect to a list of personality traits such as loyalty, promptness, and willingness to work. All too frequently this approach may again become a reflection of the rater's personality, and he describes the subordinate in terms of his own strengths and weaknesses. Occasionally a superior is asked to rate the performance of each subordinate against that of each of the other subordinates—a man-to-man rating. The shortcomings of this method are obvious, particularly when subordinates have different jobs requiring different abilities and levels of achievement. A third type of criteria is defined in terms of the goals of the job itself. However, for job goals to be effective standards of performance, they must be clearly stated, measurable, and within the control of the subordinate.

The Appraisal Interview. Most formal appraisal systems require an interview between subordinate and superior. The interview is supposed to offer an opportunity for the subordinate to discover where he stands, at which time his superior should outline steps to be taken for the improvement of job performance and self-development. An extensive study of the typical appraisal interview conducted at General Electric shows that praise has little effect, either positively or negatively, that criticism has a negative effect on future achievement, and that defensiveness results from criticism with no improvement of performance.[18] The same study indicates that discussions concerning salary should be held at a separate time and not as a part of a performance review. It is questionable whether the typical line manager is capable of conducting a broad evaluative interview in terms of his training or inclination. As McGregor has noted, there is a reluctance to "playing God," with the result that the typical interview is resisted by both superior and subordinate and usually becomes a mere formality, with little of the developmental benefits that should result from it.

IMPROVING PERFORMANCE APPRAISALS. The weaknesses of the typical performance appraisal are attributable to failure to define the purpose of the appraisal, the need for a well-defined set of criteria, and the inadequacy of the appraisal interview. Appraisals may be conducted to determine the potential of a member of management, to evaluate performance in his present job, or to develop a plan for self-improvement. Criteria may consist of a list of illusive personality traits, the performance of a subordinate's peers, or a statement of job goals. The inadequacy of the interview may result from the superior's having to evaluate performance and justify salary action at the same time, or from being required to assess personality and potential development— tasks he is not trained to do. The following five-step program eliminates the conflicting points of view in regard to purpose and criteria, and as a result places the appraisal interview on much safer ground.[19]

> Step #1: The individual discusses his job description with his superior and they agree on the content of his job and the relative importance of his major duties—the things he is paid to do and is accountable for.
> Step #2: The individual establishes performance targets for each of his responsibilities for the forthcoming period.
> Step #3: He meets with his superior to discuss his target program.
> Step #4: Checkpoints are established for the evaluation of his progress; ways of measuring progress are selected.

---

[18] Herbert H. Meyer, Emanuel Kay, and John R. P. French, Jr., "Split Roles in Performance Appraisal," *Harvard Business Review,* Vol. XLIV (January-February, 1965), pp. 123-124.
[19] Alva B. Kindall and James Gatza, "Positive Program for Performance Appraisal," *Harvard Business Review,* Vol. XXXXI (November-December, 1963), p. 157. This article presents a brief statement of the shortcomings of the typical appraisal program and then develops a plan for the installation of the five steps.

Step #5: The superior and subordinate meet at the end of the period to discuss the results of the subordinate's efforts to meet the targets he had previously established.

The five-step program suggested by Kindall and Gatza corrects the major weakness of the usual performance appraisal since the purpose of the appraisal is clearly defined as the appraisal of current performance, the goals of the job are determined and agreed upon by both superior and subordinate, and the interview is confined to a discussion of performance with superior and subordinate equally interested in improving that performance. General Electric uses an appraisal system, called the Work Planning and Review program, that incorporates these five steps and finds the new program to be far more effective than the traditional approach to appraisals in improving the level of job performance.[20]

New Trends in Management Development

Even before the early Greeks coined the expression "Know Thyself," man has been exploring various ways of gaining greater insight into himself. Today there are literally thousands of American executives who are alumni of management development programs designed specifically to enable the individual executive to know not only himself but also his impact upon other people. The training these men have received is referred to as *sensitivity training* or the *laboratory training method.*[21]

Let us look first at sensitivity training and find out what it is, how it is conducted, and its effect upon the individual executive; then we will examine what appears to be a major breakthrough in organization development—the application of a laboratory training method to every member of management in an industrial organization.

---

[20] Herbert H. Meyer, Emanuel Kay, and John R. P. French, Jr., *op. cit.,* pp. 127-129.

[21] Robert Tannenbaum, Irving R. Weschler, and Fred Massarik, *Leadership and Organization: A Behavioral Science Approach* (New York: McGraw-Hill Book Company, Inc., 1961). See Part 2, pp. 119-238, for a complete discussion of sensitivity training.

For a brief article on sensitivity training, see Chris Argyris, "T-Groups for Organizational Effectiveness," *Harvard Business Review,* Vol. XXXXII (March-April, 1964), pp. 60-74.

A detailed summary of research concerning sensitivity training is as follows: Dorothy Stock, "A Summary of Research on Training Groups," in *T-Group Theory and Laboratory Method: Innovation in Education,* edited by Leland Bradford, Kenneth Benne, and Jack Gibb (New York: John Wiley & Sons, Inc., 1964).

Sensitivity Training. As the phrase suggests, the goal of sensitivity training is to heighten a person's awareness of himself and his effect upon others, to increase his sensitivity toward the feelings and attitudes of others, and to understand how other people influence him. Sensitivity training is not the acquisition of more knowledge about human relations, nor is it directed primarily toward the improvement of skills in human relations. Instead, it is an emotionalized experience of interpersonal relationships. The result of this experience is often a change in attitudes and feelings toward one's self and toward others. The three-step model of change—(1) unfreezing, (2) changing, (3) refreezing—serves as a basis for understanding sensitivity training.[22]

Unlike most management development training activities, the environment in which sensitivity training takes place is an almost completely controlled laboratory situation. Usually the training sessions are held in an isolated resort atmosphere with freedom from interruption by family, friends, and the telephone. About 50 men attend each of the two- or three-week training sessions. They are strangers to each other, and seldom are two executives from the same company enrolled in the same training session. On the opening day there is an orientation session for the entire group. The group is then subdivided into five T-groups (T for training), with each T-group consisting of ten members and a leader. The leader, a trained psychologist, is from the staff of the training laboratory.

THE T-GROUP. As the T-group meets for the first time on the opening day of the training session, they may be greeted with the following abbreviated introductory remarks from the leader:

> Gentlemen, I am here as your leader, but I won't be doing much leading. If you think I am an instructor, you will find that I don't do much teaching. This is your training session. It is up to you to organize it, plan the program, and decide how to execute it. You decide upon the goals and purposes of the group and how to get there. In sensitivity training we concentrate on the 'here and now.' We are not particularly interested in your family life, your past, or your problems except as they affect the here and now. From time to time I'll interrupt the meeting so you can rate each other and the effectiveness of the lab session. That's all I have to say now.

The net result of this opening statement is the creation of an immense vacuum. Here is a leader who does not lead and a teacher who

---

[22] Edgar H. Schein, *op. cit.*

does not teach. There is no leadership, authority, or power; nor is there a plan, a program, or an agenda. The situation, like the Rorschach inkblots, is purposely unstructured; but the members of the T-group are all executives accustomed to working in highly structured situations with clearly stated objectives, defined lines of authority, and a plan to be executed. Any questions directed toward the leader are fruitless and are met with comments such as "I don't know" or "It's your program." Eventually someone hits upon the idea of each one introducing himself to the other members of the group. The first executive who tries to assume control of the group is sure to be charged later in the training sessions with "railroading" or "trying to cram something down our throats." Nor is the man who says nothing safe. He is usually described as a "free-loader" or "just along for the ride, with no real qualities of leadership."

The first few days of the T-group are the *unfreezing* step of Schein's model of change. The old patterns of authority are not effective, nor are the usual concepts of power and leadership working. The executive who tries to direct the group as he does his company is rejected; the jovial back-slapper is referred to as a clown. Nothing seems to work. There is a need for the unfreezing of present attitudes and feelings about one's self and about others.

FEEDBACK. From time to time during the first week, the leader of the T-group asks for comments on the effectiveness of the group and how each member reacts to the others. The following is typical of a feedback session.[23]

> "Ken, you intimidate me," says Charles. "You get sarcastic. You sulk when anyone disagrees with you. When you walk into the room, I feel like standing at attention and saluting. I wonder if your employees feel that way."
>
> Ken answers, "I certainly don't want them to."
>
> "Don't you?" Charles continues. "I wonder if you really know how you want them to feel. And I wonder if you know as much about what's going on in your company as you think you do."
>
> Then, again, it may be Ken who is the critic and Charles who is on the receiving end.
>
> "Charles, why do you go on pretending that you're so damned relaxed? You're nowhere near as calm and collected as you pretend to be."

[23] Alfred J. Marrow, *Behind the Executive Mask* (New York: American Management Association, 1964), pp. 40-41. Alfred J. Marrow, holder of a Ph.D. in psychology, is chairman of the board of the Harwood-Weldon Company. This rather brief book is a very readable account of sensitivity training.

"What makes you say that?"

"Why, it's obvious. You talk about keeping cool, but you have a lot of nervous habits. You talk about being happy with your family and happy in your job; yet some of the things you let slip this morning and the way you said them make me feel you have a grudge against the world."

Charles shakes his head. "You couldn't be more wrong."

"Come on, Charles. Why not be honest with yourself? If you're mad or impatient or angry, let it come out. Why pretend to be what you aren't?"

Charles answers sharply, "You don't have to worry about ulcers. You're not the type that gets them. You just give them."

Through feedback the unfreezing process is hastened and the process of change begins. New responses may be tried, and these may be evaluated in subsequent feedback sessions. The members of the group are removing their "executive masks" and perceiving how they really affect others and how others, in turn, affect them.

REFREEZING. The first week of the laboratory session is directed toward the individual. He sees himself, possibly for the first time, as others see him. He may perceive the need for change and try new methods of working with the group. The second and third weeks of the laboratory session are concerned with improving the effectiveness of the group, sometimes in competition with other T-groups. There is an opportunity for refreezing and making permanent the newly found forms of leadership and group participation. Although the organizational climate in their respective companies to which these men return has a marked effect upon the permanence of their newly acquired understanding of themselves and others, the fact that laboratory training is an emotional as well as an intellectual experience results in a heightened sensitivity toward one's self and toward others that seems to be relatively permanent.

A Breakthrough in Organization Development. From time to time we have commented upon the importance of organizational climate in respect to its effect upon the permanence of skills and attitudes acquired during training programs. What would happen if it were possible to alter organizational climate by having all members of management participate in a program designed to change attitudes towards one's self and toward others? In effect, what would happen if we could achieve *organizational* development as well as individual *executive* development? In a study that appears to be a major breakthrough in *organization* development, all members of management (a total of some 800 line, staff, and technical personnel) participated in a laboratory training program comparable to sensitivity training.[24]

The T-group sessions of sensitivity training are unstructured; however, the laboratory sessions of the Managerial Grid Program are structured to a degree. Although both laboratory methods utilize feedback, the T-group member engages in an introspective analysis of himself. The Managerial Grid Program directs attention toward managerial styles. Five basic types of managerial styles, as shown in Figure 20-2, are identified:

1.1—Minimum effort to get work done but sufficient to maintain organization.
9.1—Emphasis on work with minimum interference from human factors.
1.9—Primary attention to needs of people, a comfortable place to work.
5.5—Balance between attention to work and attention to people.
9.9—Work is accomplished by people committed to the organization; a high degree of congruence between the goals of the organization and the goals of its members.

Managerial Grid training can be broken down into six phases; the first two are directed toward *manager* development and the last four are concerned with *organization* development. The first phase is the *laboratory-seminar training* directed toward the analysis of management style, and the second phase is an on-the-job application of phase one resulting in *team development*. The organization development phases, also conducted on the job, are: *Intergroup development, organizational goal setting, goal attainment,* and *stabilization*. In the "breakthrough" study, Dr. Blake, the developer of the Managerial Grid Program, trained four of Sigma's top management, including the plant manager. These four trained 22 instructors chosen from management, and in turn, the instructors trained the remaining 800 members of management. Thus, with the exception of the four trained initially by Dr. Blake, the development program was administered internally by Sigma's management.

---

[24] R. R. Blake, J. S. Mouton, L. B. Barnes, and L. E. Greiner, "Break-through in Organization Development," *Harvard Business Review,* Vol. XXXXII (November-December, 1964), pp. 133-155. The first part of the article is a description of the Managerial Grid Program and is written by Drs. Blake and Mouton. As a consultant, Dr. Blake introduced the concepts of the Managerial Grid to a few top managers of the plant known as Sigma. These managers then administered the program to the entire management group. The second part of the article is an independent audit of the program conducted by Dr. Barnes and Mr. Greiner. This is an unusual, comprehensive study well worth careful attention.

For a complete description of the Managerial Grid, see: Robert R. Blake and Jane S. Mouton, *The Managerial Grid* (Houston: Gulf Publishing Company, 1964).

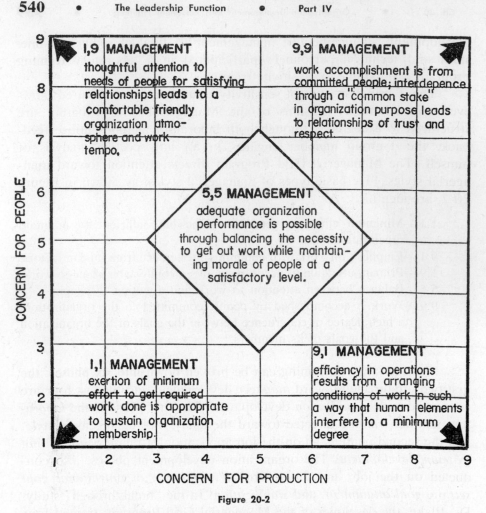

Figure 20-2

MANAGERIAL STYLES OF THE MANAGERIAL GRID PROGRAM

The problems involved in measuring organizational effectiveness are complex; nonetheless, the following changes in Sigma's organizational performance are attributable to the Managerial Grid Program of organizational development.

PROFIT. It must be remembered that profits are a function of some factors that are uncontrollable by local plant management, such as cost of raw materials, taxes, depreciation, and revenues; and factors that are within the control of management—controllable costs. Profits more than doubled during the first full year following the introduction of the Managerial Grid Program. Fifty-six percent of the increase in profits was attributable to noncontrollable factors, but the remaining 44 percent resulted from a reduction in controllable costs. Sixty-nine percent of the reduction in controllable costs came from the elimination of excess manpower—600 employees, with 520 of them accepting early retirement. Those who were laid off did not express bitterness toward the company. The balance of the reduction in controllable costs resulted from a 31 percent increase in productivity per man-hour without the introduction of new machinery or radical innovations in technology. Follow-up projects (phases four and five of the program) were established and are expected to yield substantial savings in the future.

CHANGES IN MANAGEMENT PRACTICES AND BEHAVIOR. There was a marked increase in the number of meetings held, an indicator of increased group effort in the solution of problems. There was a downward shift in the age of the 50 most valuable managers, thereby emphasizing youth and ability rather than seniority as a criterion of managerial effectiveness. Also, a greater mobility of managers was evidenced by an increase in the number of in-plant transfers and an increase in the number of transfers to corporate units outside the plant. The net result of the increase in transfers was an increase in promotional opportunities, a strong motivational factor.

CHANGES IN ATTITUDES AND VALUES. A shift in values and attitudes toward the 9.9 style of management as introduced in phase one of the grid program was noted. This shift in values was reflected by the acceptance or rejection of items descriptive of various management practices contained in a questionnaire. Overall ratings of the Managerial Grid program were obtained. Only 16 percent of those participating in the program rated the grid training as somewhat low or very low, while 84 percent rated the program as high or very high. There seemed to be a thoroughgoing respect for, and the establishment of, a set of operational ground rules approaching the 9.9 concept of management.

The organizational development program as conducted at Sigma seems to answer a question that has arisen among behavioral scientists and practicing managers alike: Are the findings of behavioral science applicable to large-scale industrial operations? The answer, based upon this study, is an unqualified "yes." However, for an organization development program, an application of what we know concerning leadership, communications, and motivation, to be as successful as Sigma's program it is necessary that top management not only give their enthusiastic support to the program but also become the internal administrators of the program. Only then will there be created an organizational climate that permits the application of our knowledge from the behavioral sciences.

PERSONNEL POLICIES

In our study of the personnel function, designated as "directing" in the management process, we have examined the nature of leadership, the process of communication, employee motivation, and the role of the supervisor particularly as a motivating force. In this chapter we have studied the problems in the development of the individual executive and a method that has the potential of developing an entire organization. If maximum benefits are to be realized from the personnel function, a careful planning of that function is necessary. Further, the manner in which the personnel function is performed has its effects upon the extent to which financial policies (Chapter 5), sales policies (Chapter 6), and production policies (Chapter 7) are realized. Financial policies are concerned with the acquisition of capital, the employment of capital, and the distribution of profits. Sales policies are directed toward the product, pricing, the channel of distribution, and the type of sales promotion. Production policies also consider the product, and in addition include questions concerning facilities for production and the selection of vendors. In a similar manner the policies of the personnel function are broad in scope. Personnel policies determine: (1) the organizational climate, (2) motivational systems, and (3) organization development. The scope of the policies of the personnel function—along with those for finance, sales, and production—are summarized in tabular form in Figure 20-3.

Organizational Climate

It might be argued that organizational climate is the result of the manner in which all policies are executed, and consequently the establishment of the climate of an organization is not the result of a specific policy decision. However, Blake and Mouton's "Breakthrough in Organizational Development" shows that a determined leadership can modify its style of management and in so doing effect a major change in organization climate. In addition to management style, the company's position in regard to labor-management relations is another important aspect of organizational climate. These two areas of the policy that determines organizational climate—*management style* and *labor-management relations*—are discussed briefly.

Management Style. The managerial grid illustrated in Figure 20-2 shows several management styles that may result from varying combinations of concern for production and concern for people. The 1.1

FINANCE	PRODUCTION
Acquisition of Capital	Product Selection
Long-Term Capital	Diversification
Stock	New Products
Bonds	Integration
Mortgages	Make or Buy
Long-Term Notes	Quality
Short Term Capital	Standardization
Commercial Credits	Inventory
Bank Loans	Facility Policies
Commercial Factors	Location
Employment of Capital	Capacity
Fixed Assets	Maintenance of Facilities
Ratio of Working Capital	Selection of Vendors
Inventory	Number of Vendors
Credits and Collections	Reciprocity
Depreciation	
Distribution of Profit	
Dividends	
Re-Investment	

SALES	PERSONNEL
Product Selection	Determining Organizational Climate
Product Diversification	Management Style
Obsolescence and Style	Labor-Management Relations
Quality	The Motivational System
Standardization	Compensation
Pricing the Product	Employee Benefit Plans
Produce Costs	Work Design
Competition	Employee Mobility
Pricing New Products	The Role of the Supervisor
Terms of Sale	Organization Development
Channel of Distribution	Responsibility of the Organization
Selecting the Channel	Responsibility of the Individual
Market Penetration	
Sales Promotion	
Direct Selling	
Advertising	
Special Promotional Devices	

Figure 20-3

SUMMARY OF THE SCOPE OF POLICIES FOR EACH FUNCTIONAL AREA

style of management shows a minimal concern for both production and people—just enough to get by in both respects. The 9.1 style of management represents major concern for production and minimal concern for people, while the 1.9 emphasizes maximum concern for people and a minimal concern for production. The 5.5 position in the center of the grid is an approach to management that attempts to balance concern for both production and people—a "middle-of-the-road" position. The 9.9 style, shown in the upper right-hand corner of the grid, represents a high degree of concern for production and at the same time a high concern for human relations values, with effort made to achieve organizational goals by developing within the members of the organization an understanding of what must be accomplished.

In Chapter 10, "Organization Theory," the propositions of Theory Z—a systems approach—are interpreted in terms of their effect upon organization structure and the effectiveness of stated patterns of leadership. For purposes of discussion, leadership patterns are described as being primarily authoritative or participative in nature. In Chapter 16, "Leadership Patterns," the systems concept is applied specifically to determine an effective pattern of leadership (pages 408 to 413). It is noted that as the size of an organization increases, there is a tendency for leadership patterns to become more formal and authoritative. The need for interaction between the members of an organization is shown for the most part to be a function of the technology of the organization; if the problems to be solved are routine in nature, there is little need for interaction. As a result, little need for participation exists. But if the problems are varied and complex in nature, interaction and participation between members are aids in the problem-solving process. Similarly, the personality of the members of the organization, the congruence of the goals of the organization and those of its members, the organizational level of decision making, and the state of the system relative to the achievement of organizational goals all contribute to determining the style of leadership that is most effective.

Admittedly, a systems concept of organization precludes the possibility of, and casts doubt upon, the desirability of all organizations achieving and utilizing effectively a participative form of leadership. However, much can be done to modify and shape management style so that there is maximum movement toward the 9.9 position on the managerial grid, with the highest possible concern—within the limits of the organizational system—for the achievement of organizational goals and, at the same time, the highest possible concern for human relations values. It is this type of management that will enable an organization to sustain effectiveness over a long period of time.

Labor-Management Relations. Another facet of organizational climate that is at the same time a reflection of management style is the labor-management relations existing between a company and the union or unions representing its employees. Frequently the nature of these relationships is described as ranging from a style of open hostility to one of cooperative effort between management and labor. Conditions of open hostility between management and labor are most likely to occur within the framework of a 9.1 management style. In this instance management's concern for production is manifested by an intense resentment toward any infringement upon management rights. The 1.1 style of management—a minimal concern for both production and people—may result in a "follow-the-leader" or "pattern" concept of bargaining. Here, management takes the course of least resistance and follows the patterns set by other companies and other unions in the community or industry, with little regard for the ultimate effect of such practice upon production or the welfare of its employees. Primary concern for the immediate welfare of people at the expense of production and the achievement of other organizational goals—the 1.9 position in the managerial grid—may result in acceding to the pressures of the union, an attitude of fear and resignation. A more mature relationship between labor and management is associated with a 5.5 management style. This relationship is often described as a business relationship and is similar in many respects to the relationship that exists between a company and its suppliers and customers. The 9.9 grid position—a high regard for production and the achievement of organizational goals as the result of cooperative effort—results in labor-management relations evidenced by complete cooperation and understanding on the part of both the union and the company. It is recognized that a mature cooperative relationship between a company and a union is dependent upon factors other than management style; for example, the goals and strength of the union and the economic condition of the company; but the style of management sets the upper limits of the extent to which cooperative effort may be realized.

Motivational Systems

In addition to retaining and motivating present employees, motivational systems are important in attracting new employees. In Chapter 18, "Motivating Employees," it is stated that some of the methods intended to motivate employees are actually not motivators; instead, they are hygienic factors. Hygienic factors are important for two reasons: first, when absent or not present in sufficient quantity, they tend to operate as dissatisfiers and become a source of unrest. Second, hygienic factors are significant in that they must be maintained at competitive levels in order to retain present employees and to attract new employees. Factors intrinsic to the job itself serve as motivators. Also, opportunities for advancement and the way in which a supervisor performs his job are important as motivators. The hygienic factors— *compensation plans* and *employee benefit plans*—are discussed first. The true motivators are discussed under the headings of *job design, mobility of employees,* and the *role of the supervisor.*

Compensation Plans. *Compensation* is defined as money paid for work performed. In establishing compensation policies, there are two major considerations. First is the selection of criteria to determine the level or amount of compensation; and second, a determination must be made concerning the method of payment.

AMOUNT OF COMPENSATION. Determining the amount of money to be paid for a given job is not an easy task since there is no single criterion applicable to all companies or even to the same company over a period of time. At least three criteria are used by most companies in determining the level of compensation; however, the significance assigned each criterion varies considerably. The three criteria most frequently used are: area rates, industry rates, and internal rate structure equity.

For many businesses the rates paid in a given geographic area are the controlling factor in determining wage levels. The geographic area encompasses the labor market that a company draws upon; thus, it may consist of a single, small community or a vast metropolitan complex. The prevailing rates for each of several key jobs, usually 15 to 25, are determined by means of a wage survey. A company can thus determine what it must pay to attract and retain the type of employee it needs. When rates higher than those paid in the immediate area are established, it may be possible to secure a better class of employee; when rates lower than those of the area are adopted, increased turnover, absenteeism, and poor performance may result. Area rates are the chief determinant in setting the level of payment of many clerical workers and for those employed in local retail establishments.

For larger industrial firms the prevailing rates of the specific industry may be the factor given the most weight. Industry patterns are prevalent in the manufacture of steel, autos, chemicals, and aircraft. To a large extent, industry rates are the result of collective bargaining agreements between the member firms of an industry, for example, the automobile companies, and a single union—the United Automobile Workers—representing a large number of employees in each of the companies in the industry.

Wage levels determined by either area or industry rates utilize criteria external to the company; however, there is an internal criterion that also must be satisfied. Within each organizational unit, such as a plant or a corporate headquarters office, there should be an equitable relationship between the amounts paid for jobs requiring different levels of skill, responsibility, and training. For example, what should the mail clerk's rate of pay be in comparison to the rate paid an accountant, and what should the accountant's pay be in comparison to that of a programmer for an integrated data processing system? The same questions arise at the plant level. What are the proper relationships for the rate of pay for the janitor, a skilled machine-tool operator, and a tool and die maker? Equitable pay structures are developed through the use of *job evaluation* procedures, a technique of weighting the various factors necessary for the performance of each job.

Thus, the amount of pay is a policy decision resulting from the weighting of three separate criteria: area rates, industry rates, and an internally equitable rate structure between each of the several jobs. In addition, some companies reward employees for above-average performance of their jobs and for length of service on the job. Policies governing these practices, usually referred to as merit and length of service increases, must also be determined.

METHOD OF PAYMENT. Once the amount of compensation has been determined as the result of a judicious weighting of internal and external criteria, a method of payment must be selected. Fundamentally there are two methods of payment. One method is to pay for *time* spent on the job; the other is to pay for the *amount* of work produced. There is, of course, the possibility of a combined payment for both time and amount produced. However, such combinations are usually regarded as payment for work and are classed as incentive plans.

Payment for time is applicable to all levels of the organization, even though the unit of time varies considerably. Production workers are paid for the actual number of hours worked, and the amount earned is usually computed and paid on a weekly basis. Time for non-exempt clerical employees, those who must be paid for overtime, is computed on a weekly basis and payment may be received weekly, biweekly, or semimonthly. Although clerical workers are expected to work a predetermined number of hours each week, policy decisions determine whether or not pay is received for time not worked due to absence or tardiness. Those employees who are exempt from the provisions of the law requiring payment of overtime are called salaried employees, and their time is computed on a monthly basis with payment received either monthly or semimonthly. It is a mistake to assume that there is no relationship between time payment and job performance. On the contrary, standards of performance should be set not only for production and clerical jobs but also for the managerial salaried positions.

Payment for work performed, whether it be the piece rate of the garment industry with no hourly guarantee for time spent or an hourly rate with additional pay for work produced in excess of a stated standard, rests upon two assumptions. First, it is assumed that the worker has control over the amount of work that can be produced; and second, that he will respond to the opportunity to earn more money by increasing his output. The validity of the first assumption can be determined only by a systematic analysis of each work situation. The findings discussed in Chapter 18, "Motivating Employees," cast doubt upon the extent to which the second assumption is applicable. Whyte's estimate that only 10 percent of the production workers respond to monetary incentives, a point of view supported by Zaleznik's analysis of "frozen groups" in industrial plants, certainly does not encourage the widespread use of incentive plans. However, the analysis presented by Gellerman indicates the conditions that must be present if policies establishing incentive plans are to be successful. Gellerman describes four groups of people in respect to their expectations for reward and their perceived power to control their environment. These four groups are: (1) those who have a high reward expectation and a high degree of perceived power over the environment; (2) high expectations, but a low degree of perceived power; (3) low reward expectations, but a high degree of perceived power; and (4) those who have both low expectations and perceived power. For an incentive plan to work effectively—to motivate employees to higher levels of productivity—it should be applied to employees best characterized as belonging to groups 1 and 3, with the common characteristic of perceiving a high degree of power to control the environment.

Employee Benefit Plans. Although compensation is not a "true" motivator, it is tangible evidence of an employee's worth from both his point of view and the company's. In this sense compensation is directly related to the job. Employee benefits, shown in the outer circle of Figure 18-1, page 466, are peripheral to the job itself and are aptly called "fringe benefits." Included among the many fringe benefits are: retirement plans, educational plans and tuition rebates, various forms of insurance, sick leave, recreation programs, supplemental unemployment compensation, and other items intended to improve the welfare of the employees.

Fringe benefits are important to the employer and the employee alike. For the former, fringes are an important cost of doing business, but unfortunately benefit programs do not motivate employees to higher levels of productivity, better quality, or innovations. In addition, benefits must be maintained at competitive levels in order to attract and retain desired employees. For the employee, benefit plans are a normal, expected part of the job. When absent or not present in sufficient quantity in a present job, fringe benefits are a source of annoyance that colors the entire work situation. If the benefit programs of a potential employer do not meet preconceived minimal levels of acceptability, that employer has little chance of attracting discriminating personnel.

Formulating policies governing employee benefit plans is primarily an economic matter. As is the case in setting compensation levels, surveys of the area and the industry should be used as a guide to determine current practice. A company has little to gain by offering the most expensive benefit plan, but there is much to lose if the plan is too little and too late. A sound communications program on a continuing basis is an aid in keeping employees informed of the value received from the many benefit programs.

Job Design. We know that the satisfaction of the needs for achievement, growth, responsibility, and recognition serves to motivate people to even greater achievement. We also know that the satisfaction of these needs in an industrial situation is intrinsic to the job itself; therefore, job design is an important aspect of any motivational system. For the professional worker—the engineer, the scientist, the accountant—minor changes in company policy and administration often permit these motivators to operate more effectively. For example, recognition of achievement in company publications and encouragement to belong to and participate in professional organizations help to motivate the professional worker.

The problem of designing clerical and production jobs so that motivation comes from the intrinsic nature of the job is difficult and complex. Current job design reflects policies that support an engineering approach to jobs, an approach that builds jobs around technological processes rather than the satisfaction of the needs of people. Admittedly, evidence supporting job enlargement, a means of making jobs intrinsically more meaningful, is fragmentary and consequently only suggestive at the present time. Yet the works of Marks (Chapter 18, page 468) is convincing. The assemblers of a hospital appliance, freed from the constraints of a mechanically paced conveyor and performing all assembly operations rather than one single repetitive operation, were able to produce more units at a higher level of quality with only six days' experience on the new job design. Non-Linear Systems, Inc., a 12-year old company with 300 employees engaged in the manufacture, design, and development of precision electronic instruments, reports similar results. The 80 assemblers, normally assigned to four assembly lines, were divided into groups of approximately seven members each. There was complete chaos for approximately nine months, but in the long run there was a 30 percent increase in production, improved quality, and many innovations in methods. Arthur H. Kuriloff, a vice president of Non-Linear Systems, attributes this change to the fact that under the new job design, people were able to satisfy their basic needs on the job.[25]

The work of Marks and the experience of Non-Linear Systems are not conclusive, yet these findings should force management to examine policies concerning current job design to determine whether or not they really have "the one best way." If not, policies should be established to encourage the design of jobs so that the needs of employees, as well as the requirements of production, are met.

Mobility of Employees. Employees may be motivated when there is opportunity for mobility within the organization, since for some the basic needs of growth, achievement, the desire for increased responsibility, and recognition may be satisfied. However, the extent to which employees can move from one level of an organization to another and to corresponding jobs at the same level in different organizational units is dependent upon the company's policies and practices in the selection, promotion, and termination of employees. The following discussion shows how policies in each of these areas affect the opportunity for mobility.

SELECTION. We must assume that a company has knowledge of the requirements necessary for the successful performance of jobs in respect to training, education, and prior experience, for without this information the selection process is little more than a game of chance. Knowing the qualifications of jobs to be filled, a company has three choices provided its compensation and employee benefits are at competitive levels: (1) It may select employees who are underqualified for the job—this usually happens when compensation and benefit plans are below par. (2) It may select employees qualified for the present job but limited in potential. (3) Employees may be selected who are overqualified for the current job vacancy. If those selected are underqualified,

---

25 Arthur H. Kuriloff, "An Experiment in Management," pp. 252-257. Jerome W. Blood (Ed.), *The Personnel Job in a Changing World* (New York: American Management Association, 1964).

excessive turnover may result from terminations due to poor performance, and those who do remain are rarely capable of being promoted within the organization. The same restrictions on mobility develop if candidates are selected to fit the requirements of the current vacancy but are limited in potential. Companies that select overqualified candidates may experience excessive turnover if these people become restless because they are not progressing rapidly enough. Also, it may be necessary to pay more than the entering job is actually worth in order to attract overqualified people. The recruitment of college graduates is a good example of hiring overqualified candidates in order to have available personnel with the potential for growth within the organization. At the hourly level it may be wise to hire candidates with one or two years of training beyond high school in order to insure a supply of potential supervisory personnel. When establishing selection policies, a company has to determine the degree of qualification desired—one of the three choices listed above—and the policy should be flexible for differing organizational levels and organizational units.

PROMOTION. Strictly defined, promotion is vertical movement upward in the organizational hierarchy and usually is associated with an increase in pay. In practice, however, the concept of promotion includes lateral transfers to other positions at the same organizational level since such transfers may be part of a long-range training plan. Also included in the concept of promotion are increased responsibilities in a current position with or without an increase in compensation. In any event, whether the new job is called a promotion, a transfer, or simply increased responsibilities, all represent a form of employee mobility and consequently all are potential motivators since they may satisfy the needs for growth, achievement, increased responsibility, and recognition. The effectiveness of policy statements encouraging promotion from within is dependent upon the selection policies of a company. Such statements are effective only if there is a sufficient number of employees with the potential for promotion; otherwise, it becomes necessary to fill vacancies by hiring from outside the company.

TERMINATION. Policies governing the termination of employment have a marked effect upon the mobility of employees. When the phrase "termination of employment" is mentioned, we usually think of discharge for cause, such as failure to report for work or resignation, but there are other and increasingly more frequent reasons for the termination of employment. Among the reasons for termination that are important in the formulation of personnel policy is retirement. Policies calling for retirement at a stated age definitely provide opportunities for mobility since positions in the organization become available as incumbents reach the stated age limit. However, there are factors other than those of providing an opportunity for mobility to be considered in the statement of retirement policies. A mandatory retirement age, such as age 65, may result in some employees, particularly executives, being forced to retire despite their potential contribution to the company, and other employees may have to work several years beyond their period of effective contribution. For these reasons retirement policies should be flexible, with provisions for extended service on a part-time or consulting basis and with provisions for early retirement.

Role of the Supervisor. The supervisor's position in the organization as the only member of management having direct contact with nonmanagerial personnel makes him uniquely capable of linking management and operative personnel. Hence, the role of the supervisor is best described as a "linking-pin" function. Although no consistent positive relationships have been found between productivity and morale or between productivity and compensation, there is fortunately a distinct consistent relationship between productivity and supervisory practices. Consequently, the role of the supervisor is a key element in any motivational system. There are many factors determining the effectiveness of the supervisor as a motivating force in the organization. The following four factors, each the result of policy decisions, stand out above all others.

Organizational climate, discussed earlier as a distinct policy area, is the outstanding factor that determines the extent of transfer from supervisory training programs to effective supervisory practices on the job. Also dependent upon organizational climate is the *style of management* expressed by the supervisor in the performance of his job. The most effective motivation occurs when a supervisor can practice a 9.9 style of management—a high concern for the needs and goals of the organization and a high concern for the needs and goals of the individual. The supervisor must be oriented to both production and people. Third, effective supervision calls for an organizational structure and practice that result in the *delegation of authority* so that the supervisor's position is clearly differentiated from the position of those being supervised. As a result of proper delegation, the supervisor should have the power and influence necessary to manage his department. The fourth factor in determining effective supervision, a reflection of both organizational climate and sound practices in delegation, is the extent to which the supervisor is able to use *participative methods* in the introduction of change in his department. Evidence indicates that participation contributes strongly to the motivation of employees. In summary, although the supervisor's role is a distinct element in the motivation of employees, effective supervision is heavily dependent upon organizational climate.

Organization Development

We have reviewed two broad areas of personnel policy determination: (1) the establishment of organizational climate, and (2) the scope of motivational systems. The third major area of personnel policy is concerned with organization development. The development of managerial personnel is best regarded as a process of change—primarily a change in attitudes toward one's self, toward others, and in respect to the role of managers in the management process. In setting policies that guide the development of individual managers and shape the development of the entire organization, it is necessary to delineate the responsibilities of the organization and the responsibilities of the individual manager.

Responsibilities of the Organization. Viewing the development of managers as a process of change permits the use of Schein's three-step model as a means of estimating the potential effectiveness of existing or potential plans of organization development. The three steps of Schein's model are: (1) unfreezing, (2) changing, and (3) refreezing. For the first step, unfreezing, to achieve optimum results, the organization should exercise a high degree of control over the environment. Examples of a high degree of control over the environment are the administration of a convent and the medical profession's control of the four years of medical school and the periods of internship and residency. Changes in attitudes and behavior occur most readily when there is opportunity to identify with superiors who exemplify the desired attitudes and behavior. For refreezing to be most effective, there must be continual reinforcement by the actions of both peers and superiors in the organization.

Business firms cannot approach the control over the environment to the degree exercised by convents and medical schools; however, there is much that can be done to improve the effectiveness of the second and the third steps of the change process. First, there can be developed a clear statement of the objectives of a management development program expressed in terms of the behavior and attitudes necessary to perform as a successful manager. Implied in this step is the belief that managerial skills can be transmitted to others through an educational process, a contrast to the belief that good managers, like cream, will rise to the top. A concise statement of objectives forms the substance of a management development program. Second, the scope of the program, defined in terms of the levels of the organization, must be determined. Are all personnel in the organization, including hourly clerical and production workers, to be included, or is organization development to be confined to certain levels of supervision and a few key administrators? Third, in order to execute the broad policy decisions regarding the objectives and scope of the organization development program, provision must be made for adequate administrative procedures to determine the extent to which objectives are met. Figure 20-1, page 528, serves as a useful check for the administrative provisions of the plan. The organizational breakthrough described by Blake illustrates maximum effort on the part of an organization to fulfill its responsibility in the development of all managers and can serve as an indication of what can be accomplished with a complete plan for organization development.

Responsibilities of the Individual Manager. The responsibilities of the organization include determining the objectives of the program, defining the scope of the program, and providing for the administration of the plan; yet, the responsibility for the ultimate success of management development efforts is shared by both the organization and the individual manager who participates in the program. There must be readiness on the part of those who participate in management development to put forth their best efforts in order that the desired change may be effected. Readiness to learn is characteristic of any successful educational process. Students are aware that universities fall short of their goals unless the students have clear personal objectives and a readiness to learn. Evidence indicates that one of the most frequent reasons for the shortcomings of management development programs is that those participating in such programs do not have clearly defined goals. They do not know what they want to achieve in the business world, nor do they have a clear concept of the position they expect to achieve within the organization. Some would like positions of responsibility and the prestige and money associated with such positions; yet many are unwilling to make the sacrifices that are sometimes necessary in the early years of corporate life, for example, frequent moves from one town to another, in order to gain the experience necessary for promotion and increased responsibility.

Top management must recognize the dual responsibility of the organization and the individual for the success of management development plans and consequently should be wary of formulating a policy requiring all managers to participate in a development program. Another result coming from the recognition of the responsibility of the individual manager is the statement of management development objectives so that they may ultimately be adopted as the personal objectives of each individual manager—only then may the objectives of the organization be fulfilled.

●   ●   ●   ●   ●   ●   ●   ●   ●

Case Problem 20-B, Formulating Personnel Policies, provides the opportunity for developing a set of consistent policies for a specific organization.

Questions for Study and Discussion

1. Two extreme approaches to the development of managers are described by McGregor. Evaluate each of these extremes and then describe a middle-of-the-road approach.
2. Most of us can agree on some of the basic attitudes necessary for the practice of medicine. Develop a similar set of attitudes for the successful practice of management.
3. Describe in your own terms the change process. What condition must exist prior to the beginning of this process for the change to be most effective? If this condition does not exist, how does the first step of the change process serve to induce a readiness to change?
4. In what respect do management development programs fall short of the ideal conditions necessary for the most effective change process?
5. Why are attitudes toward authority significant in determining the manner in which a person adjusts to formal organization? Where are early attitudes toward authority learned?
6. Would it be desirable for industrial organizations to exert the same degree of control over the environment and actions of new managers as that exercised by a convent in respect to noviates or a military academy in respect to cadets? Discuss.
7. Describe the essential steps of a management development program. In your opinion, which step is of the greatest importance? Why?
8. Discuss performance appraisals in respect to the following factors: purpose, strengths, weaknesses, and methods of improving performance appraisals.
9. What is meant by sensitivity training? Do you believe that this type of training has a place in management development? Why?
10. What is the significance of the organizational breakthrough of Sigma? What factors would limit such a breakthrough in other organizations?
11. Support the thesis that organizational climate is the result of all other personnel policies rather than an area for which policy can and should be stated.
12. Discuss the significance of each of the areas of personnel policy. Which seems to be the most important in your opinion? Why?

●   ●   ●   ●   ●   ●   ●   ●   ●

Joe Beck, vice-president of industrial relations for Diversified Manufacturing, has just completed some notes that he had been preparing for his conference with Bob Cox, the personnel director who reports to him.

"Bob," he began, "we have been asked to prepare a draft of proposed personnel policies to be submitted to the board of directors when they have their annual meeting here in Chicago next month. It seems that we are being criticized because of what appears to be a lack of consistency in some of the decisions made concerning the personnel function."

"Is that criticism true?" Bob asked.

"I believe there is a good basis for it. Here are some of the incidents that have been brought to my attention." Joe handed Bob the notes he had been preparing. The following is a copy of Joe's notes.

1. In the western division's Los Angeles plant, there was a 45-day strike because of the company's insistence that an incentive plan be installed as a means of raising the average earnings of employees. The union had proposed a general wage increase to bring the rates up to the average of the Los Angeles area. As the strike progressed, it became clear that the real issue was one of permitting union participation in the setting of time standards. The company stated that the determination of standards was a company prerogative and no concern of the union's. Yet, in a New York plant of the eastern division a job evaluation plan had been installed

---

Case Problem 20-B

Formulating Personnel Policies

---

with joint union-management participation.

2. The general manager of the eastern division, responsible for both manufacturing and sales, had attended one of Dr. Blake's Managerial Grid seminars at the request of the president, and as a result sent many of his middle managers to similar programs. Some of these managers were later transferred to the western division and have reported that they feel as though they were working for a different company. One even went so far as to state that if he could not return to the eastern division he would resign.

3. The basis for determining wage levels is not clear. In the eastern division the company's position is that the area wage should prevail as the basis for determining the wage level; yet, in the western division the company argues that the average of the industry, rather than the geographic area average, should determine the wage level. The union charges that the company is inconsistent.

4. Employee benefit programs are uniform throughout all plants in both divisions. As a result, there are locations where hospitalization benefits adequately cover the cost of hospitalization, and there are locations where the benefits received are inadequate. Uniform practices are also followed in respect to vacations, holidays, and leaves of absence, and, as in the case of the hospitalization benefits, there are instances where company practices are more liberal than those

of other companies in the area and there are situations where company practices fall short of area standards.

5. The eastern division reimburses all employees for expenses incurred for tuition and books after the completion of any course in an accredited school or college. This includes trade courses, secretarial courses, and degree courses. In addition, employees with five or more years' seniority are granted leaves of absence with one-half pay for periods of one year in order to complete their college work. The manager of the eastern division contends that such programs contribute to the division's ability to promote from within. The western division has no subsidies for self-improvement.

6. In the eastern division the plant supervisors, along with other members of the management, attend a regularly scheduled monthly dinner meeting to discuss production schedules and methods for the coming month and to review performance of the past month.

No supervisory meetings are held in the western division.

After reading these six incidents, Bob returned the list to Joe and commented, "It almost seems as though we are talking about two different companies."

"It certainly does, and our job is to develop some policies that will bring these two divisions together. Try and get a draft of such policies for me within the next couple of days."

Problems

1. What key determination must be made before any policies can be developed for this company?
2. Is it necessary, or even desirable, for a company to have consistent personnel policies within separate operating divisions? Give reasons to support each point of view.
3. Develop a proposed set of personnel policies.

● **CHAPTER 21**

The Basis of Control

Standard Building Service Company of St. Louis is a 15-year old company that provides janitorial services for office buildings and industrial plants. Standard was purchased five years ago by Leslie Waller and, at the time of the purchase, annual sales were approximately $500,000. In three years he was able to double the sales volume to the present level of $1,000,000, but for the past two years sales volume has remained relatively constant. Waller attributes the lack of growth for the past two years to his being unable to call on new accounts because the business has grown to such an extent that his full energies and time are required in solving the myriad of problems that arise each day. He recognizes that the few new accounts he does obtain do no more than offset the normal turnover of accounts lost each month.

Case Problem 21-A
A Need for Control

Janitorial services are usually performed after the tenants have left the building for the day; consequently, very few of Standard's employees start work before 6 p.m. Waller has found from experience that in order to keep employees, he must offer them at least 20 hours of work a week. On the other hand, very few people seem willing to work more than 25 hours a week. As a result, the work force of approximately 275 men and women are part-time employees. Waller also found that by hiring persons presently employed he is assured of stable, motivated employees. However, since his employees are working full-time elsewhere, there is considerable resistance when supervisors expect an above-average amount of work from them.

A recent analysis of the 121 accounts serviced by the company shows that

40 customers require the services of only one person working a maximum of 25 hours a week. Thirty-five accounts require two people with total man-hours ranging from 35 to 50 hours a week. Fifteen accounts require an average of 100 man-hours a week, thus utilizing the services of up to four employees. There is one large industrial plant that requires 500 hours of service each week and approximately 20 workers. The remaining 30 accounts range between 100 and 400 man-hours each week, and require between four and sixteen employees.

Mr. Waller is not sure which size job yields the most profit. Jobs are priced on a rule-of-thumb basis and depend upon the type of floor surfaces, the amount of building traffic, number and types of offices, and other similar factors. Mr. Waller and one of his two full-time supervisors estimate the manpower requirements for each new job. An analysis of company records shows that for the past five years variable costs—direct labor and materials (waxes, detergents, etc.)—average about 80 to 85 percent of total revenue.

The full-time organization consists of Mr. Waller, two supervisors, a secretary, an accountant, and a supply man who also maintains some of the larger pieces of cleaning equipment such as the floor polishers. In addition, there are five part-time supervisors, each of whom supervises 40 to 50 workers in a given geographic area of the city. Most of their time and energy is spent in delivering supplies and materials to the various buildings within a given geographic area of the city. They also reassign personnel as the need arises and collect the weekly time cards. The two full-time supervisors have no specific duties assigned to them nor is either one responsible for the work of any particular part-time supervisor.

At the present time Mr. Waller has only two sources of information to guide him in the operation of his business. One of these is customer complaints, which serve as a check on the quality of the work. The other source is the weekly payroll, which is prepared by a local bank. Each week time cards are submitted to the bank and from these records payroll checks are prepared. The bank also maintains the necessary social security and income tax records. In addition, a summary is prepared showing the total man-hours per week for each job. At present, no consistent use is made of this information. However, on the occasions when he has examined these weekly reports, Mr. Waller has found that the total hours per week run as much as 400 hours in excess of the number of hours used in computing the price of the services. There is no record of the use of supplies for each job.

Problems

1. Is there a need for control in this company? Why?
2. If controls are needed, what areas of the business are most in need of control?
3. What type of standards are now being used? What kind would you recommend?
4. How can the organization be modified to improve the control function?

The control function is one of the four major functions of the process of management. The usual sequence assigned to these functions places planning first, next is organizing, the third is the human relations function—frequently called leading or directing—and the last function is control. The word, control, and its position in the management process sequence are indicative of the nature of the control function. In this chapter we will examine, first, the nature of the control function, and second, we will study in detail the steps of the control process. The characteristics of effective controls are then discussed and from this discussion several principles of control are developed.

THE NATURE OF CONTROL

If plans were never in need of revision and were executed flawlessly by a perfectly balanced organization under the direction of an omnipotent leader, there would be no need for control. However, as Robert Burns observed years ago, "The best-laid schemes o' mice an' men gang aft agley." [1] In addition, organizations do not always work smoothly and need revision to meet changing conditions. Also, the effectiveness of leadership is often open to question. It is the purpose of the control function to take the corrective action necessary to assure the fulfillment of organizational objectives. Although control denotes corrective action that may be objective in all respects, the reactions of those subjected to controls may be highly emotionalized and tinged with resentment. The reason for this reaction is that control always touches upon the people who make up organizations, for they are charged with responsibilities and are accountable to their superiors for the performance of these duties. When determining whether or not goals are being met, it is the performance of the people of the organization that is actually being reviewed. One way of developing an understanding of the nature of control is to place the control function in perspective within the framework of a systems concept.

---

[1] The closing stanza of Robert Burns' *To A Mouse* is a statement that could be made by many of today's executives:

"Still thou art blest, compared wi' me!
The present only toucheth thee.
But och! I backward cast my e'e
    On prospects drear!
And forward though I cannot see,
    I guess an' fear!

Cybernetics and Control

The study of how dynamic systems maintain a state of equilibrium, or steady state, though subject to changing environmental conditions is called *cybernetics*.[2] Examples of cybernetic systems are numerous and familiar. The thermostat maintains the temperature of a room at a predetermined level by making or breaking an electrical circuit that starts or stops the furnace. The rotating arms of a steam-engine governor rise or fall with changes in centrifugal force, thereby controlling the input of steam into the cylinders of the engine with the result that a constant speed is maintained under varying load conditions. Another example is a photoelectric cell placed in a circuit to turn on lights in the evening when daylight illumination decreases to a predetermined level and to turn off the artificial lighting the next morning when natural illumination is sufficient.

The above examples of cybernetic systems illustrate the major characteristics of such systems. First, there is a predetermined steady state or equilibrium to be maintained. In the first example, a constant temperature is the state of equilibrium to be maintained; the second illustration focuses upon speed as the steady state, and the third example uses a predetermined intensity of light as the state of equilibrium. Second, in all of the above instances there is constant change in the environment within which the system operates, thus forcing adjustments within the system in order to maintain an equilibrium; hence, the term "dynamic system." Third, there is a transfer of information from the external environment to within the system. The "information" that activates the thermostat is a change in temperature; centrifugal force is the information transmitted by the steam-engine governor, and the intensity of light is the information received by the photoelectric cell. Fourth, there is a mechanical device so designed that corrective action is taken, with the result that the equilibrium of the system is maintained. The bimetal of the thermostat makes or breaks the electrical circuit, the moving arms of the governor open and close a valve regulating the flow of steam, and the photoelectric cell responds to the intensity of light by opening or closing the circuit. In each of these instances the

---

[2] For a complete discussion of cybernetics, see:

Norbert Weiner, *Cybernetics,* Control and Communication in the Animal and the Machine (New York: John Wiley & Sons, Inc., 1948).

Norbert Weiner, *The Human Use of Human Beings* (New York: Doubleday Anchor Books, 1954).

W. R. Ashby, *An Introduction to Cybernetics* (New York: John Wiley & Sons, Inc., 1956).

control device is engineered to perform the specific function necessary to maintain the system's equilibrium.[3]

All living organisms are by definition cybernetic systems, for they must maintain equilibrium in order to survive. It is useful to apply the concept of cybernetics—the maintenance of a steady state through the interpretation of information and subsequent corrective action—to organizations. The concept of cybernetic systems is not being introduced for the first time in this chapter. The systems concept is first discussed in Chapter 1. In Chapter 7, Figure 7-1 (reproduced here as Figure 21-1) shows how the major business functions of finance, production, sales, and personnel form a self-correcting system with a feedback loop to the external environment between the sales department and the external environment, the customer. Feedback loops with outside forces could also be shown between finance and sources of capital, between production and vendors, and between personnel and the labor supply. There is also a continual exchange of information internally between the major functions of an organization.

The Parable of the Spindle, Case Problem 8-A, illustrates how the cook performs a control function by selecting the most efficient combination of orders from information contained on tickets stored on

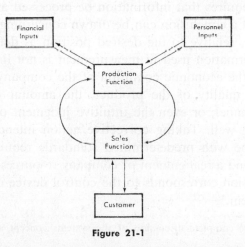

Figure 21-1

MAJOR BUSINESS FUNCTIONS AS A CYBERNETIC SYSTEM

---

[a] Robert Chin, "The Utility of System Models and Developmental Models for Practicioners," from W. G. Bennis, K. D. Benne, and Robert Chin, *The Planning of Change* (New York: Holt, Rinehart and Winston, Inc., 1961). This article discusses several types of models and their application to business situations.

a spindle. Further, the tickets can be used as a control device by the waitress and can be checked against the order received. At the close of the day the tickets may also be used as a control measure when compared with cash receipts. The schematic concept of a business as shown in Figure 21-1 and the specific illustration of the experience of a restaurant illustrate that control is the interpretation of information, from both internal and external sources, so that corrective action may be taken in order to reach desired objectives.[4]

Steps in the Control Process

There is agreement among students of management concerning the three elemental steps of the control process:

1. Establishing standards of performance.
2. Measuring current performance in relation to established standards.
3. Taking corrective action.

Let us now interpret these three steps of the control process in the light of what we know about cybernetic systems. The establishment of standards defines the desired state of equilibrium. Standards are definitions of the objectives of an organization, but it must be remembered that objectives can and do change. The second step, measurement of current performance, requires that information be processed and interpreted by someone so that a conclusion can be drawn concerning present position, or performance, relative to the desired position as defined by the standards. The information used in measurement is not limited to financial data reflecting the economic condition of the company; it also includes reports on the quality of the product, the amount of inventory, the morale of personnel, or even the intuitive judgment of a manager that all is not going well. Taking corrective action intended to bring performance in line with predetermined standards requires executive decision making and a realignment of company resources. The person who makes the decision corresponds to the control device of the mechanical cybernetic system.[5]

---

[4] For a more complete discussion of the systems concept as applied to control, see the following:

Richard A. Johnson, Fremont E. Kast, and James E. Rosenzweig, *The Theory and Management of Systems* (New York: McGraw-Hill Book Company, Inc., 1963), Chapter 4, "Control and Systems Concepts," pp. 57-72.

[5] Douglas S. Sherwin, "The Meaning of Control," *Dun's Review and Modern Industry* (January, 1956), pp. 45, 46, 83, 84.*

Edward L. Anthony, "Effective Control for Better Management," from *Management Aids for Small Manufacturers,* Small Business Administration (January, 1957), pp. 1-4.

These two articles present general discussions of the control function.

The next major section of this chapter discusses in greater detail each of the three steps of the control process; first, however, there is one more question to answer for a more complete understanding of the nature of control. Who does the controlling?

Who Controls?

Many students, particularly those majoring in accounting, consider as a personal career objective the position of controller of a business organization. Figure 21-2 presents two typical position descriptions—one, the controller of a large company, and the other, the combined position of treasurer and controller in a medium-size company. In general, the controller is closely associated with the finance function of the company, though he may or may not report to the vice-president for finance. If he does not report to the financial officer, he reports to the president or chief executive officer of the company. He is usually responsible for designing the systems and procedures necessary for management control; thus, in companies having integrated data processing systems the controller may be responsible for the design and maintenance of such systems. Traditionally the controller's function is concerned with those aspects of the business that can be reduced to dollars and cents; for this reason he is usually concerned with the efficiency of production and the cost of sales. Few companies require that the controller secure information concerning morale of employees, the status of innovations in the organization, or the quality of management; yet these factors are legitimate areas of control.

We still have not answered the question, who controls? Note in Figure 21-2 there is no statement saying that it is the duty of the controller to control by taking corrective action. Control, the act of taking corrective action, is a function of the line manager. The controller, a member of the staff organization, may design the information system, secure and interpret data concerning performance, and even make recommendations as to what might constitute the most appropriate corrective action. However, the final decision and the request for corrective action are the responsibility of the line manager. Nor is control by the line organization limited to any level of management; indeed, for effective control all levels of management must exercise control over those functions assigned to them. There is much that the first-line supervisor can control in his department that cannot be controlled directly by anyone else in the organization.

FUNCTIONS OF THE CONTROLLER IN THE LARGE COMPANY

Objectives

The Controller (or Comptroller) of Accounts is responsible for the effective financial and cost controls of the company's activities.

Functions

1. Prescription of principles and methods to govern accounting controls throughout the enterprise
2. Provision of adequate protection against loss of the company's money and property
3. Prescription of principles of accounting determining cost of product, and normal volume of production in order to compute costs and install appropriate systems
4. Verification of the propriety of expenditures
5. Providing comparison of capital expenditures and appropriations
6. Preparation of the accounts of the corporation
7. Determination of income and expenditure allocation among plants and departments
8. Proposals regarding the nature of the corporation's financial statements
9. Preparation of the financial statements
10. Preparation of analyses assisting others to improve the earnings of the enterprise
11. Observation of the manner of performing accounting responsibilities

Relationships

The Controller of Accounts reports to the Vice-President for Finance

---

Figure 21-2

FUNCTIONS OF THE CONTROLLER

THE CONTROL PROCESS

We have described the control process as consisting of the following three steps: (1) establishing standards of performance, (2) measuring current performance in relation to the established standards, and (3) taking corrective action. Standards are the basis of the control process, for without adequate standards the subsequent steps of measurement and corrective action are meaningless. Let us examine, first, the nature of standards; then, problems encountered in the measurement of performance; and last, the kind of corrective action that should be taken.

FUNCTIONS OF THE TREASURER AND CONTROLLER
IN THE MEDIUM-SIZE COMPANY

1. Accountability for the safekeeping and custody of corporate funds, securities owned by the company, and the corporate seal
2. Establishment of a General Accounting Department with the following duties:
   a. Post-audit of plant transactions
   b. Installation and maintenance of primary books of accounts
   c. Setting the policies, procedures, and standards of accounting and cost records and reports
   d. Setting up methods of cash disbursement, accounts receivable, plant and equipment records
   e. Cash management
   f. Preparation of financial statements and reports
   g. Credit approval
3. Establishment of a cost accounting department with a view to:
   a. Prescribing and administering factory timekeeping and payroll procedures
   b. Maintaining inventory controls
   c. Supervision of timekeeping methods
   d. Setting up a cost system in each plant
4. Establishing a budget department to present standards of performance to management with a view to:
   a. Showing the results of operations
   b. Establishing standards of performance
   c. Proposing a budget forecast
   d. Informing executives of variations from the budget
   e. Continuous revision of the budget

Source: Ernest Dale, *Planning and Developing the Company Organization Structure* (New York: American Management Association, Research Report No. 20, 1952), pp. 200-201.

Figure 21-2 (Concluded)

FUNCTIONS OF THE CONTROLLER

Establishing Standards

The dictionary definition of standards includes two concepts. First, a standard is a rule (unit) for measuring. It is intended to serve as a model or criterion. Second, a standard is established by authority. *Thus, a standard may be defined as a unit of measurement established to serve as a model or criterion.* The 72-stroke par for an 18-hole golf course is an excellent example of a standard. Par is a recognized level of performance or achievement established by authority —custom and the various golfing associations. Second, par demonstrates clearly that a standard is not perfection—many professional golfers consistently exceed, or break, par. Nor is par the average of the level of performance for all golfers; indeed, the average would be considerably higher than 72. Thus, par is a difficult, but attainable, level of performance. It serves as a criterion for comparing the proficiency of one golfer against that of another in terms of an objective unit of measurement—the number of strokes required to complete the course. Par is analogous to the work standards established by a company for its employees.

Scope of Business Standards. Standards in business organizations are not limited to establishing levels of performance for individual workers; instead, they are applicable to all phases of the operation. Ralph C. Davis suggests that standards be set for all activities that contribute to the primary service objectives of the organization. He recommends establishing standards of service, including the development of criteria for the particular good or service being offered by the organization. Standards of policy and function include an evaluation of the organization structure and its method of operation. Standards should also be determined for the evaluation of the physical facilities of the organization, for determining the characteristics of the kind of personnel required, and for determining the level of performance of personnel.[6] Another approach to describing the scope of standards is to set standards for each of several key result areas. General Electric uses this approach and establishes standards for each of the following eight key result areas:

1. Profitability
2. Market position
3. Productivity
4. Product leadership
5. Personnel development
6. Employee attitudes
7. Public responsibility
8. Balance between short-range and long-range goals.[7]

[6] Ralph C. Davis, *The Fundamentals of Top Management* (New York: Harper & Brothers, Publishers, 1951), pp. 28-29. Chapter 2, "Standards and Standardization," pp. 21-42, presents a complete discussion of standards in business organizations.

[7] Robert W. Lewis, "Measurement, Reporting, and Appraising Results of Operations with Reference to Goals, Plans, and Budgets," from the report, *Planning, Managing, and Measuring the Business:* A Case Study of Management Planning and Control at General Electric Company (New York: Controllership Foundation, Inc., 1955), pp. 29-41.* Mr. Lewis discusses the problems inherent in the measurement of performance in each of the eight key result areas.

The student should also review the eight major objectives of an organization described by Peter Drucker and note the similarity between Drucker's objectives and the key result areas of Lewis. Drucker suggests objectives for each of the following eight areas: market standing, innovation, productivity, physical and financial resources, profitability, manager performance and development, worker performance and attitude, and public responsibility. See Chapter 3, "Objectives and Ethics," and the following:

Peter F. Drucker, "The Objectives of a Business," from *The Practice of Management* (New York: Harper & Brothers, Publishers, 1954).*

Some of the major considerations necessary to establish standards for each of the key result areas are discussed below.

PROFITABILITY. The standard for profitability may be expressed by means of the widely used rate of return ratio, percent of profit to sales, or total dollar volume. The expression of profit as a ratio between profits earned and capital employed is useful in comparing the contribution of each of several decentralized units in respect to current performance and is also of value in determining which of several alternatives to select for future operations. Deviations from expected profit expressed as a percent of sales may indicate variations in cost or the need for changing the price of the product or service. However, profit expressed as a ratio —either return on investment or percent of sales—is not necessarily a valid measure of the contribution of personnel to the profitability of a given operation. For example, the profit of a retail store expressed as a percent of sales may be a function primarily of the cost of goods sold and the cost of renting physical facilities, factors that may be beyond the control of the manager. The expression of profits in terms of total dollars earned is a measure of the effectiveness of sales effort on the part of store personnel over a period of time. Standards of profitability should reflect the contribution of personnel in controlling costs and expanding volume as well as the utilization of physical and financial resources.

MARKET POSITION. The position of a company in a chosen market is a measure of the extent to which its product or service is accepted by the customer and an indication of the effectiveness of its sales-promotion techniques. Standards intended to measure a company's market position must be expressed in terms of the total market. A company may, for example, increase its sales at the rate of two percent a year and be the largest in its field; yet, if the total market for the good or service offered is increasing at the rate of four percent a year, that company's market position is deteriorating.

PRODUCTIVITY. Measures of productivity are immediately associated with the production function, but standards of productivity should be set for administrative and sales functions as well as for production. Typically, productivity is expressed as the relationship between total output, measured in respect to dollar volume or units produced, and units of input—for example, the number of man-hours required for a stated level of output. Standards of productivity should be determined for other units of input as well as for man-hours. Efficiency of production may be expressed in relation to the number of machine hours, and a retail establishment is interested in the dollar volume produced per square foot of floor space. The use of total payroll dollars as an index of input indicates whether or not the rate of productivity is keeping pace with the increasing cost of labor—sometimes a more significant measure than the number of man-hours employed.

PRODUCT LEADERSHIP. Standards for profitability, market position, and productivity are not too difficult to express in relatively objective, quantitative units of measurement, but corporate achievement must be measured in areas where the criteria are qualitative in nature rather than quantitative. A company's position in respect to product leadership is difficult to express quantitatively; yet an estimate of position is necessary if it is a company objective to become or remain a leader in its field. A simple count of new products or services introduced is not sufficient. The significance of new contribution should also be weighed. Standards of quality and performance for current products should be compared with those of competitors. Determination of the significance of research in the development of new products and an evaluation of research effort offer a means of estimating potential leadership capabilities. Customer surveys indicate the degree of product acceptability and may furnish suggestions for product improvement. Finally, a value judgment must be made as to whether the company is meeting its goals of product leadership.[8]

PERSONNEL DEVELOPMENT. Standards for measuring the effectiveness of management development programs are also qualitative in nature. Since management development is usually the result of long-range planning and intended to meet future needs, it is difficult to assess the success of any such program on a year-to-year basis. However, an annual reporting of developmental activities establishes a trend in this area, and when compared with projected managerial needs resulting from expected growth, an estimate may be made concerning the need for expanding the management development program. The number of people participating in formal developmental programs, the success of those who have received training compared with those who have not been trained, and the number of managers hired from outside the company should be included in annual reports of personnel development. A current inventory of personnel skills when compared with forecasts for immediate personnel needs may indicate the short-range effectiveness of a management development program.

---

[8] Barry M. Richman, "A Rating Scale for Product Innovation," *Business Horizons,* Vol. V (Summer, 1962), pp. 37-44. Mr. Richman presents a method of screening and selecting new products.

EMPLOYEE ATTITUDES. Although there is some question in regard to the existence of a positive relationship between employee attitude and short-range production goals (Chapter 18), there is no doubt that employee attitudes have their effect upon the success of an organization over a long period of time. Attitudes may be measured operationally by an analysis of labor turnover, absenteeism, grievances, and safety records. Measurement of these factors can be accomplished in an objective, quantitative manner; the difficulty lies in establishing the standard, or criterion, of what is acceptable or desirable. Year-to-year figures and comparisons between different units in the same organization or with industry experience may be used as a guide to determine expected results. Product quality, if within the control of employees, and the number of suggestions for improvements in operating methods may be used as measures of employee attitudes. Attitude surveys conducted at periodic intervals indicate the degree of progress being made in the improvement of employee attitudes. The determination of employee attitudes is significant for the company desirous of maintaining a position of respect and leadership in its community.

PUBLIC RESPONSIBILITY. The fulfillment of goals in the area of public responsibility is highly intangible and difficult to measure. Included are contributions to the life of the community in the form of stable employment, participation in community affairs, and the leadership supplied for community activities. Standards of performance are not readily expressed in quantitative terms; consequently, the results obtained in the area of public responsibility are appraised in terms of their broad contribution to the public.

BALANCE BETWEEN SHORT-RANGE AND LONG-RANGE GOALS. Again, the measure of success is subjective in nature. Implied in this measurement is the existence of long-range goals, say 15 or 20 years from now, and the existence of intermediate and short-range plans to achieve the objectives of the more distant future. The inclusion of a measurement of the balance between short-range and long-range goals forces a company to review its entire planning process and emphasizes that future success is dependent upon the execution of carefully developed plans.

Methods of Establishing Standards. It is apparent from the number and kinds of the areas for which standards may be established that one method of establishing standards cannot be applied to all areas. There are three methods used to determine the level of expected performance. One is to develop statistical, or normative, data from sources internal and external to the company; another is to appraise results in the light of experience and judgment; and the third method is to develop engineered standards.

STATISTICAL STANDARDS. Statistical standards, sometimes called historical standards, are standards based upon an analysis of past experience. The data used may be drawn from the company's own records or they may be a reflection of the experience of several companies. The particular statistic selected for the criterion may be the average or it may be a stated point above or below the midpoint, for example, the upper quartile. While an analysis of past experience may be helpful in setting standards of performance in some areas, the statistical approach has many pitfalls in setting production standards. The following example illustrates the weakness of a historical analysis.

> The accounting department of a rebuilder of automobile parts kept a careful, complete record of the number of labor hours, broken down into direct and indirect labor hours, required to rebuild each of several parts. At the end of each fiscal year, the average number of hours required to rebuild each part was determined. Thus, the average for the past year became the standard for the current year and deviations from the average were reported as above or below standard. Despite the fact that this company was producing parts well within the limits set by its own standards, its labor costs were considerably in excess of those of its competitors. A consultant called in to review the situation discovered that there were many bottlenecks in the production control department and that the output per man-hour was only 70 percent of what could reasonably be expected based upon sound time study standards.

The lesson is clear: meeting standards of past performance is not sufficient, particularly when past performance is only a fraction of potential performance.

Yet, if used as an adjunct to other sources of information, statistical data are not only helpful but sometimes the only guide available. Indexes of profitability vary widely from one industry to another, and an analysis of industry data may prove helpful in setting criteria of profitability. Analysis of the experience of competing firms and one's own historical records of growth aid in setting realistic goals relative to market position. Companies choosing to set standards in the area of employee attitudes may find it useful to analyze the results obtained by other firms using the same attitude or opinion survey. The average contribution to charities and educational institutions may be significant in setting goals of public responsibility. In all of these instances before a final criterion can be set, the information gained from statistical sources is combined with another factor—judgment.

STANDARDS SET BY APPRAISAL. Standards do not have to be expressed in units of measurement accurate to the third decimal place. Some areas of corporate performance are, in the last analysis, appraised primarily in terms of a manager's past experience and judgment. As indicated in our discussion of statistical standards, normative data are a useful adjunct in setting standards of performance in regard to profitability, market position, employee attitudes, and to some extent in the area of public responsibility. However, the final determination of what constitutes a satisfactory level of performance is a judgment based upon management's past experience. Standards set by appraisal are essentially *value* judgments and can be as realistic and attainable as statistical or engineered standards. In the absence of standards determined by formal study and analysis, every manager is expected to appraise the output of his subordinates in terms of what he, as a manager, believes to be a satisfactory day's work. In so doing, standards are being set by appraisal.

ENGINEERED STANDARDS. Engineered standards, so called because they are based upon an objective, quantitative analysis of a specific work situation, may be developed for the measurement of machine output and for measuring the output of individual workers. Machine output standards express the production capabilities of a given piece of equipment and are determined by mechanical design factors. Machine capacity figures are developed by the designers of the equipment and represent the optimum output of the equipment in normal production use. Machine capacities are significant in determining output standards in industries using automatic equipment; for example, the metal and glass container industry.

Engineered standards developed to measure the output of individual workers, or groups of workers, are called either *time standards* or *time study* standards. The reason is that time is the element of measurement and is almost always measured by means of a stopwatch.[9] The

---

[9] The student is referred to the following references for a more complete discussion of time study methods:

Marvin E. Mundel, *Motion and Time Study Principles and Practice* (3d ed.; Englewood Cliffs, N. J.: Prentice-Hall, Inc., 1960).

Claude S. George, Jr., *Management in Industry* (Englewood Cliffs, N. J.: Prentice-Hall, Inc., 1959), pp. 394-416.

Franklin G. Moore, *Manufacturing Management* (3d ed.; Homewood, Illinois: Richard D. Irwin, Inc., 1961), pp. 508-542. (*Continued*)

first time studies in this country were completed by Frederick W. Taylor in 1881 at the Midvale Steel Company.[10] His studies were directed toward an analysis of the productivity of hourly workers in a steel mill. Since then, time study techniques have been applied to all types of production jobs—including material handling and maintenance—clerical positions, and even sales jobs.

In setting time standards the actual time taken to perform a given job is determined. This value is termed the *actual* time. The standard time is the time that should be required to perform the job under certain specified conditions. These conditions are usually defined as an average worker, trained in the skills of the job, working at normal pace (rate of speed), and following the prescribed methods for the job. Determining effort, or pace, is a matter of judgment and is related to the effort expended—and the speed required—to walk three miles an hour on level ground. Standard times are usually developed for a normal eight-hour workday and include allowances for fatigue, unavoidable delays, personal time, and other interruptions of work that occur at predictable intervals. A worker who performs his work according to the standards set for his job is said to be working at 100 percent of standard. The use of the expression, 100 percent of standard, causes much of the initial misunderstandings of time study. The term, 100 percent, normally conveys the idea of perfection, of maximum effort and maximum output. A more acceptable expression would be to use the term, par.

Time study standards are essential if incentive plans are to be installed, but it does not follow that incentives are necessary to make effective use of time study. On the contrary, time standards can be used quite effectively as a means of increasing production without the introduction of incentives. The presence of time standards alone tends to increase production.[11] Time standards also form the basis of standard costs. Standard costs are composed of the cost of labor performing at standard plus standard allowances for materials and allocated overhead.

The need for establishing standards varies widely from one company to another, but any company that has labor costs greater than 30

---

[9] *Continued*

Richard N. Owens, *Management of Industrial Enterprises* (4th ed.; Homewood, Illinois: Richard D. Irwin, Inc., 1961), pp. 362-393.

For a point of view highly critical of time study methods, the following book is suggested:

William Gomberg, *A Trade Union Analysis of Time Study* (2d ed.; Englewood Cliffs, N. J.: Prentice-Hall, Inc., 1955).

[10] See Chapter 2, "The Development of Management Concepts," page 33.

[11] See Chapter 18, "Motivating Employees," page 461.

percent of its total product or service cost should investigate the possibility of establishing time standards to serve as the basis for control when measuring human output.

Measuring Current Performance

There is an intermediate step in the control process between the first step of the process, establishing standards, and the final phase of the process, the taking of corrective action. The middle step is that of measuring current performance. To a degree, the problems of measurements are defined, and sometimes partially solved, by the manner in which standards are defined. Standards of profitability, for example, imply that the measuring unit be one of dollars; but the statement of criteria in the areas of product leadership and public responsibility requires ingenuity in developing satisfactory methods of measurement. The variety and the number of performance factors for which standards may be set make it virtually impossible to discuss problems of measurement by describing units of measurement applicable to all business situations. Nonetheless, there are certain characteristics of effective control measurements to be examined. In addition, further elaboration of the significance of the measurement of current progress to the entire control process is helpful in assessing the worth of measuring devices.

Fundamental to sound control measures is recognition that management control systems are cybernetic systems, defining cybernetics as the processing and the interpretation of information. Thus, control systems are best regarded as information systems. The appropriateness of corrective action, the end point of the control process, is dependent almost entirely upon the kind of information received. Information intended to measure and describe current performance can be evaluated by seeking answers to the following five questions:

1. Is the information timely?
2. Are the units of measurement appropriate?
3. How reliable is the information received?
4. Is the information valid?
5. Is information being channeled to the proper authority?

Let us discuss each of these questions so that the problems of measuring performance are better understood.

Timeliness of Information. Control information, to be of greatest use, must reflect present position. Typically, managers rely too much on data supplied by the accounting department and as a result fail to develop other sources of information. Accounting statements are prepared at the end of a given time period, for example a calendar month, and even with efficient procedures seven to ten working days are required to prepare statements of the preceding month's operations. Though this information may have historical significance and be of value in the preparation of annual reports, it is of little or no value to the manager responsible for the efficiency of day-to-day operations. Ideally, the manager of each operating unit should have information presented to him during the course of each working day so that he might have an adequate basis for corrective action. Is such timeliness possible? The following example suggests that it is.

> The manager of a plant producing stamped automobile parts devised the following method of securing information concerning the quantity produced by each of several production departments on an hourly basis. Departments were designated by the operations performed and included the following: shearing, stamping, chrome plating, and buffing and polishing. The manager placed in his office a large blackboard ruled into vertical columns for each production department. Horizontal lines were drawn for each hour of the day. A production clerk checked with the foreman of each production department at the end of each hour, received the quantity produced by each department, and posted the information on the board in the manager's office. In this way the manager became immediately aware of trouble spots and could anticipate future difficulties likely to arise resulting from a shortage of parts or from a breakdown in earlier operations in the production sequence.

Another result of the control procedure described in the above incident is that the foremen of the various departments confer more frequently with each other and with the plant manager to minimize delays in production. Timely control information can be obtained through telephone calls, daily reports, or personal observation without having to wait for information prepared and distributed by formal reporting systems.

Appropriate Units of Measurement. One of the most difficult tasks in measuring current performance is the selection of an appropriate unit of measurement. Occasionally the use of several different units offers a partial solution to this problem. For example, profit is expressed as a percentage of sales, the percent return on capital invested, and as total dollars. Similarly, production may be measured and described as a ratio of output to input or as total units produced. Market position is also measured by several different methods. The use of multiple measures to describe performance is sound because each measure serves as a cross check on the information provided by the other measures and at the same time emphasizes one particular aspect of the performance under review.

The measurement of performance against standard for profits, productivity, and sales utilizes quantitative units of measurement. However, much of the evaluation of a company's progress is dependent upon qualitative, rather than quantitative, units of measurement. In the absence of quantitative measures, the manager, drawing upon past experience and his own set of values, must judge for himself whether or not standards are being met. Such judgments must be made in the areas of personnel development, public responsibility, and determining the balance between long-range and short-range goals. Attempting to express achievement in these areas by relying solely upon quantitative units can be misleading. For example, measuring personnel development by a head count of the number of persons who have completed a given training program does not answer the question of the effectiveness of the program in improving performance on the job. Even though qualitative measures are difficult to apply and generally unreliable when compared with quantitative units, it is a mistake not to set standards in those areas where measurement must be made in qualitative terms.

Reliability of Information. Reliability of information pertains to its degree of accuracy. It is assumed that the data are accurate in the sense that clerical errors are not involved. Thus, the accuracy referred to by the term reliability is in respect to the consistency of data and the extent to which all aspects of the problem being considered are measured. Almost always a compromise must be made between reliability and timeliness. Usually the reliability of information is positively related to its completeness. Computer predictions of election returns illustrate the increasing accuracy of predictions as more and more data are reported and interpreted. However, most managerial interpretations of operations—and the subsequent corrective action—are based upon incomplete information. A sales manager having reports for only the first two weeks of a calendar month may be required to take corrective action even though his data are not fully reliable because they are not a complete description of the month's activities. Even so, partial information on recurring time cycles, such as monthly sales and production reports, can be analyzed and related to the entire cycle and provide a relatively accurate basis for analysis and action.

In addition to decreased reliability of information resulting from utilizing incomplete data that do not reflect performance for the entire reporting period, there is a marked decrease in the reliability of data covering the initial phases of an operation. The reason for this type of loss in reliability is best explained by the old adage, "practice makes perfect." At the beginning of a new operation the quality and the quantity of performance are at their lowest point; but as time progresses, there is improved individual performance and better methods of doing the job are usually developed. Graphic representations of improved performance are called *learning curves*. The aircraft industry, constantly faced with changing products, short runs, and the ever-present threat of contract cancellation, has developed techniques to predict with considerable accuracy the average level of performance by projecting an improvement or learning curve. Data secured at the beginning of an operation are not characteristic of the entire operation or its latter phases and are a highly unreliable source of information unless interpreted as part of a learning curve. Though the use of learning curves is most highly developed in the aircraft industry, the same techniques are applicable to the prediction of final performance in maintenance operations, the building of heavy equipment, the construction industry, and the performance of salesmen when introducing a new product. The danger lies, not in using the initial data of a new operation, but in failing to recognize that there is a predictable improvement factor.[12]

Validity of Information. It is possible for information to be highly reliable, yet not valid. Likewise, the appropriate unit of measurement, either quantitative or qualitative can be established, and yet the information received may not be valid. The validity of a measurement refers to the degree that a measurement actually reflects the phenomenon that it is intended to measure. An example of a highly reliable, quantitative measure with virtually no validity is the experience of a printing company in trying to determine the quantity of daily production. The figure used was the total number of pounds of finished materials shipped each day. There were several reasons why the total number of pounds shipped is not a valid measure of the company's productivity. First, the total number of pounds bore no consistent relationship to dollar volume of sales, profitability, or man-hours required for production because of

---

[12] Winifred R. Hirschmann, "Profit from the Learning Curve," *Harvard Business Review*, Vol. XXXXII (January-February, 1964), pp. 125-139. Mr. Hirschmann's article discusses the characteristics of the learning curve, the reasons why it has not been accepted widely, and suggests some practical applications of the concept.

the diversity of product line, which included cellophane and pliofilm packaging materials, lithographed products, foil wrappings, and fibre board cartons. Second, the pounds shipped bore only an indirect relation to production for any given day since up to 40 percent of the orders shipped on any given day came out of a warehouse and not directly from that day's production. Thus, the number of pounds shipped did not measure what it was intended to measure—the amount of goods produced in a given day.

Another example of a measurement that may or may not be valid is the use of gross sales as an index of profitability. Whenever the performance being reviewed is complex and composed of many different elements, it is extremely difficult to develop one single unit of measurement that adequately portrays what it is intended to portray. In these situations it is best to measure each segment of performance separately rather than use a single indicator that may not be valid.

Channeling Information to Proper Authority. The timeliness of information, the appropriateness of the unit of measurement, and the reliability and validity of control data are directed toward having the right information at the right time. A fifth requirement must be met, the channeling of information to the proper authority. Only then do we have all ingredients of a good information system for control—the right information at the right time and at the right place. What constitutes the proper channel for information flow varies with each company organization structure, the kind of information to be interpreted, and the kind of corrective action required to attain expected standards. Even so, the following generalization can be made: control information should be directed toward the individual designated as being responsible for the operation and at the same time having the authority to take corrective action.

There is much discussion concerning the effect that integrated data processing systems have upon the flow of information. Some argue that integrated systems encourage centralized control, with the result that the control of an organization ultimately rests in the hands of a few at the top of the organization. Others point out that the speed with which information can be handled and the variety of information processed make it possible to supply control information to first-line supervisors and middle management never available to them before. Although there seems to be a trend toward centralized control, the trend is not necessarily a function of integrated data processing systems. Rather, it may be an expression of a desire to place control information in the hands of those possessing the authority to take action.[13]

In summary, the measurement of organizational performance in respect to stated standards is not precise; yet, measure we must if we are to improve the quality of corrective action. An awareness of the difficulties inherent in measuring current position eventually leads to the development of meaningful control information.[14]

Taking Corrective Action

The third and last step of the control process, taking corrective action, epitomizes the busy, efficient executive. Here is a man making things happen and getting things done. Without action there is no control. The actions taken are the result of executive decisions and as such reflect the personality of the person taking the action as well as being determined by the situational, or environmental, factors. Thus, the personality of the person in control has much to do with the kind of control. Before discussing the range of action available to the controlling executive, it is well to examine more closely the influence of personality upon corrective action, to determine who should take corrective action, and to make sure that causes—not symptoms—are being corrected.

Personality and Control. Personality factors, rather than the demands of the situation, are the cause of the extremes in control. One extreme is typified by the Captain Queeg approach to management— too much control. The other extreme might be called the Will Rogers approach to management—too little control.[15] Captain Queeg, as described by Herman Wouk in the *Caine Mutiny,* hewed to the letter of the law and insisted that his men do the same. He had to know every detail of what every man aboard his ship did and rationalized such excessive control as a means of assuring himself, and the Navy, that all

---

[13] Garry E. Morse, "Pendulum Swing of Management Control," *Harvard Business Review,* Vol. XXXXIII (May-June, 1965), pp. 158-160, 162, 164. Mr. Morse discusses the trend toward more centralized control and stresses that information systems do not necessarily determine the degree of centralization.

[14] Paul Kircher, "Fundamentals of Measurement," *Advanced Management,* Vol. XX (October, 1955), pp. 5-8. Mr. Kircher's article contains a thorough discussion of the theoretical problems involved in establishing any system of measurement. As yet we have not developed for business organizations a system of measurement comparable in effectiveness to the systems used in the measurement of length.

[15] Arnold F. Emch, "Control Means Action," *Harvard Business Review,* Vol. XXXII (July-August, 1954), pp. 92-98. Mr. Emch uses Captain Queeg and Will Rogers as the extremes in control. His article sets forth rules and guides for effective control and emphasizes good delegation as the key to good control.

regulations were being carried out. The same approach in an industrial organization results in a mass of paper work, so much so that the real work of the organization is neglected.

What motivates a Captain Queeg to check on every last detail? The answer is simple: The same personality that makes it impossible to delegate effectively. When effective delegation is practiced, there is little need for tight control. In Chapter 13, four personality characteristics that interfere with effective delegation are discussed. They are worth recounting at this point. First, there are those who by vocational choice —notably engineers and accountants—are trained to attend to details and as a result find it difficult to delegate effectively when placed in a supervisory position. Next, there are those managers who want to avoid the major issues and occupy themselves by attention to petty detail. Third, there are those who, for either real or imagined reasons, fear failure; and last, there are those who have a mistrust of others.[16] These are the traits that prevent effective delegation and at the same time result in excessive control over the relatively unimportant. The effect on an organization is stultifying. Initiative, innovation, and creativity on the part of subordinates are stifled.[17]

The other pole in control, the Will Rogers approach, is equally ineffective in achieving organizational goals. Here everything is assumed to be going along just fine, there is no need to check because these are wonderful people in the organization, and things are bound to work out just right in the long run. Also, there is a hesitancy about offending someone by questioning him about his performance. The Will Rogers type is a defender of the Theory Y approach to organization. Eventually, however, he wants to know more about the operation than the mere fact that he has a certain amount of money in the bank at the end of each month. With no clearly defined organization, the inevitable happens —he creates an "assistant-to" to do his controlling for him. It is quite possible that the assistant-to might become another Captain Queeg. But more importantly, the creation of an assistant-to leads us again to the question, "Who controls?"

Who Controls? The payoff of the control process is not the setting of standards, nor is it the measurement of performance against standards.

---

[16] See Chapter 13, page 322, for a more complete discussion of these personality traits.

[17] Lyman K. Randall, "Organizational Paradox," *Harvard Business Review*, Vol. XXXXIII (July-August, 1965), pp. 86-87, Mr. Randall presents a little quiz to determine whether one is control oriented or creatively oriented. He also mentions Captain Queeg as typical of excessive control and suggests the architect, Howard Roark, of Ayn Rand's *The Fountainhead* as typifying the creative personality.

It is taking the corrective action necessary to bring performance in line with the standards. The logical person to take this action is the manager who has had assigned to him the responsibility of managing a particular aspect of the business and who has had delegated to him the authority necessary to fulfill the assigned responsibilities. Thus, effective control is the result of sound organizational structure and the practice of an important organizational process—delegation. Taking corrective action is executive action and as such is in the hands of the line manager. The controller's office may be involved in the setting of standards and almost always participates in the measurement of current position against standard, but the taking of corrective action belongs to the manager of an organizational unit.

Symptoms or Causes? Prior to taking corrective action it is necessary to differentiate between symptoms and causes. Most of us have had the experience of taking an antihistamine drug at the first sign of a cold, and after a day or so we stop taking the medicine. Sometimes, much to our disgust, the sniffling and sneezing return and we discover that we have done an excellent job of treating symptoms but not getting at the cause of the cold. A manager must learn to recognize a symptom for what it is and to devote his attention to the cause of the problem. Cost control, or the control of expenses, often falls into the category of treating symptoms rather than causes.

Excessive costs are an indication that something has gone wrong; they are the result of someone's performance and if costs are to be brought in line it is the performance that must be corrected. First, it is wise to examine the standard to determine whether or not the costs in question are in fact excessive. Next, try and determine the contribution of each factor that makes up the total cost. How much of total cost is attributable to direct labor, to materials, and to overhead? Finally, examine each of these factors separately and determine how performance can be improved in each area. The same analytical procedure can be applied to the sales function. The answer to a declining sales volume is not necessarily more salesmen or better performance on the part of the present sales force; instead, the decline in sales may be the result of a poorly designed product or the failure to meet the challenge of competitors.

The Management Process Cycle. After determining the cause for poor performance, corrective action is in order. It is impossible to formulate a list of actions available to the manager; each situation is unique and calls for its own solution. There is, however, a frame of reference of value to the manager in evaluating his proposed action. That framework is the management process cycle—replanning, reorganizing, redirecting, and continued control since in a going organization all these functions have been performed in one way or another. Failure to meet expected levels of performance is sometimes unavoidable and calls for the development of new plans with the possibility of revised standards of performance. Though there is merit in the adage, "the difficult we do immediately; the impossible we do tomorrow," there are times when one must recognize that the impossible cannot be accomplished in accordance with present plans. Delays in a construction schedule resulting from inclement weather necessitate a revision of plans dependent upon the completion of the scheduled construction. Failure to meet a marketing objective may mean allocating more money for advertising or a restatement of expected results.

The present organization may need revising. Is the organization structured in such a manner that there is clear-cut responsibility for each organizational unit, or is there need for the creation of a new unit? What about the people in the organization? Are they performing their assigned duties satisfactorily? A change in either organizational structure or personnel may be necessary to correct the causes of poor performance. Or the difficulty may lie in directing. Sometimes a restatement of what is expected brings the desired results. Finally, there is the control process itself—it must be exercised continually. The management cycle is not composed of the four discrete steps of planning, organizing, directing, and controlling; instead, it is a continuous process, with control functioning as a catalyst to produce an integrated continuous process.

CHARACTERISTICS OF GOOD CONTROL

In the preceding discussion of the steps of the control process, many of the characteristics of an effective control system are implied and touched upon briefly. Control is an extremely critical factor in the achievement of organizational objectives, with the effectiveness of the control function dependent upon the information received. Control systems, to be of greatest use, must possess certain characteristics. Again, we are unable to describe all control systems since each control situation is unique. Despite this difficulty, there is general agreement that good control has the following characteristics: timeliness, follows organizational lines, strategic, economical, shows both trends and status, and stresses the exception.[18] Each of these characteristics is discussed separately.

Timeliness

Accounting records are relatively precise, detailed statements of a company's activity for a stated period and are historical in nature since they are prepared after the period has closed. Frequently these reports are of great value to the planning process, but they are often inadequate as control reports because they are not timely. Ideally, the optimum form of control information should forecast deviations from standard prior to its occurrence. In practice, such forecasting is seldom achieved, but every effort should be made to report deviations from standard while the event in question is still in process. We mentioned the control device developed by the plant manager of an automobile parts manufacturer that enabled him to keep abreast of the output of each production department at hourly intervals. Supervisors of production departments frequently find it necessary to develop control information during the course of the day. One supervisor in a large printing company placed a small blackboard at the end of each press, with the cumulative standard production posted for each hour. He requested the pressmen to post actual production for each hour alongside the posted standard. One immediate result of this procedure was that the pressmen called the supervisor when trouble began to develop, thereby permitting the rescheduling of work to other presses.

Another means of focusing upon timely information is to require unit managers, such as plant managers and sales managers, to prepare monthly forecasts and to submit revisions of these forecasts on either a weekly or a biweekly basis. While it is true that the information used in these forecasts may not be accurate when compared with the accounting records prepared at the close of the period, the process of forecasting and revising forces the manager to develop and rely upon timely information. If a choice must be made between timeliness and accuracy of control information, timeliness should be emphasized for the control of current operations.

---

[18] John Richard Curley, "A Tool for Management Control," *Harvard Business Review*, Vol. XXIX (March, 1951), pp. 45-86. General characteristics of tools for control based upon the experience of RCA are presented. A brief discussion of accounting controls and their limitations is also included.

Harold Koontz and Cyril O'Donnell, *Principles of Management* (3d ed.; New York: McGraw-Hill Book Company, 1964), pp. 541-544. Professors Koontz and O'Donnell discuss 10 requirements of adequate control.

Follows Organizational Lines

The excessive control of a Captain Queeg and the hands-off attitude of a Will Rogers, with the eventual inevitability of an assistant-to, reflect the same organizational shortcoming—a failure to delegate. Responsibility is not assigned nor is authority delegated, with the result that clear-cut accountability to superiors in the organization is not established. The control function can in no way substitute for poor organizational practices and structure. Good controls are closely related to organizational structure and reflect organizational structure and processes in their design and function.

Accumulated total product costs are of great significance to the sales department in the pricing of a given product, yet such figures may not be meaningful to manufacturing personnel charged with the responsibility of controlling costs. To be meaningful to manufacturing departments, cost data must reflect the portion of total cost added to the product by each department. Only then is the manager aware of the costs chargeable to his department and in a position to control those costs. Defects in quality should be traced to component parts and reported to the operating department responsible for the production of the defective part. Wage and salary plans can be utilized for control by reporting the average rate paid for each job classification and each salary grade. The information should be prepared for each organizational unit as well as for the entire company. Directing information to the responsible manager is an effective way of making it possible to exercise control at the lowest possible echelon of the organization.

Strategic Placement

It is impossible to establish controls for every aspect of even a small to medium-size business because of its complexity. Thus. it becomes necessary to establish controls at certain points of the operation selected because of their strategic value. A company whose primary contact with customers is through letters written by the correspondents in the sales order department may experience difficulty in maintaining good customer relations as the result of inconsistencies from the many sources of contact with customers. A strategic control of correspondence is the requirement that all letters be prepared for the signature of the sales manager, a step that permits the manager to sample all outgoing correspondence. Most governmental agencies require the signature of the chief administrator on all outgoing mail.

Quality control programs rely heavily upon the selection of strategic points where inspection approaches the 100 percent level as a means of meeting quality standards. A major appliance, such as a refrigerator, is checked after final assembly by connecting it to a test circuit to see if it cools properly. Also, the components of the compressor are subjected to complete dimensional checks prior to assembly to insure proper fit. Establishing key control points prior to the assembly of a critical component and after final assembly minimizes the likelihood of expensive rework and the possibility of defective products reaching the customer.

A few well-chosen measures of performance are often sufficient for the overall control of medium-size business operations. The owner-manager of a firm manufacturing trays for use in cafeterias and drive-in restaurants received weekly reports containing the following information: the backlog of orders, finished goods inventory, number of units shipped, and total hours of factory labor. A change in the order backlog with the other measures remaining relatively constant indicated the effectiveness of sales effort, and the number of units shipped was closely related to gross sales for the month. Total labor hours when balanced with inventory and units shipped let him know something about manufacturing efficiency, and a rising inventory indicated the need for either increasing sales effort or decreasing direct labor hours. To this manager, changes in the interrelationships of these four measures revealed potential trouble spots and enabled him to take immediate corrective action.

Economical Administration

In addition to its stifling effects on human effort, the excessive control of a Captain Queeg can be expensive. The story is often told of a consultant encountering strategic controls similar to those used by the manager of the tray manufacturing company. The consultant suggested that in addition to these overall controls there was a need to control overhead costs. The recommended controls were put into effect. At the end of several months a marked decline in profits was noticed, and the amount of the decline corresponded to the additional costs of administering the new controls. Figure 7-2, page 174, presents a graphic model showing the relationships between total cost, the cost of taking managerial action—for example, quality control—and decreasing costs resulting from managerial action. This model serves well as a means of judging the economic cost of proposed controls.

There is an old saying, "You can inspect yourself out of business." Yet, failure to detect defective products results in the loss of customers.

One method of balancing the cost of quality control against the cost of not taking action is the use of sampling techniques where every 10th or 100th item is checked thoroughly. Another area deserving careful attention is the use of incentives as a means of reducing unit labor costs. Although incentives may reduce the cost of direct labor, the indirect costs of maintaining up-to-date time studies by the industrial engineering department may more than counterbalance any savings in direct labor. Some companies have found measured day work—the use of time standards to determine a fair day's work—to be satisfactory since the standards do not have to be maintained with the same degree of accuracy as required when standards are used as the basis for incentive pay. Accuracy of measurement is an important factor in determining the cost of a given set of controls. Sometimes the presence of a deviation from standard and its direction, rather than the precise amount of the deviation, is sufficient for control purposes.

Reveals Trends As Well As Status

Controls that show the current status of a specific phase of an operation are relatively easy to prepare since all that is needed are periodic statements of the particular activity in question. Although such measures show present status, they do not necessarily reveal the trend of performance; i.e., monthly production reports do not show whether production is increasing or decreasing. This limitation of periodic reporting is overcome by using a graphic method of presentation that shows successive measures, thus forming a trend line, or by presenting the data in tabular form and including year-to-date or month-to-date figures. However, establishing and showing the trends of specific business functions do not always provide sufficient control information. It is necessary to include supporting information that is closely related to the primary function under observation. In the case of production, concentration on the number of units produced without the inclusion of a measure of the units of input gives no indication of the cost or efficiency of production—an aspect of production that may be more important for control purposes than the total produced.

Interpreting trends in the light of related happenings is of special significance in the development of control information for the measurement of market position. There is the well-known example of a soap manufacturer who recorded continuous gains in the sales of soap, but neglected to focus attention on the increasing share of the home-laundry market claimed by detergents, with the result that the company discovered too late that it was last in the newer and larger market. One of the largest and oldest manufacturers of men's suits measured market position not only in respect to the market for suits but also in respect to the total amount spent for men's outer wear. As a result, the company discovered that an increasing share of the money spent for outer wear was spent on sports clothes and thus established plants for the manufacture of men's sportswear. Control data showing market position should show position in relation to competitive items as well as the market position relative to that of competitors.

Stresses the Exception

In Chapter 2, "The Development of Management Concepts," Jethro's recommendations to Moses are presented. The three recommendations are: teach "ordinances and laws" to the people; select leaders and assign them "to be rulers of thousands, and rulers of hundreds, and rulers of fifties, and rulers of ten"; and those rulers should administer all routine matters and bring to Moses only the important questions. The third suggestion is often referred to as the *principle of the exception*. There are two reasons why effective systems of controls stress the exception. First, the amount of information generated in even small organizations is so great that it becomes difficult, if not impossible, to determine the significance of all information. To review every action of subordinates or to consult with them prior to taking action consumes too much of the time and energy of the manager. Second, when information stressing the exception is presented to the manager, his attention is directed toward those items that require corrective action.

Examples of controls that point up the exception are numerous in all functions of management. The sales data presented to a national sales manager should specify those districts that deviate from predicted standards of performance beyond a predetermined range; for example, those districts that vary more than plus or minus 5 percent. The exceptions must include those areas that exceed expected performance as well as those that fail to meet the standard. It is quite possible that the reasons for successful performance can be applied to those districts whose performance is below par. The reporting of the exception is of value in the control of quality, cost, production, or any other measure of performance for which standards have been set. Usually acceptable performance is defined as performance within the limits of a predetermined range, with the breadth of the range varying for each performance factor, rather than satisfactory performance as a point value with no tolerance allowed.

Control by exception is closely related to the process of delegation and is not necessarily the exercise of corrective action after the function in question has been performed. Instead, effective control is exercised by either approving or disapproving the exceptional action prior to its occurrence. When responsibilities are assigned, authority within prescribed limits is delegated in order that these responsibilities may be fufilled. Occasionally a manager requires greater authority so that he may fulfill his responsibilities. When need arises, he requests his superior to recognize the exception and grant additional authority. For instance, the supervisor of a manufacturing department may have the authority to spend $100 for the repair of any one piece of equipment in his department and $1,000 per month for total repairs in the department. Deviations beyond these maintenance cost standards require prior approval from his superior, the plant manager. The plant manager, in turn, may be permitted to spend $1,000 on any single item of general plant maintenance and $5,000 in any month. For the expenditure of sums exceeding these limits, he must secure prior approval from his superior, the manufacturing vice-president. Clearly defined limits of authority and the requirement of prior approval to exceed these limitations permit the control of the exception prior to its happening. Thus, the concept of control by exception is used to control deviations from standard before the exception occurs as well as to emphasize those areas in need of corrective action.

PRINCIPLES OF CONTROL

Each of the six characteristics of an effective control system—timeliness, follows organizational lines, strategic placement, economical administration, showing both trends and status, and stressing the exception—is important to the control of operations. These characteristics are descriptive of two different aspects of the control process and as such can be condensed and stated as two principles of control.[19] The establishment of controls that present information while it is still timely, that reveal information that is of strategic value in the control of operations, and that follow established organizational lines is

---

[19] Harold Koontz and Cyril O'Donnell, *Principles of Management,* 3d ed. (New York: McGraw-Hill Book Company, Inc., 1964), pp. 620-625. Professors Koontz and O'Donnell present 14 principles of control grouped into three general categories: (1) those reflecting the purpose and nature of control, (2) those emphasizing the structure of control, and (3) those emphasizing the control process. The following reference presents a more complete discussion of control principles:

Harold Koontz, "Management Control: A Suggested Formulation of Principles," *California Management Review,* Vol. I (Winter, 1959), pp. 47-55.

descriptive of the purpose and structure of the control system. The characteristics of economy of administration and the reporting of trends as well as current status are also a function of the purpose and structure of the control system. The last of the six characteristics, stressing and reporting the exception, leads directly to the essence of control— corrective action. Thus, logically there are two fundamental principles of control, one that emphasizes the nature and design of the control system, and the other that emphasizes the essence of the control process —taking corrective action. The first of these principles is called *The Principle of Control Design;* the second is referred to as *The Principle of the Exception.*

Principle of Control Design	{	Effective control systems are designed to be economical in their administration and to reflect organizational structure. Such systems should provide management with information that is timely, of strategic value, and descriptive of the trends of operations as well as current status.
Principle of the Exception	{	The most efficient use of managerial time and energy is possible when control information stresses the exception and focuses attention upon those functions that need corrective action.

●   ●   ●   ●   ●   ●   ●   ●   ●

Case Problem 21-B, Controlling Sales Expense, describes two widely divergent degrees of control within the same organization and offers an opportunity to determine the proper degree of control that is needed and the methods to be utilized in establishing such control.

Questions for Study and Discussion

1. Define in your own terms the meaning of the word "cybernetics." Give an example of a cybernetic system and show why it is so classified.
2. Comment on the following statement: All dynamic systems involve the transmission of information.
3. Relate the three steps of the control process to the concept of a cybernetic system.
4. What are the major functions of a person holding the title of controller in an organization? In an organization, whose responsibility is it to take the corrective action?
5. Describe the relationship between the controller and the manager of an organizational unit.
6. What are the characteristics of a standard? Does the concept of par, borrowed from the game of golf, provide a good analogy for the understanding of the concept of standard? Why?
7. How are standards and objectives related? Illustrate by example.
8. Evaluate the three methods for establishing standards by indicating which methods are most likely to be appropriate in establishing standards for each of the eight key result areas.
9. Discuss each of the major problems encountered in the measurement of performance.
10. What relationship, if any, exists between the process of delegation and the control process? Explain fully.
11. As a manager, what steps would you take to assure yourself that you were able to distinguish symptoms from causes?
12. If it is true that each control system is unique, how is it possible to develop the characteristics of a good control system? State briefly why each of these characteristics is necessary.
13. How are the principle of control design and the principle of the exception related to the characteristics of a good control system? What are the likely results when these principles are violated?

●   ●   ●   ●   ●   ●   ●   ●   ●

Frank Anchor, a district manager for Paper Products Company, has been in charge of the Chicago district sales office for two months. Prior to his transfer to Chicago to replace Tom Aderly, who has been in Chicago for 30 years as a salesman and for the last 20 years as sales manager, Anchor had been assistant manager of the New York sales district. When reviewing his new assignment with the vice-president in charge of sales, Anchor was told that the Chicago sales expenses were 50 percent higher than those in New York and that sales volume had not kept pace with the rate of increase shown by other large offices. He was advised that he should first reduce the cost of operating the Chicago office and that as soon as costs were under control he should take steps to increase sales volume.

Anchor arrived in Chicago a month prior to Aderly's retirement and had occasion to review with him the operations of the office. Aderly recognized that the Chicago expenses were higher than those for New York but attributed this difference to the size of the district, which covered many more square miles than New York. When Anchor asked to see the records of daily calls made by each salesman, a list of potential customers, and the names of the new customers for each month, Tom Aderly answered as follows:

"Frank, I don't bother much with things like that. Every morning I visit with each of my eight salesmen when they come into the office. I've known every one of these men since the first

---

Case Problem 21-B
Controlling Sales Expense

---

day he started to work here. I know that they have the best interests of the company at heart, and I'm sure that each man is doing his very best. I help them when they ask for it, but otherwise I let each man follow his own lead. Makes for a nice friendly atmosphere."

After Aderly formally retired, Anchor had the opportunity to examine more closely the salesmen's expense accounts. He found that the average expense advance was $250 instead of the $100 maximum allowed by company policy, and that one salesman had drawn a $500 expense advance. Anchor realized that, in order to bring expenses and sales volume in line with those of other districts in the company, a radical change in the method of managing the Chicago office was needed. He decided to present these changes in memo form and to discuss the change in the first of the newly instituted weekly meetings scheduled for Friday afternoons. The following is a copy of the memorandum.

To: Salesmen, Chicago District, Paper Products Company.

Re: Expense Control.

You are all aware that the expenses of the Chicago District sales office are much higher than those of offices in other large cities. For example, our expenses are 25 percent higher than those of Los Angeles, a district of comparable size. It is necessary that we get our expenses in line with those of similar offices in the company. The following procedures are effective beginning next Monday.

1. Expense advances will be limited to the $100 per week as outlined in the company sales policy manual. Those of you who have outstanding balances of more than $100 will not be permitted to draw additional advances; further, the amount in excess of $100 must be paid by the end of this month. If not paid by that time, authorization will be asked for to deduct the balance in excess of $100 in three equal monthly installments from your salary.

2. Salesmen will no longer report to the office each morning; instead, each of you is expected to telephone the office between 9 and 9:30 each morning and give my secretary a schedule of the calls you intend to make that day. You are also asked to call between 1 and 1:30 p.m. so that we may relay messages from customers that have been received during the morning.

3. Each salesman is expected to report to this office in person between 4 and 5 p.m. every day to review with me the calls made during the day and arrange appointments for calls on large accounts so that I can make the calls on these customers with you.

4. Daily expense records will be kept and are to be completed each afternoon when you are in the office.

5. Prior approval must be obtained for any entertainment expense exceeding $25.

6. Monthly time and expense reports must be summarized by the 25th of each month, showing total number of sales calls made, total expense, and total dollar volume of orders received. These summaries will then be forwarded to New York. No salary checks will be issued to any salesman until monthly time and expense reports have been received by the New York office.

Problems

1. How would you characterize Mr. Aderly and Mr. Anchor in respect to their methods of exercising control?

2. Is there need for stricter controls in the Chicago office? Why?

3. Do you agree that there is need for the controls set forth in Anchor's memo? Do you approve of the method he is using in establishing these controls?

4. How would you have handled this situation? Explain.

CHAPTER 22

Budgetary Control

Ray Barr retired from the Air Force and within a month found himself in the retail business as the result of the unexpected death of his father-in-law, who owned and managed the Avenue, a men's clothing and furnishings store. Barr was appointed acting manager by the executor of the estate and served in that capacity during the peak sales period that normally occurs during the last three months of the calendar year. When the estate was settled in mid-December, Ray and his wife decided to continue managing the store rather than selling it. The records kept by Ray's father-in-law were rather sketchy and incomplete, but they did indicate that net sales had been $200,000 a year for the past three years and that net profit before taxes had varied between 4 and 5½ percent of net sales for the same period.

Ray had worked with budgets as an officer in the management control section of the Air Force and decided that the development of a revenue and expense budget would serve as a useful guide during the coming year. After studying the information made available to him by the Small Business Administration and the publications of the National Association of Retail

Case Problem 22-A
Developing a Revenue
and Expense Budget

Clothiers and Furnishers, he decided to use the percentages for revenue and expense items as shown in Exhibit I. He considered dividing the total for each of these accounts by 12 to develop a budget for each month, but later decided that the variation in sales volume and advertising costs from month to month was great enough to require that these items be computed on the basis of the variations shown in Exhibit II. Both Exhibit I and Exhibit II are based upon an annual net sales volume of $200,000.

Problems

1. Develop an annual monthly revenue and expense budget for the store owned and operated by Ray Barr.
2. What additional information would you need to prepare a cash budget? a balance sheet budget?
3. What kind of standards has Ray used in determining budgeted performance?
4. Would flexible budgets be of any value in allocating monthly sales volume and advertising expenses?
5. Of what value will this budget be in succeeding years?

Exhibit I

BUDGETED OPERATING REVENUE AND EXPENSES FOR
ANNUAL NET SALES OF $200,000

Account	Percentage of Net Sales
Sales:	
1. Gross sales	102.6
2. Customer returns and allowances	2.6
3. Net sales	100.0
Cost of goods sold:	
4. Beginning inventory	30.9
5. Net purchases plus transportation charges paid	66.1
6. Total cost of merchandise handled	97.0
7. Ending inventory	32.3
8. Net cost of merchandise sold	64.7
9. Net busheling (alterations) cost	2.1
10. Total cost of merchandise sold	66.8
11. Gross margin	33.2
Operating expenses:	
12. Payroll:	
A. Salary of owner	7.3
B. Salaries and wages of employees	9.0
Total payroll	16.3
13. Rent expense	2.9
14. Taxes and license fees (omit real estate, Federal income and sales taxes)	1.1
15. Insurance	.6
16. Depreciation and amortization	.8
17. Repairs	.2
18. Supplies (omit repair materials)	1.0
19. Services purchased	.9
20. Traveling (business trips)	.3
21. Communication (include parcel post)	.4
22. Advertising and publicity	2.8
23. Professional services (outside professional agencies)	.2
24. Unclassified (all expenses not under other headings):	
A. Losses from bad debts	.3
B. Other unclassified expenses	.5
Total unclassified expenses	.8
25. Total expenses	28.3
26. Net profit (or loss) before Federal Income taxes	4.9

Exhibit II
BUDGETED NET SALES AND ADVERTISING COSTS FOR EACH MONTH

Month	Percentage of Annual Net Sales	Percentage of Annual Advertising Costs
January	8%	9%
February	5	7
March	6	6
April	6	7
May	8	7
June	9	8
July	7	7
August	7	8
September	7	9
October	9	8
November	10	10
December	18	14

•   •   •   •   •   •   •   •   •

The budget is without doubt the most widely used control device in both business and government; indeed, it is used so extensively that for many persons the word budget is synonymous with control. Yet, the preparation of budgets originates as part of the planning process, and the budget itself is the end point of the planning process—the statement of a plan. Some companies, in order to avoid the negative reactions often associated with the concept of control, refer to their budgetary controls as either *profit plans* or *profit paths*.

In our discussion of budgetary controls we shall examine, first, the nature of budgets and review the types of budgets used most frequently. Although budgets are an application of accounting techniques, their success or failure is dependent upon their acceptance by the people in an organization; consequently, consideration shall be given to the human factors in budgetary control. In the last part of the chapter, guides for the effective use of budgets are presented.

THE NATURE OF BUDGETS

A *budget* may be defined as a plan expressed in quantitative terms. However, this overly simplified definition of a budget does not tell us much about the nature of budgets or of budgetary control. The process of preparing a budget is planning in every sense of the word, and the budget itself is the resultant plan. As such, the budget, like any other plan, should possess the characteristics of objectivity, structuralization, and flexibility. The extent to which a budget reflects these characteristics is a measure of its probable success.[1]

Even so, there are certain aspects of budgets that differentiate them from other plans. First, the reason for preparing a budget is to provide a means for controlling operations. Second, as a means of controlling operations effectively, a separate budget is usually prepared for each organizational unit, and individual budgets may be prepared for each of the several functions within an organizational unit. Third, a budget is designed to cover a specific period of time. The fiscal year is the unit of time used most frequently, but this unit may be subdivided into semiannual, quarterly, or monthly periods. Also, budgets may be prepared for periods of time greater than one year; for example, capital expenditure budgets. Finally, budgets are expressed in financial terms since dollars serve well as a common denominator and thereby permit the comparison and coordination of all phases of a company's operations.

Though planning is an essential ingredient in the process of preparing budgets, the preparation of budgets is more closely related to the control process than it is to the planning process. The budget itself is the stated standard of performance. Thus, preparing budgets is, in effect, setting standards—the first step of the control process. The measurement of current performance against standards, the second step in the process of control, is facilitated because the budget expresses standards of performance in quantitative terms—dollars. Deviations from budgeted or expected results are readily identified and show the need for corrective action, the last step in the process of control. Undoubtedly, the preparation of budgets refines the planning process necessary for the establishment of standards, or goals; however, the greater value of budgeting lies in its contribution to improved coordination and control. When budgets are prepared for all organizational units and the various functions performed by these units, a basis is provided for the coordination of the efforts of the organization. At the same time, budgets establish a basis for the corrective action of control since deviations from expected results are more readily identified and measured. Thus, the preparation of budgets may be expected to result in better planning and improved coordination, and to provide a basis for control— the primary purpose for establishing budgets.

---

[1] See Chapter 4, pp. 90-95.

Types of Budgets

Virtually every aspect of the operations of an organization can be budgeted. A business firm may prepare budgets for sales, inventory, shipments, production, maintenance, direct labor, and indirect labor. Budgets may also be used to forecast the operations of the industrial relations department, the cost of industrial engineering, and the needs for research and development. The list of organizational units and functions susceptible to budgetary control is almost endless. Fortunately, there is a logical framework that provides an easily remembered classification of budgets. This classification follows roughly a time sequence in the operation of a business and results in the following four types of budgets:

1. Revenue and expense budget
2. Cash budget
3. Capital expenditure budget
4. Balance sheet budget

As we shall see, each of these major types of budgets may be further subdivided so that the individual needs of each company may be fully met.

Revenue and Expense Budget. If one were starting a new business or beginning to prepare the initial set of budgets for a going concern, his first need would be a summary statement of the company's operations. The *revenue and expense budget,* sometimes called an *operating budget,* provides a bird's eye view of operations. Since revenue from the sale of products or services is the main source of income, the revenue budget is often referred to as the *sales budget.* All other budgets must be coordinated with the sales forecast since revenue from sales defines the upper limits of expenses and profits.

SALES BUDGET. In preparing a sales forecast, careful consideration must be given to external environmental factors as well as to conditions within the company itself. General economic conditions, the availability of credit, and the action of competitors are illustrative of the external factors that influence a company's level of sales. Accurate sales forecasts are difficult to achieve, at best, but the experience gained from the preparation of successive annual sales budgets gradually narrows the gap between budgeted and actual sales.

The content and the format of the sales budget vary with each company; however, certain generalizations are possible. For companies with multiple products or services, the expected revenue from each product or service should be stated separately. For large companies, a breakdown of expected sales by territory is essential. Sometimes the forecast should reflect expected sales for each class of customer. Since sales are seldom the same for each month of the year, the expected revenue for each calendar month should be stated to show clearly the seasonal variations. A forecast of revenue by month is necessary for the preparation of cash budgets.

EXPENSE BUDGET. The second part of the revenue and expense budget is a statement of expected expenses. Two considerations guide the preparation of expense budgets. First is a determination of the classification of items to be included in expense budgets; and second, the allocation of expense items according to organizational unit. Expense budgets may be prepared for every item listed in the expense division of the company's chart of accounts. In manufacturing firms, a manufacturing budget is prepared to show the expenses anticipated in the manufacture of the company's product. Included are the cost of material, the cost of inventory, direct and indirect labor charges, factory overhead including the cost of supervision, and the cost of maintaining equipment and other manufacturing facilities. General administrative costs and the cost of sales are shown separately.

If the budget is to be an effective tool in the control of expenses, a budget must be prepared for each organizational unit and placed in the hands of the managers of those units. Manufacturing budgets are prepared for operating departments and become a statement of expense responsibilities for the manager of each department. Managers of territorial or product divisions of the sales department are charged with the responsibility of keeping the cost of sales within budgeted limits. Difficulties encountered in controlling expenses are often a result of ill-defined organizational structure rather than an unwillingness on the part of departmental managers to cooperate in reducing expenses.

Cash Budget. The *cash budget*, derived from the basic data included in the revenue and expense budget, shows the cash requirements needed for the operation of the business during the budget period. The need for a specific budget detailing cash requirements arises from the fact that rarely does the flow of cash into the firm from sales coincide with the amount and frequency of disbursements necessary to pay expenses. For example, if too little cash is on hand to purchase materials in order to increase inventory levels to meet seasonal sales requirements, it may be necessary to borrow and thereby incur the added cost of interest. Also, having sufficient cash on hand makes it possible to take advantage of cash discounts offered by suppliers. On the other hand, excess cash may be used for short-term investments, or it may make possible an earlier than expected fulfillment of capital expenditure plans. When the amount of cash falls below budgeted expectations, it may be an early warning that accounts receivable are running too high. Budgeting cash requirements may not alter significantly the amount of profit earned by a firm, but it does assure a liquid position and is considered one of the hallmarks of prudent management.

Capital Expenditure Budget. If the planning and the control of the revenue and expense budget are successfully managed, revenue should exceed expenses. A part of this balance is reinvested in the company to insure the continued existence and growth of the firm. Since these expenditures produce revenue, they are classed as capital expenditures and are included in the *capital expenditure budget*. Typically, one finds in the capital expenditure budget allotments for the replacement of present facilities, including plant and equipment, and funds for the expansion of facilities for increased production of the present product line or the development and manufacture of a new product.

However, there are expenses other than those for physical facilities and equipment that require the appropriation of fairly large sums of money and the passage of a relatively long period of time before the anticipated results become apparent. Executive development programs, including the recruitment of college graduates, require support on a continuing basis; and it may take many years before the results of such personnel programs can be assessed. The decision to spend a greater than usual amount in advertising in order to develop new markets is another long-range investment of company funds. Research and development plans for new and improved products require continued appropriations for their completion. Institutional advertising intended to establish a desired public image also requires special budgetary appropriations. Consequently, some companies develop a single *appropriation budget* to reflect intended expenditures for capital equipment, personnel development, the development of new markets, research and development programs, and institutional advertising.

Budgeting capital or appropriation expenditures poses some rather difficult problems not directly related to the control of expenses. Since emergency needs in the five areas mentioned above arise infrequently, the control of expenses is relatively easy to achieve—one simply does not spend more than the budgetary allowance. Instead, the difficulty in preparing budgets for special appropriations arises from the long-term nature of these investments and the limited amount of money available for such expenditures. Because these projects are long term, their true worth cannot be computed until completed or until their useful life, in the case of capital equipment, is exhausted. Even then one is not sure that the course selected is of more value than some of the rejected alternate courses of action. But alternate courses must be weighed and choices made since the funds available to a company are never unlimited. Difficult as the appraisal of the results of capital expenditure budgeting may be, there are, nonetheless, several important benefits to be gained from this class of budget. First, capital or appropriation expenditures should be controlled and can be controlled relatively easily once they are budgeted. Second, budgeting the major appropriations forces an improvement of the planning process in each of the functional areas so that a careful weighing of alternate forms of investment may be accomplished. Third, capital expenditures require cash and as a result must be budgeted if the cash budget is to be of maximum value as a control device. Fourth, special appropriations must be included so that the greatest degree of coordination of the company's resources, especially financial, is achieved.

Balance Sheet Budget. The *balance sheet budget* is a forecast of expected financial status as of the last day of the budget period, usually the close of the fiscal year. The balance sheet forecast, a statement of the relationships between assets and liabilities, does not require the preparation of any additional budgets; rather, it is a consolidation of all preceding budgets. Preparing a balance sheet forecast shows what might be expected if performance meets the standards defined in the other budgets. By preparing a forecast of anticipated financial position, management may discover that the other budgets when consolidated do not result in an entirely favorable financial condition as revealed by certain key ratios. For example, the ratio between current assets and current liabilities or expected earnings and current market price per share may be such that the value of the company's stock would be adversely affected. When this happens, the other budgets have to be recast. The balance sheet showing the actual financial position at the close of the budget period serves as a useful check on the accuracy of preparation and the degree to which all other budgets have been met. Also, deviations between the actual and the forecasted balance sheets may show the need for preparation of special budgets to improve control over performance in certain areas; for instance, accounts receivable, accounts payable, or finished goods inventory.

Securing Flexibility with Budgets

Several disadvantages may arise as the result of an overzealous application of budgetary controls. In the administration of budgetary controls, it is all too easy to emphasize conformance to the budgetary goals of the organization. For example, a regional sales manager who is experiencing difficulty in meeting sales objectives may have every reason to believe that a market research study would be of help in solving his problem; yet, he may find it impossible to conduct such a study because there is no provision for it in his budget. Another criticism arising from the use of budgets is that the statement of objectives in numeric terms lends a degree of precision and exactness that is seldom warranted. After all, goals stated numerically are no more reliable than the original estimates from which they are drawn. However, the greatest potential danger of budgetary control is that it may lead to inflexibility. Budgets are statements of plans and, like any other plan, if they are to be successful, they must be flexible as well as possess the characteristics of objectivity and structuralization. Flexibility in budgetary control may be achieved by either one of two methods: *periodic budgetary reviews* and *flexible budgets*.

Periodic Budgetary Review. Normally, budgets are prepared in advance for a 12-month period. However, changes in operating conditions may occur that make the attainment of stated bugetary goals a virtual impossibility. Some of the factors frequently subject to change during the course of the budget period are labor costs, selling price, and the predicted volume of business. Periodic budgetary reviews are intended to incorporate and reflect changes in any of the first two factors, while flexible budgets are designed specifically to reflect changes in the anticipated volume of business.

Periodic budgetary reviews may be prepared on a monthly basis, prior to the beginning of the new month. Then, during the third month of the budgetary period, a revised quarterly estimate is prepared. For example, a company whose fiscal year is the same as the calendar year would prepare revised estimates of the budget for the months of January, February, and March prior to the beginning of each of these months. During the month of March, a revised quarterly budget for the second quarter might be prepared in addition to the revised estimate for April. Also, revised quarterly budgets may be prepared for the third and fourth quarters prior to their beginning, along with the usual monthly revisions.

However, there is a danger inherent in the use of periodic budgetary reviews as a means of recognizing changing conditions. If changes are made too frequently and if the magnitude of these changes is too great, it is quite possible for the original budget to become meaningless. Also, the other extreme is possible; that is, periodic reviews of the budget, backed by ample evidence, may show the need for a restatement of budgeted goals but may not be permitted because the original budget is considered inviolate. One way of minimizing the variation between the annual budget and the revised budget resulting from periodic reviews is to anticipate in the preparation of the annual budgets the changes that might reasonably be expected in labor rates, raw materials, and selling prices. Past experience is a good guide in these areas. Changes suggested as the result of periodic reviews must not only be substantiated, but reasons must also be given showing why it was impossible to anticipate these changes in the preparation of the original budget. In this manner the accuracy of the original budget is improved over a period of years.

Flexible Budgets. Periodic budget reviews allow management to compensate for changes in labor costs, selling price, the cost of raw materials, a change in technology, or the method of operation. In many respects the amount of change resulting from these factors is unpredictable, with the result that the extent of their effect on the budget can be determined only after the change has begun. However, the effects of changes in the volume of business of a company upon the revenue and expense budgets can in many instances be predicted in advance. When budgets are prepared for the coming fiscal year, they are prepared on the basis of an assumed or predicted level of revenue or volume—a statement of expected expenses for an expected amount of revenue. Flexible or variable budgets show the effect of changes in the volume of business upon certain expense items in the revenue and expense budget.

From our study of break-even analysis (Chapter 5), we know that some costs regarded as fixed or standby do not vary proportionately with the volume of business and that other costs vary proportionately with changes in volume. Good examples of fixed and variable costs are the costs incurred in operating an automobile. The cost of depreciation, insurance, and garaging the automobile is not a function of the number of miles driven (volume). Rather, these costs are incurred at the time the car is purchased and do not change appreciably as a result of the number of miles driven. For this reason these costs are termed fixed, or standby, costs. On the other hand, the cost of tires, oil, gasoline, and repairs varies directly with the number of miles driven; hence, these costs are called variable costs. Similarly, a company's costs for depreciation, insurance, and administration remain relatively unchanged within wide ranges of volume and are termed fixed costs. Labor costs, the cost of materials, and variable selling expenses such as commissions are representative of those costs that vary directly with changes in volume and are called variable costs.

Figure 22-1 shows in graphic form the relationship between the fixed and the variable expenses of a flexible budget. The determination of the nature of the relationship between variable costs and the level of volume may be accomplished by one of two methods: (1) a historical analysis of costs incurred at varying levels of volume and (2) the development of standard costs.

HISTORICAL ANALYSIS OF COSTS. The historical approach is an effective tool for determining the relationship between variable costs and volume when the company's product line is limited to a few products and when each product contributes a relatively constant percentage to total sales volume. In its simplest form, historical analysis may consist of determining actual costs incurred in producing the company's historical maximum volume and the costs incurred for the lowest point of the sales record. These two points, the high and the low, may be plotted on a graph and a straight line drawn to connect them; thus, by interpolation, a prediction may be made concerning expected costs for each level of volume between the historical high and low points. More sophisticated techniques include plotting sales and cost data for each year and determining by the method of least squares the line of best fit. For those companies with diverse product lines, it becomes necessary to analyze the variable costs for each product.

STANDARD COSTS. Standard costs for each product may be developed and may show the predicted cost for labor, materials, and supplies that might be expected for each unit produced. The predicted standard costs become the budgeted amount of variable costs, and the total cost for varying levels of volume can be readily computed.

Evaluation of Flexible Budgets. Variable budgets, particularly those utilizing standard costs, are often criticized as being too costly from the standpoint of both time and money in their preparation. Another criticism of variable budgets is that in practice they are extremely difficult to apply in a manner that results in savings in variable expenses. Part of the difficulty arises from an inability to predict short-term variations in volume. Even when this can be done, it is sometimes impracticable to take advantage of this information. For example, a department supervisor may normally supervise a work force of 15 machinists. A decline in volume for a period of two months does not necessarily result in a

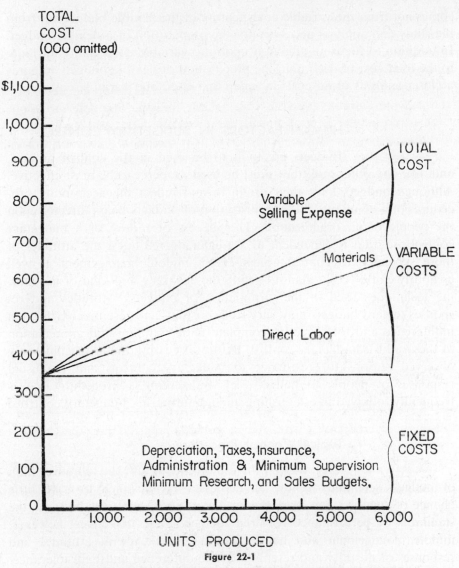

Figure 22-1

GRAPHIC REPRESENTATION OF A VARIABLE EXPENSE BUDGET

reduction in force since it may be more economical in the long run to retain highly skilled employees instead of running the risk of losing their services as a result of a layoff. Also, a sudden upturn in business may be handled more efficiently by assigning overtime work rather than incurring expenses resulting from training new employees. An advantage of variable budgets is that there is a budgeted goal for varying levels of volume without having to rework the entire budget each time a significant change in activity occurs. However, a greater advantage comes not from the variable goals feature of the flexible budget but from the study and analysis necessary for the preparation of a flexible budget. In addition to focusing attention upon the variable costs that contribute to the total cost of each unit, the preparation of flexible budgets requires a closer analysis of all costs in separating fixed and variable costs.[2]

HUMAN FACTORS IN BUDGETARY CONTROL

Budgets are tools to be used in the control process, and, like any other tool, they must be used properly to be most effective. Although budgets have their origin in and reflect the accounting procedures of a company, the administration of budgets bears directly upon the people of an organization. The success or failure of a budgetary control program is dependent to a greater degree upon the attitudes of those subjected to control—members of middle management as well as hourly employees—than it is upon the accuracy and kind of accounting techniques used in the formulation of budgets. Attitudes and responses toward budgets may vary from hostility and resentment, through indifference and tolerance, to complete understanding and appreciation of the need for budgetary control. Before discussing the most commonly observed reasons for resistance to budgetary controls and the usual responses of people to budgets, let us examine a procedure that is frequently followed in establishing and administering budgetary controls.

Typical Control Procedure

All too often the establishment and the administration of budgets seemingly follow an endless cycle destined to have little chance of success. Top management determines objectives and sets the standards of performance required to meet these objectives; however, middle management and hourly employees react with attitudes and responses of hostility and resentment or indifference and bare tolerance. Such reactions are interpreted by top management as evidence of the need for additional and firmer controls. Robert Katz describes this cycle of control, resistance, and more control as follows:[3]

---

[2] Adolph Matz, Othel J. Curry, and George W. Frank, *Cost Accounting,* 3d ed. (Cincinnati: South-Western Publishing Company, 1962), pp. 461-556. The three chapters on budgets, Chapters 16, 17, and 18, provide a discussion of the nature of budgets and offer many problems and examples of budgetary controls.

[3] Robert L. Katz, "Toward a More Effective Enterprise," *Harvard Business Review,* Vol. XXXVIII (September-October, 1960), pp. 86-87. Although Dr. Katz's comments are not directed specifically toward the establishment of budgetary control programs, they do provide a description that is typical of many budgetary control installations.

1. The predetermined program is implemented. It is characterized by general, nonpersonal rules, division of labor, specialized competences, and continuous checking to assure compliance.
2. Here the program immediately encounters unsought-for behavior as employees and subordinate managers seek to maintain their feelings of self-worth, their potential for self-determination, and their needs to have others acknowledge these capabilities.
3. Employees' reaction—Management's unilateral imposition of rules and detailed programming of behavior conflicts with employees' needs for self-determination and self-respect.

    Employees feel misunderstood, unappreciated, manipulated. They develop behavior patterns which enable them to resist rigid task pressures and permit some degree of self-regulation through informal social relationships.

    Performance stabilizes at the minimum level tolerated by management. Employees tend to produce well below their capacities, have low involvement in their tasks, show little initiative, do only what they are directed to do.
4. Subordinate manager's reaction—Expected by top management to obtain the employees' compliance in the program without deviation, subordinate managers are likely to feel helpless, asked to do the impossible, and misunderstood. They try to escape their feelings of inadequacy by blaming "unreasonable and uncontrollable" employees or "unreasonable and unsympathetic" superiors.

    Depending on their temperament, individual managers will tend either to (a) insist on more precise performance of the program, instituting closer controls, closer supervision, more rigorous use of rewards and punishments, or (b) abdicate, contacting subordinates as little as possible, giving instructions, and then busying themselves elsewhere.
5. In either case, whether the subordinate manager cracks down or withdraws, his employees tend to react to his response by developing new behavior patterns. These patterns tend to stabilize at a new level of minimal performance and minimal satisfaction so that all of the old problems remain while new anxieties are created.
6. At this point, top management becomes apprehensive and convinced that things are "out of control." Seeing widespread deviation from its predetermined program, top management is likely to respond to its anxieties by replacing the subordinate manager, applying more pressure for compliance, establishing more elaborate controls, or trying to train the subordinate manager in "how to get people to do what he wants them to."
7. Top management's action only serves to heighten the subordinate manager's anxieties and feelings of inadequacy. The proverbial "man in the middle," he finds his superiors expecting that he *should* be

able to get his employees to perform strictly according to plan, and his subordinates expecting that he should attend to *their* needs which underlie their deviation.

8. No matter what the subordinate manager does, the likely outcome is that employees will feel more unappreciated and misunderstood than before, the subordinate manager more helpless and insecure, and top management more anxious about its lack of control.

9. Top management responds by devising new predetermined programs, installing new controls, shuffling personnel, but *not* by questioning any of its original assumptions. Thus, the cycle of unanticipated consequences starts all over again.

Obviously something is wrong. The cycle of control, resistance, and more control cannot go on endlessly. Usually a compromise, or more accurately, a stalemate, is reached. Top management settles for standards of performance that fall short of budgeted expectations; and subordinates, including middle management, tacitly recognize but do not wholly accept or understand the need for budgetary control. An understanding of the reasons for resistance to budgetary controls enables us to prepare and install budgets in such a manner that the cycle of control, resistance, and more control never begins.

Why Resistance Develops

Seemingly, most of us have a built-in resistance to any form of control; perhaps such reactions are necessary for the preservation of one's own individuality. Nonetheless, as managers, we must learn not only to cope with our own reactions to control but also to meet and minimize the resistance of subordinates to control. Although the discussion that follows is directed primarily toward an analysis of the reasons for resistance to budgetary controls, it is equally applicable to the nonbudgetary controls described in the next chapter—particularly those devices designed specifically to measure and control the behavior of the individual members of an organization.

The three steps of the control process—setting standards, measuring performance, and taking corrective action—provide a logical outline for our discussion of resistance to controls.

Standards Are Too Tight. A frequent initial reaction to budgets or other forms of control is the complaint that the standard of performance is unreasonable or too tight. There are several reasons why people respond in this manner. There may be no understanding of or desire to meet organizational objectives expressed by the standard. Such reactions occur when standards are imposed without any explanation concerning their need. Budgetary allowances for waste or scrap are not only standards for the control of costs but also an expression of the quality demands of customers. Unless the reasons for standards can be presented in such a way that they become personal objectives for persons who are expected to meet such standards, complaints that the goals are unreasonable are sure to arise.

Another reason for objecting to standards is that historically they have a way of moving in only one direction—up. Consequently, is it any wonder that the initial reaction to them is the belief that they are unreasonable or too tight? A sales budget may show that a higher dollar volume is expected from each salesman for the current year; however, the increased volume may be the result of higher prices rather than the result of an increase in the number of units sold. In a like manner, an increase in the number of units expected from a production worker is often the result of improved methods or more efficient production equipment that actually call for less effort on the worker's part. Since budgets are prepared annually and usually show a steady increase in expected performance, it is necessary that those affected by standards understand not only the reasons for the changing objectives but also how the new standards can be met.

The third reason for resistance to standards lies in the way in which they are administered on a day-to-day basis. Regardless of how carefully standards may have been developed, unexpected conditions arise that make their attainment impossible. Materials that fail to meet stated specifications or machine breakdowns lower the output of the production worker. Unexpected product developments by competitors or even unseasonable variations in the weather can affect the performance of a salesman. In such cases the wise administrator notes the reasons for variances from budgeted goals and does not place undue pressure upon subordinates.

Measurements Not Accurate. Many times standards of performance are accepted, but the methods used in measuring performance are considered inaccurate. When control measures are criticized as not being accurate, more often than not factors other than accuracy are involved. The real complaint on the part of a supervisor operating under budgetary controls may be that the information provided is not timely enough to be of use to him in the operation of his department. Also, a supervisor's superior may criticize control measurements because they are not timely enough to aid in the coordination of the activities of several departments.

The comment is often heard that the measures used are satisfactory as far as they go, but they do not begin to measure all that is being done. The implication is that the measurements being used are not measuring those things that are important. The production foreman may agree that the unit count is an accurate statement of what is produced but reveals nothing about the decline in the number of units rejected by final inspection and the consequent decrease in the cost of rework. A salesman may readily admit that the dollar volume statement of his sales is correct and at the same time complain that the information used to measure his performance is unfair because it does not reflect the number of new accounts or the miles that he has to travel in his territory in order to call on customers. Before corrective action is taken, it is well to make sure that all the significant aspects of performance are being measured.

However, the bitterest complaint of all concerning measurements used in the control process is that they do not measure effort. Students may receive a grade of C on an assignment that in their opinion was worth at least a B in terms of the amount of effort expended. Unfortunately, for those whose work is subjected to measurement and comparison to standard, the information required for control purposes is an accurate statement of the amount of variance from standard. A good supervisor will note the effort spent in doing a job and should commend his subordinates for such effort. By so doing, he may be able to minimize the normal resistance of subordinates to having their work subjected to measurement—particularly when performance does not meet expected goals.

Dislike of Corrective Action. In the first paragraph of this section on human factors in budgetary control, it is stated that although budgets have their origin in and reflect the accounting procedures of a company, the administration of budgets bears directly upon the people of an organization. Specifically, it is the corrective action taken as the result of failure to meet budgeted expectations that is disliked and sometimes even feared. Somehow there is the belief that where there are no budgets there is always the possibility that poor performance will not be noticed and, if detected, plausible excuses can be offered and will be accepted. Budgets are a means of putting goals in writing and there are no columns in a budget for excuses.

One reason for disliking corrective action, even a mild form of admonition, is that it is a form of criticism directed toward an individual. Criticism of a person can never be completely impersonal even though such criticism might be based upon an objective analysis of all the facts.

Consequently, we all have a tendency to reject at least a part of any criticism and interpret what is said with some degree of animosity.

Another reason for disliking corrective action is that it exposes a person's shortcomings to his peers and sometimes to subordinates and superiors in the organization as well. Such exposure is practically unavoidable when demotion or discharge is the corrective action taken. None of us like to admit failure to ourselves, to say nothing about having others in the organization know about our inability to do a job properly. It is the dislike and the fear of potential corrective action more than resistance to standards and criticisms of the methods of measurement that lead to most of the undesirable reactions frequently associated with budgetary control.

Unfavorable Responses to Budgets

Our analysis of the resistance to budgetary control shows that any of the three steps in the control process may serve as a focal point for resistance. To some observers, resistance is regarded as a reaction to the pressures created by budgets and their application as a control instrument. Before studying the specific form of resistance demonstrated by either an individual or a group, let us find out why budgets are commonly regarded as pressure devices.

Budgets As Pressure Devices. There are two major reasons why budgets are commonly regarded as pressure devices. First, a budget is a statement of standards of performance. The standards, like the 72-stroke par of golf, should be difficult but attainable. It is expected that the amount of effort expended by an individual in attaining standard is somewhat greater than the amount he would expend if there were no stated standards. Thus, a certain degree of pressure is inherent and intended in any statement of standards. The second source of pressure arises from the procedures frequently followed in the installation and administration of budgets. More often than not, budgets are developed solely by top management and imposed upon the middle and the lower echelons of the organization. Supervisors and hourly employees alike cannot help but believe that budgets imply that top management is not entirely satisfied with the usual level of performance. Many times top management candidly affirms their subordinates' view of budgets as a means of pressure by pointing to the increases in productivity that occur after the installation of budgets. Often the reaction to budgets imposed from above results in the control, inadequate response, more control cycle described earlier in this section.

Improperly conceived and administered budgets can result in serious human relations problems. One writer has summarized what may happen as follows:[4]

1. Budget pressure tends to unite the employees against management, and tends to place the factory supervisor under tension. This tension may lead to inefficiency, aggression, and perhaps a complete breakdown on the part of the supervisor.
2. The finance staff can obtain feelings of success only by finding fault with factory people. These findings of failure among factory supervisors lead to many human relations problems.
3. The use of budgets as "needlers" by top management tends to make each factory supervisor see only the problem of his own department.
4. Supervisors use budgets as a way of expressing their own patterns of leadership. When this results in people getting hurt, the budget, in itself a neutral thing, often gets blamed.

Note that the pressure of budgets can affect both individuals and groups in an organization.

Effects on Individuals. Unfavorable individual responses to budgets on the part of supervisors are essentially reactions resulting from their failure either to understand or to meet stated budgetary goals. Occasionally the tensions and pressures created by budgets may result in a supervisor suffering a complete breakdown. Apathy, loss of interest in the job, and compliance to "the letter of the law" are forms of behavior that reflect a withdrawal from an unpleasant situation. Some supervisors respond with overt aggressiveness that is intended to shift the responsibility for failure to meet standards from themselves and their department to other departmental managers or to members of the staff organization.

Budgetary controls always contain the potential threat of disrupting cooperative relationships between members of the line-and-staff organizations. When imposed from above, the budget is developed and administered by a specialized staff group—usually a part of the controller's office. The measure of success of the budget staff is the extent to which the line managers meet the budgeted goals. Failure to meet these goals is interpreted as failure on the part of the line organization rather than the result of poorly stated or unattainable goals by the budget group. When budgets are fulfilled, ensuing budgets can be tightened so that they are more difficult to attain; thus, the line manager is once again

---

[4] Chris Argyris, "Human Problems with Budgets," *Harvard Business Review,* Vol. XXXI (January-February, 1953), p. 108. Argyris' article is a report of a research study undertaken for the Controllership Foundation to determine the effects of budgets on human relationships in an organization and the extent to which budgets accomplish their purpose. Suggestions are given to improve the effectiveness of budgets.

faced with the threat of failure. Under these conditions, it is understandable why the relationships between the line manager and the budget staff are in a state of perpetual conflict.

The departmental supervisor may generalize his conflict with the budget staff and attempt to shift the blame for his difficulties to other staff groups. The personnel department may be criticized for failure to enforce disciplinary action and for not supplying qualified and sufficient manpower. Quality control may be accused of setting quality specifications that make it impossible to meet budgeted cost and production standards. The production control staff comes under attack for failure to schedule long production runs and for scheduling unreasonable sequences in the production of different products. Plant maintenance departments receive their share of criticism for not maintaining production equipment and other facilities at peak levels of efficiency.

The reactions discussed so far are descriptive of how the individual supervisor might react when budgets are interpreted as a means of exerting pressure. He may withdraw from the situation through sickness or apathy or he may become aggressive and strike out in any and all directions. He may try to shift the blame to other operating departments, to the budget staff, or to other staff groups. Unfavorable reactions to budgets do not remain individual reactions indefinitely; instead, individuals form cohesive groups and the strength of the group is utilized to combat the pressures of control.

Group Reaction to Pressure. Organized group resistance to budget pressures, or for that matter to any other kind of external control pressure, does not develop immediately; nor is it planned. However, the formation of group resistance is inevitable and follows a consistent evolutionary pattern. Argyris describes this process well:[5]

1. First, the individuals sense an increase in pressure.
2. Then they begin to see definite evidences of the pressure. They not only feel it, they can point to it.
3. Since they feel this pressure is on them personally, they begin to experience tension and general uneasiness.
4. Next they usually "feel out" their fellow workers to see if they too sense the pressure.
5. Finding out that others have noted the pressure, they begin to feel more at ease. It helps to be able to say, "I'm not the only one."
6. Finally, they realize that they can acquire emotional support from each other by becoming a group. Furthermore, they can "blow their top" about this pressure in front of their group.

---

[5] *Ibid.*, p. 100.

When leadership crystallizes and emerges, the group is ready to act in unison. Let us see what happens; first, on the hourly level; then, within the ranks of management.

THE HOURLY LEVEL. Assume that the production of a manufacturing department, or the output of a clerical section, is stabilized at a rate that time study shows to be 65 percent of standard. Certain conditions or forces are holding production at this level. Perhaps supervision is satisfied, and an output of 65 percent of standard may be the most comfortable pace considering the methods used in performing the work. The individual worker has no reason for deviating from this pattern since conformance assures continued membership in the group and enables him to assume the protective coloring of the group. Now, incorporate the time study data into standards and express these standards as part of a budget—unannounced and imposed from above. Pressure is felt first by the supervisors, who, in turn, attempt to enforce the newly stated standards by requiring an increased level of production. The development of group cohesiveness as described by Argyris begins. Eventually a static state of balance between the pressures of the budget and the pressures of the group may be reached; a level higher than the original 65 percent but still short of the budgeted 100 percent. These are the *frozen* groups of Zalesnik or the *sick* groups described by Gellerman.[6] When the informal group achieves cohesiveness and adopts the leadership and resources of a formal organization—the union—the groundwork is laid for labor-management strife.

GROUPS WITHIN MANAGEMENT. The formation of groups whose primary purpose is to combat the pressures exerted by top management is not limited to groups composed of hourly or clerical employees. Informal groups may develop within the ranks of management as well. The first-line supervisors of a plant may feel themselves caught between the pressure of the budget from above and the resistance of their subordinates from below. They are literally caught in the middle and seek the support offered by others who are in the same position. When talking to subordinates, the supervisor blames the "budget people" for the pressures of production. When reporting to his superior, the incompetence and the uncooperativeness of his subordinates are offered as the cause for failure to meet budgeted expectations. There are instances of supervisory groups having become so firmly solidified that they eventually became formal unions of supervisors. Many supervisory

---

[6] See Chapter 18, "Motivating Employees," p. 460.

or management clubs have been formed to nullify the cohesiveness of informal groups of supervisors and forestall their becoming formal union organizations. The labor unions of engineers and scientists, though not directly the result of budgetary controls, are another example of resistant to top management that has led to the formation of groups so that group pressure may be applied in opposition to the pressure exerted by management.

Informal groups may develop within either the line or the staff organization and make it almost impossible to achieve the benefits that might be realized from the application of budgets or other forms of control. When line management unites as a group and opposes the recommendations of the staff organization, one can be sure that the staff, as a group, will oppose any suggested modifications of their programs that come from members of the line organization.

EFFECTIVE USE OF BUDGETS

Our review of those aspects of the control process that cause resistance, the concept of pressure associated with the administration of budgets, and the responses of individuals and groups to pressure does not seem to offer much encouragement for the successful application of budgetary control. Fortunately, there are ways to minimize resistance to budgetary controls. The following suggestions have been found helpful in making the application of budgets more effective.

Establish Proper Attitudes

The attitudes of the members of an organization toward budgets are dependent upon the underlying motivation of top management when first establishing budgets. Budgets can be established as a device to goad managers into better performance, or they can be used by the managers themselves as an instrument for measuring and guiding performance. These two divergent uses of budgets are analogous to the uses that may be found for two long pieces of wood. At the end of one piece of wood, there is a sharp point. This piece of wood is used as a prod to keep managers in line and moving in the right direction. Another piece of wood—the same length, is divided into 36 equal segments and becomes the familiar yardstick, a tool that can be used to measure progress. For budgets to be most effective, they must be regarded as yardsticks developed to measure performance rather than prods intended to keep people in line.[7]

Gain Top Management Support

The key to developing attitudes toward budgets that result in their being regarded as a means of measuring and guiding performance is the kind of support given by top management. Top management can provide lip service only, or its support can come as the result of a true understanding of the nature of budgetary control. Superficial support of budgets may result when the top management of a company has been sold a bill of goods by the controller of the company and accepts budgets without really understanding them. Lack of understanding is evidenced by continually questioning the accuracy of items included in the budget, by making budgets so detailed that they become a straight jacket, or by denying a manager's request for more money by stating that the budget does not permit any additional expenditures. These attitudes are reflected throughout the entire organization. The departmental manager who has been denied additional funds soon learns to pad his budget requests; and when this happens, the budget ceases to be a valid tool for measurement.

Place Budgets in the Hands of Managers

One of the best ways top management has of expressing its understanding of budgetary control is by placing the responsibility for the preparation and administration of budgets in the hands of departmental managers. True, a well-trained controller's staff is valuable in consolidating and coordinating company-wide budgets, but the preparation and administration of budgets at the operating level are best accomplished by the responsible manager. In preparing budgets, managers should make the first draft; then if revisions are needed, cooperative effort between the controller's office and line management is required to reach a final statement of goals. In order to administer budgets properly, managers must have adequate standards of performance, timely information concerning their performance, and freedom to manage. Standards serve as a measure of performance and form the backbone

---

[7] James L. Pierce, "The Budget Comes of Age," *Harvard Business Review*, Vol. XXXII (May-June, 1954), pp. 58-66. Mr. Pierce discusses some of the problems encountered in improving budgetary controls.

of any budget. In manufacturing departments, standards should be developed for labor, materials, supplies, and the maintenance of equipment. Standards of performance and cost can also be determined for administrative and sales units. The controller should provide departmental managers with timely information so that necessary corrections may be made and so that performance conforms to budgeted expectations. A budget is not intended to restrict the activities of a manager; he must have freedom to manage. So that freedom in operations may be increased, some companies state only the total of the expense items and leave to the discretion of the manager the allocation of the amount to be spent for each item. Finally, procedures must be clearly stated to set forth steps to be followed in securing budgetary revisions, and practice must demonstrate that such revisions are possible.

Follow Organizational Lines

Fundamental to effective budgetary control is a clear concept of organization structure. The manager of each department must know the superior to whom he reports and the subordinates who report to him, and his relations with other departments must be clearly defined. When organizational lines are clearly stated, the budgets become the yardstick capable of measuring performance; however, when organizational lines are fuzzy and ill defined, there is a tendency to use the budget as a prod since there is no means of defining duties and assigning responsibilities. The clarity of organizational definition marks the upper limit of the effectiveness of budgets as a means of controlling organizational performance.

Advantages of Effective Budgetary Control

Although budgets are one of the most widely used control techniques, it must be remembered that they are but one of several control devices. There are potential dangers as well as distinct advantages resulting from the use of budgets. Oddly enough, one of the strengths of budgets—the conversion of all aspects of organizational performance into a single comparable unit of measurement, dollars— can become its greatest weakness because it may result in measuring only those things that are easy to measure; i.e., those aspects of organizational performance readily converted into dollars. Equally important factors, such as manager performance and plans for organizational development, may be ignored because achievement in these areas is not readily convertible into dollar units. Second, there is a danger of identifying symptoms as causes. A decline in revenue from sales does not necessarily call for greater sales effort; instead, the real cause may result from a poor product, the action of competitors, or general economic conditions. And finally, there is a danger of autocratic control by the staff organization. The function of the controller or the budget director is to coordinate and guide the development of budgets, but the actual control of performance must remain in the hands of the line managers.

The obvious advantage of budgetary control is that a comparable statement of goals is provided for all organizational units; and since the budget serves as a standard of performance, deviations from this standard are readily measurable and provide the basis for necessary corrective action. However, there are indirect advantages resulting from the proper use of budgets. The consistent and uniform application of budgets results in a more clearly defined organizational structure since budgets measure the performance of organizational units. Second, more meaningful accounting systems and terminology are developed. Traditionally, accounting has a deep preoccupation with the preparation of historical and tax records rather than focusing upon the reporting of current operations and the forecasting of future performance. Third, better planning of all phases of the company's operations results from the use of budgets. Budgets are carefully structured plans and serve to emphasize the continuous nature of the planning-control-planning cycle. Lastly, a clearer statement and understanding of organizational goals comes from the use of budgets because each manager is forced to develop and state attainable goals for his organizational unit. Wishful thinking in respect to organizational objectives is minimized.

● ● ● ● ● ● ● ● ●

Case Problem 22-B is a continuation of Case Problem 22-A. All did not go as planned, and now there is need for corrective action. Two points are illustrated in this closing case. First, even though performance did not measure up to expectations, the presence of a budget pinpoints the areas requiring corrective action. Second, though each variation from budgeted performance may be small, the aggregate can sometimes be alarming.

Questions for Study and Discussion

1. How are budgets different from other kinds of business plans? Show why each of these differences is necessary.
2. Are the terms budget and standard synonymous? If so, what type of standards are utilized in the development of the four major types of budgets?
3. Discuss the following statement: Flexible budgets make periodic budgetary reviews unnecessary.
4. Should expense budgets be stated at a lower figure than that actually computed in order that final expenses will not exceed the budgeted amount? Support your answer.
5. Why are budgets often regarded as "pressure devices"?
6. Of what worth would a budget be if it did not create pressure? Discuss.
7. What are the attitudes essential for the effective use of budgetary control?
8. Describe the steps you would take to offset the usual resistance that develops when budgets are installed.
9. Describe the steps you would take in establishing an effective sales budget.

• • • • • • • • •

It was the latter part of January before Barr completed the proposed revenue and expense budget described in Case Problem 22-A. Only then did he know he would not make a profit during the first quarter of the year and that the best he could expect would be to break even by the end of June. In an attempt to offset the normally slow months of February, March, and April, he decided to increase advertising outlays and to gain a competitive advantage by lowering his prices slightly. During the year he hired additional sales personnel to offset his own lack of sales experience and knowledge of the men's clothing business. Also, the lease expired during the year, and a new one was negotiated at a somewhat higher figure. The results of Barr's first full year as manager of the Avenue men's clothing and furnishings store are shown in Exhibit I.

Case Problem 22-B

A Need for Corrective Action

Problems

1. Are the results shown in Exhibit I attributable to poor budgeting techniques or to poor management? Explain.
2. What corrective action would you take as manager of this store?

Exhibit I

BUDGETED AND ACTUAL PERFORMANCE—Avenue Men's Store

Account	Budgeted % of Net Sales ($200,000)	Actual Dollar Rev./Exp.	Actual Percentage of Budgeted Net Sales ($200,000)
Sales:			
1. Gross sales	102.6	$206,000	103.0
2. Customer ret. & allow. ..	2.6	5,000	2.5
3. Net sales	100.0	201,000	101.0
Cost of goods sold:			
4. Beginning inventory	30.9	61,800	30.9
5. Net purchases plus transportation charges paid ..	66.1	137,000	68.5
6. Total cost of merchandise handled	97.0	198,000	99.4
7. Ending inventory	32.3	66,800	33.4
8. Net cost of mdse. sold ..	64.7	132,000	66.0
9. Net busheling (alterations) cost	2.1	6,000	3.0
10. Total cost of mdse. sold ..	66.8	138,000	69.0
11. Gross margin	33.2	62,000	31.0
Operating expenses:			
12. Payroll:			
A. Salary of owner	7.3	14,600	7.3
B. Salaries and wages of employees	9.0	21,000	10.5
Total payroll ..	16.3	35,600	17.8
13. Rent expense	2.9	6,000	3.0
14. Taxes and license fees (omit real estate, Federal income and sales taxes) .	1.1	2,200	1.1
15. Insurance	.6	1,200	.6
16. Depreciation & amort. ..	.8	1,600	.8
17. Repairs	.2	200	.1
18. Supplies (omit rep. mat'ls.)	1.0	2,400	1.2
19. Services purchased	.9	1,400	.7
20. Traveling (business trips) ..	.3	400	.2
21. Communications (include parcel post)	.4	1,200	.6
22. Advertising and publicity .	2.8	6,400	3.2
23. Professional services (outside professional agencies) ..	.2	200	.1
24. Unclassified:			
A. Losses from bad debts	.3	800	.4
B. Other unclassified ..	.5	1,200	.6
Total unclassified expenses	.8	2,000	1.0
25. Total expenses	28.3	60,800	30.4
26. Net profit (before Federal income taxes)	4.9	1,200	.6

CHAPTER 23

Nonbudgetary Control

Tom Olafson, long a manager for a Chicago-based national moving and storage company, has recently been assigned the position of manager of a newly acquired company, Sunshine Moving and Storage Company. Sunshine's annual sales are approximately $850,000. Though the company is not as profitable as similar companies in the national system, Sunshine was considered a good buy because it is well located in a West Coast city of one million persons, the rolling equipment is relatively new, and the two warehouses are modern and well kept. The parent corporation believes that increased sales efforts should produce an annual sales volume of at least $950,000 and a net profit before taxes of six percent of annual sales.

After studying the operating statement for the previous year, shown in Exhibit I, Tom prepared a summary of the major operating ratios used as guides by the parent company in evaluating the performance of company-owned moving and storage facilities and in advising those privately owned companies that operate under a franchise system. In regard to reve-

Case Problem 23-A
Improving Operating Ratios

nue sources it is recommended that companies located on the West Coast derive no more than 25 percent of their revenue from long-distance moving, with at least 27 percent of their revenue coming from local moving. It is important to control the ratio between long-distance and local-moving revenues because the direct operating expenses incurred by long-distance moving approximate 80 percent of long-distance revenue, while local-moving operating expenses are about 77 percent of local-moving revenue. It is also recommended that storage and warehousing revenue account for at least 18 percent of total revenue, with 20 percent of total revenue from this source being entirely possible. Similarly, packing and crating revenues should range between 14 and 16 percent of the total, and commissions earned from business booked for vans from other terminals should account for at least 10 percent of total revenue. Commissions are regarded as a particularly valuable source of revenue because little capital equipment is utilized and there is usually additional income resulting from required packing and crating.

Exhibit I

ANNUAL OPERATING STATEMENT
Sunshine Moving & Storage Company

Revenue Sources:

1. Long distance $301,750
2. Local moving 204,850
3. Commissions 85,000
4. Storage & warehousing 128,350
5. Packing and crating 130,050

    Total revenue $850,000

Expense Items:

6. Traffic & sales
   Supervision, sales, and clerical salaries .... $ 34,000
   Advertising 12,750
   Other expenses 12,750

    Total traffic & sales .... $ 59,500

7. Administrative & general expense
   Salaries (officers & managers) .... $ 42,500
   Other administrative salaries 45,900
   Other general administrative expenses 90,950

    Total administrative & general expense $179,350

8. Trucking expense (includes long distance and local moving)
   Equipment maintenance .... $ 39,515
   Insurance and safety 19,757
   Depreciation 20,264
   Taxes and licenses 15,705
   Transportation—supervisor, wages, fuel oil 331,316

    Total trucking expense $426,557

9. Storage & warehousing expense
   Supervision and clerical employees .... $ 5,519
   Building expense 34,783
   Insurance, taxes, maintenance, & supplies 11,423
   Wages 25,625

    Total storage & warehousing expense .... $ 77,350

10. Packing & crating expense
   Supervision & office employees .... $ 2,601
   Depreciation, insurance, taxes 11,835
   Materials and supplies 22,499
   Wages 41,265

    Total packing & crating expense .... $ 78,200

Profit or Loss:

11. Profit .... $ 29,043

Recommended ratios for major expense items are summarized as follows:

Department	Percentage of Total Revenue
Traffic and Sales:	
Supervision, sales, and clerical personnel	5.7%
Advertising	3.0
Other expenses	.9
	9.6%
Administrative and General:	
Salaries (officers and managers)	4.5%
Other salaries	5.5
Other general expenses	10.5
	20.5%

	Percentage of Departmental Revenue
Trucking Department:	
Equipment and maintenance	6.0%
Insurance and safety	3.5
Depreciation	3.5
Taxes and licenses	2.5
Transportation (including fuel, wages, and subsistence) ..	62.0
	77.5%
Storage and Warehousing:	
Supervisory and office personnel	4.5
Building expense	28.0
Depreciation, insurance, and taxes	9.5
Wages	20.0
	62.0%
Packing and Crating:	
Supervision and office personnel	3.1%
Depreciation, insurance, and taxes	9.5
Materials and supplies	15.0
Wages	29.0
	56.6%

Problems

1. Are company expectations for sales and profits reasonable? What action would you take to increase sales?

2. Analyze each of the operating departments—trucking, storage and warehousing, and packing and crating—in respect to company recommendations for such operations and indicate the steps you would take as manager of Sunshine Moving and Storage Company in order to bring performance in line with expected results.

3. How profitable is each of the four sources of revenue—commissions, trucking, storage and warehousing, and packing and crating—when traffic and sales expense and administrative and general expense are apportioned to each in the same percentage amount that the source is of total sales?

In Chapter 21, "The Basis of Control," it is stated that standards may be set for each of the following key result areas: (1) profitability, (2) market position, (3) productivity, (4) product leadership, (5) personnel development, (6) employee attitudes, (7) public responsibility, and (8) balance between short-range and long-range goals. Since the nature of the goals and the kind of performance required to meet stated objectives in each of these areas are different, it seems highly unlikely that a single control device can be used with equal effectiveness in all areas. Such is the case. Budgets, discussed in Chapter 22, are a very effective means of controlling expense and revenue items; thus, they are particularly useful in controlling performance in the areas of profitability and productivity. However, there are other means of control, conveniently referred to as *nonbudgetary,* that are necessary to establish an effective and complete system of control. These techniques of nonbudgetary control, arranged in order from the simple to the more complex, are as follows: personal observation, reports, audit programs, ratio analysis, break-even analysis, and time-event-network analysis.

PERSONAL OBSERVATION

Personal observation is a means of securing control information applicable to all key result areas and is used by all levels of management. The supervisor in charge of a manufacturing department or a clerical section relies to a great extent upon impressions gained as the result of personal contact with subordinates. He is able to judge output by observing the pace of his workers; quality can be evaluated by personally inspecting the work in progress; and an estimate of morale and attitudes results from seeing employees, listening to their spontaneous remarks, and obtaining responses to questions. The plant manager who makes a daily tour of the plant is able to obtain firsthand information concerning conditions in the plant that are not revealed by formal reports. Similarly, many presidents and chief executive officers visit all company installations at least once each year so that the personal impressions thus gained may become a part of the basis for their decisions.

Personal observation as a means of gaining information is time consuming and is often criticized for this reason. Also, there is the possibility that subordinates may misinterpret a superior's visit and consider such action as meddling or failure to delegate. Finally, the value of firsthand information obtained from personal contact is limited by the perceptual skills and interpretative ability of the observer. Even so, personal observations are often the only means of substantiating impressions gained from other sources, and personal contacts almost always have a salutary effect upon subordinates since the presence of one's superior reveals his interest in the operation.

REPORTS

In designing or evaluating control reports, two closely related questions arise: (1) What is the purpose of the report? and (2) Who should receive the report?

Purpose of Control Reports

The primary purpose of control reports is to supply information intended to serve as the basis for corrective action if needed. At the same time, the significance of control reports must be kept in proper perspective. Control reports are only a part of the planning-control-planning information cycle that is necessary for a complete management information system. Refer to Figure 17-2, Anatomy of Management Information, on page 425. Note that control information includes nonfinancial as well as financial data, that it measures performance, and isolates variances from standard. Control information also provides feedback so that planning information may be updated and corrected. An example of a set of relatively simple control reports that contribute to the control process as well as provide a basis for updating the planing process is presented in Chapter 21, page 586. In this illustration the owner of a company manufacturing trays for cafeterias and drive-in restaurants receives reports containing information that shows the current backlog of orders, finished goods inventory, number of units shipped, and total hours of factory labor. A decline in the backlog of current orders, with the other three measures remaining relatively constant, indicates the need for corrective action resulting in increased sales. In this instance, the information provided serves primarily the control function. However, an increase in the order backlog, again with all other measures remaining constant, signals the need for additional planning so that production may be increased to meet the increased demand. Whenever possible, control reports should be designed so that they provide feedback for the planning process as well as provide information of immediate value to the control process.

Distribution of Control Reports

Since the culmination of the control process is the taking of necessary corrective action to bring performance in line with standards, it follows that control information must be directed to the person who is organizationally responsible for taking the required action. Usually the same information, though in a somewhat abbreviated form, is given to the responsible manager's superior. The supervisor of a manufacturing department requires detailed information that describes the performance of equipment and personnel in his department, but the plant manager may receive condensed summary statements showing performance in relation to standard, expressed as a percentage, for each of several operating departments. A district sales manager needs a complete daily record of the performance of each of his salesmen; yet, the report forwarded to the regional sales manager summarizes only the performance of each sales district in his region. In preparing reports for higher echelons of management, summary statements and recommendations for action should appear on the first page; substantiating data, usually the information presented to the person directly responsible for the operation, may be included if needed.

Characteristics of Good Reports

Since control reports are an integral part of a control system, they should incorporate the characteristics of an effective control system as described in Chapter 21, pages 583 to 589. They should be timely, particularly those prepared for a unit supervisor. When reports provide information intended primarily for the purpose of control, they should follow organizational lines; yet, it must be remembered that for the same information to become effective as a basis for additional planning, it is necessary to cross organizational lines. Reports should be prepared to reveal activity in the more sensitive or strategic areas of the business. In organizations where progress depends upon new products, frequent periodic reporting of research and development activities may be required. A firm whose chief concern is manufacturing efficiency may emphasize a detailed reporting of the production process. Reports should be economical, and their costs should be measured in terms of the extent to which they actually contribute to the control process. In preparing reports, sufficient data should be included so that trends as well as current status are reflected. Finally, reports should be prepared so that the exception is emphasized. Summary statements should stress performance that deviates from standard and show clearly both the direction and magnitude of the deviation.

AUDIT PROGRAMS

Traditionally, auditing, an independent appraisal of a company's financial records, seeks to test the reliability and validity of financial records by determining the degree of accuracy and the extent to which financial statements reflect what they purport to represent. As a result, audit programs are often regarded as a means of encouraging honesty on the part of employees and safeguarding the company's financial resources. This concept of auditing, the verification of company financial records, is limited in scope and is associated with *external audits* conducted by outside agencies such as bank examiners or a firm of public accountants. When conducted by a specialized staff made up of company personnel, auditing can be an effective means of control as well as a means of verifying financial records. This form of auditing is known as the *internal audit*. In addition, it is possible to apply the techniques of auditing as a means of assessing the overall effectiveness of management, an application of auditing often referred to as the *management audit*. Each of these forms of auditing, the external audit, the internal audit, and the management audit, is discussed in turn.

External Auditing

The external audit is usually conducted by a firm of public accountants. Its primary purpose is to determine whether or not company records of financial transactions present a true statement of the company's financial condition. It is essentially a verification of the accuracy of the records and a determination of the consistency of application of accepted accounting procedures. In order to make a summary statement of the financial condition of a company, it is necessary for the auditors to spot check all types of basic financial transactions to determine their accuracy. It is the checking phase of the auditing process that causes many to regard external auditing as a means of encouraging honesty on the part of employees. For example, a review of inventory records, a part of the process of verifying assets, may reveal shortages that may be the result of dishonesty.

The contribution of the external audit to the control process is indirect and limited in its nature. For instance, a company might wish to allocate certain capital expenditures as expense items, but independent auditors will not certify such allocations unless they are consistent with previously established accounting procedures. The same indirect form of control may be exerted if a company attempts to modify its statement of assets by altering established practices of evaluating finished goods or raw material inventories. The value of the external audit as a means of assessing financial position is limited by the appropriateness, or validity, of existing accounting procedures. When the summary information of the audit—usually a verification of the balance sheet items of assets, liabilities, and net worth—is used as a basis for formulating the corrective action of the control process, its worth is no greater than the validity of the accounting techniques used to record the financial condition of the company.

Internal Auditing

As the phrase, internal auditing, implies, the internal audit is conducted by a specialized staff made up of company personnel. Like the external audit conducted by an outside source, the internal audit verifies the accuracy of company records and determines whether or not such records are what they purport to be. However, the purpose of the internal audit is to provide a means of internal control. It seeks to determine the effectiveness of other controls; consequently, the internal audit may be regarded as a master control over all other forms of control.[1]

The potential benefits of an effective internal auditing program are many; however, there are three contributions that stand out above all others. First, internal auditing provides a way of determining whether established procedures and methods are effective in meeting stated company objectives and insuring compliance with stated policies. If, for example, it is the objective of a company to build a product having the highest possible quality, procedures are established to insure that component parts of the product are the best available. In reviewing purchase requisitions, the internal audit team goes beyond the accuracy of the records of the purchasing department and seeks to determine whether or not, in fact, components are of the highest available quality. The determination of the extent to which company policies are observed leads directly to the second major contribution of internal auditing— formulating recommendations for the improvement of policies, procedures, and methods so that they are more effective in the attainment of stated objectives. It may be necessary to modify existing controls, establish new controls, or change present procedures or methods. Deviations from established procedures may arise because someone believes that he has discovered a short cut, or there may have been an honest misunderstanding of the procedure due to its complexity.

---

[1] William T. Jerome, III, "Internal Auditing As an Aid to Management," *Harvard Business Review,* Vol. XXXI (March-April, 1953), pp. 127-136.

Whatever the reason, it is the task of the internal auditor to recommend those changes necessary to insure compliance, including the recommendation for additional or improved controls.

The third benefit of an internal auditing program may seem paradoxical at first glance. Internal auditing provides a means of providing a greater degree of delegation of authority and, if desirable, a means of facilitating the decentralization of operations. Delegation of authority and its broader organizational counterpart, the decentralization of authority to operating units, do not imply an absence of centralized control. On the contrary, the extent of delegation and decentralization is dependent to a large measure upon the effectiveness of central control. Internal auditing offers a means of continually checking the effectiveness of established controls and recommending needed improvements.

The use of the internal audit as a means of control has been increasing, particularly in large companies. One study reveals that in 1920 only 9 of 132 large companies had internal auditing departments; in 1940, only 58 of these companies had such departments; but by 1950, all of the 132 companies studied had internal auditing departments.[2] Even though many small and medium-size companies do not have internal auditing departments, the functions of internal auditing can still be accomplished to a degree by emphasizing that one of the functions of control is to determine the extent to which procedures and methods are being observed and to recommend improvements.

The success of internal auditing is dependent not only upon the attitude of top management but also upon the degree of acceptance accorded the audit team by lower and middle echelons of management. Acceptance by other members of management is more readily attained when internal auditors perform the functions of consultants and act as special staff advisors concerned with the improvement of all operations rather than appearing as custodians of company resources.

The Management Audit

The external audit is concerned chiefly with verifying the reliability and validity of financial records. Internal auditing goes a step further and determines the degree of compliance with company policies, procedures, and methods, and, if necessary, makes recommendations to insure the observance of established company practices. An even broader form of auditing is the *management audit*, a systematic approach to the appraisal of the overall performance of management.

---

[2] F. A. Lampert and J. B. Thurston, *Internal Auditing for Management* (Englewood Cliffs, N. J.: Prentice-Hall, Inc., 1953), pp. 84-86.

One of the better known methods of appraising managerial performance is the management audit developed by Jackson Martindell of the American Institute of Management (AIM).[3] The AIM management audit evaluates the performance of a company in relation to the performance of other companies in the same industry and in relation to the performance of outstanding companies in other industries. Some of the information needed for the management audit is a matter of public record, but much of it comes from the answers to a 300-item questionnaire. Point values for the answers given to each question are assigned, with the maximum number of points being 10,000. Managerial performance in each of the following 10 categories is evaluated: [4]

1. *Economic Function.* The economic function determines the public value of a company. Economic function is related to the product or service chosen by the company and is evaluated in a moral or ethical sense. To a degree, economic function is a measure of stature in the eyes of the public.

2. *Corporate Structure.* The organization of the company is evaluated in respect to its appropriateness for that particular company. Lines of authority, the allocation of responsibility, and the locus of decision making are some of the factors considered. Also important is the extent that the organization structure permits effective control of the enterprise.

3. *Health of Earnings.* The health of earnings record of a corporation is measured not only in terms of the dollar profit before taxes— expressed as total dollars, as a percentage of sales, and as a percentage of capital invested—but also in terms of the potential that might be realized with full utilization of company resources. The growth of earnings and their stability during periods of economic recession are also rated.

4. *Service to Stockholders.* Three basic questions are raised in determining the service rendered by a company to its proprietors, the stockholders. Has their investment in the company been subjected to an undue degree of risk, to what extent has their equity in the company appreciated in value, and has there been a fair return on investment in the form of dividends? The nature and openness

---

[3] Jackson Martindell, *The Scientific Appraisal of Management* (New York: Harper and Row, Publishers, Incorporated, 1962). This book is a revised statement of Martindell's original program that was first published under the same title and by the same publisher in 1950.

Jackson Martindell, "Management Audits Simplified," *The Corporate Director,* Special Issue, No. 15, (December, 1951), pp. 1-6.

[4] Jackson Martindell, "The Management Audit," *The Corporate Director,* Vol. IX, (December, 1962), pp. 1-4. This is a paper presented to the Academy of Management at the annual meeting held at Pittsburgh in December, 1962.

of communications between the company and its shareholders through annual reports and meetings is also important in determining service to stockholders.

5. *Research and Development.* It is axiomatic that companies must improve present products and develop new products if they are to maintain their competitive position. Consequently, investment in research and development is important. By measuring R&D investment, the potential for future growth may be inferred. As defined by AIM, research and development is more than product research. The development of new markets, improving methods of distribution, and selecting the most efficient advertising media are developmental activities considered in this category.

6. *Directorate Analysis.* The major function of the board of directors is that they should function as trustees for the shareholders. The membership of the board is analyzed to determine whether or not there are conflicts of interests rising as the result of other business activities on the part of board members. The potential contribution of each member of the board to the operation of the company is considered, and the degree of teamwork evidenced by the board is important. Finally, the board's method and degree of influence on management is assessed.

7. *Fiscal Policies.* Poor fiscal policies, rather than economic recessions, cause most corporate financial debacles. Thus, fiscal policies are rated in respect to the organization structure available for the establishment of fiscal policies, the soundness of the capital structure of the company, and the effectiveness of corporate fiscal policies and their attendant controls in insuring the financial well-being of the company.

8. *Production Efficiency.* The application of the concept of production efficiency is readily understood in appraising the performance of manufacturing organizations. However, the concept is equally applicable to the evaluation of organizations whose primary function is that of providing a service; e.g., banks, insurance companies, and airlines. Production efficiency may be expressed as a ratio between sales dollars and the number of production (or nonsupervisory) employees, between sales volume and payroll cost, and between the value of production and invested capital. The production efficiency of a company relative to that of competitors in the same industry is also of significance.

9. *Sales Vigor.* Comparative rating of the sales policies and practices of several companies is difficult because there are marked variations between companies within the same industry and even wider variations in sales methods in different industries. The method of distribution is appraised, the media and amount spent for advertis-

ing is considered, and the capabilities and size of the sales force is analyzed. The method of pricing and evidence of the ability to develop new markets is also weighed in appraising sales vigor.

10. *Executive Evaluation.* AIM considers executive evaluation to be the most important of the ten categories rated in arriving at the overall index of the performance of a company's management. Three qualities are considered to be requisites for industrial leadership and each executive of a company is rated in respect to these factors. The factors are: ability, industry, and integrity. Other measures considered in evaluating the top management of an organization are executive turnover, compensation in comparison to other companies in the industry, methods of selecting executive personnel, developmental or training programs, and the extent of participation by key executives in public affairs.

There has been much criticism of the AIM audit. For many, it is oriented too much toward the investment concept of business management. Of the 10,000 total points, only 500 are allowed for corporate structure; 2,200 for executive evaluation; and 800 for directorate analysis—making a maximum of 3,500 points for these categories. Production efficiency and sales vigor comprise a maximum of 2,000 points; the remaining 4,500 are distributed among the categories of economic function, health of earnings, service to stockholders, research and development, and fiscal policies. Another criticism is that the audit rates past performance too heavily and does not attempt to evaluate future performance.[5] In support of these criticisms, instances are cited of companies with recent ratings of "excellent" that have experienced severe financial difficulties. For example, Douglas Aircraft Company received the rating of "excellently managed" for 1957, 1958, and 1959, and then suffered severe financial reverses during the latter part of 1959 and 1960. In 1957 Allis Chalmers Manufacturing Company and Olin Mathiesen Chemical Company received "excellently managed" ratings that were immediately followed by marked financial difficulties.[6]

Despite the shortcomings of the management audit, the audit program developed by the American Institute of Management establishes firmly the concept that the performance of management can and should be subject to evaluation as a part of an overall control program. The management audit focuses attention upon many aspects of man-

---

[5] Robert B. Buchele, "How to Evaluate a Firm," *California Management Review,* Vol. V (Fall, 1962), pp. 5-16. Mr. Buchele presents a method for evaluating a firm that attempts to weight the future more than the past.

[6] The ratings are presented in *Manual of Excellent Managements* (New York: American Institute of Management, 1957).

See *Business Week* (April 9, 1960), p. 79, and (April 15, 1961), pp. 147-149 for a discussion of the companies mentioned.

agerial performance rather than upon one or two easily measured performance areas. Second, the audit emphasizes the measurement of the results of managerial performance rather than appraising the purpose of managerial performance. Third, individual companies that work seriously with the concept of auditing management's performance may develop as the result of experience within their own organization a means of assigning weight to the various performance categories that will prove a valid predictor of future performance.

RATIO ANALYSIS

A *ratio* is a way of expressing the proportional relationship that exists between two measures. Ratios may be expressed as:

1. A proportion, by using a colon to separate the two measures—1:2.
2. A fraction—½.
3. A percentage—½ × 100 = 50%.

Whatever the method of expression—proportion, fraction, or percentage —a ratio shows the magnitude of the relationship between two measures. The analysis of ratios existing between various measures of organizational performance is a useful and necessary control technique.

Single measures of organizational performance seldom have much meaning. For example, the statement that a company earned $100,000, after taxes, during the past fiscal year expresses only the dollar volume of earnings. For a statement of earnings to have more meaning, it is necessary to compare and describe the earnings of a competitor. In a like manner, the fact that a salesman sold $5,000 worth of goods last month or that a production worker produced 50 units yesterday conveys little information. We have to know the performance standards for salesmen and production workers before drawing conclusions concerning the adequacy of their performance.

Ratio analysis is not new, and much has been written about it as a control technique.[7] It is beyond the scope of this chapter to survey all or even a majority of the ratios used in analyzing and controlling business operations since there are many of them and the usefulness of a given set of ratios varies considerably from one industry to another. However, a few of the most frequently used ratios are presented and discussed briefly. For convenience, the ratios discussed are classified

---

[7] Spencer A. Tucker, *Successful Managerial Control by Ratio-Analysis,* (New York: McGraw-Hill Book Company, 1961). Mr. Tucker discusses the relatively simple first-degree ratios obtained by comparing two variables and also reviews the analysis of relationships between more than two variables.

as *financial ratios*—contributing primarily to a greater understanding of the financial condition of a company—and *operating ratios*—providing greater understanding of the operational aspects of a company. Some of the difficulties encountered in interpreting ratios are also presented.

Financial Ratios

Admittedly, financial ratios tell us something about the manner in which a company is operated as well as reveal financial condition. Yet, these ratios may be regarded as primarily financial in nature since much of the basic data is derived from the balance sheet and the information provided by these ratios is descriptive of a company's financial condition. The first and second ratios discussed below are statements of profitability; the last two ratios are statements of liquidity and are of particular significance to creditors.

Profit As a Percentage of Capital Invested. Many consider the relationship between profit (after taxes) and invested capital to be the most important single ratio. In the use of this ratio, profit is expressed as a percentage of invested capital, and when computed annually, a trend line is established. Profit as a percent of invested capital reveals how well the capital resources are being utilized. Comparisons may be made with other companies in the same industry, but the value of such comparisons is limited because the method used in evaluating invested capital varies from one company to another. Although there is no means of determining the optimum level of profitability, a realistic minimum level can be defined. The return on invested capital, after taxes, should be greater than the return guaranteed by other forms of investment—for example, tax-exempt municipal bonds. In addition to the basic rate of return offered by securities, there should be some compensation for risk and managerial effort.

Profit As a Percentage of Sales. Again, it is necessary to compute profitability from year to year so that a trend may be established. Also, comparisons with other companies in the same industry are valuable. Expressing profit as a percentage of sales volume is particularly helpful when analyzing the possible contribution of new product lines or when considering the deletion of current products. The profit-to-sales ratio is of value in measuring managerial effectiveness in the control of variable or controllable costs. For instance, within a retail chain, units of similar sales volume and fixed costs can be compared and differences in profitability may be attributed to the control of variable costs.

Current Ratio. The *current ratio* is of particular significance to credit men because it is an indication of a company's ability to pay its bills promptly. Current ratio is determined by dividing current assets by current liabilities as stated on the balance sheet. Unlike the measures of profit, which are usually expressed as a percentage, current ratio is expressed as a ratio; i.e., 2:1 or 2.5:1. Although there seems to be general agreement that a company should have a current ratio of assets to liabilities of at least 2:1 to insure ability to pay current obligations, the determination of what constitutes a satisfactory ratio is much more complex than it appears to be. Some of the problems encountered in interpreting the current ratio are discussed later under the heading, "Interpreting Ratios."

Quick Ratio. The *quick ratio,* sometimes called the *acid test ratio,* is found by dividing the company's quick assets, usually cash and negotiable securities, by current liabilities. Accounts receivables and inventory, generally a part of current assets and used in computing the current ratio, are excluded since there may be considerable time required to convert these items into cash. A minimum quick ratio of 1:1 indicates that there is sufficient cash to meet maturing obligations.

Operating Ratios

There are several ratios that contribute more to an understanding of the operations of a company than they do to an appreciation of the financial structure of a company; thus, they are referred to as operating ratios. Three of these ratios contribute to our knowledge of the sales function of a company. The fourth ratio is a generalized concept of input-output functions.

Net Sales to Average Inventory. Dividing net sales by average inventory value yields a measure of inventory turnover. For instance, net sales of $600,000 with an average inventory evaluation of $200,000 indicates that the inventory turnover rate is three times a year. If desired, the average number of days required for a complete inventory turnover can be computed as follows: $\dfrac{\text{Average Inventory} \times 365}{\text{Net Sales}}$. In the example above, the average number of days is 121. The net sales to average inventory ratio is an indication of how well the working capital invested in inventory is being utilized; consequently, the ratio should be interpreted in conjunction with profitability expressed as a percentage of sales. A profit of two percent on net sales, typical of many retail food operations, does not seem very great; but with an average inventory of $100,000 and an annual inventory turnover rate of 35, the absolute dollar volume of profit is considerable in relation to the amount of capital invested in inventory. The sales to inventory ratio provides the control information that is needed to insure maximum inventory turnover.

Net Sales to Total Market. Expressing net sales as a percentage of the total market—defined either geographically or by product line—indicates whether or not a company is maintaining its share of an ever-changing market potential. Dollar volume of sales does not provide such information since it is quite possible for a company's sales to show an annual increase, yet the rate of increase may be less than the market's rate of growth. Thus, a firm with an annual sales increase of four percent in a market expanding at a rate of six percent shows an increasing sales volume and a decreasing share of the potential market.

Selling Expense to Net Sales. Expressing selling expense as a percentage of net sales offers a means of determining the efficiency of the selling function. Selling expense may be broken down into greater detail by specifying the costs of maintaining a sales force, of advertising, or of administrative costs.

Input-Output Ratios. The number and the kind of input-output ratios used as control measures vary a great deal from one company to another. Such ratios are almost always expressed as percentages and are measures of efficiency in the utilization of inputs. Some of the more common measures of inputs and outputs are as follows:

Inputs	*Outputs*
Payroll dollars	Net sales
Man-hours worked	Units produced
Square feet of floor space	Units sold
Advertising costs	

Each input can be paired with any one of the outputs.

Interpreting Ratios

Although ratios are widely used, there are certain difficulties encountered in their interpretation that limit their value as a means of providing precise control information. First, a ratio is a quotient obtained by the arithmetic process of dividing a numerator by a denominator. A change in the value of a quotient may result from a change in the value of either the numerator or the denominator. There is no way of determining which member of the fraction changed in value by noting the change in the quotient. An analysis of the current ratio illustrates this point. Assume that a company has current assets of $60,000 and current liabilities of $30,000, thereby producing a comfortable current ratio of 2:1. Do we know what has happened if we read that the company now has a current ratio of 3:1? Fixed assets may have been sold in the amount of $30,000 and added to current assets to yield the 3:1 ratio. Or the amount realized from the sale of assets may have been $10,000 and applied to the reduction of current liabilities, again creating a 3:1 ratio. When changes occur in a ratio, it is necessary to inspect the original data used in arriving at the numeric values of the numerator and the denominator in order to have a sound basis for determining the significance of the change that has occurred.

Second, it must be realized that there is no precise means of determining what constitutes a good or a satisfactory ratio. Ratios should be used over a period of time so that trends may be established. Only then can a determination be made as to which ratios offer significant information for the control process. Occasionally it is helpful to compare ratios with those of similar companies in the same industry. Even so, there must be some assurance that the accounting systems used by the several companies are comparable.

The third danger inherent in the use of ratios is that of inferring causal relationships that are not warranted. A sales manager may conclude that an increase in selling expense as a percentage of sales indicates a decrease in the number of units sold by the sales force, but the real reason could be due to a decrease in unit price. Most faulty inferences result from a failure to examine closely the direction and magnitude of change in both the numerator and denominator and failure to evaluate the validity and reliability of the data used in computing the ratio.

Despite the difficulties encountered in interpreting ratios, they remain a useful control device when there is a thorough understanding of the manner in which they are developed and when there are several related ratios presented so that the significance of any one ratio may be checked by comparing it with another.

BREAK-EVEN ANALYSIS

Break-even analysis utilizes the same concepts employed in the construction of variable budgets (Chapter 22, pages 603 to 606). There are striking similarities between the break-even chart (Figure 23-1) and the graphic representation of a variable expense

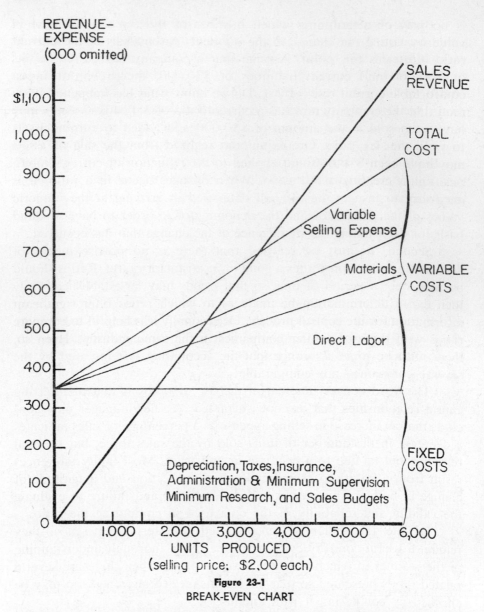

Figure 23-1
BREAK-EVEN CHART

budget shown in Figure 22-1, page 605. However, there are two important differences: first, the vertical axis of the break-even chart is designated as a revenue-expense axis rather than being labeled an expense axis; and second, the sales revenue line of the break-even chart shows the expected revenue for each level of sales volume. The point where the revenue line intersects the total cost line is the break-even point.

Break-even analysis is discussed in considerable detail in Chapter 5, "Planning for Profit," as a means of analyzing the interrelationships of various factors that influence the profitability of a company. An understanding of the dynamic relationships existing between the factors included in the break-even chart enables one to forecast and plan for profit. We know that the break-even point and consequently the amount of profit vary with changes in any one of four factors: unit volume, fixed cost, variable cost, and unit selling price. Further, the precise effect upon the break-even point resulting from a change in one or any combination of these variables can be determined by means of the following formula:

$$\text{Break-Even Point} = \frac{\text{Fixed Expense}}{P/V \text{ ratio}}$$

$$\text{when } P/V = \frac{\text{Sales} - \text{Variable Costs}}{\text{Sales}}$$

The ability to predict changes in profits under various operating conditions has obvious applications to the process of planning. A knowledge of the relationship of the factors that influence profit is equally applicable to the control process, a re-emphasis of the continuous nature of the planning-control-planning cycle. Specifically, break-even analysis provides information that aids in the control of costs and underscores the importance of sales volume.

Cost Control

Break-even charts can be prepared so that they contribute to overall control by showing both fixed and variable costs for the entire company. They can also be prepared for smaller operating units such as manufacturing departments or sales districts. In either case, fixed costs are segregated from variable costs. Fixed costs move slowly and show little variation as the result of changes in sales volume. Variable costs, on the other hand, vary directly as a function of volume. By their very nature, variable costs are subject to some degree of control. By clearly separating these variable costs, attention is directed toward those areas where corrective action is possible. When presented in the graphic form of a break-even chart, deviations from budgeted expenses are readily recognized.[8]

---

[8] Fred V. Gardner, "Breakeven Point Control for Higher Profits," *Harvard Business Review,* Vol. XXXII (September-October, 1954), pp. 123-130. Mr. Gardner discusses the need for flexible control and develops the specific control data needed so that the break-even point can be used as an effective means of control.

Sales Volume

An analysis of the break-even formula (page 639) shows clearly the effect of sales beyond the break-even point upon profit. The P/V ratio, the denominator of the fraction on the right side of the equation, expresses the profitability of an operation after the break-even point has been reached. Too many small and medium-size firms tend to express profitability as a percentage of total sales rather than as a percentage of sales beyond the break-even point. The following operating statement indicates a net profit of 10 percent of total sales:

Revenue from sales		$1,000,000
Variable costs	$500,000	
Fixed costs	400,000	
Total costs		900,000
Net profit		$ 100,000

However, the P/V ratio $\dfrac{\$1,000,000 - \$500,000}{\$1,000,000}$ indicates that the profitability of each unit sold beyond the break-even point is 50 percent. By emphasizing the contribution to profit of additional sales beyond the break-even point, there is greater incentive to stimulate and control sales effort.

TIME-EVENT-NETWORK ANALYSIS

In Chapter 7, "Planning for Production," the Gantt chart is presented as an aid in production planning (Figure 7-3, page 181). The Gantt chart is useful for both the planning and the control of repetitive operations—the industrial setting for which it was developed. The horizontal bars of the chart show clearly the scheduled and the actual time for each of the operations required to produce a relatively standardized product. As effective as it is for the planning and control of recurring manufacturing operations, the Gantt chart has serious shortcomings as a means of controlling the multitude of activities required for the design and development of a weapons system or the construction of a suburban shopping center. There are two reasons for these shortcomings. First, the usual methods of charting production require a relatively accurate statement of the time required for each operation—a situation that cannot be fulfilled in building either a weapons system or a shopping center for the first time. Second, the horizontal bars of the Gantt chart, or its many derivatives, fail to show the interrelationships of a complex production system. To meet the requirements of what has been called "an age of massive engineering"—in contrast to repetitive production—a number of fairly sophisticated techniques for the analysis of networks have been developed.[9]

Two time-event-network analysis techniques were developed separately and published almost simultaneously in 1959. One of these methods, Program Evaluation Review Technique—commonly referred to as *PERT*—was developed by the Special Projects Office of the U. S. Navy Bureau of Ordnance, with the assistance of staff members of the management consulting firm of Booz, Allen, and Hamilton. It was first used in the development of the Polaris Fleet Ballistic Missile.[10] The other method of network analysis, the Critical Path Method—referred to as *CPM*—was developed by DuPont as a means of reducing the downtime required for periodic maintenance.[11] PERT is credited with saving two years' time in the development of the Polaris missile, while the CPM method that DuPont used cut its downtime for maintenance in the Louisville plant from 125 to 93 hours.[12] Before discussing the relative merits and applications of PERT and CPM, let us review some of the fundamentals of network analysis.[13]

Fundamentals of Network Analysis

In order to use network analysis for purposes of planning and control, several conditions must be met:

1. *A clearly recognizable end point or objective.* One-of-a kind projects, such as developing and building the first prototype of the Polaris missile or the construction of a shopping center, meet this requirement. The installation of a data processing system, the construction of a highway interchange, or the building of a piece of special machinery all have clearly definable and recognizable end points. In contrast, the 100,000th car from an assembly line is difficult to distinguish from its immediate predecessor or successor.

---

[9] Se "Thinking Ahead: The Age of Massive Engineering," *Harvard Business Review*, Vol. XXXIV (January-February, 1961), p. 138.

[10] Donald G. Malcolm, John H. Rodrboom, Charles E. Clark, and Willard Fazar, "Applications of a Technique for Research and Development Program Evaluation," *Operations Research*, Vol. VII (September-October, 1959), pp. 646-699.

[11] James E. Kelley, Jr., and Morgan R. Walker, "Critical Path Planning and Scheduling," *Proceedings of the Eastern Joint Computer Conference*, (Boston: December, 1959).

[12] F. K. Levy, G. L. Thompson, and J. D. Wiest, "The ABCs of the Critical Path Method," *Harvard Business Review*, Vol. XXXXI (September-October, 1963), p. 100. On pp. 102-103 there is a discussion of how to determine the critical path through the use of a relatively simple algorithm.

[13] The term, review, is used advisedly since the network analysis required by PERT and CPM is similiar to the analysis of information systems required in the design of an integrated data processing system. See p. 202, Chapter 8, "Management Information Systems."

2. *A series of events.* There should be a series of clearly defined, separate, but interrelated, events leading up to the completion of the final project. In constructing a highway interchange, temporary routes must be built, bridges constructed, drainage facilities installed, service roads prepared, and many other distinct subprojects completed before the interchange is ready for use.

3. *Time for each activity.* The time required for the completion of the work or activity preceding each event must be calculated. Herein lies one of the major differences between PERT and CPM. PERT employs a method of estimating probable time, even though there has been no prior experience to serve as a basis for estimating time. CPM implies some prior experience or knowledge of the time estimated for the completion of activities leading to each event.

4. *A starting point.* There must be a recognizable starting point—the issuance of a sales order for a piece of special machinery, notification from the government to begin the development of a weapons system, or the date of a scheduled plant shutdown as the beginning of an annual maintenance program.

Figure 23-2 is a schematic diagram of a network analysis. Each event is designated by a square, although circles may be used. In each square there is a number and a letter. The number is a statement of the amount of work, expressed in days, that must be completed so that the event in question can occur. Events, as such, require no time; they merely serve as milestones. The letter in each square designates the event and is explained in the legend included on the chart. The arrows indicate the sequence of events. Unlike vector analysis, the length of the arrow has no particular significance. The shaded area is the *critical path,* the longest route in time from start to finish. If the duration of the project is to be shortened, it must be shortened by reducing the time intervals necessary for the completion of each event along this pathway. To reduce the work time along another path would not reduce the total time required for the project; instead, it would merely create more "slack"—excess time in the other pathways.

Let us assume that the project represented by the network in Figure 23-2 is a piece of special-purpose machinery including both electrical and mechanical components. In charting a network, the analysis of the project commences with the end result, the finished machine, and then works backwards, step by step, until the origin of the project is reached, the issuance of a sales order. The machine is ready for shipment when it has passed final inspection (J), a process that takes one day after the completion of final assembly (I). Thus, the number 1 and the letter J are entered in the square designating the completion of the

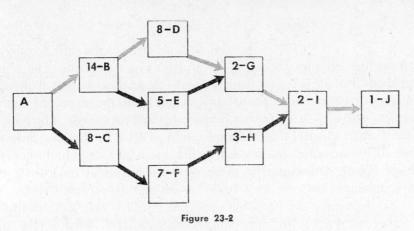

Figure 23-2

SCHEMATIC NETWORK ANALYSIS

project. Final assembly takes two days to complete but cannot be started until the subassembly of all electrical components (H) and all mechanical components (G) is finished. To perform the mechanical subassembly, components must be released by the milling department (D) and the lathe department (E). The largest single requirement for time in this network is the 14 days required for the procurement of mechanical components (B). The entire project starts with the issuance of the sales order (A). The same procedure is followed in analyzing the sequence of operations in the production of the electrical components of the manufacturing process.[14]

Two major advantages result from the use of time-event-network analysis techniques. First, breaking a project down into its component events, specifying the time required for the completion of each event, and designating the sequence of events force a degree of planning that · improves any production process. Presenting this information pictorially as a network offers the second advantage—a clear understanding of the interdependence and relationships that exist between the various events. We know that the critical path, by definition, is the longest route in time. In the example discussed, the critical path is 27 days. If the duration of the project is to be shortened, attention and control effort must be directed toward the critical path.

With this introduction to network analysis, let us examine PERT.

---

[14] E. T. Alsaker, "The Basic Technique: Network Analysis," in Gabriel N. Stilian and others, *PERT: A New Management Planning and Control Technique*, (New York: American Management Association, No. 74, AMA Management Reports, 1962), pp. 37-60. *PERT* presents in concise form a series of papers on PERT theory, the applications of PERT, and a discussion of related techniques such as the CPM and the Line of Balance system of control.

PERT

PERT in its original form stresses the time required to perform the activities necessary for a given event to occur. The unique contribution of PERT as a form of network analysis is that it provides a means of obtaining a probability estimate of the expected time to complete activities that have not been performed previously. The building of the Polaris missile, the first application of PERT, is a case in point. None of the activities leading up to the specified events had been performed before; consequently, there were no historical records or time study standards to serve as a basis for estimating expected times.

To determine the probable expected time for activities leading up to an event, PERT requires three time estimates. First is the most optimistic time—the time that is required if everything goes right. The probability of a most optimistic set of circumstances occurring is about 1 out of 100. Second, the most likely time is estimated—the time required in the normal course of events. The third time estimate is the most pessimistic—the time required if everything that could go wrong does go wrong. Again, the probability for the most pessimistic set of circumstances occurring is 1 out of 100; however, catastrophies such as floods, fires, and strikes are excluded. Designating the most optimistic time as *a*, the most likely time as *m*, and the most pessimistic time as *b*, the expected time, T_e, is found by substituting estimated times in the following formula:

$$T_e = \frac{a + 4m + b}{6}$$

There is also a formula to determine the standard deviation of the expected time, thus making it possible to state a statistical probability that the expected time will fall within a stated range.[15]

CPM

The difference beween PERT and CPM (Critical Path Method) is one of degree rather than kind. PERT emphasizes time and

---

[15] There has been much discussion concerning the mathematics of the PERT time estimate. The following report discusses the Beta distribution, a fundamental assumption of the estimated time computation.

PERT Summary Report, Phase I, (Washington, D. C.: Special Projects Office, Department of the Navy, July, 1958).

A brief description of the mathematics of PERT, along with a discussion of its application, is presented in the following article:

Robert W. Miller, "How to Plan and Control with PERT," *Harvard Business Review,* Vol. XXXX (March-April, 1962), pp. 93-104.

provides a way of computing the most probable time; however, CPM emphasizes cost as well as time.[16] CPM differs from PERT in three respects. First, only one time estimate is given for each set of activities leading up to a given event, instead of the three time estimates required by PERT. Second, with CPM, a cost estimate is included along with each estimated time for both *"normal"* and *"crash"* operating conditions. Normal operating conditions are usually defined as the least-cost method for the performance of an activity; and "crash" conditions represent the time and cost incurred in the performance of activities in less than the normal time. For example, under normal operating conditions two men assigned to the day shift take three days to complete a job. The time can be shortened under "crash" conditions by assigning two men to each of three consecutive shifts—a reduction in elapsed time but with a resultant increase in cost because of premium pay for the second and the third shifts. Third, CPM assumes some prior experience with the work necessary for the completion of each event; otherwise, it would be impracticable to state a single time and cost estimate.

These differences explain to a large degree why PERT is used primarily for one-of-a-kind projects involving an extensive amount of research and development prior to the building of a prototype and for similiar projects where time is of greater importance than cost. CPM, on the other hand, is widely used in complex construction and maintenance projects where cost is a significant factor and prior experience offers a basis for making a reliable estimate of both time and cost.[17]

Evaluation of PERT and CPM

There are three major benefits to be derived from the use of either PERT or CPM in the planning and control of certain production functions. First, the application of network analysis techniques forces of high degree of planning and results in plans that are objective, structured, and flexible. In so doing, either PERT or CPM approaches the optimum conditions described in the Principle of Planning, page 95.

---

[16] F. L. Levy, G. L. Thompson, and J. D. Wiest, op. cit., pp. 98-108.

For another discussion of the critical path method, see Walter Cosinuke, "The Critical Path Method," in Gabriel N. Stilian and others, *op. cit.,* pp. 147-163.

[17] The above discussion refers to PERT in its original form. Since its original introduction, there have been many variations of PERT. For this reason the original PERT is often referred to as basic PERT or PERT/Time to differentiate it from later variations such as PERT/Cost. The following article discusses the application of PERT/Cost.

Hilliard W. Paige, "How PERT-Cost Helps the General Manager," *Harvard Business Review,* Vol. XXXXI (November-December, 1963), pp. 87-95.

The second advantage of network analysis is that the establishment of a network system makes it possible to determine the critical path. The significance of the critical path to the control process is that knowledge of the key elements in a complex production system makes possible the design and administration of a set of forward-looking controls so that corrective action may be taken before serious deviation from schedule occurs. Third, network analysis shows clearly the interrelationships between the various organizational components of a complex production system, thereby making it possible to improve both communications and organizational structure.

Nonetheless, there are two limiting conditions that must be fulfilled before the advantages described above can be realized. First, network analysis is most effective when applied to one-of-a-kind projects that include several subprojects. Further, both the main project and the various subprojects must be fairly well defined and recognizable. They cannot be too nebulous. Examples of activities amenable to network analysis are construction projects, research and development programs, the installation of an integrated data processing system, the design and construction of a weapon systems, and the design and manufacture of special machinery or equipment. The second factor that limits the effectiveness of network analysis is organizational structure. Experience has shown that a task force or project form of organization is necessary to obtain maximum benefits from either PERT or CPM (See Chapter 12, page 306). Task force organization requires organizational flexibility and highly trained personnel. In summary, both the project and the organization must be appropriate if full benefit is to be realized from the application of either PERT or CPM as a means for planning and control.

● ● ● ● ● ● ● ● ●

Case Problem 23-B offers an opportunity to determine how the critical path in building a house can be shortened. Though a contractor might include more separate events than shown in the case problem, there are sufficient events presented to enable you to see for yourself how CPM points up the interrelationships of the various phases of a complex process.

Questions for Study and Discussion

1. What factors in the situation and what factors in the manager would tend to either increase or decrease the value of personal observations as a means of securing control information?
2. What points should be considered when designing or using control reports? Develop examples to illustrate both effective and ineffective control reports.
3. Comment on the following statement: Control reports are primarily a part of an information system rather than a control system.
4. Differentiate between internal and external auditing and show by example the strengths and weaknesses of each type of audit.
5. Discuss the similarities and differences of the 10 areas of the AIM management audit and the eight areas of control presented at the beginning of this chapter.
6. Give an example of each of the more common forms of operating ratios and financial ratios.
7. How can the difficulties encountered in interpreting ratios be minimized?
8. How do the techniques of break-even analysis contribute to the effectiveness of the control process?
9. In your opinion, does break-even analysis and P/V analysis have greater impact in the area of manufacturing through cost control than in the area of sales planning? Why?
10. How does network analysis differ from the Gantt chart? Is it possible for a schematic analysis of a network to be ultimately presented as a Gantt chart? Under what conditions?
11. Under what conditions would you recommend the use of PERT as opposed to CPM?

• • • • • • • • •

Ralph Billings, an independent building contractor, has completed building the fifth house of a projected development of 25 homes in the $30,000 price range. Recently he read of an application of the Critical Path Method to the building of a shopping center and became interested in applying the method to his own business. Currently he employs four carpenters and two laborers. Much of his work, such as excavating, plumbing, grading, cement work, bricklaying, and electrical work, is performed by subcontractors who base their charges on a combination of materials and man-hours required for each job. Ralph hopes that the application of CPM to his operation will result in a reduction of the total number of days required to build a house and in better utilization of the labor he now has.

Case Problem 23-B

Shortening the Critical Path

As a first step in applying the critical path method to his own building efforts, Ralph determined the average time required for each phase of the building of the first five houses. These values, along with the sequence of each building operation, are shown in Exhibit I.

Problems

1. Using the information presented in Exhibit I, construct a schematic network analysis similar to Figure 23-2 and determine the critical path.
2. What recommendations would you make to shorten the critical path?

Exhibit I

SEQUENCE AND TIME REQUIREMENTS OF JOBS

Job No.	Description	Immediate Predecessors	Normal Time (Days)
a	Start		0
b	Excavate and Pour Footers	a	4
c	Pour Concrete Foundation	b	2
d	Erect Wooden Frame Including Rough Roof	c	4
e	Lay Brickwork	d	6
f	Install Basement Drains and Plumbing	c	1
g	Pour Basement Floor	f	2
h	Install Rough Plumbing	f	3
i	Install Rough Wiring	d	2
j	Install Heating and Ventilating	d, g	4
k	Fasten Plaster Board and Plaster (including drying)	i, j, h	10
l	Lay Finish Flooring	k	3
m	Install Kitchen Fixtures	l	1
n	Install Finish Plumbing	l	2
o	Finish Carpentry	l	3
p	Finish Roofing and Flashing	e	2
q	Fasten Gutters and Downspouts	p	1
r	Lay Storm Drains for Rain Water	c	1
s	Sand and Varnish Flooring	o, t	2
t	Paint	m, n	3
u	Finish Electrical Work	t	1
v	Finish Grading	q, r	2
w	Pour Walks and Complete Landscaping	v	5
x	Finish	s, u, w	0

Source: F. L. Levy, G. L. Thompson, and J. D. Weist, *op. cit.,* p. 100.

APPENDIX A

How to Analyze a Case

Each chapter of this book begins and ends with a case problem, thus making a total of 46 case problems. In addition, a comprehensive case is presented in Appendix B. As a student you may logically ask the following questions: (1) Why is case material used in every chapter? (2) How do I analyze the case problems? The following discussion answers these two questions.

THE PURPOSE OF CASE PROBLEMS

A case problem is a descriptive statement of a business situation. Case problems portray an incident or a brief series of related incidents, in contrast to the comprehensive case or case study that generally describes most of the events that occur in a company or other form of organization over a relatively long period of time. The difference between a case problem and a comprehensive case is one of degree, not of kind. Case problems are used as an integral part of this textbook for two reasons. First, case problems are a way of making the text more meaningful; and second, they provide a means of improving one's ability to solve business problems.

Case problems make the information presented in the text more meaningful by relating that information to a specific business situation. As a result, the student has before him an example that shows how the concepts of the text can be transformed from an abstract statement to a practical situation. The abstract concepts of management are more readily remembered when they are described in the context of an easily remembered business experience. Case problems also make the text more meaningful by offering an opportunity to apply management concepts and principles as tools in the solution of specific business problems —another method of facilitating learning. In addition, case problems simulate a real business situation and provide the basis for improving one's skill in problem solving—a requisite for the successful manager.

THE ANALYSIS OF CASE PROBLEMS

Although there is no one way of analyzing a case problem, the following suggestions have proven to be of value in developing skill in the analysis of cases. Before reading the case in its entirety, note the title of the chapter and the title of the case. The title of the chapter tells you what the chapter is about. For example, the title of Chapter 1, "Management Defined," should convey to you that the chapter deals with the definition of management. Similarly, the title of Chapter 2, "The Development of Management Concepts," lets you know that the chapter is concerned with the historical development of management. Since the case problems in this textbook are an integral part of the chapter in which they appear, identifying the subject matter of the chapter often reveals the central theme of the case.

Second, the title of the case itself is of significance. Unlike many case problems, the name of the company in which the incidents described in the case occurred is not used as the title of the case. Instead, the title is a descriptive phrase related to the central theme of the case. Thus, the title of Case Problem 1-A, A Problem in Management Definition, informs you immediately that the problem is one of defining management. The title of Case Problem 2-A, Symptoms or Causes?, infers that the problem is one of differentiating between symptoms and causes. Since the case problem is a part of the chapter concerned with the presentation of the historical development of management thought, one might reasonably expect the solution to lie within the framework presented in the historical development of management concepts.

Reading the Case

After noting the clues offered by the titles of the chapter and of the case, read the problems at the end of the case so you will know what is expected. Then read the entire case rapidly to gain a first impression of the total situation. Next, a careful reading and a detailed analysis are necessary.

Knowledge of the structure of case problems is helpful in the detailed analysis of the case. Usually the first and second paragraphs are a statement of the setting in which the incidents described in the case occur. In these paragraphs the central characters of the case are introduced, the name of the company is given, and if relevant the product or services and the geographical location are mentioned. Information required for the definition and solution of the problem is presented in differing ways. Sometimes data are presented in the form of exhibits at the end of the case. Exhibits may be financial statements, organization charts, tables, or similar summaries designed to present a large amount of information in concise form. However, in most of the case problems the relevant facts of the situation are presented in the form of discussions among the central characters of the case. Thus, the titles of the persons described are significant since the title of the position one holds in a company indicates the role that may be expected. For instance, the title of president or general manager indicates that the major functions, and consequently the role that may be expected, are those of planning and coordinating. On the other hand, a title that designates a person as being in charge of one of the functional areas, such as finance, sales, production, or personnel, indicates that that person is responsible for a given function and may be expected to have that specific function as his major concern—sometimes to the detriment of other functions and to the achievement of overall organizational objectives.

There will be times, even after having read the case thoroughly, when you will say that more information is needed to define the problem and develop a solution. Admittedly, limitations of time and space require that the situation be described in broad strokes and rarely does a student reading a case have at his disposal the same information possessed by a manager of a company. Yet, every effort has been made to provide all the information needed for the definition and solution of the problem. All too often the criticism that a case does not contain sufficient information may become an automatic excuse for not coming to grips with the problem. It must be remembered that rarely does the executive in practice have all the information that he would like to have prior to making a decision, but the exigencies of the situation require a decision despite the incompleteness of the information upon which that decision is based.

Analyzing the Case

The following specific steps aid in the systematic analysis of a case.

1. State the Problem. After reading the case thoroughly and after studying the problems at the end of the case, write a statement of the problem—what is the case about, what is there to be done, what action has to be taken, or what questions have to be answered. It may be necessary to state several problems; and, if this is required, you must then decide which of the problems is the most important. For example, in the last paragraph of Case Problem 1-A a request is made of the personnel director that he prepare a report indicating the name of the proposed management club, a definition of who is eligible to join the club, and a statement of the objectives of the club. Thus, there are three problems: title, membership, and purpose. Which of these is the most important? In this instance the last item is the most significant since the objectives, or the purpose, of a club may well determine the title and the membership of the club. The right answer to the wrong problem is of little value.

2. Collect Data. In most instances the data required for the definition and solution of the problem are contained in the case. Marginal notes and underlining are helpful in identifying and summarizing relevant data. Occasionally it may be necessary to prepare a summary on a separate sheet of paper.

3. Analyze Data. In order to analyze and evaluate effectively the data presented in the case, the data must be arranged in a systematic manner. Figure 15-5, Checklist of Organizational Effectiveness (page 381), and the accompanying discussion, "Evaluating Organizational Effectiveness," (pages 380 to 386), present one way of arranging such information. Read this section of the text *now*. Even though you are not expected to be thoroughly familiar with all the terms and concepts used in the discussion, there is much that you can understand and apply. Note that many problems can be categorized within one of eight problem areas, ranging from overall planning to provisions for control. Reviewing the checklist on the right-hand side of Figure 15-5 provides a quick way of identifying problem areas.

4. Formulate Tentative Solutions. It is well to develop the habit of regarding initial solutions as tentative. By so doing the danger of assuming a rigid position is minimized and at the same time the door is left open for other, and sometimes better, solutions. In Case Problem 1-A there are four possible solutions in regard to membership—all persons whose names appear on the published organization chart, all who have supervisory responsibility, all exempt personnel, and all who have earnings greater than $500 per month. In a like manner the range of objectives and the proposed names of the club should be regarded as tentative. There are several tentative solutions available and all should be given due consideration.

5. Select a Recommended Solution. From the list of tentative solutions, a single solution has to be selected. The final solution should offer the best answer to the problem as stated in Step No. 1, and it should be based upon the data collected in Step No. 2. However, of greatest importance in the selection of a recommended solution is the extent to which that solution is capable of execution. Ultimately solutions to business problems require the commitment of company resources if they are to be executed.

Preparing Written Reports

When a student prepares a written report for a case problem, the report should be regarded as a project assigned by an employer rather than a class assignment. As a task to be performed as part of your job, the report will have its effect upon pay and advancement within the company. The mechanical aspects of the report—spelling, punctuation, neatness, and grammatical style—should be above reproach; yet the format of the report may vary considerably. It may take the form of a memo as requested in Case Problem 1-A. If so, the memo should indicate clearly the person to whom it is directed, its origin (including the name and title of the author of the memo), and the subject of the report. The body of the report is then presented in narrative form. When reports exceed one or two pages in length, it is well to present the conclusions or recommendations on the first page, with the body of the report containing the substantiating data from which the conclusions were drawn.

APPENDIX B

Comprehensive Case

BACKGROUND OF THE OMEGA RUBBER AND PLASTICS CORPORATION

The Omega Rubber and Plastics Corporation was incorporated in 1946 under the laws of New York as the Omega Rubber Company. The present name was adopted in 1959 to reflect the broadened nature of the company's business. The company has its executive offices and manufacturing operations at Olean, New York.

The company has operated under the same management since its founding. The major changes have been in additions to operating capacity, types of products, and processing, and a reorganization of the financial structure of the company.

Reorganization of the financial structure of the company in 1952 was for the purpose of providing securities that fitted the capital requirements of the company. Since reorganization, the company has had a very satisfactory sales and earnings record, as shown in Exhibit 1.

Exhibit 1

SALES AND NET INCOME FOR YEARS 1952-1960

Year	Sales	Net Income
1952	$2,321,385	$ 201,200
1953	2,643,105	205,475
1954	2,748,200	209,985
1955	3,125,080	325,428
1956	3,698,588	364,286
1957	2,621,143	207,330
1958	3,194,953	275,558
1959	4,361,529	491,407
1960	6,892,359	1,023,795

The decline in net sales and net income from the fiscal year 1956 to 1958 was a primary result of a decline in the output of the company's principal customers, the automobile manufacturers. While more recently the dollar volume of sales to the automobile industry has increased, the percentage of such sales to the total sales of the company has decreased. The diversification policy of the company has helped sales stability considerably.

The company's balance sheet as of December 31, 1960, is given in Exhibit 2.

Exhibit 2

OMEGA RUBBER AND PLASTICS CORPORATION
BALANCE SHEET
December 31, 1960

ASSETS

CURRENT ASSETS:		
Cash		$1,042,792
United States Treasury notes (short-term)—at cost and accrued interest		652,588
Trade accounts receivable	$ 950,871	
Less allowance for doubtful accounts	10,000	940,871
Inventories—at lower of cost (generally first-in, first-out method) or market:		
Finished products	$ 188,520	
Work in process	65,210	
Materials and supplies	187,426	441,156
Prepaid expenses		11,028
TOTAL CURRENT ASSETS		$3,088,435
OTHER ASSETS		$ 8,380
PROPERTY, PLANT, AND EQUIPMENT—on the basis of cost:		
Land	$ 53,786	
Buildings	1,638,830	
Machinery and equipment	1,073,696	
	$2,766,312	
Less allowances for depreciation	618,451	$2,147,861
		$5,244,676

LIABILITIES

CURRENT LIABILITIES:		
Trade accounts payable		$ 156,360
Accrued expenses		113,840
Federal taxes on income—established		875,690
TOTAL CURRENT LIABILITIES		$1,145,890
STOCKHOLDER'S EQUITY		
Common stock, par value $100 a share; 1,000 shares authorized, issued and outstanding	$ 100,000	
Retained earnings	3,998,786	4,098,786
		$5,244,676

PRODUCT AND PROCESSING BACKGROUND OF THE COMPANY

The company operates two divisions—the sponge rubber division and the urethane foam division—in Olean, New York.

Sponge Rubber Division

Open-cell sponge rubber is molded in various shapes and sold for use as seals around doors and windows of automobile vehicles; doors and lids of refrigerators and deep freezes; household weather stripping, etc. Adhesives, both dry-back and pressure-sensitive, are somtimes used to bond sponge rubber to other materials such as metals, woods, and fabrics. Sponge rubber is also sold in rolls for use by customers as underpadding for rugs. The company has facilities for applying various coatings to sponge rubber, such as neoprene and hypalon, to produce desirable exterior surfaces.

In 1958 the company began the manufacture of closed-cell sponge rubber. This material has moisture-resisting and thermal-insulating qualities useful for shock-absorbing and vibration-dampening purposes, required in refrigeration processes where humidity or condensation is a problem. In open-cell sponge rubber the cells are interconnected with air passages, while in closed-cell sponge rubber the cells are closed to prevent absorption or retention of moisture.

Closed-cell sponge rubber is used where the article is exposed to weather. For such purposes, it is sold for soles and heels of shoes, protective padding in athletic equipment, etc.

Urethane Foam Division

Urethane foam is a synthetic, cellular, plastic material formulated from several chemicals under controlled conditions of mixing temperatures and pressure. This material can be produced as soft, flexible, cushioning material or as light-weight rigid, or semirigid material. It also may be controlled to varying degrees of density, resiliency, tensile strength, and resistance abilities.

The company produces, in slab form, a full line of flexible urethane foams that are marketed under the trade name "Polylite." The company at present does not produce urethane foam in molded form. It produces polyether-type and polyester-type foam, but during the past year 95 percent of the total urethane sales were of the polyester type.

The polyether-type urethane foams are sold for seat and back cushions and for arm and head rests to the furniture and automotive industries. The polyester-type foams are sold for carpet underpadding and lining for packaging of delicate electronic parts and missile components.

The manufacture of urethane foam in commercial volume is a relatively new industry. The company's sales of urethane foam have increased rapidly during the last three years as indicated in Exhibit 3.

Exhibit 3

SALES OF URETHANE FOAM, 1958-1960

	1958	1959	1960
Open-cell sponge rubber	$3,052,480	$3,395,071	$4,984,555
Closed-cell sponge rubber	. . .	263,300	541,624
Urethane foam	142,473	703,158	1,366,180
Total	$3,194,953	$4,361,529	$6,892,359

During the current year the company plans to produce rigid-type urethane foams that may be used as insulation in house trailers, refrigerated truck bodies and freight cars, refrigerators, and other products. At present these markets are being supplied, for the most part, by other forms of insulation and, accordingly, there is no assurance that the company can compete successfully in such a field.

DISTRIBUTION

The products of the company are sold by its own executives and other personnel and through manufacturers' representatives. During the last fiscal year, the manufacturers' representatives accounted for 42 percent of the net sales. Foreign sales were not significant.

During the same period, the company's products were sold to about 350 customers. The three largest customers, all in the automotive field, accounted for 25 percent, 9 percent, and 7 percent of the net sales; no other customer accounted for more than 5 percent of such sales. The company's customers in the automotive industry accounted for 52 percent of such sales, of which less than four percent were of urethane foam.

COMPETITION

The company competes with other producers of the same materials and of alternative products. In addition to the Omega

Rubber and Plastics Corporation, there are two other major and a number of smaller producers of sponge rubber. Goodyear Rubber Company is the largest producer of sponge rubber. It and perhaps the other major competitor sell a larger volume of sponge rubber than Omega.

There are approximately 15 producers of urethane foam slab and about seven producers of molded urethane foam. At present, the company is engaged only in the production of urethane slab. Many of the company's competitors in this field are approximately the same size or smaller than Omega, but certain of the large integrated rubber producers are also in the production of urethane slab and are, or may be in the future, in the production of molded urethane. The company's sales of urethane foam are comparatively small in relation to total industry sales. However, Omega believes that it is the largest producer of polyester urethane foam, the production of which has not to date been undertaken by any of the large integrated rubber companies. In view of the relatively recent origin of the urethane industry and the expanding usage of urethane foam, the market for such products has not as yet stabilized and, accordingly, the company is not in a position to predict the type of competition with which it will be confronted in the future.

PRODUCT DEVELOPMENT

Omega is actively engaged in developing new applications for its present products as well as improving its manufacturing techniques. These efforts have led to increasing acceptance of its new closed-cell type of sponge rubber, and preparations are being made for its production in tubular form as thermal insulation around liquid-carrying tubing and pipes.

Omega does not operate a separate product development department as such and, accordingly, does not keep records to indicate the amount expended by the company on such operations. However, in view of the nature of the company's products, all the company's key personnel (averaging 25 persons) are continually engaged in developing new uses for the company's products, in addition to their regular duties as officers of the company or as operating personnel in the production or sales departments.

PURCHASES

There are several sources from which Omega may purchase its chemicals and other raw materials so that the company is not dependent upon any single supplier. The basic ingredients for sponge rubber are synthetic and natural crude rubber, oil, whiting, zinc, oxide, soda, sulphur, accelerators, and carbon black. The basic ingredients for urethane foam are toluylene diisocyanate, resins, and catalysts.

EMPLOYEE RELATIONS

Omega employs approximately 520 persons. There are no collective bargaining agreements with any labor union. Employee benefits consist of life and hospitalization insurance, six paid holidays, vacation plans, and participation in a Christmas bonus, which amounted to $112,000 last year.

PROPERTY

The sponge rubber division operates in a modern two-story plant of approximately 185,000 square feet. The urethane plant is a modern one-story building of approximately 96,000 square feet. The total aggregate area of these buildings is 30 acres. The plants are equipped with well-maintained modern machinery and equipment.

MANAGEMENT

The management of the company, shown in Exhibit 4, has been the same since its incorporation. All the managers are fairly competent and know their jobs well.

THE PLASTICS INDUSTRY

Initially one of the most serious problems facing the plastics industry was the consumer attitude that plastics connote lower quality than other material. In part this attitude was caused by the fact that growth in plastics had come from a substitution of familiar products previously made of metal, wood, or glass. In many cases the plastic substitute did cost less but did not stand up under usage as did the other materials. The initial misapplication of plastics was caused by the weak dimensional stability and low resistance to heat, often disregarded by early product designers. Initially, because of the insurge of many companies into the use of plastics and their desire to cut costs and prices, products were made from mixed thermoplastic scrap and

Exhibit 4
MANAGEMENT ORGANIZATION CHART

with thinner wall sections than were necessary to withstand long usage. Since 1954 the industry has undergone a quality campaign for higher standards. This campaign has been fairly successful.

The major uses of plastics by type are compared in Exhibit 5. The growth of the plastics industry, in comparison with several other industries, is shown in Exhibit 6.

The plastics industry is made up of two distinct groups of companies—the materials producers and the processors of finished products. There are approximately 110 materials producers and an estimated 5,500 processors of finished products including molders, fabricators, laminators, and sheeting concerns.

The patent situation in the industry is extremely complicated. The basic patents on many plastics are still in force, and there are many conflicting patent claims that have not yet been adjudicated by the court.

Nearly all plastic materials are produced by about 30 large, diversified companies. Seven of these companies enjoy about 80 percent of the total market. The large size of the materials producers has been attributed to the chemicals required, which include phenol, formaldehyde, ethefene, urea, benzol, and propylene. The major companies and the percentage of sales for the year 1959 were as follows: Dow Chemical, 30 percent; Monsanto, 29 percent; Eastman Kodak, 23 percent; Hercules Powder, 22 percent; B. F. Goodrich, 14 percent; American

Exhibit 5

MAJOR USES OF PLASTICS BY TYPE, 1960
(In Relative Volume)

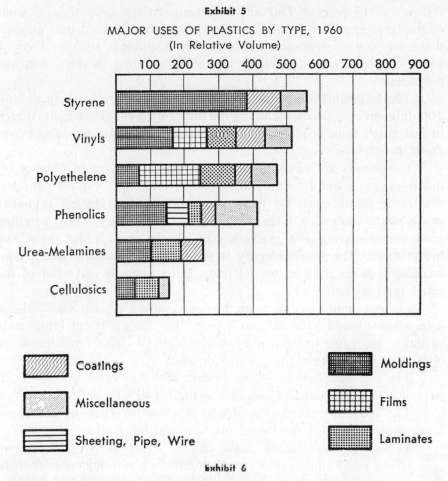

Coatings   Moldings

Miscellaneous   Films

Sheeting, Pipe, Wire   Laminates

Exhibit 6

GROWTH INDEX

Index of Employees in Selected Industries: 1950-1959
(Growth Index Jan., 1952-Dec., 1952 = 100)

Year	Plastics Mat'l.	Plastics Fabricated Parts	Furniture	Textile	Television	Steel	Oil
1951	99	99	101	100	109	104	100
1952	100	100	100	100	100	100	100
1953	101	101	99	100	91	96	100
1954	104	129	111	104	123	105	96
1955	129	128	107	103	132	113	104
1956	130	127	106	96	172	114	106
1957	149	145	115	96	222	116	110
1958	144	157	114	90	228	112	111
1959	148	161	109	90	226	118	110
1960	151	167	113	88	221	117	109

Cyanomid, 13 percent; DuPont, 8 percent. At the same time as some of the large chemical companies were integrating forward into plastics, there was some integration backward by companies such as General Electric, which started supplying and manufacturing its own resin and polysteene.

The fragmentation begins at the raw material level, where at least 200 different companies, including the major blue-chip chemicals, shared in last year's total production of more than six billion pounds of synthetic resins.

Fabricators are vastly more numerous; the Society of Plastics Industry counts about 1,600 alone. A few of these are "captive" molders that make plastic parts for their own products, but are not primarily in the plastic business. Others belong in the "proprietary" class, handling both manufacturing and marketing of plastic items under their own brand name. The third category is the "custom" molder, which does molding jobs on contract for outsiders but ordinarily stays out of the retail market itself.

Custom molding is fairly big business, with a current sales volume somewhere around $500 million a year. But this pie is cut into scanty helpings; according to one survey, only about 14 custom molders score annual sales of more than $2.5 million each.

The big, established molders lament that they often develop business only to see it snatched away by a small rival who undercuts prices.

The industry includes hundreds of concerns such as extruders, laminators, makers of reinforced plastics, and fabricators.

Technique changes are slow. During the past 10 years or so, change has come more rapidly to the industry's raw materials than to the processing techniques it uses. These have been refined but not basically altered. In custom molding, probably the most important change is injection molding, whereby the plastic is heated and then pushed through a small nozzle into a mold that may be quite intricate. Injection presses have increased in speed and capacity, and newer machines have better controls for handling skittish materials. There also have been advances in the art of blow molding, which in plastics is analogous to glass blowing.

Much of the technology of plastics molding flows out of the laboratories of the raw materials suppliers. They devote time and cash to research and development in hopes of expanding markets; the average molder is too absorbed in competition and beset by thin margins to conduct his own engineering and development.

COMPANY OUTLOOK

As explained previously, Omega is vitally interested in progress and growth; particularly they are interested in a new process called "Thermofusion," which was developed in England by the Spencer Chemical Company. This process, which is basically explained below, is licensed to only five United States companies. The management of Omega feels that it would be necessary to extend their manufacturing capacity with a new building if they were to adopt the new process.

BASIC PROCESS OF THERMOFUSION

The basic process consists of starting with polyethylene powdered to the consistency of table sugar. (Eventually, polypropylene and several other plastic materials may also be used.) The powdered plastic is poured into a metal mold built the same shape as the desired end product—a brine tank, say, or a boat hull. Then, the mold full of plastic is shoved into an oven and baked. When it emerges, some of the plastic has adhered to the mold; the amount that sticks can be controlled by varying the time and temperature of baking. The plastic that is still loose is poured out, and the mold is returned to the heat for a final treatment that smoothes the surfaces.

The most shining beauty of the process is the low cost of the molds, which, because they are not subject to much stress, can be made of much lighter material than is necessary with other techniques. The cost can run as low as five or ten percent of the bill for matched metal molds—a dramatic savings in a business that has paid $50,000 and more for some of its molds.

Problems

Recognizing the potentialities of the thermofusion process, the executives of the Omega Rubber and Plastics Corporation are very desirous of expanding and incorporating the process. Also recognizing that overanxiety on their part could jeopardize their capital and position in the industry, they call upon you as a consultant. Specifically, they want the following questions answered:

1. Is facility expansion for the thermofusion process warranted? If so, should the source of funding be from within or without the company? If without the company, should the financing take the form of stocks, bonds, or a bank loan? Would the relationship of marginal input be larger or smaller than marginal output? On what are your conclusions based?

2. What do you feel the relative position of the company is in relation to the overall competitive aspects of the industry? Can you foresee any change in the near future?

3. What general recommendations and remarks do you have relative to this company's operations?

▓▓▓▓ Index

A

Absoluteness of accountability, principle of, 317

Accountability, absoluteness of, principle of, 317; creation of, 316; lack of, in committees, 347

Action, corrective, 580

Ad hoc committee, 349

Administration, emphasis upon, 37; principles emphasizing, 40

Administration approach to management, 26

Advertising, 152

Advisory authority, 299

Affection needs, 452

Alternate solutions, development of, 217

Analysis, 216; break-even, 121, 637; historical, of costs, 604; network, fundamentals of, 641; organizational, 368; profit to volume, 124; ratio, 633; semantic, 421; time-event-network, 640

Appraisal interview, 533

Appraisal performance, 531

Appraisals, purpose of, 532

Appraising performance, problems in, 532

Appropriation budget, 600

Assets, fixed, 118

Attitudes, change in, 524; unfreezing of, 523

Audit, management, 629

Audit program, 627

Auditing, external, 627; internal, 628

Authoritative committee, 348

Authority, 289; advisory, 299; and responsibility, parity of, principle of, 316; committee, as a check on, 344; decentralization of, 257, 326; delegation of, 315; effectiveness of, 293; functional, 299; in Theory X, 241; in Theory Y, 246; institutional source of, 290; line, 294; meanings of, 290; overlapping, 293; service, 299; sources of, 290; staff, 294, 297; subordinate-acceptance, source of, 290; superior, 293

Authority relationship, 295

Automatic data processing, 200

Automatic vs. manual operations, 32

Automation, 182; economic factors, 185; evaluation of, 185; social implications, 186

B

Balance sheet budget, 601

Bank loans, 117

Benefit plan, employee, 548

Benefit programs, employee, 466

Board of directors, 353; composition of, 356; functions of, 354; in small companies, 358; inside, 357; outside, 356

Bonds, 115; secured, 116; unsecured, 116

Brainstorming, 232

Break-even analysis, 121, 637

Break-even chart, 638

Break-even point, 639

Budget, 596; appropriation, 600; balance sheet, 601; capital expenditure, 600; cash, 599; expense, 599; flexible, 603; operating, 598; revenue and expense, 598; sales, 598; variable, 603

Budgetary control, human factors in, 606

Budgetary review, periodic, 602

Budgets, as pressure devices, 611; effective use of, 615; effects on individuals, 612; group reaction to pressure, 613; nature of, 596; securing flexibility with, 602; types of, 598

Business standards, 568

Buying power, consumer, 140

C

Capital, acquisition of, 114; long-term, 115; short-term, 117; utilization of, 118; working, 118

Capital expenditure budget, 600

Capital goods, 143; demand for, 143

Cash budget, 599

Center, profit, 331

Certainty, concepts of, 83

Chain of command, 242, 295

Change, and the individual, 525; and the organization, 526

Channel of distribution policies, 150

Chart, break-even, 638; Gantt, 180, 640; organization, 375

Checklist, of organizational effectiveness, 381

Circular organization chart, 375

Climate, organizational, 507, 542

Cluster chain, 434

Coaching, in management development, 527

Code of ethics, 72
Command, chain of, 242, 295; unity of, principle of, 318
Commercial credits, 117
Commercial factor, 117
Committee, 340; ad hoc, 349; advantage of, 342; authoritative, 348; compromise decisions, 346; cost of, 345; disadvantages of, 345; evaluation of, 341; function of, 348; general management, 348; in use, 347; lack of accountability, 347; nonauthoritative, 348; restricted, 348
Communication, 417; and information systems, 424; barriers to, 429; horizontal, 431; improving, 435; line of, 269; oral, 427; principle of, 422; problems in, 423; superior-subordinate, 428; written, 427
Communication media, 427
Company records, in selecting supervisors, 496
Compensation, 546
Compensation plan, 546
Competition, 148
Compromise decisions, in committees, 346
Conflict of interest problems, 61
Congruence of goals, of an organization, 280
Consumer buying power, 140
Consumer durable goods, 142
Consumer goods, demand for, 139
Consumer nondurable goods, 140
Continuous production, 168
Continuum of leadership behavior, 407
Control, and cybernetics, 562; and personality, 580; budgetary, human factors in, 606; cost, 639; good, characteristics of, 583; nature of, 561; nonbudgetary, 624; principles of, 589; span of, 269; resistance to, 608
Control design, principle of, 590
Control procedure, typical, 606
Control process, 566; steps in, 564
Control reports, distribution of, 626; purpose of, 625
Control unit, of information system, 196
Controlling, 6, 85
Coordination, 37; improved, through use of committee, 344
Corporate purchasing power, 144
Corrective action, 580
Cost, fixed, 121, 126; product, 148; standard, 604; variable, 121, 126
Cost control, 639
Cost, historical analysis of, 604
CPM, 644
Creative process, steps in, 227
Creative thinking, group participation in, 231
Creativity, in decision making, 226

Credits, and collections, 119; commercial, 117
Criteria for evaluating plans, 89
Critical Path Method, 641
Current performance, measuring, 575
Current ratio, 635
Curve, learning, 578
Curvilinear variable costs, 129
Customer, basis of departmentation, 267
Cybernetics, 562; and control, 562
Cycle, management process, 582

D

Data, external, 92; internal, 92
Data processing, 200; automatic, 200; electronic, 200; integrated, 199
Debenture, 116
Decentralization, 281; and integrated data processing, 334; definition of, 326; of authority, 257, 326; profit, 331
Decision, selection of, 217
Decision making, 82, 214; aids in, 220; creativity in, 226; level of, in an organization, 281; location of, in Theory X, 241; location of, in Theory Y, 247; problems relating to, 60; training for, 505
Decisions, compromise, in committees, 346
Degree of structuralization, of plans, 93
Delegation, aspects of, 314; improved, 507; personality and, 322; principles of, 316; process of, 313
Demand, determinants of, 139; elastic, 149; for capital goods, 143; for consumer goods, 139; inelastic, 149
Demography, 141
Departmentation, 257, 264, 326; bases of, 265
Depreciation, 119
Description, position, 373
Design, job, 467, 549
Determinants of demand, 139
Determinants of ethical standards and practices, 70
Development, executive, 520
Diminishing returns, law of, 96
Direct selling, 152
Directing, 6, 85
Directors, board of, 353
Discipline, 503
Dispersion, geographic, 327
Dissatisfaction, job, 472
Dissatisfier, 463
Distribution, channel of, 150
Diversification, 171; product, 145
Dividends, 120
Durable goods, consumer, 142
Dynamics, personality, in leadership, 400

E

Economic effectiveness, of plans, 96; principle of, 100; principle of, applied to planning sales, 158; principle of, applied to production planning, 182; principle of, applied to profit planning, 134
Economics, 96
Elastic demand, 149
Electronic data processing, 200; development of, 200; evaluation of, 205
Empathetic listening, 438
Empathy, 438
Employee benefit plan, 548
Employee benefit programs, 466
Employees, mobility of, 550; promotion of, 551; selection of, 550
Employment, termination of, 551
Engineered standards, 573
Enlargement, job, 468
Esteem needs, 452
Ethics, 58; code of, 72; principle of, 72
Ethical standards and practices, determinants of, 70
Evaluating plans, criteria for, 89
Evaluation, personnel, 497
Exception, principle of the, 588
Execution, of decision, 219
Executive, plural, 352
Executive development, 520
External auditing, 627
External data, 92
External objectives, 53
Expense budget, 599

F

Facility policies, 176
Factor, commercial, 117; hygienic, 462; motivating, 463
Financial policy, planning, 114
Financial ratios, 634
Fixed assets, 118
Fixed cost, 121, 126; static, 130
Fixed costs concepts, reliability and validity of, 128
Fixed expense area, 123
Flexibility, of plans, 95
Flexible budget, 603
Foreman, 482
Function, basis of departmentation, 266; linking pin, 249, 491; planning, 82; production, 167
Functional authority, 299
Functional-teamwork, 305
Functions, of management, 5

G

Game theory, 224
Gantt chart, 180, 640

General management committee, 348
Geographic dispersion, 327
Geography, basis of departmentation, 267
Gordon technique, of creative thinking, 232
Graicunas, theory of, 270
Grapevine, 434
Group judgment, 342
Group participation, in creative thinking, 231

H

Hawthorne studies, 26, 29
Historical analysis of costs, 604
Horizontal communication, 431
Horizontal organization chart, 375
Human relations, 25, 26; approach to leadership, 393; principles emphasizing, 38; training in, 501; training methods in, 501
Hygienic factor, 462
Hypotheses, 11

I

Identification, in the change of attitudes, 524
Illumination, in the creative process, 230
Incident process method, 502
Income, marginal, 125
Income-expense line, 123
Income line, 124
Incubation, in the creative process, 227
Individual, and change, 525; role of, in Theory X, 244; role of, in Theory Y, 249
Inelastic demand, 149
Information system, 195; and communication, 424; components of, 195; designing an IDP, 202; functions of, 195
Inkblot test, 400
Input device, of information system, 195
Input-output ratios, 636
Inside board of directors, 357
Institutional source of authority, 290
Integration, 172; vertical, 172
Integrated data processing, 199, 200; and decentralization, 334; information system, designing an, 202
Interaction, degree of, 277; social, 231
Intermittent production, 168
Internal auditing, 628
Internal data, 92
Internal objectives, 54
Internalization, in the change of attitudes, 524
Interpersonal relationships, 62
Interview, 496; appraisal, 533
Inventory, 119, 175; management personnel, 529

J

Job, supervisor's, 482
Job complexity profile, 492
Job design, 467, 549
Job dissatisfaction, 472
Job enlargement, 252, 468
Job evaluation procedures, 547
Job satisfaction, and motivation, 462; and productivity, 252, 470
Jobbing, 168

K

Ken, 391

L

Labor, division of, 32
Labor-management relations, 544
Laboratory training method, 535
Law of diminishing returns, 96
Law of supply and demand, 139
Law of variable returns, 97
Leadership, 391; a continuum, 406; components of, 396; effective, determinants of, 408; human relations, 393; personality dynamics in, 400; scientific management, 392; situational factors in, 397; the revisionists, 393; theories of, 392; trait approach to, 396
Leadership pattern, selecting a, 405
Leadership training, 503
Learning curve, 578
Line-and-staff relationships, 294; problems in, 301
Line authority, 294
Line organization, 294
Linear programming, 223
Linear variable costs, 129
Lines of communication, 269
Linking pin function, 249, 491
Listening, empathetic, 438
Long-term capital, 115
Long-term note, 117
Loss area, 124

M

Maintenance, preventive, 177
Maintenance seeker, 465
Manageable departments, creating, 269
Management, as a group, 6; as a profession, 7; as a science, 8; as an art, 8; definition of, 9; functions of, 5; nature of, 3; need for, 3; principles of, 10; principles of, summary of, 43; process of, 12; scientific, 33; span of, 257, 269; universality of, 10
Management audit, 629
Management development, trends in, 535

Management development program, 527
Management manpower requirements, 529
Management personnel inventory, 529
Management process, 12
Management process cycle, 582
Management style, 542
Management task force, 306
Manager, responsibilities of, 554
Managerial grid training, 539
Manpower requirements, management, 529
Manual, organization, 377
Manual vs. automatic operations, 32
Marginal income, 125
Marginal product, 98
Market, replacement, 142
Market penetration, 150
Market research, scope of, 157
Market research information, sources of, 156
Meaning, of meaning, 417; triangle of, 418
Media, communication, 427
Memory unit, 197
Method, Critical Path, 641; laboratory training, 535
Methods, 89
Mobility of employees, 550
Money, and motivation, 458
Monte Carlo technique, 224
Morale, 471
Mortgage, 116
Motivation, and job satisfaction, 462; and money, 458; basis of, 449; improved, from use of committee, 343; in industry, 457
Motivational systems, 545
Motivator, 462
Multiproduct manufacturers, applying break-even analysis to, 131

N

Needs, affection, 452; esteem, 452; hierarchy of, 450; physiological, 451; safety, 451; self-actualization, 452
Net sales to average inventory ratio, 635
Net sales to total market ratio, 636
Network analysis, fundamentals of, 641
Nonauthoritative committee, 348
Nonbudgetary control, 624
Nondurable goods, consumer, 140
Note, long-term, 117

O

Objective, principle of, 51; principle of, applied to planning sales, 154; principle of, applied to production planning, 178; principle of, applied to profit planning, 132

Objectives, 50; characteristics of, 51; external, 53; internal, 54; statement of, 55; suboptimization of, 178; types of, 53; value of, 51
Objectivity, of plans, 91
Observation, personal, 624
Obsolescence, and style, 146
Operating budget, 598
Operating ratios, 635
Operations research, 220; limitations of, 226; techniques and applications, 223
Oral communications, 427
Organization, 239; and change, 526; effect of, in Theory Y, 245; line, 294; participative, 245; responsibilities of, 553; size of, 276; staff, 295; task force, 306
Organization chart, 375; circular, 375; horizontal, 375; vertical, 375
Organization development, 553; breakthrough in, 538
Organization manual, 377
Organization questionnaire, 371
Organization structure, in Theory X, 242; in Theory Y, 247; systems approach to, 275
Organizational analysis, 368; advantages of, 379; disadvantages of, 379; evaluation of, 378; procedures for, 369; tools of, 371
Organizational climate, 507, 542
Organizational effectiveness, checklist of, 381; evaluating, 380
Organizing, 5, 84
Orientation, systems, 509
Output device, of information system, 196
Outside board of directors, 356
Overall planning, 380
Overlapping authority, 293

P

Parity of authority and responsibility, principle of, 316
Participation, and change, 510; and productivity, 253
Participative belief, 341
Participative organization, 245
Path, profit, 596
Payment, method of, 547
Penetration, market, 150
Perceptanalytic Executive Scale, 402
Performance appraising, problems in, 532; current, measuring, 575; standards of, 533; supervisory, 506
Performance appraisal, 531
Periodic budgetary review, 602
Perseveration, in the creative process, 229
Personal need, in the creative process, 228
Personal observation, 624
Personal staff, 298

Personality, and control, 580; and delegation, 322; of members of an organization, 278
Personality dynamics, in leadership, 400
Personnel evaluation, 497
Personnel inventory, management, 529
Personnel policies, 542
PERT, 641, 644
Pervasiveness, of planning, 84
Plan, 82; profit, 596; standing, 220
Planning, 5, 81, for profit, 107; importance of, 84; of financial policy, 114; overall, 380; pervasiveness, 84; primacy of, 84; principle of, 95; principle of, applied to planning sales, 156; principle of, applied to production planning, 180; principle of, applied to profit planning, 133; production policies, 171; purpose of, 83; sales policies, 144
Planning function, 82
Plans, classified by function, 87; classified by scope, 88; classified by time, 86; criteria for evaluating, 89; degree of structuralization, 93; economic effectiveness of, 96; flexibility of, 95; objectivity of, 91; types of, 86
Plural executive, 352
Policies, 88; channel of distribution, 150; facility, 176; personnel, 542; pricing, 147; product, 145, 171; production, planning, 171; sales, planning, 144; sales promotion, 152
Policy, financial, 114
Position description, 373
Preparation, in the creative process, 228
Preventive maintenance, 177
Price, 141
Pricing, new products, 149
Pricing policies, 147; analysis of, via break-even analysis, 131
Primacy, of planning, 84
Primary source, of market research information, 156
Principle, of absoluteness of accountability, 317; of communication, 422; of control design, 590; of economic effectiveness, 100; of effective delegation, 316; of ethics, 72; of parity of authority and responsibility, 316; of planning, 95; of supervision, 512; of the exception, 588; of the objective, 51; of unity of command, 318
Principle of economic effectiveness, applied to planning sales, 158; applied to production planning, 182; applied to profit planning, 134
Principle of planning, applied to planning sales, 156; applied to production planning, 180; applied to profit planning, 133

Principle of the objective, applied to planning sales, 154; applied to production planning, 178; applied to profit planning, 132
Principles of control, 589
Principles of management, 10; Fayol, 38; summary of, 43; Taylor, 36
Probability theory, 225
Problem, definition of, 215
Problem solving, 215
Procedures, 89
Process, basis of departmentation, 267
Processing unit, of information system, 196
Product, basis of departmentation, 267; marginal, 98
Product costs, 148
Product diversification, 145
Product policies, 145, 171
Production, continuous, 168; emphasis upon, 31; jobbing, 168; intermittent, 168; part of a servo system, 170; to order, 169; to stock, 169; types of, 168
Production approach to management, 25
Production function, 167; characteristics of, 183
Production policies, planning, 171
Productivity, and job satisfaction, 252, 470; and participation, 253; and supervision, 252
Products, new, 172
Profile, job complexity, 492
Profit, analysis of, 120; definition of, 108; dynamics of, 124; effect of fixed costs, 126; effect of price, 127; effect of variable costs, 126; effect of volume, 124; meaning of, 107; measurement of, 108; planning for, 107
Profit analysis techniques, evaluation of, 128
Profit area, 124
Profit as a percentage of capital invested, 634
Profit as a percentage of sales, 634
Profit center, 331
Profit decentralization, 331
Profit path, 596
Profit plan, 596
Profit ratios, 110
Profit to volume analysis, 124
Profit to volume (P/V) ratio, 124
Profits, distribution of, 120
Program, audit, 627; management development, 527
Program Evaluation Review Technique, 641
Programming, linear, 223; quadratic, 223
Projection, 401
Projective technique, 401

Promotion, of employees, 551
Purchasing power, corporate, 144
P/V ratio, 124, 639

Q

Quality, production planning, 173; sales planning, 147
Quadratic programming, 223
Questionnaire, organization, 371
Queuing theory, 223
Quick ratio, 635

R

Random access unit, 197
Rank and file employees, 242
Rate buster, 461
Ratio, 633; current, 635; profit as a percentage of capital invested, 634; profit as a percentage of sales, 634; profit to volume (P/V), 124; quick, 635
Ratio analysis, 633
Ratios, financial, 634; input-output, 636; interpreting, 636; operating, 635; profit, 110
Reasoning, 215
Reciprocity, 178
Reference, in triangle of meaning, 418
Referent, in triangle of meaning, 418
Refreezing, 525
Reinvestment, 120
Relations, labor-management, 544
Reorganization, 264
Replacement market, 142
Reports, 625; control, 625; good, characteristics of, 626
Resistance, to control, 608
Responsibility, 315; of manager, 554
Restricted committee, 348
Revenue and expense budget, 598
Review, periodic budgetary, 602
Revisionists, approach to leadership, 393
Risk, 83
Role playing, 502
Rorschach Inkblot Test, 400

S

Safety needs, 451
Sale, terms of, 149
Sales budget, 598
Sales effort, 141
Sales policies, planning, 144
Sales promotion policies, 152
Scale, Perceptanalytic Executive, 402
Scientific management, 33; approach to leadership, 392

Scientific method, 91
Secondary source, of market research information, 156
Secured bonds, 116
Self, and environment, concepts of, 453
Self-actualization needs, 452
Selection, of employees, 550; of supervisors, 491
Selling, 152; direct, 152
Selling expense to net sales ratio, 636
Semantic analysis, 421
Semantics, 418
Sensitivity training, 535
Sequence, basis of departmentation, 267
Service authority, 299
Servo system, 13; production, as part of, 170
Short-term capital, 117
Signs, in triangle of meaning, 418
Simulation, 224
Situational factors, in leadership, 397
Social interaction, 231
Span of control, 269
Span of management, 257, 269; Hamilton's recommendations, 270; in practice, 273; theory of Graicunas, 270; Urwick's principle, 272
Special promotional devices, 152
Specialized staff, 298
Staff, personal, 298; specialized, 298
Staff authority, 294, 297
Staff organization, 295
Standard, 567
Standard costs, 604
Standardization, production planning, 174; sales planning, 147
Standards, business, 568; engineered, 573; establishing, 567; methods of establishing, 571; of performance, 533; set by appraisal, 573; statistical, 572; time, 573; time study, 573
Standing plan, 220
Statement of objectives, 55
Static fixed costs, 130
Statistical standards, 572
Stock, 115
Storage unit, of information system, 195
Style, and obsolescence, 146; management, 542
Suboptimization, 179
Suboptimization of objectives, 178
Subordinate acceptance, 294
Subordinate-acceptance source of authority, 290
Subsystem, 195
Superior authority, 293
Superior-subordinate communication, 428
Supervision, and productivity, 252; principle of, 512; sources of, 493

Supervisor, 482; legal definition, 483; performance of, 489; role of, 552; role of, in Theory X, 242; role of, in Theory Y, 248; selection and training of, 491; selection methods, 495; training of, 498
Supervisor's job, 482
Supervisory performance, 489; improving, 506
Supply and demand, law of, 139
Symbols, in triangle of meaning, 418
System, 195; cybernetic, 562; information, 195; information, functions of, 195; servo, 13; state of, in an organization, 281; motivational, 545
Systems approach, to organization structure, 275
Systems concept, 12
Systems orientation, 509
Systems theory, 12

T

T-group, 536
Task force organization, 306
Termination, of employment, 551
Terms of sale, 149
Test, inkblot, 400
Testing program, 496
Theories X and Y, evaluation of, 250
Theory, of Graicunas, 270; systems, 12
Theory X, a work-centered approach, 240
Theory Y, a people-centered approach, 244; assumptions of, 245
Theory Z, a systems approach, 254; application to decentralization, 328; assumptions of, 255
Time-event-network analysis, 640
Time standards, 573
Time study standards, 573
Total cost line, 123
Training, for decision making, 505; in human relations, 501; leadership, problems in, 503; managerial grid, 539; of supervisors, 491, 498; sensitivity, 535; technical and administrative skills, 500
Training methods, in human relations, 501; laboratory, 535
Trait approach to leadership, 396
Transmission, 417
Triangle of meaning, 418

U

Uncertainty, concepts of, 83
Unfreezing, of attitudes, 523
Unity of command, principle of, 318
Unsecured bonds, 116

V

Variable budget, 603
Variable cost, 121, 126; curvilinear, 129

Variable costs, linear, 129
Variable costs concepts, reliability and validity of, 128
Variable expense area, 123
Variable returns, law of, 97
Vendors, selection of, 177
Verification, in the creative process, 230

Vertical integration, 172
Vertical organization chart, 375

W

Waiting-line theory, 223
Working capital, 118
Written communications, 427

Author Index

A

Ackoff, R. L., 221
Allen, L. A., 263, 296, 304, 314, 320
Alsaker, E. T., 643
Andrews, K. R., 524, 531
Anthony, E. L., 564
Anthony, R. N., 133
Argyris, C., 395, 405, 535, 612, 613
Arnoff, F. L., 221
Ashby, W. R., 562

B

Babbage, C., 31, 32, 186, 200
Barnard, C. I., 292
Barnes, L. B., 539
Baumhart, R. C., 59, 60, 65, 67, 69
Bavelas, A., 398, 399
Beason, P. B., 15
Bennis, W., 43, 251, 392
Blake, R. R., 539
Blau, P. M., 433
Blauner, R., 473
Borko, H., 201
Bray, D. W., 531
Brayfield, A. H., 474
Buchele, R. B., 632
Burek, J., 105
Burns, R., 561
Burtt, H. E., 507

C

Cannon, W. B., 451
Carpenter, R. N., 156
Carroll, S. J., 523
Carzo, R., 304
Chandler, A. J., 276
Chase, S., 418
Chin, R., 12, 563
Christensen, C. R., 459
Churchman, C. W., 221
Clark, C. E., 631
Clay, H., 497
Coch, L., 253, 511
Collings, A. O., 157
Cosinuke, W., 645
Crockett, W. H., 474
Curley, J. R., 584
Curry, O. J., 606

D

Dale, E., 273, 274, 277, 297, 322, 342, 346, 372
Dalton, M., 303
Daniel, D. R., 425
Danielson, L. E., 503, 504
Davis, K., 434, 435
Davis, L. E., 467
Davis, R. C., 90, 204, 568
Dean, J., 172
Dewey, J., 214
Dickson, W. J., 29, 30
Drucker, P. F., 55, 60, 207, 214, 568

E

Emch, A. F., 580
Evans, M. K., 202

F

Faunce, W. A., 433
Fayol, H., 37-43, 72
Fazar, W., 641
Fisch, G. G., 305
Fisher, L. H., 530
Flanagan, J. C., 492
Fleming, G. J., 205
Fleishman, E. A., 507
Flesch, R., 430
Floor, I., 252
Follett, M. P., 37
Fox, W. McN., 296
Frank, G. W., 606
French, J. R. P., 253, 511, 534, 535

G

Gaiennie, L. R., 492
Gallagher, J. D., 203
Gardner, B. B., 482
Gardner, F. V., 124, 639
Gatza, J., 534
Gellerman, S. W., 454, 522
George, C. S., 573
Georgopoulus, B. S., 499
Gomberg, W., 574
Gordon, O. J., 471
Graicunas, A. V., 270-272
Greiner, L. E., 539
Guest, R. H., 252, 468, 485, 486, 487, 498

Guion, R. M., 471
Gurin, G., 252
Guzzardi, W., 360-65

H

Habbe, S., 522
Hague, L. R., 202
Hall, G. L., 377
Haire, M., 497
Hamilton, I., 270
Harder, D. S., 183
Harrell, T. W., 526
Harris, E. F., 507
Henning, D. A., 90
Herrmann, C. C., 221
Herzberg, F., 462
Hitch, C. J., 96, 179
Hirschmann, W. R., 578
Hoffman, L. R., 252, 428, 429
Hooven, J. J., 428, 429
House, R. J., 523

J

Jasinski, F. J., 379, 432
Jennings, E. E., 391
Jerdee, T. H., 523
Jerome, W. T., 628
Johnson, R. A., 199, 564

K

Kahane, M., 253
Kahn, R. L., 471, 474, 475, 508, 510
Kast, F. E., 199, 564
Katz, D., 252, 474, 508
Katz, R. L., 606
Katzell, R. A., 255
Kay, E., 534, 535
Kelley, J. E., 641
Kendrick, C., 62
Kennedy, J. E., 473
Kindall, A. B., 534
Kircher, P., 580
Koontz, H., 43, 314, 344, 584, 589
Korzybski, A., 418

L

Lampert, F. A., 629
Le Breton, F., 90
Leavitt, H. J., 341, 409
Levinson, H., 526
Levitt, T., 234
Levy, F. K., 641, 645, 648
Lewis, R. W., 568
Likert, R., 245-46, 249, 252, 482, 491, **513**
Littlefield, C. L., 370
Logan, J. P., 204
Lohman, M. R., 347-48
Lunt, P. S., 475

M

Maccoby, N., 252
Magee, J. F., 221
Mahoney, T. A., 523
Maier, N. R. F., 428, 429, 503, 504, 505, 515
Malcolm, D., 641
Mandeville, M. J., 292
Mann, F. C., 252, 499
March, J. G., 255
Marks, A. R. N., 468-69
Marriott, R., 472
Marrow, A. J., 537
Martin, E. W., 206
Martindell, J., 630
Marting, E., 225
Maslow, A. H., 450
Massarik, F., 535
Matz, A., 606
Mayo, E., 27-29
McDermid, C. D., 498
McDermott, W., 15
McGregor, D., 240, 245, 291, 394, 395, 521, 522, 532
McMurry, R. N., 395
McKean, R. N., 96
Mee, J. F., 51
Meyer, H. H., 534, 535
Miller, E. C., 15
Miller, R. W., 644
Moore, F. G., 573
Moore, R. F., 522
Morell, R. W., 217
Morse, G. E., 580
Morse, N., 252, 253
Mouton, J. S., 539
Mundel, M. E., 573
Murphy, T. P., 102
Murray, H. A., 497
Myers, M. S., 463, 466
Mylander, W. H., 352

N

Newman, W. H., 204, 314
Nichols, R. G., 438
Norris, L. W., 60, 69

O

Odiorne, G. S., 532
O'Donnell, C. J., 291, 314, 344, 584, 589
Ogden, C. K., 418
O'Neill, H. E., 473
Orwell, G., 423
Osborn, A. F., 232
Owen, R., 26-27
Owens, R. N., 574

P

Paige, H. W., 645
Parker, S., 105
Patchen, M., 510
Pelz, D. C., 495, 507
Peres, S. H., 489
Pierce, J. L., 616
Pigors, F., 502
Pigors, P., 502
Piotrowski, Z. A., 389-90, 397, 400, 403, 414-15
Porter, L. W., 484
Porter, W. H., 191-94
Powell, R. M., 524

R

Rachel, F., 370
Randall, L. K., 581
Reed, W. H., 428-29, 431
Reimer, E., 253
Richards, I. A., 418
Richman, B. M., 570
Rieser, C., 208-11
Rimms, H. L., 168
Robinson, H., 472
Rock, M. R., 389-90, 397, 400, 403, 414-15
Rodrboom, J. H., 641
Roethlisberger, F. J., 29-30, 439, 459, 482
Rogers, C. R., 439
Roos, C. F., 144
Rorschach, H., 400
Rosensweig, J. E., 199, 564
Rothe, H. F., 492, 494

S

Schein, E. H., 523, 536
Schmidt, W. H., 406-408
Sheehan, V., 324
Sherwin, D. S., 564
Siegelman, L., 83, 107, 159
Simon, H., 255
Simpson, R. I., 433
Spencer, M. H., 83, 107, 159

Stock, D., 535
Stogdill, R. M., 396
Strunk, W., Jr., 423
Suojane, W., 274

T

Tannenbaum, R., 253, 294, 406-08, 535
Taylor, F. W., 33-37
Thompson, G. L., 641, 645, 648
Thurston, J. R., 629
Tilles, S., 14, 199
Tillman, R., Jr., 349
Tucker, S. A., 633
Turner, A. N., 485

U

Urwick, L. F., 84, 272-73, 297

W

Walker, C. R., 252, 468, 472, 485
Walker, M. R., 641
Wallis, G., 227
Warner, W. L., 475
Weber, C. E., 292
Weiner, N., 562
Weitz, J., 495
Wechsler, I. R., 253, 535
White, K. K., 350-51, 369, 370
Whiting, C. S., 232, 233
Whyte, W. F., 191, 459, 482
Whyte, W. H., Jr., 404
Wicksberg, A. K., 306-07
Wiest, J. D., 641, 645, 648
Wolff, H. A., 520, 521
Worthy, J. C., 278
Wray, D. E., 482

Y

Yoder, D., 240, 448

Z

Zaleznik, A., 459
Zerfoss, L. F., 503, 515